A History of Israel
in Old Testament Times

Siegfried Herrmann

A History of Israel in Old Testament Times

Revised and Enlarged Edition

FORTRESS PRESS   Philadelphia

Published in the United Kingdom by SCM Press, London

First American Edition by Fortress Press 1975

Second Revised and Enlarged Edition 1981

Library of Congress Catalog Card Number 81–43092

ISBN 0–8006–1499–2

9111D81   Printed in the United States of America   1–1499

To Albrecht Alt (1883–1956)
with gratitude

Preface

THERE IS A LONG tradition of describing and interpreting the history of Israel in the Old Testament, which strictly speaking starts from the Old Testament itself. However, studies have chiefly been made by later Jewish and Christian historians, attracted by the problems of constructing a detailed account of events. The pioneer who deserves special mention here is the Jewish history-writer Flavius Josephus, who died about AD 100. The dominant viewpoints have sometimes been religious and sometimes 'historical'. Historical interest has grown particularly in the modern period, after an understanding dawned of the way in which the once tiny people on the eastern shore of the Mediterranean became involved in the political history of the leading oriental empires. To the historian's eye, Israel's destiny seemed to be at a crossroads of political, cultural and religious spheres of influence. Israel settled in the territory of Syria and Palestine, which form a corridor between Mesopotamia and Egypt, beside the wilderness of Syria and Arabia, itself an important factor whose significance should not be underestimated. As the decipherment of cuneiform and hieroglyphic sources during the nineteenth and the first half of the twentieth century became more assured, it too provided material for a fresh view and interpretation of Israel's history. We may recall the great multi-volume work of Heinrich Ewald from the 1860s; it was followed by the profound and pioneering books on the same subject by Julius Wellhausen, Eduard Meyer and finally Rudolf Kittel, to mention only these names. A remarkable new orientation in the investigation of the history of ancient Israel began to develop after the twenties and thirties of the present century. Its characteristic feature is a consistent combination of the literature of the Old Testament and other written sources with insights into the territorial history, archaeology and historical topography of Palestine. The full force of the results obtained in this way only made its impact on the consciousness of other scholars and on the wider public interested in the subject after the Second World War. For all the difference between their presuppositions, three names may be put side by side as representative of this new orientation: Albrecht Alt, William Foxwell Albright and Roland de Vaux. Martin Noth, a thoroughgoing pupil of Albrecht Alt, produced a compact outline in German in 1950 in his *History of Israel* (translated into English 1958, ²1960); this gave rise to a school, but also encouraged other conceptions. John Bright, *A History of Israel* (1959, ²1972), is indebted to both American and German stimuli. The ambitious *The Early History of Israel* by R. de Vaux (1971, translated into English 1978) remained incomplete.

In the face of such numerous and extensive researches, it is bold, yet nevertheless necessary, to present a new account of this history. Specialist scholars use a variety of different methods and therefore need to be reminded of their basic material and their presuppositions; a compressed account of the framework and the wider context in which they work will remind them also of those whom they should serve. Above all, however, this work is meant as an introduction for those who are concerned with the history of Israel and research into it, for whatever purpose.

The approach which is followed here, to combine investigation and description in a way that is as comprehensible as possible, requires restraint and sacrifice. Some fellow-scholars will find that too little attention is paid to their work; a number of themes should really have been given more thorough treatment. A number of academic details have been simplified. The specialist will lament the inconsistent treatment of proper names. As a rule they appear in the form used in English translations of the Bible, but these are not consistent in their revised forms and in many cases come nearer to the Hebrew original. Transcription of words from other oriental languages has been simplified, not least to make them fairly readable at first glance.

This book is dedicated to the memory of Albrecht Alt, whose assistant I was during the last years of his life (he died in 1956). It will not escape the notice of those who know the subject how strongly I have also been influenced by Martin Noth's work. I am very conscious of my obligations to these two men. The first stimulus towards the work came from a suggestion by Hans Walter Wolff. Christian Kaiser Verlag, and especially Fritz Bissinger, followed the progress of the book, which was expected much earlier, with patience. I must also thank them for their understanding.

I am much indebted to my colleagues, but the book had its best advocate in my wife, who, especially in the last eventful years, which have made such unusual demands on German teachers, never grew tired of reminding me of the need to finish the *History*.

Pentecost 1973

Preface to the Second Edition

IN THIS SECOND edition, the historical account has been extended as far as the appearance of the Romans in Jerusalem and Judaea in 63 BC. That does more than justice to the title *A History of Israel in Old Testament Times*, as the latest parts of the Old Testament are to be assigned to the second century BC. Roman rule opens up a new chapter in the history of Israel. It called forth the most stubborn resist-. ance offered by the oppressed people since the days of the Babylonian exile. It is also the background for the ministry of Jesus. To give a worthwhile account of the complex circumstances of the time would have made the book very much longer. I have deliberately left the text of the first edition unchanged down to the third chapter in Part Three; corrections have been made where necessary, and in the notes to the English edition references have been altered to take account of translations which have appeared in the meantime.

The time seems to have come when academic books dealing with large areas of the history of Israel appear largely as communal efforts. This, of course, is because of increasing specialization. What I have said is true in the first place of the monumental study *The World History of the Jewish People*, the authoritative work of Israeli scholars which began to appear as early as the 1960s. Beside it may be placed *Die Geschichte des jüdischen Volkes*, edited by H. H. Ben-Sasson and now appearing in German: the first volume goes down to the seventh century AD and has been written by four authors. No less than fourteen authors contributed to *Israelite and Judaean History*, edited by J. H. Hayes and J. M. Miller, published in London and Philadelphia in 1977. In the face of such riches, the individual author may well wonder about his competence. However, even in the future there will also be a place for the work of an individual author, dealing with extended periods of history, in order to maintain a unitary approach and to produce a historical work which does not sink to the level of chronicle and the consideration of minor details. Of course the individual must be aware of his limitations. The post-exilic period in particular, during which the foundations of Judaism, with all its different connections, were really laid, still poses many unanswered questions because of source material which is often complicated and fragmentary.

A full bibliography replaces the shorter one included in the first edition. It is particularly concerned with books and monographs which have appeared since the publication of the first edition. I am grateful to a new group of colleagues and not least to Christian Kaiser Verlag, and especially Herr Manfred Weber.

21 August 1979

Contents

Abbreviations

BIES	*Bulletin of the Israel Exploration Society*, Jerusalem
BJRL	*Bulletin of the John Rylands Library*, Manchester
BK	Biblischer Kommentar, Altes Testament
BM	British Museum
BRL	K. Galling, *Biblisches Reallexikon*, 1937
BVSAW	Berichte über die Verhandlungen der (Königlich) Sächsischen Akademie der Wissenschaften zu Leipzig
BWANT	Beiträge zur Wissenschaft vom Alten und Neuen Testament
BZ	*Biblische Zeitschrift*, Paderborn
BZAW	Beihefte zur *Zeitschrift für die Alttestamentliche Wissenschaft*
CAH	*Cambridge Ancient History*
CAT	Commentaire de l'Ancien Testament, Neuchâtel
CBC	Cambridge Bible Commentary
CPJ	*Corpus Papyrorum Judaicarum*, Cambridge 1957
EAE	*Encyclopaedia of Archaeological Excavations in the Holy Land*, ed. M. Avi-Yonah and E. Stern, Vols. I–IV, English Edition 1975–78
ETL	*Ephemerides Theologicae Lovanienses*, Louvain
EvTh	*Evangelische Theologie*, München
FRLANT	Forschungen zur Religion und Geschichte des Alten und Neuen Testaments, Göttingen
HAT	Handbuch zum Alten Testament
HdO	*Handbuch der Orientalistik*, ed. B. Spuler, Leiden
HK	Handkommentar zum Alten Testament
HSAT	Die Heilige Schrift des Alten Testaments (Kautzsch), ⁴1922/23, ed. A. Bertholet
HTR	*Harvard Theological Review*, Cambridge, Mass.
HUCA	*Hebrew Union College Annual*, Cincinnati
IEJ	*Israel Exploration Journal*, Jerusalem
IJH	*Israelite and Judaean History*, ed. J. H. Hayes and J. M. Miller, London and Philadelphia 1977
JBL	*Journal of Biblical Literature*, New York, New Haven, Philadelphia
JEA	*Journal of Egyptian Archaeology*, London
JJS	*Journal of Jewish Studies*, London
JNES	*Journal of Near Eastern Studies*, Chicago
JPOS	*Journal of the Palestine Oriental Society*, Jerusalem
JSJ	*Journal of the Study of Judaism in the Persian, Hellenistic and Roman Period*, Leiden
JSS	*Journal of Semitic Studies*, Manchester
KAI	H. Donner-W. Röllig, *Kanaanäische und aramäische Inschriften*, I, ²1967; II, ²1968; III, ²1969
KAT	Kommentar zum Alten Testament
KuD	*Kerygma und Dogma*, Göttingen
LCL	Loeb Classical Library

LXX	Septuagint
MDAIK	*Mitteilungen des Deutschen Archäologischen Instituts*, Cairo
MDO	*Mitteilungen der Deutschen Orient-Gesellschaft*, Berlin
MDPV	*Mitteilungen des Deutschen Palästinavereins*, Wiesbaden
MIO	*Mitteilungen des Instituts für Orientforschung*, Berlin
OLZ	*Orientalische Literaturzeitung*, Berlin
Or.	*Orientalia*, Rome
OTL	Old Testament Library, London
OTS	*Oudtestamentische Studien*, Leiden
PEFQS	*Palestine Exploration Fund Quarterly Statement*, London
PEQ	*Palestine Exploration Quarterly*, London
PJB	*Palästinajahrbuch*, Berlin
RA	*Revue d'Assyriologie et d'Archéologie Orientale*, Paris
RB	*Revue Biblique*, Paris
REJ	*Revue des Études Juives*, Paris
RGG	*Die Religion in Geschichte und Gegenwart*, Tübingen
RHPR	*Revue de l'Histoire et de Philosophie Religieuses*, Strasbourg and Paris
SAM	Sitzungsberichte der Bayerischen Akademie der Wissenschaften
SAT	Die Schriften des Alten Testaments
SBS	Stuttgarter Bibelstudien
SBT	Studies in Biblical Theology, London
SGV	Sammlung gemeinverständlicher Vorträge aus dem Gebiet der Theologie und Religionsgeschichte, Tübingen
SSAW	Sitzungsberichte der Sächsischen Akademie der Wissenschaften
SVT	Supplements to *Vetus Testamentum*, Leiden
TGI	K. Galling, *Textbuch zur Geschichte Israels*, ¹1950, ²1968
THAT	*Theologisches Handwörterbuch zum Alten Testament*, ed. E. Jenni and C. Westermann, I, 1971; II, 1976
TLZ	*Theologische Literaturzeitung*, Leipzig
TZ	*Theologische Zeitschrift*, Basel
UF	*Ugarit-Forschungen. Internationales Jahrbuch für die Altertumskunde Syrien-Palästinas*
VT	*Vetus Testamentum*, Leiden
WHJP	*The World History of the Jewish People*, Jerusalem 1970ff.
WO	*Die Welt des Orients*, Göttingen
WMANT	Wissenschaftliche Monographien zum Alten und Neuen Testament Neukirchen
ZÄS	*Zeitschrift für Ägyptische Sprache und Altertumskunde*, Berlin
ZAW	*Zeitschrift für die alttestamentliche Wissenschaft*, Berlin
ZDMG	*Zeitschrift des Deutschen Morgenländischen Gesellschaft*, Wiesbaden
ZDPV	*Zeitschrift des Deutschen Palästinavereins*, Wiesbaden

INTRODUCTION

The Scene

ISRAEL'S HISTORY IS inextricably bound up with the land, indeed the lands, in which it took place. Without qualification, that is the case with the people of Israel in the Old Testament. We can see the rudimentary beginnings of Israel on the one hand in northern Syria and neighbouring Mesopotamia, and on the other in north-east Egypt, before Israel found a homeland in Palestine, 'the promised land', possession of which was never undisputed. The widest dimensions of the scene of the history of Israel take in the land mass on the north side of the Arabian peninsula, bounded by two territories which are very different in their structure.

To the north-east of this peninsula, and immediately accessible from the wilderness of Syria and Arabia, an extensive area of cultivated land spreads out as far as the southern foothills of the Iranian mountains. It owes its fertility to the rivers Euphrates and Tigris, which flow south-east to the Persian Gulf. The central and southern part of this arable lowland, where Sumerians and Babylonians once founded their empires, was already called Mesopotamia, 'the land between the rivers', in antiquity. On the north-west boundary of the Arabian peninsula the situation was very different. Along the eastern coast of the Mediterranean Sea rose a stretch of hill-country, broken in a number of places, but acting so to speak as a barrier which hindered free access from the wilderness to the sea. The northern part of this territory is called Syria, and it is usual to assign the name Palestine to the southern part. On average, the coastal strips of Syria and Palestine are little more than seventy miles wide; they are settled land of very variable fertility. Hills run from north to south, on the whole in considerable ranges, interrupted by plateaus and plains. This produces different climatic conditions. There is no lack of rivers, but these are much more modest than the Euphrates and Tigris, and often are only partly suitable for agricultural purposes because of the depth of their beds. There are no extensive areas within the hill-country which they could irrigate; there is no basis on which a river-valley culture could develop.

Nevertheless, the course of the rivers already gives an approximate picture of the physical conditions of Syria and Palestine. The sources of the largest of these rivers lie in the area of the Lebanon, the extension of two massifs[1] which in some degree also separate the territories of Syria and Palestine. To the north, the Nuseiriyeh mountains (*jebel el-anṣārīye*) join the Lebanon, and in their hinterland the greatest Syrian river, the Orontes (*nahr el-ʿāṣi*), is capable of irrigating lowlands which are at least fertile in parts.[2] The Leontes (*nahr el-līṭāni*) flows in exactly the opposite direction, southwards, and as the *nahr el-qāsimīye* breaks through the hill-country to the south of the Lebanon in a westerly direction, at the level of Tyre, and soon reaches the Mediterranean. The Eleutheros (*nahr el-kebīr*) is also quite important: it emerges from the hill-country in central Syria flowing in an east-west direction, and also reaches the Mediterranean north of Tripolis after passing through a broad coastal plain.

South of the Lebanon and Hermon, which adjoins the Antilebanon to the south, rise the limestone hills of Palestine, divided into a western half and an eastern half by the Jordan rift. This rift is the most interesting geological phenomenon of the whole area. It is part of the so-called Syrian rift which begins in Syria with the valley of the Orontes, continues in the great depression of *el-beqāʿ*, between the Lebanon and the Antilebanon, becomes the Jordan rift and finally reaches its deepest point in the Dead Sea.[3] It continues south of the Dead Sea through the *wādi el-ʿaraba*, and finally goes through the gulf of *el-ʿaqaba* (Gulf of Elath) and the Red Sea to East Africa. This impressive phenomenon, geologically unique, is said to have come into being at the beginning of the Tertiary age. It catches the eye especially in the imposing and sometimes bizarre landscape south of the Dead Sea, where formations of the oldest stone, dominating the rosy Nubian sandstone, form solitary bare hills of austere beauty, at least on both sides of the *wādi el-ʿaraba*. Areas of steppe and desert extend eastwards and westwards; to the west they already form part of the Sinai peninsula, the southern portion of which is dominated by powerful massifs which are traditionally given the name of the Sinai mountains. The Sinai peninsula is hardly inhabited at all. It forms a bridge between the mighty Arabian peninsula and the African continent, or, more accurately, it is like a 'hyphen' (A. Alt) between Palestine and Egypt. It was once possible to enter Egypt in the eastern delta region of the Nile from the Sinai peninsula without hindrance. Today the Suez Canal cuts across this border territory.

Egypt stands on its own. The Nile country has its own peculiar structure and is far more self-contained than all the areas described hitherto. In a single stretch, say from the rapids of the First Cataract in the south down to the delta, Egypt consists of one narrow river landscape which barely reaches further than the hills bordering the Nile valley. The Nile provides irrigation and makes cultivation possible. As Herodotus once put it, in words which are apt for all periods of history, 'Egypt is a gift of the Nile'. The development of focal points within this area, places where culture and political power have been concentrated one after the other, chiefly around Thebes in the south and Memphis in the north (roughly where Cairo was built at a later time), follows from geographical conditions, and is even more the end-result of ethnographic and political trends. In contrast to the border territories of the Arabian peninsula, Egypt is geographically independent. Because of its natural conditions, the area which includes Syria and Palestine together with

Mesopotamia is a complex whose situation and structure draw it together; it has only loose contact with Egypt. The term 'fertile crescent', which has become a favourite cliché, thus refers only to those lands which form the northern boundary of the Arabian peninsula.

The land-mass described here has been shown to have many divisions, but its culture and civilization form a stronger unity. The conditions of life in this area are distinctive, but in essentials have remained the same. They are closely connected with both landscape and climate. As has been said, Egypt may be left on one side as having a different situation in a number of respects. Mesopotamia and Syria are by contrast areas bounding on extensive zones of desert and steppe.[4] There are no thick woods even in regions whose climate favours them; these areas present, rather, the picture of an 'open landscape' which offered the best conditions for settlement, without making widespread deforestation necessary. As a result, Mesopotamia and Syria could always find room for thrusts by the Semitic population from the steppes. The starting point for these Semitic groups is to be sought in the north of the Arabian peninsula, or more accurately, in the girdle of steppe-land bordering on the 'fertile crescent'. This girdle supported a nomadic mode of life which included the rearing of animals: principally sheep and goats, but also asses.[5] Even in prehistoric times these nomads migrated to territories which were later to become cultivated land. The migration of nomadic elements from the steppes into lands with established settlements could lead them to settle there permanently themselves. This process was set in motion by the need to alternate between winter and summer pastures, and continued down to modern times as a slow process of infiltration; in ancient times, however, it often also took the form of substantial and distinct aggressive movements.[6] This living contact between the steppe and cultivated land is not least the secret of the high and continually novel development of culture in these areas. The constant influx from the steppes was at the same time a transference and exchange of important cultural features, an exchange which was consummated in the symbiosis between settled elements and nomadic immigrants. For example, we know that the basic forms of our chief kinds of grain, wheat and barley, which are to be found on the steppe, were in all probability cultivated for the first time in Transjordania and Upper Mesopotamia.[7] Coupled with the use of the plough, these furthered the settlement of groups which were once nomadic. Where agricultural conditions were less favourable, the land at least offered the possibility of extensive cattle-rearing and pasturage on a large scale, for instance in the less fertile limestone hills of Palestine.

The influence of these geographical conditions on settlement, commerce, language and the general trend of historical development is obvious. New layers of population were constantly being added to these countries, who either came in from the adjoining steppes or were introduced through the expansion of the great powers. The plains, on which there were no forests, cried out to be occupied, and made possible military operations of considerable magnitude, often resulting in the downfall of the isolated states in the hill-country of Syria and Palestine, which were inevitably quite small. In the larger areas, there was no absolute uniformity of language, but individual idioms are related. It is, however, improper to derive the languages of Mesopotamia and Syria from one common basis, 'Proto-Semitic'. 'Proto-Semitic' is a hypothesis for which there is no evidence. As the inhabitants of the steppes came into contact with settled communities, independent local forms were introduced into the language which they shared through ethnic connections; the structure of these local forms is often similar, so they may be termed 'common Semitic' but not 'Proto-Semitic'.[8]

> The distribution of languages in the area under discussion is closely bound up with the various historical movements which will be the subject of the next section. However, the general point may be made here that those languages which are traditionally called 'Semitic' are to be found particularly in territories which have a long boundary on the Syro-Arabian wilderness. These are the languages of the cultivated areas which were settled from the steppes of the Syro-Arabian wilderness.[9] They include in the first place Akkadian (Babylonian/ Assyrian), the language of Mesopotamia, which has a variety of individual dialects, and is now usually called 'East Semitic', but not Sumerian, which rests on a different basis. The origin of Sumerian is unknown. As the different geographical features of the area already suggest, the languages of Syria and Palestine are more strongly differentiated. For the earlier period, going back into the second millennium BC, 'Canaanite' has become the comprehensive designation of a series of North-west Semitic dialects. Knowledge of these varies, depending on the fortunes of archaeological discoveries. They include Ugaritic, Phoenician-Punic, Moabitic and not least Hebrew, which is a relatively well-attested dialect group of Canaanite. Those who entered Palestine were assimilated to the language which they found there to a much greater degree than the Aramaeans who set foot in Syria proper at the same time and established Aramaic there. However, Aramaic was to gain increasing influence in the first half of the first millennium BC. It gradually suppressed the Canaanite dialects and after the sixth century, in the form of 'Imperial Aramaic', even became the official language of the Persian chancery and the administrative language of the Achaemenidean kingdom, including Syria-Palestine and Egypt to the south- west. In addition, numerous local dialect forms of Aramaic developed; their end was sealed principally by the spread of Arabic after the seventh century AD. Arabic (which is divided into North and South Arabic), together with Abyssinian-Ethiopic, belongs to the southern group of West Semitic languages. Egyptian is usually said to be a Hamitic language with only a few Semitic components, which can be seen only in some vocabulary and in a number of grammatical peculiarities. This difference in language confirms the special geographical situation of Egypt noted above: it is to be distinguished from the 'Semitic' lands of the fertile crescent.[10]

As the scene of the history of Israel, Palestine is inextricably involved in the geographical conditions of the areas which border on it. It is itself part of this larger whole, albeit a relatively independent and complex part. Its size is usually overestimated. The strips of cultivated land are hardly longer than 70 miles in an east-west direction. The Old Testament itself usually denotes the northernmost and southernmost points of Israelite territory aptly by the phrase 'from Dan to Beer-sheba': from one place to the other is less than 150 miles as the crow flies. According to an exact calculation made after the First World War, the cultivated land of Palestine west of the Jordan is rather smaller than what used to be Württemberg.[11] The following example may illustrate the unusual difference in land-level. The surface of the Dead Sea is almost 1300 feet below the surface of the Mediterranean;[12] Jericho, at the northern end of the Dead Sea, is 820 feet below, whereas Jerusalem, only 14 miles to the west, is already 2500 feet above the Mediterranean, and the neighbouring Mount of Olives is as high as 2658 feet. These considerable differences of height have been caused by geological movements.

Palestine consists of deposits once built up by the sea: in some places horizontal stratification is still easily recognizable. The formations are of the Cretaceous and Jurassic eras. The strata of the Upper Cretaceous era are most evident, particularly the harder limestone of the Cenomanian and Turonian periods with an average thickness of 1800 feet. One striking feature of them is the terrace formation which often determines the landscape. The topmost stratum of the Cretaceous era, above the Cenomanian and Turonian levels, is the soft limestone of the Senonian period, which shines a blinding white in the sun. The landscape of the Senonian period is marked out by gentle rolling hills, especially in the hill-country of Judah and Samaria. Towards the end of the Tertiary period there were volcanic eruptions in the north-east of the country, especially around the Hauran (*jebel ed-drūz*) and in the area of *jōlān* north of the Yarmuq. As a result, the whole of the northern third of Transjordania and even the south-eastern part of the Galilean hill-country was covered with a layer of basalt.

Geological disturbances have determined the present character of the surface of the land. Lateral pressure after the deposits which produced the Cretaceous strata led to disturbances in this layer in the form of geological folds or distortions (so-called 'flexures'). This development is particularly evident on the east side of the hill-country of Judah and Samaria. In the second half of the Tertiary period (between the Miocene and Pliocene age), the strata were split in a north–south direction. This produced the present Jordan rift, and at the same time the coastal plain was broken up on the western side of the hill-country west of the Jordan (Cisjordania). As a result, the whole of the Cisjordanian hill-country remained as a kind of 'eyrie', extending over a considerable area. The most important of the faultings from a later period is that running from south-east to north-west, which formed the plain of Jezreel. In the subsequent period, wind and water played their part in producing even sharper contrasts in this landscape. Thus it is characteristic that the Senonian strata on the west side of the hill-country have been worn away where the rain-clouds coming in from the Mediterranean have fallen. Larger and smaller watercourses had their effect on the unusually varied landscape and have often resulted in that profusion of varied conditions which make the reconstruction and exact location of a number of historical events so very difficult. As a result of these great geological disturbances, the following profile of the land emerges, seen from east to west. Transjordania rises gently from the flat Arabian wilderness and falls sharply in the west towards the Jordan rift; the west side of the Jordan rift rises sharply to the heights of the hill-country of Judah and Samaria, and for some distance this eyrie falls rather less steeply towards the coastal plain.

The characteristics of individual parts of Palestine can only be understood from this basic structure of the country. The best place from which to begin a brief description is the south-east, where some of the Israelite tribes moved into the cultivated land at the time of the settlement. The most important border river in southern Transjordania is the Arnon (*sēl el-mōjib*), the deep valley of which once separated the Moabites in the south from the Ammonites in the north. It runs into the Dead Sea almost exactly in the centre of its eastern side. The land to the north of the Arnon is almost all over 2000 feet high and is only fertile in parts; to the east it merges into the belt of steppe and wilderness. To the north it joins hill-country which extends as far as the Jabbok (*nahr ez-zerqa* = the blue river). The area between the Arnon and the Jabbok is known today as *el-belqa*. The most important place on these highlands is Medeba (*mādeba*), known from its mosaic map. On the upper reaches of the Jabbok, where it describes a great circle southwards, lies the ancient Rabbath-Ammon, now *'ammān*, the capital of Jordan, in the centre of a stretch of hill-country. Four miles to the west of *mādeba* is one of the highest points of the Transjordanian hill-country, the peak of Nebo (*en-neba*, 2630 feet), which is almost like an advance post giving a view over large areas of Transjordania and far over the other side of the Jordan. This is the place from which Moses is said to have had his view of the promised land at last (Deut. 34).[13]

To the west, the territory of *el-belqa* joins the Dead Sea and the lower Jordan rift. The Dead Sea[14] is a tideless inland lake, subject to a constant high temperature which causes evaporation. As a result, it has an excessively high salt and mineral content,[15] which makes life impossible in its waters. However, all the streams flowing into the Dead Sea bring fresh water, so that some vegetation is possible in the surrounding country. This is particularly luxuriant in the area of the hot springs on the eastern bank, and in the Hellenistic-Roman period a place called Callirrhoe was sought after as a spa which effected cures.[16] The fertile district of *'ēn feshka*, less than a mile south of the ruins of *ḥirbet qumrān*, well-known from the scrolls discovered in the area, is less extensive. The hill-country on the eastern side of the Dead Sea, split by deep valleys, was called Pisgah in Old Testament times.[17] The hills on the western side are formed of outrunners from the hilly wilderness of Judah; in parts they fall directly into the Dead Sea. Climate and geographical features make normal settlement in the region of the Dead Sea impossible. Nevertheless, from time to time it has acquired a significance of its own as a boundary or a place of refuge. David used the oasis of Engedi (*'ēn jidi*) on the south-west side of the Dead Sea as a retreat (I Sam. 24), and both Maccabaeans and Herodians thought that they could protect themselves against the danger posed by the Nabataeans by constructing a triangle of fortresses, Machaerus (*el-mashnaqa* at *ḥirbet el-mukāwer*) on the east side, and Hyrcania (*ḥirbet mird*) and Masada (*es-sebbe*) on the west side of the Dead Sea.[18] Finally, at different times Jews sought refuge in this area: the community of Qumran in the pre-Christian period, and large sections of the Jewish people in the early-Christian period, during their desperate war against Rome (AD 70–73 and 132–135).

A large complex of country makes up the hill-country of Judah, in the area south of Jerusalem. At its heart lies the 'hill-country of Judah' (*har-yᵉhūdā*) in the narrower sense. This is situated in the area between Hebron (*el-ḥalīl*), the chief town of the area, and Bethlehem (*bēt laḥm*), which lies to the north. The eastern parts of the hill-country of Judah lie in the rain shadow and there form the 'wilderness of Judah' (*midbar yᵉhūdā*). On the western side, on the other hand, a great fault separates the hill-country from the coastal plain. Here the country takes the form of hills only about 1000 feet high. The hill-country also falls away increasingly to the south-west and the south. The steppe and wilderness once to be found here, around Beer-sheba (*bīr es-sebaʿ*), is at present the object of Israelite projects for cultivation. The area round Hebron has always been fertile, as the Israelite spies once reported (Num. 13; 14).

It is impossible to give exact boundaries to Judah on all sides, but it is an independent, self-contained area, with marked differences from other territories. The road from Bethlehem up to Jerusalem gradually reveals a different kind of landscape. The gently rolling highlands of Judah take on a much sharper profile around Jerusalem. Deep valleys reach right up to the city, whose oldest part, the south-east hill (now outside the Old City), between the Kidron valley and the valley of Hinnom, is relatively low in comparison with the walled Old City to the north. Modern Jerusalem has been built up to the north and west.

Largely open country extends to the north of Jerusalem, with a number of chains of hills; on the heights of today's *el-bīre* and near *rāmallah*, however, it is bordered by a clearly visible ridge. To the east and west, this area north of Jerusalem, which in Old Testament times was settled by members of the tribe of Benjamin, is again bounded by ridges and outrunners from the hill-country. Among these, to the west, is the striking elevation called *en-nebi samwīl*, supposed to be the burial place of Samuel. Gibeon (*el-jīb*) lies at its foot, separated by a valley. From here the hill-country gradually rises more steeply to the west, interrupted by several plateaus; in some stretches it becomes quite stark. One of the most important routes from the interior to the coastal plain ran through this district, the road via Beth-horon, attested in biblical times as 'the ascent of Beth-horon'; it also played a significant role in the Maccabaean and Roman periods.[19] It went near *ʿamwās* (probably the

Emmaus of the New Testament) and Gezer (*tell jezer* by *abu shūshe*) and down to the coastal plain. In parts this hill-country is very fertile, unlike the hilly eastern border of the great plateau to the north of Jerusalem. A deeply-fissured and difficult hill region separates it from the Jordan rift. The deepest and best-known *wādi* in this area, leading in the direction of Jericho, is the *wādi el-qelt*.

From Jerusalem there is a direct link with the north, the Jerusalem 'north road', which touches Saul's Gibeah (*tell el-fūl*), Samuel's Ramah (*er-rām*), the Mizpah of I Kings 15 (*tell en-naṣbe*) and the present-day *el-bīre* (Beeroth ?) within Benjaminite territory; it leaves Gibeon on the left and Anathoth (*ʿanāta*), Geba (*jebaʿ*) and Michmash (*muḥmās*) on the right. It leads right into the heart of the hill-country of Ephraim and Samaria, stretching from the heights of Bethel (*burj bētīn*) in the south to the plain of Jezreel in the north. This is the real heart of central Palestine, the territory of the northern kingdom of Israel. The natural character of the country favoured historical developments. The hill-country is not as high as that of Judah, so that the zone of the rains coming from the west reaches further east than in Judah. The fertility of the whole area is great. Its real centre is the area round Shechem (*nāblus*, the old site *tell balāṭa*), lying in the centre between Mount Ebal (*jebel islāmīye*) in the north (3083 feet) and Gerizim (*jebel eṭ-ṭōr*), in the south (2889 feet).

The varied character of the hill-country allows a whole series of interconnecting routes, especially in the north. The Jerusalem north road forks in the centre of the hill-country near Shechem. From there it is possible to make quick progress to Samaria (*sebaṣtye*), lying high above a valley basin, and on to *jenīn* in the plain of Jezreel. A road also leads north-north-east from Shechem through the *wādi bēdān* to Tirzah (*tell el-fārʿa*), which goes on to the eastern extremities of the plain of Jezreel at Thebez (*ṭūbāṣ*) through the north-eastern part of the hill-country. South of Tirzah it is possible to cross in the opposite direction to the *wādi fārʿa*, a broad and fertile valley which provides a direct link south-east between the heights of the hill-country and the Jordan rift. In particular, it leads to the Jordan fort of Adam (Josh. 3.16: *tell ed-dāmye*), near to the mouth of the Jabbok. It is also worth mentioning the route across the hill-country through the *wādi-ʿāra*, made famous especially by Thutmoses III before his siege of Megiddo; this provides a link between the coastal plain and the southern plain of Jezreel on the west side of the hill-country.

The broad and fertile plain of Jezreel, which divides the hill-country of Ephraim and Samaria from the Galilean plateau, takes its name from the town of Jezreel (*zerʿīn*) which lies on its eastern edge; sometime it is also called the plain of Megiddo, from the old fortress which lay on its south side. To the west there is a narrow tongue between the ridge of Carmel, which extends right to the sea, and the edges of the Galilean hill-country, which ends in the bay of Acco. The important modern port of Haifa lies between Acco and Carmel. On the eastern side, the plain of Jezreel has a connection with the Jordan rift, or more accurately, with the plain of Beth-shean (*bēsān*) in the *nahr jālūd*, north of the hill-country of Gilboa (*jebel fuqū'a*). The broadest and deepest break in the hill-country west of the Jordan, the plain of Jezreel was the scene of many battles. Important fortresses were already being constructed on its borders during the second millennium BC, both to serve as an operational basis for further thrusts into the interior and to supervise traffic between the coastal plain and the northern hill-country as far as Syria. From north-west to south-east these fortresses were Jokneam (*tell qēmūn*), Megiddo (*tell el-mutesellim*), Taanach (*tell ta'annak*), Ibleam (*ḫirbet bel'ame*) and Beth-shean in the Jordan rift (*bēsān*: the old site *tell el-ḥuṣn*). Jezreel was only occasionally the residence of the kings of Israel.

The Galilean hill-country which adjoins the plain of Jezreel to the north is the last piece of hill-country west of the Jordan which is usually assigned to Palestine. The southern and south-western part of Galilee is characterized by a hill-country like that of Samaria: in contrast to the hilly north it is known as Lower Galilee. Leaving aside the area round Lake Gennesaret to the east, this was the chief sphere of Jesus' work in Galilee: the towns of Nazareth, Cana and Nain lie side by side here. The imposing bulk of Mount Tabor (*jebel eṭ-ṭōr*) rises in the south-eastern part of Lower Galilee (1929 feet). On the eastern side of the highlands lies the town of Hazor (*tell waqqāṣ*), which has attracted increasing attention through modern excavations. The highest mountain west of the Jordan, *jebel jermaq* (3962 feet), is in the hill-country of Upper Galilee, five miles north-west of the town of Safed.

Something must still be said about the lower-lying land, which has not yet been described. The coastal plain extends on the west side of the hill-country, becoming increasingly broad. Less than 2 miles in breadth south of Carmel, it becomes almost 25 miles wide at the level of Gaza; ultimately it merges almost imperceptibly with the wilderness of Sinai. It offers good communications along the coast, and therefore in the course of time has been the route taken by the great conquerors. Of course, the flat coastline offers hardly any possibilities for natural harbours.

We have already given an extensive account of the origin of the Jordan rift. The Jordan itself rises from a number of sources which come down from the southern edge of Hermon; it first flows through the marshy (now drained) area of what used to be called the upper Lake of Jordan or Lake Merom (*baḥret el ḥūle*), and after breaking through basalt hill-country reaches Lake Gennesaret.[20] The chief scenes of Jesus' activity were on the western bank, where the hill-country does not descend so abruptly to the lake, especially in the plain south of Capernaum. Between the southern end of the lake and the Dead Sea (about sixty miles as the crow flies), the Jordan flows through a broad rift (*el-ġōr*, 'the descent'), which narrows only south of the bright of Beth-shean to a mile and a half; south of the mouth of the Jabbok, however, it reaches its greatest width of twelve miles. This last section is occupied by the fertile oasis called *kikkar hayyardēn* in the Old Testament, with Jericho (*erīḥa*: ruins of *tell es-sulṭān*) as the most significant town on its south-western edge. The Jordan itself flows sinuously round constant bends, between dazzling white banks of marl through which it has made its way. Its deep-lying bed makes it almost impossible to draw off water for irrigating the adjoining fields, so the Jordan rift is largely wilderness. The oases of Beth-shean and Jericho are fed with water by streams from the edges of the hill-country.

One last word needs to be said about central and northern Transjordania. North of the Jabbok, the territory of *'ajlūn* adjoins the area of *el-belqa*; it lies between the Jabbok and the Yarmuq (*sheri'at el-menāḍire*). This hilly country, which rises to nearly 4000 feet, is still the most wooded part of Palestine, and even has considerable oak forests. These oaks are not, however, as tall as those in Europe, nor do the forests have the density and fullness to which we are accustomed.

To the north of the *'ajlūn* is the area of *jōlān* (once Gaulanitis and now familiar as the Golan heights), which reaches as far as the southern outrunners of Hermon. This is the district of Bashan (*habbāšān* = 'level ground'), often mentioned in the Old Testament, which also embraces the plain of *en-nuqra* ('the hollow') adjoining Golan to the east. The area owes its fertility to the weathered basalt lava which once poured down from the then volcanic hill-country of the Hauran, on the outermost edge of the wilderness. Remarkably enough, the Hauran mountains (*jebel ed-drūz*) in the extreme north-east of Palestine, rising to a height of 5970 feet, are never mentioned in the Old Testament. They found a place in political and church history only in Roman and Christian times. To some degree that is also the case with the whole of Transjordania. This is evident from the impressive ruins of Gerasa (*jerash*) in the south-eastern *'ajlūn*, of Bosra (*boṣra*), former capital of the Nabataean kingdom on the extreme south-western side of the Hauran, and the countless remains of church buildings in *umm el-jemāl* on the edge of the cultivated land near the modern road to Bagdad. North-west of the Hauran is the broad and sparsely populated district of *el-leja*, the extreme north-eastern boundary of what we normally call Palestine. The chief route to Damascus, the capital of Syria, runs between *leja* and *jōlān*, passing through an oasis on the eastern side of the Antilebanon.

The character of the country today, the bareness of the hills, the poorness of the ground (which can only be utilized for agriculture after extraordinary effort, like that expended by the modern state of Israel, and the maximum use of available water), raises the question whether there has been a fundamental change of climate between ancient and modern times. Formerly, it is thought, the country could have been much more fertile, attractive and pleasant, a view which can appeal to the 'promised land, flowing with milk and honey'. The short answer to this is that there is no biblical or scientific basis for supposing such a change of climate in the last millennia.[21] Like the rest of the Mediterranean world, Palestine enjoys a 'sub-tropical' climate, characterized by the change from a rainless summer to a period of rain in the winter. The Old Testament already gives evidence of the scorching summer heat and the ensuing periods of winter rain, so extraordinarily important for agriculture. The latter are aptly described by the terms *yōreh*, 'early rain' (end of October); *gešem*, the chief winter rain (January/February); and *malqōš*, 'late rain' (about May). All other inferences that can be drawn from the Old Testament and the Mishnah about meteorological and agricultural conditions are in accord with modern circumstances.

The Dead Sea provides a particularly impressive argument against any climatic change. Lakes without outlets react very quickly to changes in humidity and sometimes can flood their banks to a considerable degree. However, the Dead Sea has never altered its form since antiquity. Had there been only a slightly higher degree of humidity in earlier times, the surface of the sea would have risen considerably, flooding the peninsula of *el-lisān*. But this never happened, as information in Pliny shows.[22]

The extensive decline in the fertility of the land is only partly connected with natural developments. Certainly in the course of the centuries fertile agricultural land has been washed away, exposing the bare limestone. But this is a consequence of bad agriculture, and follows not least from variations in the density of population. Historical reasons, including shifts in the balance of power, the neglect of the whole area in the power-play of great historical developments, the decline of the Roman empire, invasion by Persians and Arabs, changes in landowners, have all brought about the rise and fall of cultural centres and have also resulted in ongoing negligence in cultivating the land. Confirmation from the opposite side comes from the consistent use of modern methods in agricultural development of the country which have been carried out particularly successfully in the modern state of Israel. In any case, 'the promised land' was no more a 'land flowing with milk and honey' in ancient times than it is today – at least in its natural characteristics. This phrase, the details of which are so difficult to interpret, is in all probability an ideal conception, the sort of picture of cultivated land which could arise among the inhabitants of the steppe.[23]

There is no comprehensive account of the geography of Palestine which takes the most recent data into account. Most books are works of historical geography: F. M. Abel, *Géographie de la Palestine* I, 1933; II, 1938, reprinted 1967; D. Baly, *The Geography of the Bible*, ²1974; Y. Aharoni, *The Land of the Bible. A Historical Geography*, 1967. M. Noth, *The Old Testament World*, 1966, with its numerous references to specialist literature, is important, and for German readers H. Guthe, *Palästina*, Monographien zur Erdkunde 21, ²1927.

Illustrated books continue to increase in number. The fault with most of them is that the pictures are described either inadequately or not at all. Older books are: L. Preiss and P. Rohrbach, *Palästina und das Ostjordanland*, 1925; P. Volz, *64 Bilder aus dem Heiligen Lande*, n.d. A modern presentation, with good pictures but inadequate comment on them, is L. H. Grollenberg, *Atlas of the Bible*, 1957. Of the three illustrated books by H. Bardtke, *Zu beiden Seiten des Jordans*, 1958; *Vom Roten Meer zum See Genezareth*, 1962; and *Vom Nildelta zum Sinai*, 1967, the last is the most original. H. Cazelles, J. Bottéro, E. Lessing et. al., *Vérité et poésie de la Bible*, 1969, contains a series of fascinating colour pictures. H. Guthe, *Bibelatlas*, ²1926, is still unsurpassed for its historical cartography; more recent works are: H. G. May and G. N. S. Hunt (eds.), *Oxford Bible Atlas*, ²1974; *Atlas of Israel, Cartography, Physical Geography, History, Demography, Economics, Education*, ²1970; D. Baly and A. D. Tushingham, *Atlas of the Biblical World*, 1971.

For the exact location of sites in Palestine the '1 : 100,000 South Levant Series', provided with a special grid, will be found useful; the Israeli edition (24 sheets) '1 : 100,000 Palestine' is overprinted with modern Hebrew place names. There are details of older maps in Noth, *Old Testament World*, 2f.

NOTES

1. The Lebanon in the west and the Antilebanon in the east, divided from the former by plains (*el-beqāʿ*). A full description, of course limited to the modern state of Syria, is to be found in E. Wirth, *Syrien*, Wissenschaftliche Länderkunden, Vols. 4/5, 1971.

2. The *qara ṣū* and the *ʿafrīn* flow into the Orontes from the Amanus mountains lying to the east. They join it at almost its most northerly point. They draw their waters largely from the marshy plain of *el-ʿamq* and the Lake of Antioch.

3. It is the deepest depression on earth, almost 1300 feet below sea level.

4. In the wilderness areas proper, rainfall is less than four inches per year; it is four to ten inches in the steppe and ten to twenty inches in areas nearer to cultivated land. This distinction is made on the instructive map of North Syria in R. de Vaux, 'Les patriarches hébreux et les découvertes modernes', *RB* 56, 1949, 13. There is similar information, though with less differentiation, in the basic study by R. Gradmann, *Die Steppen des Morgenlandes in ihrer Bedeutung für die Geschichte der Menschlichen Gesittung*, Geogr. Abh. 3, 6, 1934, 22ff., with accompanying maps; id., 'Palästinas Urlandschaft', *ZDPV* 57, 1934, 161–85.

5. Present source material has led to different estimates of the date and extent of the rearing and use of camels among the Semites. The camel may have been used for riding and as a beast of burden at least in some instances in the early second millennium; a marked increase is attested only towards the end of the second millennium. The problem has often been discussed. Cf. the brief survey in J. Henninger, *Über Lebensraum und Lebensformen der Frühsemiten*, AGF-G 151, 1968, 24–8; id., in *Viehwirtschaft und Hirtenkultur*, Ethnographische Studien, ed. L. Foldes, 1969, 33–68.

6. There are numerous monographs on Semitic nomads. Surveys are to be found in: J. Henninger, *Frühsemiten*; M. Weippert, *The Settlement of the Israelite Tribes in Palestine*, SBT II 21, 1971, 102–26; R. de Vaux, *Ancient Israel*, 1965, 3–18. Investigations prompted by the Mari letters have been particularly important: J.-R. Kupper, *Les nomades en Mésopotamie au temps des rois de Mari*, 1957; M. Rowton, 'The Physical Environment and the Problem of the Nomads', in *XVᵉ Rencontre Assyriologique Internationale, Liège 1966*, 1967, 109–21. Cf. also S. Moscati, *The Semites in Ancient History*, 1959; the symposium *Das Verhältnis von Bodenbauern und Viehzüchtern in historischer Sicht*, Deutsche Akademie der Wissenschaften zu Berlin, Institut für Orientforschung, Veröffentlichung no.69, 1968, reports on similar phenomena in other cultural areas.

7. R. Gradmann, *Die Steppen des Morgenlandes*, 59.

8. The concept of 'Proto-Semitic' is used by H. Bauer and P. Leander, *Historische*

Grammatik der hebräischen Sprache des Alten Testaments, 1922, reprinted 1965, as one of the main themes of their researches. The results, however, are often hypothetical. Closely related to the question of Proto-Semitic is that of the 'Proto-Semites' and their homeland. To introduce some differentiation into these extremely problematical considerations, ethnologists have recently begun to distinguish between the 'primal homeland' and the 'centre of diffusion': the earliest tangible sphere of diffusion is separated from what seem to be the earliest settlements. J. Henninger, *Über Lebensraum und Lebensformen der Frühsemiten*, cf. esp. 8–13, therefore uses the substitute term 'early Semites'.

9. This is the largely accepted view. There is a brief account of other theories (with an extensive bibliography) in J. Henninger, op. cit., 9–13.

10. Further details of Semitic languages are to be found in B. Spuler (ed.), Handbuch der Orientalistik, Vol. 3, *Semitistik*, ²1964; Vol. 2, *Keilschriftforschung und alte Geschichte Vorderasiens*, sections 1 and 2, esp. fasc. 1, *Das Sumerische*, ²1964; fasc. 3, *Akkadische Grammatik. Einzelstudien in Linguistica Semitica*, Studi Semitici 4, Rome 1961. Cf. also the introductions of relevant grammars; for Hebrew, R. Meyer, *Hebräische Grammatik* I, ³1966, 1–5; for linguistic relationships in Syria in connection with historical factors see A. Alt, *Kleine Schriften zur Geschichte des Volkes Israel* (= *KS*) III, ²1968, 25–42; for North-west Semitic see E. Y. Kutscher, 'Contemporary Studies in North-Western Semitic', *JSS* 10, 1965, 21–51.

11. Further details of the extent of the country and its inhabitants appear in M. Noth, *The Old Testament World*, 1966, 24–7. It need only be mentioned in passing that since the foundation of the modern state of Israel there have been considerable changes in the use of land and in the make-up of the population. This development is likely to continue.

12. The Dead Sea is up to 1300 feet deep at the northern end; the southern part, from about the *el-lisān* peninsula on, is extremely shallow.

13. The Nebo traditions proper, however, are attached to a point rather further west of *en-neba*, called *rās es-siyāga*; with a height of 2307 feet, it affords a good view.

14. About 52 miles from north to south and up to 9 miles wide. Its surface is about 575 square miles.

15. The salinity is about six times that of our oceans (between 20% and 26%); magnesium chloride and calcium chloride also predominate.

16. Even by Herod the Great shortly before his death (4 BC). Remains of old buildings can still be seen at modern *'ēn ez-zāra*. H. Donner, 'Kallirrhoe', *ZDPV* 79, 1963, 59–89.

17. Num. 21.20; 23.14; 34.1, etc.

18. O. Plöger, 'Die makkabäischen Burgen', *ZDPV* 71, 1955, 141–72, reprinted in O. Plöger, *Aus der Spätzeit des Alten Testaments*, Studien, 1971, 102–33, where there is also a discussion of the fourth of the constructions discussed here, the Alexandreion (*qarn ṣarṭabe*), near to the mouth of the *wādi fār'a*.

19. Josh. 10.10; cf. also I Macc. 3. 13ff.; 7. 1ff. For the route and significance of the Beth-horon road see T. Oelgarte, 'Die Bethhoronstrasse', *PJB* 14, 1918, 73–89, and plates 6 and 7.

20. Its Old Testament name is *yām kinneret* (after a place Kinnereth on the north-western side above the site of later Capernaum, Num. 34.11; Josh. 12.3; 13.27). The designation 'Lake Gennesaret' is principally supported by the New Testament (cf. esp. Luke 5.1), and probably derives from the name of the small plain on the west side of the lake, which is called Gennesar (thus in Josephus, the Talmud and I Macc. 11.67). The lake is also called Lake Tiberias (*baḥret ṭabarīye*), after the city of Tiberias (*ṭabarīye*). It is 12 miles long and about 6 miles wide at the broadest point; it is almost 700 feet below sea level.

21. R. Gradmann, *Die Steppen des Morgenlandes*, 55ff.; on the problem of desiccation in Asia Minor see most recently K. W. Butzer, 'Late Glacial and Postglacial Climatic Variation in the Near East', *Erdkunde* 11, 1957, 21–35; H. von Wissmann, 'Ursprungsherde und

Ausbreitungswege von Pflanzen- und Tierzucht und ihre Abhängigkeit von der Klima-
geschichte', ibid., 81–94, 175–93. The most important result of recent research is that with
minor deviations the climate remained constant from about 2400 BC, J. Henninger,
Frühsemiten, 10f.

22. Pliny, *Hist. nat.* V, 72; see J. Partsch, 'Über den Nachweis einer Klimaänderung der
Mittelmeerländer in geschichtlicher Zeit', *Verhandlungen des 8. Deutschen Geographen-
Tages*, 1889, 124f.; id., 'Palmyra, eine historisch-klimatische Studie', *Berichte über die
Verhandlungen der Sächsischen Akademie der Wissenschaften*, phil.-hist. Kl. 74, 1, 1922, 2–4;
Gradmann, *Die Steppen*, 58.

23. In one place the Old Testament even applies the phrase to Egypt (Num.16.13). Cf.
H. Guthe, *Palästina*, ²1927, 50–73; see also the impressive account of conditions in
Palmyra and Damascus from a geographical and climatic aspect by I. Burton, cited in
Partsch, *Palmyra*, 16f.

The Time

IT IS POSSIBLE without too much difficulty to project the outlines of historical movements in the area which has just been described. With varying degrees of intensity, they remained the same over the millennia, right down to the Christian period. One direction of movement was from the wilderness of Arabia and Syria in a north-easterly, northern and north-westerly direction into the adjoining cultivated lands. Following the rhythm of changing pastures, or concentrating in aggressive groups, elements of population from the wilderness and the adjoining steppe took possession of fertile and cultivable areas, either in the broad plains of Mesopotamia or in the hill-country of Syria and Palestine. The latter was in some respects more arduous. Another movement took precisely the opposite course. From time to time the 'mountain people' invaded from the north-east, north and north-west. They came from the highlands of Iran/Persia, what later became Armenia and Asia Minor, down into the plains of Mesopotamia and the cultivated land of Syria and Palestine. The corridor formed by the latter meant that it was equally exposed to a threat from the south, when the kings of Egypt were intent on expansion. They were able to launch an invasion through the Sinai peninsula, and at the peak of their power penetrated beyond the Euphrates.

Such considerable expansions could elevate particular nations to the status of 'world powers', at least within the framework of the international politics of the time, for shorter or longer periods. This happened for the first time in the seventh century BC, when the Assyrians were able to penetrate as far as Egypt. A century later the Babylonians made a similar show of power, but they had to halt before the gates of Egypt. The Persians again gained control of an empire which included Egypt, the most extensive realm acquired by a nation in the Near East; this, however, fell victim to the armies of Alexander. The Roman empire had variable success in governing the East. After the seventh century AD, finally, it was the Arabs under the banner of Mohammed who won over the territories with which we are concerned. This last aggressive thrust from Arab lands also went far beyond the 'fertile crescent'.

When Israel first entered on the scene among these movements, towards the end of the first millennium BC, a number of momentous changes in the balance of power were taking place. We can only fully understand their importance if we also see the situation from which they developed and the events which led up to them. This is an essential preliminary towards understanding Israel in the context of the history of the ancient Near East. Brief reference must therefore be made to the beginning of this history.

General accounts of the history of the ancient Near East, or parts of it, often vary considerably in scope and quality. Over the last few decades the number available has risen astonishingly. Here only a few important works will be mentioned, which provide further bibliographies. 1. General accounts: A. Scharff/A. Moortgat, *Ägypten und Vorderasien im Altertum*, [3]1962; Fischer, *Weltgeschichte*, Vols. 2–4: *Die Altorientalischen Reiche* I–III, 1965–67; cf. also Vols. 5–8: *Die Mittelmeerwelt im Altertum* I–IV. The *Cambridge Ancient History*, revised edition of Vols. I and II, 1962ff., is appearing in individual fascicles; it provides a detailed treatment by periods, and takes into account the archaeological material, giving extensive bibliographies. The periods of the history of the ancient Near East are described in more general accounts of world history, though more superficially than in the works listed above and often within much wider terms of reference; see in particular the relevant volumes of the Propyläen Weltgeschichte and the Saeculum Weltgeschichte; a classical account is E. Meyer, *Geschichte des Altertums*, 5 vols. in 8, reprinted 1965–69.

Monographs on the history of particular countries and peoples are as follows: E. Otto, *Ägypten – der Weg des Pharaonenreiches*, [4]1966; A. H. Gardiner, *Egypt of the Pharaohs*, [3]1962; E. Drioton and J. Vandier, *L'Égypte*, [4]1962; W. Wolf, *Das alte Ägypten*, 1971; W. Helck, *Geschichte des alten Ägypten*, Handbuch der Orientalistik, Div. 1, Vol. 1, Section 3, 1968; H. Schmökel, *Geschichte des alten Vorderasien*, Handbuch der Orientalistik, Div. 1, Vol. 2, Section 3, 1957; W. Helck, *Die Beziehungen Ägyptens zu Vorderasien im 3. und 2. Jahrtausend v. Chr.*, Ägyptologische Abhandlungen, Vol. 5, [2]1971.

Accounts of cultural history: H. Kees, *Ägypten*, 1933; A. Goetze, *Kleinasien*, [2]1957 (both volumes appeared in the Handbuch der Altertumswissenschaft); H. Schmökel, *Kulturgeschichte des Alten Orient*, 1961; S. Moscati, *Storia e civiltà dei Semiti*, 1957.

The foundation of the power relationships which were later to be expressed in imperial terms goes back to the third millennium BC in both Egypt and Mesopotamia. By tradition, the primal datum of Egyptian history is the 'union of the two lands', Upper and Lower Egypt, under king Menes.[1] This took place rather earlier than the decisive rise of Sumerian civilization in southern Mesopotamia, at the beginning of the third millennium. In Mesopotamia, the victory of king Sargon I over the Sumerian Lugalzaggisi (about 2350 BC) is an equally decisive foundation for further developments. Sargon I was part of one of those great Semitic movements invading from the Arabian wilderness; under his leadership it attained independent rule in Akkad. Of course it must be conceded that the

Semites of Akkad did not achieve the impressive degree of state unity to be found at the same period in Egypt during the Third to Sixth Dynasties, in the so-called Old Kingdom (about 2650–2200 BC). This was the time when Egypt's most impressive symbols, the pyramids of Giza, were already being built. However, the cultural contributions made in both regions are not to be underestimated. The first complete systems of writing were developed in both areas almost simultaneously, though they were quite different from one another;[2] other contributions were made in the sphere of graphic art and in the technical and mathematical treatment of numerous questions.[3]

Crises began to arise towards the year 2000, which were not originally connected. While Egypt was undergoing a period of severe internal unrest (the so-called First Intermediate Period, from about 2200–2050 BC), a new Semitic wave of extraordinary complexity was advancing not only on Mesopotamia, but also on Syria and Palestine. It is widely known as 'Amorite' in academic literature, but unfortunately this term is ambivalent.[4] Consequently the term 'West Semite', which has also become a convention, is to be preferred, for all the arguments that can be advanced against it.[5] The struggles between Mesopotamian rulers which broke out in the first centuries of the second millennium are extremely confused; they are connected with the advance of the West Semites on the one hand and the invasion of Elamite tribes on the other. The dynasties of Isin and Larsa attained particular heights of power. However, all the rival forces were finally put in the shade by the Semites of the so-called First Dynasty of Babylon, whose sixth king Hammurabi (1728–1686 BC), famous for his collection of laws, overcame Rimsin of Larsa and ended the rule of Mari (*tell ḥarīri*) on the central Euphrates.[6] It should not, however, be forgotten that the same period saw the first significant beginnings of Assyria, a new Mesopotamian centre of power which developed on the Tigris and went on to threaten even Babylon. Of course, its great hour in world history only came at a later date.[7]

Meanwhile, shortly after the year 2000 BC, Egypt had returned to a state of relative stability which lasted through the so-called Middle Kingdom (1991–1786 BC). At this time events in Mesopotamia had no effect down by the Nile: this was to come later.[8] Egypt reconstructed its considerable administrative system and developed it further; its chief military successes were against the Nubians in the south. However, the end of the Middle Kingdom was engineered by forces from Semitic territory; the invaders are termed 'rulers of the foreign lands' (*ḥq3.w ḫ3sw.t*) in Egyptian, an expression more familiar in its Greek form, 'Hyksos'. The origin of the Hyksos is still disputed. The most probable solution to the question will be that which does most justice to the varied ethnic, political and military situation in the first half of the second millennium. In this case, it seems very likely that the so-called Hyksos movement was composed of West Semitic groups which were already making successive incursions into the eastern delta of the Nile from Syria and Palestine during the Middle Kingdom. However, it can be shown that Hurrian elements, coming to Syria from the north, were also involved. This association of West Semites and Hurrians evidently enabled a small ruling class first to establish independent rule in the northern areas of Lower Egypt, and then to extend it into Upper Egypt. This means that the so-called Hyksos invasion of Egypt was not a single aggression, but a long-drawn-out process.[9] It explains on the one hand the presence of Semitic elements in Egypt as early as the Middle Kingdom,[10] and on the other hand the way in which the Hyksos, with their limited sphere of influence, could gradually rise to power. They were unable to sustain their position and in general had no tangible influence on Egyptian culture as a whole. The deposition of the Hyksos in Egypt, which is usually described as an 'expulsion',[11] brought to an end the so-called Second Intermediary Period, which is reckoned as being from the decline of the Middle Kingdom during the Thirteenth Dynasty (from 1785 BC) down to the end of the Seventeenth Dynasty.

With the Eighteenth Dynasty (1580–1314 BC) the Egyptians were able to rise again to the brilliance of their New Kingdom (1580–1085 BC). This was the period of great expansion, during which they succeeded even in subjecting Palestine and large areas of Syria for centuries. Almost all the significant Pharaohs of the New Kingdom, the most famous names among whom are Thutmoses III, Amenophis II, Thutmoses IV, Sethos I and Rameses II, fought in Syria and Palestine and maintained these northernmost Egyptian possessions. Ultimately, however, this was only possible for them as long as they were not involved with forces who disputed their advance. These new powers, which began to emerge about the middle of the second millennium, were the so-called mountain peoples, centred in the highlands from Elam to Asia Minor.[12] The Cassites, whose derivation is still uncertain, penetrated as far as Babylon; a second large group was the Hurrians (*Hurri*) who invaded northern Mesopotamia. The most significant contribution of the latter was the formation of the kingdom of the Mitanni,[13] which in turn was the starting-point for further expansion extending at least as far as Syria. The Mitanni brought the Assyrians to a nadir of their history in the fifteenth century BC when they even made them dependent. About 1365 BC the kingdom of the Mitanni was overthrown by the Hittites, the third great group of peoples,[14] enabling the Assyrians once again to rise to power. At the same time the Hittites came so far south that they clashed with the Egyptians. The two spheres of interest met in Syria. Finally, a now-famous battle took place at Kadesh on the Orontes (*tell nebi mend*) between Pharaoh Rameses II (*c.* 1290–1223 BC)[15] and the Hittite king Muwatallis. Extensive Egyptian documents and Hittite sources give different accounts of the outcome of this encounter. Both powers measured their strength and did not venture any further moves. A little later the Egyptians under Rameses III and the Hittites under Hattusilis III came to an agreement in the hitherto unique form of a regular peace treaty, and gave assurances of peaceful relations in the future.[16] The time seemed to have come for north and south to maintain a balance of power, and a policy embracing the whole of the ancient Near East seemed in sight. Within this balance of power, peace and order appeared possible.

But this situation was not to last. The last centuries of the second millennium saw the rise and appearances of completely new forces, to which the Hittite empire very soon succumbed.[17] The 'Sea-peoples' invaded the eastern Mediterranean from the west, possibly from different parts of Greece and Italy.[18] The highly-developed Cretan-Minoan civilization most probably fell victim to their aggression on land and water; they penetrated Asia Minor as far as Syria and threatened Egypt from the west by setting some of the peoples of Libya in motion against Lower Egypt. Almost simultaneously with this conquest by the Sea-peoples from the west, a new Semitic wave began to take possession of the cultivated regions from the interior, moving in from the wilderness of Arabia and Syria. These were Aramaean tribes who spread out right over the fertile crescent and laid claim to rule the territory between Syria and Babylon. Here was a new crisis for Babylon and Assyria; the balance of power in Syria and Palestine was completely changed. Under Egyptian domination, individual cities and city states had managed to flourish relatively easily, as is indicated by the letters from the archives of Amenophis III and Amenophis IV (Akenaten) found at *tell el-'amārna* in Middle Egypt[19] and from the excavations at Ugarit (*rās shamra*) in northern Syria.[20] Now, however, elements of the Sea-peoples increasingly gained ground, especially in the coastal areas. Among them were the Philistines, who established themselves on the Palestinian coastal plain without any Egyptian resistance worth mentioning; by contrast, the hilly interior stood open to the Aramaeans, who soon founded their own city states in Syria. To the south, in Palestine, a unique development took place. Here the land east and west of the Jordan was taken over successively, and not without resistance, by those tribes and groups of tribes who were ultimately to become a unity under the name 'Israel'. There finally emerges from their midst king David, who both founded an empire and increased its extent. However complex his apparatus of state may have been, he is the first figure in early Israel who has to be taken seriously in world politics; after conquering the Philistines he united Palestine in a single power complex and was even successful in extending his sphere of influence into Syria. This made Israel a factor in world politics for the first time. It is clear how David was aided by the contemporary world situation. In the south, Egypt had been weakened through battles with the Sea-peoples and Libyan demands, added to which the kingdom had now split apart into two halves with separate rulers.[21] In the north, the Sea-peoples had shattered the power of the Hittites, Syria had been torn apart by the Sea-peoples and the Aramaeans, the Assyrians were threatened by the creation of Aramaean states and the Babylonians were too weak for independent political and military initiatives. In the context of this break-up of power, in which it too had a share, after various tribulations Israel began to become a nation. It was able to assert its national existence through a series of crises, though not for an unlimited period. All too quickly the initiative grasped by David for the young state was taken away and passed on in a north-easterly direction, first to the Syrians, then to the Assyrians and finally to the Babylonians, who caused Israel its greatest crisis. Only the generous imperial policy of the Persians saved Israel from going under completely. At one time or another, in their most successful efforts at expansion, all these powers plundered Israel as a whole or in part. They had to fight hard for predominance over neighbouring states and peoples and defend it once it had been achieved. The narrow corridor between the great powers, the strip of cultivated land on the east coast of the Mediterranean which makes up Syria and Palestine, remained a through route and for that reason was sought after by these powers. Confronted with them, the petty local potentates could never put up resistance for long.

This is the stage for the history of ancient Israel. Israel's territory and its potential as a world power were necessarily limited. Its fate was bound up in a network of unavoidable dependent relationships. However, what took place almost in a corner of the world and its history was to have far more influence on world history than might ever have been suspected. Tiny Israel, historically weak and really insignificant, unleashed forces which were stronger than any calculations in world politics. This Israel became a phenomenon pointing beyond itself and raising in paradigmatic fashion the fundamental question of the nature of historical existence. The answer to that question seems to lie beyond any understanding which merely registers causal connections.

NOTES

1. Later Egyptians believed that king 'Menes' stood at the beginning of their history. The Egyptian king-lists began with him, and these have been confirmed by the Greek tradition, i.e. by extracts from Manetho's history of Egypt. Our division of Egyptian kings into dynasties goes back to Manetho. For the historical problems of the beginning of Egyptian history see W. Helck, *Geschichte*, 24–39; for problems of tradition see S. Morenz, 'Traditionen um Menes', *ZÄS* 99, 1972, x–xvi.

2. In Egypt hieroglyphics, and in Mesopotamia cuneiform. For a first introduction see A. Erman, *Die Hieroglyphen*, [2]1923; B. Meissner, *Die Keilschrift*, [3]1967, which are still instructive. More recent works are: S. Schott, *Hieroglyphen*, 1950; G. R. Driver, *Semitic Writing from Pictograph to Alphabet*, The Schweich Lectures 1944, [2]1954; Handbuch der Orientalistik, Vol. 1, Section 1, *Ägyptische Schrift und Sprache*, 1959; Vol. 2, Sections 1 and 2, fasc. 1, *Das Sumerische*, 1964, 1–13.

3. See A. Scharff, *Die Frühkulturen Ägyptens und Mesopotamiens*, Der Alte Orient (AO), Vol. 41, 1941; id., *Wesensunterschiede ägyptischer und vorderasiatischer Kunst*, AO, Vol. 42, 1943; W. von Soden refers to scientific achievements in Mesopotamia, especially the lists transmitted there, in *Die Welt als Geschichte* 2, 1936, 417ff. and *Sitzungsberichte der Österreichischer Akademie der Wissenschaften*, Phil.-hist. Kl., Vol. 235, 1, 1966, 3–33.

4. *amurru(m)* in Akkadian means 'the land in the west', so that the name can be applied sometimes to west Mesopotamia, sometimes to Syria and the Syrian wilderness, and even as a designation for nomadic groups in this area. The inner cohesion of the so-called Amorite movement after the year 2000 has chiefly been recognized from common features of nomenclature which still provide the most important support for describing the whole movement. The most important literature is: S. Moscati, *I predecessori d'Israele, Studi sulle più antiche genti semitiche in Siria e Palestina*, 1956; D. O. Edzard, *Die 'Zweite Zwischenzeit' Babyloniens*, 1957; J.-R. Kupper, *Les nomades en Mésopotamie au temps des rois de Mari*, 1957. T. Bauer, *Die Ostkanaanäer. Eine philologisch-historische Untersuchung über die Wanderschicht der sogenannten 'Amoriter' in Babylonien*, 1926, is a basic study, though its

interpretation of the material is controversial. K. M. Kenyon describes the situation in Palestine and Syria on the basis of archaeological material in 'Syria and Palestine *c.*2160–1780 BC', *CAH* I, ch. 21, 1965, 38–61; see also C. H. J. de Geus, *UF* 3, 1971, 41–60. Some of the Canaanite inhabitants of Palestine are called 'Amorites' in the Old Testament. However, this is connected with a state Amurru in Syria, for which there is evidence in the fourteenth and thirteenth centuries BC; its inhabitants were incorporated into the pre-Israelite population of Canaan; cf. R. de Vaux, *The Early History of Israel*, 1978, 67f.

5. Cf. S. Moscati, *The Semites in Ancient History*, 1959, 57.

6. More than 20,000 cuneiform tablets were discovered in the royal palace at Mari, which was excavated by A. Parrot between 1933 and 1939. Not all of them have yet been published. They are extremely instructive for the history of the whole period and are also relevant to certain Old Testament questions (movements of nomadic groups, prophecy, law). Between 1933 and 1963 A. Parrot directed 13 campaigns of excavation in all. Texts are published in A. Parrot–G. Dossin, *Archives royales de Mari*, 9 vols, 1946–60. See especially W. von Soden in *WO* I, 3, 1948, 187–204; I, 5, 1950, 397–403; J. R. Kupper, *Les nomades*, 1957; *XVe Rencontre assyriologique internationale, Liège 1966 : La civilisation de Mari*, 1967.

7. W. von Soden, *Der Aufstieg des Assyrerreiches als geschichtliches Problem*, AO 37, 1, 2, 1937.

8. For the whole period see G. Posener, J. Bottéro, K. M. Kenyon, 'Syria and Palestine *c.* 2160–1780 BC', *CAH* I, ch. 21, 1965; W. C. Hayes, 'The Middle Kingdom in Egypt', *CAH* I, ch.20, 1961. H. E. Winlock, *The Rise and Fall of the Middle Kingdom in Thebes*, 1947, is a specialist study; the period of transition between the Old Kingdom and the Middle Kingdom was a classic period for Egyptian literature, G. Posener, *Littérature et Politique dans l'Égypte de la XIIe dynastie*, 1956.

9. A. Alt emphatically favoured the 'local' thesis, that Syria and Palestine were the main area of recruitment for the Hyksos, in contrast to earlier views that there was a Hyksos empire (for which there is no evidence), which was often sought far to the north of Syria. See Alt's 'Die Herkunft der Hyksos in neuer Sicht' (1954), *KS* III, 72–98. W. Helck sees the Hyksos as part of a great Hurrian expansion; he gives reasons for his view and defends it in *Die Beziehungen Ägyptens zu Vorderasien*, ²1971, 89–106; cf. also W. Helck, *Geschichte*, 113–40. R. de Vaux, *Early History*, 75–81, agrees with Alt in seeing Palestine as the starting-point for the Hyksos.

10. G. Posener, 'Les Asiatiques en Égypte sous les XIIe et XIIIe dynasties', *Syria* 34, 1957, 145–63.

11. Cf. the restrained remarks by T. G. H. James, 'Egypt: From the Expulsion of the Hyksos to Amenophis I', *CAH* II, ch.8, 1965, 9f.

12. Indo-Germanic elements entered the Near East among their number. This is true, above all, of the Hittites. However, we already find the phenomenon of regular cavalry (*maryannu*) among the Hurrians as part of a dominant Indo-Iranian ruling class there. The Hurrians will be primarily responsible for the spread of the horse as an animal used in war; at first it was predominantly used with chariots. This took place from the middle of the second millennium on. See R. Hauschild, *Über die frühesten Arier im Alten Orient*, BVSAW, phil.-hist. Kl. 106, 6, 1962.

13. Probably under the leadership of the Indo-Iranian (Arian) ruling class within the Hurrians, Hauschild, op. cit., 1of.

14. A. Goetzê, *Hethiter, Churriter und Assyrer*, 1936; id., *Kulturgeschichte des Alten Orients, Kleinasien*, ²1957; R. Hauschild, *Die indogermanischen Völker und Sprachen Kleinasiens*, SSAW, Phil.-hist. Kl.109, 1, 1964.

15. The chronology of this period is still under research. E. Hornung, *Untersuchungen zur Chronologie und Geschichte des Neuen Reiches*, Ägyptologische Abhandlungen, Vol.11, 1964.

16. The original text was engraved in cuneiform on a silver plate; we know of two copies on monuments in Egypt (in Karnak and in the mausoleum of Rameses II, the Ramesseum); there is also a copy on a clay tablet from Boğazköy – Hattusa, the capital of the Hittite empire. The two texts are compared by S. Langdon and A. H. Gardiner, *JEA* 6, 1920, 179–205; see also *ANET*, 199–201.

17. H. Otten, *Neue Quellen zum Ausklang des Hethitischen Reiches*, MDO 94, 1963, 1ff.

18. P. Mertens, 'Les Peuples de la Mer', *Chronique d'Égypte* 35, 1960, 65–88; G. A. Wainwright, 'Some Sea Peoples', *JEA* 47, 1961, 71–90; W. Helck, *Beziehungen*, ²1971, 224–34; W. F. Albright, 'Syria, the Philistines and Phoenicia', *CAH* II, ch.33, 1966, 24–33; R. D. Barnett, 'The Sea Peoples', *CAH* II, ch. 28, 1969.

19. The significance of the Amarna letters for the history of Syria and Palestine has been stressed in countless studies. See the literature listed in *ANET*, 483, and the work by A. Alt, not mentioned there, in *KS* I, 89–175; III, 57–71; 99–140; 158–75. There is a summary in W. F. Albright, 'The Amarna Letters from Palestine', *CAH* II, ch. 20, 1966.

20. However, hardly any real historical texts have appeared in Ugarit; apart from administrative documents, the texts have been largely religious and mythical. For the first decade of research see O. Eissfeldt (ed.), *Ras Schamra und Sanchunjaton*, 1939. The texts are essential for an understanding of Canaanite religion; there is still controversy over the degree to which they further the understanding of Old Testament texts. See J. Gray, *The Legacy of Canaan. The Ras Shamra Texts and their Relevance to the Old Testament*, SVT 5, 1957; the Ugaritic material is now treated in a wider context by H. Gese, *Die Religionen Altsyriens, Altarabiens und der Mandäer*, Die Religionen der Menschheit, Vol. 10, 2, 1970.

21. In the Twenty-first Dynasty, from about 1085, Thebes was the centre of southern Upper Egypt and Tanis the capital of northern Lower Egypt. The difficult conditions at the end of the Egyptian New Kingdom and the transition to the late Egyptian period are discussed in J. Černý, 'Egypt from the Death of Ramesses III to the End of the Twenty-first Dynasty', CAH II, ch. 35, 1965.

Witnesses and Evidence

IT HAS ONLY been possible to give a comprehensive survey of the history of the ancient Near East and the role played in it by Israel since international oriental scholars have discovered, investigated and interpreted a great variety of source material. This has happened over the last generation. The material comprises not only an abundance of texts, but also cultural artefacts which were only brought to light through excavations. We begin with the latter.

No matter where it begins, archaeological work in Syria and Palestine is involved in a variety of remains from every period of the long history of these countries. The first things which strike the eye of the visitor to Palestine chiefly testify to its more recent history: the enormous buildings constructed by the civilization of Islam, some monuments witnessing to the period of the Crusades, and above all ruins from the Graeco-Roman period, like the Roman theatres in Amman, Gerasa and and Bosrah. It is also possible to recognize the plans of Roman cities, some of which have been reconstructed, the remains of ancient waterworks and in favourable circumstances milestones from the old Roman roads.[1] Hardly any buildings worth mentioning survive from an earlier period. As a rule, pre-Hellenistic material has first to be brought to light by systematic excavation. There is only one exception: fragments of early pottery can be found (or could be found up to the middle of the present century) on the surface at the sites of old ruins, often in astonishing concentrations, where modern methods had not yet been adopted. With luck it has been possible even to find sherds from the Bronze Age.

Down to the Hellenistic period, Palestine largely shared in the same cultural development as Syria. The chief periods were as follows:[2]

Prehistoric periods

Early Stone Age (Palaeolithic)	down to 9000 BC
Middle Stone Age (Mesolithic)	9000–7000
Late Stone Age (Neolithic)	7000–3600
Copper Stone Age (Chalcolithic)	3600–3100

Historical periods

Early Bronze Age	3100–2000

Middle Bronze Age	2000–1550
Late Bronze Age	1550–1200
Iron Age I	1200–900
II	900–600
III	600–300
Hellenistic period	300–63 BC
Roman-Byzantine period	63 BC–AD 636
Islamic period	from AD 636

We know of pottery from at least the Neolithic period. Study of it plays a dominant role in the archaeology of Palestine in determining the dates of early sites. Historical topography makes a considerable contribution towards the reconstruction of historical events, as it is able to illuminate periods of settlements and their crucial points; it also makes possible inferences about particular features of the distribution of population. Because the history of the country has been so eventful and varied, it is desirable also to investigate the more distant sites because of their former significance. Not all the biblical sites have preserved the same name down to the present, even when they have been occupied subsequently. Some places were destroyed or abandoned, biblical names disappeared or were attached to a new foundation away from the old ruins. The Arabic place names used today do not always go back to biblical models. Countless new sites have contributed towards confusing the picture of historical topography. These difficulties need to be noted. A great many expedients and calculations are necessary for a reliable reconstruction of the network of ancient sites.[3] Mention in the Bible or, if possible, in other contemporary documents, offers the first step towards establishing the site of a place which is no longer known; onomastica, itineraries and reports afford more certainty, but do not provide a final answer. Thus in cases of doubt, an investigation of the site itself is indispensable. If a place was settled in at a later period, and perhaps was given a name similar to that in the Bible, at least a beginning has been made. If no excavations are possible because of extensive settlements, fragments of pottery may give some indication of the date of the settlement. Scholars attach most importance, however, to the mountains of debris which conceal the remains of abandoned sites, unconnected with any modern settlement. In Arabic, these hills, which are easily recognizable for what they are, are called *tell* (plural *tulūl*), or *ḫirbe*, if the remains of walls can still be clearly recognized. Both designations are often connected with proper names, from which it is possible to draw conclusions about biblical sites.[4] When interest is concentrated on such a *tell*, for historical or topographical reasons, any pottery which may be lying around is of decisive significance in making a first assessment of the age and extent of the old site. If the sherds lying on the surface go back as far as the earliest period of the civilization of the area, it is possible to conclude with a fair degree of certainty that the place was founded in an early period. Sometimes it may even be identified with a biblical location. Sometimes, however, a number of ruins may make it more difficult to decide in favour of one particular place. More frequently, a lack of pottery prevents more wide-ranging conclusions. It follows from this that the distribution of pottery can be an extraordinarily important indication of the age and importance of a site; often it is the only evidence of a particular territorial history. Of course, pottery cannot be an independent historical source. Nevertheless, a sum of observations can at least contribute towards the reconstruction of greater events. When taken in conjunction with written sources, the evaluation of pottery discovered on the surface attains the status of an almost indispensable supportive discipline.[5]

However difficult it may be to establish all the details of historical topography in particular instances, we do have a sufficiently reliable picture of even the earlier settlement of the country to locate the chief historical movements with some degree of certainty. Nevertheless, it is useful to know at least the basic reasons why it may be difficult to establish the location of a small place.[6]

Unfortunately, systematic archaeological excavations have only been carried on in a limited number of places in Palestine in the course of time. Modern Palestinian archaeology only began towards the end of the last century, with the foundation of archaeological and historical societies in a number of European countries and in America. Even then, the amount of excavation carried out depended on the means at the disposal of the society and the character of its leaders.[7] On this basis, excavations which have had to be interrupted from time to time, have led to more detailed knowledge of the following biblical sites. The list extends as far as the 1960s:[8] Jerusalem (soundings in the temple court 1867–70; south-east hill 1881, 1894–97, 1923–25, 1961–65); Gezer, 1902–05, 1907–09, 1934; Taanach, 1902–03, 1904, 1963–64; Megiddo, 1903–05, 1907–09, 1934; Jericho, 1907–09, 1913–14, 1930–34, 1952–58; Samaria, 1908–10, 1931–33, 1935; Shechem, 1913ff., 1926ff., 1956ff.; Bethshean, 1921; Gibeah, 1922–23; Mizpah (?) (*tell en-naṣbe*), 1926; Shiloh, 1926, 1929; Lachish, 1932ff.; Ai, 1933–35.

Some excavations have attracted special attention in most recent times. Among them are the excavations and investigations of the site of Qumran (*ḥirbet qumrān*) and its surroundings, triggered off by the discovery of manuscripts on the north-west side of the Dead Sea in 1951–56 and 1958;[9] the extensive excavation in Jericho from 1951 to 1958, where it was possible to demonstrate at a considerable depth traces of a compact Neolithic settlement from the seventh millennium BC;[10] and excavations at Gibeon (*el-jīb*), which brought to light not only an extensive system for the supply of water but also a sort of 'winery', an 'industrial area' with facilities for storing wine jars in bell-shaped hollows in the rock. This last seems to date from the period of the Israelite monarchy.[11] Excavations in Gibeon took place between 1956 and 1962. At almost the same time (1955–58), excavations in search of ancient Hazor, undertaken on Israeli territory at *tell el-qedaḥ* (earlier called *tell waqqāṣ*) in Galilee, aroused considerable attention. These were continued in 1965 and 1968. They once again raised fundamental questions about the Old Testament tradition of the settlement of Palestine.[12] Excavations at *tell el-fār'a* (1946, 1950–51, 1954, 1958),[13] which is probably – but not certainly – to be identified with the ancient royal city of Tirzah, investigated important periods in the Middle and Late Bronze Age and also the beginning of the Iron Age.[14] Excavations on the south-east hill of Jerusalem which were begun in 1961 produced almost sensational results. They disproved earlier views that during the monarchy Jerusalem was restricted to the summit of the hill and made it almost certain that it extended down the slope towards the Kidron valley, just as the modern village of *silwān* extends down the slope opposite the south-east hill.[15]

Among most recent Israeli excavations, the greatest interest has been aroused by researches in the Negeb which have discovered ancient Arad;[16] most publicity was attracted by the archaeological investigation of the fortress of Masada on the south-west shore of the Dead Sea, from 1963 to 1965. The chief reason for this was the impact made on Israeli national feelings by the desperate resistance of the Jewish people against the Romans in AD 73.[17]

The most valuable find in any archaeological investigation is, of course, written sources. Palestine is not very well situated in this respect. Apart from a few un-important discoveries, the best-known and most important written evidence from Palestine is made up of the so-called agricultural calendar from Gezer,[18] the tablets from *tell ta'annak*[19] and Shechem,[20] the ostraca from Samaria, [21] the stele of king Mesha of Moab,[22] the inscription in the Siloam tunnel in Jerusalem[23] and the ostraca from Lachish.[24] The manuscripts found at Qumran belong to a much later period and, as far as the Old Testament is concerned, have merely confirmed the canonical writings that we already have. The real significance of Qumran arises from writings connected with the religious community which settled in Qumran between the second century BC and AD 69 and the way of life which it adopted. The documents hidden in the adjacent wilderness of Judah, principally in the *wādi murabba'āt*, chiefly come from the period of the last desperate war of the Jewish people against the Romans between AD 132 and AD 135. They are of inestimable value, but for that particular period.

It may still be asked why the material remains of Israelite and Jewish history are so relatively sparse, why they have to be laboriously extracted from the soil, and why they are only partially representative. They bear no comparison with the mighty buildings by the Nile, the Tigris and the Euphrates; no such extensive original writing has been found in Palestine as is presented by the great papyri and inscriptions of Egypt and the archives of clay tablets from Mesopotamia.[25] This is because of the historical and natural circumstances of the country. Very few centres were open to any degree of traffic. Most of them lay away from the great through routes. For all their favourable locations, Jerusalem, Shechem and Samaria are cities built in the hills. Prominent buildings may have been constructed in them during brief periods of prosperity, but they repeatedly fell victim to alien conquer-ors. Even the most significant building in the country, the Jerusalem temple, did not survive catastrophes. Both the temple of Solomon and the temple of Herod were destroyed; the splendid buildings of the Assyrian period in Samaria were rased to the ground. Sections of wall dating from the end of the Bronze Age and the first periods of the Iron Age, the chief periods of the early history of Israel, remain here and there to hint at former greatness,[26] but today they are almost unnoticeable alongside the more imposing remains from Hellenistic and Roman times. Archives were destroyed in the sack of state capitals, containing the state acts of the kings of Israel and Judah, the official correspondence of these rulers on matters of home and foreign policy. We have none of the papyri which were written in Palestine in the Old Testament period. The only writings we possess are inscribed on stone or clay, although we know from the Old Testament that scrolls were in existence.[27] Lack of care or turbulent events have led to their destruction. No writings have emerged from among the objects placed in graves. Consequently we only have very limited original written material relating to Palestine itself.

This situation makes those documents from outside Israel which can illuminate or enrich the history of Israel in some way all the more important. During their conquests, as part of their well-organized administration, the great powers kept a record of their invasions and also made reports on conditions in Palestine and the changes which took place there. This material is extensive and very varied. It comes principally from Egypt and Mesopotamia, but also from Syria and from Canaan itself. Discoveries in recent generations have been furthered not only by the increasing number of excavations in these countries, but also by the growing skill of scholars in deciphering hieroglyphic and cuneiform texts. The material extends over all the periods of Palestinian history, and consequently can also provide valuable information about Palestine in the pre-Israelite period. At the same time, events in the history of Israel itself have been confirmed either directly or indirectly and have been set in a more exact context.

Only the most important of these sources and collections of sources can be mentioned here.[28] The earliest account of conditions in Syria and Palestine is contained in the story of the Egyptian court official Sinuhe, who escaped from Egypt on the death of Amenemhet I (1991–1962 BC). He risked his life crossing the so-called 'Prince's Wall', the system of Egyptian border fortifications on the eastern side of the Nile delta, and fled into the wilderness of Sinai. For many years of his life he was exiled in Palestine and Syria. King Sesostris I pardoned him and gave him safe conduct back to Egypt.[29] The next documentation is much rougher. It consists of the so-called Execration Texts, lists of hostile rulers, tribes, countries and objects on Egyptian potsherds. The vessels on which the texts were inscribed were presumably broken deliberately, to bring about the annihilation of the persons and objects listed by means of sympathetic magic. In addition to the sherds there are small pictures of prisoners who also bear the names of foreign rulers and countries. Palestinian names, too, have been handed down to us in this way and provide an approximate picture of the principalities and districts of the time. The texts certainly come from the Middle Kingdom; whether from its beginning or its end is disputed.[30]

At the same time, we also begin to hear from Akkadian sources. Babylonian legal documents, above all the great stele of Hammurabi's law, provide material which, in a somewhat different form, was later to form the basis of Canaanite and Israelite legislation.[31] Letters from the archives of the kings of Mari on the central Euphrates report hard and wearisome struggles against invading nomads and also against Hammurabi's great opponent Shamshi-Adad I. At present, only part of the extensive material is available; it also provides instances which are significant for the assessment of early prophecy in Israel.[32]

On the invasion of the mountain people, in the period around the middle of the second millennium BC, the Akkadian sources again fall silent. This is the period of the New Kingdom in Egypt, from about 1580 BC on, the time of the great Egyptian expansion towards Syria, and Egyptian sources become more extensive. In addition to annals of individual campaigns,[33] so-called city-lists are of exceptional value for the historical topography of Palestine.[34] Here we have a genre which describes the triumphs of the Pharaohs over conquered enemy places. The great walls of Egyptian temples usually depict dramatic scenes in which the king drags behind him rows of captives, roped together, each carrying a shield, covering half the body, which bears the name of their city. In this way the Egyptian masons were able to give a vivid demonstration of the extent of the Pharaohs' conquests; at the same time they shaped the features of the captives in a way appropriate to the cities which they represented. Lists of conquered places composed in this way were left behind by kings Thutmoses III, Amenophis II, Thutmoses IV, Amenophis III, Haremheb, Sethos I, Rameses II and III, and Shishak I.[35] However, it can be demonstrated that in some cases one list is dependent on another, so that not all of them provide reliable historical information. Nevertheless, the latest of these lists, that of Pharaoh Shishak I, who invaded Palestine a short time after the death of Solomon, gives far more information about the event than can be inferred from the biblical account alone (I Kings 14.25ff.; II Chron. 12.2ff.).[36]

The extensive archive of letters from *tell el-ʿamārna*, the site of the former residence of Amenophis IV – Akenaten (1364–1347 BC), is of a very different nature. This contains the greater part of the diplomatic correspondence of Amenophis III and IV. On the whole, the letters are from Palestinian and Syrian princes and governors who are complaining to the central Egyptian administration. Unfortunately, we have none of the Pharaohs' letters in reply. The letters are written in Akkadian, the diplomatic language of the time, and provide an unusually vivid picture of political conditions in Palestine during the fourteenth century BC.[37]

The account of the travels of Wen-Amun (about 1076 BC) gives an incomparable picture of the decline of Egyptian power in Syria at the end of the New Kingdom. Wen-Amun is an Egyptian official who is visiting the Phoenician coast to purchase wood for the construction of a sacred barge in Egypt; he clashes with the local rulers and finally is threatened by ships belonging to the Sea-peoples. Unfortunately the account is incomplete.[38]

Numerous minor inscriptions from Phoenicia and Syria, some of them written in Aramaic, illuminate later developments. They give some indication of the balance of power in Syria before the Assyrian invasion.[39] From the ninth century BC on we rely chiefly on Assyrian and Babylonian sources, annals and campaign reports, which clearly reflect the *modus operandi* of these great powers and allow us to assess the foreign pressures on Israel during this period. It is important that these sources also extend beyond the Babylonian exile and illuminate the historical circumstances which led to the end of the Babylonian empire and thus to the end of the exile.[40]

The most important group of non-Israelite texts from the post-exilic period which have a bearing on the history of Israel is that of the Aramaic papyri from the Jewish military colony of Elephantine from the sixth and fifth centuries BC. They bring us evidence from Diaspora Judaism during the period of Persian supremacy – legal documents, official writings and lists – which is of particular importance not only for politics but also for religious developments.[41]

We have almost no original non-canonical documents for the period from the beginning of the fifth century to the beginning of the crisis in the second century BC, caused by the threat posed to Palestinian Judaism by Hellenism. There is nothing to illuminate the course of events. At best, arguments can be constructed to and from historically significant documents in the context of wider historical accounts.[42] In principle this is also true down to the period of the Roman conquest and occupation, the chief events of which are essentially related in the historical works of Josephus.

The term 'non-canonical' recalls the chief source for the history of Israel and the development of Judaism which has yet to be mentioned, the Old Testament and – for the later period – the Apocrypha. The omission was deliberate. The reason why this source occupies last place here is not only because of its great value but also for profound reasons relating to its content. It is quite different from all the other evidence so far mentioned. The Old Testament is a collection of sources from all periods of the history of Israel, which have been assembled not to present an unbroken history but consistently to present the acts of Yahweh, the God of Israel, who at all times showed himself to be living, present and uniquely powerful. These documents witnessing to Yahweh from about a millennium of Israelite and Jewish history have successively contributed to the formation of a vivid picture of this history. Naturally, the process of collecting and working over the individual sources underwent a long development. We encounter the results first in the form of the Pentateuch,[43] and then in the so-called Deuteronomic history work and the work of the Chronicler, two accounts which in parts are related but which have differences in emphasis.[44] These works are confirmed and complemented in a number of ways by reports from the prophetic books. The poetic books of the Old Testament by contrast offer relatively few criteria for dating the sources and contribute little to illuminating the historical development of Israel. Among the apocryphal books, the books of Maccabees enjoy the status of independent historical accounts.

It is important to note and observe within the Old Testament the pattern of historical value which can be detected in a critical examination of individual documents. This pattern is also to be found, quite naturally, in a similar way among other peoples and in other cultures. First come brief and highly pictorial pieces of poetry, from the earliest period. In the next stage they are entwined with historical saga. This forms a rounded whole and usually centres on a single person, a particular hero and his family, or even a particular object, a single city or a sanctuary. Individual scenes are combined in larger contexts and subordinated to particular themes only at a later stage. Groups of sagas emerge; the narrow framework of stories about heroes and families is expanded and comes to represent the history of larger communities. The saga tradition develops into the traditions which one day the whole people will proudly present as their national tradition. Only the growing nation, on the threshold of saga and history-writing, can contribute a sufficient degree of critical reflection on events to discover problems in the history itself. This is when history-writing proper begins, in which the account covers not only people and their actions but also the motives behind events and particular constraints which result from them. The history-writing which Israel produced in the period of David and Solomon was the first writing deserving of the name from a cultured nation; it can even claim a high degree of excellence.[45] Of course this did not mean that from this point on sagas and legends were forced to fall mute. They can, however, be clearly distinguished from the historical perspective. For the period of organized monarchies also produced official material, notes from journals and annals, lists of officials and institutions, remarks about battles and victories, about territorial gains and losses. The picture becomes increasingly clear, at least in its main features; details may continue to be obscure because of inadequate or tendentious description.

It should be remembered that this differentiation of source material may be noted in the Old Testament, but that it does not always become apparent at first glance. Careful analyses and a judicious use of form criticism are often necessary first.[46] The whole of this material has been included in the great composite works of the Pentateuch and the historical books, often without consideration of its genre, and on occasion even without regard for exact chronological sequence. For their part, the Pentateuch and the historical books were arranged in particular theological perspectives which governed the choice of material. Thus any assessment of the relationship of the patriarchs to Moses or of the giving of the law on Sinai to the rise of a legal system in Israel depends on the degree of historical reliability which is attached to each one of these traditions. This is in turn impossible without consideration of the hypothetical conditions under which these traditions arose and of the interests which they were first meant to serve. Thus the historical evaluation of every source must be preceded by a literary assessment. This is not an expression of notorious scepticism or a pseudo-scientific complication; it is the appropriate course to take in view of the state of the Old Testament sources. The aim of the method is to secure the greatest amount of true information from the sources and also to establish the basis of their theological perspective.

But why do the sources of the Old Testament in particular require such a complicated investigation? The question is a reasonable one. The procedure is required by the particular way in which the Old Testament presents its material. From a very early stage Israel believed itself to exist under divine leadership and based its judgments, with astonishing assurance, on this belief. During the course of its development it regarded the exodus from Egypt, even more than the giving of the law on Sinai, as the fundamental presupposition of its history. In reflection on the event, sometimes the oppression by a foreign power and sometimes Israel's own failure came to the forefront. But in either case, the liberating and indeed redeeming act of its God was seen here. Israel understood the occupation of the cultivated land of Palestine to be the fulfilment of a promise; it did not seek to lay claim to the land either by right of conquest or on the basis of treaties. It defended the land with a good conscience, because the land had been 'given' by Yahweh, the God of Israel, in other words by a treaty on a higher plane. It would be wrong to describe convictions of this sort as historical fictions or dogmatic prejudices. These considerations were basic to the very existence of Israel, even if they may have arisen in the first place from the sense of a threat to the people's existence. In the last resort, Israel was not seeking its own rights; its rights were grounded on an indissoluble bond with its God, who differed from the gods of the neighbouring peoples in appearing as the one who held the nation's historical destiny in his hand, rather than placing himself at their disposal in the cult.

It is almost certain that these views arose after the beginnings of Israel's history. They will have emerged as norms of historical self-assessment only after long and wearisome processes, or have been forced on Israel by historical events. But they became the norms by which Israel did judge history, and they are the norms which we meet in our sources. The conscientious historian will therefore have to be able to distinguish, or will at least have to try to distinguish, between what actually happened and what is to be attributed to an often highly pragmatic view of history. As he does this, he will not become sceptical about his sources, but he will find in the sources themselves a particular history, the history of an independent presentation and assessment of what has happened, and through this he will make a way, almost against his original limited historical concern, not only for a 'political' history of Israel but also for a history of the spiritual growth of this former people, which in this case amounts to an account of its theological development. The common view that only 'pure facts' are the appropriate and fundamental material of history is based on the delusion that there are 'pure facts', or that they can be reliably discovered in the course of historical processes. Writing history also means judging history. For who can guarantee that the motive of the 'pure fact' is also recognized by the historical writer? Concern with the history of Israel in this context may therefore confront us in paradigmatic fashion with the basic questions of historical research and historical writing.[47]

Given these presuppositions, it is out of the question that a modern history of Israel should proceed in the same manner as the first writer of a history of Israel to use the Old Testament as his source, Flavius Josephus (who died about AD 100). In the first half of his ἱστορίαι τῆς Ἰουδαικῆς Ἀρχαιολογίας⁴⁸ he essentially limited himself to retelling the events of the period from Adam, the 'first' man, to Nehemiah, the organizer of the post-exilic community, along the same lines as the account given in the Old Testament, with a few expansions and additions. By contrast, the present state of our historical knowledge, which has been increased not least by the countless non-Israelite sources which have come to light in the meantime, has compelled us to adopt a more comprehensive and in many respects a modified view of the nature of the history of Israel. The modern historian will have to make critical use of all the witnesses and evidence for this history, taking account of their particular provenance; he will have to be aware of the most recent results and methods of modern scholarship, and finally he will have to feel himself bound to the scriptures in such a way that he cannot take his work lightly, but is compelled to do justice to the πολυμερῶς καὶ πολυτρόπως in which the revelation was vouchsafed to the fathers, until it came to completion, according to the New Testament witness, in the Son (Heb. 1.1–2).

NOTES

1. The same is also true for Syria. See the very brief, but instructive survey by E. Littmann, *Ruinenstätten und Schriftdenkmäler Syriens, Länder der Turkei* 2, 1917. G. Lankester Harding, *Antiquities of Jordan*, 1959, gives important information about the part of Palestine which was Jordanian when he wrote, and about its most important archaeological sites; K.-H. Bernhardt, *Die Umwelt des Alten Testaments I, Die Quellen und ihre Erforschung*, 1967, is a full source book of non-Palestinian archaeology; H. Bardtke, *Bibel, Spaten und Geschichte*, 1969, provides an introduction to Palestinian archaeology (and also for a wider area).

2. G. E. Wright, 'The Archaeology of Palestine', in *The Bible and the Ancient Near East* (Albright Festschrift), 1961, 73–112, gives a very detailed survey; there are short accounts in Harding, op. cit., 26–53; de Vaux, *Early History*, 833. Kenyon and Lapp in particular postulate an 'Intermediate Period' after the Early Bronze Age: K. M. Kenyon, 'Syria and Palestine', in *CAH* I, ch. 21, 1965, 38–61; see also C. H. J. de Geus, 'The Amorites in the Archaeology of Palestine', *UF* 3, 1971, 41–60.

3. M. Noth uses a particular example to explain the difficulties in 'Jabes-Gilead. Ein Beitrag zur Methode alttestamentlicher Topographie', *ZDPV* 69, 1953, 28–41.

4. *Ḥirbe*, then in the form *ḥirbet*, e.g. *ḥirbet teqū'* = Tekoa; *ḥirbet sēlūn* = Shiloh. It is often impossible to recognize direct connections with biblical originals in proper names compounded with *tell*, e.g. *tell balāṭa* = Shechem; *tell el-mutesellim* = Megiddo; however, *tell ta'annak* = Taanach.

5. Courses given by the Deutsches Evangelisches Institut für Altertumswissenschaft des Heiligen Landes deal almost exclusively with surface exploration; cf. the detailed reports and researches in the *Palästinajahrbuch* (*PJB*), after the Second World War in *ZDPV*; an example of wide-ranging surface exploration is to be found in N. Glueck, 'Explorations in Eastern Palestine I–IV', in *AASOR* 14, 1934; 15, 1935; 18/19, 1939; 25/28, 1951.

6. Comparative finds at the great burial places are decisive for dating small material like pottery. In them, pottery and small objects appear successively in individual strata of the

tell and thus provide a basis for dating in a sufficiently reliable archaeological context.

7. In addition to accounts of excavations see the survey given by Noth, *Old Testament World*, 125–44, and by P. Thomsen, *Palästina und seine Kultur in fünf Jahrtausenden*, AO 30, 1932, 5–19; K. M. Kenyon, *Archaeology in the Holy Land*, [2]1965, 305–22 (with numerous bibliographical references).

8. The chief works on the archaeology of Palestine are: P. Thomsen, *Palästina und seine Kultur* (see note 7); C. Watzinger, *Denkmäler Palästinas* I/II, 1933/35; W. F. Albright, *The Archaeology of Palestine*, [4]1960; A. G. Barrois, *Manuel d'archéologie biblique* I/II, 1939, 1953; K. M. Kenyon, *Archaeology in the Holy Land*, [2]1965. Archaeological discoveries are set in the wider context of history, religion and the history of culture in W. F. Albright, *Archaeology and the Religion of Israel*, [2]1946; id., *From the Stone Age to Christianity*, [2]1946; excavations and finds are presented in the form of a lexicon by K. Galling, *Biblisches Reallexikon (BRL)*, 1937. Bo Reicke/L. Rost, *Biblisch-historisches Handwörterbuch (BHH)* I–III, 1962–66, has many illustrations; pictorial material is also to be found in Gressmann, *AOB*; Pritchard, *ANEP*; and in L. H. Grollenberg, *Atlas of the Bible*, 1957.

9. See R. de Vaux, *RB* 60, 1953, and *RB* 66, 1959; also summarized in Harding, op. cit., 185–98.

10. K. M. Kenyon, *Excavations of Jericho* I/II, 1960, 1965; id., *Digging up Jericho*, 1957; Harding, op. cit., 165–9.

11. Cf. the short survey by the archaeologist concerned, J. B. Pritchard, in SVT 7, 1960, 1–12, and id., *Where the Sun Stood Still. The Discovery of the Biblical City*, 1962; see also *ZDPV* 79, 1963, 173f.; 80, 1964, 160. However, not all scholars have accepted the identification of *el-jib* with Gibeon without qualification.

12. Y. Yadin et al., *Hazor* I, 1958; II, 1960; III–IV, 1961; id., 'Hazor', in *Archaeology and Old Testament Study*, ed. D. Winton Thomas, 1967, 245–63; more recent investigations are: Y. Yadin, *IEJ* 19, 1969, 1–19; summarized in Y. Yadin, *Hazor, The Head of all those Kingdoms*, Schweich Lectures 1970, 1972; for the biblical Hazor see F. Maass, 'Hazor und das Problem der Landnahme', in BZAW 77, 1958, 105–17; J. Gray, 'Hazor', *VT* 16, 1966, 26–52.

13. R. de Vaux gives an account of his excavations in *RB* from 1947 onwards.

14. Cf. the survey (with full bibliographical details) by U. Jochims in *ZDPV* 76, 1960, 73–96.

15. See the brief surveys in *ZDPV* 79, 1963, 174–6, and *ZDPV* 80, 1964, 166–8, with indications of more extensive reports; summarized in K. M. Kenyon, *Jerusalem. Excavating 3000 Years of History*, 1967.

16. Total duration of the excavation 1962–67; preliminary report by Y. Aharoni and R. Amiran, 'Excavations at Tel Arad, Preliminary Report on the First Season, 1962', *IEJ* 14, 1964, 131–47 (Hebrew in *BIES* 27, 1963, 217–34); cf. also the brief reports by M. Weippert in *ZDPV* 80, 1964, 180–5, and *ZDPV* 82, 1966, 286f. Also V. Fritz, 'Arad in der biblischen Überlieferung und in der Liste Schoschenks I', *ZDPV* 82, 1966, 331–42.

17. Y. Yadin, *Masada, Herod's Fortress and the Zealots' Last Stand*, 1966 (with excellent illustrations and references to further literature). M. Weippert gives brief, and sometimes more extensive accounts of more recent archaeological investigations in Palestine in his 'Archäologischen Jahresberichte', *ZDPV* 79, 1963, 164–79; 80, 1964, 150–93; 82, 1966, 274–330.

18. H. Gressmann, *Altorientalische Texte zum Alten Testament (AOT)*, [2]1926, 444; J. B. Pritchard, *Ancient Near Eastern Texts relating to the New Testament (ANET)*, [2]1955, 320a; H. Donner–W. Röllig, *Kanaanäische und aramäische Inschriften (KAI)*, I (Texts), [3]1971; II (Commentary), [3]1973; III (Glossary, indices and plates), [2]1969, no. 182.

19. Tentative translations in *AOT*, 371; *ANET*, 490b.

20. F. M. T. Böhl, *ZDPV* 49, 1926, 321–7, tablets 44–46.

21. K. Galling, *Textbuch zur Geschichte Israels (TGI)*, 1950, 50; *ANET*, 231; *KAI*, nos. 183–8; see M. Noth, *PJB* 28, 1932, 54–67; K. Galling, *ZDPV* 77, 1961, 173–85.

22. *AOT*, 440; *ANET*, 320f.; *TGI*, 1950, 47–9 (Hebrew text with commentary); ²1968, 51–53 (translation); *KAI*, no.181.

23. *AOT*, 445; *ANET*, 321b; *TGI*, 1950, 59 (Hebrew); ²1968, 66f. (German); *KAI*, no. 189; see H. J. Stoebe, *ZDPV* 71, 1955, 124–40; the two *silwān* inscriptions, *KAI*, no. 191 AB, are also worth noting.

24. *ANET*, 321f.; *TGI*, 1950, 63–5 (Hebrew); ²1968, 75–8 (German); *KAI*, nos. 192–9.

25. This is one of the principal reasons why archaeological material can provide only limited historical evidence for investigation into the history of Israel. The archaeology of Palestine is largely 'dumb archaeology', which is principally supported by cultural artefacts, and not also by contemporaneous documents, inscriptions, letters or other lists. There are very few exceptions to this rule. The evidence about historical events to be obtained from excavation reports is extremely relative and in every case needs to be tested by dated documents, often those found outside Palestine, and the historical accounts in the Old Testament. American archaeologists have often attached more weight to the external evidence than it can bear in the question of verifying historical events. On this see especially M. Noth, 'Der Beitrag der Archäologie zur Geschichte Israels', in SVT 7, 1960, 262–82 = *Aufsätze* 1, 17–33; id., 'Hat die Bibel doch recht?', in *Festschrift für Günther Dehn*, 1957, 7–22; R. de Vaux, 'On Right and Wrong Uses of Archaeology', in *Near Eastern Archaeology in the Twentieth Century* (Glueck Festschrift), ed. J. A. Sanders, 1970, 64–80.

26. This is true, to give just a few examples, for the remains of a wall from the early Iron Age in Gibeah (*tell el-fūl*), for the Solomonic stratum of Megiddo and the walls of the royal palace(?) in Samaria. The latter are extremely well constructed and made from stones which have been particularly carefully prepared. The famous 'Weeping Wall' in Jerusalem is of a later date and was part of the wall surrounding the courts of the temple of Herod. Cf. Noth, *Old Testament World*, 147–51; *BRL*, 371–4; *BHH* II, 1174–6.

27. The best-known example is Jer.36.

28. Translations of texts from outside Israel can easily be found in large collections. Gressmann, *AOT* and *AOB*, are still indispensable; more recently the same intention has been followed by J. B. Pritchard, *ANET* and *ANEP*, ³1969; there is also an independent supplementary volume to the first two editions, *The Ancient Near East, Supplementary Texts and Pictures relating to the Old Testament*, 1969. The most important inscriptions can be found with a German translation and full commentary in H. Donner–W. Röllig, *KAI* I–III. Older collections of translations of historical texts are: J. H. Breasted, *Ancient Records of Egypt* I–V, 1906/07; and D. D. Luckenbill, *Ancient Records of Assyria and Babylonia* I/II, 1927.

29. Translated in *ANET*, 18–22. See especially A. Alt, 'Die älteste Schilderung Palästinas im Lichte neuer Funde', *PJB* 37, 1941, 19–49; G. Posener, *Littérature et politique dans l'Égypte de la XIIᵉ dynastie*, 1956, 87–115.

30. K. Sethe, *Die Ächtung feindlicher Fürsten, Völker und Dinge auf altägyptischen Tongefässscherben des Mittleren Reiches*, APAW, Phil.-hist. Kl., no. 5, 1926; G. Posener, *Princes et pays d'Asie et de Nubie. Textes hiératiques sur des figurines d'envoûtement du Moyen Empire*, 1940; for the texts found in Mirgissa (Sudan), see G. Posener, *Syria* 43, 1966, 277–87; W. Helck, *Die Beziehungen*, ²1971, 44–67; for the discovery of historical connections see Alt, *KS* III, 49–56, 62–71, 90–8.

31. *AOT*, 380–411; *ANET*, 159–80; *Suppl.*, 526–8; further bibliography there.

32. *Archives royales de Mari*, ed. Dossin, I–V, 1941ff.; for the prophetic texts see now especially F. Ellermeier, *Prophetie in Mari und Israel*, 1968. For a first orientation see the survey by W. von Soden in *WO* I, 3, 1948, 187–204.

33. *AOT*, 80–99; *ANET*, 234–64; *TGI*, 1950, 12–19; ²1968, 14–21, 28–34.

34. J. Simons, *Handbook for the Study of Egyptian Topographical Lists relating to Western Asia*, 1937; cf. also the survey of the names of places and districts mentioned in the lists in *ANET*, 242f.; detailed examination of individual lists by M. Noth, *ZDPV* 60, 1937, 183–239; 61, 1938, 26–65, 277–304; 64, 1941, 39–74; *Gesammelte Aufsätze* 2, 1–118.

35. In addition, there is a series of smaller lists and numerous scattered fragments, partly of ornamental character, on the bases of pillars. Detailed treatment of the material in W. Helck, *Beziehungen*, 167ff.

36. B. Mazar, SVT 4, 1957, 47–66; S. Herrmann, *ZDPV* 80, 1964, 55–79.

37. Selected translations in *AOT*, 371–9; *ANET*, 483–90; *TGI*, [1]1950, 19–29; [2]1968, 24–8; for an edition of the texts see J. A. Knudtzon, *Die El-Amarna-Tafeln*, 1907–15 (usually cited as *EA*), 1–538; further letters were published by F. Thureau-Dangin in *Revue d'Assyriologie* 19, 1922, 91–108, cited according to the museum numbers, AO 7093–98.

38. Translations in *AOT*, 71–7; *ANET*, 25–9; *TGI*, [2]1968, 41–8.

39. The chief inscriptions are those from Zinjirli, Afis (inscription of ZKR of Hamath) and the stelae of *sefire*; see the texts in *KAI*, sections A I, II, F I; *AOT*, 440–4; *ANET*, 499–505.

40. Translations with copious bibliographies in *AOT*, 339–70; *ANET*, 274–317; *Suppl.*, 558–64; *TGI*, [1]1950, 45–72; [2]1968, 49–84; note especially the 'Wiseman Chronicle': D. J. Wiseman, *Chronicles of Chaldaean Kings (626–556 BC) in the British Museum*, 1956; the most important parts of the text are in *Bibl.* 37, 1956, 389–97.

41. The greater part have been published: E. Sachau, *Aramäische Papyrus und Ostraka aus einer jüdischen Militärkolonie zu Elephantine*, 1911; see also the edition of the texts by A. Cowley, *Aramaic Papyri of the Fifth Century BC*, 1923; a further part of the find at Elephantine has been made available by E. G. Kraeling, *The Brooklyn Museum Aramaic Papyri*, 1953; selected translations are in *AOT*, 450–62; *ANET*, 222–3, 427–30, 491f.; *Suppl.*, 633; *TGI*, [1]1950, 73; [2]1968, 84–8; for the historical problems see E. Meyer, *Der Papyrusfund von Elephantine*, 1912. A further find from Egypt from the same period is worth noting (exact provenance unknown): documents on leather, some of which come from the archive of a Persian satrap of the time of Darius II; G. R. Driver, *Aramaic Documents of the Fifth Century BC*, 1954, [2]1957.

42. See the extracts from Josephus' *Antiquities*, II Maccabees and Polybius collected in *TGI*, [1]1950, 74–80.

43. Extensive study of the Pentateuch is still by no means finished and the literary problems have yet to be completely clarified. M. Noth, *A History of Pentateuchal Traditions* (1948), 1972, dominates the field; cf., however, the indications of the many literary problems in O. Eissfeldt, *The Old Testament. An Introduction*, 1965, 182–241; G. Fohrer, *Introduction to the Old Testament*, 1970, 103–92 and the long article by H. Cazelles, 'Pentateuque', *Supplément au Dictionnaire de la Bible* VII, 1964, 687–858.

44. At least the books from Joshua to II Kings in the Hebrew canon are assigned to the Deuteronomistic history work. The work of the Chronicler embraces I and II Chronicles, Ezra and Nehemiah. M. Noth, *Überlieferungsgeschichtliche Studien*, 1943, [2]1957, is fundamental for the study of both works. However, in more recent times questions have been raised more frequently about the unity and independence of the Deuteronomistic work; at least it must be acknowledged that within the work there has been a very complex redaction of varied traditional material.

45. Chiefly G. von Rad, 'The Beginnings of Historical Writing in Ancient Israel', in *The Problem of the Hexateuch and Other Essays*, 1966. See also L. Rost, *Die Überlieferung der Thronnachfolge Davids*, 1926, reprinted in *Das kleine Credo und andere Studien zum Alten Testament*, 1965, 119–53. Matters are different in Egypt, but Egypt is very important for the purpose of comparison; see E. Otto, 'Geschichtsbild und Geschichtsschreibung in Agypten', *WO* 3, 1964–66, 161–76.

46. K. Koch, *The Growth of the Biblical Tradition*, 1969, discusses the problems of method and gives examples.

47. For the problem of the accuracy of the historical tradition on a broad basis see J. Hempel, *Geschichten und Geschichte im Alten Testament bis zur persischen Zeit*, 1964, though he is not completely convincing.

48. Usually called 'Jewish Antiquities', *Antiquitates Iudaicae* (in the sense of 'Jewish History'), twenty books in all, from the first man to the outbreak of the Jewish rebellion in AD 66. Josephus' other historical work, 'The Jewish War', *De Bello Judaico*, is more valuable as a historical work because it is independent. Its seven books cover the period from the appearance of Antiochus IV and the Maccabaean revolt to the destruction of Jerusalem in AD 70, and depict the crushing of the Jewish rebellion by Vespasian. Where the account runs parallel to that in the *Antiquities*, there are a number of discrepancies, and the treatment is less careful. The works of Josephus are available in a Greek and English text in nine volumes, LCL, ed. H. St J. Thackeray, 1926–65.

_____

PART ONE

The Birth of the People of Israel

I | *The Patriarchs*

IT HAS SEEMED impossible to begin more recent scholarly discussion of the problems of the early history of Israel without consideration of what 'Israel' is – tribal confederacy, people, state, nation or idea.[1] However, it is premature to embark on an account of the facts of Old Testament history of the kind to be presented here with a discussion of this question. What applies to all other 'peoples' also applies to 'Israel'. Israel does not begin where this designation for the whole people appears for the first time in documentary evidence; it begins with the first groups who are later to form themselves into a people which understands itself as 'Israel'. The Israel which emerged from a series of common destinies and experiences over the course of time is the result of a historical process not unlike that which can be noted in the formation of the states of Europe. They too began from movements of peoples which made possible consolidations into politically effective groups. From the early period one may think of the Angles, the Saxons, the Franks, the Alemanni or the tribes of Central Germany. A history of Israel must first show how Israel came into being and from what constituent parts; how such a complex beginning could produce a totality which attained world-historical importance.

The Old Testament itself gives us a document which does not mention 'Israel', but nevertheless sets Israel's origins in the context of the world history of the time in a suitable form which we are able to check. It offers a convincing picture of the forces operative at the beginning of what was later to become Israel, those forces which made it possible for 'Israel' to enter world history. This document is the so-called 'table of nations' in Gen. 10.

Semitic thought tended to understand historical periods and relationships in terms of genealogy; the progress and development of an event and its consequences were depicted through the sequence of generations. In this perspective, Gen. 10, coming immediately after the story of the Flood, has a disconcerting consistency. The one man to survive the Flood, Noah, becomes the ancestor of the new humanity, a humanity which already demonstrates natural distinctions in issuing from the three sons of Noah: Shem, Ham and Japheth. Thus this new humanity is no uniform mass, but is already divided as a result of its origin from three different ancestors. Genealogy becomes the means of expressing historical relationships which have already been noted.

While Gen. 10² displays a few striking traditional elements, the survey of the sons of Japheth is headed by figures who bear the names of peoples in the north and west of the ancient world. They range from the Medes to the people of Javan (Ionians) on the west coast of Asia Minor, and probably even go as far as Spain.³

The sons of Ham are introduced as: Cush, referring to the Sudanese territory south of Egypt; Mizraim, i.e. Egypt itself; Put, a country adjoining Egypt on east or west;⁴ and lastly Canaan. Here progress is made in succession northwards from the furthest territory in the south then known; the one remarkable feature is that Canaan is the northern pillar of this group. The peoples understood to be the sons of Shem embrace the broad area from Elam in the east through Asshur to the most westerly component of this group, the Aramaeans, who may possibly also include the Lydians of Asia Minor.⁵

On the basis of this survey it seems legitimate to speak of Japhetic, Hamitic and Semitic peoples. To some degree these designations have also become part of modern academic nomenclature, especially in philology, where it has become customary to talk of Hamitic and Semitic languages.⁶ However, the biblical division was probably based on neither ethnographic nor linguistic affinities. It is much more likely that historical and political factors will have been determinative. Within the three groups we can see power blocks which played their own part in the course of history, gaining in influence at least after the second half of the second millennium BC and remaining influential thereafter. This can be seen most clearly in the southernmost group, which reckons Canaan among the lands of Africa and thus describes the sphere of power gained by the Pharaohs during the Egyptian New Kingdom. While it is impossible to read out the details of events and situations from this tradition, we can at least recognize and comprehend the essential dimensions of historical spheres of action and their annexes.

This insight is deepened by the fact that the list first presents the Japhetic peoples as the powers of the north and in immediate succession introduces the Hamites as the powers of the south. Here is a picture of power politics about the middle of the second millennium, that confrontation which never reached a real balance, however near the balance may seem to have come in the peace treaty between the Hittites and Egypt at the time of Rameses II.⁷ It is all the more significant that the Semites appear last in the table of peoples, inserted between the classical power blocks, announcing as it were a 'third power' which was in fact to have its effect on history. This corresponds to the new historical situation towards the end of the second millennium BC. The formation of the Aramaean states is the most visible expression of the new period. Those in power in Mesopotamia were concerned with them, whereas at the end of the New Kingdom the influence of Egypt was perceptibly on the decline. The time had come when the corridor of Syria and Palestine was beginning to have potentialities of its own. The table of nations ends with the Semites. It is 'a document of the youthful self-awareness' (A. Alt) of these nations.

It is clear that not all the parts of Gen. 10 are a product of the early period; it is hardly a 'contemporary' document. It presupposes a degree of reflection capable of forming an estimate of historical powers and comparing them with one another. The question of the date of the composition of this text remains secondary in comparison with its superb evaluation of the groups covered in it.

It should be stressed once again that Gen. 10 does not describe a particular historical situation at one point of time, nor did it grow out of such a situation. The lists collected here, together with all their additions, reflect an increasing growth in philosophical and political observations and experiences which presumably only came to an end in the post-exilic period. This would even fit the time of the composition of P, which took over the earlier traditions (presumably J) with their more limited geography. Nevertheless, the considerations advanced here continue to be valid because Gen. 10 is a testimony of the Old Testament about the geographical and political distribution of power in the ancient Near East which over the centuries made its impact on the people of the Old Testament in varying ways.

Quite rightly, the name 'Israel' is completely absent from the table of nations. The ancestors of Israel did not belong among the first generation of descendants of the sons of Noah: Shem, Ham and Japheth. Historical intermediaries were required, together with their appropriate genealogies. There was an awareness that 'Israel' entered on a world which already had an existing order of peoples, that it emerged from one of the great groupings of mankind. Consequently in Gen. 11.10–32 the genealogy of Shem comes down to Abra(ha)m,[8] with whom a special development within the world of nations is introduced. The character of this genealogical sequence, which is maintained consistently and apparently one-sidedly in the Old Testament text, is not purely fictitious. Further lists of this kind are distributed throughout Genesis, each beginning from a tribal ancestor and extending to well-defined groups. In addition to Gen. 11.10–32, the lists in Gen. 22.20–24 and 25.1–4, together with Gen. 25.13–16 and 36.10–14, should be noted. They are complicated and refined by the fact that some of the patriarchs have several wives. Thus a gradation is achieved within the groups, capable of expressing the varied historical relationships.

It is in accord with the logic of the book of Genesis that all the kindred mentioned in the lists are sub-members of the Shem group, which is first extended further in Gen. 11.10ff. From v. 20 onwards, the immediate forebears of Abraham are given as Serug, Nahor and Terah; the latter's children are Abram, Nahor and Haran; Haran's son is Lot. These lists and their names cover a particular area. The names are typical of north-west Mesopotamia.[9] It is also stated that Terah, Abram and Lot set out from Ur Chasdim, reached Haran, and had the land of Canaan as their goal.

Ur Chasdim, which may be translated 'Ur of the Chaldaeans', is often identified with ancient Ur (*el-muqeiyar*) in southernmost Mesopotamia, the centre of ancient Sumeria.[10] In that case, it would be necessary to suppose extensive travelling right across Mesopotamia to reach a destination of Haran in the north-west. Such a movement is conceivable, but not compelling.[11] 'Ur of the Chaldaeans' does not play a further role in the Old Testament. By contrast, in Gen. 11.28 the Greek text of the Septuagint offers the reading 'in the land' instead of the Hebrew 'in Ur'. This could easily have arisen from the omission of a single letter: אר instead of ארצ. That would mean that the ancestors of Abraham came 'from the land of the Chaldaeans', i.e. from Babylonia. This would bring them nearer to Haran. Haran lies on the great bend of the Euphrates at the exact spot which was later occupied by the Aramaean state of Bit-adini. Of course, this is not the last word on 'Ur Chasdim'. But it is by no means the case that Sumerian Ur is the only possible location.

The list of the twelve sons of Nahor (Gen. 22.20–24) also points in the direction of Haran. It is divided between two wives, Milcah (cf. Gen. 11.29) and Reumah. Among the sons is Bethuel, the father of Rebecca, and a man with the significant epithet 'the father of Aram'. Nahor and his family are most closely related to Abraham within a limited area. By contrast, the lists in Gen. 25.1–4 and 25.13–16 point towards southern Palestine and north-western Arabia. Among the six sons whom Abraham had by a wife named Keturah (Gen. 25.1–4), we also find Midian, the name of a people distributed widely in the region of the gulf of Aqaba. They were camel nomads. Later descendants of the sons of Keturah include the Sabaeans along the coast of the Red Sea[12] and the Dedanites[13] who lived north of them. The twelve sons of Ishmael, a son of Abraham (Gen. 25.13–16), also belong to the south; they are said to dwell 'opposite Egypt'.[14] Further details confirm that this is an allusion to the west coast of the Arabian peninsula.[15]

This genealogical distribution thus shows that the descendants of Abraham occupied a broad area, one corner of which was in upper Mesopotamia and the other in southern Arabia. The derivation of these groups of peoples from Abraham and their internal arrangement in terms of six or twelve members may be called schematic and artificial, but the governing factor was the conviction that the groups were in a closer or more distant relationship to Abraham, and had to be seen and assessed together. This fact, and the possibility of verifying the names in the various geographical areas, allow us to conclude that no matter from what period the genealogy may derive, within the limitations of its system it shows us historical circumstances which are to be taken seriously. Here is the interaction of a complex of peoples who include, not least, those elements from which one day 'Israel' was to emerge. How else could one explain the interest which the Old Testament took in these particular groups?

In accordance with the genealogical system, this system is supplemented by a central group which now leads directly to Palestine. Gen. 36.10–14 mentions the alliance of the twelve sons of Esau, giving a list of Edomite tribes which established themselves principally in southern and south-eastern Palestine.[16] Next, in Gen. 29.31–30.24, the family of Abraham's grandson Jacob is developed in broad outline. The twelve sons of Jacob are distributed between two chief wives and two subsidiary wives. They bear the names of the twelve tribes of later Israel; in addition there is a girl called Dinah. The name Israel does not appear. The twelve sons of Jacob are listed and arranged in exactly the same way as the twelve sons of Abraham or the children of Nahor. The complex which was one day to be called Israel is first seen within the genealogical framework of Genesis as a group of twelve members, set alongside the descendants of Abraham. The only difference is in the choice of the other tribal ancestor, Jacob. This should be noted. However, in its final form, the genealogical and geographical arrangement of the whole system is rounded off as follows: Terah, in Upper Mesopotamia, has three sons, Abraham, Nahor and Haran. Nahor is given twelve sons, covering upper Mesopotamia and northern Syria. From his union with Hagar Abraham gets Ishmael, whose twelve sons belong in the south and south-west of the Arabian peninsula, whereas the six sons of Abraham by Keturah occupy the adjoining area to the north-west. The geographical centre is more complicated: from Isaac's union with Rebecca come Esau and Jacob, who in turn produce the twelve sons of the Edomites and the Israelites respectively as their eponymous descendants. Abraham's nephew Lot becomes the tribal ancestor of the Moabites and the Ammonites (Gen. 19.30–38).

What was said about the table of nations also holds good for this system. It presupposes knowledge of a wide area and of the complicated relationships between peoples. It is not possible to transfer the genealogical system into a historical context with complete exactitude, but the system itself is hardly an arbitrary product. It is clear that the 'Semites', assigned in this way to their various tribal ancestors, were aware of sharing a common destiny, if not a considerable degree of ethnic affinity. This awareness was sufficiently strong for them to believe that they had an independent historical potentiality. So we cannot escape the question of the historically verifiable context into which such an over-arching genealogical system can be set. The best solution would seem to be offered by the wide-ranging but nevertheless essentially simple process of the arrival of Aramaean tribes towards the end of the second millennium BC. This solution has the advantage of accommodating the genealogies of Genesis plausibly and convincingly as a unit of tradition and restricting them to a relatively limited period of time. The patriarchal age is no long-drawn-out epoch, the beginning and end of which are lost in obscurity,[17] nor has it to be investigated on the basis of hypothetical caravan routes.[18] It is a quite clearly definable period within an ethnically limited framework, of considerable dimensions, but in the last resort limited to the western flank of the 'fertile crescent'.

However, this relatively unitary picture should not be exaggerated. We should assume that there is a piece of independent history behind each of the groups contained in the genealogies of Genesis. The relationships between the groups remain questionable. It is hardly probable that there were contacts between the people in Haran with Terah and Abram and the southern groups, the people of Keturah and Ishmael. The genealogical system has its limitations when it comes to inferring particular historical movements and developments. We should also assume a process of growth within the groups. Their formation into alliances of sixes or twelves may be the final stage of particular processes. Only in a single instance are we in a position to make a closer examination of these internal relationships within a group of tribes, namely with the sons of Jacob. Not only the tradition in Genesis but also the further course of the history of Israel makes it clear that the tribes of Israel who bore the name of sons of Jacob did not form an active unit from the start, but finally found a common abode in different ways.

The complexity of this beginning is shown in a compressed but appropriate form in the so-called 'brief historical creed' (Deut.26.5b–9) which is quoted so often.[19] It makes the Israelite farmer of a later period say, 'An Aramaean doomed to perish was my father when he went down to Egypt . . .' Here is explicit evidence that the patriarchs were Aramaean, with an indication at the same time of the problem of the semi-nomads who came in from the steppe and at first had varied success in existing on the borders of cultivated land.[20] That the 'father' (who is not described more closely here) went down to Egypt and evidently also failed there before reaching Palestine may be seen simply as a reference to the extremely complicated events which made up the Aramaean invasion.

Although it is impossible to identify the Aramaean 'father' 'doomed to perish' from Deut.26,[21] the question remains why the independent groups of the Genesis genealogies were clearly made dependent on the patriarchs. Who were these patriarchs, and how did they attain their superiority? The three great figures of Abraham, Isaac and Jacob, who are associated in a series of father-son relationships, are hardly literary inventions to form a great framework for the other relationships of affinity. There is evidence that Abraham at least is rooted in the northern group from upper Mesopotamia, whereas Isaac and Jacob stand outside larger groupings. They hardly attain supreme importance for the reader of Genesis as intermediaries in the genealogical framework for the nations; rather, they achieve prominence through their role in the impressive series of narratives about them and their encounters with God, mostly at Palestinian sanctuaries which are mentioned by name. In their original form, these brief anecdotal accounts, which H. Gunkel characterized as small units and with some justice entitled the 'sagas of Genesis',[22] are almost exclusively the encounters of a patriarch with a deity; only at a later redactional stage have they been combined in 'saga cycles'[23] and provided with the theme of a multitude of descendants in the promised land.[24] In this way the texts have been given an emphasis of promise, markedly directed towards the future.[25] However, we should not allow this later, over-arching theme to blind us to the original forms of the encounter of the patriarchs with local deities of Canaanite Palestine, which can still clearly be recognized. This encounter in fact provides the key to historical insights into the nature of the individual figures of the patriarchs. It must be seen against a wider background.

One of the striking features of the patriarchal narratives is the wandering life of the patriarchs and their families. Quite apart from the fact that the theme of wandering often serves to link one narrative to another, which may take place in a different area, we have an overwhelming impression that the patriarchs do not possess land but are at best in search of it. Many comparisons with nomadic forms of existence have been introduced to illuminate the wanderings of the patriarchs. Reference is made to transhumance, the annual change from winter to summer pasturage, to the great amount of livestock owned by the patriarchs and the extensive grazing which they seem to continue even in Palestine itself.[26] Without doubt these patterns of life, which were also characteristic of the border area between the steppe and the cultivated land, played a significant role in the existence of the patriarchs. But in their case we must refine and differentiate this whole form of approach. The traditions about the patriarchs which have come down to us are not set in the wilderness and the steppe, nor even in the border territory of the Palestinian hill-country, but right in the centre of areas of later settlements. Thus although the nomadic form of life may be their characteristic mode of existence, they seem to be in a final stage before at last settling down.[27] We are in possession of many traditions not least because they clearly show the goal of later habitation. In Gen. 13, Abraham and Lot consult about how to divide the land; Lot goes into the apparently more fertile Jordan region, while Abraham goes into Judah. Abraham acquires land in Hebron (Gen. 23) and has Rebecca brought for his son from his homeland. She lives in distant upper Mesopotamia, where the union could be arranged in more favourable circumstances. Isaac seems still to be on the edge of a settled form of life. His whole way of life is a fight for wells in the southern wilderness around Beersheba (Gen. 26). Characteristically, his son Jacob serves Laban in upper Mesopotamia and there gains the basis for his future prosperity. Finally he enters Transjordania, where he has to mark out territory for himself in competition with his brother Esau, the ancestor of the Edomites; he also moves over into central Palestine, as his sons tend cattle near Shechem, and Joseph is sold at Dothan (Gen. 37.17).

The narratives depict and presuppose successive settlements in the land, not of course in the increasingly heavily populated coastal plain, but in the hilly hinterland, in the fertile centres of the hill-country west (and sometimes east) of the Jordan. The most striking narratives are associated with the chief sanctuaries of this stretch of land. The central sanctuary of Shechem plays a part in both the Abraham and the Jacob stories (Gen. 12.6; 35.4); however, the Abraham tradition seems to be concentrated on Hebron and the sanctuary of Mamre (Gen. 18.23), whereas Jacob appears in Bethel (Gen. 28) and in Transjordania, on the Jabbok (Gen. 32.23–33) and at Mahanaim (Gen. 32.2f.).[28] A characteristic of all these sanctuary narratives is that God appears each time to the patriarch concerned, or more accurately, that each patriarch feels the overwhelming power of a God who overcomes other, evidently more ancient beings which have a numinous influence at the same place. The God of the patriarchs triumphs.

These observations allow us to draw decisive conclusions for the history of the patriarchs. During the process of their settlement, the patriarchs and their gods displace the local gods of the country. They gain possession of the ancient holy places and there found their own cult, legitimated by an appearance of 'their' God. In fact this is already a final stage of 'patriarchal belief'. Decades ago, A. Alt explained the form of patriarchal religion in a way which has still to be refuted.[29] Beginning from the linguistic observation that the designation of the God and the name of the patriarch are often closely connected by the use of the genitive, as in 'the God of Abraham', 'the God of my father', 'the God of his father Isaac', but also 'the God of Nahor',[30] and still more bluntly 'the fear of Isaac'[31] and 'the mighty one of Jacob',[32] and making use of later comparative material,[33] Alt was able to demonstrate that the individual patriarchs were subjects of particular experiences, not to say manifestations, of a god which befell each one independently at particular times. To these their descendants referred. This type of religion is understandable among non-sedentary groups. The divinity does not reveal himself at the holy place of a permanent sanctuary, but makes himself known to a person who, as the guarantor of a valid experience of God, also determines the belief of members of the group and their descendants. A persuasive conclusion to this theory is that the formula 'the God of NN' not only communicates faith in a deity, but also indicates that the person who received the revelation is a historical personality, and not a fiction.

The patriarchal narratives in Genesis fit these observations. There, too, the patriarchs are revealers of revelation, not only providing a foundation for the faith of their clan but also experiencing in holy places the superiority of their God to the local deities[34] attached to them. With this, a decisive new stage in patriarchal belief begins. The God who once, at the nomadic stage, had only personal associations, is given a particular location and is attached to a sanctuary which he takes over. The settlement of the patriarchs and their people is accompanied by an appropriation of the land and its cultic institutions which is legitimated by their deity.

It is often asked whether this 'God of the fathers' is identical with Yahweh, as the Genesis account supposes. Logically, the answer to this question must begin in the negative. The patriarchal deities and faith in Yahweh were originally independent phenomena. On the other hand, at a later stage, when the worshippers of the patriarchal deities came in contact with Yahweh, Yahweh was able to embody these patriarchal deities in such a way that they could figure as a legitimate ingredient of Yahwistic faith. Of course we shall only be able to see the full extent of this development when we consider the nature of faith in Yahweh and its role in the history of Israel, and this is only possible in the context of the Moses tradition. However, the absence of any such title as 'the God of Moses' may already be taken as an indication that in the case of Yahweh we are dealing with a different type of deity from the God of the fathers.

The possibility of comparing the names of the patriarchs with West Semitic nomenclature is often used as an emphatic argument in favour of their historicity as well as to establish their date. The archive of correspondence from Mari has also provided illuminating material.[35] The three-character root with a prefixed *yod*, as in the names Jacob and Isaac, is regarded as being West Semitic. Whereas extensive comparative material can be demonstrated for 'Jacob' or the fuller form 'Jacob-El',[36] there are no parallels for 'Isaac'. The name 'Abraham' has a different structure, but only the shorter form 'Abram' can be used for any philological comparison. This is formed on the principle of noun + verb, in which the noun can be the theophorous element.[37]

Speculations that the names belong to particular groups of people among the West Semites continually tempt scholars to make bold attempts at dating the 'patriarchal age'. Whereas Noth uses the appearance of this type of name in the letters from Mari to support his thesis that here we have 'proto-Aramaean' phenomena and wishes to use this conclusion to illuminate the earliest history of Israel,[38] de Vaux rejects the conception and regards the alleged 'Aramaean character' of the patriarchs as an 'anachronism': in his view the patriarchs emerged earlier than the first evidence about the Aramaeans.[39] However, it should be clear that individual observations about the form of patriarchal proper names or about their context in cultural and legal history should not be treated in isolation and should certainly not be over-emphasized.[40] As has been shown, we cannot illuminate the very beginnings of the patriarchal history; we have evidence only of its final stages, which are limited to Palestine. Nor can we ever make a start by recognizing rudiments which allow us to draw conclusions in the direction of a much older substratum of tradition which might be dated centuries before the settlement. There are no indications which point backwards towards the free-ranging existence on the steppe of those who were later to invade the cultivated land. It is impossible to find an unexceptionable date even for Abraham, Isaac and Jacob. For they are seen as the last members of the Shem genealogy and appear as representatives of the groups who settle in the cultivated land. To this degree, they too could convincingly be found a place within the genealogical system of Genesis. And while this subordination of the various ethnic groups to the great patriarchal figures certainly took place at a later stage by a deliberate process of reflection, we are not compelled to see here a process which took place with total disregard of historical relationships. It seems most likely that the Aramaean movement in the second half of the second millennium BC was the wider context for the patriarchs. But there is no firm foundation for the view that some or all of these invaders from the steppe called themselves *ḫapiru*, or were so called at a slightly later date, even if this hypothesis is not completely to be ruled out.[41]

One single narrative in Genesis seems to lie outside the chronological and geographical framework which has been indicated here. At the same time, it is one of the most difficult passages of the Old Testament to assimilate. This is Gen. 14 and the traditions which it combines. Here Abraham appears as a warrior and, like

Lot, only seems to have been combined with the much earlier saga material as an afterthought. Four kings, evidently the rulers of considerable territories and peoples,[42] lead a punitive expedition against five treacherous vassals who are to be located in the immediate neighbourhood of the Dead Sea. The kings win a victory and take a great deal of plunder; the captives include Lot, who was living at the southern end of the Dead Sea. This leads Abraham to intervene; he robs the kings of their plunder and frees Lot. The connection of this Lot–Abraham episode with the saga tradition, which has quite a different character, is clearly secondary. Presumably it is based on a local saga current in the neighbourhood of the Dead Sea, which was associated with Lot and then enlarged by the inclusion of Abraham.

This is confirmed by a further remarkable scene which has been added at the end. The king of Sodom and the king of Salem, Melchizedek by name, a priest of the God El Elyon, come to meet Abraham after his victory. Melchizedek blesses him; in humble recognition Abraham pays him a tithe of the plunder and in proud superiority accedes to the greedy demands of the king of Sodom.

The historical events presupposed by these reports remain obscure; it is impossible to date them. But in an exemplary way they show the degree to which the patriarchs were able to absorb local traditions and transform them in such a way that in the end they themselves emerged as victors. What was originally an account of the defeat of local vassals by the Dead Sea becomes a triumph for Abraham. Even the city-king of Jerusalem, who possibly stands behind Melchizedek of Salem, cannot ignore the new development brought about by the entry of the patriarchs into the land. Of course, Abraham remains strictly subordinate to him.[43] But this itself is an apt reflection of the new situation in the land. The patriarchs cannot vie with the potentates of established city states. They remain at the gates of the great cities and represent a new way of life and a new culture.

It is almost superfluous to say that the traditions about the patriarchs, as we see them from afar, do not allow us to construct a continuous historical account or to portray a series of events into which a well-rounded 'biography' of the patriarchs might be fitted. They owe their particular function in Genesis to an on-going development. To balance the Yahweh tradition, which later became dominant, and which is essentially bound up with the mediatorship of Moses, they were given the role of the great forerunners, the 'forefathers' of the future people. It is significant that no special revelation of the God Yahweh was attributed to them, but rather that they reflect the knowledge of a former connection with the El deities of Canaan. Indeed, even the promise of land and descendants assumed a specific form in their case. A prototype on these lines is to be found in summary form in Gen. 12.1–3. The later form of the promise of a land 'flowing with milk and honey' does not appear with the patriarchs, but only emerges with Moses.[44] Nevertheless, it remains an open question whether or not the patriarchs themselves already lived and acted in the light of a future community, whether national or religious. Certainly the texts about the promise speak of many descendants and the blessing associated with them, but all terms are avoided which might indicate particular forms of organization or government over and above the physical assurance of existence.

Thus from a historical point of view the patriarchal traditions prove to be evidence of no more than the first small, but extremely complex stages of a settlement by individual unknown Aramaean groups which is set about with many problems. However, it remains striking that the name 'Israel' is already associated with the patriarchal period. Jacob is given the name after his fateful struggle by the Jabbok (Gen. 32.23–33). This means that the name was originally alien to the patriarchs and had to be given to them subsequently, naturally and significantly to the father of the twelve sons who later bore the names of the twelve tribes of 'Israel'. This would, however, presuppose the experience of the later entity 'Israel'. On the other hand, though, we cannot reject out of hand the possibility that the name 'Israel' was the designation for a group of tribes in central Palestine, at the very point where the Jacob traditions were concentrated, round Bethel and Shechem. But this must remain no more than a hypothesis.[45] Still, the only appearance of the name outside Israel at an early period is on the stele of Pharaoh Merneptah in this very area, and seems intended to designate a particular group of men as 'Israel'.[46] Of course the full importance of this Egyptian evidence for the existence of early patriarchal clans or groups in Central Palestine can only be assessed when its content is related to those events which are connected with the arrival of tribes from the south. Thus we are now compelled to evaluate those texts which dominate the end of the book of Genesis and the rest of the Pentateuch.

NOTES

1. Explicitly since M. Noth, *History of Israel*, 1–7; cf. now the introductory remarks in R. de Vaux, *Early History*, 4–7.

2. The text of Gen. 10 displays two styles, a simple enumeration in the form of a list, and a verbal sentence with the names in the accusative after a form of the verb *yld*, usually in the sense 'he begat'. The change of style is not fortuitous. Larger groups appear in the style of a list; sub-groupings, which introduce further sons, are usually in the form of a verbal sentence. As a rule the pure lists are assigned to P, the later tradition, and the constructions with a verb to J. This produces the following picture: P: vv. 1a, 2–7, 20, 22, 23, 31, 32; J: vv. 1b, 8–12, 13, 14, 15–19, 21, 24–30.

3. One son of Javan was Tarshish, the Greek colony Tartessus in south-west Spain. The agreement with the tradition in Herodotus I, 162, 163 is striking. It is generally true that we have to reckon on a successive growth in the tradition of Gen. 10, but this is hard to date. Cf. the attempt to produce a map based on the table of nations in H. Guthe, *Bibelatlas*, ²1926, pl.6.

4. Probably Libya (see Jer. 46.9; Ezek. 27.10; 30.5; 38.5 according to LXX), and not the Punt of the Egyptian texts (the African coast of the Red Sea and Somaliland); cf. J. Simons, *The Geographical and Topographical Texts of the Old Testament*, 1959, 149, 198, 1313, 1601.

5. To this degree the identification of 'Lud' before 'Aram' in Gen. 10.22 with the Lydians is apt; cf. J. Simons, *Texts*, 150, 151, 1601.

6. The designation 'Semitic' goes back to A. L. Schlözer; accordingly those who had a Semitic type of language were called Semites; cf. J. G. Eichhorn, *Repertorium für biblische und morgenländische Litteratur* VIII, 1781, 161; see also R. Meyer, *Hebräische Grammatik* I, [2]1966, 12–17.

7. See the detailed account, above, 20f.

8. Abram is the older form; only the later strata of the Old Testament know the form Abraham, expanded by the addition of a Hebrew *hē*, presumably under Aramaean influence (Gressmann); see also Noth, *Die israelitischen Personennamen*, 1928, reprinted 1966, 145 n.1.

9. The area is that round the city of Haran (*ḥarrān*) in the area of the upper Balikh. In the Old Testament, the whole area is called Paddan-aram ('the plains of Aram') or Aram-naharaim, the land between the upper course of the Euphrates and the Tigris, watered by the Balikh and the Habor. The city of Haran is associated with the patriarchs in Gen. 11.31f.; 12.4f.; 27.43; 28.10; 29.4. In this area the names of persons often appear as names of places, e.g. Serug in *serūj*, lying west of Haran. There is evidence of Nahor in the Mari texts in the form *naḥur*; it occurs later in Assyrian texts as *til-naḥiri* and lies in the neighbourhood of Haran. The name Terah appears in *til-turaḥi*, south of Haran, in the Balikh valley. Cf. R. de Vaux, 'Les patriarches hébreux', *RB* 55, 1948, 323f.; id., *Early History*, 193–8.

10. To call Sumerian Ur 'the home of Abraham' is a favourite cliché which has been taken over and given wider circulation in secondary, journalistic writing like that of Marek-Ceram, W. Keller and P. Bamm, without further examination.

11. R. de Vaux, *Early History*, 187–92, attempts to demonstrate the historical probability of contacts between Ur and the Haran region against the wider background of the 'age of Abraham'.

12. Merchants, in possession of rich caravans; cf. I Kings 10; Jer. 6.20; Ezek. 27.22ff.

13. Cf. Isa. 21.13; Ezek. 27.20. The *'aššūrim* of Gen. 25.3 does not refer to the Assyrians but to a tribe which was a neighbour of the Ishmaelites, cf. Gen. 25.18.

14. For the juxtaposition of Nebaioth and Kedar (v. 13) cf. Isa. 60.7.

15. The mention of Havilah, known from Gen. 2.11, 12, is remarkable. In Genesis it is celebrated as the land of gold and other mineral treasures. This also points to Arabia.

16. Cf. F. Buhl, *Geschichte der Edomiter*, 1893, which has become a classic description.

17. R. de Vaux, *Early History*, 263–6, maintains that the first contacts of patriarchal groups with Palestine took place in the wider context of Amorite movements in the intermediate period between the Early and the Middle Bronze Age, in the nineteenth and eighteenth centuries BC; on the other hand, he feels compelled to assign the patriarchs to a period before the thirteenth century, in view of the history of individual Israelite tribes. Thus it is only possible to speak 'in very general terms of an "age of the patriarchs" and . . . it is impossible to give exact dates either to the beginning or to the end of that period'.

18. W. F. Albright put forward the thesis that the patriarchs travelled established international routes as merchants at the beginning of the second millennium BC, and were in charge of donkey caravans: 'Abram the Hebrew: A New Archaeological Interpretation', *BASOR* 163, 1961, 36–54; id., *Yahweh and the Gods of Canaan*, 1968, 47–9. Against: R. de Vaux, *Early History*, 225–9; id., *Die Patriarchenerzählungen und die Geschichte*, SBS 3, [2]1968, 23–5; there is a full discussion with references to extensive literature in M. Weippert, *Bibl.* 52, 1971, 407–32.

19. G. von Rad, 'The Problem of the Hexateuch' (1938), in *The Problem of the Hexateuch and Other Essays*, 1966, 1–78; criticized by L. Rost in *Das kleine Credo und andere Studien zum Alten Testament*, 1965, 11–25.

20. J. Henninger, 'Zum frühsemitischen Nomadentum', in *Viehwirtschaft und Hirtenkultur*, ed. L. Földes, 1969, 33–68; id., *Über Lebensraum und Lebensformen der Frühsemiten*, AFLNW/G, Vol. 151, 1968.

21. Cf. the critical study by H. Seebass, *Der Erzvater Israel und die Einführung der Jahweverehrung in Kanaan*, BZAW 98, 1966, which is in many respects consciously hypothetical. It is often said that the Aramaean 'father' is Jacob, but this is not in the text and is based on a free combination with the Genesis tradition, which brings Jacob down to Egypt.

22. By 'saga' Gunkel primarily meant ancient oral tradition. A fundamental study is the introduction to his commentary on Genesis, reprint of the 6th edition, 1963, with the subtitle 'The Sagas of Genesis'.

23. The combination of individual narratives in larger complexes, partly with the characteristic of the Novelle, can be seen in the cases of Abraham (the Abraham–Lot tradition) and Jacob (Jacob and Esau, Jacob and Laban), quite apart from the elaboration of the Joseph story at the end of Genesis. Following Gunkel, see the work by O. Eissfeldt, 'Stammessage und Novelle in den Geschichten von Jakob und von seinen Söhnen' (1923), now in *Kleine Schriften* I, 84–104; the early stages and the composition of the Abraham narratives have been investigated by R. Kilian, *Die vorpriesterlichen Abrahamsüberlieferungen*, BBB 24, 1966.

24. The plan is formulated in Gen. 12.1–3 (see von Rad, 'The Problem of the Hexateuch', 65ff.; H. W. Wolff, *Gesammelte Studien*, 351–61; O. H. Steck, in *Probleme biblischer Theologie*, 1971, 525–54) and in Gen. 15 and 17; cf. also J. Hoftijzer, *Die Verheissungen an die drei Erzväter*, 1956.

25. S. Herrmann, *Die prophetischen Heilserwartungen im Alten Testament*, BWANT 85, 1965, 64–78.

26. For conditions in Israel see, in addition to the study by J. Henninger already mentioned on p. 14 n.5 above), which is written from the standpoint of modern ethnographic knowledge, especially A. Alt, 'Erwägungen über die Landnahme der Israeliten in Palästina' (1939), *KS* I, esp. 139–53; summary in M. Weippert, *The Settlement of the Israelite Tribes in Palestine*, SBT II, 21, 1971, esp. 5–46.

27. R. de Vaux, *Early History*, 229–33, attractively suggests a 'dimorphous society' in a 'transitional state' which fluctuates between tribal culture and city culture. 'The patriarchs, then, followed a way of life which was transitional, halfway between a nomadic life and a settled one' (231).

28. The local traditions are especially stressed by A. Jepsen, 'Zur Überlieferungsgeschichte des Vätergestalten', *Wiss. Zeitschrift d. Karl-Marx Universität*, Leipzig, Ges. und sprachwiss. Reihe 3, 2/3, 1953/4, 267–81.

29. A. Alt, 'The God of the Fathers' (1929), in *Essays on Old Testament History and Religion*, 1966, 3–77; J. Hoftijzer, *Die Verheissungen an die drei Erzväter*, 1956, 83–99, is a critical study, if not always convincing; de Vaux, *Early History*, 268–74, is on the whole positive, and takes more recent work into account.

30. Gen. 31.53.

31. Gen. 31.42, 53.

32. Gen. 49.24.

33. This consists principally of Nabataean and Greek inscriptions from the first century BC to the fourth century AD; they are to be found in the border country of Syria and Palestine and come chiefly from the region of the Hauran, from the area of *leja*, ancient Trachonitis, and from Palmyra and Petra. Alt expanded his collection of material translated in 'The God of the Fathers', op. cit., 67–77, by communications in *PJB* 36, 1940, 100–3.

34. The local deities are usually deities whose designations contain the element *'ēl*, a widespread designation of God in Canaan. This 'El' is associated either with a proper name of a particular kind (e.g. *'ēl 'elyōn*, Gen. 14.22; *'ēl shaddai*, Gen. 17.1) or with the name of a place. The instances used here make it clear that these Canaanite divine epithets recur in a rudimentary form in the patriarchal traditions, but are there closely connected with the

patriarchal God, or Yahweh. The problem which arises here, of the conflict between nomadic forms of religion and those of Canaan before and during the Israelite settlement, has given rise to a considerable scholarly literature, especially since Canaanite religion has become better known through the discoveries of Ugarit and Ras Shamra. However, the last word in this sphere has yet to be spoken. See H. Gese, *Die Religionen Altsyriens, Altarabiens und der Mandäer* (from the series Die Religionen der Menschheit, Vol. 10, 2), 1970, 3–232; L. Rost, 'Die Gottesverehrung der Patriarchen im Lichte der Pentateuchquellen', SVT 7, 1960, 346–59; J. Gray, *The Legacy of Canaan*, SVT 5, 1957; W. F. Albright, *Yahweh and the Gods of Canaan: A Historical Analysis of Two Contrasting Faiths*, 1968; O. Eissfeldt, 'Der Gott Bethel' (1930), *Kleine Schriften* I, 206–33; id., 'El und Jahwe' (1956), *Kleine Schriften* III, 386–97; R. Rendtorff, 'Die Enstehung der israelitischen Religion als religionsgeschichtliches und theologisches Problem', *TLZ* 88, 1963, 735–46.

35. M. Noth, 'Mari und Israel. Eine Personennamenstudie' (1953), *Aufsätze* 2, 213–33; id., 'Die Ursprünge des alten Israel im Lichte neuer Quellen' (1961), *Aufsätze* 2, 245–72.

36. Cf. e.g. the form *Ya(h)qub-ila*, which is often attested in West Semitic, and the equally frequent shorter form *Ya-qu-bi*; probably to be translated 'may he (God) protect'; Noth, 'Mari und Israel', 142–4; de Vaux, *Early History*, 199.

37. The two elements *'b* and *rm*, 'father' and 'raise, exalt', certainly occur frequently, but a translation of the whole name can only be guessed at, e.g. 'the father (a deity?) has exalted (him)'; the possibility put forward by de Vaux, 'he is exalted as to his father; he is noble by birth', *Early History*, 197, is problematical; Noth, op. cit.

38. M. Noth, 'Die Ursprünge des alten Israel im Lichte neuen Quellen' (1961); earlier, in *Die israelitischen Personennamen*, 43–7; for a time he expressed a different view, in *ZDPV* 65, 1942, 34 n.2.

39. De Vaux, *Early History*, 200–9; however, it is necessary to be sceptical about the new use of the term 'proto-Aramaean' proposed by de Vaux, as a comprehensive designation for the ethnic movements of the second millennium, from the 'Amorites' to the Ahlamu and Aramaeans. This can certainly lead to misunderstanding.

40. It is wrong to apply particular parallels which fit the patriarchs directly to them without consideration of their chronological or sociological situation. In nomenclature, custom and law, common Semitic presuppositions are conceivable which extended back to the patriarchs through a number of intermediaries. Particular reference must be made to the customs of family law which are attested in the Nuzi texts and are often compared with the situation in the patriarchal families. Differences should be noted here. Cf. de Vaux, 'Les patriarches hébreux', RB 56, 1949, 5–36; id., *Die Patriarchenerzählungen*, 27–33; id., *Early History*, 241–56; R. Martin-Achard, *Actualité d'Abraham*, 1969, 27–32.

41. The difficulty lies in giving a clear definition of the term *ḥapiru*. In contrast to earlier attempts to describe it in sociological terms, there is a growing tendency to understand *ḥapiru* to be people from a common racial background. It is worth noting a text from the time of Amenophis II (Urk.IV 1309, 1) in which *ḥapiru* (there in the Egyptian form *'prw*) stand with the Shasu alongside the Syrian groups of the Hurrians and the people of Nuḥasse. Here the *ḥapiru* are clearly distinguished from other groups. Cf. W. Helck, *VT* 18, 1968, 479; de Vaux, *Early History*, 110f. It has been insufficiently noted that the term *ḥapiru* underwent a change in the course of time and was adopted and used differently in different areas. K. Koch, 'Die Hebräer vom Auszug aus Ägypten bis zum Grossreich Davids', *VT* 19, 1969, 37–81, notes this emphatically; similarly de Vaux, *Early History*, 111. Koch would go still further, and associate the whole genealogical complex in Genesis with the *ḥapiru* as a general ethnic designation, speaking of 'Hebrew peoples'. However, this would seem to be a generalization which brings down to one level elements which the texts themselves present in more differentiated form.

42. There is no evidence that the kings mentioned were individual historical person-

alities, much less that they were ever in action together. Only elements of their names are approximately comparable with others from the wider sphere of the East, but not with any certainty. The name of Arioch of Ellasar is probably Hurrian; identification with Arriwuk, a son of Zimrilim of Mari, has been disputed. The name Tidal cannot be separated from the Hittite royal name Tudḫaliya, which was borne by four kings. Chedorlaomer is in fact composed of elements of two Elamite names (Kudurlagamar?), but the appearance of Elamite alliances in Palestine is improbable. Amraphel, the king of Shinar (Babylonia) is most problematical of all since any identification with Hammurabi has been abandoned; identification with Amatpiel of Qatna (Böhl, von Soden) has been disputed. Cf. W. von Soden, *WO* I, 3, 1948, 198; K. Jaritz, *ZAW* 70, 1958, 225f.; F. Cornelius, *ZAW* 72, 1960, 1–7; de Vaux, *Early History*, 218.

43. Various interpretations have been given of the scene with Melchizedek. The history of religion is primarily interested in the relationship between priest and king, the history of Israel in a pre-Israelite monarchy in Jerusalem, usually assessed in conjunction with Ps. 110 and the handing over of the kingship to David. More recently, the possibility has also been raised of Melchizedek being partner in a covenant. See H. H. Rowley, 'Melchizedek and Zadok (Gen. 14 and Ps. 110)', *Festschrift A. Bertholet*, 1950, 461–72; H. E. Del Medico, 'Melchisédech', *ZAW* 69, 1957, 160–70; W. F. Albright, 'Abram the Hebrew', *BASOR* 163, 1961, 36–54, esp. 52; L. R. Fischer, 'Abraham and his Priest-King', *JBL* 81, 1962, 264–70; R. H. Smith, 'Abram and Melchizedek (Gen. 14.18–20)', *ZAW* 77, 1965, 129–53.

44. Exod. 3.8. For the two types of promise see S. Herrmann, *Die prophetischen Heilserwartungen*, 64–78.

45. Cf. also L. Wächter, 'Israel und Jeschurun', *Schalom* (Festschrift A. Jepsen), 1971, 58–64.

46. The name 'Israel' occurs after the mention of the cities of Ashkelon, Gezer (*tell-jezer*) and Jenoam (*tell en-nā'am*, south-west of Lake Gennesaret), and unlike these cities is distinguished by the hieroglyphic determinative for 'men'; it therefore refers to a group of people and not to a city constitution. The text of the stele is in W. Spiegelberg, *ZÄS* 34, 1896, 1–25; translations: *AOT*, 20–5; *ANET*, 376–8; the 'Israel' section alone, with more detailed comment, in *TGI*, ²1968, 39f.

Semitic Elements in Egypt and the Tradition of the 'Exodus'

AT LEAST FROM the beginning of the book of Exodus, the dominant tradition in the Old Testament is that the Israelite tribes did not invade Palestine from the north and east, like the patriarchs, but largely entered from the south. In connection with this, belief in Yahweh came from the south and those who handed on the tradition were able to establish it in Palestine. Thus these southern traditions later also became significant for the whole of Israel. This process is quite essential for understanding the theology of the Old Testament,[1] but it had catastrophic consequences for understanding the history of Israel. It suggested the view that in fact the whole of Israel had been in Egypt and had its origins there. But this is historically improbable. Only one component of later Israel can have had contact with Egypt, but its reminiscences and experiences were so persuasive that in the end they even attained credal character in the formula 'Yahweh, the God who brought us out of Egypt'.[2] This conviction is the final product of an extremely complex process of tradition, the historical foundations of which can, however, still be reconstructed, not least from the Old Testament itself.

Genesis begins consistently from its genealogical system and the framework of family history which that provides. It makes a move to the southern group of traditions with the statement that Jacob's second youngest son, Joseph, was sold into Egypt. Significantly, the intermediaries are Midianites or Ishmaelites, peoples who have already been assigned to the southern groups in the genealogy.[3] Joseph makes a position for himself in Egypt and causes Jacob and his sons also to come to Egypt. They settle there and are finally able to become a great and powerful people (Exod. 1.9, J), which later tradition promptly develops into the perfect Israelite twelve-tribe system (Exod. 1.1–7, P). The contradiction which results is readily tolerated. The patriarchs again leave the land which was promised to them in Genesis, and instead settle in Egypt. From here they have to embark on a new 'conquest', which again takes them to Palestine and fulfils the promise for the second time. From this the Priestly writing (P) develops the theory that for the patriarchs Palestine was at first 'a land of sojourning' (Exod. 6.4). The historical improbability of this course of events is obvious, and details in the narrative in fact point in another direction.

The actual historical picture begins to take shape and gain plausibility when the consequences of the Aramaean wanderings and the genealogical record of them in Genesis are taken in full seriousness. Whereas the groups which entered Syria and Palestine found a foothold in the less populated hill-country through a lengthy process and eventually settled there, the groups which entered in the region of the Sinai peninsula found themselves confronted with a harder task. They found only a few watering-places there, and at best an oasis like Kadesh, which allowed some of them to settle for a while. Other elements pressed further westwards, but did not find territory which they could take over without any problem, as in Syria and Palestine. In the eastern delta they reached the frontier of the Egyptian empire and had to deal with its administrative apparatus. The consent of Pharaoh made it possible for some tribes seeking pasture to stay for a period, but a longer settlement was impossible, especially as this was the time when Rameses II was constructing a residence of considerable dimensions in the eastern delta. It is extremely probable that Semites, too, were used in the work of building, though of course there is considerable disagreement about their origin. The Old Testament suggests circumstances (for which, however, there is no evidence outside the Old Testament) which led to the departure or flight of Semites who had settled in the eastern delta. They moved into the wilderness of Sinai, where presumably they made contact with groups of similar ethnic background, perhaps in Kadesh. Independently, or together with the latter, they later took the way which brought them to Palestine. We may assume that there they met up with groups which had already settled and who may be supposed to have handed down the patriarchal traditions.

This framework may be hypothetical in many places, but it does give some indication of the context in which we may understand — and indeed demonstrate – in historical terms how some of the groups which were later to become Israel spent a period in Egypt. Some indication has been given of the circumstances which provoked the 'exodus' and at the same time also created the presuppositions for the so-called journey through the wilderness, the central point of which was the encounter with Yahweh on the mount of God. Some indication has also already been given of the bases from which the conquest 'from the south' was launched, and of the possibly greater potency which enabled these groups to attain a position of dominance and pave the way for the establishment of the religion of Yahweh.

The probability of the picture outlined here can now be increased by the introduction of detailed material.

The person of Joseph, who was sold into Egypt, poses to Old Testament scholars the problem whether he is to be regarded simply as a patriarch, the son of Jacob, as a high Egyptian official and a significant historical personality, or as an ideal figure of Old Testament literature, the chief hero of the Joseph story of Gen. 37;39–50, which has been expanded and given the form of a romance. Correct observations lie behind each of these possibilities, and each possibility has been specially favoured.[4] There are many sides to the problem and no straightforward solution can be presented. At its heart lies the question of the possible means and circumstances by which Semitic elements could have entered Egypt and remained there.

With some justification, it is continually stressed that in historical times Semitic groups entered the eastern delta at a very early stage, demonstrably at the latest about the end of the third millennium BC, and very soon presented a threat which required counter-measures to be taken. A classical account of this is given in the so-called 'historical section' of the *Teaching for King Merikare* (*c.* 2070–2040).[5] At the beginning of the Middle Kingdom, Amenemhet I erected the 'Prince's Wall', a system of border fortifications on the edge of the eastern delta, to provide protection against invading nomads. The royal official Sinuhe gives an impressive account of the way in which he fled to Syria-Palestine after hearing of the death of Amenemhet I and broke through the barrier of 'the Prince's Wall' by himself at risk of his life.[6] Nevertheless, after the Middle Kingdom, trade and the exchange of peoples between Syria and Egypt must have grown, so that 'Asiatics' were largely accepted in Egypt and could be utilized to provide services of various kinds.[7] Here we find an important basis for the subsequent establishment of Hyksos rule,[8] which introduced a 'Second Intermediary Period' for Egypt.[9]

In the New Kingdom, the eastern delta became the starting-point for the great military operations of the Egyptian kings against Palestine and Syria. In addition to the system of border fortifications there was a regular 'military road', with fortifications and defences especially at watering places. This led from the eastern zone of the delta into the steppe of southern Palestine, at some distance from the coast.[10] Prisoners of war were now brought back to Egypt in large numbers and settled there wherever it was possible. This led to a considerable expansion of the Semitic element in the population of Egypt.[11] Trade with the vassals of Syria was lively and well-organized. We have evidence of this not only in the Amarna letters from the time of Amenophis III and Amenophis IV (Akenaten) but also in a number of other individual documents.[12] One which continues to arouse great interest is the letter from a frontier official stationed at the edge of the eastern delta to his superior (*c.* 1190). It affords a first-hand glimpse at the situation in this area at a time near to the 'exodus' of the groups later to become Israel. The letter runs:[13] 'Another communication to my [lord], to [wit : We] have finished letting the Shasu tribes of Edom[14] pass the fortress [of] Merneptah, which is (in) *Ṯkw*,[15] to the pools of the temple of Atum (*pr-Itm* = 'Pithom') of Merneptah, which are (in) *Ṯkw*,[16] to keep them alive and to keep their cattle alive, through the great *ka* of Pharaoh, the good sun of every land, in the year 8,[17] five [intercalary] days, [the birth of] Seth.[18] I have had them bring in a copy of the report[19] to the [place where] my lord is, as well as the other names of the days when the fortress of Merneptah which is in *Ṯkw*, may be passed . . .'

The letter gives an impression of the routine registration of border traffic which was evidently connected with a change in the pasturage of nomadic groups. These groups are given no further description, but the places in which they are allowed to graze their flocks are mentioned. The groups are Shasu tribes from Edom, members of those nomadic groups which came to the eastern zone of the delta after crossing the north of the Sinai peninsula from southern Palestine.[20] Here they sought pasturage, for either a shorter or a longer period, but were allowed it only with the Pharaoh's consent. All this takes place in the very area in which the Old Testament indicates that the 'Israelites' stayed.

This very brief survey of contacts between elements of the population of Syria, adjacent on the east, and Egypt, opens up possibilities, but also shows the limits of the certainty with which Egyptian material can be related to an 'Israelite stay' in Egypt. Nevertheless, the apparently broad range of possibilities reduces itself to a plausibly small geographical area and an appropriate and convincing period of time. The most important geographical reference is in Exod. 1.11 and is at the same time bound up with the possibility of establishing a date which could not simply be invented. In Exod. 1.11 we are told that the Israelites built 'store cities', namely Pithom and Ra'amses, for the Pharaoh under the supervision of 'taskmasters'. Pithom may be identified with *pr-Itm* in *Ṯkw*, mentioned in the letter of the frontier official, and is situated in the fertile area of the *wādi eṭ-ṭumēlāt*.[21] The name of the famous Pharaoh Rameses clearly underlies the name Ra'amses, but here it denotes a place. The rulers of the Nineteenth Dynasty did in fact build a residence in the east delta and gave it, among other names, the all-embracing name 'house of Rameses (*Pr-R'mśśw*), beloved of Amun, great in victorious power'. In that case the short form 'House of Rameses' would be limited in the Old Testament to the reproduction of the proper name Rameses only.[22] But this residence cannot have been restricted to the area of the *wādi eṭ-ṭumēlāt*. Archaeologists have believed that they have discovered the city of Rameses, or at least parts of it, both in the ruins of Tanis, lying in the north-east of the delta (*ṣān el-ḥagar*) and also in *qantīr*, lying twelve miles further south, and the buildings excavated there.[23] There is an attractive thesis that this delta residence of the Ramessids was a large estate extending over a considerable area, of the same kind as the residence of Amenophis IV–Akenaten, which has been discovered at modern *tell el-'amārna*.[24] In that case the scattered remains, including those of Pithom, would fit into a comprehensible total picture,[25] which in the end would also clarify the nature of 'store cities'. These must have been administrative quarters and store-areas attached to the residence. It is hard to imagine that this juxtaposition of the names Pithom and Rameses, in such a correct order, rests on secondary tradition and does not reproduce any historical circumstances which need to be taken seriously.[26] Thus it is hard to separate the Old Testament reminiscence of 'servitude' in Egypt from the employment of Semitic groups in the building of this new residence of Pharaoh. To this degree, the biblical account, and especially Exod. 1.11, provides concrete and appropriate historical material.

Unfortunately, however, for all further details we move completely into the realm of hypothesis, however much the relatively long account in Exod. 1–15 seems to know about the stay of the later Israelites in Egypt.[27] The legal status of the foreign workers is doubtful, for a start. Difficulties arise in view of the approach adopted by Egyptian administration. The theory that a group of workers, presumably composed of different elements, finally escaped from Egypt and, despite their probable ethnic complexity, attached themselves to groups in the Sinai desert who later went on to Palestine, seems to be logically correct.[28] This theory of the 'fugitive workers' could also find a certain amount of support in the Old Testament. For it is striking that in the account of the exodus in particular, the oppressed people are called 'Hebrews'.[29] Given that here we have a recollection of the *ḥapiru* (Egyptian *ʿprw*), and accepting the widespread view that those described had a sociological status with lower privileges, this designation could be the right one for a group of workers composed of different elements. On the other hand, supposing that these people shared a common racial background and the inner coherence which that provided, and also that the designation 'Hebrew' was to be understood in ethnic rather than in sociological terms, an identification of these 'Hebrews' with the nomadic Shasu, like the Shasu from Edom in the letter of the frontier official, would not have to be ruled out completely. In that case, the question would be whether a group of Shasu seeking temporary pasture could be pressed into building a residence for Pharaoh.[30]

However, these are considerations which begin from the presupposition that in any event analogous circumstances or events are needed, or have to be adduced, for a correct explanation of this stay in Egypt. At all events, it seems advisable not to neglect completely the Old Testament and the statements it contains. The Old Testament makes it clear that this employment in building 'store cities' was felt to be harsh oppression which did not accord with the self-understanding of free nomads who were used to living on the steppe. Observations in the Joseph story in Genesis already give vivid evidence of such a feeling.[31] The connections between this group and the 'wilderness' are also emphasized by the fact that Moses is able to convince the Pharaoh that they want to go a three days' journey into the wilderness to sacrifice to their God (Exod. 3.18). This pretext remains remarkable, even if one supposes it to have been conceived in the light of a later situation.

In the circumstances, the best explanation for the event in Egypt would seem to be one which can reconcile the heterogeneous elements in the traditions both within and outside the Old Testament. It is conceivable that one group of Shasu with an Aramaean background approached the east delta, passed the Egyptian frontier legally and was allotted favourable pasturage for their livestock for a period. They may well have visited the pasturage regularly and therefore have been allowed it on privileged terms.[32] The extent of contact with the Egyptians must remain open. We have no parallels for the conscription of people to build the neighbouring residence of the Ramessids from among these nomads living on the frontier of the cultivated land. Nor is there any evidence from authentic sources to attest the flight of discontented construction workers. But it seems almost certain that free nomads would feel the labour of building in Egypt to be shameful and oppressive and would try to avoid it. Thus if the Old Testament traditions contain a historical reminiscence of oppression and exodus, this must be understood in terms of the conflict situation between the nomadic groups and the administration concerned with the construction of the Ramessids' residence. We can explain these events all the better if the group which left Egypt was characterized not only by a common destiny but also by a particular ethnic background which made it hard for them to adapt to the unpalatable conditions imposed by a foreign power.

The man Moses towers above all others involved in this conflict at the time of the exodus. Despite his Egyptian name,[33] we learn nothing about him from Egyptian sources.[34] He emerges as an intermediary between the two sides, between the power of the Egyptian state and the oppressed aliens. He evidently has good connections in both directions. He is said to have been involved in Egyptian civilization from earliest childhood through adoption;[35] he makes representations on behalf of his unprivileged 'brethren', even commits murder, and leaves the country from fear of the Egyptians.[36] Like the court official Sinuhe at an earlier date, he escapes from Egypt eastwards into the territory of the nomadic Midianites; there he marries, but later returns to Egypt to fulfil a divine commission which is imparted to him in the wilderness at a hallowed place.[37] He is to free his countrymen from Pharaoh's bondage.

The many-sidedness of this man and the multiplicity of functions which he performs have long suggested that the tradition has exaggerated the contribution of one man, who could not possibly have been all these things himself in a single person.[38] After all, Moses bears an Egyptian name, is spokesman for his oppressed brethren, son-in-law of a Midianite priest, the receiver of a revelation, a hard-headed politician at court and a successful liberator. Here too, only a construction in some form calculated to approximate to historical probability can take us a step further. At any rate, however, an attempt should be made.

There is evidence at the latest after the Middle Kingdom that people from the region of Syria bore Egyptian names which they acquired as foreigners who were either active in Egypt or born there.[39] Moses may have risen to a privileged position in some way. There can be no doubt that he later exploited it or acted without regard for it. However, it is more difficult to explain the background to his flight and marriage, his contact with the Midianites. The sphere of activity of these camel nomads was great and can have extended as far as the delta region. Contacts between Midianites and subject peoples in Egypt cannot be completely ruled out. The appearance of the Shasu of Edom in the letter of the frontier official suggests considerable traffic between the large area south of Palestine and the delta. Thus for all the uncertainty over the details of the historical Moses, a sphere of action should be considered which neither binds him one-sidedly to Egypt nor genuinely associates him with the Midianites. Moses had an Egyptian name, and this is hardly pure invention; he was regarded as a kinsman of the Midianites by marriage, and this cannot be without foundation. However these contacts between the wilderness and Egypt may be assessed in Moses' case, the man only had some prospect of success if he were sufficiently familiar with the difficulties on the frontier of the Egyptian empire and could establish sufficient solidarity with those who were leaving Egypt. This intermediate position of Moses between the two spheres of wilderness and cultivated land is made credible by the biblical account, and it fits the historical conditions on the edge of the eastern delta at the time of Rameses II well. So we should think in terms of a Semite who left Egyptian service and headed for the wilderness with the fugitives, no matter whether a point of contact with the Midianites may be found then or at an earlier stage.

These considerations raise the question of the possible length of the stay of these Semites in Egypt. The Old Testament itself has different views on the matter. These fluctuate between the doubtless artificial number of 430 years and the assumption that only four generations separated the patriarchs and the time of Moses.[40] There is nothing against assuming that the 'oppression' lasted only a fairly short time; perhaps it began during the reign of Rameses II and did not extend far beyond it, if at all. The usual formula that Rameses II was the Pharaoh of the oppression and his successor Merneptah the 'Pharaoh of the Exodus' rests on a combination of passages in the book of Exodus which is not compelling.[41] In view of the uncertainty of an absolute calculation of time during the Nineteenth Dynasty, absolute figures are not appropriate.[42] Still, we can begin from the fact that the exodus took place at the end of the thirteenth century BC.

The event itself is described in the book of Exodus in broad terms, which tend towards the dramatic. The Egyptian king is never named in the Old Testament text, but is constantly called Pharaoh;[43] he refuses to allow the people to depart, as they request. The negotiations carried on by Moses and Aaron are supported by the outbreak of a series of terrifying plagues which are visited on the land; last of all the firstborn of the Egyptians are killed. It has rightly been pointed out that the passover rite, into which the account of the plagues leads, is the heart of the complex of plagues. The Israelite firstborn are spared: the angel of destruction passes over the houses of the 'Israelites' (Exod. 12). The fearful happening among the Egyptians and the sacrifice of the Israelites lay the foundations for the exodus. This complex of traditions has an end in itself. It rests on a cultic development which only took place at a later period and was given a historical explanation by the event of the exodus. The passover lamb and the eating of unleavened bread were originally elements in a nomadic and agricultural festival which in Israel was associated with grateful remembrance of the exodus. Thus part of the exodus tradition could be built up and dramatized through the passover legend.[44]

The exodus itself took place *via* a series of places which can only be identified very approximately.[45] But it leads up to a last dramatic climax which acts as an echo of the difficulties and tribulations experienced in Egypt. Pharaoh regretted his decision to allow the exodus.[46] He sent his chariots in pursuit of the Israelites, and at the Reed Sea a last dangerous threat was posed to those who had been released with apparently supreme authorization, but who were in reality almost certainly fugitives.[47] The catastrophe which befell Pharaoh's troops is depicted in two extended units of tradition which in the course of time have increasingly been endowed with miraculous features.[48] The disaster is brought about through a natural miracle. The earlier tradition tells how the sea was dried up and then suddenly returned, swallowing up the unit that was manoeuvring there; the later tradition, on the other hand, depicts the sea as standing like walls through which Israel passed, while the Egyptians were annihilated. In addition there is a short verse which is put in the mouth of Miriam:[49]

Sing to the Lord for he has triumphed gloriously;
the horse and his rider he has thrown into the sea.

This Song of Miriam is regarded as one of the oldest pieces of tradition in the Old Testament. It celebrates a victory of Yahweh over his enemies and those of Israel. As before, the lively interest taken by the Old Testament tradition in this event is striking; historical research has seized hold of the question of the location of the miracle at the sea and by considering local conditions has also attempted to demonstrate the probability of a historical event.

With the support of the evidence of ancient sources in conjunction with the relatively exact topographical details in Exod. 14.2, O. Eissfeldt has stated that the miracle took place on the eastern tongue of the Sirbonian sea, a tongue of land about six miles west of Pelusium on the Mediterranean coast between Egypt and Palestine.[50] The treacherous coast, partly marshy and partly visited by periodic floods, often swallowed up whole armies in this region, according to the reports of ancient writers.[51] This country therefore provided the natural conditions against which the miracle at the Reed Sea might be imagined.

M. Noth disagreed with Eissfeldt and put forward another suggestion.[52] He stressed the uncertainty of the term 'Reed Sea' and regarded the surprisingly exact topographical details of Exod. 14.2 as the work of a later tradition which was interested in the exact location of the event and which transferred the miracle at a secondary stage to the area of the Sirbonian sea.

Although his examination of the Old Testament tradition is in no way comparable to that of Eissfeldt and Noth, W. Helck would see one of the Bitter Lakes in the present-day Canal Zone as the place of the miracle of the Reed Sea.[53]

Many questions remain open about the miracle at the Reed Sea which, in view of the different elements in the tradition, should not simply be spoken of as the 'passage of the Israelites through the sea'. However, it is at any rate certain that an incautious advance beyond the eastern delta in the region of the old Egyptian military road to Palestine, well guarded and fortified, was dangerous. Egyptian monuments testify to this.[54] The pursuing force of Egyptian chariots probably did not set out from Egypt itself, say from the eastern zone of the delta; it could have been stationed at one of the forts on the military road and have been dispatched from there. We may assume that it was only a small contingent. The failure of the technically superior Egyptians has been stylized as a great defeat in the memory of those who escaped and were delivered; perhaps it may even have been associated with the catastrophe of the water at a later stage, and explained in that way. Details are hard to arrive at, but true reminiscences of battle experiences of Semites who escaped from Egypt or of nomadic Shasu may have been the factor which gave rise to the complex group of traditions about the miracle at the sea. The Old Testament is well aware (Exod. 13.17f.) that the direct route to Palestine from the east of the delta, parallel to the sea, was well guarded and dangerous. Hence the fact that those who left Egypt now turn in a south-easterly direction and move from the Reed Sea into the interior of the Sinai peninsula.

NOTES

1. Now markedly stressed in W. Zimmerli, *Grundriss der alttestamentlichen Theologie*, Theologische Wissenschaft 3, 1972; the difficulties are outlined in G. von Rad, *Old Testament Theology* 1, 1962, 3–14. For the whole of this chapter see also S. Herrmann, *Israel in Egypt*, SBT II, 27, 1973.

2. M. Noth coined the phrase 'the primal confession of Israel'. At the same time it is, he says, 'the kernel of the whole of subsequent Pentateuchal tradition', M. Noth, *A History of Pentateuchal Traditions*, 1972, 47–51.

3. Midian as Abraham's son by Keturah, Gen. 25.2; the sons of Ishmael, Gen. 25.12–18. The sale of Joseph by Ishmaelites, Gen. 37.25–27, 28aβ; by Midianites, Gen. 37.28aα; the two traditions are usually interpreted as elements of two narrative traditions and assigned to J. and E.

4. O. Kaiser, 'Stammesgeschichtliche Hintergründe der Josephsgeschichte', *VT* 10, 1960, 1–15; H. H. Rowley, *From Joseph to Joshua*, 1950, 109–23, offers a great deal of material, but his historical conclusion, that Joseph should be set in the time of Akenaten, is problematical; G. von Rad, 'The Joseph Narrative and Ancient Wisdom', in *The Problem of the Hexateuch and Other Essays*, 1966, 292–300; from the Egyptological standpoint, J. Vergote, 'Joseph en Égypte. Genèse Chap. 37–50 à la lumière des études égyptologiques récentes', 1959; for criticism of Vergote's book see S. Herrmann, *TLZ* 85, 1960, 827–30; more recent literary-critical investigations are: L. Ruppert, *Die Josephserzählung der Genesis. Ein Beitrag zur Theologie der Pentateuchquellen*, 1965; D. B. A. Redford, *A Study of the Biblical Story of Joseph (Genesis 37–50)*, SVT 20, 1970.

5. A. Scharff, *Der historische Abschnitt der Lehre für König Merikare*, SAM, Phil.-hist. Abt. 1936, 8. These are lines 69–110 of the text of the 'Instruction'; lines 91–100 are important here; translated in S. Herrmann, *Israel in Egypt*, 9; see also *AOT*, 34–6; *ANET*, 414–8.

6. *TGI*, ²1968, 2f. The name 'Prince's Wall' is often used: a literal translation is 'the walls of the ruler'. The 'bitter lakes' (*km-wr*) mentioned in the Pyramid Texts of the Old Kingdom may be a forerunner of the 'walls of the ruler'; in the hieroglyphic text they are given the determinative for a wall (I am grateful to G. Fecht for this reference).

7. The picture of a caravan arriving in Egypt, found in an excavation at Beni Hasan and dating from the time of the Twelfth Dynasty, is impressive. The leader, named Ibsha

(*Ibsh*') bears the title *ḥq' ḫ'š't*, 'ruler of a foreign land'; thus he is, so to speak, a Hyksos; cf. also Helck, *Beziehungen*, 41f. The lists published by W. C. Hayes, *A Papyrus of the Late Middle Kingdom in the Brooklyn Museum [Papyrus Brooklyn 35,1446]*, 1955, are illuminating for the provision of services in the Middle Kingdom; see also *ANET Suppl.*, 553f., and Helck, *Beziehungen*, 77–81; a fundamental study with further material is J. M. A. Janssen, 'Fonctionnaires sémites au service de l'Égypte', *Chronique d'Égypte* 26, no. 51, 1951, 50ff.

8. Cf. A. Alt, 'Die Herkunft der Hyksos in neuer Sicht' (1954), *KS* III, 72–98; G. Posener, *Syria* 34, 1957, 145–63; for discussion and criticism of other views see W. Helck, *Beziehungen*, ²1971, 89–106.

9. H. E. Winlock, *The Rise and Fall of the Middle Kingdom in Thebes*, 1947; J. von Beckerath, *Untersuchungen zur politischen Geschichte der Zweiten Zwischenzeit in Ägypten*, Ägyptologische Forschungen 23, 1964.

10. A. H. Gardiner, 'The Ancient Military Road between Egypt and Palestine', *JEA* 6, 1920, 99–116.

11. Helck, *Beziehungen*, 342–69; cf. also the mention of *'pr* people in Egyptian texts in *TGI*, ²1968, 34–6.

12. Cf. here the register of a frontier official in *TGI*, ²1968, 37–9.

13. *TGI²*, 40f.; *AOT*, 97; *ANET*, 259; detailed commentary in R. A. Caminos, *Late-Egyptian Miscellanies*, 1954, 293–6.

14. Probably the Edomite territory south of Palestine: Edom presumably also occurs in the list of Pharaoh Shishak; see Noth in *ZDPV* 61, 1938, 295.

15. This is a frontier fortification in the city *Tkw*.

16. The centre of the city *Tkw* was a temple of Atum, to whose lands the pools also belonged, so that the whole terrain could be given the name *pr-Itm* ('Pithom'). The remains of *Tkw* are to be located in *tell el-mashūta* in the *wādi eṭ-ṭumēlāt* east of modern Ismaelia. W. Helck, '*Tkw* und die Ramsesstadt', *VT* 15, 1965, 35–40, arguing against D. B. Redford, *VT* 13, 1963, 403–8. Cf. also H. Cazelles and J. Leclant, 'Pithom', *Supplément au Diction-naire de la Bible* VIII, fasc.42, 1967, cols. 1–6.

17. The eighth year of the reign of Sethos II (about 1203–1194).

18. The five intercalary days are days which were added to balance the calendar of twelve months of thirty days with the solar year. The day of the birth of Seth is the third intercalary day.

19. Refers to the official registration of the arrivals.

20. It is worth noting the important observation by W. Helck, that Shasu (*sh'św*), 'nomads', is a term applied to those moving in the south of Palestine south of a line from Raphia to the southern end of the Dead Sea and on its eastern bank, disturbing the military road from Egypt to the north. Those living north of this line appear in Egyptian sources as *'prw* (to be identified with *ḥapiru*). This 'linguistic rule' applies from the middle of the Eighteenth Dynasty down to about the time of Rameses II. W. Helck, 'Die Bedrohung Palästinas durch einwandernde Gruppen am Ende der 18. und am Anfang der 19. Dynastie', *VT* 18, 1968, 472–80. For the Shasu in general see the extensive work by R. Giveon, *Les bédouins Shosou des documents égyptiens*, 1971.

21. H. Bardtke, *Vom Nildelta zum Sinai*, 1968, gives some idea of the present appearance of the country described here; his pictures were taken in 1966.

22. For the abbreviation of the name and the way in which it is written in Hebrew see W. Helck, *VT* 15, 1965, 40–7, disagreeing with Redford, *VT* 13, 1963, 408–13.

23. Tanis: P. Montet, *Tanis: douze années de fouilles dans une capitale oubliée au Delta égyptien*, 1942; id., *Les énigmes de Tanis*, 1952; J. Yoyotte, 'Les fouilles de Tanis (XXIIIᵉ campagne 1966)', *Comptes rendus de l'Acad. d. Inscr. et Belles-Lettres*, 1967, 590–601. Qantir: Labib Habachi, 'Khatā'na-Quantīr: Importance', *ASAE* 52, 1954, 443–562; R. North, *Archeo-Biblical Egypt*, 1967, 95–9.

24. The surviving boundary stelae show that the extent of the residence of Amenophis IV was about 9 miles from north to south and 12 from east to west.

25. Ruins of a temple have been found in Tanis, but not a palace; a palace was discovered in Qantir, but not a temple. This is some of the evidence on which A. Alt based his theory of a 'great residence', 'Die Deltaresidenz der Ramessiden' (1954), *KS* III, 176–85. Qantir is preferred as the real site of the delta residence by E. P. Uphill, 'Pithom and Raamses: Their Location and Significance', *JNES* 27, 1968, 291–316; 28, 1969, 15–39.

26. The late date of Exod. 1.11 put forward by Redford in *VT* 13, 1963, 414–8, is not convincing, and the arguments which he produces are insufficient to demonstrate it. Cf. S. Herrmann, *Israel in Egypt*, 75.

27. Cf. G. Fohrer, *Überlieferung und Geschichte des Exodus. Eine Analyse von Ex. 1–15*, BZAW 91, 1964, which is primarily literary, with limited historical reference. See now also G. W. Coats, 'A Structural Transition in Exodus', *VT* 22, 1972, 129–42.

28. W. Helck, *Beziehungen*, 581; id., *VT* 18, 1968, 480, and *TLZ* 97, 1972, 180.

29. Exod. 1.15, 16, 19; 2.6, 7, 11, 13; 3.18; 5.3; 7.16; 9.1, 13; 10.3; and on them K. Koch, 'Die Hebräer vom Auszug aus Ägypten bis zum Grossreich Davids', *VT* 19, 1969, 37–81.

30. W. Helck, *TLZ* 97, 1972, 180, regards the idea of conscripted nomads as improbable and suggests a 'group of prisoners of heterogeneous ethnic composition', predominantly Shasu. Apart from the fact that this is a hypothesis, the question remains whether it can be demonstrated that Shasu were prisoners in Egypt and were in the service of Egyptian overlords there. The fragment of a stele from Tanis of the time of Rameses II perhaps (the text is damaged) provides evidence for the taking of prisoners: R. Giveon, *Les bédouins Shosou*, 1971, 108f. (document 30).

31. Cf. Gen. 46.31–34.

32. This could be seen as the historical nucleus of the tradition of the 'land of Goshen', which the Pharaoh assigned to Jacob and his sons; cf. Gen. 45.10; 47.4, 6, etc.; see also Exod. 8.18; 9.26. It is significant that this is also given the name 'the land of Rameses' (Gen. 47.11). Thus Goshen must be part of the residence of Rameses, most probably around the *wādi eṭ-ṭumēlāt*; thus confidently R. de Vaux, *Early History*, 302. Cf. also the survey of the most recent scholarship, with a precise proposal for the situation of Goshen within the north-east delta, in R. North, *Archeo-biblical Egypt*, 1967, 80–6.

33. The attempt at an explanation of the name in Exod. 2.10 is a Hebrew 'popular etymology'. In fact 'Moses' is the same element as appears in many Egyptian names after the New Kingdom, as in Thutmoses, Ramoses and even in Rameses. Here the name of a god is linked with the Egyptian root *mśy* 'born', though with different grammatical connections. Thus Ramoses means '(the God) Re is born', but Rameses '(the god) Re bore him'. The theophorous element has been broken off from the name Moses, producing an abbreviated name for which evidence can also be found in Egyptian. J. W. Griffiths, 'The Egyptian Derivation of the Name Moses', *JNES* 12, 1953, 225–31; for a number of philological details see also Helck in *VT* 15, 1965, 43–7, esp. 46f.; E. Edel, 'Neue keilschriftliche Umschreibungen ägyptischer Namen aus den Bogazköytexten', *JNES* 7, 1948, 11–24; for a summary see also S. Herrmann, *Israel in Egypt*, 43–5.

34. The miscellany by F. Cornelius, 'Mose urkundlich', *ZAW* 78, 1966, 75–8, rests on uncritical harmonizations, details in S. Herrmann, *Israel in Egypt*, 68.

35. Exod. 2.1–10 uses the more common literary theme of the exposed child which is destined for great things. See my remarks in *Israel in Egypt*, 44f., which are not meant to argue that Exod. 2.1–10 are directly historical, but are intended to illuminate the Egyptian background.

36. Exod. 2.11–22.

37. Exod. 3.

38. Cf. the critical historical works by R. Smend, *Das Mosebild von Heinrich Ewald bis Martin Noth*, 1959, and E. Osswald, *Das Bild des Mose in der kritischen alttestamentlichen Wissenschaft seit Julius Wellhausen*, 1962.

39. G. Posener, 'Les asiatiques en Égypte sous les XIIe et XIIIe dynasties', *Syria* 34, 1957, 145–63; Posener here also gives a detailed discussion of the Papyrus Brooklyn 35, 1446, edited by Hayes (cf. now *ANET Suppl.*, 553f.). For details and consequences for the Old Testament cf. S. Herrmann, 'Mose', *EvTh* 28, 1968, 301–28, esp.306–8; id., *Israel in Egypt*, 45.

40. For details see Exod.12.40f. (430 years); Gen.15.13 (400 years); Gen.15.16 (the fourth generation after Abraham may return to Palestine; Exod.6.13ff. (four generations from the sons of Jacob to Moses); R. de Vaux, *Early History*, 388–92; S. Herrmann, *Israel in Egypt*, 48–50.

41. The death of the king responsible for the oppression is reported in Exod.2.23. One might conclude from this that the Exodus took place under the successor of Rameses II, king Merneptah. This possibility is not to be excluded, though Exod.2.23 (P) does not necessarily require it. A. Alt, *KS* I, 162–8, still considers an exodus under Rameses II; similarly de Vaux, *Early History*, 392.

42. Cf. primarily E. Hornung, *Untersuchungen zur Chronologie und Geschichte des Neuen Reiches*, 1964; developed in id., *ZDMG* 117, 1967, 11–16, and summarized in his book *Einführung in die Ägyptologie*, 1967.

43. This is remarkable, but can be explained. The title Pharaoh (from *pr-ʿ3*, properly 'great house', like 'sublime Porte' in Ottoman Turkish) was current in later Israel; but the proper names of Egyptian kings only appear during the monarchy in the Old Testament, i.e. when court annals were kept. The proper names of Egyptian kings may not have been known in an earlier period because of the complexity of their titles (which contained five elements), and on occasion may not even have been understood.

44. For the complex of questions concerned with the passover see J. Pedersen, 'Passahfest und Passahlegende', *ZAW* 51, 1934, 161–75. Noth took over Pedersen's theory with some qualifications, *A History of Pentateuchal Traditions*, 65–71; see further L. Rost, 'Weidewechsel und altisraelitischer Festkalender' (1943), reprinted in *Das kleine Credo*, 1965, 101–12; de Vaux, *Early History*, 359–70; see also S. Herrmann, *Israel in Egypt*, 54–6; article 'Plagues', in *Suppl. au Dict. de la Bible*.

45. Exod.12.37: from Rameses to Succoth; Exod.13.17–18a: no direct route to Palestine, but through the wilderness in the direction of the Reed Sea; Exod.13.20: from Succoth to Etham; Exod.14.2: camp by the Reed Sea (the exact location is said to be before Pi-hahiroth between Migdol and the sea before Baal-zephon); Num.33.5–8: probably a later systematic summary of all the places whose names are known from the book of Exodus. Cf. especially H. Cazelles, 'Les localisations de l'Exode et la critique littéraire', *RB* 62, 1955, 321–64; de Vaux, *Early History*, 376–81.

46. More accurately, Yahweh hardened Pharaoh's heart. For an analysis of the extremely complex tradition of the happening at the Reed Sea in Exod.14; 15, cf. the literature in de Vaux, *Early History*, 381–8; special reference should be made to M. Noth, *Exodus*, OTL, ²1966, 102–26. Most recently, questions have been raised about the traditio-historical background to Noth's considerations, with particular reference to the relationship between the Reed Sea tradition and the tradition about the stay in Egypt; G. W. Coats, *VT* 17, 1967, 253–65; B. S. Childs, *VT* 20, 1970, 406—18; cf. also G. W. Coats, *VT* 22, 1972, 129–42.

47. This is expressly stated in Exod.14.5.

48. The prose tradition in Exod.14 is followed by the great complex of Exod.15.1–21, which has a poetic form.

49. Exod.15.21.

50. O.Eissfeldt, *Baal-Zaphon, Zeus Kasios und der Durchzug der Israeliten durchs Meer*, 1932.

51. Diodore, Strabo, Polybius.

52. M. Noth, 'Der Schauplatz des Meerwunders', *Festschrift Otto Eissfeldt zum 60. Geburtstag*, 1947, 181–90.

53. W. Helck, *TLZ* 97, 1972, 182. A Bedouin tradition supposes the miracle of the Reed Sea to have taken place at the Red Sea in the neighbourhood of *jebel hammām*; cf. the impressive photograph in *Vérité et poésie de la Bible*, ed. E. Lessing, 1969, 114–5; this tradition surely rests on false presuppositions. Moreover there are no reeds there!

54. A. H. Gardiner, 'Military Road', *JEA* 6, 1920, 99–116.

3 | Tribal Operations in the Sinai Peninsula. The Mountain of God and Kadesh

THE OLD TESTAMENT text of the book of Exodus gives the impression that those who were saved at the Reed Sea penetrated the interior of the Sinai peninsula in a south-easterly direction by a single route of march; after a number of difficulties they reached Sinai, the mountain of God and spent some time there. This group again sets out in the book of Numbers, from ch. 10 onwards, this time in a northerly direction towards the cultivated land of Palestine. A stay in the oasis region of Kadesh, half way between the mountain of God and the promised land, stands out particularly. This interlude between Egypt and Palestine is usually called 'the journey through the wilderness' or 'Israel's stay in the wilderness'. On several occasions the people murmur against their God, wish they were back among the 'fleshpots of Egypt',[1] criticize their leader Moses and even allow themselves to be led astray into forsaking the God of Moses at the very mountain of God. There they speedily cast a 'golden calf' and worship a representation of God which they have made themselves.

These well-known details, the list of which can be further increased by a number of other anecdotes, clearly begin from the presupposition that in Egypt Israel was a self-contained unit which left Egypt as such, gradually approaching Palestine with the clear goal of the promised land before their eyes. However, this well-defined conception is obviously the work of a later unification of the traditions of the tribes who came from the southern wilderness. It has long been recognized that the 'wilderness journey', with its continuous march through a series of places to which an exact geographical location can apparently be given, is to be found in passages in the Pentateuch which are to be assigned to the latest literary stratum, the Priestly writing (P). It is also striking that the number of places increases, and their location becomes clearer, the nearer 'Israel' comes to the cultivated land of Palestine. Of course more importance was attached to the latter traditions, and they were more firmly fixed in memories, since they lay closer to the land where the settlement was eventually made. The uncertainties are greatest for the period between Egypt and the mountain of God. This is the most difficult and the 'earliest' stage of the supposed route. On the other hand the author of the introductory chapter to Deuteronomy has presented the local traditions known to him from the area between Kadesh and Palestine as far as possible in the form of an organized march. The terseness and comprehensiveness of his account has done a good deal to deepen the picture of Israel operating as a unit and to fill it out.[2] The passages usually ascribed to the Yahwist (J) and the Elohist (E) confirm in their own way the action of the later redactors. As a rule they offer very brief anecdotes from various places and indicate virtually no deliberate plan of progress. They aptly reflect an early stage of the tradition which preserved memories of various areas quite independently of an ordered 'journey through the wilderness' and witness to the experience of individual tribes in one place or another.

To add some substance to these general remarks, it is worthwhile at least to list the most important traditional material, assigning it to the accepted sources. After Pi-hahiroth by Baal-zephon on the Reed Sea (Exod. 14; 15.1–22, JEP), J mentions the wilderness of Shur (Exod. 15.22) and the place Marah (Exod. 15.23); P mentions Elim (Exod. 15.27) and the wilderness of Sin (Exod. 16.1), goes on to Rephidim (in the *wādi refāyid*? Exod. 17.1) and into the wilderness of Sinai (Exod. 19.1f.). In Exod. 17.7 J mentions the places Massah and Meribah. After the great insertion of legal material (Exod. 20 – Num. 10), P mentions the wilderness of Paran (Num. 10.12) and then mentions Hazeroth (Num. 11.35) and the wilderness of Paran again in Num. 12.16. Between these passages we find the brief aetiological narratives of Taberah (Num. 11.3, JE) and the 'graves of craving' (Num. 11.34, JE). The wilderness of Paran appears again in Num. 13.3, JE, followed by Kadesh (Num. 13.36, JE) and Hormah (Num. 14.45, E). From now on a tradition which is essentially assigned to P comes to the forefront; it mentions the following places and areas one after the other: the wilderness of Zin (Num. 20.1), Mount Hor (Num. 20.22), the surrounding Edomite territory (Num. 21.4), Oboth, Iye-abarim, the Valley of Zered, the area beyond the Arnon, Beer (in the *wādi et-ṭemed*?), Mattanah (south-east of *mādebā*?), Nahaliel, Bamoth and through Moabite territory to the hills of Pisgah (Num. 21.10–20).[3] The assumption that the so-called wilderness wandering lasted forty years has already been mentioned. This possibly rests on old traditions, but the first certain evidence of it is in Deuteronomy and within the Deuteronomistic literature: Deut. 2.7; 8.2, 4; 29.4; Josh. 5.6, etc. It is later taken up in Neh. 9.21; Ps. 95.10. There is doubt whether Amos 2.10 is in fact to be assigned to the prophet.

The best approach to the reconstruction of historical events is from the fundamental considerations which have been mentioned several times already. The penetration of Aramaean groups into the lands of the fertile crescent towards the end of the second millennium BC was attended by various conditions. The possibilities of settling in the zones of steppe and wilderness in the region of Sinai were limited, and this inevitably meant that people moving into them became scattered. It has already been remarked that such groups advanced as far as Egypt and there had the experiences which have been described. However, this does not exclude the possibility that other groups settled in the Sinai peninsula at the same time, at least for a period. There were places where it offered sufficient accommodation, particularly at watering-places. This can be most clearly seen from the case of the oasis of Kadesh. In addition to these watering places there may also have been holy places at which deities were already found to be present, or in which they were installed. The hill-country offered particular sites here.

From this we may conclude that the recollections which appear in the Pentateuch as the tradition of the entire people of Israel on its way through the wilderness after leaving Egypt have their historical roots in various places on the Sinai peninsula. This is not because progress was made successively from place to place, but because the individual Aramaean groups had their experiences in these areas and later incorporated them in a comprehensive 'wilderness tradition'. What happened in Kadesh, on the mountain of God or in the hill-country of Seir had independent importance for those concerned, who came out of the steppes of the wilderness zone of Syria and Arabia. But the same people cannot all have been in Egypt to begin with.

Given these presuppositions, it would seem that a historical reconstruction should not look for 'wilderness journeys'[4] or seek to establish one group or another as the exclusive bearers of the tradition. A separate examination should first be made of the geographical locations and their traditions. Typical elements will emerge from the characteristics of the material which fit in with the total picture and support a historical reconstruction. The most profitable course would seem to be to begin with the best-attested locations. These are without question the oasis region of Kadesh and the so-called 'mountain of God'.

Of course, of the two it is possible to assign a certain geographical location only to Kadesh (or Kadesh Barnea). The name still survives in the spring *'ēn qdēs* in an oasis region about fifty miles south of Beer-sheba near the starting point of two valley routes running northwards. To the north-west is the *wādi el-'arīsh* (the so-called 'Brook of Egypt'), and to the north-east the *wādi fiqre*, running in the direction of the Dead Sea. Thus Kadesh lies relatively close to Palestine. Until modern times Beer-sheba was the southernmost frontier location between steppe and cultivated land. In fact Kadesh offers a number of advantages for a lengthy stay, so that we can well imagine it as a starting point or a staging post for a settlement in Palestine.[5]

It is more difficult to determine the location of the mountain of God, the place where in the traditional view the covenant was made between Yahweh and his people and the law was proclaimed. Here, too, Yahweh first appeared to Moses in the burning bush (Exod. 3). None of the names for this mountain, 'Mountain of God', 'the mountain', or 'the mountain of Sinai' (*har sīnay*), Horeb, 'Horeb the mountain of God', gives a firm indication of its geographical location. The two proper names Sinai and Horeb are usually used as criteria for distinguishing sources: Horeb is more frequent in the later strata. The common view that the names apply to peaks in the massif in the southern half of the 'Sinai' peninsula is irrelevant for understanding the Old Testament evidence for the very reason that on the basis of the biblical tradition the name Sinai is only used for this area at a later stage. The tradition comes from Christian monks and can be demonstrated from the fourth century AD onwards, though it is presumably some centuries earlier than that.[6] The monks who retreated to the solitude of the peninsula already found in the mountains sacred traditions which in their view confirmed that here was the mountain of God.

Numerous Nabataean inscriptions have been found in the rocky valleys of the southern Sinai massif, mostly composed in stereotyped form as a brief greeting, giving the name of a visitor.[7] From the second half of the first millennium BC, the Nabataeans encroached increasingly on Transjordania and the regions bounding it on the south. However, they did not gain any footing in Palestine itself. Hasmoneans, Herodians and Romans fought against them with varying success. Nabataean power reached its climax in the first century BC; it was centred on Petra, at the edge of the Sinai peninsula, where important trade routes cross. The Romans under Trajan overthrew the Nabataean state in AD 105/6 and incorporated it into the Roman empire as the province of Arabia. The inscriptions found in the south of the Sinai peninsula come principally from the second and third centuries AD, that is, from the time after the Nabataean power had been crushed. It is therefore highly probable that the inscriptions are to be taken as the work of pilgrims who could no longer visit the great sanctuaries of Petra. There is no possibility of demonstrating that the pilgrims were following already existing sanctuary traditions in this area, but it is certainly not out of the question that this was the case. The Christian monks may well have entered the Nabataean holy places in a sacral succession and there have felt themselves to be in touch with the Old Testament tradition of the scenes on the mountain of God.

Particular peaks of the massif have been claimed as the mountain of God. The local tradition of today, of Byzantine and Christian provenance, prefers the so-called *jebel mūsa*, 'Mount of Moses' (7467 feet), with the monastery of Saint Catherine lying at its foot, and *jebel qāterīn*, 'Mount Catherine' (8455 feet), not far away. The Nabataean inscriptions are to be found particularly in the valleys leading to *jebel serbāl* (6669 feet) further to the west.

It is natural to ask whether the mountain of God could be located on any other massifs than those described. When one considers the sanctuary traditions which were possibly taken over and developed by the Nabataeans, it is not difficult to imagine a sacral tradition reaching back to earliest times. And if one begins from the assumption that the mountain of God must be a high mountain peak, it is natural to seek it in the south of the Sinai peninsula. However, even that is by no means compelling. Other places, lying nearer to the cultivated land of Palestine, are also possibilities.

Hypotheses which locate the mountain of God east of the Gulf of Aqaba in the north-western part of the Arabian peninsula are, however, less probable. H. Gressmann[8] was to the fore in attempting to support this view with references to the links between Moses and Midian and the volcanic character of the landscape there. However, the area over which the Midianites moved was so great that it even reached into the Sinai peninsula; the appearance of smoke and fire need not be associated with volcanic phenomena but could equally well be explained as the phenomena accompanying the manifestation of the deity.[9]

M. Noth took a completely different starting-point, which led him to reconsider whether the mountain of God should not be located in north-west Arabia. He interpreted a list of places in Num. 33.1–49, which purports to give the staging-posts on the route from Egypt to Palestine, as part of a special tradition about resting-places for later pilgrims to the mountain of God. He therefore followed backwards the list of places given, and by his explanation of individual place names reached the volcanic area south of *tebūk* where Gressmann also wanted to locate the mountain of God.[10] However, Noth himself later declared that the arguments were not enough to transfer the mountain of God with any certainty to north-west Arabia. The Sinai peninsula was to be preferred.[11]

Some other passages of ancient tradition in the Old Testament should also be noted. These do not locate Yahweh's dwelling at the traditional mountain of God in the south of the Sinai peninsula, but in the hills south of the cultivated land of Palestine. The ancient Song of Deborah speaks of Yahweh who 'comes from Seir' and 'marches from the region of Edom' (Judg. 5.4), while a later composition in Deut. 33.2 says in parallelism that Yahweh comes from Sinai and shines forth from Seir. Seir is essentially identical with the eastern boundary of the Arabah, the *wādi el-'araba*, between the Dead Sea and the Gulf of Aqaba. This would be the area nearer to the cultivated land and nearer to Kadesh which was postulated above. Mount Paran (Deut. 33.2; Hab. 3.3) is mentioned in the same context and fits the picture; its name is still preserved in *jebel fārān* on the western side of the Arabah. There is another recollection in *fīrān*, the oasis of palms.

The Old Testament tradition is agreed that Yahweh's abode is to be sought in localities in the south of Palestine; reliable memories of the exact situation of the mountain of God must have been lost. The possibility cannot be excluded that the mountain of God was transferred or given a number of different locations in the interest of pilgrims. The pilgrimage route inferred from Num. 33 is in any case only one of several versions. The most prominent among later visitors to the mountain of God was certainly Elijah, who came from the northern kingdom of Israel and first stopped in Beer-sheba. He then made a day's journey far into the wilderness and finally reached the mountain of God after forty days and forty nights.[12] We are given no geographical details, but we do hear of the various ways in which Yahweh appeared; these do not necessarily require him to be associated with a volcano.[13]

More important than the locality is the event associated with the mountain of God. The chief report of this is to be found in Exod. 19; 20; 24 and Exod. 32–34. Literary criticism indicates that these texts were repeated down to a late period, and were worked over, often with very different results.[14] However, only a very few passages allow us to draw inferences to very old, primal happenings. The account tells how a great sacral act is carried out with all the appropriate concomitants: it is prepared for by the people; Moses speaks alone with God on the mountain, the law is read, the covenant is concluded and a sacral meal is taken in the holy place. But the complicated composition of the material does not allow us to make a clear and unbroken reconstruction of a single event or even an event which was repeated in a cultic framework. We cannot exclude the possibility that elements of this tradition could later become the ingredients of sacral actions or proceedings; however, there is no express evidence of this.[15]

Two things, however, are particularly remarkable and need to be stressed. First is the singular passage Exod. 24.9–11. Moses goes up the mountain with three companions and seventy elders. They are allowed to see God face to face without his hand being raised against them. Finally they eat and drink there at the holy place. This account seems less encumbered than the rest. It still evidently knows nothing of the exclusive strictness of the later tradition, which allows only Moses to see God and makes him the sole mediator between God and the people. A meal is mentioned, but there is nothing about the binding communication of a divine message or of a divine law, nor is there anything about a 'covenant'. Possibly in Exod. 24.9–11 we have the rudiments of an early sacral tradition which has been preserved quite by chance; it would seem to know of sacred events and a solemn festival at the mountain, but as a periodic custom rather than as a single happening. It could become the starting point and the framework for what took place between Moses and the people.

The other important fact is that the legal traditions which the book of Exodus associates with the happening at the mountain of God, for all their internal differences, are of a later date and can be derived from an original nomadic law in only a few places, and there only hypothetically. Their final form presupposes settlement in the cultivated land. This can be seen from the collections of the Decalogue (Exod. 20.1–17) and the so-called Book of the Covenant, which is probably the earliest collection of Israelite law (Exod. 20.23–23.19), both of which are strictly isolated. It can be seen even more clearly from the other legal traditions. Nevertheless, we are left with the question of the presuppositions by which law could come to be anchored on a sacral act on the mountain of God in this way. The remarkable passage Exod. 15.25b, which is quite independent of the mountain of God, gives us one indication. This passage knows of a communication of law at other places during the stay in the wilderness or on the steppe.[16] There was thus an awareness of earlier legislation in connection with nomadic existence, wherever it may have been enacted. The event at the mountain of God became the occasion for elaborating this element of the tradition of a proclamation of the law, rooted in nomadic existence, to a monumental degree, and for supporting the later law of Israel with the authority of the God of the holy mountain.

Thus, if we are careful, we can draw a number of consequences for assessing the historical events on the mountain of God. The first of these are negative. The tribes who took part did not found a new homeland on the mountain of God. Their stay was only a limited one, even if it was felt to be a particular climax. A sacral act was performed at the holy place. We cannot detect any change in the style of living of those who took part either in connection with the stay at the mountain of God or afterwards. There is nothing in the text to suggest that a cultic fellowship was established, say with the Midianites.

The question of the relationship between Israel and Midian in both earlier and later times has been raised again and again as a result of the tradition that Moses escaped to the Midianites, married there, probably also had his first manifestation of Yahweh there (Exod. 3) and later could even share in legal decisions with his father-in-law Jethro (Exod. 18). Attempts have been made, above all, to look for the origins of belief in Yahweh among the Midianites and even more among the Kenites (in connection with the important passage Judg. 4.11). The Kenites later settled south of Hebron (I Sam. 27.10; 30.29; Josh. 15.56f.). It is probable that they also had links with the Rechabites and Calebites, as the lists in I Chron. 2.50–55 seem to suggest. Significantly, the groups of Kenites and Rechabites, who were particularly zealous worshippers of Yahweh, also held fast to nomadic ideals (cf. Jer. 35). However, all attempts to seek the earliest roots of Yahweh worship in one of the tribes end in hypotheses.[17] Of course these particular traditions cannot have been completely without foundation, say among the Kenites and the Rechabites; the probability is that they, too, came into close and lasting contact with Yahweh in the southern steppes, but that this belief took its own form and produced independent traditions.

The positive conclusions that can be drawn from the event on the mountain of God are, first, that the early tradition in Exod. 24 allows us to posit periodical festivals at a mountain sanctuary which were associated with sacred meals and perhaps even with sacrifices. We cannot exclude the possibility that legal enactments were also presented, but the details are hidden from us.

Furthermore, it can hardly be disputed that the God who made himself known at the mountain was a phenomenon whose nearness could be experienced at a particular place and within certain boundaries. This conviction remained alive until later times in the traditions that Yahweh came forth from southern lands, and also in the certainty that Yahweh could be sought there, as he was sought by Elijah. The fact that this God only revealed himself to Moses after Moses had reached a certain place and that he made himself known in a burning bush would also fit this supposition (Exod. 3). Thus it is legitimate to conclude that Yahweh was the God of a holy mountain.[18] The fact that there is never any mention of a 'God of Moses' excludes any direct analogy with the 'gods of the fathers' (Exod. 3.13–15).

The prevalent association with Yahweh is local, and not personal. There is no mention of a 'God of Moses' even when he is expressly linked with the god of the fathers (Exod.3.13–15). We may perhaps have a reference to the early history of Yahweh, which may confirm his association with a particular place, in Egyptian sources.

Mentions of a 'land of the *sh'šw yhw*'' have been found in descriptions of the same kind as the well-known Pharaonic lists of foreign peoples and cities at Soleb in Nubia, about 125 miles south of Wadi Halfa.[19] The lists of Rameses II from Amara West (and Achsa), which have already been known for some time, are probably dependent on these. The Nubian examples are earlier, and date from the time of Amenophis III (say 1402–1364). The mention of the Shasu tribes takes us into their sphere of operations south of Palestine. It is highly significant that a territory of the Shasu is designated with the proper name *yhw*', the consonants of which are those of the Old Testament divine name (YHWH). Whether this proper name denotes an area, a place, a person or even a god is still obscure. The first remarkable thing is that this sequence of consonants in a neutral non-Israelite source appears in this particular neighbourhood at this particular time. This increases the possibility that the name YHWH had already emerged on the Sinai peninsula or at least on the borders of the Sinai peninsula before the events of the exodus. Other circumstances which can be recognized are sufficient to allow further conclusions. The fact that in the Egyptian view Shasu were on the move or settled in the area of this name makes it easy for us to associate them with groups which would include members of the Aramaean movement and, along with them, the Israelites. These considerations are supplemented by the further occurrence of 'the land of Shasu S'rr' in the Amarna list, which is identified with the mountain of Seir. The land of the Shasu of *yhw*' will thus have been situated in a territory or even in a neighbourhood near to Seir. These legitimate combinations immediately suggest biblical associations, where the mountain of Seir is also mentioned in connection with Yahweh coming forth from the south. There is even mention in the Bible of the fields of Edom, where the letter of the frontier official indicates that Shasu also lived. More features are thus added to a picture which justifies us in concluding that there were Shasu movements in the area south of the Dead Sea on the borders of the Arabah, at least from the time of Amenophis III to that of Sethos II. Now this is also the period when the Israelite tribes were operative in the area, and amongst them were the Shasu with their further designation *yhw*'. We are virtually forced to associate them with the Old Testament tradition. While it may be a hypothesis to see this 'land of the Shasu *yhw*'' as hill-country, one might go so far as to recognize in this *yhw*' the name of a mountain and a god; at any rate, in the Shasu of *yhw*' we at least have an element which comes surprisingly close in time and place to the Old Testament tradition.[20]

Mention should be made of a confirmation which does not consist of evidence from an early period, but belongs at the other end of the chronological development. A *'bd'hyw* often occurs among the proper names in the Nabataean inscriptions in the area of Sinai.[21] The second element of this name gives the impression of being independent, and designates the one who bears the name as a 'servant of *'hyw*'. The root is composed of the consonants of the divine name and in a striking way even recalls the *'hyh* of Exod. 3.14. If we may perhaps regard the Shasu of *yhw*' as the representatives of a very early Aramaean stratum, the Nabataeans are the representatives of a very late one. Both before and after, the name Yahweh was known within Aramaic groups in perhaps slightly different forms. At the time of the exodus, or at any rate when the Israelite tribes were beginning to form in the Sinai area, the God with the name YHWH may have been a relatively new but significant phenomenon; tribes or ethnically related groups attached themselves to him, having penetrated into this area and perhaps also having made closer contact with one another as a result.[22] Despite the element of hypothesis here, this would provide the historical roots for the Old Testament traditions about the mountain of God and Yahweh who manifested himself there. It would explain how and why Yahweh entered the lives of particular tribal groups which did not know him earlier as something new, as the God of a particular area or of a mountain. 'Yahweh's revelation of himself' (Exod. 3) was necessary for those who first came into contact with him and his holy place during their wanderings, which in the Egyptian view were movements of Shasu. In any event, these movements also included Moses and his people.

The information contained in the Kadesh traditions can reasonably be reconciled with these considerations. There are good historical reasons for detaching the tradition of the mountain of God from the high mountains in the south of the Sinai peninsula and transferring them to the region of the Arabah in the neighbourhood of Seir. Here we find ourselves in the general area of Kadesh. A fairly lengthy stay was possible there, and to visit the mountain of God, either once or periodically, presented no insuperable difficulty. Finally, Kadesh was a possible place from which to make first contact with the cultivated land lying to the north. This is in fact the content of the Kadesh traditions, though they are not as self-contained as the traditions about the mountain of God. The framework for them is Exod. 17 and Num. 10–20.[23] In this way the 'mountain of God' can virtually be incorporated into the tradition of the events at Kadesh. All this is understandable. The lengthy stay in Kadesh gave rise to various independent traditions which were only given their historical setting and their function within the framework of a more comprehensive structure. The local traditions of Kadesh confirm that there must have been a centre and a point of radiation there which played a decisive part for some of the semi-nomadic tribes; unfortunately the dominant role given to the mountain of God in the Pentateuch put Kadesh into an apparently secondary position.

Given that Kadesh served as a meeting place for individual groups which were later to form Israel and gave them cohesion, we come nearer to a comprehensible solution to the question how it could be that Yahweh became the dominant God for all the tribes entering from the south. For them, Kadesh was the decisive stage in the settlement. This does not mean that what was later to become Israel was already formed with all its members at Kadesh. At Kadesh the individual groups were still independent, in their original state of separation, nor did all depart from Kadesh at the same time in the same direction. However, whatever the individual details, their common destinies in the general region of the Arabah may well have brought them closer links to Yahweh or strengthened existing links.

We may now take up again the question of what happened to the group which left Egypt and with it the question of the historical context and ultimate significance of Moses. The dominant tradition which has been sustained in the Pentateuch makes Moses leave Egypt, lead the people through the wilderness, act as mediator at the mountain of God and finally die at the gates of Palestine on the summit of Mount Nebo, east of the Jordan. This is quite compatible with the fortunes of a group which had come out of Egypt. In the region of the Arabah and the mountain of God they will have made contact with the 'Shasu' who were living there; in more precise terms, with groups of Aramaeans who were ethnically close to them. In this way they may have established connections with Kadesh. Above all, however, they had close ties with the God of the mountain, whether these ties were strengthened, or established for the first time. We cannot exclude the possibility that Moses, the acknowledged leader of the exodus, played a special role here; indeed that is highly probable. Although there may also have been contacts with Kadesh, they were not so close that this group from Egypt took over land in Palestine in conjunction with the other tribes there. The man Caleb is particularly prominent in Kadesh in the tradition contained in Num. 13;14; later he went with his people into the Negeb and gained a footing in the territory of Judah.[24] Moses did not follow him. His way led into southern Transjordania. His death in this region is credible. The picture outlined here has the advantage of giving Kadesh and the mountain of God their due; it allows the group from Egypt to act independently, it explains their connection with the mountain of God and it does not leave Moses in an awkward isolation, as though he could only have been the leader of the exodus or only the mediator on the mountain of God. He appears with his group in a convincing historical continuum which also makes his prominent position in the tradition comprehensible. Once the people of Moses were given pride of place in the Pentateuchal tradition, other complexes were necessarily overshadowed, but did not completely disappear. Kadesh also retained a place alongside the mountain of God as an independent element.

The attempt at a historical account presented here will be challenged by German Old Testament scholars and regarded as an illegitimate harmonization. The fascination exerted by M. Noth's classic *History of Pentateuchal Traditions* continues to have its effect. Noth's observations retain their intrinsic value, but other conclusions should be drawn from them. The complexity of the tradition to which Noth pointed indicates the traditions which were alive among several groups of the Aramaean movement on the Sinai peninsula, but does not compel us to assume that Moses was incorporated simply to hold the literary tradition together. Rather, we should suppose that these traditions were permeated by an ongoing Moses tradition about a group which moved with him from Egypt to Palestine; by virtue of their dominance they also attracted other tribal traditions. Just as in the book of Joshua the Benjaminite tradition about the invasion of Palestine from the Jordan through Jericho and Gibeon and beyond could form the nucleus of an account of the settlement, so a sufficiently self-contained Moses tradition could make up the nucleus of the Pentateuchal traditions. Such a judgment of the tradition would produce a comprehensible picture of the process of the formation of the tradition which would occupy a lengthy, but not too extended period of time. Just as the patriarchal traditions are not to be spread over a wide geographical area and a considerable space of time, so it would seem appropriate not to dissolve the 'wilderness period' into countless individual destinies of an immeasurably long duration. The traditional forty years certainly does not provide a reliable indication, but at least it indicates a relatively short time. Noth has given up the possibility of accepting a continuous history and tradition by suggesting a literary arrangement of the Pentateuch into five themes. At the same time he has developed this literary hypothesis to such a pitch that each of the themes also has independent historical validity. His question of the theme in which Moses originally belonged does not dispense with critical logic, but it is insufficient for historical argument. It would also appear to be a legitimate method to examine the historical presuppositions of this complex literary composition and to test the authenticity of its statements. As has been shown, there is no obstacle to giving Moses a part in all the themes of the exodus and wilderness tradition which Noth produces. From this perspective earlier considerations also gain increased importance, like the discussion of the relationship between Kadesh and the mountain of God carried on by Eduard Meyer and others.[25]

The tribe of Levi seems to be particularly closely connected with Kadesh. The passage relating to Levi in the so-called Blessing of Moses (Deut. 33.8–11), with its abundance of themes, points to events at Massah and the water of Meribah. In the same passage, the manipulation of the oracular Urim and Thummim is associated with the house of Levi. Moses plays no part in this saying. We cannot exclude the possibility that here we have evidence of the particular fortunes of a tribe which was already exercising legal and possibly even priestly functions at Kadesh. The problem of the Levites in the Old Testament is complicated and full of contradictions. Moses is said to have been incorporated into a Levite genealogy at a later stage.[26] But this could only prove that originally he had nothing to do with the Levites. On several occasions they appear as the energetic representatives of their own views.[27] One of the roots of these developments could lie in the independent role of this tribe which developed and established itself in Kadesh; in contrast to those who became assimilated to the cultivated land, members of this tribe, whatever view may be developed of their 'priesthood', defended the originality of the nomadic tradition and a form of worship of God appropriate to the ideals of the early period. This particular case of the tribe of Levi at Kadesh may not be unique. We cannot exclude the possibility that other developments began at this point, to introduce conflicts within the history of Israel and cause those confrontations attested in the Old Testament which are otherwise so hard to explain. It may be mentioned in passing that various holy objects which are associated with the wilderness period, including the ark on the one hand and the 'tent of meeting' on the other, had their origin among different nomadic groups and, despite an apparent capacity for extension, continued to retain a relatively independent role at a later date.[28] These objects will also include the Urim and Thummim, whose place with the tribe of Levi happens by chance to be attested.

It is very clear that there must have been a direct movement north from Kadesh, or in contact with Kadesh, which aimed at settling in the general area of Judah, particularly in the neighbourhood of Hebron. The famous spies who gained such an overwhelming impression of the fertility of the land and brought back a single cluster of grapes, suspended from a pole carried on their shoulders to prove it, penetrated in that direction, more accurately into the Eshcol valley.[29] Of course their account of the fearful sons of Anak, whom they depicted as giants, aroused fear and dismay, but Caleb remained firm and later settled with his people in the neighbourhood of Hebron.

These dramatic scenes are matched by a series of further traditions which are set in the area between Kadesh and the southern part of the cultivated land which was later to become Judah. They concern tribes or tribal groups who had varying fortunes in this area. These include the Kenites, who have already been mentioned in conjunction with Caleb, the Othnielites, and finally the Jerahmeelites and not least the tribe of Simeon. All operated in the southern frontier area and are known to us only by a few scattered traditions.[30] Particular mention is made of battles against the king of Arad, and the name of the city of Hormah plays a role.[31] It is impossible to write an independent history of these southern tribes. But their difficulties with the inhabitants of the territory on the edge of cultivated land and with other tribes ring true; they represent what we must infer, namely a gradual penetration into cultivated land accompanied by resistance and fighting. This is why we only have sparse information about the tribes of southern Judah, not least about Simeon and Levi, who will have been involved in these operations.[32]

We may believe that the tribes who moved into southern Transjordania had the same difficulties as those involved in this difficult settlement in the direction of western Palestine. There was a battle with the Amalekites immediately south of the Dead Sea, which may even be the cause of a primal feud between Amalek and Israel.[33] Then the adjoining territory in the north-east had to be crossed. Edomites and Moabites offered resistance.[34] These two related groups, which later formed their own states,[35] had probably established themselves so firmly at the time of the arrival of the tribes of the future Israel that they did not want to allow uncontrolled movement within their area. Of course there was no battle. Did the newcomers somehow feel that in the end the Edomites and Moabites had some remote ethnic relation with them? On the other hand, however, the tradition is aware that Jacob and Esau, the ancestor of the Edomites, separated. The genealogical framework of Genesis unmistakably indicates the tension. At any rate, the growing independence and internal consolidation of the Edomites and Moabites provides a historical explanation why new groups coming from the south and east in search of land had to make a detour round their territory. At least they had no prospect of settling there. The advance only met with success some way north of the Arnon, in the direction of the hilly country on the east side of the Dead Sea (Pisgah). The numerous peaks of Nebo rise on its northern side, and this is the traditional place where Moses died.[36] In fact it is possible to look over considerable areas of the land east and west of the Jordan from this point. So the story that Moses was allowed to see the promised land but not to enter it is a credible interpretation of his evidently premature death.[37]

The shape of the Old Testament tradition allows us to conclude with some degree of certainty that the settlement in Palestine by the tribes coming in from the south followed at least two main advances, on the one hand from the region of Kadesh in the direction of southern Palestine lying west of the Jordan, and on the other hand from the high plains of Edom and Moab in the direction of Transjordania and the central land west of the Jordan, especially the hill-country of Ephraim and Samaria. Thus movements of tribes in the steppe surrounding Palestine were in essence a preparation for the so-called conquest; the settlement took place in successive stages, but over a limited period of time and in connection with the Aramaean movement. Of course acceptance of details depends on assessments of the sources and their reliability. It is only to be expected that the earliest memories of the conquest of the promised land were swallowed up in ideal conceptions and the justification of claims to territory in which particular tribes were interested. A historical account of the settlement cannot do more than follow the movements of the nomadic groups in the wilderness and the steppe as closely as possible; even after they entered the cultivated land, the tribes did not deny their original nature and their understanding of it.

NOTES

1. Exod. 16.3.
2. For an assessment of the literary nature and content of Deut.1–3 see M. Noth, *Überlieferungsgeschichtliche Studien*, ²1957, 27–40; J. G. Plöger, *Literarkritische, formgeschichtliche und stilkritische Untersuchungen zum Deuteronomium*, BBB 26, 1967, 1–59.

3. For individual sites cf. J. Simons, *The Geographical and Topographical Texts*, 1959, 416–59; cf. also H. Cazelles, *RB* 62, 1955, 321–64; Y. Aharoni, *The Land of the Bible*, 1967, 178–84; O. Eissefeldt, 'Palestine in the Time of the Nineteenth Dynasty (*a*) The Exodus and Wanderings', *CAH* II, ch. 26 (*a*), 19–26.

4. R. de Vaux, *Early History*, 370–6, gives a schematic picture of two exodus traditions, but acknowledges that he himself regards it as a hypothesis. His starting point is that according to J Israel was 'driven out' of Egypt, but according to E the exodus was a 'flight'. To this double form of the tradition he attaches two chains of tradition, the final result of which corresponds to the two 'entry traditions': according to J, he argues, the Leah tribes entered southern Palestine *via* Kadesh, whereas according to E the Rachel tribes under Moses wandered from the Reed Sea to Sinai and later entered the cultivated land from the east. A redactor later superimposed these two traditions. More will have to be said about the division of the tribes which is attached to Gen. 29.31 – 30.24 and which understands them as children of the two wives of Jacob, Leah and Rachel, along with two concubines. The context for this will be the places where the tribes settled in Palestine.

5. For the history of Kadesh and some further watering-places in that area see R. de Vaux, *Early History*, 423f.; of the older literature, H. C. Trumbull, *Kadesh-Barnea*, 1884, is still worth considering.

6. H. Gressmann, 'Der Sinaikult in heidnischer Zeit', *TLZ* 42, 1917, 153ff.; S. Mowinckel, 'Kadesj, Sinai og Jahwe', *Norsk Geografisk Tidsskrift* 9, 1942, 1ff.

7. Many difficulties accompanied the discovery and decipherment of the inscriptions. Work on them was done almost entirely by Julius Euting, whose edition was a model for its period: J. Euting, *Sinaitische Inschriften*, 1891.

8. H. Gressmann, *Mose und seine Zeit*, 1913, 409–19; some of the perspectives which he opened up still have a part even in more recent publications, e.g. in O. Eissefeldt, *CAH* II, ch. 26a, 1965, 20–2. H. Gese has put forward new considerations in the same direction, in *Das ferne und nahe Wort* (Festschrift L. Rost), BZAW 105, 1967, 81–94; but see G. I. Davies, *VT* 22, 1972, 152–60.

9. Reference may be made to Yahweh's presence in a pillar of smoke and a pillar of fire during the wilderness period, to the ascension of Elijah in a fiery chariot and to the screen of smoke associated with Yahweh's presence in the account of Isaiah's call; the burning bush must also be taken into consideration, and the phenomenon of the fire connected with ritual acts like that in Gen. 15.12, 17.

10. M. Noth, 'Der Wallfahrtsweg zum Sinai (Num. 33)' (1940), *Aufsätze* 1, 55–74.

11. M. Noth, *History of Israel*, 130ff. M. Harel, *Masa'ey Sinai*, 1968, 274ff. (in Hebrew), conjectures that *jebel sin bisher* in the north-west of the Sinai peninsula could be Sinai, the mountain of God.

12. I Kings 19.1–8. The forty days and forty nights seem to be connected in v. 8 with the miraculous food which enabled the prophet to undertake this long journey without further sustenance; cf. also Matt. 4.2. This makes it all the more difficult to base topographical considerations on the information. For an assessment of this tradition see now K. Seybold, 'Elia am Gottesberg', *EvTh* 33, 1973, 3–18.

13. I Kings 19.11, 12. Storm, earthquake and fire are phenomena which accompany the appearance of Yahweh, and are not descriptions of the local character of the place where he appears.

14. M. Noth, *Exodus*, OTL, [2]1966; W. Beyerlin, *The Origins and History of the Oldest Sinaitic Traditions*, 1965; O. Eissefeldt, 'Die älteste Erzählung vom Sinaibund', *ZAW* 73, 1961, 137–46 (*Kleine Schriften* IV, 12–20); id., 'Das Gesetz ist zwischeneingekommen', *TLZ* 91, 1966, 1–6; id., *Die Komposition der Sinai-Erzählung Exodus 19–34*, Sitzungsberichte Sächsischen Ak. d. Wiss, Phil.-hist. Klasse, 113/1, 1966; H. Schmid, *Mose, Überlieferung und Geschichte*, BZAW 110, 1968, 55–73; R. E. Clements, *Exodus*, CBC, Cambridge 1972.

15. Thus S. Mowinckel, *Le décalogue*, 1927, sought the cultic elements of the Israelite New Year Festival in the account of the events on Sinai. G. von Rad took Mowinckel's idea of a covenant festival further and sought to rediscover in the Sinai tradition the festal legend of a covenant renewal festival in Shechem. G. von Rad, 'The Problem of the Hexateuch' (1938), in *The Problem of the Hexateuch and other Essays*, 1966, 1–78, esp. 20–40. Cf. also H.-J. Kraus, *Worship in Israel*, 1966, 141ff.

16. Earlier scholarship already attached great importance to this passage and associated it with Kadesh. See J. Wellhausen, *Prolegomena to the History of Israel*, reprinted 1957, 342–5; E. Meyer, *Die Israeliten*, 1906, 61–3; the 'spring of judgment' (En-mishpat) in Gen. 14.7, which is already identified with Kadesh in the Hebrew text, was put in the same context.

17. Cf. H. H. Rowley, *From Joseph to Joshua*, 149–55; id., 'Moses and Monotheism', in *From Moses to Qumran*, 1963, 35–66; H. Heyde, *Kain, der erste Jahwe-Verehrer*, 1965; A. H. J. Gunneweg, 'Mose in Midian', *ZTK* 61, 1964, 1–9.

18. There is plenty of evidence for the worship of deities in connection with mountains and for the identity of the names of the two; mention need only be made of Baal Zephon, Baal Hermon, Baal Lebanon, and also the god of Mount Carmel, about whom Tacitus remarks with classic simplicity: '*est Iudaeam inter Syriamque Carmelus: ita vocant montem deumque*', *Hist.* II, 78, 3. Cf. O. Eissfeldt, *Baal Zaphon, Zeus Kasios und der Durchzug der Israeliten durchs Meer*, 1932; id., 'Der Gott des Tabor und seine Verbreitung' (1934), *Kleine Schriften* II, 29–54; id., *Der Gott Karmel*, Sitzungsberichte d. Deutschen Akademie der Wissenschaften, Kl. f. Sprachen, Literatur und Kunst, 1953, 1; K. Galling, 'Der Gott Karmel und die Ächtung der fremden Götter', *Geschichte und Altes Testament* (Festschrift A. Alt), 1953, 105–25.

19. The material is now easily accessible and there is a detailed commentary on it in R. Giveon, *Les bédouins Shosou des documents égyptiens*, 1971, documents 6a and 16a and cross-references. Giveon translates *t' shśw yhw* (his transcription) as 'Yahwe en terre de Shosou', thus understanding 'Yahwe' as a place-name in Shasu territory. Helck, *Beziehungen*, 266, remains closer to the Egyptian text: 'Land schá-śu ja-h-wa', using the group writing of the New Kingdom. Copies of the texts and transcriptions are offered by Jean Leclant, who is familiar with recording inscriptions in Soleb, *Les fouilles de Soleb* (*Nubie soudanaise*). *Quelques remarques sur les écussons des peuples envoûtés de la salle hypostyle du secteur IV*, Nachrichten der Akademie der Wissenschaften in Göttingen I, Phil-hist. Kl. 1965, no. 13, 214ff.

20. The summary remarks in Giveon, op. cit., 267–71, are extraordinarily confident; S. Herrmann, 'Der alttestamentliche Gottesname', *EvTh* 26, 1966, 281–93, is more restrained; id., 'Der Name JHWЗ in den Inschriften von Soleb. Prinzipielle Erwägungen', *Fourth World Congress of Jewish Studies, Papers*, Vol. 1, 1967, 213–6; R. de Vaux, *Histoire*, 316f., 325. There is criticism in M. Weippert, *ZAW* 84, 1972, 491 n. 144, but in principle he is now positive.

21. J. Euting, *Sinaitische Inschriften*, no. 472, 156 [80?].

22. We cannot take up here the enticing question whether the ambivalent, but certainly changeable term *bᵉrīt* was used at the adoption of a local god in conjunction with other groups of worshippers. E. Kutsch, *Verheissung und Gesetz*, BZAW 131, 1973, 75–92, answers this question in the negative as far as Exod. 19–34 is concerned, both on the basis of literary and terminological investigations and in connection with his scepticism about the translation 'covenant'.

23. Earlier Old Testament scholars had already taken into account passages to do with disputes over water, as well as mentions of the name 'Kadesh'. More exactly, these passages include the names Meribah and Massah, and also 'Me Meribah' ('Waters of Strife'), and expressly Meribath-Kadesh. See Exod. 17.1–7; Num. 20.1–13; 27.14 = Deut. 32.51; Num.

33.36; Deut.33.8; Ezek.47.19 = 48.28; Ps.95.8. It is very probable that all these places are connected with Kadesh; cf. also the 'spring of judgment' (Gen. 14.7), which is located in the same area. Following Wellhausen, the significance of Kadesh was stressed especially by E. Meyer, *Die Israeliten und ihre Nachbarstämme*, 1906 (reprinted 1967), 51–82; there is no basis in the primary traditions of the Pentateuch for a lengthy stay in Kadesh by the 'Israelite tribes', according to Noth, *History*, 132; von Rad disagrees with Noth and finds that some evidence about the stay in Kadesh is very old, *Old Testament Theology* I, 11f.; see also de Vaux, *Early History*, 419–25.

24. Alongside the Kenizzites, Kenites and Othnielites, Caleb belongs among those tribal groups which later attached themselves to Judah and were assimilated into its territory to such a degree that they no longer played any independent historical role. The chief passages of the 'Caleb traditions' are Num.13.6; 32.12; Josh.14.6–15; 15.13–19; Judg. 1.12–20; cf. also I Sam.25.1–3; 30.14; Caleb himself is a Kenizzite, Num.32.12.

25. This does not mean that the theories put forward by Wellhausen in his *Prolegomena to the History of Israel* and taken further by E. Meyer in his book on the Israelites can simply be adopted without question. Over recent decades they have merely been forced into the background by the predominance of other points of view and consequently their importance has been underestimated. C. A. Simpson, *The Early Traditions of Israel*, 1948, believed himself to be following Wellhausen and Meyer; he was criticized by O. Eissfeldt, *Die ältesten Traditionen Israels*, BZAW 71, 1950; the Kadesh traditions have again been stressed by E. Auerbach, *Moses*, 1953; for criticism see O. Eissfeldt, 'Mose', *OLZ* 48, 1953, 490–505 = *Kleine Schriften* III, 240–55. The difficulties are chiefly those of procedure, since there is no agreement over methods of approach; H. Schmid, *Mose, Überlieferung und Geschichte*, BZAW 110, 1968, gives some indication of this, though of course his book is again over-burdened by hypotheses.

26. For details, see K. Möhlenbrink, 'Die levitischen Überlieferungen des Alten Testaments', *ZAW* 52, 1934, 184–231. Exod.2.1 can only be understood as a later note; in Judg. 18.30, which is often quoted, 'Manasseh' is usually conjectured instead of 'Moses' in the genealogy of the priesthood of Dan, but this conjecture is not convincing; cf. Möhlenbrink, op. cit., 223. E. Meyer, *Die Israeliten*, 72–82, differs.

27. Cf. chiefly Gen.49.5–7; Exod.32.25–29.

28. These objects are discussed with varying tendencies by J. Maier, *Das altisraelitische Ladeheiligtum*, BZAW 93, 1965; M. Görg, *Das Zelt der Begegnung. Untersuchung zur Gestalt der sakralen Zelttraditionen Altisraels*, BBB 27, 1967; W. Zimmerli, 'Das Bilderverbot in der Geschichte des alten Israel (Goldenes Kalb, Eherne Schlange, Mazzeben und Lade)', in *Schalom* (Festschrift A. Jepsen), 1971, 86–96.

29. Num.13.23f.; 32.9; Deut.1.24f.; H. Guthe, *Mitteilungen und Nachrichten des DPV*, 1912, 65–71, gives an instructive account.

30. 'Cities of the Jerahmeelites' alongside 'cities of the Kenites', I Sam.30.29; cf. also I Sam.27.10; Jerahmeel as brother of Caleb in the late list I Chron.2.9, 42. Simeon appears in the shadow of Judah in Judg. 1.1ff., within the episode relating to the conquest; his tribal area in the south of Judah appears in later accounts as a subdivision within Judah (Josh. 19.1–8); for Judg. 1.17 cf. the next note.

31. Num.14.40–45; 21.1–3; the only specific report about Simeon is in Judg.1.17, according to which he took possession of the city of Hormah; its earlier name is said to have been Zephath, and it is probably identical with present-day *tell el-mushāsh* east of Beer-sheba; cf. Y. Aharoni, *The Land of the Bible*, 28, 148f., etc.

32. In this context there is usually a reference to the vain attempt of Simeon and Levi to settle in the region of Shechem (Gen.34). These tribes were then possibly forced further south, where perhaps their very existence came into jeopardy; for the violent action of both tribes see also Gen.49.5–7. It is not clear from the texts what historical conclusions we

should draw from these passages. Possibly we have the same sort of forays without immediate historical effect as those reported of Judah in Judg.1.4–11. V. Fritz, *Israel in der Wüste*, Marburger Theologische Studien 7, 1970, considers the problem of the southern tribes and their traditions against the background of the Yahwistic wilderness tradition.

33. Exod.17.8–16.

34. Num.20.14–21; 21.4; Deut.2; Judg.11.17f.

35. Gen.36.31–39; Num.20.14; 22.14 mention their independent kingdoms; there are comments on their earlier history in connection with the interesting stele of *bālū'a* (*ANEP*, 488) in A. Alt, 'Edomiter und Moabiter' (1940), *KS* I, 203–15.

36. Deut.34. The historical reliability of this tradition about Moses' grave, which is detached from the areas where the tribes settled, is also stressed by Noth, *Überlieferungsgeschichte*, 186–9; of course his conclusions about the history of the tradition in ibid., 190f., are not convincing; he deals with the topographical problems of Deut. 34 in *Aufsätze* 1, 398–401.

37. On the basis of parallel evidence, D. Daube, in *Von Ugarit nach Qumran* (Festschrift O. Eissfeldt), BZAW 77, 1958, 35, suggests that Moses' 'view from the mountain' can also be understood against a juristic background: Yahweh is already making Moses the owner of the country by showing him its full extent.

4

The Penetration of the Tribes into the Land East and West of the Jordan

WHEN WE ALMOST unthinkingly use the simple phrase 'the entry into the promised land', we are very much involved in the terminology and conceptuality of the Old Testament. After their stay in the wilderness and the steppe, the individual tribes moved into the areas which were to become the scene of their further history. However, the process was complex and varied, and it is also necessary to take into account the earlier history of the tribes and groups involved, in the regions of the steppe from which they came. Moreover, they came into a country which was by no means simply there for the taking; it had long been visited by numerous historical movements. However, not all parts of this country were equally focal points for particular events. The broken hill-country with its valleys and highlands, divided by the Jordan rift, was naturally overshadowed by more prominent events. The coastal plain, which had always been a through route, was more appealing as a place to settle. The nature of the first encounters of embryo Israel with their later abodes varied, depending on the nature of the country and the distribution of the population. Conditions were often harsh and severe, and arrangements with the existing inhabitants were made in accordance with circumstances. In some places it may have come to fighting, but on the whole a foothold was gained in the less densely populated areas without any resistance; of course, at first the coastal plain and a number of through routes were inaccessible.

It was, and probably still is, a mistake to suggest that the settlement of the tribes generally took place on the same basis. Earlier scholarship in particular was swayed by the idea that the Israelite tribes essentially entered the country together and at the same time. Even the terminology reveals different emphases. Wellhausen already used the neutral expression 'settlement in Palestine', and Strack spoke of 'entering the land west of the Jordan'; H. Guthe spoke of the 'occupation of Canaan', whereas E. Meyer and R. Kittel spoke more cautiously of the 'penetration' of Palestine or Canaan. By his epoch-making study 'The Land-taking of the Israelites in Palestine', A. Alt introduced a new term (*Landnahme*) which has been influential in German scholarship right down to the present, though it has not been universally accepted, and has not found its way into English, where the German word appears as the less distinctive 'settlement'. M. A. Beek again speaks of the 'conquest of the land', and Gunneweg uses the neutral term 'becoming settled in Canaan'. The German terminology, which, as has been indicated, cannot entirely be reproduced in translation, is rather more sophisticated than the English, which just has 'Israelite settlement' or, more crudely, 'conquest of Palestine' (Bright, Kaufmann, Yeivin); Bright even talks of the 'Israelite occupation of Canaan'. In French, the tendency towards neutral forms of expression like 'l'établissement' (J. Pirenne) or 'l'installation en Canaan' (de Vaux) seems to be greater. These are only a few examples. The terminology simply indicates a tendency and is not the whole story.

According to the evidence of the Old Testament, the individual tribes took possession of the cultivated land of Palestine from the south and east. It is in the very nature of occurrences of this kind that virtually no direct source material is available. Tribes and tribal groups on the move do not usually keep careful annals. What has been said about the period spent on the steppe also applies to the settlement. What we know largely consists of a collection of individual episodes and brief narratives; most of them are set in particular places which were reached by the invading tribes. These more or less scattered notes are the only material which enables us to draw conclusions about the actual course of the settlement. However, there is also an indirect source which allows us to make inferences, namely the way in which the tribes were distributed through Palestine and their final locations once the settlement was at an end.

The fact that we have two very different views of the nature of the settlement in the Old Testament itself makes it all the harder to form a judgment. According to the view of the book of Joshua, the occupation of the land was achieved in a single, almost military operation. Under the leadership of Joshua, Moses' official successor, the tribes advanced. They first crossed the Jordan on the heights of Gilgal and Jericho. Jericho itself was captured, not by military power but most probably by a ruse. The story that Yahweh himself brought the walls of the city down is the more famous version. The tribes once again took up military formation and moved up into the hill-country of Judah and Samaria, destroying the city of Ai en route, after making use of another military stratagem. Finally they encountered the inhabitants of Gibeon, who handed themselves over to the Israelites and along with some other cities in their neighbourhood entered into a treaty with the invading tribes.

From this sequence, Jordan–Jericho–Ai–Gibeon, we can reconstruct within the book of Joshua a fairly clear route of march into the plateau between the hill-country of Judah and that of southern Ephraim. At that point, however, the movement ceases to have cohesion and can no longer be traced. There follow individual accounts of events which take place in different areas of the country and do not have any immediately obvious interconnection. They already include the great battle at Gibeon and in the neighbouring valley of Aijalon (Josh. 10.1-15), made famous by the appeal to the sun and moon to stand still until the end of the battle. The opponents of the Israelites fled along the Beth-horon road, the ascent of Beth-horon, a kind of pass, which was later to acquire strategic significance. They reached Azekah (*tell ez-zakarīyeh*) and Makkedah, moving in a south-westerly and southerly direction along the western edge of the hill-country of Judah. The pursuing Israelites joined battle with five local kings who were imprisoned in the cave of Makkedah (Josh. 10.16–27). These far-reaching military operations seem to indicate that Joshua maintained a kind of headquarters in the Jordan rift a little to the north of Jericho, at Gilgal, but his next move seems to suggest that this is no longer the case. Joshua 10.28–43 records an advance into the south of Judah, in the area of Libnah, Lachish and Eglon, and also into the heart of Judah: Hebron and the surrounding area.

A second unconnected and unmotivated move follows this digression into the south. It leads northwards. Joshua 11 records a military expedition into Galilee, where the city of Hazor is destroyed after a battle against a coalition of local rulers at the 'waters of Merom'.[1]

It is quite evident that the purpose of the book of Joshua in presenting this series of episodes, often in the form of vivid sagas, is to offer a loosely constructed narrative of an 'occupation' or even a 'conquest' of the land west of the Jordan. For this purpose it primarily uses a chain of local traditions from the area which was later assigned to Benjamin, extending from the area of Jericho and Gilgal westwards into the highlands beyond Ai and Gibeon as far as the hill-country to the west along the coastal plain. But as soon as the book of Joshua goes beyond these Benjaminite traditions, its local traditions lose all continuity and the occupation of the whole territory of Israel is hinted at rather than described. The only highlights are the account of the sally into the south of Judah and the action round Hazor in Galilee. Joshua 10 and 11 give representative incidents relating to the whole of Palestine, whereas chs. 1–9 provide a continuous account relating to part of it.

The fiction of a conquest made by the whole of Israel is continued through the book of Joshua. From ch. 13 on we have a list of tribal areas and tribal boundaries given as the result of a planned distribution of the land, carried out by lot, made under the authority of Joshua.[2] The settlement of the land east of the Jordan (Josh. 22) and the death of Joshua, which also indicates that the occupation of the whole country is complete (Josh. 23), form an organic conclusion to this account. Chapter 24 has a character of its own and serves as a kind of appendix. After the territorial needs of the tribes have been satisfied, the ceremony at Shechem indicates their obligations to Yahweh as the God of all the tribes.

The aim of the account in the book of Joshua is unmistakable. It sets out to bring together the episodes of the settlement on the one hand and the religious and legal consequences of this settlement on the other: the demarcation of the tribal territories and the guarantee by Yahweh of his gift of the land, which fulfils his promise for all Israel. This unified composition is no doubt intended to fulfil the needs of a time which is already far removed from that of the settlement. Yahweh indeed gave this promised land to all his people; he made it possible for them to possess it and he assigned parts of it to the individual tribes through the authority of Joshua. We may conclude from this that there was a time when such a well-constructed guarantee of the land was thought to be necessary and that it was possible to go back to material, to accounts and traditional lists, which laid down and secured the religious and legal framework of the settlement and the occupation of the land. The individual narratives with the character of sagas may in fact have their roots in the events of the settlement itself, whereas the lists will have come from practical administration which was established for individual territories in the course of time and required clear boundaries to be drawn. There is much to support the view that this interest in the clear demarcation and comprehensive assignment of Israelite territory was not possible before the time of David at the earliest, and only assumed a precise and fixed form towards the end of the monarchy.[3]

A contrast to the more extended account of the settlement in the book of Joshua is provided by the fragment of a shorter account in Judg. 1, which knows nothing of the figure of Joshua. Sometimes the tribes act in isolation, sometimes together. Judges 1.1–15 gives details about actions of Judah and Simeon in the south and about smaller groups close to Judah like Caleb and Othniel. Judges 1.16–21 also mentions the Kenites, the tribe of Simeon and the area of Benjamin. Judges 1.22–26 narrates a brief episode from the history of the 'house of Joseph', the occupation of the city of Bethel by treachery.[4] The rest of Judg. 1, after these narratives and anecdotes about the settlement, offers a traditional list of cities and adjoining places of which it is explicitly said that the Israelites were unable to take possession of them because the Canaanites were settled there. A. Alt described this remarkable tradition in Judg. 1.27–36 impressively as a 'negative index of possessions'.

The list of course presupposes that the settlement had already been brought to some sort of conclusion. But it cannot come from a time far removed from the settlement, since by then interest in 'negative possessions' would already have faded. This points to the early period of the monarchy up to David as the most likely time, especially as David's victory over the Philistines at the latest robbed the list of its validity. Allusion is often made to this increase in the strength of Israel with a reference to the fact that in some areas the Canaanites were put to forced labour.[5] The significance of this list is of such extraordinary importance for an assessment of the structure of the country at the time of the conquest and for the distribution of the tribes in their particular areas that we must consider it in some detail. Judges 1, with its reports of the history of various territories, has virtually a key function for the further course of the history of Israel in Palestine.

Judges 1.27ff. begins with the statement that the tribe of Manasseh was unable to take possession of the cities of Beth-shean, Taanach, Dor, Ibleam and Megiddo and their neighbourhoods, and that the Canaanites persisted in remaining in these areas. All these places formed a single chain which extended from Dor on the Mediterranean eastwards to the southern boundary of the plain of Megiddo and then down into the plain of Beth-shean by the Jordan. Here a girdle of cities went straight across the country. These were all old foundations, which were already fortresses in Egyptian hands about the middle of the second millennium BC.

> Mention is made of the following in Thutmoses III's Palestinian list on the temple of Amon at Karnak: no.2, Megiddo (*Mkt*); no.42, Taanach (*T⁽nk*); no.43, Ibleam (*Ybʿrm*); no.110, Beth-shean (*Bt Šr*); also no.38, Shunem (*Šnm*), and no.113, Jokneam (*ʿnqnʿm*).⁶ There is also later evidence that the two extremities, Dor⁷ and Beth-shean,⁸ were Egyptian administrative centres. That means that on the northern margin of the Ephraimite hill-country there was an ancient system of cities which lay across the land like a wall. Beth-shean and Shunem occur in the Amarna letters.⁹

There was also a chain of cities in the south, corresponding to that in the north, so to speak a southern 'wall' across the heights of Jerusalem and Bethel: Gezer (Judg. 1.29); Aijalon and Shaalbim (Judg. 1.35).

> No. 104 (*qḍr*) in Thutmoses III's Palestinian list is usually interpreted as Gezer; however, some other explanation is more probable.¹⁰ Still, both Gezer and Aijalon are attested in the Amarna letters.¹¹ But from the same neighbourhood we already know from an earlier period of a considerable number of cities which continued to exist and are not fully covered in Judg. 1.¹² From Thutmoses III's Palestinian list we hear of the following places in this area: no.61, *Yp* (*yāfa*), about 6 miles from Ono; no.64, *Rṭn* (*lidd*), 5 miles from Ono; no.65 *In* = Ono (*kufrʿāna*), about 6 miles from Aphek; no.66, *Ipqn* = Aphek (*tell rās el-ʿēn*), 13 miles from Soco; no.67, *Šk* = Soco (*rās esh-shuwēke*), 3 miles from *Yḥm*; no.68, *Yḥm* (*yemma*). Finally, Jerusalem itself also belongs in this series of southerns states; at any rate it was impregnable at the time of the Israelite invasion, as Judg. 1.21 already indicates.

> It is impossible to be so certain about the rest of the cities in the list in Judg. 1, but they do afford us an adequate indication of the general situation. Kitron and Nahalol belong in southern Galilee, in the territory of the tribe of Zebulon (Judg. 1.30). We do not hear of them elsewhere. A series of coastal cities in the territory of the tribe of Asher are said to be impregnable; the most important of them are Acco, Sidon, Ahlab and Achzib.¹³ We do not know the exact location of any of the other cities on the list. Unfortunately this is also true of the places in the territory of the tribe of Naphthali in Galilee, mentioned in v.33; among them, Beth-shemesh and Beth-anath are probably to be located on the plains of the Jordan.

It must be added that this picture of the settlement of Palestine which can be gained from early non-Israelite sources dating from the middle of the second millenium BC did not undergo any considerable change before the end of the millennium, especially when the Egyptians were in the ascendant. This was the case until the time of Rameses III (about 1184–1153) at the latest. He was responsible for one of the last late resurgences of Egyptian power in Palestine. Traces of his building activity can be found in Beth-shean. Objects which bear his name have also been found in Gezer and Megiddo.[14] The base of a statue of Rameses VI which came to light at Megiddo, dating from the middle of the twelfth century, may be the last sign of Egyptian representation at the end of their centuries-long rule.[15]

The successors to the rule of the coastal plains of Palestine were not the Egyptians, but the Sea-peoples, who gained a footing before the arrival of the Aramaeans from Asia Minor and Syria. We know the names of the two chief peoples in the coastal plains of Syria and Palestine, the Zeker[16] and the Philistines. As far as we can see, the former remained in the area of Syria and Phoenicia, but the Philistines penetrated further south, finally establishing the well-known 'five cities of the Philistines',[17] Gaza, Ashkelon, Ashdod (*esdūd*), Ekron (*'āqir*) and Gath as their principalities. This only seems to have become possible after the gradual decline of Egyptian power in these areas; we cannot rule out the possibility that the Egyptians even allowed the Philistines to settle on the flat land outside the great cities. As far as we can see, however, the area of Philistine influence did not extend further north than Joppa and the *nahr el-'ōja*. It is unlikely that the arrival of the Philistines introduced an essential change in relationships between the inhabitants of the Palestinian coastal plain, especially as the change from Egyptian to Philistine supremacy was gradual and essentially peaceful.[18]

Thus individual features of the geographical picture of the settlement to be found in Judg. 1 can be confirmed by accounts of historical topography from the middle of the second millennium BC onwards. It demonstrates the starting point for a historical reconstruction of the Israelite settlement. The Old Testament is the only source for this settlement, but it fits perfectly into the general historical picture which can be constructed from non-Israelite evidence. According to Judg. 1, the chief areas where the incoming tribes found it difficult to gain a footing were the plains, both the coastal plains and the plain of Megiddo, the area from Acco northwards, and probably also parts of the upper Jordan rift and its immediate surroundings. They were able to gain access to the hill-country which rose alongside and beyond the plains, but which was cut through at decisive points by the two chains of cities west of the Jordan, supported by the structure of the country.[19] Consequently it was impossible to achieve a coherent occupation of territory immediately after the settlement.

As far as we can see, the settlement in the country west of the Jordan must have taken the following form: Judah moved into its territory around Hebron and Bethlehem from the south;[20] smaller groups like Caleb and Othniel arrived in approximately the same way.[21] The hill-country of Judah was occupied in this fashion; to the east, the wilderness of Judah was a natural barrier, and the southern chain of cities brought settlement to a halt in the north. This chain included the Jebusite area round the city of Jerusalem and the territory adjoining it to the north and west.

There were difficulties in settling in the land between the two chains of cities. Simeon and Levi had already encountered resistance in the area of Shechem, not least because from the middle of the second millennium Shechem had been the centre of an independent and expanding city state, as we know from the Amarna letters.[22] It seems to have been able to sustain a particularly aristocratic constitution, even down until Israelite times.[23] The tribe of Dan attempted to settle west of Jerusalem; however, in Judg. 1.34 we find the characteristic remark: 'The Amorites pressed the Danites (Amorites here is probably a generic description for the pre-Israelite population of the country) back into the hill-country, for they did not allow them to come down to the plain.' In the end, the tribe of Dan could no longer survive in this area. It probably migrated north in the period before the monarchy, and there settled at the extreme end of the country, at the foot of Hermon (Judg. 17;18).[24]

Even the 'house of Joseph', which was composed at least of the tribes of Ephraim and Manasseh, and finally gained possession of the country between the two chains of cities, had its difficulties. These are indicated very vividly in Josh. 17.14–18. Complaints are made to Joshua. The people are so many and they have so little land. Joshua advises them to climb still further into the hill-country and clear ground there. The Josephites reply: 'The hill-country is not enough for us; yet all the Canaanites who dwell in the plain have chariots of iron, both those in Beth-shean and its villages and those in the valley of Jezreel.'[25] This gives a clear enough indication of the limits set by the northern chain of cities and the coastal plain. What remains is still uncultivated hill-country, which must be made cultivable by some form of colonization.

One of the particular problems of the settlement was the occupation of the area on the southern border of the hill-country of Ephraim. This was a central but relatively self-contained area. It is dominated by the highlands which extend beyond Mount Scopus, north of Jerusalem, and stretches at least as far as the high road bounded by the modern places *rāmallāh* and *el-bīre* (Beeroth?). In the east this plateau is bounded by the hill-country leading to the Jordan rift and on the west by the last mountain barrier before the transition to the hills, where the pass of Beth-horon lies and south of which the valley of Aijalon begins. This relatively narrow strip of land, which belongs geographically neither to Judah in the south nor to Ephraim in the north, was the area where the tribe of Benjamin settled. The dramatic account of the first chapters of the book of Joshua, with its stages at Jericho, Ai and Gibeon, leads here. By way of anticipation it should be noted that in occupying this unique intermediate position Benjamin was also able to play a special historical role – and did so. Israel's first king, Saul, was a Benjaminite, and when Ephraim in the north was to be joined with Judah in the south in the time of David, the Benjaminites were specially asked for advice (II Sam. 3.19). After the division of the kingdom, Benjamin remained essentially with Judah.[26] The geographical basis of the settlement was hardly sufficient to break up these historical constellations.

The same fundamental unity is confirmed in the case of the tribes in the neighbourhood of the northern chain of cities, on the border of the plain of Megiddo and above all in Galilee. None of this territory ever played a prominent role in the history of Israel. It lay outside the centres of Israelite history.[27] It is understandable how a city like Hazor could gain a position of prominence by taking a military and political initiative, being able to make dependencies of the smaller places in its area. Hazor is called 'head of the kingdoms' in Josh. 11 because its environs enabled it to achieve a special political status in Galilee, however limited that status inevitably was. In the south, the chain of fortresses in the plain of Megiddo formed an impassable barrier; the Phoenicians were settled in the coastal plain and Lebanon rose to the north. The only possible area for expansion was Syria, to the east and north-east.

However, we have no details about the course of the settlement in Galilee, apart from Joshua's alleged attack on Hazor. We are quite in the dark about the early history of the tribes of Asher (in the western hill-country near to the Philistines), Zebulon (chiefly on the southern boundary of the hill-country of Galilee) and Naphthali (in Galilee, to the east). Surprisingly enough, however, light is shed on the fate of the tribe of Issachar in a critical frontier area where the plain of Megiddo joins the Jordan valley by Beth-shean. At least, that is so if it is permissible to compare notes from the Amarna correspondence with the early history of this Israelite tribe.

The saying about Issachar which has been handed down in the context of the 'blessing of Jacob' (Gen. 49.14, 15) is quite remarkable. He is said to be a strong ass, crouching between the sheepfolds, who found the land so attractive that he bowed his shoulder to the burden; consequently he became a 'slave at forced labour' (*mās-'ebed*). The name of the tribe itself seems to correspond well with this characterization; it is usually translated 'man for hire'.[28] Can this be an allusion to the fortunes of Issachar as a member of the Israelite tribal alliance? Could a tribe have been so 'degraded' within Israel? What is true in general for all the tribal sayings, namely that they largely reflect the fortunes of the tribes in the early period, will also apply to Issachar, which must have found itself in a particular situation. If we can assume that its territory extended from south-eastern Galilee, including Tabor, into the southern plains, and perhaps even had the Jordan as its eastern frontier, that will indeed have been a 'pleasant land', quite suitable for agricultural development. On the other hand, for that very reason, it had already been occupied and opened up, and was immediately adjacent to the northern chain of cities.

The Amarna letter Louvre AO 7098 fits this situation exactly.[29] It probably dates from the fourteenth century BC and tells the king of Egypt that the sender, the prince (Biridiya) of Megiddo, has sole rights to ploughing in the territory of the city of Šunama (Shunem) and is bringing *mazza* people there; none of the other princes of his district have permission. Shunem lies east of Megiddo, on the opposite side of the plain to the area in which Issachar is later to be located. Another Amarna letter explains the sending of *mazza* people, i.e. forced labour (cf. Hebrew *mās*), to Shunem.[30] According to this, Labaya, the city-prince from central Palestine, destroyed and depopulated the city of Shunem. Labaya's plans for expansion came to nothing; Shunem returned under the sovereignty of Megiddo, and from there attempts were renewed to make its land fertile. Biridiya of Megiddo brought forced labour from the Yapu in south-western Galilee,[31] who achieved what could not be done from local resources after the destruction of Shunem and the loss of its inhabitants.

It would be over-hasty to seek to draw a direct conclusion from the fourteenth century to Issachar simply on the basis of this account. But the hypothesis is not to be ruled out[32] that the tribe of Issachar followed the former *mazza*-people at a later stage in a kind of legal succession, first purchasing the right to settle[33] by being prepared to contribute labour in the area of Shunem and Jezreel. The tribe remained in the 'pleasant land', but at the cost of becoming a 'slave at forced labour'. Genesis 49 would describe its fortunes at an early period; there can hardly be any doubt that it was later able to extricate itself from this dependent position, once foreign rule in its territory came to an end.

The suggestions put forward here rest on a combination of very different sources, but they do reflect the conditions of a particular well-defined area in a time to which we can gain access. They make it possible to assess the difficulties with which an individual tribe had to struggle in gaining a foothold in Palestine, especially when it was involved with the pre-Israelite administrative structure. They indicate a pattern from a time of particular crisis. The fate of Issachar may be extreme, like the saying about the tribe which was current, but it also allows us to draw conclusions about other similar problems of which we have no knowledge.

The particular case of the tribe of Issachar makes it clear that there can be no thought of an account of the course of the Israelite settlement. That is why our description so far has had to be limited to a demarcation of the territories which were especially suitable for the settlement of newly-arriving elements of population in Palestine. In view of the present state of our knowledge, nothing can be said about the way in which the individual tribes approached cultivated land, their equipment, the number of their possessions, their size or the exact period of their arrival. For some tribes we must consider the illuminating theory of A. Alt, that the process must have been connected with the annual change between winter and summer pastures; there is also another possibility, that to a limited degree individual tribes attempted to make room for themselves by force, attacking the population already in possession.[34] Here, however, the fact that in the first stage of the settlement the incoming tribes were not in a position to occupy fortified cities is an important criterion. This is clear from the way in which the places within the two chains of cities were avoided, and can also be seen from the fortunes of cities in the hill-country and in the Jordan valley. If a city was overcome in these areas it was usually as a result of special circumstances rather than through a clear military victory. We have details of individual instances, for example the use of trickery or the exploitation of treachery. Sometimes such a happening was elaborated with miraculous details and celebrated as a victory of the deity.

A characteristic instance of this is the occupation of Jericho. The story of the fall of Jericho is well known, with the walls falling down during a march round the city, accompanied by the blowing of sacred instruments. But this tradition can be clearly detached from an earlier report in which a woman named Rahab, presented as a prostitute, agrees with two spies to put a scarlet thread in her window on the city wall (Josh. 2.21), evidently to mark the place where it will be possible to enter the city. The degree to which the theme of the 'harlot story' is involved here is a quite separate question,[35] and it is unnecessary to seek to check the detail about the falling walls from the archaeological evidence.[36] The mere fact that what has been handed down is not a decisive military victory but a tradition about the occupation of the city which has been developed in a variety of ways, not ruling out favourable circumstances and miracle, is proof enough of the difficulties which were usually too much for the incoming tribes.

The occupation of Bethel by the house of Joseph (Judg. 1.22–26) looks like almost an exact parallel to Jericho. A man is taken who will show the way into the city, or more accurately, the weak place where it is possible to break through the defences.

There is mention of ambush and stratagem in connection with the destruction of Ai (Josh. 7; 8). The great battle at Gibeon (Josh. 10) also has a miraculous character. Its outcome is victorious because Yahweh plays a part in it. Sun and moon stand still until he has wreaked vengeance on his enemies.[37]

From this perspective, the occupation and destruction by Joshua of Hazor in Galilee is also extremely suspicious (Josh. 11). First, the location of the city in the far north, in an area about which we have no other accounts of a settlement, raises questions; so does assumption of a military potential capable of bringing down so strongly fortified a city. The excavations carried out there in recent decades really make it even more improbable that we should suppose a clear Israelite victory. We must rather assume that what happened was a different matter. Hazor was the centre of the most significant city state in Galilee. This is already clear from the Mari texts and the Amarna letters; it really was 'formerly the head of all these kingdoms', as Josh. 11.10 puts it. Hazor had the aura of the great dominating centre in the north. Solomon built fortifications there (I Kings 9.15). Accordingly Hazor was among the cities which were acquired later and whose territory was made part of Israel. The city may have lost its independence as Egyptian influence waned and during the advance of the Sea-peoples, or in other local circumstances; in Israelite eyes it may have seemed obvious to associate the gain of Hazor retrospectively with the battle by the waters of

Merom and to bring the account to a climax with the fall of the famous fortress. It is possible to provide archaeological proof of a partial destruction of the city in the thirteenth century BC, but there is no reason why this should be attributed to the Israelite tribes. The significance of the battle at the waters of Merom remains an open question. The obvious thing is to assume that we have here a local tradition of those tribes which settled in Galilee, quite independent of the process of settlement in the rest of Palestine. In that case, in the end these groups could also have had a hand in the destruction of Hazor.[38] However, it must readily be conceded that these are constructions which cannot be given any strict proof, although the situation at the time seems appropriate, and it can be shown that Hazor was burnt after the last Bronze Age settlement.[39] So while we can survey the wider framework of the Israelite settlement to some degree, gaps remain in our knowledge on the periphery of Palestine which can only be filled by hypothesis.

Significantly, the book of Joshua says nothing about the capture of Jerusalem. This city was a Jebusite stronghold in the immediate proximity of the area settled by Judah and Benjamin, and as such remained quite independent to begin with. Only David was in a position to capture it at a later stage, with his mercenary troops. Even then, however, a stratagem seems to have been involved. Use was probably made of a shaft connected with the waterworks of the city, which had an opening outside the walls.[40] This is also an indication of the tactical and technical considerations which could be helpful at that time towards capturing a city.

While from time to time there may have been battles at particular stages of the settlement, it essentially seems to have remained a slow and peaceful process, the result of which was summed up by A. Alt in words which are still valid:[41] 'The Israelites did not adopt the urban culture of Palestine as soon as they had occupied the country, but as it were dwelt at first before the city gates.'

So far, nothing at all has been said about the historical role of Joshua, the dominant figure of the settlement and the leader of almost all undertakings. Joshua is regarded as Moses' successor in office; he continues and completes the programme of the occupation of the promised land foretold by Moses. The Old Testament sees Joshua in this wider context; it has been produced from the traditions of individual tribes and the process which made these traditions the common possession of all the tribes. Chapters 1 and 23 of the book of Joshua, the framework provided by the Deuteronomists, reflect this perfectly. They deliberately and consistently include all the individual traditions in the programme entrusted to Joshua, which involves the whole of Israel. Supposing that the tribes in fact acted independently, and that the book of Joshua is merely a redactional compilation and unification of the traditions, where, if anywhere at all, did Joshua have his original setting? Alt has declared that the note in Josh.24.30, about the inheritance and grave of Joshua in Timnah in the hill-country of Ephraim,[42] cannot possibly have been invented and is without bias.[43] He therefore regards Joshua as a man from Ephraim and finds this confirmed by the tradition of the expansion of the house of Joseph in Josh. 17.14ff. and by the leading role played by Joshua at the assembly at Shechem in Josh. 24. Joshua was included in the Benjaminite traditions only subsequently, as a result of his valuable co-operation in the battle at Gibeon in Josh. 10, and consequently in the end achieved a significance for all Israel. Thus Joshua was an Ephraimite hero whose particular personal achievements in the settlement of the tribes of central Palestine laid the foundation for his exceptional role.[44]

None of these arguments of Alt's really needs to be changed. However, his conclusion from the tradition that Joshua was buried in Ephraim, that he must have belonged without question and exclusively to the tribe of Ephraim, which settled north of Benjamin, is excessively specific, and compels him to seek a missing link to explain why Joshua had achieved such a leading position in the Benjaminite traditions. This bridge in the tradition has to be provided by the battle at Gibeon. But we cannot exclude the opposite possibility, that Joshua is to be associated with the allegedly exclusively Benjaminite traditions which are only regarded as 'Benjaminite' because the places mentioned, between Jericho and Gibeon, later belonged to Benjamin. Moreover, Joshua's grave in Timnah, in south-western Ephraim, is only about seven miles away from Benjaminite territory. It is an open question whether this Timnah belonged to Ephraim at the time of Joshua's death. Thus it could be that Joshua played a determinative role among the tribes which settled in the territory which was later to belong to Benjamin, and in southern Ephraim. The reference to the grave tradition may be of regulative, but not exclusive historical significance.[45]

The problems of method indicated here are connected intimately with the judgment on early Israelite traditions made by Alt and Noth. Because this is so significant for subsequent scholarship, a brief explanation is called for. The starting-point of their reflections is the concept of the 'aetiological saga'.[46] In fact this concept was first tested and defined by Alt in connection with the sagas of the book of Joshua.[47] He says that the aetiological saga gives a causal explanation of striking phenomena by deriving their origin from events of the past. As examples he gives the twelve sacred stones in the sanctuary at Gilgal (Josh. 3f.), the 'hill of the foreskins' (Josh. 5.2ff.), the depopulated hill on which the city of Jericho stood and the isolated dwelling of Rahab's family (Josh. 6), the *tell* of Ai (Josh. 8.1–29), the treaty with Gibeon and three further cities and the appointment of the Gibeonites as cultic personnel (Josh. 9), and finally the five trees above the blocked entrance to the cave of Makkedah (Josh. 10.16ff.). These were taken up by sagas and understood as the consequences of historical events from the time of the conquest. They aroused a zeal for narrative whose aim was the disclosure of historical causes (aetiologies), in a very dramatic and impressive form. Alt believed that each of these sagas originally had a life of its own, was complete in itself and was at first independent of the context in which it was later set. Even Joshua may have been dispensable in the first version of these narratives.

This approach carries within it the beginnings of an extensive literary and critical fragmentation of the traditions. Once they were assumed to have had an independent life of their own, it was very quickly supposed that the accounts had to be derived from historically independent and isolated events. Now it is true that this method is quite consistent, and cannot be rejected out of hand. On the other hand, it is by no means compelling in every respect. The observation of aetiological characteristics, usually introduced or explained in the narrative with the formula 'until this day',[48] cannot have set each and every saga in motion with an automatic inevitability. Rather, two poles of the process should be noted and taken into account: first, a known course of history, primarily independent of the 'circumstances of the present' which are to be given an aetiological explanation, and secondly a striking object in the locality of this event, which could be regarded as a 'remembrance' of what once happened there. So while the aetiological saga is without doubt concerned with an object 'until this day', it derives its real substance from a historical recollection which not only remembered isolated events at particular locations, but was also capable of embracing larger complexes. If we apply this argument to the book of Joshua, that would mean that the events by the Jordan, at Jericho, Ai and Gibeon belong, in that order, to a successive process of settlement in a particular area and that the recollection of this process provided the basic substance for aetiological explanation of striking objects at a later time. In so far as Joshua played a role in this total process, he necessarily also became involved in the shaping of the individual sagas. We may therefore legitimately argue that Joshua was associated with the central Palestinian tribes, though we cannot make out an originally more limited circle of activity with any certainty. At any rate, he has no place among the southern tribes nor in Judg. 1, even in connection with the house of Joseph (Judg. 1.22–26); his role in the destruction of Hazor, in the north, remains disputed.

The difficult problems of the early history of Israel in Palestine which have been discussed above come to a head in the question of the nature and function of the so-called 'twelve-tribe system'. In even the most recent histories of Israel, immediately after accounts of the settlement, a survey is given of the final territories of the tribes in the cultivated land, not least because the central part of the book of Joshua also records the boundaries of tribes and gives lists of cities.[49] Maps of the historical topography of Israel apparently support such accounts by dividing Palestine into twelve tribal territories, often shown in different colours.

In the present account, the main outline of the territories in which individual tribes settled has already been given. The account has paid close attention to the historical circumstances which the tribes encountered, especially where fortified cities made a peaceful occupation impossible. Nothing further need be said here in addition. The apparently exhaustive tribal system with its tribal territories has been shown with sufficient clarity[50] to rest on administrative measures connected with the development of land laws; while these may well have begun in the period before the formation of the state, they will only have been perfected and given statutory form during the period of the monarchy. This will be the case with lists of boundary points and cities in Joshua 13–19. It is clear that the authors of these lists found it extremely difficult to give exact details of the settlement of twelve tribes all at the same time. Either they did not have sufficient material for some of the tribes, or they had to extend boundary points themselves, sometimes arbitrarily, on an inadequate basis.[51] It is particularly striking that the territory of the tribes in the west of the country is regularly extended as far as the coast, although historically this was never the case. Thus the ideal conception that the whole of Israel must also possess the whole land has unmistakably been at work here.

Behind these theories about the division of the country is the idea that 'all Israel' consists of twelve tribes, not all the same size, but together making up a fixed number. Consequently every tribe had to be assigned territory. Historical reality falls short of this conception. The numbers six and twelve were figures for the complete membership of a tribal alliance, as is clear from the groups of six and twelve tribes in the genealogical system in Genesis. However, the Israelite system does not always achieve the figure twelve in the same way. It is particularly striking that while the tribe of Levi originally[52] appears along with Simeon as an independent tribe, it is later said to be a 'tribe of priests' and is assigned no land.[53] The number twelve is rescued by the division of the 'house of Joseph' into Ephraim and Manasseh. Leaving aside other minor differences, for example in the order in which the tribes are listed,[54] it is clear that the pressure towards the number twelve did not derive from historical causes alone; it must be regarded as an attempt to systematize all Israel and to represent its completeness. The emergence of new groups after the completion of the system, or while it was being worked out, shows the internal difficulties of the theory. For example, there was an unwillingness to remove the tribe of Simeon, which had no historical influence, and replace it, say, with Caleb; a group like 'Machir' was not included;[55] and there was no room alongside Gad[56] for the inhabitants of 'Gilead'. When this theory of the twelve tribes emerged, and what historical influence it exercised, is a disputed question which we shall have occasion to reconsider more than once. A fundamental presupposition must almost certainly be the conclusion of the settlement and the incorporation of the southern and northern tribes in a single alliance. This, however, had not happened completely before the formation of the state.

In Gen. 29.31–30.24, the twelve tribal ancestors of Israel are presented as sons of Jacob by his two wives Leah and Rachel and his concubines Zilpah and Bilhah. Both earlier and more recent scholarship has used this genealogical material to build up tribal affinities or territorial connections. Thus it has become usual to talk of Leah and Rachel tribes, the former comprising the four southern tribes, Reuben, Simeon, Levi and Judah, and the latter the two central Palestinian groups, Joseph and Benjamin. But there is no such obvious reason for assigning the other tribal ancestors to the various wives.[57] It will, of course be considered possible that the connection of four tribes with Leah and two with Rachel is not fortuitous and in principle already represents that 'dualism' within Israel which was later to have its historical effect in the formation of 'Judah' and 'Israel'. On the other hand, however, the schematic assignation of the other six tribes to the various wives shows the pressure that existed towards completing the system, by introducing tribes from the outer areas.

In the course of the present account, it will transpire that individual tribes in fact worked closely together and already engaged in common actions during the period of the judges. In individual cases, it is not impossible that tribes were associated with a common sanctuary, claimed by an alliance of, say, three tribes. This is not, however, to accept the preconceived notion of a 'tribal system'; rather, such a grouping will have had its historical roots in the fact that the territories occupied by the tribes were limited and the dangers they had to face were common to all. The hypothesis of the existence of an 'early Israelite amphictyony', developed in detail by M. Noth on the basis of earlier suggestions, is reasonably correct in its starting-point.[58] Noth attempted to explain the 'twelve-tribe system' on the pattern of the sacral tribal alliances to be found in Greece and Italy. These also often had twelve members, who regarded the care of a central sanctuary as their common task. Noth regarded the sanctuary in which the ark stood as this central Israelite sanctuary; it was to be regarded as the real centre for the Israelite tribes and at the same time functioned as a kind of collecting point for the legal and historical traditions of early Israel. Noth believed that this amphictyony functioned in the period of the judges. His penetrating investigations of territorial history, always in contact with historical events, did not prevent him from believing that such a functional system, going beyond all boundaries, was already possible shortly after the settlement, despite the hill-country and the gaps in occupied territory. The twelve tribes, he believed, were involved in it.

Noth put forward his theory in 1930. In fact he never revised it, nor even partially retracted it on the basis of his later investigations into territorial history. Had he done so, he would doubtless have developed a much more differentiated picture of early Israelite history than is to be found in his *History of Israel* and even more in his later commentaries. In view of the influence which Noth's theory has had on Old Testament scholarship, reference will constantly be made to it in the following paragraphs.

The problems in allocating the tribes over the whole of the cultivated land of Palestine become particularly clear when we consider the settlement in Transjordania. Noth laid the foundations for this territorial history and carried out fundamental investigations into it.[59] According to the Old Testament tradition, this settlement took quite a simple form. The tribes moving directly north from the area east of the Dead Sea had no difficulty in defeating the two kings of what appear to be the leading territories east of the Jordan, Sihon king of Heshbon and Og king of Bashan.[60] This is not only a simplified account of historical events, but an irresponsibly abbreviated schematization of the territories east of the Jordan and of their allocation. The names preferred in other passages in the Old Testament are, from south to north, 'the tableland' (Hebrew *hammīšōr*), 'the land of Gilead', 'the (land of) Bashan'. These therefore essentially presuppose a threefold division of Transjordania facing the land west of the Jordan.[61] 'The tableland' means the plateau beyond the hills which rise east of the Dead Sea, to the degree that it was the scene of Israelite history, that is, with the Arnon as its southern boundary. 'Gilead' denotes the wooded hill-country through which the Jabbok flows: primarily the area south of the Jabbok, but then also the area adjacent on the north side. Similarly, 'Bashan' is the land alongside the Yarmuq, which for Israel was the northernmost part of Transjordania. It includes the fertile plains of the landscape which is now called *en-nuqra*. The watercourses of the Jabbok and the Yarmuq certainly help to divide the relatively narrow strip of cultivated land east of the Jordan, but they are not necessarily well-defined boundaries which will have determined the structure of the settlement.

In contrast to the dominant later Old Testament conception of a first Israelite settlement in these areas which took place exclusively from the south and the south-east, there is evidence that Transjordania was gradually settled from west of the Jordan.[62] It is difficult to describe in detail here the complicated process which can be reconstructed from a number of scattered reports and observations.[63] However, the chief features may easily be seen. At the time of the Israelite settlement, and well beyond it into the period of the monarchy, other peoples had gained a firm footing on the periphery of Transjordania, in the territories regained from the wilderness of Syria. Presumably they founded states even earlier than the Israelites, and developed a military potential. Mention has already been made of the Edomites and Moabites in the south, who stood in the way of tribal movements there; in the east the Ammonites were to be a severe threat to Israel, and in the north the Aramaeans, who were beginning to consolidate themselves. The 'promised land' was chiefly the land west of the Jordan. Moses died before the crossing of the Jordan, and therefore still outside the land which had been promised to Israel for the future. The land available in Transjordania was essentially a narrow and restricted area on the west side, beginning with 'the tableland' east of the Dead Sea and extending over wooded Gilead towards the Aramaean sphere of influence in Bashan. But this free area to the east in no case seems to have extended as far as the end of the cultivated land, because these boundary areas adjacent to the steppe were already occupied.[64] In this way, access to the remaining part of western Transjordania was virtually barricaded on the eastern side; and even in that limited territory, city states must already have begun to form. These had to be overthrown if a permanent Israelite settlement was to be made possible. Representatives of this kind of rule will have been king Sihon of Heshbon (*ḥesbān*) on the northern edge of the 'tableland', immediately south of the 'land of Jasher', later settled by the Israelite tribes, and king Og of Bashan, who was slain by the Israelites at Edrei (*der'a*), almost on the eastern edge of cultivated territory (Deut. 3.1–3). There is every probability that these undertakings began west of the Jordan, when the Israelite tribes had become so strong that they faced the need to move over into Transjordania. This was certainly not one single movement, but a process which will have differed from place to place and which will have lasted at least until early in the period of the monarchy.[65]

Here the so-called 'mountain of Gilead' seems to have been an important starting point for an early Israelite settlement. According to Gen. 31, Jacob already concluded a treaty with the 'Aramaean' Laban there; this is the location for which the name 'Gilead' will first have been used.[66] The territory in question is the hill-country lying south of the Jabbok, bounded in the east by the *wādi rumēmīn* and in the south by the *wādi abu quṭṭēn*.[67] Presumably Israelite tribes will also have moved out into the hill-country lying north of the Jabbok and will have settled there. At first sight, this seems to suggest a movement from the east; but the inhabitants of Gilead were Ephraimites (cf. Judg. 12.1–6), which means that Jacob, from central Palestine, found a way into the area of the Jabbok.

Now 'Gilead' is not an independent tribe.[68] The area we have just described appears, rather, in allocation of tribal territories as the possession of Gad. Reuben is almost always mentioned as Gad's nearest neighbour. As far as anything certain can be said about the territory of Gad,[69] it was to be found south of the Jabbok in the area adjoining the land occupied by Gilead, but at least on the heights at the north end of the Dead Sea it made contact with the Moabite sphere of interest. That means that both Nebo and the place described as 'Peor', from which Balaam cursed the Israelites,[70] remained outside this Israelite country. We have virtually no reliable reports of the tribe of Reuben, which is mostly mentioned along with Gad as a tribe east of the Jordan.[71] However, the tribe of Gad still had a role in later times, when king Mesha of Moab forced back Israelites who had evidently attempted to assert their influence as far as the neighbourhood of the Arnon. Mesha mentions Gad on his famous memorial stone from the ninth century BC.[72]

At all events, the Israelite associations described as the tribes of Reuben and Gad hardly moved from the east into the areas they occupied. At one time they may have undertaken the crossing from west of the Jordan, as other elements already occupied both sides of the Jabbok and they will really only have been left with the northern part of the 'tableland'.

Developments in the north, in the area of the Yarmuq, seem to have been different yet again. Here parts of the central Palestinian tribes, presumably because of their size, sought refuge on the other side of the Jordan. Chief among these was the group Machir, from the tribe of Benjamin, still shown to be an independent entity at the time of the Song of Deborah, which moved into the area north of the

Jabbok.[73] We must also mention links between the tribe of Benjamin and the city of Jabesh.[74]

These complicated events have been described in a simplified form in the Pentateuch and elsewhere, in that what was in fact a movement of individual tribal groups from west to east over a relatively long period and in different areas, was incorporated in the book of Numbers into a virtually direct movement from south to north, under the leadership of Moses and before the occupation of the land west of the Jordan. In this way the settlement of Transjordania appears as a first partial success in the attempts of all Israel to occupy the promised land. The Deuteronomic literature schematized this process to the highest degree and developed the theory that able-bodied men of the tribes of Reuben, Gad and 'Half-Manasseh' first took part in the conquest of the land west of the Jordan before finally being allowed to take up their own dwelling-places in Transjordania.[75]

The account of the settlement can be concluded here. It was remarked earlier that the details given in Judg. 1, and especially the so-called 'negative index of possessions', are a key factor not only in assessing the situation immediately after the settlement, but also in describing the whole future development of Israel. This being so, it would seem appropriate to give a brief summary of the result of the settlement, not least in view of the later course of events.

The southern part of the land west of the Jordan was occupied by tribal groups which also came directly from the south, presumably from the area round Kadesh. Among them was the strong contingent which is known to us after its settlement under the name 'Judah' and which may have had close contacts with the smaller groups of Othnielites, Calebites, Jerahmeelites and parts of the Kenites. They settled in the hill-country of Judah in the fertile area round Hebron, particularly in the land adjacent to the north, extending about as far as Bethlehem. In the southern boundary-areas of this 'greater Judah' the tribe of Simeon and perhaps also an independent tribe of Levi seem to have had fortunes of their own, about which we know no details.

The settlement in central Palestine took in, to the south, the narrow Benjaminite territory on the heights of Jericho and Gilgal in the Jordan valley as far as Gibeon and Aijalon in the area north of Jerusalem, but excluding the city itself. The centre of this settlement extended as far as the heart of the hill-country of Ephraim and Samaria, with Shechem at the centre and the plains of Megiddo as a northern boundary. The 'house of Joseph' was the chief participant in this movement; it was made up of the dominant groups Ephraim and Manasseh, and the clan-association of Machir also belonged to the latter. We cannot say with any certainty whether the tribe of Benjamin in the south had a closer relationship to 'Joseph' from the very beginning, as is suggested by the fact that they share the same mother, Rachel. They may only have formed a loose alliance once they had settled in the cultivated land. The first areas to be settled were the less densely inhabited areas on the hills and in the valleys and plains, but not the coastal plain, the territory round the chain of cities on the plain of Megiddo and the heights of Gezer. In all probability the main thrust of this settlement in central Palestine was from the south-east, the territory from which the book of Joshua begins and which also includes the neighbourhood of the lower Jabbok valley.

We know virtually nothing of the early history of the tribes of Asher, Zebulon and Naphthali beyond the plain of Megiddo; in all probability they first settled for the most part on the borders of the hill-country of Galilee. The tribe of Issachar possibly managed to establish itself at the south-east end of the plain of Megiddo in difficult conditions and in the closest proximity to the existing Canaanite population. The tribe of Dan was not so fortunate; they were not able to remain on the heights west of Jerusalem, near the southern chain of cities, and finally managed to settle right in the north, near the source of the Jordan.

It is extremely probable that Transjordania was settled from west of the Jordan; Israelite tribes were able to find a footing in the hilly border country to the west and some way up the river valleys, especially those of the Jabbok and Yarmuq. The tribes of Reuben and Gad occupied the area adjoining the territory of the Moabites; north of them were some individual groups in Gilead and in the area of the Yarmuq, among them the Manassite group of Machir.

This originally loose structure of self-contained tribal alliances grew closer together in later times, but did not give up its characteristics completely. Even the transition to the monarchies and the rise of state alliances could not change this. On the contrary, the growth of state organizations seems to have provided an impulse to define Israel as a tribal alliance and to see the number of twelve tribes as an ideal and permanent guarantee for all Israel. Even the total catastrophes which brought about the end of the so-called 'northern kingdom' of Israel in 722 BC and the collapse of the southern state of Judah in 587 BC did not put an end to the idea of the people of the twelve tribes.

It will emerge even more clearly in due course that the division of Israel into the two independent kingdoms of Israel and Judah was the natural consequence of the geographical distribution of the tribes which followed from the period of the settlement. In the south, Judah was an entity in itself and remained so; the apparently 'unified kingdom' under David and the state of Solomon with their defences against the outside world were in reality complex entities, containing contrary tendencies and a will for independent self-determination. Galilee and Transjordania were overshadowed by these developments, the focal points of which were in the hill-country west of the Jordan and south of the plain in Jezreel. In fact the southern chain of cities remained a dividing line between Israel and Judah.

The negative index of possessions in Judg. 1 not only delineates territories but also indicates coming developments. The battle with the Philistines in the coastal plain could be foreseen; it came to a provisional conclusion in the time of David. But the incorporation of this territory into the Israelite state made necessary a symbiosis with the Canaanite way of life. This led to confrontation, delimitation and self-assertion in economics, politics, religion and not least in legal matters;

it also led to adaptation, intermingling, adoption and transformation. The struggle against Baal in Israel is only one of the more prominent symptoms. Like a flash of lightning, Judg. 1 illuminates the busy landscape of Israelite life until well into the period of the monarchy and enables us to understand the geographical and political basis underlying the struggles in which the Israelite tribes were involved after the settlement, both on the frontiers and within their territory.

It would be wrong to imagine a self-contained tribal alliance already functioning immediately after the settlement. As will soon appear, the theory of the amphictyony has only a semblance of truth about it. The survey of developments must be pursued in detail in the way in which it has been begun, as the development of particular groups, each on its own territory. Collaboration between these groups is usually only of an occasional nature. Hardly had the tribes arrived when they had to defend themselves against hostile attacks on their borders, surprisingly soon, and it is this that seems to have furthered and strengthened the awareness of a common destiny, without leading at first to a complete union. The period of transition to the formation of the state is given a disputed title, 'the time of the judges'.

NOTES

1. A watering-place by the village of *mērōn* in Upper Galilee, north-west of *ṣafed*.
2. Division of land: Josh.13.7; 14.5 etc.; assignment by lot: 14.2; 15.1; 16.1, etc.; both views in juxtaposition: 18.10.
3. This argument will be substantiated in the course of the present account. It needs more than a few words of explanation.
4. Someone shows a way in; this is comparable with what was presumably the original function of Rahab in Jericho (displaying a scarlet thread, Josh.2.18).
5. Judg.1.28, 30, 33, 35. For Judg.1 as a whole see G. Schmitt, *Du sollst keinen Frieden schliessen mit den Bewohnern des Landes*, BWANT 91, 1970, 46–80.
6. A. Alt, 'The Settlement of the Israelites in Palestine', *Essays in Old Testament History and Religion*, 1966, 146–9; the numbers for the cities are taken from the edition of the text by K. Sethe, *Urkunden* IV, 781–6. The names given here from the list of Thutmoses III may serve as an example; other names could be added from other lists, and the mentions of these places would have to be followed through the period of the Egyptian New Kingdom up to the appearance of the Israelites; see M. Noth, *Aufsätze* 2, Part 1; W. Helck, *Beziehungen*, [2]1971, 107–327; cf. also the survey of the places mentioned by the Egyptians, *ANET*, 242–3; the hieroglyphic texts are collected in J. Simons, *Handbook for the Study of Egyptian Topographical Lists relating to Western Asia*, 1937 (second edition in preparation). The map in Helck, *Beziehungen*, 135, covers the places mentioned in the lists in the neighbourhood of Megiddo, but extends a good way south and also includes the 'southern chain of cities' (see below).
7. But Dor first appears in Wen Amun 1, 8ff. (*el-burj* by *eṭ-ṭanṭūra*, cf. Galling, *TGI*[2], 42), where it is included among the possessions of the *Ṯkr*, a tribe of the Sea-peoples; see the remarks by Alt, *KS* I, 227 n.3.
8. A. Alt, 'Zur Geschichte von Beth-Sean 1500–1000 BC' (1926), *KS* I, 246–55.
9. See Knudtzon, 289; *AOT*, 377 (Beth-shean); AO 7098, *AOT*, 738, and *TGI*[2], 28 (Shunem); for details see below in connection with the tribe of Issachar.

10. See Helck, *Beziehungen*, 128.

11. Both cities in Knudtzon, no.287 (*AOT*, 375f.; *TGI*[1], 24–6; *ANET*, 488); the prince of Gezer plays a role in a series of letters (Knudtzon, nos.249f., 254, 267–73, 286–300); cf. Galling, *TGI*[2], 24f.

12. Cf. A. Alt, 'The Settlement of the Israelites', op. cit., 145.

13. For the independence of the coastal cities and a mention of Acco (Akka) cf. the Amarna letter AO 7096, *TGI*[2], 27; *ANET*, 487; cf. also the explanations of A. Alt, *KS* III, 161–5.

14. A. Rowe, *The Four Canaanite Temples of Beth-Sean* I, 1930; F. W. James, *The Iron Age of Beth-shean*, 1966; for small objects see A. Rowe, *Catalogue of Egyptian Scarabs in the Palestine Archaeological Museum*, 1936; for material from Megiddo see G. Loud, *The Megiddo Ivories*, 1939, esp. pl.62; there is a summary with further details by A. Malamat in *The World History of the Jewish People*, First Series, Vol. III, 1971, 32–6; cf. also *ANET*, 260–3.

15. G. Loud, *Megiddo* II, 1948, 135ff.; A. Malamat, op. cit., 36.

16. Egyptian *Tkr*, more recently also transcribed as *Tkl*.

17. Josh.13.3; Judg.6.16–18; M. Noth, *Old Testament World*, 78.

18. A. Alt, 'Ägyptische Tempel in Palästina und die Landnahme der Philister' (1944), *KS* I, 216–30; B. Mazar, *The Philistines and the Rise of Israel and Tyre*, The Israel Academy of Sciences and Humanities, Proceedings, Vol. I, no.7, 1964; W. F. Albright, 'Syria, the Philistines and Phoenicia', *CAH* II, ch.33, 1966; A. Malamat, 'The Egyptian Decline in Canaan and the Sea Peoples', in *The World History of the Jewish People* I, Vol. III, 23–38 (further literature on p.347).

19. This is true not only for the plain of Megiddo but also for the southern chain of cities. It is relatively easy there to cross the hill-country of Gibeon westwards to Gezer by the Beth-horon road (cf. T. Oelgarte, *PJB* 14, 1918, 73–89, and maps 6 and 7); after crossing the hills, the road on the heights of *'amwās* and *latrūn* into the area of Gezer (*tell jezer*) and on into the coastal plain is no longer any problem.

20. Bethlehem lies 5 miles south of Jerusalem and Hebron about 14 miles south of Bethlehem; it is easy to move from one place to the other. Gen.13 seems to suggest a movement in the opposite direction during the Israelite settlement. After joining Lot, Abraham moves there from the north, entering Judah from the area round Bethel. However, a different approach must be adopted towards the tradition and the history of the movements of the patriarchs in the land from that made to the geographical details of the settlement in Joshua and Judges. An invasion of Judah through the lower Jordan valley can be conjectured, but not proved.

21. According to Judg.1.11–15 (= Josh.15.15–19), the dwelling-places of the Othnielites are connected with the city of Debir (formerly Kiriath-sepher, Judg.1.11, or Kiriathsannah, Josh.15.49). The exact site of the city is not certain. It has been sought south-west of Hebron; suggestions have been: *tell bēt-mirsim* (Albright), *tell ṭarrāme* (Noth), *ḫirbet er-rabūḍ* and also *eḍ-ḍaharīye*; cf. W. F. Albright, *The Archaeology of Palestine and the Bible*, 1932, 77ff.; M. Noth, *Aufsätze* 1, 204–9.

22. Particularly the expansionist policy of a certain Labaya, who seems to have had his base at Shechem; for a first introduction see Alt, 'The Settlement of the Israelites', op. cit., 149ff.

23. Judg.9.2 mentions 'all the lords of Shechem'.

24. Dan is the most interesting example of a tribe which first made a successful settlement and then had to move on before finally gaining a firm foothold (in a border region!). In the upper reach of the Jordan valley it captured the city of Laish (*tell el-qāḍī*) and later gave it a different name (Judg.18.27–29). The expression 'from Dan to Beersheba' later described the full extent of Israelite territory from north to south. Samson, who performed

deeds of valour against the Philistines (Judg.13–16), came from Dan; at that time Dan doubtless dwelt in its old tribal territory. For the form of the tradition of the migration of Dan and the foundation of its sanctuary, and for an assessment of it, see M. Noth, 'Der Hintergrund von Richter 17–18' (1962), *Aufsätze* I, 133–47.

25. The specific references to Beth-shean and the plain of Jezreel are usually regarded as explanatory glosses (cf. *BH*³; Noth, *Joshua*, HAT I, 7², 102); however, the text is informative enough with or without this information! For Josh.17.14–18 see now also G. Schmitt, BWANT 91, 1970, 89–97.

26. Cf. above all I Kings 11.30–32, 36; 12.20 (LXX), 21; for a discussion of these passages and the problems involved see K.-D. Schunck, *Benjamin, Untersuchungen zur Enstehung und Geschichte eines israelitischen Stammes*, BZAW 86, 1963, esp.139–53; see also his p.169 with an instructive map with the boundaries of Benjaminite territory during the monarchy.

27. A. Alt, 'Galiläische Probleme' (1937–1940), *KS* II, 363–435, in his account of territorial history, significantly deals chiefly with the later periods of the country, especially in post-exilic and Hellenistic times.

28. It is assumed that the name is made up of '*iš* and *śākār*, which may be indicated by the strange orthography *yiśśaskār*; cf. e.g. Gen.30.18 and the apparatus in *BH*³. Noth, *History of Israel*, 66, even supposes that Gen.49.14, 15 has the character of a taunt and that consequently 'Issachar' is a nickname first given to these tribes by the Israelites. That would mean that the original name of this tribe or its members has been lost. In fact, however, the translation 'hired man', which follows the Hebrew etymology, cannot be right; the name may rest on earlier elements which can no longer be interpreted in their present form.

29. Cf. Galling, *TGI*², 28; *ANET*, 485; the connections discussed here have been recognized and described by A. Alt, *KS* III, 169–75.

30. Am.250, 41ff. (Knudtzon edition).

31. The modern *yāfa*, near to Nazareth. It is no longer possible to locate the place Nuribda, which is mentioned alongside it.

32. The evidence mentioned illuminates a historical situation connected with the territory; of course its association with particular features, known by name, like the tribe of Issachar, rest on a combination of evidence; in this respect, H.-J. Zobel, *Stammesspruch und Geschichte*, BZAW 95, 1965, 87, is too confident.

33. Shunem and Jezreel are given as dwelling places of Issachar in Josh.19.18; cf. II Sam.2.9; I Kings 4.17.

34. A. Alt, 'The Settlement of the Israelites in Palestine' (1925), *Essays on Old Testament History and Religion*, 1966, 135–69; 'Erwägungen über die Landnahme der Israeliten in Palästina' (1939), *KS* I, 126–75; significantly, Alt divides the latter study into 'warlike events' and 'the peaceful development'. M. Weippert, *The Settlement of the Israelite Tribes in Palestine*, SBT II, 21, London 1971, gives a detailed account of other assessments of the Israelite settlement, represented by names like those of Albright and Mendenhall; reference must be made to this book, because a detailed discussion of the theories of the nature of the settlement would go beyond the bounds of the present account. Weippert agrees in principle with the solutions of Alt and Noth.

35. Material from Greece and Rome is indicated in Windisch, *ZAW* 37, 1917/18, 188–98; G. Holscher, *ZAW* 38, 1919/20, 54–7; F.-M. Abel, *RB* 57, 1950, 327f.

36. J. Garstang, *PEFQS*, 1931, 187, 192–4, believed that he had discovered the walls of late Bronze-Age Jericho destroyed by earthquake and fire. The excavations of Miss Kenyon proved that these walls came from the early Bronze Age; only fragments of a number of houses survive from the late Bronze Age. It can be stated with some degree of certainty that the city was resettled about 1400 BC, but was again abandoned about 1325 BC.

Considerable erosion has wiped out important traces for what is supposed to be the period of the Israelite settlement. It is therefore impossible to draw any firm conclusions about the Israelite occupation of the city from the archaeological evidence. Cf. the comprehensive account by K. M. Kenyon, *Archaeology in the Holy Land*,[2] 1965, 209–11. The account given above provides confirmation for the situation in its own way. Thus possibly the Israelites were not involved with a 'fortress' at all, but only with an insignificant settlement. What is presumably the earlier report, which has the family of Rahab living in relative isolation near the ruins of the city (Josh. 6.22–25), could rest on old recollections.

37. In Josh. 10.13 the Old Testament text itself refers to an ancient tradition in which these words can be found, i.e. the 'Book of the Upright'. Conclusions can be drawn from this to a very old tradition from the time of the settlement which made use of cosmic phenomena; their connection with the events at Gibeon need not be unique, but they are the only instance which has been handed down to us.

38. R. de Vaux, *Early History*, 789–92, 794–6; he is primarily thinking that members of the tribe of Naphtali were involved.

39. In the discussion between Y. Yadin and Y. Aharoni, the problem is concentrated principally on the assessment of the late Bronze-Age strata XIV and XIII, which indicate an extensive destruction of the city and which are succeeded by stratum XII, with Iron-Age pottery; the last-named is like that found in Upper Galilee, regarded by Aharoni as Israelite and belonging to the twelfth century BC. To this point Yadin is in agreement with him. But Aharoni concludes that the Israelite settlement in Galilee preceded the fall of Hazor and therefore cannot have taken place before the twelfth century. Yadin disagrees with this on the basis of his archaeological observations: according to him, in view of stratum XIII, the thirteenth century is the only possible date; the rest of Galilee was only settled then. This group of questions goes on to be very complicated and hypothetical because Aharoni's argument is that the fall of Hazor was a consequence of the victory of Deborah in Judges 5/4; the battle at the waters of Merom was a last defence of the territory surrounding Hazor, which then finally fell like a ripe fruit into Israelite hands. For Yadin, both the settlement of Galilee and the victory of Deborah took place after the fall of Hazor. See the summaries in Y. Yadin, *Hazor*, 1972, 129–32; Y. Aharoni, *The Land of the Bible*, 1967, 205–8. By no means the least reason why the two scholars come to blows is that they both accept the unproven premise that the fall of Hazor is to be connected in some way with the settlement in central Palestine.

40. II Sam. 5.6–8; cf. also I Chron. 11.4–6 and the account of the occupation of Jerusalem by David which follows.

41. A. Alt, 'The Settlement of the Israelites', 169.

42. Present-day *ḥirbet tibneh*, on an old Roman road east of *'abūd*, in the south-western part of the hill-country of Ephraim (Thamna in the Hellenistic–Roman period). The Old Testament tradition speaks more accurately of Timnath-serah or Timnath-heres (Judg. 2.8f.).

43. A. Alt, *KS* I, 186.

44. A. Alt, 'Joshua' (1936), *KS* I, 176–92.

45. It may be mentioned in passing that Alt, with his thesis of the tradition about the grave of Joshua in Ephraim and the introduction of the figure of Joshua into allegedly Benjaminite traditions in the narrower framework of the book of Joshua, anticipated Noth and his attempt to use the tradition of the grave of Moses in connection with Pentateuchal traditions. According to Noth, Moses, whose tomb is located in Mount Nebo, only found his way into the mass of the Pentateuchal traditions at a later stage. Of course, Noth did not go so far as to declare that the tradition of Moses' tomb was Reubenite, although the neighbourhood of Nebo was presumably inhabited by portions of the tribe of Reuben at a later date. At least during the period of the settlement, there are problems in inferring

membership of a particular tribe from the situation of a tomb; later, of course, the Israelite usually wished to be buried in his ancestral city.

46. A detailed and sometimes polemical discussion of this complex of questions can be found in J. Bright, *Early Israel in Recent History Writing. A Study in Method*, SBT 19, 1960; for a critical review, particularly of the parallels drawn by Bright from American history, cf. especially M. Noth, *Aufsätze* 1, 48–51; M. Weippert, *The Settlement of the Israelite Tribes*, 136–143; the same problems are dealt with, in connection with Y. Kaufmann, *The Biblical Account of the Conquest of Palestine*, 1953, in a short article by A. Alt, 'Utopien', in *TLZ* 81, 1956, 521–8 (prepared for publication after Alt's death by O. Eissfeldt).

47. A. Alt, *KS* I, 182–92.

48. B. S. Childs, 'A Study of the Formula "Until this Day" ', *JBL* 82, 1963, 279–92, attempts to demonstrate that the formula largely denotes a redactional expansion of already existing traditions.

49. M. Noth begins his *History of Israel* with a detailed account of the places where the Israelite tribes settled in cultivated land; R. de Vaux devotes the third part of his *Early History* to 'the Traditions concerning the Settlement in Canaan', but develops this section geographically and discusses in succession the tribal traditions which belong to individual Palestinian territories.

50. A. Alt, 'Das System der Stammesgrenzen im Buche Joshua' (1927), *KS* I, 193–202; cf. also the series of articles in *KS* II, 276–315; M. Noth, 'Studien zu den historisch-geographischen Dokumenten des Josua-Buches' (1935), *Aufsätze* 1, 229–80; id., *Das Buch Josua*, HAT I, 7, ²1953, esp. 13–15. Alt's and Noth's studies were a stimulus and a starting point for more recent studies, among which are: F. M. Cross Jr and G. E. Wright, *JBL* 75, 1956, 202–26; Z. Kallai-Kleinmann, *VT* 8, 1958, 134–60; id., *VT* 11, 1961, 223ff.; Y. Aharoni, *VT* 9, 1959, 225–46; K. D. Schunck, *ZDPV* 78, 1962, 143–58; cf. also the commentaries or summary accounts from more recent times: Y. Aharoni, *The Land of the Bible*, 1967; J. A. Soggin, *Joshua*, OTL, 1972; S. Yeivin, *The Israelite Conquest of Canaan*, 1971; R. de Vaux, *Early History*, 523–680.

51. Cf. A. Alt, *KS* I, 195–7.

52. Levi after Simeon as a child of Leah, Gen. 29.34; Simeon and Levi regarded as brothers, Gen. 49.5.

53. Thus in the list of Israelite clans in Num. 26.5–51 and in the list of heads of Israelite tribes in Num. 1.5–15; for the tradition of the twelve tribes of Israel see M. Noth, *Das System der zwölf Stämme Israels*, BWANT 52, 1930, 3–38. Further discussion of the important question whether the so-called 'priestly tribe' of the Levites is identical with or akin to the 'secular' tribe of Levi from the early period of Israel, or whether it is possible that the designation 'Levite' led to an improper identification with members of the tribe of Levi, which was later held to be historical, is impossible here. For a rapid introduction to the relevant literature see M. Weippert, *The Settlement of the Israelite Tribes*, 43 n.139.

54. Remarkably enough, in Num. 1 and 26 Gad takes the place of Levi, which in Gen. 49.19 follows Dan and precedes Asher; in Gen. 30. 9–13 Gad and Asher are sons of Leah's maid Zilpah; further differences have now been worked out and evaluated by Helga Weippert, 'Das geographische System der Stämme Israels', *VT* 23, 1973, 76–89.

55. Machir, an independent entity among the central Palestinian tribes in the Song of Deborah, Judg. 5.14, probably migrated later into northern Transjordania. Manasseh seems to have expanded in its original dwelling in northern Ephraim, but is not mentioned in the Song of Deborah. A summary evaluation of the material about Machir can now be found in A. Elliger, *Die Frühgeschichte der Stämme Ephraim und Manasseh*, Diss. Rostock 1972, 113–36, so far unpublished.

56. The 'Gileadites' were taken up into Gad. There is an interesting process here. What was originally the name of an area (Gilead) became a kind of ethnic title and assumed the

character of a tribal designation; Ephraim and Judah, too, were presumably originally the names of areas. For this process and its relationship to the Israelite tribal system see the remarks of Noth in *Aufsätze* 1, 361–3.

57. Gad, east of the Jordan, and Asher, in western Galilee, appear as sons of Leah's maid Zilpah; Dan, in northern Galilee, and Naphthali, in western Galilee, are assigned to Rachel's maid Bilhah. However, Dan originally lived in central Palestine, so that in this case there would be an explanation for a closer association with Rachel's sons Joseph and Benjamin. Issachar, Zebulon and the girl Dinah were born to Leah later. Thus in essentials the Galilean tribes are the ones which are regarded as children of the maids, or as having been born later.

58. M. Noth, *Das System der zwölf Stamme Israels*, 1930; id., *History of Israel*, ²1960, 85–109. The idea was taken over by John Bright in his *History of Israel*, ²1972, 140–76, though he puts the accents differently. Meanwhile, the transference of the amphictyony theory to Israel has been criticized in various ways; cf. R. Smend, *Jahwekrieg und Stämmebund. Erwägungen zur ältesten Geschichte Israels*, FRLANT 84, 1963; S. Herrmann, 'Das Werden Israels', *TLZ* 87, 1962, 561–74, and the critical survey by G. Fohrer, 'Altes Testament – "Amphictyonie" und "Bund"?', *TLZ* 91, 1966, 801–16, 893–904. R. Smend gave a positive evaluation of the idea of the amphictyony along the lines set out by Noth in *EvTh* 31, 1971, 623–30; de Vaux does not concern himself explicitly with the amphictyony in his *Histoire*, but see his contribution 'La Thèse de l'Amphictyonie Israélite', *Studies in Memory of Paul Lapp* (*HTR* 64, 1971, 415–36). H. M. Orlinsky, 'The Tribal System of Israel and Related Groups in the Period of the Judges', *Studies and Essays in Honor of A. A. Neuman*, 1962, 375–87 (also reprinted in *Oriens Antiquus* 1, 1962, 11–20). See now the detailed critical study by C. H. J. de Geus, *De Stammen van Israel. Een onderzoek naar enige vooronderstellingen van Martin Noths amfiktyonie-hypothese*, Proefschrift Groningen, 1972.

59. M. Noth, *Aufsätze* 1, Part IV, 'Beiträge zur Geschichte des Ostjordanlandes'; southern Transjordania has been opened up in particular by the surface explorations of N. Glueck, 'Explorations in Eastern Palestine I–IV', *AASOR* 14, 1934, 1–114; 15, 1935, 1–202; 18/19, 1939, 1–288 and tables 1–22; 25–28, 1951, 1–711; cf. also R. de Vaux, 'Nouvelles recherches dans la région de Cadès', *RB* 47, 1938, 89–97; id., 'Exploration de la région de Salt', *RB* 47, 1938, 398–425.

60. Sihon of Heshbon: there is an old victory song in Num. 21.27–30 within the narrative Num. 21.21–31; a mention within the speech of Moses in Deut. 2.26–37; see Noth, *Aufsätze* 1, 414–7. Og of Bashan: Deut. 3.1–3 (almost literally = Num. 21.33–35); further mentions, together with Sihon of Heshbon, in Deut. 1.4; 4.47; 29.6; 31.4; Josh. 2.10; 9.10; 12.4; 13.12, 31; see also Ps. 135.11; 136.20; Neh. 9.22; also Noth, *Aufsätze* 1, 441–9.

61. Deut. 3.10, 12, 13; 4.43; Josh. 20.8; II Kings 10.33.

62. It is no coincidence that the dominant term used to describe Transjordania is 'beyond the Jordan'. This presupposes (like the English equivalent) a perspective from west of the Jordan.

63. Note the works already mentioned above by Noth, de Vaux and N. Glueck, though they often pay little attention to possible movements and usually restrict themselves to a description of material that has been discovered. Cf. also A. Alt, *KS* I, 193–215.

64. See M. Noth, 'Die Nachbarn der israelitische Stämme im Ostjordanlande' (1946–51), *Aufsätze* 1, 434–75.

65. Cf. the considerations advanced by Noth, *Aufsätze* 1, 445f.

66. Cf. here the instructive sketch maps in Noth, *Aufsätze* 1, 348 and 425.

67. In addition, it should be noted that the well-known struggle of Jacob with an unknown being (Gen. 32.23–33) is set on the lower course of the Jabbok, only a little way east of the heart of Israelite territory here named 'Mount Gilead'. 'Penuel' is usually

identified with the place *tulūl ed-ḏahab*, where the Jabbok valley narrows once again in a striking way before flowing out into the Jordan plain.

68. Cf. Noth's remarks in *Aufsätze* 1, 361–3, and his article on Gilead and Gad, ibid., 489–543.

69. M. Noth, 'Israelitische Stämme zwischen Ammon und Moab' (1944), *Aufsätze* 1, 391–433.

70. Num. 22–24; there is later a theme that Balaam must overlook the whole Israelite camp from a prominent place in order to achieve maximum effect for his curse, cf. Num. 22.41; 23.9, 13; 24.2. The narrative presumably takes it for granted that the land around Peor was once a boundary between Israelites and Moabites; Noth, *Aufsätze* 1, 402–8.

71. According to Num. 32.1, the tribes of Reuben and Gad occupied 'the land of Jasher and the land of Gilead', with a great multitude of cattle. Defining the land of Jasher is a topographical problem of a special kind; it is sought north of the *wādi ḥesbān* in an area which lies on the height of present-day Amman. Noth, *Aufsätze* 1, 408–14; R. Rendtorff, 'Zur Lage von Jazer', *ZDPV* 76, 1960, 124–35; Y. Aharoni, *The Land of the Bible*, 189; R. de Vaux, *Early History*, 570–3.

72. Lines 10f.; Galling, *TGI*¹, 47–9 (Hebrew); *TGI*², 51–3; Donner–Röllig, *KAI* no. 181; for the topographical problems of this area north of the Arnon see also A. Kuschke, in *Verbannung und Heimkehr* (Festschrift W. Rudolph), 1961, 181–96; W. Schottroff, *ZDPV* 82, 1966, 163–208; K.-H. Bernhard, *ZDPV* 76, 1960, 136–58.

73. Noth, *Aufsätze* 1, 368–70.

74. Cf. Judg. 21.1–14; I Sam. 11; 31.11–13; II Sam. 21.12; Noth, *Aufsätze* 1, 369f.

75. Josh. 1.12–18; 22.1–9 (10–34); cf. also Deut. 3.12, 13, 18–20.

5

The Life of the Tribes before the Formation of the State. The 'Judges'

EVERYTHING THAT WE know indicates that the Israelite tribes which took possession of the cultivated land of Palestine from different points and at different times were not at first united or led and organized under a common leadership. Relations between them were loose; only a few of the tribes, perhaps the southern tribes round Judah or the central tribes in the hill-country of Ephraim, can have made closer contact, at least during the latter stages of their settlement. Their first forms of organization were those of the tribe, and whether tribes facing the same difficulties united for common action depended on the time and the conditions in the land. From the beginning, the settlement was governed by the conditions which had arisen from the ethnic and political developments following the invasion of the Sea-peoples on the one hand and the Aramaeans on the other. Growing Israel had to win its territory and defend it against the interests of its neighbours, constantly prepared for attacks and crude threats from surrounding areas. The first stage for the Israelite tribes in Palestine was a stage of self-assertion; forces had to be organized to defend the land, so as to be able to resist opponents who in some respects were better equipped.

On the new territory, distributed over its dwelling-places and forced to scatter, the individual tribe, no longer the original entity made up of families and clans wandering in search of pasture, was less able to resist outside attack and was often dependent on the contours of the variegated hill-country. The internal organization of the tribes demanded new forms; it required central authorities, new forms of communication; it needed institutions for a permanent guarantee of settled existence.

The Old Testament clearly indicates the growing difficulties involved. The tradition indicates the drive towards leadership rather than the internal constitution of the tribes. We are given the names of men who primarily took over the rule of their tribe in a threatening situation, or better, who were called to come to the rescue, to mobilize their own tribe or a group of tribes, to remove the threat and bring the warriors home again. Once safety had been restored, their task was fulfilled; the man of the day returned to his family and became a member of the tribe again as before. He had temporary authority, which he had to use, as had the dictators of Rome, in accordance with the needs of the situation. We are not told of any fixed period for this temporary exercise of power; fulfilment of the appointed task set a limit to the function.

These prominent personalities were designated *šōpᵉṭîm*, from the Hebrew root *špṭ*, usually translated 'judges'. This, however, can lead to misunderstanding. It inevitably gives the impression that these men were the supreme legal authority within their tribes. In fact the range of meaning of *špṭ* is wider, and means nothing less than the exercise of the transferred authority of leadership and government. The office of the Carthaginian 'suffetes' is often cited as a parallel; that was an office of government, and the designation rests on the same Semitic root *špṭ*.[1] This does not exclude legislative functions in the narrower sense. It can be demonstrated that the Israelite *šōpᵉṭîm* also administered the law within their sphere. How the office arose has still to be explained. The 'judge' Deborah, who did in fact administer the law (Judg.4.4, 5), was prominently involved in raising Israelite forces to take the field against the Canaanites in the area of the northern chain of cities; Jephthah was victorious against the Ammonites, but is also introduced as a man who 'judged' Israel (Judg.12.7). It is remarkable that as a saviour from distress he is also called *qāṣîn* (Judg.11.6), and this archaic expression is applied only to him. The variations in terminology and the difference in the spheres of function indicate that as the tribes became consolidated, the leading figures were regarded and assessed in different ways, depending on their character and their task. It must be allowed that on the one hand men (and women) who had already achieved a prominent position as lawgivers would also emerge as capable leaders in a crisis, while on the other hand external pressures would produce such people whose reputation might possibly continue after a successful struggle so that subsequently they acquired functions, including legal ones, within their tribe which found undisputed recognition.

The Old Testament tradition does not make it easy to form many clear ideas. In the book of Judges it has been simplified and generalized in a number of respects. Thus e.g. in the case of Gideon we have a regular call which singles this man out for the fight against the Midianites (Judg.6.11–24);[2] the outsider Jephthah is apparently called by the majority of the men of war in his tribe (Judg.11.1–11); the hero Samson seems to be singled out from his very birth to do great things for his people (Judg.13). Finally, however, there is a series of men who are enumerated in a brief list; this tradition says that in their time they exercised the function of *špṭ* in Israel, but does not add whether they proved themselves as military leaders in times of acute threat, or indicate where this may have taken place. It seems most likely that they were only active within the tribe in times of peace.[3] The rise and fall of Abimelech as usurper shows yet another situation (Judg.9).

All these men fall under the general heading of 'judge', but each clearly needs to be assessed separately, in terms both of the functions that they acquired and of the tasks that they were set. The reader of the book of Judges naturally remembers more vividly those who had great success in war and who are the subject of more detailed narrative. And because these are the ones who are shown to have received a call from Yahweh, it has been customary to call them 'charismatic leaders', following a definition of Max Weber's.[4] Those who are simply included in the lists and have no military reputation usually have to be content with the designation 'minor judges', while the charismatic leaders are the judges proper. By adopting this working hypothesis, Old Testament scholarship makes a distinction that takes note of the tradition which is to be found in the book of Judges and has grown out of it, but which in terms of the historical situation is completely arbitrary.[5]

> These peculiarities of tradition and terminology in the book of Judges associated with the general designation 'judge' have become even more complicated historically since M. Noth, in his study on 'The Office of the "Judge of Israel"',[6] made the 'minor judges' included in the lists into amphictyonic officials who 'judged Israel', and in a scrupulously observed succession helped to frame and preserve legal traditions which were binding on Israel. According to Noth, here in this early period was an office which involved all Israel, even if it is the only one of which we know.[7] As a consequence it is also supposed that there was always only one judge for the whole alliance at any one time. On the basis of traditio-historical considerations, Noth suggested how it came about that the 'title' of 'judge', originally associated with this 'official position', could also be transferred to charismatic leaders. In his argument the figure of Jephthah plays a decisive role, but significantly, again only on traditional grounds. Jephthah is clearly a 'major judge', but in Judg. 12.7 he has found a way into the schematic list of 'minor judges'. This fact itself suggested the transference of the official term 'judge' to the other charismatics.[8] The understanding of *špt* as being limited to the juristic sphere, and the developed stylization of the *šōpᵉṭîm* as bearers of a fixed office with juristic functions which embraced all the tribes, prepared the ground for the conception of a tribal alliance which was already well organized and functional before the rise of the state. The book of Judges is then seen to confirm it at every point. In fact the schematic account of the period of the judges in the book of Judges has been historicized too hastily. In reality the tribal alliance was very much looser; particular events were needed to strengthen it in some areas and to tighten up its organization.[9]

Not only has the book of Judges been the cause of the classification into 'major' and 'minor' judges by its incorporation of different traditions, but it has followed other schematic patterns which make it difficult to write a reliable continuous 'history of the period of the judges'. In an independent, pragmatic introduction, the redactor,[10] who is probably a member of the Deuteronomistic school, attempts to explain what happened with the charismatic leaders (Judg. 2.11–3.6). Israel had repeatedly forsaken its God and gone after Baal and cultic practices involving fertility symbols, the Asheroth and the Astartes. Yahweh had to intervene. He sent a foreign nation to oppress Israel. Thereupon the people cried to their God, who sent them a 'deliverer', a 'saviour', to follow the translation that Luther rightly used in Judg. 3.9 (*mōšīaʿ*).[11] But once the enemy had been repelled, Israel again apostatized from its God, as the redactor knows. God then for some inconceivable reason resolved on a new act of deliverance.

This pragmatic introduction to the book of Judges suggested the view that one 'judge' followed another, that it was always all Israel that was threatened, that all Israel could always be saved from disaster thanks to the saviour destined for them all. Exact details about the period of office of each 'judge' made it possible to produce a relative chronology for the period of the judges, which supported the conception of a successively progressive development.[12] The reasons for this mode of description lay in the generalizing approach of the redactors, whose leading points of view had to coincide with the fundamental idea of Deuteronomy, which was convinced that all Israel acted as a whole and thus had to serve their one God.[13] Earlier traditions have been incorporated into the book of Judges within this framework. The consistency of approach is emphasized by a fact which may not be immediately evident: leaving aside Barak, who is made subordinate to Deborah, and the usurper Abimelech, twelve judges are introduced, including the so-called 'minor judges'. This number twelve is hardly a coincidence; on the other hand, we do not have one judge for each of the tribes known to us. There was probably not enough appropriate material for this. But almost without exception the 'judges' each come from a different tribe and appropriately enough are always involved only with hostile neighbours in their immediate proximity.

The series of twelve produces the following picture: 1. Othniel (probably from Judah) fights against king Cushan Rishathaim, who is supposed to have come from Aram-naharaim, i.e. from upper Mesopotamia (Judg. 3.7–11); the events are obscure and cannot be interpreted properly.[14] 2. Ehud from Benjamin fights against an alliance of Moabites, Ammonites and Amalekites who occupy Jericho, the city of palms (Judg. 3.12–30). 3. A single verse (3.31) commemorates Shamgar, who went out against the Philistines with an ox-goad, in a way somewhat reminiscent of Samson. 4. The 'judge' Deborah came from the hill-country of Ephraim and Barak from Naphthali; resistance was offered to the Canaanites (Judg. 4;5) in a great coalition in which it is certain that six tribes took part. 5. Gideon (Jerubbaal) leads an expedition in alliance with Asher, Zebulon and Naphthali (i.e. a Galilean coalition) from Ophrah in Manasseh against the Midianites who were launching an invasion westwards from Transjordania (Judg. 6–8). 6. Tola from the hill-country of Ephraim is no charismatic leader (Judg. 10.1, 2) and is a so-called 'minor judge', like 7. Jair from Gilead. 8. Jephthah's main thrust is against the Ammonites; he himself comes from Gilead (Judg. 10.6–12.7); 12.7 seems to have integrated him in what is called the list of 'minor judges'. He was followed by 9. Ibzan from Bethlehem,[15] 10. Elon from Zebulon, and 11. Abdon from Pirathon 'in the land of Ephraim, in the hill-country of the Amalekites',[16] all three of them 'minor judges'. 12. The hero Samson from Dan has a special character and concludes the series of independent narratives about the judges. They make it clear that, with the exception of Jephthah and perhaps Abdon, all these men come from west of the Jordan. Their actions are chiefly directed against strong inhabitants of the coastal plains, but also against threats from Transjordania. From the latter come Moabites, Ammonites and even Midianites, increasingly interested in expansion. Samson is involved with the Philistines; it seems to be taken for granted that at that time Dan still remained in its first abode west of Jerusalem.

This survey makes it clear that the 'judges' each had their local sphere of activity. The charismatic leaders, in particular, came from those areas most exposed to danger. When a particular threat arose, coalitions of tribes developed. These strengthened the consciousness of togetherness which may also have continued after a common victory, but sometimes also gave rise to rivalries and feuds, as in the remarkable war of the Gileadites against Ephraim in the time of Jephthah (Judg. 12.1–7). With the best will in the world, however, we cannot say that a 'tribal system' emerged as a well-organized, active unit. Rather, the traditions indicate with credible impressiveness the difficult situations in which the newly-arrived tribes were involved and the way in which they gradually had to take up formation, driven by immediate threats to their very existence. Among the sanctuaries in the country, Tabor, on the south-eastern border of the Galilean hill-country, had a special role; here the tribal areas of Issachar, Zebulon and Naphthali met (cf. Judg. 4.6, 14). We can see how this prominent peak on the boundaries of these three territories will also have become the place for common worship. To this degree, we might look for an 'amphictyonic' centre here, though it would only have had limited relevance for 'all Israel'! We are given flashes of insight into the turbulent and variegated period after the settlement only through very careful observation of further details in the different narratives. Here it is important to keep the hypothesis of forms of organization relating to the whole of Israel as much on one side as possible. The period was characterized not so much by a continuous succession of great charismatic figures as by a considerable uncertainty. Calamitous consequences made just as much a mark as those struggles and battles in which Israelite tribes came out on top, often against their expectations. There are no chronicles to record their defeats, as the sagas and traditions about heroes from all over the world tend only to celebrate successes!

We have a considerable amount of information about the great charismatic leader Gideon (Judg. 6–8). The occasion for his rise was an invasion of Midianite camel nomads, who came from Transjordania.[17] They occupied the height of Beth-shean beyond the Jordan and from there posed a direct threat to the area west of the Jordan. It is said that they camped in the plain of Jezreel (Judg. 6.33). Thereupon Gideon sent messengers throughout Manasseh, and to the tribes of Asher, Zebulon and Naphthali (6.35; 7.23); later also to the inhabitants of the hill-country of Ephraim (7.24, 25). Here we can see clearly how the action continued to develop; in the face of the great danger, increasingly large contingents were summoned and involved in the fight. At first these were the tribes north of the plain of Jezreel, then those living in the hill-country of Ephraim, probably all the central Palestinian tribes.

Unfortunately we cannot tell Gideon's precise origin. It is said that he lived in Ophrah, which was earlier sought in *tell fārʿa*, about ten miles east of Samaria.[18] In that case, he will almost certainly have been a Manassite. However, it would fit the area invaded by the Midianites better if we could identify Ophrah with *eṭ-ṭayibeh* between Tabor and Beth-shean.[19] That would be in the territory of the tribe of Issachar, who must have felt the Midianite threat most acutely. Gideon attacked the Midianite camp at the spring of Harod (*ʿēn-jālūd*) on the north-west side of Mount Gilboa, a most critical point at the entry to the plain of Jezreel, and only about six miles from Ophrah if it is identified with *eṭ-ṭayibeh*. Thereupon the Midianites retreated back over the Jordan. The operation in which Gideon pursued them is reported in some detail;[20] an exact knowledge of the fords over the Jordan was required. These were occupied by men from the hill country of Ephraim, who evidently used them often (Judg. 7.24). Finally, there were individual groups from the hill-country of central Palestine who had moved over into Transjordania and settled there. They include the group of Machir, already mentioned above, which was probably Manassite.

We can only understand the peculiar story told in connection with Jephthah's victory over the Ammonites (Judg. 12.1–6) against this background of the connection between Ephraim and Transjordania. The tribe of Ephraim felt slighted, because it had not been summoned to battle by the Gileadites. A bitter and bloody fight broke out, during the course of which Ephraimite fugitives were recognized at the fords over the Jordan by the way in which they spoke the word 'shibboleth' (שבלת), prompted by the Gileadites (Judg. 12.6). If the person challenged pronounced the word 'sibboleth' (סבלת) in his own dialect, he was recognized as an Ephraimite and killed. This is possibly a reference to a difference in dialect which was known not only in the early period, but also at a later date. The details of the narrative may have been prompted by current differences in pronunciation. The problem of a confederate army becomes a dramatic cause of conflict between Ephraim and Gilead, but it also plays a major role in the context of one of the earliest pieces of tradition in the Old Testament, the Song of Deborah in Judg. 5. Here a song of victory, like Miriam's 'Song of the Reed Sea', is put on the lips of a woman who judged Israel at that time, 'sitting under the palm of Deborah between Ramah and Bethel in the hill country of Ephraim'. She summoned Barak from Naphtali to assemble the neighbouring tribes for battle on Tabor. The problem whether the prose account in Judg. 4 deals with the same events as the poetic Song of Deborah in Judg. 5 need not be discussed here. It is possible that accounts from different sources underlie the tradition and are now set side by side without any apparent contradiction.

The focal point of the two chapters is a dispute with Canaanite kings, most probably city rulers, which does not have any obvious cause; even the consequences of the battle can only be inferred. The scene of the war is the plain of Megiddo and Jezreel, which often appears as a battlefield; the part of it involved this time is to the north-west, north of Carmel, in the area round the 'Brook of Kishon'. Thus the battle takes place north of the chain of fortifications, of which the cities of Taanach and Megiddo are specifically named. It is more difficult to establish the time of the conflict. The Song of Deborah mentions a certain Shamgar, in whose time 'the paths were idle'. Shamgar is a Hurrian name, so he clearly belongs on the Canaanite side. Since the text goes on to speak of 'the days of Shamgar', he will have been an influential figure, reminiscence of whom was associated with a kind of barricading of paths and roads (the 'idleness of the paths'). This may have had unpleasant effects, particularly in the area of the northern chain of fortifications. To put this in the time of the Philistine invasion is sheer conjecture. Taking into account the fact that the Israelite tribes had meanwhile grown strong enough to join arms against the Canaanite kings, we should put the battle at some time from the Philistine invasion, probably towards the end of the twelfth century. It will hardly have been as early as the thirteenth.[21]

The Canaanite coalition was under the command of Sisera, a man with presumably an Illyrian name. That Sisera is named commander of the army of king Jabin of Hazor presents a problem (Judg. 4.2). This combination introduces a number of chronological difficulties to which there is no simple answer.[22] It is quite possible that the king of Hazor is simply introduced as the type of ruler in that area, especially as he himself played no part in the fight. At any rate Barak, whom Deborah summoned to the battle against Sisera, came from Kedesh in the tribe of Naphthali, a place very near to Hazor. He is said to have gathered people from Naphthali and Zebulon to Mount Tabor (Judg. 4.6). In addition, the Song of Deborah tells how Issachar was summoned and how Ephraim, Machir (not Manasseh) and Benjamin took part. This coalition of six Israelite tribes clearly included the three important Galilean tribes centred on Tabor and the whole extent of the hill-country of Ephraim. However, the most remarkable thing about the Song of Deborah is that groups are also mentioned which did not take part in the fight. First we have the curse on the city of Meroz, probably a place with a predominantly Canaanite population in the territory of Manasseh, which did not answer the summons.[23] It is also said that Reuben, Gilead, Dan and Asher did not take part. The first two are probably the inhabitants of the southern part of Trans-jordania, whereas Dan and Asher, in the north and west of Galilee, possibly felt it better to keep out of the quarrel with the Canaanites because of their contacts with the Phoenician cities on the coast.

With some justification the Song of Deborah has been regarded as a basic document for the existing, or better the growing collective consciousness of 'Israel' because of its remarkable summary of the tribes which did or did not take part. However, the document should not be over-estimated or seen in the context of a 'system' of tribes. The six tribes round the plain of Megiddo clearly take part; all the other tribes are on the periphery, and were probably not considered for the army. There is no mention at all of the groups beyond the southern chain of fortified cities, Judah and Simeon, who were obviously right outside the field of vision. Nevertheless, the Song of Deborah does represent one stage and gives an occasion which will have been of far-reaching significance for the cohesion of the leading Israelite tribes and their common action. They call themselves 'Israel', but there is no mention of the groups in the territory of Judah. This is worth noting. It was suggested earlier that this name 'Israel', which figures in the Jacob traditions and in the places listed on the stele of Merneptah, was most likely to have its roots in southern Ephraim, or at least that the basis of it was to be found there. It only seems consistent that when the 'northern kingdom' later took shape it should have borne the name 'Israel'.

In addition, the Song of Deborah says that Yahweh, 'the God of Israel', went forth from the mountain of Seir, from the fields of Edom, to take part in the battle. Thus the idea of the local association of this God with the south has not yet faded. He still dwells outside the country, but his actions are directed against 'thine enemies, Yahweh', whom he can annihilate when his people need him. The conception of Yahweh as the supreme war lord, who wages his wars and bestows victory, gave rise to the misleading formula of the 'holy war' which was and is used for military conflicts in the Old Testament.[24] It is more appropriate to speak of 'Yahweh's war',[25] or better still, to avoid applying such specific terms to Israel altogether. The participation of the gods in battle is a theme to be found throughout the East, irrespective of whether the wars are defensive or aggressive.[26] The outcome of the so-called 'battle of Deborah', depicted in the song with vivid poetical colours and dramatic imagery, which includes the stars 'fighting in their courses against Sisera', may have exceeded many expectations. The Canaanites employed a powerful contingent of chariots; we hear of the beat of the hoofs of the horses, who at that time were especially used for war, and were specialized in chariot fighting. But the waters of the Kishon came to the help of the Israelites. There was probably marshy land here, like that round the Reed Sea, which hindered the chariots. Nevertheless, we may say that this battle by the waters of Kishon was one of those instances in the history of war where troops equipped with different weapons were involved in a fight in which the technically inferior combatants gained the victory.[27]

The tactical and political result of this battle will have to be assessed in relative terms. True, the Israelite contingents were the victors in the field, but the great fortresses like Taanach and Megiddo remained Canaanite.[28] The acute threat directed at the tribes seems to have been removed, but there was no fundamental change in the balance of power in the land. However, the paths were no longer 'idle' as in the days of Shamgar. Free trading conditions could have been established in the plain of Megiddo, so that the northern chain of cities did not have so sharply divisive an effect. This simplified communications between the Galilean tribes and those in the hill-country of Ephraim. It was perhaps at that time that the tribe of Issachar gained its complete independence.

The Song of Deborah is a document of a unique kind.[29] Its language retains its original power and is often hard to understand where events are summed up or merely hinted at in extreme brevity. Its imagery is extraordinarily artistic and has an unusual tension. The departure of Yahweh at the beginning is monumental, and the death of Sisera by a woman's hand at the end is almost macabre, given the effect of bitter irony with the picture of his waiting mother and her women. But this must be the end of all the enemies of Yahweh. There is more here than a unique form for the celebration of the triumph of the victors and their God Yahweh; here is the expression of a self-awareness which has either dawned or found its deepest confirmation among the participants as a result of battle and victory. There is a tendency to see here the birth of the ethnic self-awareness of 'Israel', which would be justified if we could be certain that we have all the documents of early Israel. Even the song of Deborah is no more than a searchlight, albeit a significant one. 'Israel' took shape as a 'people', as the sum of its tribes, with a common destiny, in this period of charismatic leaders. This did not happen through an idea or through the compulsion of an amphictyonic 'system', but through the experience of the guiding power of a God who set out from his distant abode to smite 'his' – and that means 'Israel's' – enemies. We can see both the justification for the theory of the early Israelite amphictyony and its limitations. The link with Yahweh and the common action in the face of threats helped to bring about a 'self-awareness' in the nation. The process seems to be quite natural, but the basis of the experience seems to be not only 'national' but religious. The period of the so-called 'judges' does not take its contours from the perfect functioning of an amphictyonic tribal alliance but from the awareness of being a 'people' which increasingly seizes hold of individual tribes. This people feels able to defend its newly-won territory and its existence in the certainty that God is its leader. Of course, such a feeling was first to be found among those tribes mentioned in the Song of Deborah; the tribes in the south still maintained a degree of detachment. Here there is a further explanation for the development of an independent history of Judah, which had already been introduced by the settlement. The assimilation of Judah in the south to Israel in the north was a lengthy process, which can be found in the sources only during the rise of the state. None of the charismatic leaders seems to come from Judah.[30] In the view of the book of Judges, the danger from the coastal plains adjacent to Judah was warded off by the Danite Samson who, with his completely personal charisma and the unique power of a great hero, is less a charismatic leader than a champion. The elaboration of the saga in which he appears does not allow the historian to draw any reliable conclusions.

The historical credibility of the narrative in Judges 19–21, in the so-called appendix to Judges, which tells of a 'shameful act' in Benjaminite Gibeah, is often doubted. The narrative should not, however, be overlooked. An Ephraimite is travelling through Gibeah with his wife, on their way from Bethlehem in Judah, and stays with an Ephraimite who is living in Bethlehem. This insignificant occurrence gives rise to a shameful orgy held by men from Gibeah, who dishonour the Judaean wife of the Ephraimite in a shocking way, so that she eventually dies. The parts of her body are sent round 'Israel' and are the occasion for a punitive expedition against Benjamin. After a number of unsuccessful attempts this ends with the burning of Gibeah and leads the Israelites to swear that they will never give their daughters to any Benjaminite. The decision is later regretted; there is anxiety that a tribe may be lost. Jabesh in Gilead did not take part in the assembly which made the decision, and becomes the goal of a second expedition, in the course of which the virgins are spared so that they can be handed over to Benjamin. As there are not enough to go round, it is suggested to the Benjaminites who have gone away empty-handed that they should try to seize and take away the maidens who usually go to Shiloh in Ephraim to join in a cultic dance there. The advice is followed, and the dispute seems to be settled. We are explicitly told that all this took place when there was still no king in Israel. Each one acted as he thought fit.

What we have here is clearly a conflict between the tribes of Ephraim and Benjamin which is personified in the narrative about the 'shameful act' and developed so that it becomes a dramatic climax. There is no mention of the deeper causes of the conflict, so that scholars so far have had to resort to hypotheses.[31] Noth found the theory of the amphictyony confirmed in the summons issued by 'Israel', and therefore considered this to be an amphictyonic war.[32] Eissfeldt rejected this hypothesis and suggested that the cause of the dispute was a rebellion by Benjamin or a number of cities against the heart of Ephraim, which began from Gibeah.[33] In that way Benjamin would finally have won its independence. K.-D. Schunck summed up the results of his research in a different way.[34] He saw these chapters as proof for the complete loss of Benjaminite independence. It is impossible to achieve complete clarity on this question. However, a number of observations are worth noticing. The text has certainly been expanded at a later date, but it contains elements which cannot have been invented and which remain significant for the later history of the tribes in this area. Benjamin plays a unique role, and its relationship to its neighbours was problematical. The early tribal sayings call Benjamin a 'ravenous wolf' (Gen. 49.27). Ephraim was oppressed by bowmen; the Benjaminites were in fact good archers.[35] The contacts between Benjamin and Jabesh-gilead also rest on facts which emerge even more strongly in the story of Saul.[36] The absence of the people of Jabesh from the assembly of the tribes in Mizpah is also certainly connected with their close relationship to Benjamin and their defensive attitude towards Ephraim (Judg. 21.8). Finally, the mention of the ark in Bethel (Judg. 20.27f.) and the tradition of the annual feast in Shiloh are not irrelevant. From this we can infer close connections between the central Palestinian tribes and these sanctuaries, and light is also shed on the problematic role of Benjamin on the southern border of the Ephraimite hill-country: either it found the right contacts with its neighbours difficult or it attempted to detach itself from

Ephraim and assert a political and military independence. All this points to tensions in central Palestine, the effects of which can still be seen during the monarchy; for this reason we are compelled to accept the vivid accounts in Judg. 19–21 as a much-revised record of local conditions and moods in the time before the formation of the state, rather than to dismiss them as pure fiction. At all events, the 'Israel' which is often mentioned is not the amphictyonic organization rising as one man,[37] but the same central Palestinian contingent, or more exactly the contingent including Ephraim and its (nearest) northern neighbours, which took part as 'Israel' in the battle joined by Deborah.

Despite the uncertainties over details which still remain, the narrative of the shameful act in Gibeah serves as a topographical instrument which makes more comprehensible the complicated developments in the political relationship of the tribes during the period of the monarchy which is soon to follow.

Even more interesting than the conflict over Gibeah in Benjamin are the attempts to acquire independent and permanent power in the territory of Ephraim and Manasseh, which were played out against a background of conflict with the Canaanite city rulers. It is no longer possible to make a historical assessment of the offer of permanent leadership to Gideon, the victor against the Midianites (Judg. 8.22–35). Gideon rejects this both on behalf of himself and on behalf of his son Abimelech. But in the same context there is mention of some kind of strange cult; this suggests closer contact which may have developed between the Israelites and the native Canaanites and which may have furthered the idea of claims to hegemony on both sides.

Unlike his father Gideon, Abimelech is demonstrably not called to be a 'judge'. Rather, he is related on his mother's side to the indigenous leading class in Shechem, and seeks to seize power for himself in Shechem in alliance with the aristocratic leaders of the city (Judg. 9). He exterminates his kinsmen on his father's side in his home town of Ophrah, so as to exclude them as potential opponents; only Jotham escapes. He is the singer of the 'fable of Jotham', which later became famous (Judg. 9.8–15);[38] it warns against making the most inappropriate person king. But Abimelech won the confidence of the upper class of the city and was made prince. However, opponents emerged who would not be obedient to him. Abimelech succeeded in retaining the upper hand by military means, but at the price of destroying the greater part of the city. This seems to have emboldened him to extend the fighting to the strong city of Thebez (*ṭūbāṣ*), only about nine miles north-east of Shechem. Victory seemed assured. But there was a fortified tower in the middle of the city which offered a haven to the defenders. Abimelech stormed it. Then a woman suddenly appeared high on the walls, threw down a millstone and hit Abimelech on the head. The battle came to an abrupt end. The Israelites immediately scattered and returned home. The death of Abimelech marked the end of a one-man political career which is unique in our traditions of the period before the formation of the state.[39]

These events are symptomatic. The individual Israelite tribes were in process of securing their existence in the land. They were in a position to defend themselves against outward attacks; in particularly threatening situations they combined in a coalition. However, in their midst there were fortified cities, chiefly dominated by the indigenous Canaanite ruling classes. The confidence of these had still to be shattered, and a readiness to make arrangements with the invaders had yet to be completely developed. The late heritage of the power politics of Shechem as practised at the time of the Amarna letters by the man called Labaya does not seem as yet to have lost its attraction. To transfer this power to an individual who could mediate between Canaanites and Israelites by virtue of his origin was a novel but ultimately unsuccessful attempt, and we know of no one who followed Abimelech by re-establishing the supremacy of Shechem, or who even undertook to install a central authority over Ephraimite territory with the aim of tightening the inner organization of the tribes. The case of Abimelech remains limited to Shechem, and was ultimately seen from a Canaanite rather than an Israelite perspective. The struggle of this man did not arouse any 'national' feelings. Abimelech's claim to leadership and his exercise of it stood and fell with his person. In the background lay opposition to Canaan, opposition to indigenous elements of the population distinct from Israel. To live with them seemed possible; to fight against them was beyond the power of the Israelite tribes, at any rate over the long term. In a word, the time for the monarchy, the time for an alliance of the tribes in the form of a fully organized state, had not yet come. In contrast to a number of wide-ranging hypotheses, our starting point must be the assumption that at first the tribes in the cultivated land had few administrative and cultic institutions; on the whole the arrangement by family and clan still continued. As far as we know, almost every tribe had control over at least a sanctuary of its own; in one case we see interest in installing such a sanctuary and maintaining it in proper order. There is explicit testimony to this in connection with the migration of the tribe of Dan.[40] These sanctuaries were not subject to any central authority. The assembly of a group of tribes at a sanctuary was an extraordinary action which did not in principle extend the validity of the holy place concerned beyond the tribe in whose territory it was situated. Rather, the power and reputation of a tribe also increased the significance of its sanctuaries.

If there is any historical event at all underlying the summary tradition of an assembly of Israelite tribes at Shechem, which is said to have taken place as early as the time of Joshua (Josh. 24), it may well be that Ephraimite groups originally sought to bind to belief in Yahweh indigenous groups and other arrivals who did not belong to the tribe. The conflicts with Transjordanian settlers in Gilead which broke out in the time of Jephthah, or with the tribe of Benjamin, show something of Ephraim's claim to leadership, which possibly also contributed to victory in the battle in which Deborah was involved. On the whole, however, the course of the assembly at Shechem and the details in the tradition show a high degree of reflection, which already presupposes a comprehensive conception of the history of Israel. There was no basis for this either at the beginning or at the end of the period of the judges. Joshua 24 can hardly be regarded as the reflection of an action which was constitutive for the entire amphictyony of early Israel.[41] Those approaches which consider the assembly in the context of the Deuteronomic and Deuteronomistic view of history seem more to the point.[42] In the view of the book of Joshua, once the tribes had taken possession of the whole of the land, and no part remained unoccupied, it was appropriate that in the last chapter they should all bind themselves to the one God. The isolated position of Josh. 24 confirms its exclusive and programmatic character, which serves to further the purpose of a history writing with a pragmatic concern, rather than to record history itself. In the history work which extends from Joshua to II Kings, Josh. 24 serves as an interlude to provide a summary and an evaluation. The same function is performed by the speech of Samuel (I Sam. 12) and the reflection after the fall of the northern kingdom (II Kings 17).

The transition from local actions on the part of the tribes to the creation and recognition of more far-reaching forms of organization is best seen as having been provoked and brought about by events external to the tribes. The development was not abstract, the result of administrative decisions. These external pressures eventually forced the Israelites to the unexpected decision to make a man of merit king. The Israelite monarchy is not the result of careful planning; from the beginning it was under pressure to preserve and protect the existence of the tribes. In the end it was only possible to survive in the settled land when a consistent leadership could ensure speedy reactions beyond the individual tribal groupings. It seems to have been taken for granted that the person in question could not function without the explicit legitimation of Yahweh. The loose associations of tribes in the period before the formation of the state, which can still be clearly recognized from the texts that we possess, were certainly not transcended or fused together by a clearly defined monarchical constitution. Rather, we shall see how this new office, which really also introduced the title 'king' as a designation of office, grew organically out of the existing practices and institutions within the tribes.

NOTES

1. The Phoenician word for 'suffetes' matches the Hebrew form precisely (cf. J. Friedrich, *Phönizisch-punische Grammatik*, Analecta Orientalia 32, 1951, §198b); there are both differences from and interesting parallels to the rough beginnings of the office in Israel. In Carthage the 'suffetes' were officials at a time when a hereditary monarchy was lacking; the range of their functions could therefore include strategic as well as political and

juristic authority. It cannot be shown that the office was hereditary in every respect; it was administered by several officials at the same time and underwent various stages of development over the centuries. See the article 'Sufeten' (V. Ehrenberg), *Pauly-Wissowa, Realencyclopädie der classischen Altertumswissenschaft* IV A 2, 1932, 643–51. W. Richter has recently introduced material from Mari, Ugarit and Phoenicia/Carthage in support of the argument that designations of office made up of the root *špṭ* 'had the same areas of meaning, which can be described as those of civil administration and legislation. Thus the root is a West Semitic term connected with rule, close to *mlk* and *šarrum*. Its nomadic derivation is not improbable' (W. Richter, *ZAW* 77, 1965, esp. 58–72).

2. In most recent times this report has often been used and evaluated as a paradigm for a genre of 'call account': E. Kutsch, 'Gideons Berufung und Altarbau Jdc 6, 11–24', *TLZ* 81, 1965, 75–84; see also N. Habel, *ZAW* 77, 1965, 297–323; W. Beyerlin, *VT* 13, 1963, 1–25; W. Richter, *Traditionsgeschichtliche Untersuchungen zum Richterbuch*, BBB 18, ²1966, 112–55; id., *Die sogenannten vorprophetischen Berufungsberichte. Eine literaturwissenschaftliche Studie zu 1. Sam.9, 1–10, 16, Ex.3f. und Ri.6, 11b–17*, FRLANT 101, 1970; M.-L. Henry, *Prophet und Tradition*, BZAW 116, 1969, 11–41.

3. Judg.10.1–5; 12.7–15.

4. M. Weber, *Aufsätze zur Religionssoziologie* III, 1923, 47f., 93f.; id., *Wirtschaft und Gesellschaft*, ²1925, 140ff., 753ff., 662ff.

5. For the problem of the 'judges' and the historical problems of 'the period of the judges' see A. Malamat, *The World History of the Jewish People* I, 3, ch.7, 'The Period of the Judges', 1971, 129–63; 314–23, 350, with full bibliography.

6. M. Noth, 'Das Amt des "Richters Israels"' (1950), *Gesammelte Studien* II, 71–85.

7. Noth, op. cit., 81f.

8. Noth, op. cit., 74.

9. The two main critical discussions of Noth's conception are to be found in R. Smend, *Jahwekrieg und Stämmebund*, FRLANT 84, 1963, 33–55, and W. Richter, 'Zu den "Richtern Israels"', *ZAW* 77, 1965, 40–72; the latter is inclined to give up the contrast between 'minor judges' and 'charismatic leaders' altogether, and defines the 'judges of Israel' as follows: 'They came from the city (sic!) or from the tribes and were the representatives of an order in transition from the constitution of a tribe to that of a city, appointed for the civil administration and legislation in a city and its territory by the elders (of the tribe). Further developments led to a monarchical constitution' (op. cit., 71). Richter explains the succession as 'an analogy to the royal annals'. 'If the succession falls due, so too does the need to accept a judge, that is, a central office, only for a particular period' (op. cit., 56). Over against this markedly 'civil' definition of the 'judge', K. D. Schunck, 'Die Richter Israels und ihr Amt', SVT 15, 1966, 252–62, stresses its indisputably military function.

10. See M. Noth, *Überlieferungsgeschichtliche Studien* I, ³1967, 47–50; W. Richter, *Die Bearbeitungen des 'Retterbuches' in der deuteronomischen Epoche*, BBB 21, 1964, 26–49; 87f., etc.

11. M. Luther, *Die gantze Heilige Schrifft Deudsch Wittenberg 1545*, ed. H. Volz, 1972, I, 455. See also Judg.3.15.

12. The function of this information within the chronological framework of the Deuteronomistic history work is explained by M. Noth, *Überlieferungsgeschichtliche Studien*, 18–27; criticized by W. Vollborn, 'Die Chronologie des Richterbuches', in *Festschrift F. Baumgärtel* (Erlanger Forschungen A, 10), 1959, 193–7.

13. This fundamental conception of Deuteronomistic theology cannot be disputed even by those who are sceptical about Deuteronomy as a total conception. Cf. the details in G. Fohrer, *Introduction to the Old Testament*, 1970, 192–5; O. Kaiser, *Introduction to the Old Testament*, Oxford 1975, 131–3.

14. See now A. Malamat, *The World History* I, 3, 1971, 25–7.

15. Not necessarily Bethlehem in Judah; this could be a place of the same name in the territory of the tribe of Zebulon.

16. The expression 'in the hill-country of the Amalekites' is probably wrong (see also LXX). For further details in the list of the 'minor judges', many of which must remain ex-explained, cf. the article by Noth, *Gesammelte Studien* II, 71–85; cf. also W. Richter, *ZAW* 77, 1965, 41–5.

17. This is the first written evidence of camel nomads being involved in war. The camels probably had one hump (dromedaries), cf. J. Henninger, *Über Lebensraum und Lebensformen der Frühsemiten*, 1968, 18–23.

18. M. Noth, *Aufsätze* 1, 167.

19. A. Alt, *KS* I, 160 = *Grundfragen*, 170.

20. Cf. the account and the maps in A. Malamat, *The World History* I, 3, 141–7; id., 'The War of Gideon and Midian. A Military Approach', *PEQ* 85, 1953, 61–5.

21. Thus after taking into account archaeological arguments and the differing views of Aharoni and Yadin, A. Malamat, op. cit., 135–7; A. D. H. Mayes, 'The Historical Context of the Battle against Sisera', *VT* 19, 1969, 353–60, suggests a late date towards the end of the eleventh century BC.

22. It might be relatively easier if the name Jabin occurred more often in the dynasty of Hazor; cf. A. Malamat, op. cit., 135, 315; id., 'Northern Canaan and the Mari Texts', in *Near Eastern Archaeology in the Twentieth Century*, ed. J. A. Sanders, 1970, 168, 175 n.22.

23. A. Alt, 'Meros' (1941), *KS* I, 274–7.

24. The 'school' was founded above all by F. Schwally, *Der heilige Krieg im alten Israel*, Semitische Kriegsaltertümer 1, 1901; G. von Rad, *Der heilige Krieg im alten Israel*, ⁴1965.

25. R. Smend, *Jahwekrieg und Stämmebund. Erwägungen zur ältesten Geschichte Israels*, FRLANT 84, 1963; F. Stolz, *Jahwes und Israels Kriege. Kriegstheorien und Kriegserfahrungen im Glauben des alten Israel*, ATANT 60, 1972.

26. M. Weippert, ' "Heiliger Krieg" in Israel und Assyrien', *ZAW* 84, 1972, 460–93.

27. Y. Aharoni, 'New Aspects of the Israelite Occupation in the North', in *Near Eastern Archaeology in the Twentieth Century*, 1970, 254–67, esp.259, suggests that the 'Philistines' were really a group of mercenaries serving the Egyptians and based at Beth-shean; however, this theory is forced on him by other considerations, primarily of an archaeological nature.

28. There is a striking gap in settlement falling in the first half of the eleventh century BC. There is archaeological evidence for it in Megiddo between strata VI and V. This has given rise to a number of explanations which might also settle arguments over the dating of the Deborah battle. Of course we cannot expect complete clarity over historical circumstances as a result of such observations, especially since in the time in question at least Egyptians, elements of the Sea-peoples and Israelites must be seen as having been involved in the political and ethnic developments in this area. The problems are discussed in detail by A. Alt, 'Megiddo im Übergang vom kanaanäischen zum israelitischen Zeitalter' (1944), *KS* I, 256–73; in a more restrained manner now by A. Malamat, *The World History*, I, 3, 136, 316.

29. From the extensive literature reference might be made to the differing editions of the text by E. Sellin, 'Das Debora-Lied', in *Procksch-Festscrift*, 1934, 149–66, and O. Grether, *Das Deboralied*, 1941; see also A. Weiser, 'Das Deboralied', *ZAW* 71, 1959, 67–97; R. Smend, *Jahwekrieg und Stämmebund*, 1963, 10–19.

30. The judge-ship of Othniel (Judg. 3.7–11), a kinsman of Caleb, presents problems. He has been associated with the puzzling figure of Cushan Rishathaim and, like the latter, cannot be interpreted with any certainty. Othniel's position at the head of the judge figures in the book of Judges may correspond to the intention of the Deuteronomistic

redaction to stress the predominance of Judah at this point. The form of the verse is almost exclusively Deuteronomistic. However, we cannot rule out in principle the emergence of 'judges' in Judah.

31. O. Eissfeldt, 'Der geschichtliche Hintergrund der Erzählung von Gibeas Schandtat (Richter 19–21)' (1935), *Kleine Schriften* II, 64–80, also gives a detailed survey of earlier conceptions and interpretations.

32. M. Noth, in connection with a literary analysis of Judg. 19–21 in his book *Das System der zwölf Stämme Israels*, 1930, 162–70: a member of the amphictyony had 'transgressed against the amphictyony', and as a result an 'amphictyonic war' broke out.

33. O. Eissfeldt, op. cit., esp. 77–9.

34. K.-D. Schunck, *Benjamin*, BZAW 86, 1963, 57–70.

35. For these details see Eissfeldt, op. cit., 76f.

36. I Sam. 11; 31.11–13; II Sam. 2.4b–7.

37. The sudden mention of Judah in Judg. 20.18, where it is supposed to be the first tribe to take the field against Benjamin, proves precisely the opposite of what was intended by this brief and probably secondary note. Judah did not even take part, and yet was mentioned at least once, in a leading position!

38. There is a detailed literary discussion of the fable in W. Richter, *Traditionsgeschichtliche Untersuchungen zum Richterbuch*, 282–99.

39. There is a literary-critical investigation of Judg. 9 in W. Richter, *Traditionsgeschichtliche Untersuchungen*, 246–318; see also E. Nielsen, *Shechem*, 1955, 142–71; for a historical evaluation of the events see A. Alt, *KS* I, 129; II, 6f. = *Grundfragen*, 139, 263f.

40. Judg. 17; 18. The nucleus of the account is the erection of the Danite sanctuary and the legitimation of its levitical priesthood. C. Hauret, 'Aux origines du sacerdoce danite, à propos de Jud. 18, 30–31', in *Mélanges A. Robert*, 1957, 105–13; M. Noth, 'Der Hintergrund von Ri. 17–18' (1962), *Aufsätze* I, 133–47.

41. Thus in particular M. Noth, *Das System der zwölf Stämme Israels*, 1930, 65–86, esp. 70; see also the literary analysis, ibid., 133–51; Noth repeats that Josh. 24 is a history of the 'ceremonial founding of the sacral twelve tribe alliance' in *Joshua*, HAT I, 7, ²1953, 139; Götz Schmitt, *Der Landtag von Sichem*, Arbeiten zur Theologie I, 15, 1964, attempts corrections to most recent scholarship on Josh. 24; for a clarification of Noth's position see R. Smend, *EvTh* 31, 1971, 623–30; cf. now the opposed position of R. de Vaux, *HTR* 64, 1971, 415–36: on Shechem, 425f.

42. Now in pointed form in L. Perlitt, *Bundestheologie im Alten Testament*, WMANT, 36, 1969, 239–84.

PART TWO

The Kingdoms of Israel and Judah

I | *The Kingdom of Saul*

ALTHOUGH INDIVIDUAL ISRAELITE tribes made temporary alliances under the pressure of acute threats, and there was an increasing awareness that at least the group of tribes in central and northern Palestine formed an entity under the name 'Israel', characterized by a common origin, the same God and the same destiny, in the period of the judges 'Israel' did not as yet form a 'state' in any way. There was no question of an active political policy in the modern sense of the phrase, and while we may sense the beginnings of the equally modern conception of a united 'people', no clear lines had yet been drawn. The stimuli towards a new development came from outside.

The attacks made on Israelite territory by hostile neighbours, which were countered by the charismatic leaders, were limited in scope and duration. These threats became a chronic danger with the arrival of the Philistines. Their settlement had preceded that of the Israelites; it was limited to the coastal plains. But the consolidation of their power, in the form of city kingships, heightened a desire to expand and possibly also to aim at an independent kingdom in a clearly-defined territory. Thus an organized power gradually developed all along the western side of Israelite territory, beginning from the coastal plain, thrusting its advance posts eastwards into the hill-country. At that point it inevitably clashed with the Israelites.[1]

The charismatic leadership was no longer an adequate answer to such a massive and permanent danger: it was limited to a summons issued to the tribes in a particular situation and dependent on the initiative and the direction of a man who was 'called by Yahweh' and who therefore had to be waited for or found in each particular instance. None of this was sufficient answer to the increasing pressure from the Philistines or that from the Ammonites in the east and the Amalekites in the south. What seemed appropriate was so to speak the permanent commissioning of a charismatic leader, a 'lifetime judge-ship';[2] this could also provide the basis for a tighter organization of the army raised from the tribes, which would increase its fighting efficiency. In practice, this amounted to the birth of the idea of the monarchy, and was the nucleus of a fixed and mutual bond between the tribes under a single leader, combined with a military concentration of what was still a tribal union with central leadership rather than a 'state' in the strict sense of the word. This careful choice of terms will indicate how the Israelite tribes gradually moved over to a different form of organization and with it to a new degree of mutual awareness.

These observations and considerations find confirmation in the fact that, as far as we can see, Saul, the first king of Israel, was originally himself a charismatic leader and to some degree remained one all his life. He was primarily the leader in the mobilization of the tribes, a 'military king' whose task consisted in not much more than the leadership and maintenance of a powerful defensive force. In practice, the conditions of the 'period of the judges' prevailed; the only difference was that the man in charge was a person equipped with a permanent authority.

It accords with this that Saul did not create any formal apparatus of state; he does not even seem to have made any attempts in this direction. He constructed no residence, did not enlarge his seat at Gibeah in Benjamin (*tell el-fūl*) or regard it as a 'royal city', and did not have any permanent officials to act as a central authority responsible for the area over which he ruled.[3] We hear nothing of a change in cultic institutions or of interventions in religious life.

> The massacre of the priesthood of the sanctuary of Nob, whose high priest had taken David's side, shows a degree of insecurity on Saul's part over domestic politics. He took the doubtful advice of an outsider and seems to have paid no attention to the sacral status of the priesthood of a leading sanctuary (I Sam. 22.6–23).[4]

All this confirms the common view that the monarchy was a late phenomenon in Israel, forced on it by historical circumstances and essentially alien to its original nature.[5] Israel was by nature a tribal alliance, and remained so ideally and to a large degree in practice. Sooner or later it was felt that the monarchy needed its own justification. From the beginning, the office of king in Israel was burdened with tensions introduced by its link with the basic structure of the tribes, tensions which could not completely be overcome. Later prophecy gives examples, and this is the reason why the monarchy was not renewed in the post-exilic period once it had collapsed. Other factors may also have played a part in this later period, but among them was certainly the conviction that the monarchy was not indispensable for Israel.

The tensions and problems surrounding the Israelite monarchy have found credible expression in the Old Testament tradition, but they often dominate the account to such a degree that it is difficult to distinguish between reliable historical information and reflection and criticism. Unfortunately this is also true for the narrative complex of I Sam. 8–12, which sets out to record the founding of the monarchy and the choice of Saul. It is obvious that these accounts have already been moulded by a particular attitude to the institution of the monarchy, whether that was coming into being or was already established; they are not contemporary, but to a considerable degree reflect later experiences of the Israelite kings. It has been recognized that I Sam. 11 is relatively independent, and it alone offers a basis for setting the figure and activity of Saul in a wider context. The details in it can hardly have been invented.

Jabesh in Gilead, east of the Jordan, was threatened by the Ammonites, whose historical power must have grown in parallel to the Israelite settlement.[6] Before the Ammonites were able to attack their city, the Jabeshites managed to send messengers into Israelite territory west of the Jordan. This they did in the hope that a 'saviour', a *mōšiaʿ*, would arise for them (I Sam. 11.3)! Thus the account follows the pattern of the 'period of the judges', even though it is right outside the book of Judges.

The messengers also reach Gibeah in Benjamin, Saul's home town. He is in the field, behind his plough, pulled by oxen. When he hears the news from Jabesh, he becomes furious. The spirit of God (*rūaḥ 'elōhīm*) comes upon him. He seizes a couple of oxen, cuts them up, and has the pieces sent round the territory of Israel. Unfortunately we do not have a more exact description of the area. His message is: the fate of anyone who does not follow Saul will be like that of these butchered oxen. The impact is tremendous. A 'fear of God', a 'fear of Yahweh' (*paḥad yhwh*) falls on those who are summoned. Yahweh has affected them so strongly that they follow Saul and march out 'as one man' (11.7).

Saul assembles this army at Bezek (*ḥirbet ibzīq*), where the road from Shechem comes down to Beth-shean,[7] immediately before the fords over the Jordan through which Gideon presumably pursued the Midianites. From there it is not far to Jabesh.[8] Saul and his army are able to inflict a resounding defeat on the Ammonites and thus to achieve a successful relief of the city.

So far, there is no difference from the situation of a charismatic leader and the success granted him with the help of Yahweh. While in the field, Saul experienced a regular, albeit extremely ecstatic call; holy anger seized him; in a short time he collected an army and attacked the invaders. It is worth noting that it is the Benjaminite Saul who comes to the help of the people in distant Jabesh. The existing links between Benjamin and Jabesh are confirmed; we may assume a genealogical basis for them in the theme of the rape of the women in Judges 20.

The account in I Sam. 11 ends with the people going to the sanctuary of Gilgal after their victory and there electing Saul king. This happens at the ancient Benjaminite sanctuary, i.e. not in Transjordania, nor on the other hand on Ephraimite territory. There is no indication which individuals were involved in this proclamation. In any case, it was certainly more than the tribe of Benjamin; it may have been all those who followed Saul to battle and who gathered at Bezek. These were the Ephraimites and perhaps also Galilean tribes. At best, they were the 'Israel' of the Song of Deborah. Gilgal not only played the role of an 'amphictyonic centre' but was also Saul's native sanctuary, to which he had every reason to go in gratitude after the victory. Here, whether spontaneously or after some preparation, what was already in the air became reality: a proven charismatic figure was elevated to a position of permanent power.[9]

Thus I Sam. 11 depicts in a spirited but brief sequence of events Saul's career from charismatic leader to king. It becomes clear how the new office grows out of the presuppositions of charismatic leadership, supported by the victorious army of the tribes who took part in the battle. Spontaneity predominates. However, there will doubtless have been preparations for the resolve to appoint a king. We have no reliable information here. All we have is a narrative tradition which concerns itself from a later perspective with the problems of the development of the monarchy and the higher determination of the chosen man, and does so in a vivid account with a rich variety of themes. It has been preserved in a number of variants in I Sam. 8–12 without concern for the contradictions and tensions within the complex tradition. The intermediary function of Samuel alone seems to provide a connecting link.

We can deal fairly easily with what is probably the latest stratum of tradition in I Sam. 8 and 12. According to I Sam. 8, Samuel was administering law in Israel. Because his end was near, the elders of Israel asked him, as lawgiver, to appoint a king for them. This took place at Samuel's abode in Ramah, that is, only a few miles north of Gibeah. Samuel did not take the demand well. But Yahweh asked him to accede to the wish of the elders, for, as Yahweh states explicitly, in expressing this wish 'the people has not rejected *you*, but *me*, as a ruler over them'.

The monarchy is presented as an enterprise in direct competition with the kingly rule of Yahweh, which should alone claim validity. Thus for Israel the office of earthly kings appears in the worst light conceivable. In complete accordance with this, Samuel tells the people during the course of ch. 8 what they are to expect from a king in their midst. Nothing good will come of him, only disadvantages, burdens, conscription, provisions for the court, crown possessions, taxes. The elders remain unimpressed. They demand a king, and Samuel receives divine confirmation that they are to have one. At first, however, nothing happens; after presenting their proposal to Samuel the men of Israel return home. Now Samuel has to take the initiative and find a suitable man. Chapters 9 and 10 in fact describe such an initiative, but in narratives of quite a different character from the artificial and reflective programme of I Sam. 8. This latter style only returns in I Sam. 12, where in a great discourse Samuel returns to the problems associated with the choice of the king and repeats the arguments of ch. 8. Evidently chs. 8 and 12, with their awareness of the problems, are the framework for the account of the rise of the monarchy in Israel, into which three other forms of tradition, I Sam. 9.1–10.16; 10.17–27; 11, have been incorporated; the last-mentioned reports the events of the Jabesh expedition.

The complex contained in 9.1–10.16 presents a series of idyllic, but illuminating scenes. While searching for the runaway asses of his father Saul by chance meets the 'seer' Samuel, who hitherto has been unknown to him. Samuel, who similarly has not known of Saul before, anoints him *nāgīd* over Israel. This is evidently a preparation for the kingdom, but at first nothing further is to be said about it. In every detail Samuel acts at Yahweh's behest, but the occasion for his actions arises almost incidentally, when Saul comes to meet him by chance. In complete contrast to ch. 8, any form of excessive human demand is excluded. In 10.17–27 Samuel takes the initiative in quite a different way. He summons a tribal assembly to Mizpah,[10] makes the tribes and clans come forward one by one and discloses the king by a process of lot which is not described in further detail. It falls upon Saul, the son of Kish, who for some remarkable reason is hidden with the baggage. When he appears, it emerges that he is a head taller than all the rest, perhaps a welcome confirmation of the choice that has been made.[11] The people acclaim him with 'Long live the king!' Samuel thereupon proclaims to the assembly a 'law for the king' which he lays up in writing at the sanctuary. Saul returns with his people to Gibeah. But some sceptics appear and wonder 'How can this man help us?' They despise Saul and bring him no presents, thus refusing him their loyalty.

The scene in Mizpah is now followed in ch. 11 by the report of Saul's battle against the Ammonites in Jabesh, in which Samuel's figure is completely superfluous.[12] Evidently 11.12–14 are meant to attach this report about Jabesh to the scene at Mizpah. There death is required for those who doubted Saul as king. But Saul declares that on this day on which Yahweh has given a victory, no one is to die. Thereupon Samuel, who is present in 11.14, sets in motion a march to Gilgal, to 'renew' the kingship there; this is perhaps because in the view of 10.17–27 Saul was already king. But 11.15, which is part of the Jabesh account and reports Saul's elevation to kingship quite independently, conflicts with 11.14.

The problems of composition which have just been discussed make it clear that the redactor of the books of Samuel already had trouble in combining the traditions about the rise of the monarchy for the purpose of forming a consistent account. It is quite clear that these traditions were originally separate, expressing different interests and not seeking to narrate a consecutive history. Nevertheless, the concern of the Old Testament scholar is often to combine the disparate material in a continuous narrative sequence and to distil from it what is historically probable or at least credible. One particular school has followed Wellhausen in putting forward the following division:[13] I Sam. 7; 8, followed by 10.17–27 + 11.12–14; 12 is a source 'hostile to the monarchy', whereas I Sam. 9.1–10.16 together with ch. 11 are based on an account 'favourable to the monarchy'. These are seen to be the main complexes.[14] Numerous attempts have been made to refine this result or to identify individual strata of tradition which in turn may be claimed to be historically significant.[15] These have not, however, produced widely accepted conclusions, important though it would be, for example, to know more of Samuel's role as alleged 'king-maker'.[16] We must content ourselves with stating that the beginnings of the monarchy can be discerned only with a relative degree of certainty, but that Israel itself evidently reflected on these beginnings to a considerable degree and already incorporated into the narratives about its origin the chief contributory factors which led to the monarchy and the problems which arose in the later course of its development. To this extent the significance of I Sam. 8–12 is not only for history but also for the problems posed by the monarchy.

We should not overlook the fact that the accounts of the origin of the monarchy agree on important points. In every instance it is Yahweh who chooses the person of the king. He it is who lets loose the divine fury which enters into Saul while ploughing; he enlightens Samuel on his sudden encounter with the unknown Saul and gives him the assurance that this is the *nāgīd* who is to rule Israel; the will of God also stands tacitly behind the business with the lot and the 'taller by a head'. Secondly, all the accounts are aware that the king needs the consent of the people. This is given in the form of the acclamation 'Long live the king!' Here we have two basic presuppositions which were important for the later period and which were never abandoned: they legitimate the king in Israel. Alt has reduced them to short formulae which at the same time mark the constitutive acts of king-making, the 'designation by Yahweh' and the 'acclamation of the people'.

This means that no one could become king in Israel on the basis of his own power. He needed the divine assent made visible in the act of anointing and then the consent of the people, the free men of the Israelite commonality. Anointing was always performed by prominent men versed in cultic service; they were very often cultic personalities. Samuel, a figure predestined in a number of respects,[17] anointed Saul; later, the designation of future kings chiefly came through prophets, principally in the so-called northern kingdom of Israel. There has often been a concern to find the 'democratic principle' represented in the Israelite monarchy in the form of the acclamation of the people. This is correct in principle, though in practice the sacral and legal foundation of the office ruled out any possibility that the people could exclude a man designated by Yahweh. This would have had extremely unfavourable effects. Conversely, on the one occasion when an acclamation took place without a designation, it promptly proved to be a wrong decision.[18] At the least, the acclamation of the people means that the king could not rule on the narrow basis of a decision which had been made by only a few people. From the beginning, an absolute monarchy in Israel was ruled out. The kingship was that of Yahweh on a basis recognized and confirmed by the people, and to this degree was not a rule exclusively based on 'God's grace'. The king stood in the centre between Yahweh and the people and was ideally the representative of both equally.

It was not in the nature of Israelite thought and the literary form which it took to present such distinctions in abstract terms. Rather, problems were incorporated in the course of an event, a report or a dialogue. Thus we cannot expect to find an account of the Israelite monarchy anywhere in the form of a statement of its nature. However, the redactor of the books of Samuel has taken account of the difficulty by collecting the traditions about the election of Saul as king which were at his disposal and has at least made a beginning of linking them together to establish the various aspects of this moment of historical significance.

Particular interest is usually expressed in the act of anointing which, in the case of Saul, is also combined with a formula that recurs later, namely that he has become a '*nāgīd* over (my people) Israel'. The anointing is performed by pouring oil on the head of the man designated. In the view of the ancient East, oil contained the power of life; anointing communicates the divine charisma as well as the authority of the office. The custom of anointing was possibly taken over by Israel; it was known in Syria and Palestine, possibly under Hittite influence. An Amarna letter[19] describes the appointment of a king in northern Syria with the words, 'oil has been poured on his head'. In passing it may be mentioned that the custom of calling the Israelite king 'the anointed one' (in a fuller form, 'the anointed of Yahweh')[20] originally referred merely to the king reigning at the time; 'the anointed one' only became an eschatological title gradually, after the end of the monarchy. In the Hellenized transcription of the Hebrew משיח it appears as 'Messias', and in the Greek translation of the word as *Christos*.[21] The roots of the designation 'Christ' for Jesus lie in the act of anointing the Israelite king and in the later Priestly tradition. The fact that Jesus was given the name 'Christ', which especially links him to the Old Testament tradition,[22] should be noted particularly by all those who want to detach the 'Christ'-ian tradition too much from its Palestinian and Israelite presuppositions.[23]

The exact definition of the title '*nāgīd* over Israel' is still disputed.[24] As no clear description of the function can be given, a translation of *nāgīd* is virtually impossible. Out of expediency, titles of people in middle or higher administration with wide-ranging responsibilities are used, like 'excellency', 'count' or 'prince', while the expression 'designate' is an *ad hoc* translation derived from the interpretation of the structure of the Israelite monarchy. It is of little use seeking the earlier history of the title within the tribal organization or in the military leadership of Israel before the formation of the state.[25] One would expect a *nāgīd* to appear alongside the *šōpēt* and the *qāṣīn*, but this is not the case. Remarkably enough, however, the designation lasted into the later period and was then presumably extended and used in a more general way.[26] We can only endorse the suggestion that in the period of the first kings it was a current designation among the Ephraimite tribes, the content of which was transferred at least to the monarchy in northern Israel, where it lived on uncurtailed. It would be bold to suppose that it was the original Ephraimite-Benjaminite designation for king, before the kingship of David finally confirmed the status of king for the rulers of what was later to be the northern kingdom of Israel also. There is no basis for such a theory in the sources that we have.

At the moment of his elevation to the throne Saul must have seen himself confronted with a whole series of tasks. The most pressing were those of foreign policy. For the moment the Ammonite danger seemed to have been removed. The conflict with the Philistines would be of longer duration. Saul must have made immediate preparations for battle at Gilgal. He assembled a select detachment from the conscript army and put part of them under the command of his son Jonathan.[27] However, the first clashes were not battles with the full Philistine fighting force, but chiefly sallies against fortified posts and border guards which the Philistines had pushed far into Israelite territory. The long narrative in I Sam. 13.2–14.46 gives a report of this. However, it is extremely anecdotal, and particularly interested in and oriented on the achievements and transgressions of Saul's son Jonathan. I Samuel 17.1–58; 18.6, 7; 23.1–13 report further battles of this kind against the Philistines; significantly, however, these accounts are really already narratives of the successes and fortunes of the young David, which are very closely connected with the Saul traditions. There are traditio-historical problems here which are of more general interest because the report of the triumph of the young David over the so-called 'giant' Goliath also belongs in this narrative complex.

Goliath was a typical champion of the Philistine army. The Philistine leaders had under their command small but powerful detachments, some of which were made up of select mercenaries. It was customary at that time for a full-scale battle to be preceded by single combat between champions; these issued challenges, taunted each other and finally engaged in hand-to-hand fighting.[28] The word translated 'giant' is *'îš habbēnayim* in Hebrew, literally meaning 'the man between', i.e. between the lines of battle. This understanding would fit the champions who fought in the full view of both armies. Whether Goliath was very tall is quite a different question, which has nothing to do with the question of single combat. It is interesting that he had a wooden spear with an iron head.[29] Iron was known in Palestine at that time and was at first a monopoly in the hands of the Philistines. Their iron chariots were a sign of their superiority.

We can understand the Israelite fear of such well-equipped opponents. It is significant that David overcomes the Philistine champion by a stratagem rather than in regular combat. The young man comes into the Israelite camp almost by chance and finds an opportunity there to accomplish his well-known act of heroism. With sling and stone he brings down the formidable man and is said finally to have slain him with his own sword.

Saul is extremely surprised. He has the young victor brought to him and asks where he comes from. This is clearly in tension with I Sam. 16.14–23, according to which Saul had David brought to him on special recommendation, without having made his acquaintance earlier in military operations. In fact the tradition about the victory over Goliath will only have been transferred to David at a later stage.[30] For according to II Sam. 21.19, the man who slew Goliath was someone quite different, a man from Bethlehem called Elhanan. David may have reaped Elhanan's reward because of his great and well-known victories over the Philistines, which later aroused Saul's envy. What the maidens sang in I Sam. 18.6, 7 could easily have influenced the tradition.

The battle in which Goliath was involved fits into the series of local encounters between the Philistines and Israel under Saul. These were often surprise attacks made by one side on the other. The great encounter was still to come. The tradition in I Samuel sees it as being closely connected with the personal destinies of Saul and David. More will be said about the rise of David later. At first he emerges between the Israelite and Philistine fronts not least because of unmistakable difficulties with Saul. David's rise runs parallel to a clear 'decline' of Saul, the deeper reasons for which we can only illuminate to a limited degree. I Samuel 15 presents the battle against the Amalekites, Israel's primal enemy since wilderness days,[31] as the turning-point in the development of Saul's kingdom. Apparently Saul allowed the Israelites to seize booty without seeing to Yahweh's share. Samuel declares that Saul has forfeited his kingdom. The king sinks into melancholy, along with pathological envy of David, and finally comes his defeat by the Philistines and his death. It is not easy to give a historical explanation of this reversal in Saul's development. There are factors that can be adduced independently of the person of the king, objective difficulties which it might be beyond the power of a single individual to overcome.

In all his undertakings, Saul could only rely on the tribal army, and that means on the conscription of men which was not possible without the consent of the tribes. There is no indication that Saul introduced changes in the constitution of the tribes or even attempted such changes. When it was desirable and necessary for him to take steps to consolidate his kingdom and to safeguard his territory, he had no personal following ready for action at all times. Tensions were inevitable between Saul and the tribes, who found it difficult to become used to the new ideas of stricter organization and central government.

We may leave aside the question whether Noth[32] is to be followed in assuming a personal quarrel between Saul and Samuel, who may then have taken sides with the tribes. This would be to take seriously in historical terms the personalization of objective difficulties which the Old Testament presents in the construction of a clash between Samuel and Saul. Such a personal conflict is, however, quite conceivable as another unwelcome element in the situation.

We must discuss another important question for future developments here, because it is inevitably among the characteristics of Saul's kingdom. What was the exact size of the area over which he ruled? If we could begin by assuming that he was recognized by an intact 'system' of ideally twelve tribes, there would be no difficulty in picturing his kingdom as extending from Judah in the south to the foothills of Hermon in the north. But closer examination of the tradition shows that to be improbable. All the decisive events in the life of Saul take place in what later became the territory of the northern kingdom of Israel. David's origin in Bethlehem and the extension of Saul's persecution to the territory of the tribe of Judah, as at the oasis of Engedi by the Dead Sea (I Sam. 24), are exceptional features, and do not force us to conclude that Saul was also king over Judah. David's birthplace lay well to the north of the territory of the tribe of Judah, so that we can easily imagine a pull towards Benjamin;[33] Engedi lay outside the central area of Judah and may not yet have been included in it in a 'political' sense.

II Samuel 2.9 offers some evidence of the size of the territory under Saul's control. The verse describes the area over which Saul's successor Ishbaal was appointed. It includes Gilead, and therefore at least the centre of Transjordania; also Ephraim and Benjamin and some frontier areas in the north, extending as far as the plain of Megiddo.[34] Judah is not mentioned. This confirms the theory that Saul had no political influence south of Benjamin. When he became king, he did not take over a clearly defined territory; he was merely acclaimed by a group of tribes about whom unfortunately we know no further details. Saul's 'kingdom' was a national state in the original sense of the word, a hegemony over clans and tribes of the same origin; it was not at the same time a territorial state with fixed boundaries and an independent administration.

Saul's kingdom was thus at first still vague. It had not developed any systematic official structure, and was supported only by the consent of the tribes, being quite independent of them. This was as yet no adequate basis for a proper defence of the land. Saul could not cope with the power of the Philistines and fell victim to them. After a number of local battles and skirmishes the Philistine leaders prepared a massive attack on the area over which he ruled. This will not have taken long, especially as Saul is said to have ruled for only two years. The Philistines skilfully attacked at the point where the Canaanite territory penetrated most deeply into that of Israel, in the area of the northern chain of cities. This at the same time separated the Galilean tribes from the contingents of Ephraim and Benjamin. The Philistines achieved their aim completely. According to I Sam. 31.7 the Israelites 'on the other side of the valley and those beyond the Jordan' took no part in the battle.

For Saul and his central Palestinian followers the situation was almost lost from the start. The Philistines were extremely well equipped and assured in their tactics. Saul was weaker and had lost confidence after a number of bitter experiences with the tribes. His uncertainty is reflected in the well-known narrative of his visit before the battle to the necromancer (not 'witch') of Endor, in the immediate vicinity of the battlefield. He wanted to see the spirit of Samuel and talk with him (I Sam. 28.3–25). Samuel was successfully conjured up; he prophesied the end for Saul's army and his kingdom.

The battle between Israelites and Philistines did not last long (I Sam. 31). The Israelites fled in the direction of the mountains of Gilboa, to the east of the plain of Jezreel. Losses were high. The dead included a number of Saul's sons including Jonathan, David's friend. David himself could not take part in the battle. There will be more to be said about this later. Saul himself was pursued, and archers wounded him. Cornered, he asked his armour-bearer to stab him. But the latter did not dare to lay hands on the Lord's anointed. So Saul took his own sword and killed himself. The armour-bearer followed his example and died at his side.

The Philistine victory was complete; the Israelite situation was hopeless in every respect. Those who lived on the other side of the plain and beyond the Jordan are said to have fled when they heard the news of the fearful defeat; from then on the Philistines are said to have lived in their cities (I Sam. 31.7). Unfortunately we have no exact details. Presumably the Philistines occupied places in Galilee and Transjordania; we do not hear anything of further inroads into the hill-country of Ephraim. Saul's head and weapons were sent round the Philistine cities as trophies of victory; his body and the corpses of his sons were hung on the walls of Beth-shean.

The gruesome story ends with an honourable action. The inhabitants of Jabesh in Gilead, whose city Saul had once saved from the Ammonite threat, felt a debt of gratitude to him even after his death. Armed Jabeshites went secretly to Beth-shean by night, took the corpses of Saul and his sons from the wall and buried them in Jabesh. The wheel had come full circle. Israel's first king found his resting place where he first won fame.

We may leave aside discussion of the personality of Saul, about which there has been much reflection and much puzzlement. He was king of an army and did not have the organizing ability to adapt the old tribal alliance, limited and partly scattered over Palestine, to the new conditions of the incipient monarchy. Existing or developing tensions may have complicated matters. An army mobilized by levy was too narrow a basis on which to strengthen Israel internally and externally. Saul was a charismatic leader appointed for life, without a court or a working administration, at the end perhaps abandoned by the man whom he trusted, his sponsor and protector Samuel, and mistrustful of the successes of David. In the end he was tried beyond his abilities in being required to found a state on a permanent basis under the eyes of hostile neighbours. Saul left behind him a tribal alliance weakened and in disarray, which would have found it difficult to establish itself again out of its own resources. The new development was influenced from outside. David became king in Judah. This opened up new possibilities.

NOTES

1. Apart from the sagas of encounters of the 'judge' Samson with the Philistines (Judg. 13–16), we have occasional reports of local conflicts in the narratives at the beginning of the book of Samuel (I Sam. 1–7). They are centred on the sanctuary of Shiloh (*ḫirbet sēlūn*) in southern Ephraim, where the ark of Yahweh stood, and at which the young Samuel served. The occasion on which the ark, which was used as a palladium in war, fell into Philistine hands was a series of skirmishes between the Israelite tribes and the Philistines in the

region of Aphek (probably *tell el-muḥmar* by *rās el-'ēn* on the western border of the hill-country of Ephraim). In the course of these conflicts the ark was lost (I Sam.4.10, 11), and the sanctuary of Shiloh was probably destroyed also (much later, this is recalled by the prophet Jeremiah, in whose time the ruins could still be seen, Jer.7.12, 14; 26.6, 9). For the narrative about the ark see L. Rost, *Das kleine Credo und andere Studien zum Alten Testament*, 1965, 122–59; for Shiloh see also O. Eissfeldt, 'Silo und Jerusalem' (1957), *Kleine Schriften* III, 417–25.

2. The continuity in development is worked out and stressed by A. Alt, 'The Formation of the Israelite State in Palestine' (1930), in *Essays on Old Testament History and Religion*, 1966, 173–237; J. A. Soggin, *Das Königtum in Israel*, BZAW 104, 1967, is near to Alt's position. G. Buccellati, *Cities and Nations of Ancient Syria. An Essay of Political Institutions with Special Reference to the Israelite Kingdom*, Studi Semitici 26, 1967, is written on a broader basis, often following the intentions of Noth and Alt; it pays more attention to political perspectives than to religious ones. Cf. the abundant literature mentioned in these works, and also K. Galling, *Die israelitische Staatsverfassung in ihrer vorderorientalischen Umwelt*, AO 28, 3, 4, 1929.

3. Whatever our verdict on the scene in I Sam.22.6ff., Saul's sitting under the tamarisk in Gibeah, spear in hand, in the midst of his people, is more a confirmation than a refutation of the provisional nature of his monarchy.

4. However, note the position of the narrative in the context of I Samuel. Saul avenges himself because help has been given to his rival David. This also increases the alienation between Saul and Yahweh in the context of the narrative as a whole. Cf. now H. J. Stoebe, *Das erste Buch Samuelis*, KAT 8, 1, 1973, 407–16.

5. Buccellati, *Cities and Nations*, 1967, takes a diametrically opposed view. For him the monarchy in Israel is 'the natural development of forces present among the Israelites and stimulated by circumstances such as the conquest of Palestine and the fight against the Philistines' (241). This is hardly to be disputed. But it is equally certain that the Israelite understanding of the monarchy was based on different presuppositions and that the tribal structure did not give way to the monarchy without problems. To this extent, comparison with circumstances in Syria can only be a partial help.

6. M. Noth, *Aufsätze* I, 463–70, esp.468f.

7. The favourable situation of Bezek in terms of communications was already described by A. Alt in *PJB* 22, 1926, 49f.; on the basis of new surveys see now the detailed article by P. Welten, 'Bezeq', *ZDPV* 81, 1965, 138–65.

8. The topography is discussed by M. Noth, 'Jabes-Gilead, Ein Beitrag zur Methode alttestamentlicher Topographie' (1953), *Aufsätze* I, 476–88, with reference to I Sam.11.

9. For the numerous matters of detail see K. Möhlenbrink, 'Sauls Ammoniterfeldzug und Samuels Beitrag zum Königtum des Saul', *ZAW* 58, 1940/41, 57–70; also W. Beyerlin, 'Das Königscharisma bei Saul', *ZAW* 73, 1961, 186–201; J. A. Soggin, 'Charisma und Institution im Königtum Sauls', *ZAW* 75, 1963, 54–65; id., *Das Königtum in Israel*, 1967, 29–45.

10. Supposing that Mizpah is identical with *tell en-naṣbe*, about six miles north of Jerusalem on the main route leading into Ephraimite territory (cf. now H. J. Stoebe, *KAT* 8, 1, 1973, 215), the territory lay in Benjamin. However, according to I Sam.11.15 the king-making took place in Gilgal, which was also in Benjamin. It is clear only that there were competing traditions about the decisive events in the rise of the monarchy. The significance of Mizpah in the time of the kings (cf. I Kings 15.22; II Kings 25.23; Jer.40;41) may have favoured the transference of the saga-like events of I Sam.10.17–27 there.

11. O. Eissfeldt assigns this theme of Saul's size to what is presumably an independent earlier tradition; cf. *Die Komposition der Samuelisbücher*, 1931, 7, 10.

12. In I Sam. 11.7 'and behind Samuel' is an insertion for which there is no reason in the context.

13. J. Wellhausen, *Die Composition des Hexateuchs und der historischen Bücher des Alten Testaments*, reprinted 1963, 240–3.

14. For details see the accounts in the various Introductions to the Old Testament, and more recently the detailed commentary on the chapter with a historical introduction by H. J. Stoebe, KAT 8, 1, 176–240.

15. See especially H. Wildberger, 'Samuel und die Enstehung des israelitischen Königtums', *TZ* 13, 1957, 442–69; K.-D. Schunck, *Benjamin*, 1963, 30–138; G. Wallis in the collection of his articles, *Geschichte und Überlieferung*, Arbeiten zur Theologie II, 13, 1968, 45–87; H. J. Boecker, *Die Beurteilung der Anfänge des Königtums in den deuteronomistichen Abschnitten des I. Samuelbuches*, WMANT 31, 1969; see also M. Buber, 'Die Erzählung von Sauls Königswahl', *VT* 6, 1956, 113–73. There is a traditio-historical investigation of the prior history of the election of Saul as king in three studies by H. Seebass, *ZAW* 77, 1965, 286–96; 78, 1966, 148–79; 79, 1967, 155–71.

16. A. Weiser, *Samuel. Seine geschichtliche Aufgabe und religiöse Bedeutung*, FRLANT 81, 1962; R. Press, 'Der Prophet Samuel. Eine traditionsgeschichtliche Untersuchung', *ZAW* 56, 1938, 177–225; E. Robinson, 'Samuel and Saul', *BJRL* 28, 1944, 175–206. See also M. Noth, 'Samuel und Silo' (1963), *Aufsätze* 1, 148–56.

17. I Sam. 1–3 gives an account of Samuel's youth, which was bound up with his service at the sanctuary in Shiloh. On the whole it is difficult to put this man and his functions in a convincing historical setting. He is pictured as a 'judge', but also as a 'seer', and in addition must have been an extremely influential person, at least in Benjamin (cf. I Sam. 7.16). He even contradicted the king, who feared Samuel's answers. See particularly A. Weiser, *Samuel*, 1962; M. Noth, 'Samuel und Silo' (1963), *Aufsätze* 1, 148–56; K.-D. Schunck, *Benjamin*, 1963, 80–138; G. Wallis, 'Die überlieferungsgeschichtliche Forschung und der Samuelstoff', in Wallis, *Geschichte und Überlieferung*, 1968, 67–87.

18. This seems to have been the case with Tibni, Omri's counterpart, although the tradition does not allow us to draw any exact conclusions (I Kings 16.15–22): cf. also A. Alt, *KS* II, 121 = *Grundfragen*, 353.

19. EA 51, Knudtzon, 318f.

20. I Sam. 24.7, 11; 26.9, 11, 16, 23; II Sam. 1.14, 16; 19.22; see also Ps. 18.51; 20.7; 84.10; 89.21, 39; 132.10; II Sam. 23.1.

21. See the explicit translation of the title Messiah in John 1.41; 4.25.

22. Cf. e.g. Rom. 1.1–4, which is also the earliest passage about the Davidic sonship of Jesus. The composite phrase *Christos Kyrios* (or *Kyriou*) is illuminating; the Hebrew genitive *mōšiaḥ yhwh*, 'anointed of Yahweh', underlies it, cf. Ps. Sol. 17.32; 18.7; Luke 2.11.

23. For problems associated with anointing see R. de Vaux, *Ancient Israel*, 1961, 103–6; M. Noth, 'Office and Vocation in the Old Testament' (1958), in *The Laws in the Pentateuch*, 1966, 229–49; a very refined understanding of anointing the king is advanced by E. Kutsch, *Salbung als Rechtsakt im Alten Testament und im Alten Orient*, BZAW 87, 1963.

24. Cf. I Sam. 13.14; 25.30; II Sam. 5.2; 6.21; 7.8; I Kings 1.35; 14.7; 16.2.

25. W. Richter, 'Die *nāgīd*-Formel. Ein Beitrag zur Erhellung des *nāgīd*-Problems', *BZ* NF 9, 1965, 71–84, who asserts, probably aptly, that the title was limited to the northern tribes before the monarchy. The assumption that this was a designation given to the man who brought deliverance from distress remains a hypothesis; see also W. Richter, *Traditionsgeschichtliche Untersuchungen*, ²1966, 154; more recently L. Schmidt, *Menschlicher Erfolg und Jahwes Initiative. Studien zu Tradition, Interpretation und Historie in Überlieferungen von Gideon, Saul und David*, WMANT 38, 1970, 140–71; J. van der Ploeg, 'Les chefs du peuple d'Israel et leurs titres', *RB* 57, 1960, esp. 45–7, regards the *nāgīd* as 'l'homme éminent, le prince'; J. J. Glück, 'Nagid-Shepherd', *VT* 13, 1963, 114–50, regards him as a 'shepherd'.

26. The term is used in the plural in I Chron. 11.11; II Chron. 35.8; as a title in the case of the high priest, I Chron. 9.11; II Chron. 31.13; Neh. 11.11.

27. I Sam. 13.2; cf. also 14.52.

28. H. Donner, 'Zum "Streitlustigen" in Sinuhe B 110', *ZÄS* 81, 1956, 61f.; G. Lanczkowski, 'Die Geschichte vom Riesen Goliath und der Kampf Sinuhes mit dem Starken von Retenu', *MDAIK* 16, 1959, 214–8; R. de Vaux, 'Les Combats singuliers dans l'Ancien Testament', *Bibl.* 40, 1959, 495–508.

29. 'And with this spearhead he towered up to the Iron Age!' Thus A. Alt in his lectures.

30. For the transmission and tradition of the text, also in the later period, cf. H. J. Stoebe, 'Die Goliathperikope 1. Sam. XVII 1 – XVIII 5 und die Textform der Septuaginta', *VT* 6, 1956, 397–413.

31. Cf. Exod. 17.8–16; Deut. 25.17–19.

32. M. Noth, *History of Israel*, ²1960, 175.

33. As the king's retainer, David was not necessarily the legal subject of his king. It was not necessary for the successful warrior to belong to the tribes and clans in Saul's kingdom, especially as the kingship was still in process of consolidation; K. D. Schunck, *Benjamin*, 1963, 124, differs.

34. According to the narration these areas are expressly designated as 'Israel in its totality'. Unfortunately the text is doubtful in the middle of the verse. The tribe of Asher is probably mentioned there, and then the city of Jezreel. For the basic elements of Saul's 'empire' and its expansion in the Davidic period see A. Alt, *KS* I, 116–9 = *Grundfragen*, 126–9.

2 | *The Kingdom of David*

APART FROM THE brief note in I Sam. 31.7, that the Philistines occupied the cities in the hill-country of Galilee and beyond the Jordan, we have no account of circumstances in the heart of Israel, the hill-country of Ephraim. It does not seem as if the Philistines penetrated as far as that to claim sovereign powers there. They probably believed that they had removed all threats after their victory over the Israelite host and especially after the death of Saul. We may therefore assume that the hill-country of Ephraim remained unoccupied, and also the southern part of Transjordania. This is confirmed by the further course of events.

Abner, Saul's commander, finds one of Saul's sons who evidently did not take part in the fight against the Philistines and who survived the catastrophe. On his own initiative, Abner makes this descendant of the king, a man called Ishbosheth (or more correctly, Ishbaal),¹ king over the area outlined in II Sam. 2.9. His sphere of rule is the hill-country of Ephraim, Gilead, and a few scattered parts near the plain of Megiddo. We do not learn that Ishbaal was designated by Yahweh and acclaimed by the people. Thus he in no way fulfilled the basic conditions for being king in Israel. But Abner, now evidently the most powerful man in the state, was pursuing his own political goals; he possibly considered Ishbaal only as a shadow king, and ventured to use him to start a hereditary monarchy in Israel. At first Abner does not seem to have come up against any resistance. His initiative may even have been welcome at a time of need.

Had he been up to it, Ishbaal might in fact have been able to achieve something. However, he anxiously remained at Mahanaim in Transjordania,² the place where he had been made king, and allowed Abner and his people to depart over the Jordan. It is said that these people were the 'servants' (*ᶜᵃbādîm*) of Ishbaal, a kind of bodyguard, a group of mercenaries, probably assembled by Abner as the king's personal troops.

West of the Jordan, in Benjaminite territory near Gibeon, there were skirmishes between Ishbaal's troops under Abner and David's mercenaries under the leadership of Joab (II Sam. 2.12–3.1). These were clashes between mercenaries, it seems, and not decisive passages at arms; there were no battles involving the summoning of the tribal army, which in any case had been destroyed in the battle with the

Philistines. But what lay behind them? Were these attempts by Judah in the south to take over the north? Was Abner just looking for adventure? Ishbaal remained passive. Developments did not seem to favour Abner. He fell out with Ishbaal; private issues were involved. Then the unexpected happened. Abner began negotiations with David, who at this point was already king of Judah and was residing in Hebron. The commander was received in generous fashion. David arranged a banquet. Abner made his intentions quite clear. He was ready to encourage the Israelites of Saul's old kingdom to make an alliance with David, so that as king of Judah he could also reign over Israel. We do not have David's answer. The decisive verse II Sam. 3.21 is as good as a modern communiqué: 'So David sent Abner away; and he went in peace.' Hardly had he left Hebron, however, when Joab returned from a raid. Abner had killed a brother of Joab's in the fighting at Gibeon. The two men had accounts to settle. Joab, furious at Abner's visit, muttered vaguely about some plans, took David to task and finally had Abner recalled without David's knowledge. In the gate of Hebron, Joab stabbed the hated visitor.

Matters were brought to a head. Abner had been in process of separating from Ishbaal, and in going over to Judah had irrevocably put himself in the hands of David, who had once been zealously pursued by Saul. He had to pay for his bold attempt with his life because of Joab's personal revenge, with which he had not reckoned. David now incurred the suspicion of wanting to take over Saul's heritage by force. He recognized the danger of far-reaching complications which could ruin all his plans, although he was not personally to blame. A demonstration was called for to clarify matters. He ordered a kind of state funeral for Abner, himself walked behind the bier and uttered the well-known saying, 'Do you not know that a "prince" (*śar*) and a great man has fallen this day in Israel?' (II Sam. 3.38). David's grief and his remarks were able to convince those around him.

The reaction aroused by Abner's death among Ishbaal and his Israelites is also clear and understandable (II Sam. 4.1): 'When Saul's son heard that Abner had died at Hebron, his courage failed, and all Israel was dismayed.' Ishbaal had lost the man who meant everything to him; Israel felt compromised and robbed of their last hope. Events came in quick succession. Two mercenaries from Saul's entourage murdered Ishbaal and brought his head to Hebron in expectation of a great reward. They came before David with the fictitious declaration that this was the head of his enemy, who had sought his life. David saw through their game and had the murderers executed and their bodies publicly exhibited in Hebron. Ishbaal's head was placed in Abner's tomb.

We have reproduced the dramatic course of events in the narrative of II Sam. 3.6–4.12 in some detail. That this account is favourable to David is unmistakable, but the situation on which it is based exactly fits the internal situation of the Israelite tribal alliance after the death of Saul. Now, at the latest, it is clear how independent was Judah with its king David, and how utterly all the hopes of Saul's alliance had been dashed. In contrast to Judah, with its monarchy, Israel appeared to be virtually a different entity. The independence of Judah's existence since the days of the settlement became a powerful factor in the political landscape, which had suddenly undergone a change.

We cannot determine whether David deliberately intended to take over Saul's heritage when the opportunity was ripe. He knew from his own experience the tension, expectations and claims which were dominant in the Ephraimite north and was himself one of the factors which had made it so difficult for Saul to rule. Nothing would have been more foolish than to provoke this tribal alliance. David had to win its confidence, and unlike Saul was patient enough to allow things to develop. The acts of violence to Abner and Ishbaal were much more calculated to disrupt and even nullify his own plans and purposes than to further them. However, in reality, time and circumstances were on his side.

The Israelites under Saul's sphere of rule had had to endure in quick succession a crushing defeat, the death of two kings and the loss of their most able man. The victorious Philistines were still at their doors. What had been set in motion was now moving towards a climax. Whether or not all the tribes unanimously agreed,[3] the Ephraimite north voluntarily subjected themselves to the protection of David as the strongest man in the land.

An Israelite delegation appears in Hebron (II Sam. 5.1–3) and declares its confidence in the king in the name of Israel. 'Behold, we are your bone and flesh. In times past, when Saul was king over us, it was you that led out and brought in Israel.' This formula is chosen not to express something that is a matter of course, but to give reasons for the unusual situation. The north is yielding to the south. There were certainly bonds of kinship to justify the step, even if so far they remained ineffectual. On the other hand, however, David had already proved his loyalty. His deeds in the war against the Philistines as Saul's aide were not forgotten. The ambassadors now added as a word of Yahweh what the Israelites felt that the king of Judah still lacked: 'You will rule my people Israel and will be *nāgīd* over Israel.' David, the king of Judah, is recognized by Israel as the one designated by Yahweh, and the message of the delegation in fact includes his acclamation. He makes a treaty with these people, which is designated by the momentous term *bᵉrît*. We are not given any details of the content, but it can hardly have been anything other than the official acceptance by David of the kingship of Israel.[4] The scene ends with his anointing as king over Israel.

At this point it seems appropriate to consider in some detail the significance and application of the name 'Israel'.[5] The preceding account has made it clear that since the days of the settlement, 'Israel' was primarily used for the tribes in the Ephraimite hill-country, including Benjamin. In so far as the settlement of Transjordania took place from the west, these groups also necessarily belonged to Israel. We may therefore assume that the claim for extending the name Israel to Transjordania and perhaps also to the tribes of Galilee came from Ephraim.

In fact Zebulon, Naphthali and Issachar, from the region round Tabor, had proved themselves in alliance with Ephraim, at least in Deborah's battle, whereas Gilead had not provided the expected help. It is not surprising that in these circumstances the area outlined in II Sam. 2.9 was given and continued to bear the name 'Israel'. Judah had no role in these developments, or at any rate remained quite independent. It was never 'Israel' in the strict sense. In principle, the transference of rule over Israel to David did not change matters. He now combined the two 'kingdoms' of Israel and Judah in a personal union without expressly combining them as a whole under some such name as 'kingdom of Israel'. We do not have so clear and comprehensive a formula as this from the time of the monarchy. When the personal union broke apart again after the death of Solomon, it was natural that the 'houses' of Israel and Judah should once again lead separate lives. It was not the case that the name Israel was from now on 'limited' to the northern kingdom, while the southern kingdom 'adopted' the name Judah.

The widespread conviction that this 'people of Israel' had included Judah from an early period rests rather on a conception first developed during the course of the monarchy which was later elevated to be an ideal: from earliest times Israel had formed a single entity; the 'Israelites' had always been conscious of being one 'people', belonging together under this name, and had also thought and acted on the basis of being one 'Israelite' nation. By contrast, it must be realized that the name 'Israel' was first attached to the tribes of central Palestine and strictly speaking remained with them. The name 'Israel' was idealized and the idea of 'all Israel' (*kol-yiśrā'ēl*), as expressed in the Deuteronomistic literature, was formed only after the fall of the northern kingdom. Significantly, this phrase 'all Israel' is never explained in more detail, nor is it identified with a particular number of tribes.[6] That 'all Israel' is a 'people of twelve tribes' is an artificial construction which only appears in the testimony of late sources. The conception is never used during the monarchy.[7]

Although strict proof cannot be given, it may be that the idea of a union of twelve tribes is earlier and was promoted under the influence of David's personal union. It may even have been built up into a kind of 'national ideology' in Jerusalem to support the rule of the house of David. This may be the context of old tribal sayings like those contained in Gen. 49, which were made part of the 'Yahwist' material, usually dated in the early period of the monarchy. It is worth noting, however, that the development of the idea of twelve tribes is part of the so-called Priestly writing in the Pentateuch. Here the 'twelve-tribe system' in fact appears as a cultic postulate to establish earlier traditional conceptions.[8] The combination of 'all Israel' in Deuteronomy with the cultic alliance of twelve tribes in the Priestly writing impressed on the later period the notion of a primal unity of Israel and made 'Israel' an ideal and an honorific name for this totality. From the perspective of a later period this course was not unjustified. After the fall of the 'northern' kingdom of Israel, Josiah took over the name

'Israel' for Judah in his reform of 622 BC by recognizing the book of Deuteronomy; in so doing he introduced a development which made the men of Judah and later the 'Jews' into 'Israelites' at the same time.[9]

The significance of the moment of union between the Ephraimite tribal alliance and Judah in the south, together with the problems attached to it, has constantly been underestimated, because of the conviction that Judah had always been part of 'Israel'. In reality, quite a new stage of development began here. Israel became the 'people' we customarily envisage, naturally including Judah, as a result of Abner's bold resolve. Had he not taken this first step, the elders of Israel would hardly have found their way to Hebron. Ultimately, however, this new development was based on the historical power of a single dominant personality, David,[10] of whose effectiveness and resolution the men of Judah and the Israelites were alike convinced. He had been made king quite independently of Saul's heritage, and at first resided in Hebron. We must now trace the career of this man up to the moment when he combined Israel and Judah in a personal union. It reaches back into the time of Saul.

It has become customary in Old Testament scholarship to divide the tradition about David into two complexes, each of which has its own particular themes. One is called the 'history of the rise of David', comprising I Sam. 16.14 – II Sam. 5.25, and the other is the 'succession narrative', which includes II Sam. 6; 7; 9–20 and I Kings 1.1–2.11. I Samuel 16.1–13; 17; II Sam. 21–24 are usually regarded as later additions to these ancient traditions, and II Sam. 8 occupies an isolated position all by itself. The person of David stands at the centre of these chapters, so one could speak of almost a biographical tradition. Seen in context, however, the account is not just personal and anecdotal. It achieves its contours by disclosing deeper causes of external events through the skilful composition of smaller units: the people involved and their intentions ultimately retreat behind the pressure of events. Both the rise of David and the crises of his kingdom are described with great skill and allow the reader to forget that he is being told the history of quite a long period. Rather, he feels himself transported into a dramatic course of events with its heights and depths, inexorably moving towards a goal; first the elevation of David to be king over Israel and Judah, and then his installation in Jerusalem. Finally come the establishment of his kingdom and the problem of his successor.

This impressive account, with its almost psychological elements, led Eduard Meyer to make his often-quoted remark that 'the burgeoning of the monarchy of Judah brought real history-writing into being', and that as a result 'Israelite culture' found itself 'independently and with equal rights at the beginning of a development which was completed on Greek soil a century or two later, in a much richer and more varied form'.[11] We may leave aside the question whether the standard applied by Meyer to what he calls 'real history writing' can be applied so directly today; without question it needs to be refined, whether it is used for Greece or for Israel.[12] But the great originality of the stories about

David which we now possess cannot be denied. They took shape only a short time after the events themselves, and in any case soon after the death of David. This does not mean, of course, that no problems stand in the way of a historical understanding of the period. The course of historical development inevitably remains open to many questions. Account must be taken of contradictions and absurdities.

It is customary to attribute two narratives at the beginning of the complex concerned with the rise of David to the work of later writers: David's anointing in Bethlehem (I Sam. 16.1–13) and his fight with Goliath, which has already been mentioned (I Sam. 17). The story of the anointing seems to be a repetition from a northern perspective of the anointing of David, bringing out elements which did not emerge in the tradition from Judah: the anointing of David as *nāgīd* is described in almost the same terms as the anointing performed by Samuel on Saul (I Sam. 9.1–10.16). Jesse, David's father,[13] presents all his sons. Finally Samuel puts the proverbial question: 'Are all your sons here?' One is missing, the youngest, David, who has to be recalled from tending the flock. The dramatic technique of the narrative is obvious. There is no further reference to this anointing, nor does it appear that the kingship of David was prepared for in this way from the beginning. But the designation of the man who is to be king must be assured. Samuel, from Benjamin, must be his guarantor.

We have already mentioned the way in which the victory over Goliath was transferred to David. The traditions of the anointing and the fight with Goliath belong to David's youth and their historical reliability is problematical. On the other hand, in I Sam. 16.14–23 we seem to have firmer ground under our feet. There the handsome and gifted David is summoned as a minstrel for the melancholy Saul, a theme which has been often taken up by painters.[14]

David is promoted from being Saul's minstrel to being his armour-bearer.[15] He has his first successes as a young warrior and commander, so that the maidens sing that Saul has slain thousands, but David ten thousands (I Sam. 18.6, 7). Saul is afraid for his prestige and his authority. The famous covenant of friendship between his son Jonathan and David increases the mistrust of the unstable king. There is a quarrel. This, at any rate, is the impression which the tradition in I Samuel intends to make. David's rise shines out the more brightly against the dark foil of the decline in Saul's power and reputation. It would be a mistake to interpret too strictly in historical terms the parts of this narrative which are presented in personal and highly emotional terms. The one thing that is certain is that David drew immediate and drastic consequences. He left Saul and returned to Judah, his homeland.

One further proof of the independence of Judah, in the south, is the fact that from there David was able to build up a completely new existence for himself. This would hardly have been possible in Ephraim and Benjamin. He developed into a mercenary, maintaining and leading his own personal troops. The undertaking seems to have been attractive to a number of people. I Samuel 22.2 records that 'David assembled everyone who was in distress, and everyone who was in debt, and everyone who was discontented.' Four hundred men are mentioned, and later six hundred (I Sam. 27.2). These were people who had failed or who were near to failure, debtors who sought to avoid their obligations by entering into a mercenary troop;[16] the embittered men may also have included dispossessed sons of farmers in Judah. In any case David and his troops stood outside the ranks of those levied for the tribal army, and made their own decisions. The men were a kind of household guard for David.

David's life as a warrior has often been deprecated. He is said to have been a kind of bandit, a condottiere, an outlaw, tolerated rather than admired. In fact, however, his services will have been valued in Judah. He helped the city of Keilah[17] against the Philistines (I Sam. 23.1–13) and preserved its independence. David later appears in the service of the farmers of En-gedi and there takes the side of this presumably nomadic tribe on the south-west side of the Dead Sea (I Sam. 24–26).

The tradition associates David's operations in the territory of Judah with Saul's pursuit of him. Saul, full of envy, hatred and mistrust, seeks in vain to seize the young man, allegedly even in the territory of Judah. There were no state frontiers to prevent him. In view of the situation, David took an apparently incredible step, though it was not unusual for a free mercenary leader. He offered his services to Achish of Gath, the nearest of the five Philistine city-kings. They were accepted, and David at first remained in Gath, later asking for a city state of his own on Philistine territory. He was given Ziklag,[18] far to the south, as it were on lease, and had to provide troops for the Philistines when summoned. They knew what they were doing. Ziklag, in the south, was more exposed to invasion from the inhabitants of the southern steppes than any other city. David was to form a kind of buffer zone. He succeeded in inflicting a decisive defeat on the Amalekites (I Sam. 30). His victory over these arch-enemies of Israel attracted all eyes to him. He exploited the situation in diplomatic fashion and made friends with the southern tribes and city states in the territory of Judah, including the Jerahmeelites and the Kenites (I Sam. 30.26–31). He gave them some of the plunder from the Amalekites and even sent some to the elders of Judah, 'his friends' (I Sam. 30.26). In this convincing way David kept his men of Judah in mind. He spent a year and four months in Ziklag. The time was sufficient for him to build diplomatic bridges in all directions. Understandably, David's activity attracted the attention of the Philistines. When they were preparing for the decisive battle against Saul, David was excluded from the fight. He was spared from having to fight against Israel (I Sam. 29).

The death of Saul on the heights of Gilboa created a new situation. At first it is difficult to discern. David remained in Ziklag and waited. He enquired of Yahweh whether he should go up into one of the cities of Judah (II Sam. 2.1). Yahweh assented. The way was opened for new possibilities. David took them resolutely. He went up to Hebron, taking with him his whole family, his two wives Ahinoam from Jezreel and Abigail from Maon.[19] He was also accompanied by the men 'who were with him', each with his family, whom he settled in places around Hebron. In practice, this meant that David took up residence in the centre of Judah with all his personal power. We do not know whether he gave up Ziklag completely. Perhaps he left occupying troops behind.

David was at the disposal of his men of Judah. He was a factor, a power in the land, which could not be overlooked. The words which are added in v.4 to the brief account of this total revolution (II Sam.2.1–3) seem almost a matter of course: 'And the men of Judah came, and there they anointed David king over the house of Judah.' Was this David's ultimate intention? The possibility cannot be excluded. The signs of the time were in his favour. Saul was dead, Ephraim had been defeated. The men of Judah were not affected by what Abner did with Ishbaal in Mahanaim. They, or at any rate the troops with David, put him on the throne as being the most powerful man. They anointed him king[20] 'over the house of Judah'. He had known how to make friends by distributing the Amalekite plunder; they may have hoped that he had the trust of the Philistines and represented a kind of personal guarantee against the Philistine danger. In terms of both domestic and foreign policy the step taken by the men of Judah was understandable, well-considered and timely.

> From the very beginning, David's kingdom had a different character from that of Saul. Saul had come from the tradition of charismatic leaders. He was a military king and the king of a nation, though he did not have a secure and permanent foundation among the tribes. He had no residence, and no effective administration. David was never a charismatic leader. He was a warrior from the start, supported by his troops and their successes, and independent of tribal control and of the levy. David became king over the territory of his tribe by virtue of being so to speak a 'proven' man. He ruled over a 'national' group which was in one sense limited, but whose territory and purpose was far more closely defined than Saul's complex 'empire'. David's kingdom in Judah had a firm foundation and seemed likely to last. The Philistines did not intervene in this development. The transference of David's activities back to Judah did not limit their sphere of influence; it protected them from attacks and could only benefit them as long as it could contain the forces in Ephraim. Whether the Philistines in fact calculated in this fashion remains an open question. In any event it was important to keep an eye on the resourceful David.

There are reliable indications that David pursued further political aims. Hardly had he been anointed in Hebron when he sent men to Jabesh in Gilead with a message of gratitude to the Jabeshites for their kindness in having buried Saul in their city. He ends it with the diplomatic phrase: 'Now therefore let your hands be strong, and be valiant; for Saul your lord is dead, and the house of Judah has anointed me king over them' (II Sam.2.7). This is more than a greeting and a report. The delegation to Jabesh does not declare war, it brings a message of sympathy; but between the lines there is dynamite! David declares himself ready to fight wherever and in whatever way his intervention may be possible and necessary. Another move points in the same direction, and even more clearly. When Abner begins to detach himself from Ishbaal and seeks the first contacts with David, in II Sam. 3, the latter suddenly makes the unexpected demand that Abner is not to appear before him without bringing Saul's daughter Michal. David also makes the same request directly to Ishbaal.

> There was something special about Michal. She had been given by Saul to David during his first battles with the Philistines on certain conditions. Later, when David was waging war in Judah, the two had separated. Michal was married again to a certain Paltiel. Now, when matters had come to a head in Ephraim, David used the first opportunity to ask for Michal back again – his former wife who was also the daughter of Saul. We may guess the background. Through Michal David had married into Saul's stock and was husband to one of the true claimants to the throne of Israel. His request was a challenge to Israel and was an opportunity of testing the honesty of the other side.

Abner did in fact take Michal with him to David. Her parting from Paltiel at Bahurim is touching; he weeps. The reader does not hear of Michal's reaction, but she becomes David's wife. The marriage remains childless. This gives the problem of the succession a dramatic turn. It can hardly be disputed that David asked for this wife back again for more than personal reasons. He intended to use her one day as pledge for a policy which extended beyond Judah.[21]

With Abner's attempt at mediation in Hebron (II Sam. 3) and its consequences, which finally led to the transference of the rule over Israel to David, we reach the point at which the continuous account of David's history was interrupted earlier. It may be seen that he did not attack Saul's old kingdom by force of arms, nor did he exploit the vacuum which had arisen by the murders of Abner and Ishbaal to hasten on too actively a union of Ephraim and Judah. His careful tactics need not be suspected as a fiction put forward by a subsequent tendentious account.

Transference of rule over the northern tribes to David brought about a personal union; it did not establish a completely united state. Judah and Israel retained their independence, and also retained their own group consciousnesses. They merely accepted the sovereignty of David. No more could be expected to begin with. The tribal structure still predominated, and the monarchy was still in its infancy as a new form of rule and organization.

There is no mistaking the increased power at David's disposal, which was greater than that of any previous Israelite leader. He had his own band of mercenaries, was commander of the host of Judah and could levy the host of Israel. Of course this increase in power was not to the liking of the Philistines, who had hoped, rather, for opposition between Judah and Israel. David now confronted them with concentrated power. II Samuel 5.17 clearly reflects their reaction: 'When the Philistines heard that David had been anointed king over Israel, all the Philistines went up (into the hill-country) in search of David . . .' They take quite a different course from their battle against Saul. They do not attempt to roll forward a front line from the area of the plain of Megiddo into the hill-country, but make a thrust into the heart of David's own territory, in the area of the southern chain of fortifications. It looks as if they wanted to drive a wedge at this point between the territories of Israel and Judah, in order to split David's new constellation of power once again.

In II Samuel 5.17–25 we in fact have accounts of two clashes between David and the Philistines, both of which took place quite near to Jerusalem: west of the city, as might be expected. The Philistines first occupied the plain of Rephaim, and the attack took place on its southern edge, by the sanctuary of Baal-perazim on mount Perazim.[22] David emerged the victor in the first skirmish, probably because of his good knowledge of Philistine methods of fighting and with the help of his adaptable mercenaries. The defeat did not quieten the Philistines. 'Opposite the balsam trees'[23] in the plain of Rephaim there was a new encounter (II Sam. 5.23), but that was the last. We do not hear of any more Philistine attacks. David was finally able to remove this threat from Israel and Judah.

These clashes had indicated the danger which was still presented by the southern chain of fortifications, as these were still not completely in David's hands. The Jebusites still lived in Jerusalem; the two territories over which David ruled were still separated by a city and its terrain which had so far been able to assert its independence and which must inevitably have looked like an alien body in the context of the new constellation of power. However, David had special plans for Jerusalem. Because of its situation, the city was best suited to become his residence. Hebron, where David had been king for seven and a half years, was a brilliant centre for greater Judah. But it lay well outside the centre of the extended Israelite territory. It might have seemed possible to make, say, Shechem a residence instead of Jerusalem, as it was an old centre of power for Ephraim and central Palestine. But Shechem lay too far to the north for Judah.

Jerusalem offered the best conditions for David's plan of ruling the two parts of his state from a point which lay exactly between them. But he had to decide to which of his territories he was going to assign the city when it belonged to him. He could not neglect the interests of Judah, nor could he underestimate the claims of the Benjaminites, who could best extend their territory as far as the city. He hit upon the wise solution of assigning Jerusalem officially to neither state; he regarded it as *his* city, an independent city state which belonged to him alone. Jerusalem was given the full status of a capital, but to a certain degree it remained extra-territorial in relation to the areas belonging to the surrounding tribes. Yet how was it possible in practical terms to give Jerusalem this special status right from the beginning?

David did not take possession of the city with the help of the armies of either Judah or Israel, but with his own mercenaries alone (II Sam. 5.6, 'the king and his men'). He won the city for himself by his own means, which on the one hand guaranteed him military success and on the other excluded the claims and privileges of others, from wherever these might be sought.

The account of the conquest of Jerusalem appears in II Sam. 5.6–8. Unfortunately it is fraught with a number of difficulties which can no longer be resolved. The text contains a puzzling saying, perhaps the fragment of a proud speech by the Jebusites: 'You will not come in here, but the blind and lame will ward you off.' The Jebusites may have felt so safe in their city that if necessary it could have been left to even the blind and the lame to drive David away. Verse 8, which mentions climbing the *ṣinnōr*, prompted archaeological investigations. This will be a reference to part of the subterranean water system which had been constructed from the spring of Gihon on the eastern slope of the old city to the interior of the city. It consisted of a short tunnel and then a shaft, steep in places, leading upwards under the city wall to an entry within the city. Thus in times of war the inhabitants of Jerusalem had access unobtrusively to a spring lying well down the slope; David and his men used the shaft so to speak in the reverse direction, once they had found the entrance. David's remarks in the parallel account in I Chron. 11.6–8 are also illuminating: 'Whoever shall smite the Jebusites first shall be chief (*rōš*) and commander (*śar*). And Joab the son of Zeruiah went up first, so he became chief.' According to this, the occupation of Jerusalem could in fact have been connected with a heroic achievement involving a climb into the interior of the city. Whatever the verdict on these traditions, they remain symptomatic of the difficulties presented even to an experienced troop like that of David in the occupation of a fortified city.[24]

There is no indication that in the course of the capture of Jerusalem a city-king residing there had to be removed, as was often the case in Canaanite cities. It is not impossible that Jerusalem, like Shechem, had an aristocratic constitution. It is in accord with a generous approach to conditions and institutions existing within captured territory that David did not commandeer the so-called threshing-floor of Araunah, the later site of the temple and the palace, but obtained it by a legal purchase (II Sam. 24.20–25).[25] Another significant indication of respect for existing circumstances is the fact that David did not name the city which he had captured 'the city of David', as was probably his original idea (II Sam. 5.7), but kept its traditional name.[26]

In one respect, however, David felt it necessary to give Jerusalem a special status and a special importance in the eyes of the tribes of Ephraim and Israel. He gave it a special sacral status. One of the first actions that we hear of after the capture of the city is the bringing of the ark of Yahweh to Jerusalem (II Sam. 6). It had most recently been kept in the ancient city of Kiriath-jearim, which belonged to Benjamin, having been set up there after a number of adventures. In the meantime the sanctuary of Shiloh had probably been destroyed. We do not, of course, know of any cultic function performed by the ark there. Beyond question, it was a significant holy object for Ephraim and Benjamin; we can discover nothing about its possible significance for Judah in the period before the monarchy.[27] We may therefore assume that in taking over this object David not only promised to heighten the significance of the local sanctuary of Jerusalem but at the same time forged a sacral link between the northern tribes and his new residence. Remarkably enough, however, at a later date, after the collapse of the personal union, those who belonged to the northern state of Israel never expressly laid claim to the ark, but regarded its location in Jerusalem as final.[28]

The capture of Jerusalem by David and the elevation of the city to the status of a capital on the border between the territories of Judah and Israel unmistakably introduced a development which was of supreme significance for events in the country, and particularly for the city, long after the Davidic period. Jerusalem, high in the hills, relatively isolated, not at the crossroads of the great trade routes and geographically separated from the heart of the territory of the tribe of Judah, ultimately owed its rise solely to David's initiative. 'Almost overnight the stunted city state becomes the centre of a kingdom which embraces the whole of Palestine.'[29] The deeper reason for this revolution is to be found not least in the history of the settlement and the topography of central Palestine. At first Judah and Ephraim made no contact. The barrier of the Jebusite fortress of Jerusalem and its narrow approaches prevented the bridge-building which David achieved by force through the far-sighted calculation of political perspectives. Of course he could not realize that at the same time he was laying the foundation for the subsequent importance of the 'holy city' in world history.

From his new capital David could first rule over Israel and Judah within their traditional boundaries. In addition, he seems to have worked consistently at consolidating the area of his territorial possessions in Palestine, not least to ward off danger from his nearer neighbours. It is said that he humbled the Philistines and took the 'bridle' out of their hands (II Sam.8.1).[30] However, the way in which he exercised lordship over the Philistines remains obscure. Nothing is said about an occupation of their cities. The real evidence that makes possible the reconstruction of all David's territory is a designation of boundaries in connection with the census of all men capable of bearing arms (II Sam.24.5–7).

David sent out officers, and the course which they took is described. It begins in Arnon, in southern Transjordania, runs northwards through the territories of Gad and Gilead into the area of the *'ajlūn* and extends northwards again into the 'land of the Hittites'. [31] The land west of the Jordan is then crossed from the north: Dan, Tyre and the city states of the coastal plain north and south of Carmel, then through Judah as far as Beer-sheba. Their route took the officers 'through all the cities of the Hivites and Canaanites'. Thus they will have gone primarily through the territory occupied by the pre-Israelite population, and not through the territory of the states of Israel and Judah. According to the information that we have, they in fact moved only in the border territories of

Palestine. This probably presupposes that all these areas were in fact under David's control; possibly the purpose of his action was to form a picture of the total number of troops in the contingents from those areas which had newly come under his dominion.

We may conclude from this that David succeeded where Saul failed in taking the step from a national to a territorial state, to a 'kingdom' with more or less fixed boundaries, to a territory and not just a tribal alliance, under the authority of the king. But this state had to be purchased through the incorporation of other ethnic groups, who necessarily had different religious practices from those of the Israelites. The Canaanites and with them to some degree also parts of the Philistine population became more or less equal members of this Davidic state. As a result, the chain of fortified cities known to us from Judg. 1 lost its dangerous divisive effect in power politics and military activity, though it remained to the degree that the influence of these cities and their surrounding districts with Canaanite population was brought to bear more closely than before through the more intimate contact with Israel. The result was that the so-called 'Canaanite problem' became not only an acute domestic political difficulty but also above all a religious danger. There was an acceleration in the process of assimilation, of the mixing of religion and culture, which was necessarily bound up with closer personal and family ties.

From now on the coastal plains ceased to be significant as centres of independent political power. The focal point of state government and religious influence had finally been transferred to the hill-country. The state of Israel and Judah increased in strength and became an independent force in the development of political power in the context of the Syrian states.

Of course, this process should not be over-estimated. A complete 'assimilation' of such disparate elements did not take place so quickly within a tribal alliance comprising a number of members which had itself developed with speed towards political independence. The development of the states shows that in Judah people continued to think in terms of Judah and in Israel in terms of Israel, not to mention the surviving popular consciousness of the Philistines. Boundaries were already being shifted on the fringes of Israelite settlement in the post-Solomonic era, and independent Philistine city rulers reappeared in the Assyrian period.[32] The picture of the Davidic state alliance is a variegated one. But it was now by no means limited to the territorial state outlined above. David had reached out far beyond his boundaries, and had officially been compelled to do so.

At first he had hostile neighbours to the east and south-east. The great clash with the Ammonites appears in the well-known account of the Ammonite war in II Sam. 10.1–11.1 + 12.26–31, into which has been inserted the story of David and Bathsheba and Nathan's conversation with David ('You are the man!'), alongside the highly dramatic preparations for the choice of the successor to the throne.[33] Uriah, Bathsheba's husband, falls in the fight against the Ammonites. Their kingdom passes to David, so that Ammon now belongs in a personal union with Judah and Israel, but has a lower status: the Ammonites are made to provide forced labour.

II Samuel 8 summarizes both the expansion of the territory of the Davidic state and the territorial and political integration of the old and potentially new opponents of Israel. The distinctions it draws are convincing. Edom becomes a province under governors appointed by David. The old native monarchy is abolished. The kings of the Moabites become vassals of David and are forced to pay tribute.

Unfortunately we do not have the confirmation we would like of David's intervention in the territory of the Aramaean states in Syria, which for a long time had exercised virtually no influence on the consolidation of the Israelite tribes in Palestine. We can understand the particular occasion for the action against the Aramaeans from II Sam. 10.6. The Ammonites had summoned the troops of a series of larger or smaller Aramaean principalities to help in the fight against David; these had come into being in northern Transjordania and southern Syria. After his victory over the Ammonites, David directed his attack against their allies. Prominent among his Aramaean opponents was king Hadadezer of Zobah in the region of the Antilebanon, north of Damascus. He seems to have ruled over an area which included northern Transjordania, probably also the land round Damascus and further Aramaean territories in northern Syria as far as the neighbourhood of the Euphrates. The question is, how far could David have extended his sphere of rule northwards after he had defeated the king of Zobah? The Old Testament account (II Sam. 8.3–10) leads one to believe that David captured considerable booty in Syria, including ore in great quantity, which was controlled by Hadadezer because of the deposits in the plain between the two Lebanons. David set up his own officials in Damascus, which will already have been under the sway of Zobah's state, and exacted tribute through them. The king of Hamath on the Orontes (present-day *ḥama* in central Syria) acted in a different way. He sent congratulations and gifts of homage to David, either as a protective measure or as an offer of vassalship. The king of Hamath was an old enemy of Hadadezer of Zobah.[34]

We may imagine that the territories of Zobah and the state of Damascus, south of the state of Hamath, with which alliances were made and from which tribute was levied, formed the northern and north-eastern boundaries of David's effective sphere of influence. David's exercise of power may also have extended this far.[35] In addition, it has come to seem probable that after David's victory over Hadadezer a number of Syrian states as far as the Euphrates who had been in close contact with Hadadezer as a result of personal unions likewise acknowledged David's sovereignty, and that the one dangerous outsider, the king of Hamath, expressly demonstrated his subjection.[36] Such a considerable extension of David's influence is indeed conceivable, but it cannot be confirmed explicitly by non-biblical sources. However, the notes in the Bible themselves make a gradual differentiation in the outer areas of David's sphere of influence very probable, first through states paying tribute, and then through those who offered him peaceful recognition. This assumption is confirmed to some degree by the friendly relations which David must have had with the Phoenician coastal states; we know nothing of any clashes which he may have had with them.[37]

This seems to be sufficient definition of the apparatus of David's state with its degrees of dependence: the personal union of Judah and Israel at its heart; the securing of the coastal plains after the military defeat of the Philistines; the subjugation of Transjordania by a differentiated system of vassal and tribute-paying states, whose connection with the centre grew weaker, the greater the distance from Jerusalem. (This can be seen most clearly in connection with the Syrian city states.) At one point, in I Kings 5.1, we hear that Solomon 'ruled from the river (Euphrates) to the land of the Philistines and the frontier of Egypt'. This is an ideal extension of the empire of Israel and Judah, and does not represent the actual situation in the case of either Solomon or David without qualification. In any case, the 'frontier of Egypt' was the *wādi el-'arīsh* in the north of the Sinai peninsula, later often called the 'Brook of Egypt', although it was only half-way to Egypt. We cannot suppose that either David or even Solomon succeeded in subjugating the whole world of Syrian city states as far as the Euphrates in the sense of conquering them by military means. However, David's historical achievements certainly do not pale in the light of so ambitious an ideal. His kingdom, with its variety of territories, has rightly been called an 'empire',[38] and represents an achievement of considerable solidity and force in the context of the situation of Israel in the early days of the monarchy. At this point in history the balance between the great powers was in David's favour, and made this empire possible, at least for a short time.

The formation of the Davidic empire was the personal achievement of the king. It was aided by the crisis in the Egyptian empire to the south; after the end of the Ramessids in the Twenty-first Dynasty, this empire fell into two halves, with one complex of power to the north and another to the south.[39] Smendes and Tentamun reigned in the north, while the sacred city of Thebes developed in the south. This was the period of Egyptian weakness illustrated so vividly by the travel report of Wen-amun. Egypt had lost its influence on Palestine; the Philistine settlement had already prepared the decline of its powers. The empires in the north were likewise in no position to embark on expansionist policies. The Hittites had long been robbed of their influence; the Sea-peoples had already set foot at least on the Syrian coast, and the Aramaeans were pressing in from the east and founding their states. All these factors restricted Assyrian military power. The rise and establishment of the Davidic state, the first really Israelite constitution with independent power, took place in the shadow of this remarkable change in the history of the Near East about 1000 BC. David warded off the dangers threatening from surrounding principalities striving towards independence, the Philistines, Ammonites, Moabites, Edomites and Aramaeans in Syria, by military superiority and diplomatic skill.

David was able to establish and sustain his empire not least because he had an adequate base for his foreign policy within his kingdom. This he gradually created for himself. The development of his army was only one side of the matter; he was also concerned to found a capital and court of his own and to develop an independent state administration.

Jerusalem was to become a capital and could not remain a military base. We have only very sparse accounts of the development of the city in the time of David. He restored the city walls and had a residence built for himself. At the beginning it is certainly going too far to talk of a 'palace' (cf. II Sam.5.11). The city was narrow and the possibilities of extending it on the south-east hill were limited. According to the new excavations of R. de Vaux and K. M. Kenyon on the south-east hill,[40] we must imagine that the earliest city developed on the side of the hill in the same way as the modern suburb of *silwān*, on the opposite side of the Kidron valley. There will have been tightly-packed houses in a situation where expansion was barely possible.[41] One need only think of the scene involving David and Bathsheba. From the roof of his house the king could easily watch the intimate domestic details of life in the neighbouring houses below! This was very like suburban life in modern terms. For topographical reasons, the best direction for extending the city by constructing large buildings was northwards. Here the temple and palace were later built, on the threshing-floor of Araunah, which David himself is said to have bought.[42] To begin with, however, the ark was given emergency quarters (see II Sam. 7.1–6). At first there will have been no increase in population in the new circumstances. Mercenaries and officials will have had to be near David and at his disposal, but the peasant farmers of Israel and Judah will have had neither reason nor occasion to change their ways. We have a good, though perhaps exceptional example of this in Barzillai's refusal to accept David's offer of honourable care in the new capital.[43] Barzillai wants to die in *his* city by the tombs of his father and mother! By contrast, it is typical that Bathsheba, the wife of an army commander, lives in Jerusalem.

Lastly, Jerusalem had and retained the character of an 'international' city whose population was composed not only of the earlier inhabitants but also of quite new elements. It was a city which belonged neither to Judah nor to Israel, but was almost an alien body within the new state.

David distributed the burdens of government over a series of officials, whose names we have in two lists which hardly differ from each other.[44] Both mention two military officials, first the office of the *'al haṣṣaba'*, the one set 'over the army'. We already have similar evidence of this rank under Saul;[45] it must denote the commander of the army. Then comes the rank of the *'al hakkerētī we'al happelētī*, the man over the 'Cherethites and Pelethites'; all we know about him indicates that this was the supreme officer of the mercenary troops.[46] Both commanders were directly under the king's orders; both lists mention Joab as commander of the army and Benaiah as commander of the mercenaries.

Of the other high state officials, the most striking are the *sōpēr*, literally 'scribe', and the *mazkīr*, which is best translated 'herald'. J. Begrich saw the functions of these two officials as being parallel to those of two high Egyptian administrative posts,[47] which are there described as *sš* ('scribe') and *whm.w*. As well as the supreme royal scribe, the Egyptians had a 'spokesman' or 'herald'. He may well have been comparable to the Davidic *mazkīr* in function, if not in the etymology of the title.[48] The Egyptian official was both master of ceremonies and secretary of state, who had to be approached for an audience with the king. The office was certainly more developed by tradition in Egypt than could have been the case at the tiny court in Jerusalem, which was still in its infancy. But a comparison is also justified because the tradition and practice of foreign courts were certainly in many respects the model for the royal institutions in Jerusalem.

In the later list of officials in II Sam. 20.24 we also find the post of the minister of forced labour, the *'al hammas*. This will probably have come into being only during the course of time under the pressure of new measures, above all the building plans which may have developed in the state. Priests also appear among the state officials; these will be primarily those who were active in the temple in Jerusalem. The names include that of the priest Zadok, whose family was to rise to such exclusive priestly dignity in Jerusalem under Solomon. His derivation has been a source of much puzzlement. There is something to be said for the hypothesis that this Zadok was a member of the native priesthood of Jerusalem which was taken over by David and that his family had something to do with the ancient Melchizedek, the second element in whose name is identical with Zadok.[49] Questions remain open here.

II Samuel 8.18 mentions sons of David as priests. Possibly the king himself had priestly prerogatives, of which he made use in bringing in the ark (II Sam. 6), dancing before the ark and finally himself blessing the people. However, we do not know of any other appearance of David as priest. The priestly sons of David do not appear in the list of officials in II Sam. 20.23–25.

There would be problems in suggesting the theory of a 'priest kingship' for the sons of David on the basis of these scattered notes. There can be no question of it in the special circumstances of the Davidic court.[50] We should also remember that the particular circumstances which led to the appointment of priests to a narrow sphere of functions which was not without reference to the specific features of Yahwistic religion, in the religious isolation of the royal capital of Jerusalem, was not burdened with the fundamental problems that can be found elsewhere. Within more developed nations a cluster of ideas had arisen which defined the king as a cultic official because of the priestly function of his office.

In Judah and Israel kings played a role in the cultic sphere only in instituting state sanctuaries. Otherwise they did not. But these sanctuaries were not the real centres of religious life in the tribes; this was no more true of Jerusalem than it was later of the royal sanctuaries in Bethel and Dan. Thus the transference of cultic traditions to Jerusalem and the construction of a specifically Jerusalemite cult tradition should be regarded, at least during the monarchy, as the expression of a development originally bound up with the royal sanctuary and its sphere of influence. Only later was it seen as belonging to 'all Israel'.[51]

All the offices mentioned here are state offices within the entourage of the king of Jerusalem. They are in his charge and strictly speaking have little to do with the ongoing ordering of the tribes and their internal structure. Independently of the tribes and virtually without them, there arose on its own territory between the states of Judah and Israel a state government in Jerusalem, an administrative centre, the centre of a power with its own laws. The tribes allowed this to happen. But they lost influence over this new development; they failed to develop a political concern of their own. Apparently the initiative went over entirely to the king and his officials. The functioning of the state rested on the personality of the king, who largely also enjoyed the trust of the tribes, but himself resided in 'his city'.

David's action in the Ammonite war shows the degree to which he had given up the principles of a military kingship. He directed the decisive events from his residence without being present in person. First he observed the course of operations from the capital, had reports brought to him and had the meeting with Bathsheba. He only involved himself personally in the last stages of the war, to bring it to an end in person and enjoy the fruits of victory where they had been earned (II Sam. 12.28–31). He behaved in the same way at the end of Absalom's rebellion, when he kept out of the decisive battle at Mahanaim in Transjordania and waited for news (II Sam. 18.19–19.9). Thus the king attained a special position which on the one hand threatened to alienate him from his troops,[52] and on the other gave his office the status of an ideal. It helped to create an aura round his person which was taken up in the formation of court tradition.

These considerations are by no means irrelevant to the question of the development of a kingly ritual in Judah which deliberately took over and assimilated alien notions,[53] and also demanded something like an 'imperial ideology' which sought to consolidate the state alliance made through personal union in a single state. With some justification, the time of David, and later still more strongly the time of Solomon, was seen as a period in which the earlier traditions of Israel and Judah were collected and given fixed form; they were also regarded as the common possession of Israel and Judah. Implicitly or explicitly, behind this development stood the wish for a single Israel, which seemed to have been realized under David, and now sought expression in forms which involved 'all Israel'. This reflective activity is suggested not only by the particular form of history-writing about the period of David and Solomon, but also by the association of David and Solomon in the tradition with individual contributions in the sphere of culture. They cultivated 'poetry' and 'wisdom', which were furthered and valued as a result of the existence of the central court and its intellectual atmosphere.[54] It may be only a hypothesis, but it is highly probable that the conception of an 'all Israel' which now in fact embraced twelve tribes was only really born at this time. At first this may have been an ideal conception formed in Jerusalem, which understood the Davidic empire of the present to have grown from the traditions of history[55] and which took up the number twelve as a mark of completeness, not least in order to represent the state alliance as a work of the divine promise. We cannot rule out the possibility that principles of 'amphictyonic' collaboration from the tribal period had an influence here. But the ordering of the traditions and the formation of them into a consistent idea of a 'people' with ethnic and national contours, with its own national awareness, could only be developed to the full under the impact of the formation of the Davidic state. The evidence from the period before the foundation of the state is so constituted that it does not compel the conclusion that such ideas were developed at an earlier date.

The Old Testament tradition makes it quite clear that such a new constitution for Israel and Judah inevitably made the question of David's successor a particularly pressing one. That the solution to this problem took place in quite exceptional circumstances, one might almost say 'in the inner circle' in Jerusalem, and met with ultimate success, is a feature of the new situation where decisions were made in the court without recognizable reference being made to the tribes. The way towards the solution was fraught with difficult problems, and what was said of the independence of David's court and politics has its counterpart in the state crises which show how unstable an element northern Israel could prove to be within the state.

The historical problem of the succession to David is the subject of the tradition known as the 'succession narrative' and recognizable in II Sam.7; 9–20 and I Kings 1.1–2.11. This group of chapters is centred on the question of the successor to David, even where that is not explicitly mentioned. The rebellions of Absalom (II Sam. 15–19) and Sheba (II Sam. 20) have their own significance in this context. These were the acute crises experienced in the heart of David's empire, crises which were decisive for its survival and which in the last resort could put in question the permanence of David's achievements.

II Samuel 7 has been much discussed.[56] It sets out the programme for the succession to the throne and takes up in an independent context problems which followed from the existence of the dynastic principle in the house of David. The conviction that the ruler from David's line was accepted and legitimated as a son of Yahweh justifies the dynastic concept at the highest level, but in this form can only be the result of historical experiences. This is indicated not least by the adoption of a stereotyped literary form in which this 'dynastic promise' appears.[57] It achieved theological significance as the nucleus of the 'messianic' idea which expressed the conviction that a future ruler, often envisaged in ideal terms, would arise from the house of David. This idea even outlived the time when the monarchy was a reality in Israel and Judah.

The historical presuppositions for a dynastic succession in the house of David were by no means self-evident. David must first have intended to have as successor a son from his marriage with Michal, Saul's daughter. This would have produced a natural balance between Judah and Israel. Israel would have been able to see the heritage of Saul continued in a son by Michal.[58] But David's marriage to Michal remained childless.[59] The next possibilities seemed to be sons by the wives whom David had in Hebron.[60] But he seems never to have made up his mind completely about these men. Special circumstances led him to be cautious.

Amnon, the firstborn, was ruled out because of a misdemeanour. He made advances to his half-sister Tamar, who was a full sister of his brother Absalom. The latter took his revenge and killed Amnon (II Sam. 13). The second son, Chileab, is never mentioned again. His fate is unknown.

Matters became serious with the third son, Absalom. After killing Amnon, he at first went into exile. David made his return possible after a struggle. Absalom, a man with a good opinion of himself,[61] but not endowed in every respect with the diplomatic skill of his father, tried in his own way to gain the trust of the Israelites in the northern state. In the early morning he would intercept at the city gate of Jerusalem petitioners who came from 'one of the tribes of Israel', i.e. from the northern kingdom. Absalom promised to present their cases to the king. With his exaggerated affability he combined the wish, 'Oh that I were judge in the land!' By using the term *šōpēṭ* Absalom tried to associate himself with the best Israelite traditions. In this way he sought to 'steal the hearts of the men of Israel' (II Sam. 15.1–6). He evidently exploited a mood of hostility towards the king among the Ephraimite tribes and incorporated it in his further plans.

He obtained permission from the king to go to Hebron, allegedly to fulfil a vow. The undertaking appeared harmless, but Absalom took 200 men with him as guests to the feast. He had secretly informed the 'tribes of Israel' that on an agreed signal they should proclaim, 'Absalom has become king in Hebron'. This 'in Hebron' has given rise to the hypothesis that the whole of David's territory, in both Israel and Judah, had been instructed, and that people every-where were waiting for Absalom's signal. But in fact Absalom's journey to Hebron misled not only David and the men of Jerusalem 'but also the modern historian' (Alt). The latter might believe that in Hebron Absalom attempted to win Judah to his side, in order to take over the whole state with the help of Judah.[62] But the further course of Absalom's rebellion makes it clear that in this conflict Judah remained neutral. Absalom's plan was different. From the beginning he wanted the northern state of Israel to rise against David, so that with its help David, Jerusalem and Judah would fall into his hands. By exploiting internal differences, Absalom had conceived his rebellion in such a way that he could make a thrust against Jerusalem in the south, from Hebron, while the men of Israel could seize David in a pincer movement from the north.

This plan to encircle David in Jerusalem failed because the king surprisingly left the city and crossed the Jordan. He may have foreseen that Absalom would fail in Jerusalem. Absalom found the city open to him and was unwise enough to establish himself there, while David and his mercenaries operated outside the city and found time to gather strength. Absalom was at a loss. He rejected Ahithophel's sage advice to pursue David immediately and to strike him wherever he was, He followed the counsel of Hushai, a man from the king's entourage, who suggested that he should wait and assemble a host against David.[63] Ahithophel saw the catastrophe that would come and committed suicide. Delay on the part of Absalom could only benefit David. The Israelite host and David's mercenaries met south of the Jabbok. The decision was made in the forest of Ephraim,[64] not far from Mahanaim, where the king was staying. The forest action brought doom to the unwieldy Israelite army and not least to Absalom himself. As he fled from the fight, his long hair was caught in the branches of a tree and the horse he was riding went on from under him. Joab killed him. The trumpets were blown and the battle was broken off. Its aim had been achieved. Absalom was dead, and the threat of the rebellion was removed. There could be no further question of fighting against Israel.

The situation which had arisen was nevertheless unique. The rebellion had been overthrown, but the king was not at home in his residence, in that city which belonged neither to one state nor to the other. Israel, which for the most part had followed Absalom, found itself in a precarious situation *vis-à-vis* the king. Did it face punishment from the king? Should it pay homage to the king once again? Judah had kept out of the rebellion; it was most able to do something for David. II Samuel 19 reports the fatal situation clearly enough. There was a dispute among the northern tribes over what to do next. They knew about David's achievements, and had to take seriously the fact that Absalom was dead. There was an increasing inclination to return to David. Then the king himself intervened. He opened negotiations with the elders of Judah through the Jerusalem priests, asking them to make a demonstration by bringing him back as king. David wanted to be legitimated anew through the initiative of his men of Judah. They stood by him 'as one man' (II Sam.19.14). The king crossed the Jordan at Gilgal and received the homage of the men of Judah and also of the Israelites, who came to him in a delegation. Nevertheless, there was again a discussion as to who was to be the first to claim the king for themselves. Men of Israel and men of Judah expressed their rivalry in strong words.

Nevertheless, the situation in the northern state of Israel remained tense. David was anxious that the whole of the northern territory might not be behind him. Opposition escalated into open conflict when the Benjaminite Sheba ben Bichri produced the dangerous slogan, 'We have no portion in David, and we have no inheritance in the son of Jesse; every man to his tents, O Israel' (II Sam.

20.1). The final summons was that normally issued to the host, to return home after battle. But here it is a cry that Israel should look to itself and break off relationships with David. Sheba found a number of supporters, while Judah remained faithful to David. So David mustered both the army and his mercenaries and succeeded in pushing Sheba and his people further and further north. Sheba seems to have taken refuge in Abel-beth-maacah.[65] 'A wise woman' there negotiated with David's commander Joab and declared that Abel Beth-maacah was a peaceful and loyal city, a 'mother in Israel'. No hands were to be laid on it. Joab agreed but asked for Sheba to be surrendered. His head was thrown over the wall. The rebel was dead. The war was at an end, as with Absalom. Israel yielded and waged no new conflicts with king David.

Nevertheless, Sheba's rebellion marks an important situation. Hitherto recognition of David by the northern state of Israel had rested on a voluntary basis, and Israel had acknowledged David afresh after Absalom's rebellion. But now David had a justifiable reason for subjugating Israel by military means. Forces had emerged which would stop at nothing to break the personal union. In Israel there were evidently many people who were reluctant to accept the authority of the government in Jerusalem. What had earlier rested on a free decision now took the form of the necessary acknowledgment of the superior party. Israel remained quiet because it could do nothing against the south. This development was unsound, even if for the moment there were no further struggles.

The succession narrative, to which these accounts of Absalom and Sheba belong, makes it clear that considerable danger could confront the whole kingdom from internal crises, even from the circles of the king's own sons. The question of David's successor became more and more urgent, and more and more difficult. The concluding section of the succession narrative, I Kings 1.2–2.11, shows how it was finally decided.

We are given a glimpse of circumstances at the court in Jerusalem at the time when David had grown old. Parties had formed, concerned not least with who would hold power in the state in future. On the one side was the party of Adonijah, David's next son after Solomon, and the man who had first claim to the throne. Important people followed him: Joab, the commander of the army, and Abiathar, the priest. On the other side was a no less significant group: Zadok the priest, Benaiah, the commander of the mercenaries, and Nathan, who appeared more as a privy councillor than as a prophet, and who was evidently a minister with special responsibilities in the immediate entourage of the king. It is interesting that there was a split in both the army and the priesthood. There was one commander and one priest in each party. We are also told that the mercenaries under Benaiah followed their commander.

Developments reached a dramatic climax. Adonijah arranged a sacrifical meal with his people at the spring of Rogel,[66] right next to Jerusalem. We are given no details (I Kings 1.9, 10). In the course of the further dramatic account we are told how David, chiefly under the influence of his counsellor Nathan, who knows how to make skilful use of Bathsheba, is more or less compelled to name Solomon, Bathsheba's son, as his successor. The anointing of the new king takes place immediately at the spring of Gihon, with the participation of the royal party: Zadok the priest, Nathan and the mercenaries with Benaiah at their head. The rejoicing over the new king reaches the men of the other party, with Adonijah, who are holding their feast within earshot at the spring of Rogel in the Kidron valley. When Adonijah's followers hear that the anointing of Solomon has formally taken place, they immediately leave their claimant to the throne. He is finally excluded from the succession, and fears pursuit from the anointed ruler. He seeks protection in the sanctuary. Solomon assures him that his person will not be violated so long as he remains loyal.

The succession narrative leaves open a number of questions of detail. It is shot through with intrigue. But the decision has been made. According to the custom of Judah, Solomon, like David, was anointed by a small group of leading men, apparently without being previously designated *nāgīd*, a title which is in fact only known from Israel. Solomon's succession laid the foundation for the dynastic principle. It was not least in accordance with political necessity. David had to take care to assure the continued existence of the state and the territories dependent on it by making the course of the succession quite clear; not the least of the necessary presuppositions was the preservation of the personal union with Israel.[67] The Davidic empire was a unique creation, but a product of history, subjected to conflicting trends from within and threatened by dangers from without. David's successor took over a great heritage, but it was not without its difficulties.

David is said to have died after reigning for forty years. Solomon, too, is said to have reigned for forty years (I Kings 11.42). Given that Solomon died about 930 BC,[68] it may be said that David's rule should be put about 1000 BC.

A number of the details in the reports of David's reign are certainly tendentious, but the general political situation, the historical moment for Judah and Israel in which he was involved, compels the observer to the view that the essential details of the historical picture of David are accurate. The situation required an adaptable personality, which David certainly had. He was doubtless a complex figure, not without weaknesses, but a brilliant man with an eye for what was necessary and possible, diplomatic and full of ideas. Saul was rough, and still firmly rooted in the old Israelite tribal order and its bonds. David detached himself from this, founded a new style of life and contributed towards creating a new consciousness. The boldness of his plans and resolves may have been surprising; he held everything together with statesmanlike sagacity and convinced not only Judah, but ultimately also a reluctant Israel.

The complicated state structure created by David was held together, in essentials, by Solomon. As the territories bordering on the empire increasingly came to an awareness of their potentialities, hostile forces began to increase, but they were not yet fatal to the personal union in the heart of Palestine which had been taken over by Solomon. Solomon created an efficient internal administration. However, this very fact developed contrary to its purpose by furthering the divergent tendencies within the state, with drastic results, as we shall see.

NOTES

1. This is the correct form, to be found in I Chron. 8.33; 9.39. Ishbosheth is a later distortion, intended to suppress the theophorous element -baal.

2. In all probability identical with tel *ḥejāj*, only about two miles south of the Jabbok on the heights of *tulūl eḏ-ḏahab*; R. de Vaux, *RB* 47, 1938, 411ff.; id., *Vivre et Penser* I, 1941, 30f.; M. Noth, *Aufsätze* 1, 374–8; K.-D. Schunck, 'Erwägungen zur Geschichte und Bedeutung von Mahanaim', *ZDMG* 113, 1963, 34–40; see also S. Herrmann, *ZDPV* 80, 1964, 74 and pl. 2.

3. It is worth noting that Abner must have carried on special negotiations with the tribe of Benjamin to convince them of his intention (II Sam. 3.19).

4. E. Kutsch regards *bᵉrīt* at this point as being 'in all probability David's acceptance of an obligation towards the Israelites' and thus finds 'obligation' confirmed as a basic meaning for *bᵉrīt*; E. Kutsch, *Verheissung und Gesetz*, BZAW 131, 1973, 55f. However, at this particular point one just does not have the impression that anyone is accepting particular obligations (about which Kutsch can only advance hypotheses); rather, an understanding is arrived at between the partners, especially from the side of David, the one who was asked. Through the *bᵉrīt* a legal relationship is established, a treaty is concluded which 'binds' both sides and is to that degree (contra Kutsch) a 'covenant'.

5. On this see W. Richter, *ZAW* 77, 1965, 50–7; K.-D. Schunck, *Benjamin*, 1963, 124–7, differs.

6. See the material in A. R. Hulst, 'Der Name "Israel" im Deuteronomium', *OTS* 9, 1951, 65–106.

7. The passages which attach importance to the number twelve and define the *bᵉnē yiśrā'ēl* as a people of twelve tribes in distinction from *kol yiśrā'ēl* are almost exclusively passages from the Priestly Writing (P) or influenced by priestly tradition: Gen. 49.28; Exod. 28.21; 39.41; Num. 1.44; 17.17, 21; Josh. 3.12; 4.2. Ezek. 47.13 is the only passage from the prophetic writings.

8. Quite apart from the passages cited in the previous note those passages should be added where the twelve tribes are enumerated or where the order of the heads of the tribes follows a pattern of twelve: Gen. 35.23–26; Exod. 1.2–4; Num. 26.5–51; the list of the heads of the Israelite tribes in Num. 1.5–15, cf. the ordering of the camp in Num. 2.3–31 (repeated in Num. 10.14–28) and the list of the heads of tribes in Num. 7.12–83; the geographical list in Ezek. 48.1–29 also belongs to priestly tradition. It is natural to assign these patterns from the Priestly Writing and priestly tradition, which stress the number twelve so decisively and which often move in the realm of cultic ideals, to Jerusalemite tradition.

9. These considerations are supported by O. Eissfeldt, who regards the establishment of the system of twelve tribes as having many theoretical elements in it, even if it fits the situation; cf. O. Eissfeldt, 'The Hebrew Kingdom', *CAH* II, ch. 34, 1965, 12–17; S. Mowinckel regards the twelve-tribe system as a work of the Davidic period in BZAW 77 (Eissfeldt Festschrift), ²1961, 129–50; for more details relevant to the account given above see S. Herrmann, 'Autonome Entwicklungen in den Königreichen Israel und Juda', SVT 17, *Congress Volume, Rome 1968*, 1969, 139–58.

10. For the dispute over the interpretation of his name in recent times see J. J. Stamm,

'Der Name des Königs David,' SVT 7, *Congress Volume, Oxford 1959*, 1960, 165–83.

11. E. Meyer, *Geschichte des Altertums* II, 2, [3]1953, 285.

12. Other remarks made by Meyer in the same context are uncalled-for. He says that this history writing 'lacks all political and apologetic tendencies', and continues, 'The narrator looks back on the events with cool objectivity, indeed with supreme irony, and can therefore report them with incomparable vividness. Any religious colouring, and any idea of supernatural guidance is far removed from his thoughts . . .' But the persuasions and passions of the biblical author are visible at every step! This 'history-writing' draws its strength to a very great degree from the conviction of divine guidance which it pursues very closely into 'historical' and human detail. Meyer, who notices a positive lack of 'religious colouring', explains Israelite history-writing in terms of 'the unfathomable riddle of its innate gifts'. For criticism of Meyer which begins from these quotations see R. Smend, *Elemente alttestamentlichen Geschichtsdenkens*, Theologische Studien 95, 1968; for the nature and significance of the succession narrative see G. von Rad, 'The Beginnings of Historical Writing in Ancient Israel', in *The Problem of the Hexateuch*, 1966, 166–204; a thorough analysis of the material is presented by L. Rost, *Die Überlieferung von der Thronnachfolge Davids*, BWANT III, 6, 1926 (reprinted in *Das kleine Credo*, 1965, 119–253); see more recently R. Rendtorff, 'Beobachtungen zur altisraelitischen Geschichtsschreibung anhand der Geschichte vom Aufsteig Davids', in *Probleme biblischer Theologie* (von Rad Festschrift), 1971, 428–39; L. Delekat, 'Tendenz und Theologie der David-Salomo-Erzählung', in *Das ferne und nahe Wort* (Rost Festschrift), 1967, 26–36.

13. *yišay* = Jesse according to the Greek and Latin rendering of the name; the form Jesse was disseminated by the later poetry of the church, which sees *yišay* as the ancestor of the Messiah.

14. One example from the Romantic period is king Saul and David on a painting by Gerhard von Kügelgen (Caspar David Friedrich was the model for king Saul), reproduction in Haenel and Kalkschmidt, *Das alte Dresden*, 1934, 198.

15. David's home in Bethlehem of Judah need not tell against this. War service was not necessarily bound up with membership of a tribe or people.

16. One might think of the institution of slavery for debt which is described in Exod. 21.2–6. We cannot progress beyond hypotheses in the case of the hiring and assembling of mercenary troops. There was a similar instance earlier in the case of Jephthah (Judg. 11.3). In any case such armies must have had an international character. For the details of the relevant, but probably schematized list in II Sam. 23 see K. Elliger, 'Die dreissig Helden Davids', *PJB* 31, 1935, 29–75; B. Mazar, 'The Military Elite of King David', *VT* 13, 1963, 310–20.

17. *Ḥirbet qila*, north-west of Hebron on the western edge of the hill-country of Judah.

18. Location uncertain; probably on the inner edge of the southern part of the coastal plain; according to Josh. 19.5 it belonged to the tribal territory of Simeon. There is no clear evidence for locating it at *tell el-ḥuwēlife*, about nine miles north-east of Beer-sheba; cf. H. J. Stoebe, *BHH* III, 2238–41.

19. Ahinoam probably came from a Jezreel south-east of Hebron (cf. Josh.15.56; Simons, *The Geographical Texts*, 1959, 709); for Abigail from Maon (*tell ma'ín*), cf. I Sam. 25.

20. Would this have been necessary if I Sam. 16.1ff. were true? The wording of the phrase, that the anointing was done 'by the men of Judah', suggests a sovereign action of the men of Judah without any sacral concomitants; there is no mention of a priest or any other person with sacral authority. Does this suggest that from the start there was a 'secular' view of the monarchy in Judah as opposed to the more sacral institution in Israel? Cf. the consideration of the matter in Alt, *KS* II, 41f. = *Grundfragen*, 298f.; J. A. Soggin, *Das Königtum in Israel*, 64–6.

21. H. J. Stoebe, 'David und Mikal. Überlegungen zur Jugendgeschichte Davids', BZAW 77, ²1961, 224–43, has cast doubt on David's early marriage to Michal for traditio-historical reasons. On this view, David's request to Abner to bring the woman with him to Hebron emphasizes his political concerns even more clearly; similarly M. Noth, *History of Israel*, ²1960, 184 n. 1.

22. It is no longer possible to reconstruct the exact course of events; possibly David moved into the plain of Rephaim, *el-buqei'a*, from Judah in the south. It is sometimes questioned whether David was in full possession of Jerusalem at the time of these battles, and the position of the text in II Sam. 5 is therefore challenged, but no certain answer can be given. The location of Mount Perazim is unknown; for the sanctuary of Baal-perazim see the location suggested by A. Alt, *PJB* 23, 1927, 15f.

23. A place that was certainly very well known at the time.

24. K. M. Kenyon has happily confirmed the archaeological details by her excavations. From the point where the rising system of shafts can be shown, the tunnel leading from the spring of Gihon was continued, in the time of king Hezekiah as today, in a channel under the hill which is quite passable; it ends on the western side at the pool of Siloam. Cf. the details with sketches in K. M. Kenyon, *Jerusalem – Excavating 3000 Years of History*, 1967; for the system of shafts see also the earlier considerations by H. J. Stoebe, 'Die Einnahme Jerusalems und der Ṣinnor', *ZDPV* 73, 1957, 73ff.

25. For similar purchases of Canaanite territory by Israelites cf. the purchase of the cave of Machpelah by Abraham in Gen. 23 and of the hill on which Samaria was later built by Omri in I Kings 16.24.

26. The first literary mention of the city is in the execration texts; cf. K. Sethe, *Die Ächtung feindlicher Fürsten*, 1926, e. 27/28; f. 18; G. Posener, *Princes et pays*, 1940, E 45; W. Helck, *Beziehungen*, 48, 58. From the Amarna letters cf. the letter sent by Abdihiba, who was stationed in Jerusalem, Knudtzon edition nos. 285–90; *AOT*, 374–8; *TGI*, ¹1950, 23–9; ²1968, 25f.

27. Significantly II Sam. 7.6 mentions Yahweh's presence 'in the tent and in the dwelling'. Was there only a tent sanctuary in Judah, while the ark tradition belonged to the north? R. de Vaux, *Ancient Israel*, 1961, 297, supposes that the tent mentioned here which David erected for the ark was merely meant to recall the desert sanctuary and was not an independent sanctuary, the 'tent of meeting'. M. Görg, *Das Zelt der Begegnung*, BBB 27, 1967, questions whether there was any connection between the tent in Jerusalem erected to protect the ark and the tent of meeting, which could have stood in Gibeon.

28. Moreover, the kings of the northern state were to lend official support to the two state sanctuaries of Bethel and Dan not least to exclude competition from Jerusalem; however, the critic must ask whether the remarks made in I Kings 12.26–29 are not conceived of from the perspective of Jerusalem.

29. A. Alt, 'Jerusalems Aufstieg' (1925), *KS* III, 243–57, esp. 253 = *Grundfragen*, 323–37, esp. 333.

30. This probably means that David broke the hegemony of the Philistines so they could no longer keep anyone 'on the bridle'. The text literally reads 'rein of the forearm'; perhaps it is in some disorder. I Chron. 18.1 has another, unconvincing reading. Cf. the remarks by O. Eissfeldt, *ZDPV* 66, 1943, 117–9 = *Kleine Schriften* II, 455f.

31. This should be read, following a number of Septuagint manuscripts. However, it may already be an interpretation of the Masoretic text, which had become incomprehensible at this point.

32. O. Eissfeldt, 'Israelitisch-philistäische Grenzverschiebungen von David bis auf die Assyrerzeit' (1943), *Kleine Schriften* II, 453–63.

33. For the accounts of the Ammonite war, cf. L. Rost, *Das kleine Credo*, 1965, 184–9.

34. The form of his name, To'i or To'u (II Sam. 8.9f.), is a Hurrian coinage, or comes

from Asia Minor. The independence of the principality of Hamath is possibly connected with privileges from the time of Hittite supremacy in this area.

35. Earlier scholarship has on the whole made cautious decisions along these lines: cf. K. Elliger, 'Die Nordgrenze des Reiches Davids', *PJB* 32, 1936, 34–73; A. Alt, 'Das Grossreich Davids' (1950), *KS* II, 66–75 = *Grundfragen*, 338–47.

36. A. Malamat, 'Aspects of the Foreign Policies of David and Solomon', *JNES* 22, 1963, esp. 1–8; id., 'The Kingdom of David and Solomon in its Contact with Egypt and Aram Naharaim', *BA* 21, 1958, 96–102; see also G. Buccellatti, *Cities and Nations*, 1967, 143–5.

37. This was probably based on mutual benefit; one can see that it was almost a principle of Phoenician policy to create or to maintain good relationships with the interior, while themselves keeping to the narrow coastal plain. According to II Sam. 5.11 David is said to have had building material and workers brought from Phoenicia even before Solomon. There is some dispute about the position of the verse; does it belong after II Sam. 8.1–14? See M. Noth, *History of Israel*, 197 n. 2; see the thorough study by F. C. Fensham, 'The Treaty between the Israelites and Tyrians', SVT 17, 1969, 71–87, esp. 73–9.

38. Cf. the title of Alt's article, 'Das Grossreich Davids' ('David's Empire'), which has already become a classic.

39. J. Černý, 'Egypt from the Death of Ramesses III to the End of the Twenty-first Dynasty', *CAH* II, ch. 35, 1965.

40. Cf. the summary accounts by K. M. Kenyon, *Jerusalem*, 1967, 19–53; id., *Archaeology in the Holy Land*, ²1965, 241–3.

41. There are good coloured illustrations of modern *silwān* in M. Ronnen (ed.), *Jerusalem cité biblique*, 1968 (pages not numbered).

42. There is an impressive aerial view which shows the relationship of the south-east hill to the area of the temple court (levelled at a later period) in its modern setting in H. Reich, *Jerusalem* (in the series Terra Magica), 1968, 42–3.

43. II Sam. 19.32–9.

44. II Sam. 8.16–18 and II Sam. 20.23–25. Chapter 8 possibly reproduces an earlier stage.

45. There called *śar haṣṣābā'*: Judg. 4.7; I Sam. 14.50; 17.55; cf. also I Kings 1.19.

46. The designation of these troops as *kᵉrētī ūpᵉlētī* is possibly connected with their international character, which may also be responsible for the expression itself. The explanation that it means 'Cretans and Philistines' seems to fit, as this could allude to elements from the Sea-peoples. David could have taken over the designation from the Philistines or from his own mercenaries. But Crete is probably identical with Caphtor in the Old Testament, and the Philistines are called *pᵉlištīm* and not *pᵉlētī*. It remains a vague suggestion that the names were distorted when they were taken over from a foreign milieu. The proverbial use of the expression 'Cherethites and Pelethites' for an undifferentiated mass of lower status probably arose in circumstances in which an accurate understanding of the Old Testament was lacking.

47. J. Begrich, 'Sōfēr und Mazkir', *ZAW* 58, 1940/41 = *Gesammelte Studien zum Alten Testament*, 1964, 67–98; see also R. de Vaux, *RB* 88, 1939, 394–405, and more recently in *Ancient Israel*, 127–32, esp. 132; cf. further H. Graf Reventlow, 'Das Amt des Mazkir', *TZ* 15, 1959, 161–75; H. J. Boecker, 'Erwägungen zum Amt des Mazkir', *TZ* 17, 1961, 212–6.

48. Erman-Grapow, *Wörterbuch* I, 344, gives 'spokesman' as an official title for *whm.w*. Further mentions of the *mazkīr* appear in II Kings 18.18, 37; Isa. 36.3, 11, 22; II Chron. 34.8.

49. H. H. Rowley, 'Melchizedek and Zadok (Gen. 14 and Ps. 110)', in *Festschrift A. Bertholet*, 1950, 461–72.

50. Cf. inter alia G. Widengren, *Sakrales Königtum im Alten Testament und im Judentum*, Franz Delitzsch Lectures 1952, 1955, esp. 17; for the theme in general see A. R. Johnson,

Sacral Kingship in Ancient Israel, 1955; questioned in principle by M. Noth, 'God, King and Nation in the Old Testament' (1950), in *The Laws in the Pentateuch,* 1966, 145–78; R. de Vaux, *Ancient Israel,* 111–14, is equally critical. For the problems involved, see J. de Fraine, *L'aspect religieux de la royauté israélite. L'institution monarchique dans l'Ancien Testament et dans les textes mésopotamiens,* Analecta Biblica 3, 1954; K. H. Bernhardt, *Das Problem der altorientalischen Königsideologie im Alten Testament,* SVT 8, 1961.

51. H. J. Kraus, *Worship in Israel,* 1966, 182, estimates the situation correctly when he speaks of the 'foundation of the state cult'. However, the question when and how 'the ancient Israelite cultic calendar also began to be observed in Jerusalem' (Kraus, op. cit., 208) remains in dispute, the problems being also indicated by Kraus.

52. Joab energetically countered such a danger at a decisive moment: II Sam. 19.6–9.

53. G. von Rad, 'The Royal Ritual in Judah' (1947), in *The Problem of the Hexateuch,* 222–31; A. Alt, *KS* II, 133f. = *Grundfragen,* 365f.; see also S. Morenz, 'Ägyptische und davididische Königstitulatur', *ZÄS* 79, 1954, 73f.; J. de Savignac, 'Essai d'interpretation du Psaume CX a l'aide de la littérature égyptienne', *OTS* 9, 1951, 107–35; H. Cazelles, 'La titulature du roi David', *Mélanges A. Robert,* 1957, 131–6; R. de Vaux, *Ancient Israel,* 100–14.

54. This may perhaps still be recognizable in the sublime details of the Yahwistic work; cf. W. Richter, 'Urgeschichte und Hoftheologie', *BZ* NF 10, 1966, 96–105; M.-L. Henry, *Jahwist und Priesterschrift. Zwei Glaubenszeugnisse des Alten Testaments,* Arbeiten zur Theologie 3, 1960, esp. 7–19, illuminates the relationship between the history of the time and literary form in still further contexts.

55. Cf. also H. Schultze, *Die Grossreichsidee Davids, wie sie sich im Werk des Jahwisten spiegelt. Die politische Interpretation des geschichtlichen Credos durch den Jahwisten* (David's idea of empire as reflected in the work of the Yahwist. The political interpretation of the historical credo by the Yahwist), dissertation Mainz 1952.

56. See H. van den Bussche, 'Le texte de la prophétie de Nathan sur la dynastie Davidique', *ETL* 24, 1948, 354–94; M. Simon, 'La prophétie de Nathan et le temple', *RHPR* 32, 1952, 41–58; M. Noth, 'David and Israel in II Samuel VII', in *The Laws in the Pentateuch,* 1966, 250–9; G. Ahlström, 'Der Prophet Nathan und der Tempelbau', *VT* 11, 1961, 113–27; H. Gese, 'Der Davidsbund und die Zionserwählung', *ZTK* 61, 1964, 10–26; A. Caquot, 'La prophétie de Nathan et ses échos lyriques', *SVT* 9, 1963, 213–24; M. Tsevat, 'Studies in the Book of Samuel III', *HUCA* 34, 1963, 71–82; A. Weiser, 'Die Legitimation des Königs David', *VT* 16, 1966, 325–54.

57. S. Herrmann, 'Die Königsnovelle in Agypten und in Israel', *Wissenschaftliche Zeitschrift der Universität Leipzig* 3, 1953/4, Geschichtliche und sprachwissenschaftliche Reihe 1, 51–62; but see E. Kutsch, 'Die Dynastie von Gottes Gnaden', *ZTK* 58, 1961, 137–53; now, however, positively, M. Görg, *Der Gott vor dem König* (Habilitationsschrift Bochum 1972).

58. David felt it important to maintain his loyalty to the house of Saul; this is particularly clear in the case of Jonathan's son Meribbaal (I Chron. 8.34; 9.40); in II Sam. 9, etc., his name has been distorted into Mephibosheth.

59. II Sam. 6.21–23.

60. II Sam. 3.2–5.

61. Cf. the description of him in II Sam. 14.25–27: he only had his hair cut once a year and then it weighed 200 shekels by royal weight, an impressive contribution to the typology of revolutionary personalities. 200 shekels is about five pounds, or even double that, if this is what is meant by 'royal' weight; cf. *BHH* II, 1167. Absalom also had a chariot, certainly a war chariot on a Canaanite pattern, and a personal escort (II Sam. 15.1).

62. Cf. e.g. the remarks in W. Caspari, *Aufkommen und Krise der israelitischen Königtums unter David,* 1909, 84–90.

63. At the culmination of the narrative of the rebellion of Absalom, with its convincing construction and dramatic details, we read, 'For Yahweh had ordained to defeat the good counsel of Ahithophel, so that he might bring evil upon Absalom' (II Sam. 17.14b). This is a particularly impressive piece of evidence to tell against E. Meyer's thesis that the narrator employed no religious colouring and had no thought of supernatural guidance (*Geschichte des Altertums* II, 2, 1953, 285).

64. This must be a wooded region south of the Jabbok. Even today there are the remains of a forest in this area. A picture of mine taken from the height of *tell ḥejāj*, *ZDPV* 80, 1964, table 2, plate B, gives a minimal impression of this; cf. the text, 74 n.84.

65. *tell ābīl el-qamḥ* in the extreme north of Palestine west of Dan: J. Simons, *The Geographical Texts*, §§19, 788, 814, 889.

66. 'The fuller's spring', south of the confluence of the Kidron and Hinnom valleys, thus almost immediately adjoining Davidic Jerusalem on the south-east hill; the modern 'Job's spring' (*bir 'eyyūb*); H. J. Stoebe, *BHH* III, 1606.

67. Cf. also a series of points of view indicated by M. Noth, 'Jerusalem and the Israelite Tradition' (1950), in *The Laws in the Pentateuch*, 1966, 132–44.

68. K. T. Andersen, *Die Chronologie der Könige von Israel und Juda*, Studia Theologica 23, 1969, 69–114.

3 | David's Kingdom under Solomon

SOLOMON IS REGARDED as a peaceful king, and indeed he was. We know of no clashes with foreign powers during his reign. Of course, whether we may connect the name 'Solomon', which unmistakably contains the root of the term '*shalom*', with the particular circumstances of his life and his rule, is quite another question. It is striking that at his birth Solomon was given the name Jedidiah (II Sam. 12.25). We cannot exclude the hypothesis that 'Solomon' was a throne-name which was assigned to him; there is no certainty about the matter.[1]

The achievements of Solomon's reign lie in the religious, economic and cultural spheres. Not only did he build and complete the temple at Jerusalem; he also erected buildings in other cities and set up fortresses. He made trade alliances and economic treaties with neighbouring countries, though these essentially benefited only the new court in Jerusalem, its buildings, its splendour and its style of life, which increasingly took on international forms.

The tradition about Solomon in I Kings 2.12–11.43 is fundamentally different from that about David. Its accounts are no longer fraught with the tension involved in the growth and development of the personality of the king and his power; the tradition is completely static. It enumerates what there *was* in Solomon's time, and describes conditions in the state without consideration of the circumstances which brought them into being. It lists Solomon's officials, his administrative districts, the fortresses and possessions of the king, his wives, his riches, his relationship with foreign powers. The longest consecutive account is without doubt the account of the preparations for the temple, its building and its consecration, which is contained in chs. 5–8. Only a small amount has been preserved in narrative style, e.g. the details in ch. 2 of the way in which Solomon fulfilled David's 'last will'. We have two reports of conversations between Yahweh and Solomon, in chs. 3 and 9, which are concerned with the legitimation of his kingdom.[2] The narration elsewhere verges on the realm of saga and is somewhat intangible: the famous story of the judgment of Solomon (I Kings 3.16–28) is a widespread theme which here becomes a demonstration of the king's wisdom;[3] the visit of the queen of Sheba has the brilliance of saga, but also celebrates the king's wisdom (I Kings 10.1–13).

On the whole, Solomon was not so vigorous and creative a figure as David; there is much about him that sounds almost imitative. He waged no wars and in this respect played Augustus to David's Caesar. Israelite territory had already been marked out; David had extended the boundaries of the kingdom far beyond the area which Israel could keep permanently under control. It seems as if this varied apparatus of state remained essentially peaceful and was not exposed to any problems from outside, so that no defensive wars were necessary. Even the personal union of Judah and Israel was sustained, especially as the Israelite army was doubtless weakened after Sheba's revolt.

The way in which Solomon kept control of the kingdom he inherited was largely by vigorous diplomatic connections which he developed and sustained in various ways. One way was through his wives. The summary note in I Kings 11.1 ascribes to the king love for Moabite women, Ammonite women, Edomite women, Sidonian women and Hittite women. It is easy to see the background of foreign politics underlying this enumeration. For these are women of the very countries which Solomon would wish to see at peace, in his immediate neighbourhood and further beyond. The daughter of the king of Egypt, whom Solomon won as a spouse and for whom he had a special care, plays a prominent role. She is mentioned five times in different contexts.[4] The parenthetic note in I Kings 9.16 seems to be of particular importance; it says that 'Pharaoh the king of Egypt' occupied and burnt the city of Gezer and killed its Canaanite inhabitants; he gave the city itself to Solomon as a dowry along with his daughter. Unless we take the events summarized in this verse as a vague combination of different actions and doubt their historicity, the question arises whether an Egyptian king of the Twenty-first Dynasty in fact made a thrust into Palestine in the time of Solomon. The possibilities have been weighed in all directions.[5] Although it may be difficult from what we know to see Solomon involved in military developments,[6] it is certain that even immediately after David's reign, Philistine territory was not made so firmly dependent on Judah and Israel as were, say, the states of Transjordania. The Philistine city-states retained some life of their own which could also be expressed in the assertion of certain strong-points.[7] According to the evidence of the Old Testament, the involvement of an Egyptian king in actions against the Philistines in the time of Solomon was a very isolated event, but it did signal certain claims made by Egypt on the coastal plain and even beyond. It is quite certain that under Solomon's successor, the Pharaoh Shishak/Shoshenk, attempts were made to assert these claims in an expedition of which there is also evidence in the Bible.[8] But this probably confirms that Egypt had not yet become a serious danger for Solomon's empire.

The relationship of Solomon with the Phoenicians, and above all with the king of Tyre, is much clearer. A treaty had been arranged with the latter, which formed the basis for reciprocal aid.[9] Solomon drew on Tyre for building ·material and skilled craftsmen who knew how to deal with it. In return, Solomon agreed to cede twenty cities in Galilee to the king of Tyre (I Kings 9.11–14).[10]

In addition to his diplomatic contacts, Solomon cultivated extensive trade relationships, which in this form also represented a new development for Israel. Pride of place is taken by voyages to the land of Ophir, which brought back gold, valuable wood and other luxuries. As the Israelites themselves were no seafarers, Solomon was supported by the king of Tyre, who put shipwrights and sailors at his disposal (I Kings 9.26–28; 10.11, 22).[11] We can no longer locate the land of Ophir accurately. It is by no means certain whether Ophir was the land from which these countless riches came, or whether it was only an intermediate trading-post. At any rate, Solomon had the city of Ezion-geber constructed as a harbour for his fleet, on the north coast of the Gulf of Aqaba (*tell el-ḫlēfi*).[12] Excavations have confirmed that the city was possibly a new foundation by Solomon.[13] Facilities have also been found for the smelting of copper and iron which were mined on the borders of the Gulf and in the Arabah, and were then worked further in Ezion-geber. For this, use was made of the prevalent wind there, which blew in from the sea. However, we hear nothing of this copper and iron industry in the Old Testament. Nevertheless, Solomon doubtless took part in it with profit.

Solomon also engaged in a profitable trade in horses and chariots (I Kings 10.28, 29). The chariots came from Egypt and the horses from Cilicia.[14] They were sold on to the 'kings of the Hittites' and the 'kings of Aram'. We are probably to understand these to be the kings of smaller states in Syria.[15]

The visit of the queen of Sheba may also be connected with such far-flung connections. She perhaps came from southern Arabia, from the area of what is now the Yemen. The news of the empire of the Sabaeans may have reached as far as Jerusalem, but we know little about the person of the queen herself.[16] It is impossible to pronounce on the historical reliability of the visit to Solomon.[17]

Solomon was able to maintain David's empire, but had to make concessions at the points where political forces were developing which were to shape the long-term future. We have already spoken of the special concessions made to the Phoenicians of Tyre. They were probably connected with contributions which Solomon received from these city states. Matters turned out differently and proved more difficult in Syrian and Aramaean territory proper, from which David received tribute which was in part collected by his own envoys. An officer who was originally under the command of the king of Zobah succeeded in founding a kingdom in Damascus, which was later to prove a dangerous opponent of Israel. This kingdom of Damascus broke the former domination of the ruler of Zobah.[18] It is probably not too much to suppose that Solomon lost the whole of eastern Syria, which had formerly belonged to David's kingdom.[19] He also seems to have lost part of Edom. An Edomite prince named Hadad had fled to Egypt in David's time; after David's death he must have been made ruler of part of Edom.[20]

This balance in foreign policy during Solomon's reign may have had its negative side. But this is understandable. The change of government in Jerusalem was most likely to have an effect at the extremities of the kingdom, on the states and territories on the borders of the administration of David and Solomon. Solomon did not prove to be an active general, nor even one who preserved his possessions at any price.

He ran risks and sustained losses, but they did not shake the foundations of his power. Nevertheless, he did not neglect the military potential in domestic affairs. Of course he took over the mercenary troops from David. Extraordinarily, however, he also built up a chariot corps. This could not be recruited from the levy, but had to be an élite, the members of which should if possible already have had experience in chariot fighting. People from the Canaanite and Philistine population who were now at his disposal were most suited for this purpose. This is suggested not least by the extension of what were once Canaanite fortifications in the frontier regions.

Solomon must have seen the need to protect the state against the continuing threat of invasion, especially in the border regions. Special mention is made of Hazor, Megiddo and Gezer in a summary section (I Kings 9.15–22) which sketches out Solomon's building activity over the widest areas. In Hazor, Solomon will have been reviving part of the old city state, possibly as a protection against the purposeful Aramaeans of Damascus who were establishing themselves in the neighbourhood.[21] In view of the fact that the Phoenicians had already penetrated into the region of Carmel, the fortification of Megiddo on the southern edge of the plain of Megiddo/Jezreel, the scene of many battles, may have been an important measure.[22] We also hear of further building work at Gezer[23] and also at Beth-horon (I Kings 9.17), to protect the southern chain of cities which was once so important. Baalath, which is also mentioned, is unknown;[24] however, Tamar, about twenty miles from the southern end of the Dead Sea, may have been fortified against the Edomites.[25]

For all these measures to be put into practice, the use of forced labour had to be developed systematically. The king probably made use during the summer of people who were free while there was no work in the fields. The minister in charge of forced labour, a post which also existed under David (II Sam. 20.24), was called Adoniram in the time of both kings, but we cannot be certain that it was the same man in each case (I Kings 4.6).

We have two conflicting accounts of the recruitment of forced labour. According to I Kings 5.27, forced labour was drawn 'from all Israel', whereas in I Kings 9.20–22 it is stressed that only the non-Israelite population of the Canaanite city-states were recruited for forced labour.[26] There is much to be said, however, for the view that the 'all Israel' mentioned in I Kings 5 in fact means the inhabitants of the northern state, excluding Judah. Eventually, in David's time, after the rebellion of Sheba, Israel too had been subjected to military rule. The transference of forced labour to the northern state of Israel must finally be seen as one of the reasons for the later collapse of the personal union. This is confirmed by the fact that Solomon created twelve administrative areas which were intended to distribute the burden of supporting the court as fairly as possible over the twelve months of the year. It is significant that in the list of the administrative districts transmitted in I Kings 4.8–19, only the northern state of Israel is taken into account.[27] We know of no similar administrative division of Judah. It remains open whether Solomon included Judah in this system of provision and taxation in any way at all.

There is no need to go into the details of the list of administrative districts in I Kings 4.[28] Each district was supervised by its own administrator. The division of areas partly followed tribal territories and partly the districts which had been formed by the old city-states. As far as we can see, the districts were divided into equal halves, partly Israelite and partly Canaanite. Unfortunately we know nothing of how this administrative apparatus worked.

The administrative districts were to provide for the upkeep of the royal residence. In fact Solomon developed the city of Jerusalem considerably. He expanded it, and above all he erected the temple in conjunction with the royal palace. The exact site of these two great buildings is still being investigated. There is hardly any doubt that they will have been located on land which adjoins the south-east hill, the site of earliest Jerusalem, to the north of a small depression. Solomon will already have carried through some levelling there; during the construction of the temple of Herod an impressive plateau was formed, the 'temple place' which now bears the holy places of Islam, the so-called 'Dome of the Rock' and the Achsa Mosque. Within this area, however, we can only guess at the site of Solomon's temple, as excavations in the area have so far been ruled out. Understandably, the rock which now stands under the cupola of the Dome of the Rock, which is largely in its original state, plays a determinative role in the question of the exact location of the temple building.[29] However, quite apart from the exact site of the temple of Solomon, the post-exilic temple and the temple of Herod, which were presumably all built on the same spot, the extent, construction and equipping of these buildings are of interest. In default of archaeological remains, they have to be investigated and described chiefly on the basis of literary tradition.[30]

I Kings 6–8 gives a detailed description of the temple of Solomon and its apparatus: I Kings 5 reports the prelude to Solomon's efforts.[31] The king made use of the support of Hiram of Tyre, thus utilizing an alliance which was in all probability in existence in the time of David (cf. II Sam. 5.11). He imported building material and craftsmen for the construction of these unique buildings, which were quite new in Israelite experience. It therefore seems likely that foreign models determined both the details and the overall aspect of the palace, and particularly of the temple, albeit in a form which was appropriate to the religion of Yahweh. Phoenician involvement suggests especial Phoenician influence. Phoenician culture was itself syncretistic, with unmistakable indications of the influence of the cultures of Syria/Mesopotamia and of Egypt. This is also confirmed by the account of the building in I Kings 6 and 7, which even in outline clearly suggests that the temple followed the so-called 'Syrian temple' pattern.[32] A long building (*hēkāl*) with a vestibule (*ūlām*) is marked off from an inner shrine (*dᵉbîr*); in the temple of Solomon, the inner shrine becomes the 'holy of holies', in which the ark was set up.[33] In polytheistic religions the sanctuary was the place where the images of the gods were kept. This deliberately planned ground structure indicates that the Jerusalem temple was not really built round the ark, but was arranged in such a way that people had access to the ark.[34] It may be doubtful whether the individual believer was ever allowed to enter the temple building; it is certainly clear that its elements did not develop from specifically Israelite traditions, like that of the holy tent,[35] but were arranged according to the architectural principles of temples already existing in the surrounding world of the time. Two free-standing pillars in front of the vestibule which did not support anything were a particular characteristic of the temple; these were named Jachin and Boaz.[36] The altar of burnt offering obviously stood outside the temple building within the sacred precinct.

Building the temple was the king's affair: he determined the plan and carried it out. The addition of the palace to the temple must have heightened the impression that the temple was a state sanctuary in which even the priests functioned as royal officials. Solomon, the builder of the temple, was both its permanent owner and the one responsible for its upkeep. We do not know whether this met with the unanimous approval of the inhabitants of Judah and Israel, nor do we hear whether individuals from the two states were entrusted with permanent functions in the sanctuary. Remarkable though it may seem, this temple, like Jerusalem as a whole, was an alien body in the state, a royal undertaking, a place for the autonomous representation of the king and the God whom he worshipped.[37] It is hard to conceive what course Yahwistic religion would have taken had it been limited to these forms of a practice of worship focussed on the king. As it was, the living tradition of the tribes and their sanctuaries saw to the preservation of the worship of Yahweh in unbroken continuity and originality from the days of the wilderness.

We do not hear whether the building of the temple in Jerusalem restricted or even abolished the validity of the surviving sanctuaries elsewhere in the country. There life continued along its usual pattern. By way of anticipation, however, it must be said that the development of Old Testament religion was also moulded and accentuated to a considerable degree by the worship of Yahweh, which was bound up with Jerusalem as a result of the royal decree. At the state sanctuary, and under the patronage of the king, it was in fact possible for a cultic tradition to develop whose roots were in neither Judah nor Israel. The tribes preserved and cultivated memories of their nomadic days, narratives from their particular histories from the days in the wilderness onwards. In the course of the political union which took place during the monarchy, these traditions were developed so that they applied to 'all Israel', but there was some tension between them and state rule. This concentration of the tradition is most clearly expressed in the 'Deuteronomic' conception in which the monarchy is only one functional member, and by no means the most dominant one. Deuteronomy and its traditions confront another group of traditions which are oriented on the cultic practice of priestly ordinances; Jerusalem may be regarded as its centre. But Deuteronomy and the Priestly tradition form the two great components of exilic and post-exilic tradition in the Old Testament. Their roots lie in the 'dualism' which was unleashed by royal decision when the 'great sanctuary' in Jerusalem displaced the cultivation of tribal religion. That tribal religion survived in the form of Deuteronomy is also to the credit of a royal decision. It was made by Josiah towards the end of the seventh century when he took over the nucleus of the Deuteronomic legislation in Jerusalem. In this way the 'traditions of Israel' were also rescued to a considerable degree; the protection of the Jerusalem tradition sanctioned both their existence and their influence. The concept of 'Mount Zion' may be seen as a characteristic of the new religious sensibility which gradually established itself during the course of the monarchy, with Jerusalem as the city of the temple; the term refers to the hill on which the temple of Jerusalem is built, but at the same time contains an allusion to the connection between the monarchy and Yahweh's new abode.[38]

Solomon had made Jerusalem into a metropolis which, as the seat of government, followed its own laws. There is a list of Solomon's officials in I Kings 4.2–6. It shows that almost all the offices formed by David[39] continued in existence under Solomon, but that the administration was also extended in a number of ways.

The list is headed by a priest, Zadok's only son. From the time of Solomon only the sons of Zadok performed priestly duties in the temple. Abiathar, David's priest, is banished to Anathoth (I Kings 2.26f.).[40] The mention of Zadok and Abiathar as priests in I Kings 4.4b is presumably an error.[41] The office of the scribe is duplicated, and that of the *mazkir* ('herald') retained. Only the leader of the host is mentioned as army commander. Did the king himself take over the mercenaries in conjunction with the chariot troops?

The new offices of Solomon's administration included an official set over those who supervised the administrative districts, so to speak the chief civil servant in the state, a minister for trade and tribute, i.e. for taxation. In addition there were officials in charge of forced labour. Two additional offices in particular seem to have been created, following the pattern of foreign courts: the *reʿā hammelek*, 'the king's friend', and the *ʿal-habbayit*, the officer set 'over the house'. There are parallels for both offices in Egypt and in Akkad. The 'king's friend' had special authority. In Egypt there were a whole series of 'king's friends', in some ways comparable with secretaries of state.[42] The officer 'over the house' was the superintendent of the palace, a kind of lord chamberlain who in the course of time will also have taken over the administration of the royal estates, crown property. In any case, in some respects his duties will have extended beyond the palace and will have related to court procedure in general.[43]

None of these offices emerged from the organization of the tribal alliance; as has been demonstrated, some of them will have been modelled on the customs of foreign courts. In this way the administration of David's state will have been perfected in Solomon's hands. However, it is hard to imagine that the tribes in Judah and Israel took any vigorous part in this development which was bound up so closely with the capital, or even that they co-operated with it on their own initiative. The king guaranteed the existence of the two states, which he still united in a personal union; he was not forced into any military action, so he did not have to make contact with the army, at least with that of Judah. For Judah at any rate the reign of Solomon may have been a peaceful time, which strengthened confidence and even encouraged pride in the Jerusalem government. In Israel, the northern state, things were different. Unparalleled contributions were required of it which were exclusively connected with the concerns of the central government. We can see why we only have sources for this period from Judah and Jerusalem: Israel began to feel the burden of the monarchy in the way outlined in I Sam. 8.11–17, even if that passage was written in retrospect.[44]

We can infer how much Jerusalem went its own way and how much the king immersed himself in the 'international' milieu of the time from notes which betray its participation in a wide-ranging cultural life. Solomon was not only involved in religion. There is praise of his 'wisdom'. This is a reference to more than the personal qualities of the ruler, though here of course a son of David should not be underestimated. The term 'wisdom' covers a wider sphere of intellectual activity and also ambitious initiatives within the consolidated court. This involved more than the person of the king. In Jerusalem people were evidently occupied in the creation of encyclopaedic lists which embraced the world and what was in it, following the example of lists known to us from both Mesopotamia and Egypt.[45] One prominent Egyptian example from about 1100 BC, little more than a century earlier than Solomon, is the *Onomasticon* of Amenope, which allows a broad glimpse of the nature of this 'knowledge through encyclopaedic lists'.[46] We may infer from I Kings 4.33 that Solomon, or at least people from his court, was involved in this kind of understanding of the world: 'And he (Solomon) spoke of trees, from the cedar that is in Lebanon to the hyssop that grows out of the wall; he spoke also of beasts, and of birds, and of reptiles, and of fish.' There is an exact outline here of the principles of listing, which arranges objects by size and by type. It is surely no coincidence that in I Kings 5.10 Solomon's wisdom is compared with the wisdom of other peoples, including the Egyptians. We cannot exclude the possibility that Solomon not only had lists prepared, but also had collections made of sayings of experiential wisdom ('proverbs'), ethical and moral principles, and saw that these were written down. I Kings 4.32 mentions 1000 sayings and songs of the king. The 'saying' is described by the term *māšāl*, which even in Solomon's time may well have also included the formulation of a rule for conduct.[47] Finally, at the heart of the visit of the queen of Sheba lies a cultural exchange; it represents the international connections of the king at the highest level.

One cosmopolitan feature of the court which apparently went contrary to the exclusiveness of Israelite sensibility was the fact that Solomon also took wives from neighbouring countries and even had temples erected for their deities on the Mount of Olives (I Kings 11.1–10). It may in fact have been the gods of the women who were worshipped there. But it is no less probable that the installation of this 'pantheon' was an expression of the loyalty of Solomon's state; by accepting foreign gods it also sought to offer a guarantee of peace to the countries around. A state government acts in terms of power politics, and has a right to do so. But no one should be surprised that in view of such models there was also encouragement in Judah and Israel to take note of the wives and the gods of their neighbours, the Canaanites from the coastal plain, and to present Yahweh as one god among many. Here were the seeds of the practices which later aroused the prophets' anger. They grew during the further course of the monarchy, and could eventually be rooted out only by force, by the law enacted in the time of Josiah.

It is often said of the peaceful era of Solomon that this was the time when Israel made associations with the international world, when it became open to the spirit of the age: art and learning began to flourish, great buildings were erected, literature was collected. But where did this happen? In Jerusalem, of course, and nowhere else. The spirit of Solomon's 'enlightenment'[48] and wisdom had its effect at the court; it also found its way into the Old Testament in the form of court history-writing, and increased the fame of the king. Nevertheless, this whole development must be seen in modest terms, within a small area. It was so to speak a laborious conquest of the province! The flights of the spirit and the urge to build soon declined, especially as Judah could not provide the same contributions that Solomon exacted, where possible, from the Israelites in the north. Nevertheless, this age of Solomon should not be underestimated. The office of $s\bar{o}p\bar{e}r$ was not doubled without a purpose; acts of state were compiled, a book of Solomon's achievements (I Kings 11.41). This period probably also saw the writing of the vivid account of the time of David which E. Meyer praised as the beginning of history-writing in Israel. It may have been in the vein of the state ideology and the growing awareness of the tribes to collect the traditions from the early period and to fix them in essentials. Foundations were laid for the literature which we now call the work of the 'Yahwist', the earliest witness in the Pentateuch. With some justification, comparisons have been made between the penetrating and psychologically accurate accounts of the succession narrative and the Yahwistic tradition, say in Gen. 2; 3; their strongly anthropological side has been recognized.[49] Self-awareness grew in Judah and Israel, and with it an eye for human nature, its possibilities, its limitations and its weaknesses.[50] Of course the insights whose foundation was laid in the time of David and Solomon may not have been developed fully until later in the course of the monarchy. The tribes were often left out of the development introduced by king and court with their ambitious visions and the practices which stemmed from an anticipation of intellectual power and insight. With their burden of tradition and their conflicts, the tribes did not break out from their hallowed ordinances so quickly. In particular, violent conflicts broke out on the death of the occupant of the throne in Jerusalem, the son of great David, who to some people was also a hated figure. The palace had now reached its peak and had gone past it; the hour of the tribes was striking again.

NOTES

1. M. Noth, *Personennamen*, 165, interpreted the name 'Solomon' in the sense of 'well-being', 'peace', with ō as a hypocoristic ending. Another proposal has been made by J. J. Stamm, 'Der Name des Königs Salomo', *TZ* 16, 1960, 285–97, which takes into account the more immediate circumstances of Solomon's birth. Jedidiah = 'friend, favourite of Yahweh'; Noth, op. cit., 149.

2. Solomon is given a divine assurance of the validity and future success of his kingdom during a dream in the sanctuary; the form of the account follows the style of the Egyptian royal Novelle. Cf. S. Herrmann, 'Die Königsnovelle in Ägypten und in Israel', *Wissenschaftliche Zeitschrift der Universitäts Leipzig* 3, 1953/54, esp. 53–7; M. Görg, *Der Gott vor dem König. Untersuchung zu den Gott-König-Reden der prosaischen Literatur Altisraels im Lichte ägyptischer Phraseologie*, Habilitationsschrift, Bochum 1972.

3. H. Gressmann, 'Das salomonische Urteil', *Deutsche Rundschau* 130, 1907, 212–28; M. Noth, 'Die Bewährung von Salomos "göttlicher Weisheit" ' (1955), *Gesammelte Studien* II, 1969, 99–112.

4. I Kings 3.1; 7.8; 9.16; 9.24 (cf. II Sam. 8.11); 11.1.

5. A. Malamat, 'Aspects of the Foreign Policies of David and Solomon', *JNES* 22, 1963, esp. 8–17.

6. One insuperable difficulty is that neither the name of the Egyptian king nor that of his daughter is mentioned; Malamat suggests king Siamun (*c.* 976–958 BC), and even reckons with the possibility that this king ultimately had a conquest of Judah and Israel in mind (op. cit., 13). Malamat doubts the accuracy of the picture of Solomon as purely a peaceful king. He wants to see him as a dynamic personality who is really comparable with David, even in foreign policy.

7. A. Malamat, op. cit., 14f.; O. Eissfeldt, 'Israelitisch-philistäische Grenzverschiebungen', *Kleine Schriften* II, esp. 459–63.

8. I Kings 14.25–28.

9. See F. C. Fensham, 'The Treaty between the Israelites and Tyrians', in SVT 17, 1969, esp. 78f.

10. For 'Cabul', which is remarkable as a designation of a place or district, see M. Noth, *Könige*, 211; F. C. Fensham, 'The Treaty' (n. 9 above).

11. Cf. F. C. Fensham, 'The Treaty', 78.

12. For a summary, see now Noth, *Könige*, BK 9, 222f. He thinks of a 'particular area near the Red Sea', or at any rate of a place with access to this sea.

13. M. Noth, op. cit., 221.

14. The place names are confused in I Kings 10.28. The reading should be: 'And Solomon's import of horses was from Muzri and Kue, and the king's traders received them from Kue at a price.' Kue is the plain of Cilicia, and there is also evidence for it in cuneiform sources: Muzri should be read for Mizraim (Egypt), and is probably to be located in the region of the Taurus. All Solomon's horses probably came from districts in south-eastern Asia Minor. For details and evidence see M. Noth, *Könige*, 234f.

15. The brevity of the formulations does not allow us to draw any further conclusions about details, see also Noth, op. cit.

16. The name 'Sheba' is usually taken to indicate the kingdom of the Sabaeans. Inscriptions from this state in southern Arabia only begin in the ninth century; the kingdom came to an end about 525 BC. These dates are late for Solomon's time; however, we may suppose that the early history of the kingdom was quite extensive. Unfortunately no evidence has yet been found in the inscriptions for queens of the Sabaeans (cf. R. Borger, *Or.* 26, 1957, 8ff.). For other possibilities of interpreting Sheba in the Old Testament see M. Noth, *Könige*, 223f.

17. Cf. Noth's hypothesis, op. cit., 226f. He regards trade relationships between Israel

and southern Arabia as a possible background, especially as the exchange of goods plays quite a prominent part in the story.

18. I Kings 11.23–25, and on it A. Malamat, *JNES* 22, 1963, 5.

19. Once Solomon no longer had any influence on Damascus, it is difficult to see why areas in the heart of Syria, say within the reach of the ruler of Hamath, should continue to maintain relations with Jerusalem.

20. I Kings 11.14–22; unfortunately this tradition is fragmentary.

21. The south-west corner of the city of Hazor, at *tell waqqāṣ*, which was surrounded by a casemate wall, has been presented as a piece of fortification from the time of Solomon. A splendid gateway has also been excavated, the plans and dimensions of which correspond closely to those of Megiddo and Gezer; see Y. Yadin, *Hazor*, 1972, 135–46; K. M. Kenyon, *Archaeology*, [2]1965, 248–50.

22. There is a short summary of the results of most recent excavations in K. M. Kenyon, *Archaeology*, [2]1965, 250f.; more detail can be found in Y. Yadin, 'Megiddo of the Kings of Israel', *BA* 33, Sept. 1970; id., *Hazor*, 1967, 150–64. The stables at Megiddo were once singled out as coming from the time of Solomon; however, stratification has shown that they are probably from a later date. They are not on the same level as the gateway which is regarded as Solomonic and the casemate wall which is associated with it, Y. Yadin, 'New Light on Solomon's Megiddo', *BA* 23, 1960, 62–8; C. Wätzinger, *Denkmäler Palästinas* I, 1933, 87f. and plates 8of., is representative of an earlier stage of knowledge.

23. The excavations of Gezer by R. A. Macalister, *The Excavations of Gezer, 1902–05 and 1907–09*, I–III, 1912, still belong in the pioneering period of Palestinian archaeology. Recent excavations have disclosed a type of casemate wall which is similar to that of Hazor: Y. Yadin, 'Solomon's City Wall and Gate at Gezer', *IEJ* 8, 1958, 80–6; id., *Hazor*, 1972, 147–50.

24. It is not certain that this is identical with the Baalath of Josh. 19.44; however, a place south of Gezer has been conjectured; cf. A. Malamat, *JNES* 22, 1963, 16; M. Noth, *Könige*, 213f.

25. Identified by Y. Aharoni, *IEJ* 13, 1963, 30–42, with *'ēn ḥaṣb* on the western edge of the Arabah, the great valley south of the Dead Sea.

26. The contradiction between the two passages has been handled by commentators in different ways. See the subtle judgments in M. Noth, *Könige*, 92, 216–18; Noth would understand 9.20–22 to mean that 'only the enslaved or at most the semi-free subject population of the pre-Israelite city states' were conscripted for forced labour; his understanding is that the Israelite population itself was merely called on for 'all kinds of other royal duties', though these were also seen as an invasion of the freedom of Israelite men. Here Noth is considering 'all the territory under the direct rule of Solomon' as Israelite population; he makes no distinction between the inhabitants of the two states of Israel and Judah.

27. A. Alt, 'Israels Gaue unter Salomo', *KS* II, 76–89.

28. Cf. A. Alt, op. cit.; W. F. Albright, *JPOS* 5, 1925, esp. 25–54, nevertheless later sought to include Judah in the list by textual emendation.

29. Understandably, it has not yet been possible to verify earlier views, that the sacred rock is the site of the Holy of Holies in the temple or was the altar of burnt offering that would be expected in front of the temple building. More recently, a position north of the sacred rock has been regarded as a probable site for the temple buildings; T. A. Busink, *Der Tempel Salomos*, 1970, 20; cf. also the account of this work in H. Bardtke, *TLZ* 97, 1972, 801–10; for the discussion of the problem cf. especially H. Schmidt, *Der heilige Fels in Jerusalem*, 1933, which assumed that the Holy of Holies was above the rock; he is followed by H. Schmid, 'Der Tempelbau Salomos in religionsgeschichtlicher Sicht', *Archäologie und Altes Testament* (Festschrift K. Galling), 1970, 241–50.

30. In addition to the work by Busink, cf. the description by K. M. Kenyon, *Jerusalem*, 1967, 54–62; also K. Möhlenbrink, *Der Tempel Salomos*, BWANT IV, 7, 1932; C. Watzinger, *Denkmäler Palastinas* I, 1933, 88–97 (there is also a description of Solomon's palace here); K. Galling, *BRL*, 511–19; A. Parrot, *The Temple of Jerusalem*, 1957; G. E. Wright, *Biblical Archaeology*, 1957, 136–42; id., *BHH* III, 1940–47; cf. further the work on Jerusalem by L. H. Vincent and A.-M. Steve, *Jérusalem de l'Ancien Testament*, 1954–56, esp. II/III, 373–431.

31. The most recent detailed commentary on the text is by M. Noth, *Könige*, 95–193.

32. A. Alt, 'Verbreitung und Herkunft des syrischen Tempeltypus' (1939), *KS* II, 100–15; cf. also O. Eissfeldt, *Tempel und Kulte syrischer Städte in hellenistisch-römischer Zeit*, AO 40, 1941.

33. The division of the house into three along the 'Syrian temple' pattern has been challenged by H. Schult, 'Der Debir im salomonischen Tempel', *ZDPV* 80, 1964, 46–54; this article has rightly been disputed by A. Kuschke, 'Der Tempel Salomos und der "syrische Tempeltypus",' *Das ferne und das nahe Wort* (Festschrift L. Rost), BZAW 105, 1967, 124–32.

34. J. Maier, *Das altisraelitische Ladeheiligtum*, BZAW 93, 1965, 64–74, denies that the ark had any sacral architectonic function in the temple of Solomon. 'The temple was not built for the ark' (69). Maier is of the opinion that the ark became the symbol of the double election of Jerusalem and its dynasty. This theory has far-reaching consequences for the functions of temple and ark, and the way in which the two should be understood, which cannot be discussed here. As an equally problematical contrast see H. Vincent, 'Le caractère du temple salomonien', *Mélanges A. Robert*, 1957, 137–48.

35. For the complex form of this tent tradition, which was perhaps deliberately opposed to the traditions of the ark and of Jerusalem, cf. M. Görg, *Das Zelt der Begegnung*, BBB 27, 1967.

36. H. G. May, 'The Two Pillars before the Temple of Solomon', *BASOR* 88, 1942, 19ff.; S. Yeivin, 'Jachin and Boaz', *PEQ* 91, 1959, 6ff.

37. Against this background we can understand the thesis of J. Maier, op. cit., which makes the ark in the Jerusalem temple a dynastic symbol. However, it is worth asking whether the ark, which hitherto had symbolized the presence of Yahweh as the God of Israel only to the northern tribes, was not in fact intended to further and represent the firm association of the northern state with Jerusalem by virtue of being placed in the temple of the ruler in Jerusalem. Maier, op. cit., 70, takes a similar view, though he places the accents rather differently. For O. Eissfeldt, on the other hand, the transfer of the ark to Jerusalem represents the introduction of all the religious and theological power associated with the 'cherub throne'. The setting up of the ark at Shiloh became the pattern for Jerusalem, O. Eissfeldt, 'Silo und Jerusalem' (1956), *Kleine Schriften* III, 417–25.

38. For the association of the conception of the mountain with the throne of Yahweh and the consequences that this had in the tradition of the Jerusalem sanctuary as they have found expression in the Old Testament, see M. Metzger, 'Himmlische und irdische Wohnstatt Jahwehs', *Ugarit-Forschungen* 2, 1970, 139–58, and tables I, II.

39. Cf. II Sam.8.15–18; 20.23–26.

40. It is often supposed that the prophet Jeremiah, who came from the priesthood of Anathoth (Jer.1.1), was a descendant of this Abiathar, but there is no reliable proof.

41. These two were priests under David, cf. II Sam.20.25.

42. A. van Selms, 'The Origin of the Title "The King's Friend" ', *JNES* 16, 1957, 118–23; H. Donner, 'Der "Freund des Konigs" ', *ZAW* 73, 1961, 269–77, differs. This is possibly the translation of a foreign title into Hebrew, cf. Noth, *Könige*, 64f.; for the survival of the title in later times and its appearance in John 19.12 cf. E. Bammel, *TLZ* 77, 1952, 205–10.

43. The title appears in I Kings 16.9; 18.3; II Kings 18.18, etc. and also on an inscription in the village of *silwān* in Jerusalem (Donner–Röllig, *KAI*, no. 191), and as the legend on a seal from Lachish (S. H. Hooke, *PEFQS* 67, 1935, 195); for the function of the administrator of crown property see M. Noth, *Aufsätze* I, 159–82, esp. 163f.

44. At any rate, it is unnecessary to suppose that the burdens comprised by this royal law arose under the influence of non-Israelite monarchies. There is enough foundation for them in Israel itself. Cf. the considerations advanced by A. Weiser, *Samuel*, 1962, 38–42.

45. There is a survey of the evidence from Mesopotamia and an introduction to the character of these lists in W. v. Soden, *Die Welt als Geschichte* 2, 1936, 417ff., supplemented in *Sitzungsberichte der Österreichischen Akademie der Wissenschaften*, Phil.-hist. Kl., Vol. 235, 1, 1960, 3–33; cf. also Matouš, *Die lexikalischen Tafelserien der Babylonier und Assyrer in den Berliner Museen* I, 1933, 1ff.; there is a detailed account of tablet 14 in B. Landsberger, *Die Fauna des alten Mesopotamien* (1934) = *Abhandlungen der Sächsischen Akademie der Wissenschaften*, Phil.-hist. Kl., Vol. 42, 6. For Egypt see the survey in Spuler (ed.), *Handbuch der Orientalistik* I, 2 (Egyptology, literature), [2]1970, 187–93; there is a detailed discussion of individual texts in A. H. Gardiner, *Ancient Egyptian Onomastica* I, II, and the volume of plates, 1947; A. Alt, 'Die Weisheit Salomos' (1951), *KS* II, 90–9, is a fundamental study on the influence of these genres of literature on the Old Testament; cf. also G. von Rad, 'Job XXXVIII and Ancient Egyptian Wisdom' (1955), in *The Problem of the Hexateuch*, 1966, 281–91; see also S. Herrmann, 'Die Naturlehre des Schöpfungsberichtes', *TLZ* 86, 1961, 413–24.

46. Text, translation and commentary in A. H. Gardiner, op. cit.

47. So far it has not been possible to clarify the extent to which Israelite proverbial wisdom was shaped and written down in the time of Solomon, or to assess the degree of Egyptian influence on Israel. R. B. Y. Scott, 'Solomon and the Beginnings of Wisdom in Israel', *SVT* 3, 1955, 262–79, is too pessimistic in this respect, while Christa Kayatz, *Studien zu Proverbien 1–9*, WMANT 22, 1966, is extremely confident; see also H.-J. Hermisson, *Studien zur israelitischen Spruchweisheit*, WMANT 28, 1968; more recently, M. Noth, *Könige*, 79–84. Special reference should be made to the composite volume 'Les sagesses du Proche-Orient ancien', *Colloque de Strasbourg 1962*, 1963, and the contributions by H. Cazelles, S. Morenz, W. Zimmerli and H. Gese.

48. Cf. G. von Rad, *Old Testament Theology* 1, 1965, 48–56; he sees clearly that the spirit of this time was probably limited to the court and the upper classes (op. cit., 56).

49. G. von Rad, *The Problem of the Hexateuch*, 1966, 166–204, 292–300.

50. Marie-Louise Henry, *Jahwist und Priesterschrift*, 1960, esp. 15–19.

The Division of the Kingdom and its Immediate Consequences

INFORMATION ABOUT THE time after Solomon is sparse. Whereas the period of about eighty years which covers the reigns of David and Solomon has been recorded in documents which extend over several Old Testament books (from I Sam. 16 to I Kings 11), the second half of I Kings, from I Kings 12 on, deals with the very complicated period down to the middle of the ninth century BC. Thus eleven chapters span almost three-quarters of a century. We are told only the bare essentials of many events, and of some we hear nothing at all. The most detailed accounts are those of the successions in the divided kingdoms of Israel and Judah and of the fight of the prophet Elijah against the cult of Baal in Israel. Happenings abroad are noticed almost in passing, and then only when they have unmistakable consequences for Israel and Judah.

In principle, these considerations apply to the tradition for the whole of the 'period of the kings' down to the fall of Jerusalem in 587/86 BC. II Kings, the content of which goes as far as the exile in the case of some notes, follows the same pattern in its choice of material and its themes. Details of the succession to the thrones of Judah and Israel form the framework for the tradition,[1] which is filled out by details of domestic policies, principally the actions of the kings over cultic matters, and reports of events abroad which affected living conditions in the two states. In these main themes we can see the basic principles of the 'Deuteronomistic redaction' (undoubtedly an apt description) at work in selection from earlier material. Its interest in the problems of the monarchy and its attitude towards the true worship of Yahweh is evident; we are told what should have been done for the perspective of the ideal conceptions which are enshrined in the book of Deuteronomy. In II Chronicles the Chronicler essentially follows the Deuteronomistic account, but keeps as far as possible to events in the southern state of Judah, because the redactors were interested in the exclusive legitimation of the Jerusalem sanctuary and its cult and in the historical tradition associated with the Davidic monarchy.

These principles of selection are regrettable; they are explicitly confirmed by constant stereotyped references to the fact that more information about the reign of a particular king is to be found in the 'chronicles of the kings', whether these are 'the kings of Israel' or 'of Judah'. These chronicles may also have contained the notes about the length of the reigns of kings, which allow at least a relative chronology to be established; with the help of fixed chronological points to be obtained through comparisons with non-Israelite sources, it is also possible to establish an absolute chronology for the kings of Israel and Judah. It is in the nature of things that account must be taken of certain inaccuracies which have led to different versions of the chronology of the history of Israel and Judah. However, the differences are only slight, so that we may say that in essentials this chronology may be taken as certain.

Several outlines of the chronology of the kings of Israel and Judah have been worked out in the last decades. German scholars have largely followed the investigation by Joachim Begrich,[2] which was later re-examined and altered for the second part of the period of the monarchy by Alfred Jepsen.[3] In fixing a date, Begrich always gives two successive years, e.g. 853/2. The reason for this procedure is the principle of 'ante-dating' or 'post-dating'. There is evidence of ante-dating for at least some dynasties in Egypt. Here the time from the New Year to the day on which a ruler dies is taken as the last complete year. Similarly, the period from the accession of his successor to the end of the year is regarded as his first *full* year. Thus on New Year's Day the successor officially enters upon the second year of his reign. Post-dating, which was officially practised in Babylonia, differed from this. The year of the death of the ruler was still taken as a full year, but his successor was credited only with the first *full* year of his reign, and not with the period from the death of his predecessor to the end of the year. There is no way of being certain which of these two modes of calculation was used for the Old Testament information about the kings of Israel and Judah. Begrich regards it as possible that ante-dating was used in the first period of the monarchy and post-dating in the later period (in Judah).

Another fundamental consideration should be noted. In the early period of the monarchy of Israel and Judah a calendar was used in which the year began in the autumn; in the later period the year began in the spring. Begrich believes that it is conceivable that the earlier calendar was succeeded by the later one before 620. Jepsen, who follows Begrich in essentials, suggests that the alterations to the calendar year and to the method of dating began when the two states became Assyrian vassals, in each case at the first subsequent accession. In Israel this would have been with the accession of Pekahiah and in Judah with that of Hezekiah.[4]

In view of the numerous uncertainties in which methods of calculating dates are involved, the outline proposed by K. T. Andersen begins from presuppositions which are simpler and which in particular do not reckon with a change in methods of dating within the period of the monarchy.[5] Andersen arrives at the following results: (*a*) that the calendar year began in the autumn throughout the period of the existence of the two states of Israel and Judah; (*b*) ante-dating was always used in both states; (*c*) co-regencies and rival monarchies were not included in the official record of the years of a king's reign.[6] Here, too, corrections are needed, but in essentials this approach produces an illuminating chronological sequence which can also be reconciled with important fixed points outside Israelite history, the battle of Karkar in 853/52 and the tribute of Jehu to Shalmaneser III, probably in the summer of 841. Consequently, in the present book the chronology of Andersen is used, even though it has not been tested much hitherto; in places cross-references are made to earlier ideas, especially those of Begrich and Jepsen.

For other and earlier chronological investigations by S. Mowinckel, W. F. Albright, R. Thiele and C. Schedl,[7] see Jepsen's book; Andersen also refers to them.[8]

For the reasons given above, the historian must always be cautious in his conclusions about the course of the monarchy. In a number of places he has to be particularly careful, and at times he is reduced to comparisons or inferences. His hypotheses will be supported by sources which come from foreign powers and which sometimes note the fortunes of Israel and Judah.[9] However, all the important stages in the course of events can be reconstructed. The accounts in the 'historical books' are also supported by allusions or references in the prophetic books. But the latter themselves show that it would be impossible to reconstruct the history of Israel and thus to fix the activity of the prophets exactly without the more comprehensive material of the historical books. This gives the historical books the status of independent and credible sources, which can be assessed independently of the activity of the prophets and the witness of the cultic tradition.

The first theme of the reign of Solomon's successor, his son Rehoboam, is the question of the continuation of the personal union between the states of Judah and Israel with Jerusalem as the centre of government. The succession to the throne seems to have taken place at the Jerusalem court without any difficulty. We hear nothing of opposition from court officials or from inhabitants of the state of Judah. Things were different among the northern tribes in Israel. They did not regard it as a matter of course that the king of Jerusalem should automatically be given sovereignty over them. For this, at least an independent act of legitimation in the territory of the state of Israel was required. However, it remains an open question whether this possibility was seriously considered among the Israelite tribes, who may have decided not to recognize Solomon's successor as king in any circumstances. It is already suspicious that Rehoboam made the journey to Shechem (I Kings 12.1), allegedly to have himself confirmed as king there, instead of receiving the representatives of the northern tribes in Jerusalem. After Solomon's death Israel probably maintained a completely passive attitude, and with his personal appearance in Shechem Rehoboam may have counted on either persuading or even forcing Israel to acknowledge his rule.

Shechem was a city which once belonged to a group of vigorous Canaanite city-states in the centre of Ephraim and was the scene of the assembly over which Joshua presided (Josh. 24). Like Hebron in Judah, it must have been the focal point of the Israelite tribes. Now it was also the centre for an act of determined self-assertion against the south, and above all against the claims and ambitions of the residence in Jerusalem. Rehoboam would not be allowed to become king of Israel without conditions. The Israelites emphatically declared, 'Your father (Solomon) made our yoke too hard' (I Kings 12.10). All Solomon's extremely strict administrative apparatus was to be done away with, especially as it was particularly harsh to Israel and, as was suggested above, may even have borne down on Israel alone. When the Israelites made a clear request to Rehoboam to lighten the burden imposed by his father Solomon, it says little for Rehoboam's resolve and diplomacy that he should have asked for three days to consider the matter, should have sent the people's assembly home and should meanwhile have taken counsel with his closest advisers. We may leave aside the question whether the following scene, in which the king rejects the advice of the elders to moderate his policy and follows the advice of the younger men ('Tell them, My father chastised you with whips, but I will chastise you with "scorpions"!') is conceived on the basis of models from elsewhere.[10] One is reminded of the moment in which Absalom rejected the wise counsel of Ahithophel (II Sam. 17.14b); it is no coincidence that a similar note is inserted in I Kings 12.15, 'It was a turn of affairs (*sibbā*) brought about by Yahweh'.

What happens now is no surprise. Israel, the northern tribes, immediately breaks away from Rehoboam. They declare their intention with the very words by which Sheba once gained his following (II Sam. 20.1), and add, 'Look now to your own house, David' (I Kings 12.16). The assembly at Shechem breaks up. Rehoboam is bold enough to send Adoniram, the minister in charge of forced labour, once again, to terrify the Israelites. But their reaction is unmistakable. They stone him in the sight of the king. All the latter can do is mount a chariot and rush in headlong flight to Jerusalem![11]

That was the end of the personal union achieved by David and Solomon. The two part-states of Judah and Israel were separated again, and finally broke apart. There was no serious attempt to establish the bond of personal union afresh. Anyone who has followed carefully the course of the history of the tribes on Palestinian soil up to this event will not find the separation of the two states unduly surprising. Even after the settlement, Judah and the tribes in central Palestine remained separate entities with different pasts and independent developments. The term 'the division of the kingdom', which is conventionally used as a description for the scene in I Kings 12, may do justice to events, but it may also give a wrong impression. It may suggest that what happened was the division of an organism, an unnatural act of force. In reality, the situation was quite the reverse. This was a return to the context of tried organizations. The imperial policy of David and

Solomon, which had become possible through their resources and had been accepted by the northern tribes, proved to be no more than an episode, a vain attempt to form the tribes in the hill-country of Palestine into a unity and through their power to realize a comprehensive idea of the state and to build a kingdom. The intentions of the two kings did not have a lasting effect on the consciousness of the tribes. Judah now kept to the lineage of David. It remained under the family of the man whom it had once confidently set on the throne in Hebron. Israel thought and acted in Shechem according to its own ideas. There was a firm conviction that there would have to be a new king, from Israel, a man of passion and power, who would be resolved to develop an independent policy for Israel, apart from that of Judah. When the break took place in Shechem, he had already been found: Jeroboam.

The story of Jeroboam goes back into the time of Solomon's reign. Solomon himself had noticed Jeroboam's competence and had therefore put him in charge of forced labour in the house of Joseph. Jeroboam came from this area, from a city of Zeredah in the hill-country of Ephraim.[12] He and his people were engaged on the royal building work in Jerusalem. One day the prophet Ahijah of Shiloh met him on his way back to Israel. We are told that Ahijah was wearing a new garment. The two men were alone. Ahijah tore his garment into twelve pieces and said to Jeroboam, 'Take ten pieces!' Then he announced in the name of Yahweh that the kingdom of David would be divided. 'I will take the kingdom out of his son's (i.e. Solomon, David's son) hand, and will give it to you, ten tribes. Yet to his son I will give one tribe.'[13] This speech might suggest that the breach was already to take place in the time of Solomon. At least Jeroboam might feel called to prepare for Israel's secession from Solomon. Although we hear no more, Jeroboam must at least have made efforts in this direction. Otherwise the note in I Kings 11.40, that Solomon sought to kill Jeroboam, would be incomprehensible.

Jeroboam fled to Egypt, but seems to have returned to Israel on the news of the death of Solomon. From there he may well have stirred up feelings against Jerusalem or at least have supported movements hostile to it.[14]

Hardly had Rehoboam escaped to Jerusalem when the Israelites made Jeroboam king of the northern kingdom.[15] The Old Testament tradition considers the message of Ahijah of Shiloh to be the act of designation made by Yahweh; now the people acclaimed a new ruler in Shechem. But there is no mention of anointing. In principle, Jeroboam became king in the same way as Saul. There is mention of the two stages of designation and acclamation, whereas David and Solomon were anointed and acclaimed from the side of Judah in a single event which signified their legitimate accession. The same thing will have happened with Rehoboam. The dynastic principle was preserved; Judah and Jerusalem kept to it.

The different procedures in the two states remained determinative for the whole of the period of the kings. The house of David kept to dynastic succession in Jerusalem; in Israel, too, dynasties were often formed, but the founder of a dynasty was regularly designated king by a prophet. It is characteristic that the prophetic designation of a ruler almost always encouraged him to exterminate the whole family of the ruling king, thus excluding the possibility that the descendants of a former ruler might once again seek power.

In the northern state of Israel, then, the charismatic elements which was already evident with Saul and which was again taken up with Jeroboam, the first independent king of Israel after Saul, was kept alive. This charismatic element, which was given concrete expression in the designation of the king by a prophet, introduced an unstable and fluid element into the Israelite monarchy which was not present in Judah. Every ruler had to fear the possibility that without his knowledge a new man had already been designated who might seek to kill him the very next day. We can see this from individual instances. The bloodshed which accompanied changes in rule introduced in this way gives the impression that any charismatically motivated change in government virtually amounted to a revolution. Thus Alt arrived at his phrase that the state of Israel was a land of 'divinely-willed revolutions', divinely willed because only the prophetic designation made possible and legitimated a change in rule.[16] The course of events in general and its context makes it clear that such a change of rule only affected the ruling families and did not involve any change in social conditions or structures. Thus in view of its modern significance, the term 'revolution' may not be altogether apt as a description against the background of the Israelite constitution. More important is the fact that such changes of power were ruled out in principle in Jerusalem, where there was only one dynasty. This confirms on another level that the tribe and state of Judah may never have known designation as the independent act of a prophetic and charismatic intermediary. This ideal was probably only extended to Judah at a later stage in the Old Testament literature, when there was a desire to interpret even the early history of Judah and Israel from a unitary standpoint.[17]

These remarks are of fundamental significance not least because in the Old Testament literature, with its marked theological colouring, sweeping judgments are made on 'the' monarchy in 'Israel', and the monarchies of Israel and Judah are taken together without any distinction being made between them. In a quite unjustified way, prophetic designation is then expected of the kings of Judah, or there is surprise at the lack of dynastic consciousness in Israel. Furthermore, whereas the conception of sacral kingship can be applied to Jerusalem with some appearance of justification,[18] the situation in the north is different. Arguments which could be legitimately used for the house of David cannot be applied to the kings of Israel, because their presuppositions were so different. Moreover, there are difficulties in making general statements about a connection between the idea of the Messiah and the Old Testament kingship, since there is no basis for this idea in the northern kingdom; its presuppositions are to be found solely in Jerusalem, where the dynastic monarchy also made the renewal or rebirth of a ruler from one and the same tribe conceivable. Thus there was a tension between the monarchy in the north and that in the south, in theory and in practice, which is understandable once the fact is taken seriously that the two kingdoms were two tribal alliances each with a different structure. This tension is also one of the reasons for the constantly recurring criticism of the monarchy, which began in Israel. When it was extended to Judah, it failed to observe the historical roots of the monarchy and thus put the historical rule of the house of David in an unnecessarily bad light. For Judah stood by its kings. The general condemnation of the monarchy in the Old Testament probably begins with Deuteronomic theology, which transferred to Judah principles which were developed in the northern kingdom. Attention to these criteria could help to clarify and deepen the picture of the theology of the kingship in the Old Testament.[19]

For the most part, developments in the two part-states must now be followed separately. At first Rehoboam of Judah seems to have attempted to win back Israel through military measures, through a great levy of the men of Judah and, remarkably enough, those of Benjamin (I Kings 12.21–24). Finally, word from a prophet forbade the king to wage war against his northern neighbours. The summary (Deuteronomistic) note at the end of Rehoboam's reign (I Kings 14.30) reads rather differently. It states that there was war between Rehoboam and Jeroboam as long as they lived. It can easily be imagined that there were skirmishes between the two states throughout this period. But they do not seem to have developed into a great struggle which fundamentally threatened the independence of the northern state.

We hear a good deal about the measures taken by Jeroboam. The first question was where the new king was to reside. There was no reason to go back to Gibeah, Saul's first residence; there were several reasons against such a course. Benjamin kept with Judah, for reasons which will be indicated later. Shechem was much more suitable for a capital, as it lay in the centre of the state. The development of the city was the first item in Jeroboam's domestic policy: I Kings 12.25 states explicitly that 'he dwelt there'. There is also the additional remark that 'he went out from there and built Penuel'. Penuel is in Transjordania on the lower reaches of the Jabbok.[20]

If Jeroboam in fact built a fortified city there or made an existing town into a fortified outpost, his policy was a sound one, both geographically and tactically. It was relatively easy for the king to retreat there. Connections with Shechem were quite good. He could either cross the *wādi bēdān* and use the wide and easy *wādi fār'a*,[21] crossing the Jordan by the fords near the mouth of the Jabbok, in which case he could quickly be in Penuel; or he could reach the fords by using a valley which runs from Shechem in a south-easterly direction and descends into the Jordan valley after crossing several easy slopes in the region of present-day *mejdel beni fādil*.[22] However, we do not know of any further role played by Penuel in the course of later history.

Geographical considerations make it easier to understand why Jeroboam later (I Kings 14.17) had a footing in a third city, Tirzah, which served as a residence for a number of kings. Tirzah lies on the upper reaches of the *wādi fār'a*; archaeological investigations of it have been made in recent excavations on *tell el-fār'a*.[23] The city was much closer to Shechem; communications with it were good, but it lay much further into the hill-country than Shechem.

The question of the significance of these three successive seats of government for Jeroboam is an open one. They can certainly be seen as a further indication of the insecurity of the monarchy in Israel, which had particular difficulties in its initial stages, and at any rate to begin with did not have a residence like Jerusalem at its disposal. After all, Jerusalem was unquestionably a royal city, which was virtually the king's private possession. We shall return to this point later. The reason for the moves could be difficulties with the inhabitants of Shechem on the one hand and with the process of the fortification of distant Penuel on the other. Another event has also been given as an explanation: the expedition of the Egyptian king Shishak I, who according to the evidence of his Egyptian city-lists was very active in the northern state of Israel. In that case, the residences will have been places to which the king retreated. But this can be no more than hypothesis.

In addition to his choice of capital, the cultic measures taken by Jeroboam were also of considerable significance. It may be regarded as certain that he elevated the two sanctuaries of Bethel and Dan, on the extreme southern and northern boundaries respectively, to the status of state sanctuaries; he installed a golden calf in each of them and equipped each holy place with an independent priesthood subordinate to his needs. I Kings 12.28 gives the reason for the king's decision: 'You have gone up to Jerusalem long enough. Behold your gods, O Israel, who brought you up out of the land of Egypt.'

Old Testament research is still concerned with every element of this royal decision on the part of Jeroboam. At any rate, we hear nothing from this period of a special significance for the sanctuary at Shechem, however much it might have seemed an obvious move to build a palace and a temple there modelled on those in Jerusalem. Perhaps the plan came to grief on the Canaanite upper classes, who were still hostile to Israel, and on the traditions which they supported. Both Bethel and Dan had earlier Israelite traditions, some of which may even have gone back into the early period of the settlement.[24] These were places in the interior from the Canaanite settlements. Jeroboam gives reasons for his decision in I Kings 12.28. But was it necessary to exclude Jerusalem as the great competitive sanctuary? The formula, which takes up the Egypt tradition, suggests that we may have here a later interpretation from a Deuteronomistic perspective. The claim of Jerusalem to the God of Israel, which is defined here on Deuteronomistic lines in close association with the Egypt tradition, is put in the forefront. The reason given attributes to Jeroboam the commission of a sacrilegious act in beginning a false cult of this God. However one may attempt to explain matters, it is difficult to see I Kings 12.28 as a reliable historical explanation.

There remains the remarkable feature of the golden calves, or more accurately, the images of the golden bulls. Were these pedestals in the form of animals for the God who was invisibly enthroned above them?[25] Quite certainly they are not special features of the earliest worship of Yahweh. The resolute revolt of levitical circles against these animals which can be seen in credible retrospect in the chapter on the 'golden calf' from the wilderness period (Exod. 32), confirms that the images were an extraordinary innovation compared with nomadic traditions. If this is the case, then the step taken by the king may be explained as one governed by 'religious politics' in the truest sense. By adopting a cult object acceptable to the Canaanite population, Jeroboam was also attempting to bind the dissident Canaanite groups among his subjects to his rule. To set up an ark would have been far too esoteric a move, comprehensible only to the Israelites; the bulls seem to have been acceptable to the Israelites as well.

This unusual step required royal regulations of a comprehensive nature. Jeroboam not only excluded the levitical priests, but also developed his own festivals to make the sanctuaries functional.[26] Events show that the king intervened in the cultic concerns of the state far more crudely in Israel than in Jerusalem, and in so doing sought to remould the old nomadic form of Israelite religion which survived among the tribes into a unified pattern. Here he was also concerned about his own position. There is later evidence for the dominance of the state in the cult at Bethel, whose high priest instructs the prophet Amos that he is at a 'royal sanctuary' and in a 'royal place' (Amos 7.13). Jeroboam's state religion lay upon the developed Yahweh worship of the tribes like an alien body; it is therefore no wonder that the tribes offered criticism and resistance, that above all memories of nomadic religion survived and indeed were cherished in their midst. This is the basis for the prophetic opposition to the monarchy and the source from which it drew its original power. We may also look to these circles for those who handed down the traditions whose ideas were later to be written down in programmatic form in the nucleus of Deuteronomy.[27]

Jeroboam's religious politics were as energetic as they were shadowy. They were intended to secure his throne and his state, but they provoked serious inner tensions which not least kept summoning prophets on to the scene to designate new kings. Behind this perhaps lay the hope that it would be possible to force a reform of the existing monarchy. We can see how the Deuteronomistic editors of the books of Kings never grew weary of chastising the 'sin of Jeroboam, the son of Nebat', and of representing him as an outlaw among the kings. To Yahweh worshippers who thought on more orthodox lines, he had to appear in this light. In reality, however, he instinctively went straight to the main problem with which his successors also had to deal (with varying degrees of success), namely, the satisfaction of the heterogeneous elements within the population of the northern kingdom, which was not only made up of Israelites and which for a long period was to remain a source of danger.

We hear virtually nothing about Jeroboam's military measures. Nor do we hear of any aggressive thrusts into neighbouring states. The Israelite levy may have acquired an increased significance. But Solomon had already given Israel chariots, and some of the fortifications which Solomon built were on Israelite soil.[28] In the course of time Israel doubtless increased its chariot force; we later read of one of its commanders (I Kings 16.9). In view of Jeroboam's building measures, it seems improbable that he completely did away with forced labour. But perhaps he had difficulties in this sector.

One event must have shaken the two states of Israel and Judah to the same considerable degree, although the Old Testament account of it is very short and is completely restricted to Judah and Jerusalem. In the fifth year of Rehoboam's reign, Shishak king of Egypt went up against Jerusalem and there made deep inroads into the treasures of the temple and the royal palace; later, however, Rehoboam was able partly to make good the damage (I Kings 14.25). This is probably an extract from annals of Judah which did not give any account of the military details of the Pharaoh's invasion, merely recording its consequences and the changes it brought to the temple and the palace. It at least seems clear, however, that the king of Egypt did not capture or plunder Jerusalem. There is rather more detail in the parallel report of II Chron. 12.2–12, which lists cities of Judah which were occupied by the Egyptians; the king is then said to have reached Jerusalem, where Rehoboam did homage, so that everything was not given up to destruction. This suggests that Rehoboam purchased the relief of the city by a large payment of tribute. It was not, therefore, the Pharaoh who made inroads into the temple treasury, but the king of Judah himself, in order to secure the city and the government.

These accounts can in fact be confirmed from Egyptian material. Shishak is doubtless identical with Shoshenk I, the founder of the Twenty-second Dynasty (Bubastids). The Pharaoh is also called Sheshonk, following the Greek form Sesonchis.[29] His rule certainly falls in the second half of the tenth century, so that the fifth year of Rehoboam's reign (about 925 BC) would fit in well. Shoshenk I left behind an impressive list of cities on a wall of the great temple of Amun in Karnak, in fact the last that we have from an Egyptian king relating to an expedition to Palestine.[30] It is remarkable that Jerusalem does not seem to be mentioned on it and does not therefore belong among the places seized;[31] on the other hand, the city-list includes a series of places which belong in the northern state, Israel. Jeroboam must have been very hard pressed, but we hear nothing about this in the Old Testament account.

In clear sequence we find Gibeon, Beth-horon and Aijalon one after the other, describing an exact route from the coastal plain to the territory of Benjamin. But the name of Jerusalem does not appear. Still, Shoshenk could have come close to the city on the route described. Another equally intersting series of cities in the list runs: (Megiddo), Taanach, Shunem, Beth-shean, Rehob . . . Mahanaim (*mḥnm*). According to this the king would have advanced northwards as far as the plain of Jezreel, and ultimately even have descended into the Jordan valley, crossing the fords by the mouth of the Jabbok into Transjordania and moving on as far as Mahanaim, if the identification with *mḥnm* is correct. The details of Jeroboam's various residences can be reconciled with this operation, and make a retreat by the king understandable. The information given in Shoshenk's city-list offers an incentive to develop a regular plan of operations. The attempt has been made impressively by B. Mazar, and the persuasiveness of his theory has been heightened by the fact that he combined names of cities at one end of a line with those at the end of the next line, reading in the opposite direction (known as 'boustrophedon').[32] In this way he succeeded in reconstructing a coherent route of march for the Egyptian army through the northern state of Israel. However, this theory pays no attention to geographical conditions, which are difficult in places, nor is it compelling in every respect.[33] Quite apart from these details, however, it is evident that Shoshenk's undertaking was of limited duration. With the best will in the world he could not consider an occupation of Palestine, as in the days of Egypt's great expansion during the New Kingdom. Egypt no longer had the necessary means of power at its disposal, and in Palestine itself powers had gained ground which would prove more than a match for the Egyptians in the long run. Thus Shoshenk's expedition was probably a last attempt to represent Egyptian power on a large scale in Palestine and Syria. The second part of the city-list gives a great many names, but only a very small number of them can be interpreted. They point to an area south of Judah and probably also to Edom. Perhaps this indicates the route taken by the Egyptians on their return.

Shoshenk's expedition to Palestine was an episode which did not have any lasting results. However, the documents on it give a faithful picture of the centres of fortification at the time. They correspond in essentials and even in details with the old chain of fortifications on the heights of Jerusalem and on the plain of Megiddo. Shoshenk's expedition may have stimulated Rehoboam over his seventeen years of rule to see to the defence of his territory, particularly in the south and west. II Chronicles 11.5–10 gives a list of fortified cities which he built or developed. Only Chronicles reports this, but the list is certainly based on official documents, especially as the details give an astonishing glimpse of the territorial possessions of Judah.[34] The remarkable thing about this list of fortified cities is that it contains places which apparently lie deep in the interior, i.e. in the old tribal territory of Judah itself, and excludes both the coastal plain and the deep south.

There are fifteen cities in all. In the south, it is significant that Beer-sheba does not appear; the line of fortification is taken back some way and runs through Adoraim, Hebron and Ziph. The boundaries of the system are Lachish and Gath on the west and Aijalon in the north. All the coastal plain lies outside it, but it includes at least part of Benjaminite territory. Now it is by no means certain that these cities described a fixed boundary line for Judah; on the other hand, we must reckon with the possibility that from the time of David Judah suffered considerable losses in the south and west. In particular, the Philistines seem to have struggled to gain independence once again under the leadership of particular city rulers, and to a large degree to have succeeded. The break-away of the northern state only served to encourage them to take such steps. Very soon armed clashes with the Philistines developed once again.

Conditions on the northern frontier of Judah seem to have developed in a different way. If not during the reign of Rehoboam, at least during the reigns of his successors, it became clear that Judah had an interest in extending its territory northwards. This is understandable. After the separation of the two states, Jerusalem lay near the border with Israel. What was once an advantage for David now proved to be a considerable disadvantage. Israel could threaten Jerusalem directly. So the kings in Jerusalem had the understandable desire to establish a buffer territory to the north of their city, to protect the capital against Jerusalem.

Over a moderately high ridge, commonly known as Mount Scopus, there is a gently rolling area which comes to an end about nine miles from Jerusalem in another high ridge to the north which is clearly distinct from it. At the present day, *rāmallah* and *el-bīre* lie on this ridge. The territory was that in which the tribe of Benjamin settled; from Rehoboam onwards Judah and Israel fought over it.

The problem of the northern frontier of Judah is bound up with the situation and history of the tribe of Benjamin. Its relatively small territory came to lie between the stronger powers of Judah and Ephraim. Whether this territory originally belonged to Ephraim is a disputed question. Although Saul came from Benjamin and was recognized by Ephraim, the tribe seems to have retained some measure of independence which from time to time called for a special action (cf. II Sam. 3.19), and was able to choose freely in favour of one partner or the other. According to I Kings 12.21, Rehoboam also assembled men of Benjamin for his fight to regain Israel; in Shechem Benjamin opted for Judah. The question may also play a part in the history of the designation of Jeroboam. Ahijah promised him ten tribes; he wanted to give one tribe to the son of David. Was this one tribe Judah? Would this have been mentioned specially? It seems more likely that this one tribe was to be taken from Israel. In that case, it can only be Benjamin.[35] I Kings 11.36 gives as a reason that David is to have a light for all time in Jerusalem. Thus this separation is to take place for the sake of Jerusalem. Jerusalem will be preserved, and Benjamin will make a contribution to its safety. The war which lasted the lifetimes of Rehoboam and Jeroboam (I Kings 14.30) was a struggle for Benjaminite territory, and was continued for the same purpose by their successors.

In foreign affairs, the two kingdoms only sustained losses. The system of complicated dependencies of tributary states and governorships, which was built up by David and neglected by Solomon, completely collapsed. Israel lost its Aramaean-Syrian province in the north-east. The kingdom of Damascus developed independently and claimed the territories which were once conquered by David, reaching deep into northern Transjordania. Here Israel had a dangerous opponent for generations. The state of the Ammonites, whose crown had once been worn by David himself, gradually developed out of its dependent status. At first Moab does not seem to have withheld tribute. A new kingdom arose in Edom, which had already gained its independence under Solomon.

How quickly times had changed since David and Solomon! The personal union had been destroyed, the great patterns of wide-ranging expansion and the development of domestic administration seemed to have broken up. It was necessary to protect possessions in the central territory; a number of cities in the north were fortified with some difficulty to make them usable as residences; in the south the frontiers of old tribal possessions were drawn back for reasons of security; there were stubborn skirmishes in the attempt to establish a line of demarcation. Jerusalem, a former capital and international centre, had to be protected against a former partner in the state. Judah and Israel had become petty kingdoms which had to defend themselves, with more or less success, against attacks. They had to develop new forces, and to be on the guard against succumbing to the growing strength of neighbouring countries. Nothing illustrates the exceptional character of the heyday of David and Solomon better than this macabre regression into the competitiveness of tribal rivalry after the collapse of the personal union. There is more reason than before to consider events in Israel and Judah as separate developments. The consequences for theological issues and for the cult are evident. 'Israel' as an entity, the ideal conception of 'Israel' on an 'amphictyonic' basis, was and remained a postulate which was threatened by historical developments.

At the end of the reigns of Rehoboam and Jeroboam we are given for the first time in I Kings a synchronism for the reigns of the two kings. I Kings 15.1 runs: 'Now in the eighteenth year of king Jeroboam the son of Nebat, Abijam began to reign over Judah.' In a similar way, we read later in I Kings 15.25: 'Nadab the son of Jeroboam began to reign over Israel in the second year of Asa the king of Judah; and he reigned over Israel two years.' This is the information, already mentioned above, which provides the material for a relative chronology; in an absolute chronology, Rehoboam is assigned the years 932/31–916/15, and Jeroboam the period from 932/31 to 911/10.[36] We are told virtually nothing about king Abijam of Judah (916/5–914/3). He is praised for having established Jerusalem (I Kings 15.4), but the words used are those put on the lips of Ahijah of Shiloh in his conversation with Jeroboam (I Kings 11.36). Abijam also fought against Jeroboam. Thus the problem of the northern boundary of Judah remained paramount.

The events in which Jeroboam's son Nadab was involved seem to have been more dramatic. His reign over Israel was short (911/10–910/09). The question now arose as to how the succession to the throne of Israel was to be arranged. Jeroboam had been personally designated by Ahijah; his son Nadab had not. To begin with, his rule seems to have been tolerated, but the two years on the throne which are ascribed to him (I Kings 15.25) mean that he was only in power for just over a calendar year if ante-dating was used (the year of his reign was reckoned as a complete year). His doom was already being prepared. Baasha, a man from the tribe of Issachar, engaged in a conspiracy against Nadab and killed him in Gibbethon, where he was engaged in a battle against the Philistines. Baasha made himself king and completely exterminated the house of Jeroboam. I Kings explains the violent revolution in terms of the principle of prophetic influence on the king-dom, which has already been explained. It was no less a person than Ahijah of Shiloh who now proclaimed doom on the house of Jeroboam (I Kings 14.1–18), and it was the prophet Jehu ben Hanani who designated Baasha king and made him a *nāgîd* over Israel (I Kings 16.2). It is quite certain that the automatic character of the account, in which prophetic disqualification and qualification follow each other so harshly and so precisely, is based on pragmatic considerations which may themselves have simplified the course of events, even if the motivation is not immediately apparent. But it would certainly be wrong to see this as no more than the work of the Deuteronomist. In each instance the prophetic motives are kept secret; in the end this is meant to indicate the unfathomable will of God who chose his men in each particular instance. However, it is legitimate to enquire after the historical causes which led so quickly and unexpectedly to the fall of a king. It took some time before dynasties began to be formed in Israel. Actions there may at first have been dictated by uncertainty and a degree of turbulence. The pattern established by Jerusalem seemed to rob the idea of dynastic links of some of its savour. The charismatic principle was to remain effective. On the other hand, though, whether the men concerned maintained their rule will have depended upon their quality. Those who had to fend for themselves after the division of the state at Shechem found it difficult to renew the kingdom from their midst; in choosing the charismatic rather than the dynastic principle they were faced with a decision which over the long term was unfavourable to settled politics. A period of turbulence set in with Baasha which only had a peaceful outcome with Omri.

As the years of the reigns of the kings of Israel and Judah overlap in a compli-cated fashion during this period, a synoptic table may be useful:

Rehoboam	932/31–916/15	Jeroboam	932/31–911/10
Abijam	916/15–914/13		
Asa	914/13–874/73		

	Nadab	911/10–910/09
	Baasha	910/09–887/86
	Elah	887/86–886/85
	Zimri	886/85
	Omri	886/85–875/74
	Ahab	875/74–854/53

In the two states, Rehoboam and Jeroboam were followed by two brief reigns, those of Abijah and Nadab; in turn, these were followed by the longer reigns of Asa and Baasha. The latter are said to have spent their lives fighting each other;

their dispute was over the frontier area in Benjaminite territory (I Kings 15.16–22). At first Baasha was the more active. He advanced towards Ramah, only five miles north of Jerusalem, with the declared purpose of blockading Jerusalem on the north side, so that no one could move in or out (15.17).

The fortification of Ramah was an obvious move. As can still be seen today from *er-rām*, it was a projecting hill with a good view to the south, at the very point where it was possible to control the route leading from the coastal plain in the west through Gibeon and touching the northern route from Jerusalem. Asa, the king of Judah, did not respond to this move with war, but with diplomatic activity, which is indicative of the new balance of power. He sent a delegation to king Benhadad of Damascus, not with empty hands. He delved deep into the treasure in the temple and the palace and sent his offering with a request for an alliance against king Baasha of Israel. To comply, the king of Damascus had to break his already existing alliance with Baasha. He agreed, sent troops into Galilee and caused considerable damage there. This caused Baasha to give up the fortification of Ramah for the moment; he is said to have retreated to Tirzah. We do not hear how he dealt with the king of Damascus, but we do hear what Asa did. He advanced against Ramah, took possession of the Israelite building material which had been assembled there and used it to fortify two cities, Geba and Mizpah.

Geba (*jeba*ʿ) is about a mile and a half east of Ramah and is also a convenient site, with some good views northwards. Mizpah was in an even more favourable position, if it is to be identified with *tell en-naṣbe*, which lies further north than Ramah, right on the road coming from Jerusalem.[37]

Asa is also said to have fortified other cities; more was recorded in the chronicles of the kings of Judah. The Deuteronomist does not supply the information, but compensates the reader by giving him the important piece of news that in his old age the king had bad feet! The account of the forty-one years of Asa's reign is sadly one-sided. The only other interesting information is that to begin with, his mother Maacah reigned for him; first she probably acted as regent, but she also seems to have laid claim to the throne. Asa had to depose her, allegedly for some cultic offence. Here the role of the queen mother (Hebrew *gᵉbīrā*, properly 'mistress') becomes a problem which must be considered in the context of the institution of the monarchy against the wider background of royal law in the ancient East.[38]

Parallel developments in the northern state of Israel during Asa's reign were at first turbulent, but then took on wide-ranging significance. It is striking that the account from I Kings 16 to II Kings 10 deals at length almost exclusively with Israel; only twice are brief notes inserted about the state of Judah.[39]

As is well known, Baasha killed his predecessor Nadab when the latter was in process of laying siege to the city of Gibbethon. Gibbethon belonged to the Philistines and probably lay between the two towns of Ekron and Gezer;[40] it was thus in the area where the hill-country gives way to the coastal plain, at the very point where the southern chain of cities begins. The interests of Judah, Israel and the Philistines clashed most sharply at this point. From Gezer it was as easy to move north into the hill-country as to move south, and the town could pose a threat to the existence of both states. Shoshenk's troops operated there, which can be seen as an indication of the permanent significance of the area. It is clear that the time will inevitably have passed when Gezer was a possession of Judah, having been presented as a dowry of the Egyptian princess whom Solomon married. The Philistines had long established their independence there and defended themselves against Israel, seeking to gain an even firmer footing. The outcome of Baasha's campaign is unknown, but his successors continued it.

The very prophet who had once designated Baasha king, Jehu ben Hanani, now prophesied the fall of his whole house. Baasha died a natural death in Tirzah, but the events surrounding the death of Jeroboam now repeated themselves. First of all Baasha's son Elah ascended the throne, making a new attempt to establish a dynasty. But he is said to have reigned only two years in Tirzah, and that may mean that he only occupied the throne for a few months. Elah fell victim to a senior officer from the chariot force, Zimri. While Elah was drunk at a feast in Tirzah, Zimri murdered him (I Kings 16.9, 10).

Zimri modelled his actions as king on those of Baasha. He set out to exterminate the house of Baasha, believing that in this way he could usurp the kingdom for himself. But he was wrong. He reigned in Tirzah for only seven days. We do not hear that a prophet ever designated him king. He was a conspirator, and accordingly had to come to a speedy end.

The army heard of Zimri's conspiracy and its consequences while they were fighting the Philistines at Gibbethon. They immediately acclaimed their commander Omri as king. He left for Tirzah immediately, to lay siege to the city in which Zimri had taken refuge. The latter saw that the end was in sight. In despair he withdrew to the innermost rooms of the palace and was burnt to death along with the whole building.

Zimri, the man who made himself king, the 'real' usurper, was dead. Omri had been acclaimed king by the army in their camp. Was he also the future king? This question was also a preoccupation of the Israelites – and the Old Testament indicates that opinions in Israel were divided. Some supported a certain Tibni and wanted to make him king; others took the side of Omri (I Kings 16.21). We can see what happened when there was no prophetic designation; there were regular crises of government, and competing kings. Finally Omri gained the support of the majority. And Tibni died. We are given no more details.

Anyway, the fact is that Omri became king. He reigned for twelve years over Israel. He became king by a majority decision, first in the camp at Gibbethon, and then by the choice of all Israel. We hear nothing of any prophetic designation. But after all the confusion, the setbacks and the internal crises which had shaken and weakened the state since the time of Jeroboam, there was at last a great personality on the throne of Israel. He had a broad political vision, evidently coupled with the skill to strengthen the internal constitution of Israel. He was certainly no David, but the actions associated with his name are reminiscent of David. The first real dynasty in Israel to last more than a decade or so began with Omri, and it was Omri who gave Israel a new permanent capital, the city of Samaria. He introduced a new era for the state of Israel.

NOTES

1. A. Jepsen, *Die Quellen des Königsbuches*, [2]1956, is entirely devoted to the framework of the books of Kings; R. Bin-Nun, 'Formulas from Royal Records of Israel and Judah', *VT* 18, 1968, 414–32, investigates the information in the chronological notes. See now especially Helga Weippert, 'Die "deuteronomistischen" Beurteilungen der Könige von Israel und Juda und das Problem der Redaktion der Königsbücher', *Bibl.* 53, 1972, 301–39.

2. J. Begrich, *Die Chronologie der Könige von Israel und Juda*, 1929.

3. A. Jepsen/R. Hanhart, *Untersuchungen zur israelitisch-jüdischen Chronologie*, BZAW 88, 1964; A. Jepsen, 'Noch einmal zur israelitisch-jüdischen Chronologie', *VT* 18, 1968, 31–46; id., 'Ein neuer Fixpunkt für die Chronologie der israelitischen Könige?', *VT* 20, 1970, 359–61.

4. Jepsen/Hanhart, *Untersuchungen*, 28.

5. K. T. Andersen, 'Die Chronologie der Könige von Israel und Juda', *Studia Theologica* 23, 1969, 69–114.

6. Andersen, op. cit., 73.

7. S. Mowinckel, *Die Chronologie der israelitisch-jüdischen Könige*, 1932; W. F. Albright, 'The Chronology of the Divided Monarchy of Israel', *BASOR* 100, 1945; id., 'New Light from Egypt on the Chronology and History of Israel and Judah', *BASOR* 130, 1953; R. Thiele, *The Mysterious Numbers of the Hebrew Kings*, 1951; C. Schedl, 'Textkritische Bemerkungen zu den Synchronismen der Könige von Israel und Judah', *VT* 12, 1962, 88–119.

8. See also A. L. Otero, *Chronologia e Historia de los Reinos Hebreos (1028-587 BC)*, 1964; G. Sauer, 'Die chronologischen Angaben in den Büchern Deuteronomium bis 2. Könige', *TZ* 24, 1968, 1–14; D. N. Freedman, 'The Chronology of Israel and the Ancient Near East', in *The Bible and the Ancient Near East* (Albright Festschrift), 1961, 203–28.

9. See the introductory chapter, 'Witnesses and Evidence'.

10. A. Malamat, 'Kingship and Council in Israel and Sumer: A Parallel', *JNES* 22, 1963, 247–53.

11. For a positive assessment of the historicity of the events cf. A. Malamat, 'Organs of Statecraft in the Israelite Monarchy', *El Ha'ayin* ('Back to the Sources') 41, 1964 = *BA* 28, 1965, 34–65; M. Noth, *Könige*, BK 9, 265–87 (with further literature). For I Kings 12 see also S. Herrmann, 'Geschichte Israels – Möglichkeiten und Grenzen ihrer Darstellung', *TLZ* 94, 1969, 641–50; in detail J. Debus, *Die Sünde Jeroboams*, FRLANT 93, 1967; for the LXX tradition of I Kings 12 see H. Seebass, 'Zur Königserhebung Jeroboams I.', *VT* 17, 1967, 325–33; D. W. Gooding, 'The Septuagint's Rival Versions of Jeroboam's Rise to Power', *VT* 17, 1967, 173–89.

12. The name has presumably been retained in the designation of the spring *'ēn ṣerēda* south west of *selfīt*. One of the places near to it could be identical with Zeredah, cf. W. F. Albright, *BASOR* 11, 1923, 5f.; A. Alt, *PJB* 24, 1928, 69; Simons, op. cit., 839.

13. I Kings 11.35f. For the passage see Noth, *Könige*, 258–64; see also J. Debus, op. cit., 12ff.; S. Herrmann, op. cit., 649.

14. Taken with I Kings 12.20, I Kings 12.2, 3 are obscure; on the one hand Jeroboam

seems to have returned on his own initiative while on the other it is said that he is 'brought back'; cf. the discussion of the problems in Noth, *Könige*, 273; for the nature and origin of the historical account see I. Plein, 'Erwägungen zur Überlieferung von I Reg. 11, 26–14, 20', *ZAW* 78, 1966, 8–24.

15. He is usually called Jeroboam I in order to distinguish him from the king of the same name in the eighth century.

16. A. Alt, 'Das Königtum in den Reichen Israel und Juda' (1951), *KS* II, 116–34 = *Grundfragen*, 348–66.

17. This happened in the case of David in I Sam. 16.1–13, where Samuel performed an act of anointing on David modelled on the pattern of Saul's anointing; cf. also II Sam. 7.8–10 and the consequences associated with it in M. Noth, 'David and Israel in II Samuel VII' (1957), in *The Laws in the Pentateuch*, 1966, 250–9.

18. In so far as one observes the close connection between monarchy and state sanctuary, 'palace and temple', and regards the temple as a 'royal sanctuary', which was not to the same degree the sanctuary of the tribes of Judah (and Israel).

19. For more recent discussion of the monarchy see the works by G. Wallis, *Geschichte und Überlieferung*, 1968, esp. 45–108; H. J. Boecker, *Die Beurteilung der Anfänge des Königtums in den deuteronomistischen Abschnitten des I. Samuelbuches*, WMANT 31, 1969; W. H. Schmidt, 'Kritik am Königtum', in *Probleme biblischer Theologie* (von Rad Festschrift), 1971, 440–61; J. A. Soggin, 'Der Beitrag des Königtums zur israelitischen Religion', SVT 23, 1972, 9–26.

20. It is not possible to determine its exact situation; it is probably *tell ed-dahab el-jerqi*, cf. K. Elliger, *BHH* 3, 1478, and M. Noth, *Aufsätze* 1, esp. 518 n.71.

21. This *wādi* never plays a recognizable role in the Old Testament and has also been neglected by archaeological investigation; more recently, however, cf. the investigations by S. Kappus, 'Oberflächenuntersuchungen im mittleren *wādi far'a*', *ZDPV* 82, 1966, 74–82, and R. Knierim, 'Oberflächenuntersuchungen im Wādi el-Fār'a II', *ZDPV* 85, 1969, 51–62. The significance of the *wādi* for communications is noted in Y. Yadin, 'Some Aspects to the Strategy of Ahab and David (I Kings 20; II Sam. 11)', *Bibl.* 36, 1955, 332ff., esp. 338ff.

22. Cf. the considerations in this direction by S. Herrmann in *ZDPV* 80, 1964, 74–6.

23. Cf. K. M. Kenyon, *Archaeology in the Holy Land*, ²1965, 312, with details of further literature.

24. For Bethel cf. Gen. 28.10–22 and O. Eissfeldt, 'Der Gott Bethel' (1930), *Kleine Schriften* I, 206–33; A. Alt, 'Die Wallfahrt von Sichem nach Bethel' (1938), *KS* I, 79–88; for Dan cf. Judg. 17;18 and M. Noth, 'Der Hintergrund von Richter 17 und 18' (1962), *Aufsätze* I, 133–47; see also ibid., 235–7; A. Malamat, 'The Danite Migration and the Pan-Israelite Exodus Conquest: A Biblical Narrative Pattern', *Bibl.* 51, 1970, 1–16.

25. O. Eissfeldt, 'Lade und Stierbild' (1940/41), *Kleine Schriften* II, 282–305; M. Weippert, 'Gott und Stier', *ZDPV* 77, 1961, 99–117; W. Zimmerli, 'Das Bilderverbot in der Geschichte des alten Israel', in *Schalom* (Jepsen Festschrift), 1971, 86–96; see also L. Malten, 'Der Stier im Kult und mythischen Bild', in *Jahrbuch des Deutschen Archäologischen Institut* 43, 1928/29, 90ff.

26. I Kings 12.31–33.

27. Cf. A. Alt, 'Die Heimat des Deuteronomiums' (1953), *KS* II, 250–75 = *Grundfragen*, 392–417; H. W. Wolff, 'Hoseas geistige Heimat', *TLZ* 81, 1956, 83–94 = *Gesammelte Studien*, 232–50.

28. Namely Megiddo and Hazor.

29. E. Otto, *Ägypten – der Weg des Pharaonenreichs*, ⁴1966, 213–21; A. H. Gardiner, *Egypt of the Pharaohs*, 1961, 326–30; W. Helck, *Geschichte des alten Ägypten*, HdO I 1, 3, 1968, 221–3.

30. Impressively published in *Reliefs and Inscriptions at Karnak, Vol. III : The Bubastide*

Portal, Chicago, Oriental Institute Publications LXXIV, 1954; J. Simons, *Handbook for the Study of Egyptian Topographical Lists relating to Western Asia*, 1937, 89–101, 178–86; there is a detailed investigation by M. Noth, 'Die Schoschenkliste' (1938), *Aufsätze* 2, 73–93. Shoshenk's presence in Palestine is attested by the fragment of a relief from Megiddo which bears the king's name; Lamon-Shipton, *Megiddo* I, 6of.; P. Porter – R. L. B. Moss, *Topographical Bibliography* VII, 381ff.

31. Probably not even in the few damaged parts of the relevant sections of the list.

32. B. Mazar, 'The Campaign of Pharaoh Shishak to Palestine', SVT 4, 1957, 57–66.

33. S. Herrmann, 'Operationen Pharao Schoschenks I. im östlichen Ephraim', *ZDPV* 80, 1964, 55–79.

34. G. Beyer, 'Das Festungssystem Rehabeams', *ZDPV* 54, 1931, 113–34; see also O. Eissfeldt, 'Israelitisch-philistäische Grenzverschiebungen von David bis auf die Assyrerzeit' (1943), *Kleine Schriften* II, 453–63.

35. This view is, of course, disputed. Cf. the change of opinion over the question in M. Noth, *Überlieferungsgeschichtliche Studien*, [2]1957, 72 n. 7, and *Könige*, 259f.; see also S. Herrmann, *TLZ* 94, 1969, 647, 649; for the whole problem see K.-D. Schunck, *Benjamin*, 1963, 139–53.

36. Jepsen allots to Solomon the period from 965–926; the dates for Rehoboam (926–910) and Jeroboam I (927–907) differ accordingly.

37. For the excavations see K. M. Kenyon, *Archaeology*, [2]1965, 320 (with bibliography); for the identification with Mizpah see A. Alt, 'Neue Erwägungen über die Lage von Mizpa, Ataroth, Beeroth und Gibeon', *ZDPV* 69, 1953, 1–27.

38. G. Molin, 'Die Stellung der Gebira im Staate Juda', *TZ* 10, 1954, 161ff.; more comprehensively H. Donner, 'Art und Herkunft des Amtes der Königinmutter im Alten Testament', *Festschrift Johannes Friedrich*, 1959, 105–45. The special position of the queen mother is restricted to monarchies with a dynastic succession. Donner believes that it is possible that Hittite influence was at work through the mediation of Canaan in the development of the 'office' of the queen mother in Judah. However, no reliable statements can be made about the rights, duties and functions of the queen mother from Old Testament sources. H. Donner, op. cit., names and discusses the telling evidence from Assyria, Ugarit and the Hellenistic sphere.

39. I Kings 22.41–51 on king Jehoshaphat; II Kings 8.16–29 on Joram and Ahaziah.

40. Possibly Gibbethon is to be sought on *tell el-melāt*; G. von Rad, 'Das Reich Israel und die Philister', *PJB* 29, 1933, 30–42; he is followed by O. Eissfeldt, 'Israelitisch-philistäische Grenzverschiebungen', op. cit., 458; K. Elliger, *BHH* 1, 566f., differs: noting the sequence in Josh. 19.43ff. he recommends that *tell el-melāt* should be identified with Eltekeh and Gibbethon with *'āqir*, which lies about three miles further west. The latter was earlier identified with Ekron.

5 | *Omri and his Dynasty in Israel*

AFTER A NOTE on the accession of Omri, I Kings 16.23 states that he resided for six years in Tirzah. But where did he move after that? The continuation of the text marks the change: 'Then he bought the hill of Samaria (*šōmᵉrōn*) from Shemer for two talents of silver; and he fortified the hill, and called the name of the city which he built, Samaria, after the name of Shemer, the owner of the hill.' Here we have a report of the foundation of the city of Samaria, which from then on was to become the undisputed capital and official residence of the kings of Israel. All the details of this event need careful consideration.

King Omri bought a place where no settlement had previously been made.[1] He *bought* it, which leads us to conclude that it was a Canaanite, and not an Israelite possession.[2] Shemer was a man who belonged to the pre-Israelite population of the country; it is significant that hitherto he had been able to retain his property high in the hill-country of Ephraim. Omri bought his land and thus took possession of a territory which originally had nothing to do with Israel, but now became his personal possession. He did this with the intention of building a city on it – his own residence and the capital of the state.

All this is very reminiscent of David and the way in which he made the site of his intended capital, Jerusalem, his own property. At least Omri bought the hill of Samaria in the same fashion and with the same intention, and further developments proved him right.

Albrecht Alt, who has paid particular attention to this passage,[3] says quite openly that Omri imitated David in his actions. Omri made an even more favourable beginning. For unlike David, he did not take over a city which was already built, with its inhabitants and its institutions. He began something quite new, and as a result was able to give much clearer shape to his own ideas. He did not call the city 'The City of Omri', any more than David was able or wanted to change the city of Jerusalem into 'The City of David'. Clearly he did not wish to break off all connections with the earlier history of the place. He may have had in mind that the name of the city would retain a Canaanite element and help relations with the Canaanites.

Samaria lies about five miles north-west of Shechem, not quite in the hills, but in an area far west of the previous residences of Shechem, Tirzah and of course

Penuel. It was near to the coast and to the Canaanites. Omri may have chosen deliberately to settle there. From Samaria he may have expected to be able to exert favourable influence on those parts of the country which had mixed populations. Here too there is a parallel with David. He chose Jerusalem because it lay in a border area between Judah and Israel where he could be equally close to both the states which he governed. Omri chose Samaria, the hill of Shemer, because he saw that its favourable position, in land which could be fortified, offered the possibility of compensating for the differences between the two strata of the population, whether in ideology or in politics. In exemplary fashion he refused to go near to Shechem. Shechem was burdened with specifically Canaanite traditions and was the seat of an ancient aristocracy; internal resistance against Israel may have been too great there, and it was from there that Jeroboam had retreated.

One last consideration remains to be added. How did Omri conceive of the future constitutional relationship between Samaria and the state of Israel? Did he follow the Davidic pattern in this respect also? David ruled over Judah from Jerusalem, but as David's personal residence the city retained a special status which was later given expression in the phrase 'Jerusalem and Judah'. Granted, we never find the formula 'Samaria and Israel',[4] but the 'city' did claim an independent position over against the territory of the 'tribes' in Ephraim and Manasseh; this would emerge later in the context of Jehu's revolution. Topographical conditions were also in its favour.

The hill of Samaria has a dominant aspect on almost every side; the west side is particularly impressive, where it towers above a broad valley.[5] Isaiah 28.1 aptly addresses Samaria as a 'proud crown on the head of a rich valley'. This is not the place to go more closely into the construction of the city.[6] Above all it was the later kings who saw to the adornment of Samaria as a residence. Omri's successor Ahab built an 'ivory house' (I Kings 22.39); the phrase probably means a house which was decorated with carved ivory, interesting pieces of which have been found on the site.[7] Ahab also built a temple to Baal in the city, thus confirming that it was not merely an Israelite place; the various elements of the state were to be represented in the capital to provide so to speak a connecting link between the different elements of the population.

It is regrettable that we have no more information about domestic political problems from the time of Omri. He himself is given a black mark by the Deuteronomistic redactor because he aroused the wrath of Yahweh by apostasy. The evil he did against Yahweh surpassed all that of his predecessors (I Kings 16.25). These words may cloak a whole series of concessions towards the Canaanites, in politics as well as in the cult. Omri seems to have introduced a policy of accommodation and compromise. The choice of the hill of Samaria and the building of his own residence there were only steps on this course, albeit decisive ones. The instability of the Israelite monarchy, the charismatic ideal with its constant and unpredictable changes of rule, the permanent threat from the Philistines and the growing danger from the north-east, where the state of Damascus bordered on Israel, all required that Israel should be strengthened internally, and that there should not be clashes between the various groups of the populace and the tribes which the state contained. To achieve such an end it was necessary not only to stabilize the monarchy but also to tolerate ancestral religions. Permanent success here meant the toleration of the religion of Baal rather than its extermination. Israel paid a high price. The king was prepared to pay it, but at the same time he provoked an Israelite opposition. In the long run, the interaction of these forces dealt a death-blow to Omri's dynasty. However, this should not detract from the value of Omri's political contribution. After the time of David and Solomon he was the first to make the state of Israel into a more complex ethnic structure by incorporating other elements of the population. He saw the problems which were crucial for governing Israel and for securing its existence. The course of compromise begun by Omri, followed with considerable mistrust by those dedicated to Yahweh, met the needs of the hour. For the state could not be stabilized by permanent conflict; it was necessary to gain control of the powers at work within it, in the best fashion possible.

Omri was buried in Samaria. This is the conclusion of his life and the seal set on his programme. Omri was buried in *his* city. This fact also pointed the way for his successors. Anyone who wanted to continue the successful work of this far-seeing man could not but regard this city of Samaria as a pledge for his own success and further it to the best of his abilities. Here too there is an unmistakable parallel to the southern state: in the future, Israelite kings would be buried in their new capital, just as the house of David were buried in Jerusalem.

Omri's successor was his son Ahab, who kept his place on the throne. He did not meet the fate of Nadab or Elah, who were buried alongside their fathers after only a few months. Ahab was able to maintain his position because adequate foundations had been laid for the formation of a dynasty and the beginnings of a lasting political constitution. Ahab benefited from Omri's reputation and from the consolidation of the monarchy, in which he too played his part. He resolutely continued his father's policies and built up Samaria further. The fact that he reigned in Samaria is specially noted: his reign was twenty-two years (I Kings 16.29), ten years longer than that of Omri. Andersen puts Ahab in the period between 875/74 and 854/53 BC.

Ahab's positive and successful political activity naturally incurred the criticism of the Deuteronomistic redactors of our books of Kings. The verdict on Omri is repeated over Ahab word for word. He did more evil in the eyes of Yahweh than all who were before him. In fact he went a considerable step further than his father. He married a Phoenician princess, Jezebel, a daughter of king Ittobaal of Tyre.

In I Kings 16.31 this king is of course called Ethbaal, 'king of the Sidonians'. But in *Antiquities* VIII, 13, 2 (324) Josephus speaks of ιθώβαλος, king of Tyre. In fact the name may have been wrongly vocalized in the Old Testament; it must have been *ittōbaʿal*. Sidon is about twenty-two miles north of Tyre on the Phoenician coast; it is the nearest city state in this area. There may be an error in both the Old Testament and in Josephus, or 'Sidonian' may have been used as a generic term for the Phoenicians.

Ahab's marriage to this Phoenician princess had consequences for his domestic policy, and above all for the cult. It is said that he worshipped Baal, the deity whom the Phoenicians revered in different local manifestations as the supreme god of their city states.[8] Ahab's policy is similar to that already followed by Solomon: the royal house respected the deities of *all* subjects, and especially those of the royal family. However, Ahab's situation was different in some respects. Solomon is said to have built sanctuaries for his wives' gods on the Mount of Olives. This was a concern of the capital, and had a particular diplomatic background. But in Samaria Ahab built a temple to Baal as an official sanctuary, not just for the royal house but for members of his own state. This amounted to the official recognition of the religion of Baal in Israel. A counter-attack from those faithful to Yahweh was inevitable. We have a vivid indication of the extent of this opposition in the wide sweep of the Elijah and Elisha traditions in Kings, which displace almost everything else between I Kings 17 and II Kings 8. Even their continuation, the story of Jehu (II Kings 9 and 10), in the last resort belongs in this great opposition movement and forms so to speak its crown and conclusion. Here the Deuteronomists could use material about a development which was directed against the Canaanites, first in prophetic and then in militant fashion.

In this period we hear of both prophets of Yahweh and prophets of Baal. Jezebel directed her attention above all to the worshippers of Yahweh. She exterminated them (I Kings 18.4), or at any rate made the attempt. A rift went right through the centre of the royal court. One of the highest state officials, one of those who were set 'over the house' ('*aser 'al habbayit*), a certain Obadiah, was among those who 'feared Yahweh' (18.3). He concealed prophets of Yahweh in caves and looked after them there. We can hardly have a more vivid picture of the tense internal situation during this period. On the one hand was a 'foreign' queen bent on removing the servants of the national god whom she found so alien; on the other hand there was an Israelite minister, still with a name indicating his allegiance to Yahweh (!),[9] secretly thwarting the policy of his queen.

Among the prophets of Yahweh one figure towers above the rest. Tradition has clearly singled him out, and saga has heightened his stature, so that he seems to be raised above any conflict. With sovereignty and relentless strength he took Yahweh's part and fought for him. The man is, of course, the prophet Elijah. A whole series of Elijah stories has been handed down to us, continued in a similar group which have his disciple Elisha at their centre. The stories about Elijah appear in I Kings 17–19; 21; II Kings 1.1–2.18; those about Elisha in II Kings 2; 4.1–8.15.[10]

Tradition sees these men as determined fighters in the cause of Yahweh, the God of Israel. They defied all influences from foreign cults and all worship of foreign gods. Of course this feature appears in a more marked, more consistent, more monumental fashion in Elijah than in Elisha. The Elisha tradition is broader, often stronger in narrative detail, and has a greater interest in miracle; it is not constructed so tersely, and in parts it is dependent on the Elijah tradition. To pass historical judgment on its form and content is incomparably more difficult than in the case of the Elijah stories.

Elijah came from Tishbe, which must be located in Transjordania.[11] He made an appearance in a number of places in Israel, but never in Judah, with which he had nothing to do. Elijah is exclusively a figure from the northern state of Israel, and can only be understood against that background. We know of virtually no clashes with the religion of Baal in Judah; this does not mean that they did not occur, but possibly they were not as acute as in Israel, and did not have the same political consequences. At any rate, Elijah was an adversary of the house of Ahab and above all of Jezebel. He appeared at the flashpoints of the state, and in the border areas of Yahwistic religion. We can see him in the frontier area between Israel and Phoenicia, and Zarephath may even have been in Phoenician territory (I Kings 17.8–24).[12] We find him on Carmel, in the palace of Jezreel and finally also in Samaria, not to mention his great pilgrimage to the mountain of God in the south, which is described in I Kings 19. But the greatest and most triumphant event of his life seems to have been the contest on Carmel (I Kings 18.20–40).[13]

Carmel is the striking mountain ridge in the north-west of Israel, the foothills of which border the bay of Acre (Akko) or Haifa on the south; here they fall steeply into the Mediterranean. Running from south-east to north-west, the massif of Carmel rises over the northern part of the plain of Megiddo. The site of Carmel is particularly significant. It was part of the border territory disputed over by Phoenicians and Israelites. The king of Tyre had been able to extend his sphere of power this far south. Carmel may have had a sanctuary on it from earliest times, as was the case later. Even Tacitus mentions a sanctuary on Carmel, which was visited by Vespasian in AD 69.[14] The place was ideal for the worship of a mountain deity whose sanctuary could be reached easily, and at all times it must have attracted a wide circle of worshippers.[15]

I Kings 18.30 also bears witness to the varied history of the cult place. Elijah reconstructed an altar to Yahweh which had been thrown down. So Carmel once had a regular cult of Yahweh, which seems most likely to have been instituted in the time of David and Solomon. But if that was the case, the divine inhabitant of this border area of Carmel must have changed under the influence of Canaanites and Phoenicians. Baal again predominated where once Yahweh had had an altar. This Baal was presumably the Baal of Tyre.[16] Presumably as a result of the favourable influence of Israel's good relationships with Tyre, Ahab seems to have gained controlling rights over Carmel. This was the moment which Elijah exploited for his demonstration at this prominent site of cultic celebration, in full view of both Israelites and Phoenicians. Who was the real owner of Carmel? That was the chief question to be decided. The conflict may be said to have been a 'local' one. In the background, however, lurked the much more profound political problem for Israel in this period, namely the significance of the rapid advance of Baal under the rule of Ahab and his wife Jezebel, to which there seemed to be no limit. One cannot object to the fact that the account of the great scene on Carmel in I Kings 18 elevates this local conflict into the fundamental question which could be understood in national terms: who is the God of Israel? Is it Yahweh or is it Baal?

The decision was made in favour of Yahweh. The fire from heaven which kindled Elijah's sacrifice proclaimed the true God; the desperate dance of the prophets of Baal only magnified the extent of their defeat. We cannot know how far the cultic conflict at the sanctuary of Carmel was the occasion for extensive clashes with the prophets of Baal in the area. Elijah is said to have slain such prophets with his own hands at the foot of the mountain (I Kings 18.40).

What was the historical nucleus of the events on Carmel? It seems that there was a clash between Phoenicians and Israelites over the sanctuary on Carmel in which Elijah played a leading part. The process may possibly have had an ambivalent outcome. For the state asserted itself, and Jezebel may have lent her support to the Canaanite side, thus limiting the influence of Elijah and his followers. It is credible that the queen persecuted Elijah, as a leading figure of the opposition, so that the prophet had to go into exile. In I Kings 19 the tradition ascribes to Elijah a pilgrimage to the southern mountain of God,[17] where Yahweh is said to have appeared to him in a majestic scene reminiscent of the Moses traditions.[18] However, Yahweh was not present in the powerful manifestations of nature, but was experienced by Elijah in 'a still small voice', to use the impressive words of the familiar translation. A more apt translation of the original text would be 'in a profound and utter silence'.[19]

We do not know whether the Elijah stories in I and II Kings are in exact chronological order. For this reason the further course of Elijah's career is obscure. At any event, the instructions immediately following the scene at Horeb have caused commentators some difficulty, because they are both improbable and contradictory. Elijah is to perform three anointings: he is to anoint Hazael king of Damascus, Jehu king of Israel and Elisha his own successor. The end of the house of Ahab and thus the end of the dynasty of Omri is the background to the three events: the anointing of Israel's enemy by Elijah;[20] the anointing of Jehu, which was in fact performed later by a disciple of Elisha;[21] and the subsequent acceptance of Elisha as a disciple, reported in I Kings 19.19–21, which is signified not by anointing, but by the passing on of a mantle.[22] The Syrians of Damascus were to pose a permanent threat to Israel for the immediate future; Elisha was to anoint Jehu; and Jehu was to topple the last of the dynasty of Omri. We can well imagine that the tradition had an interest in associating this chain of events with Elijah, at least representing him as a dynamic figure and the spiritual author of a coming judgment. I Kings 19.17 regards the ideal significance of this chain of events in the same terms and builds it up into a massive programme: 'And him who escapes from the sword of Jehu shall Elisha slay.' In the last resort, this is not a political prognosis but a prophetic perspective. Judgment will come; it will fall on the worshippers of Baal; they will perish because they will be pursued by the sword that Hazael, Jehu and Elisha will wield against them, each in his own time and in his own way. I Kings 19.18 confirms this interpretation: 'Yet I will leave seven thousand in Israel, all the knees that have not bowed to Baal, and every mouth that has not kissed him.'[23]

The pattern of the Elijah tradition indicated here is directed against the domestic politics of Israel, but in the background we find two other matters: Elijah's own later career and Israel's position *vis-à-vis* its neighbours. We are given a few pointers in this direction. II Kings 1 records an extremely legendary appearance of Elijah in the time of Ahaziah, Ahab's successor. Elijah may in fact have returned to Israel, when Ahab was no longer on the throne. The narrative of Elijah's 'ascension to heaven' in a chariot drawn by fiery horses (II Kings 2.1–18) really belongs in the Elisha saga; it takes place by the Jordan, near Jericho, and by virtue of its character resists any attempt at dating. Of course, the Elijah stories are only one beam of light shed on the general situation of their time, but they are certainly appropriate. After the introduction of Omri's policy of compromise, the struggle between Yahweh and Baal came to a climax with Ahab and Jezebel. Elijah was one of the most dominant figures on the other side. The struggle did not come to an end in his lifetime, as the future was to show.

Elijah's part in the well-known story of Naboth's vineyard in I Kings 21 must be challenged on exegetical grounds.[24] The main point of this story is concerned with the law rather than with the cult.[25] In Israel, land was inalienable; the conviction of the Old Testament is that by an exclusive hereditary principle Yahweh himself is the owner of the promised land, which he grants to the individual Israelite. The Israelite does not have his own rights of possession. Ahab's attempts to appropriate a useful piece of land as crown property in Jezreel, which after his time became a secondary royal residence,[26] came to grief on the prescriptions of Israelite law. In full accordance with these, Naboth defended what he had inherited from his fathers and refused to hand it over; Ahab, too, was ready to recognize his claim. But Jezebel's appearance on the scene brought the turning-point. For her the supreme commandment was the sovereignty of the ruler, which was unlimited, even in matters of property: a conception which is understandable in view of Phoenician practices, which made possible unlimited dealings in land. In the end, this narrative presents a clash between legal ordinances rather than one between individuals; these ordinances may often have affected the climate of domestic politics and made them more difficult. The criminal outcome of the story, which brings the death of Naboth, may be a symptom of the severity of the clash. To that point the story is also an entity in itself; Elijah's appearance seems secondary, and the content of the story does not demand it.[27]

We have already pointed out that the broad sweep of the Elijah and Elisha traditions which have been included in the books of Kings has obscured the picture of foreign politics in both Israel and Judah, at the time of the dynasty of Omri and thereafter. One particular reason for this is that most of the passages about Elisha have the character of saga. Above all, there is the remarkable fact that in a whole series of texts about clashes with Damascus and its allies in Transjordania, the names of the kings involved are either not mentioned at all or are put in contexts with which originally they had nothing to do. Often the matter is connected with one or other of their successors. We gain the impression that a variety of reminiscences were current of the considerable political activities of the Aramaeans of Damascus and the battles which extended all over Transjordania, in which troops from both Israel and Judah were involved. Certainly, these reminiscences were connected with particular places and events, but the latter are not always reproduced accurately within the books of Kings. In other words, careful attention is not always paid to historical circumstances, and different events are often combined. One indication of this is the association of Elijah with king Hazael of Damascus (I Kings 19.16f.), with an eye to events in the internal politics of Israel. We can see the motives behind the literary elaboration of the work. In the last resort, for the final redactors of the books of Kings, events in foreign policy were no more than mileposts for developments within Israel; these redactors are ultimately interested in wider politics only where they have a clear effect on events in Israel itself.

One vivid illustration of this which may be mentioned here is the vivid and almost fortuitous light shed on Ahab's initiatives in foreign policy by an Assyrian royal inscription; it indicates developments about which the Old Testament says nothing at all. Ahab took part in a coalition of Syrian rulers who resisted an Assyrian invasion under Shalmaneser III. Ahab of Israel and his contingent of troops are mentioned on the so-called 'monolith inscription'.[28] The fact was probably recorded in the chronicles of the kings of Israel, which will have been known to the redactors of the books of Kings. But Ahab's involvement in Syrian enterprises was unimportant to them if it had no detectable effect on the domestic politics of Israel. We shall return later to the details of Ahab's part in fighting against the Assyrians, when it can be set against the background of the Assyrian policy of expansion. The account appears in the chapter on Jehu's dynasty.

In view of the difficulty over sources, all that can be said with any degree of certainty is that at the time of Omri's dynasty, Israel's relationship with the Aramaean state of Damascus became increasingly difficult, and the Aramaeans had to regard Israel, with its increasing strength, as a serious rival in the south. At the least, they will have been interested in extending their hegemony as widely as possible. To the north they were able to exercise considerable influence on the city states of Syria; they also seem to have sought contacts with the Phoenicians. It is an open question whether the good relationships between Israel and Tyre which Ahab had endorsed by his marriage to Jezebel had made relationships between Damascus and Israel worse. The Phoenicians, of course, needed to secure the hinterland, as they were increasingly interested in the sea. Under Omri and Ahab, Israel had been able to assert itself in the interplay between its neighbours. There were no clashes with the Philistines worth mentioning, and an astonishingly friendly relationship developed with Judah, to such a degree that the king of Jerusalem was even prepared on a number of occasions to ally his army with that of Israel. King Jehoshaphat, Asa's successor, several times appears as an ally; and king Joram, who followed him, married Athaliah, one of Ahab's daughters (II Kings 8.18).

Relationships between Israel and the state of Damascus must have fluctuated. As has already been said, Ahab took part in the great Syrian coalition against Shalmaneser III and provided troops to fight in the battle at Karkar in northern Syria. This was in 853 BC. Israel was prepared to enter into an alliance with Damascus to ward off the great enemy from the north. On the other hand, however, it was involved in disputes with the Aramaeans in Transjordania, where territorial interests had to be defended on both sides. All the Old Testament traditions which claim to fall in the period of the dynasty of the Omrides must be set, with all due caution, in this wider political and strategic framework.

At this point it is worth continuing in synoptic form the dates of the rules of the kings of Israel and Judah, adding the kings of Damascus whom we may presume to have been on the throne at the same time:

Israel	*Judah*	*Damascus*
Omri 886/85–875/74	Asa 914/13–874/73	Benhadad I
Ahab 875/74–854/53	Jehoshaphat 874/73–850/49	Hadadezer
Ahaziah 854/53–853/52		
Joram 853/52–842/41	Joram 850/49–843/42	
Jehu 842/41–815/14	Ahaziah 843/42–842/41	Hazael
	Athaliah 842/41–837/36	

I Kings 20 and 22 transpose into the time of Ahab battles with Aramaean and Syrian troops at Aphek (*fīq*) east of Lake Gennesaret and at Ramoth Gilead (*tell rāmīt*); further border fights and clashes which even affected Israel itself are difficult to date and in II Kings have been woven into the traditions about the prophet Elisha. They are to be found in II Kings 6.8–23; 6.24–7.20. Finally, Ahaziah of Judah and Joram of Israel fought as allies against the Aramaeans at Ramoth Gilead, II Kings 8.28.

There is a remarkable arrangement in I Kings 20.34, where Samaria and Damascus accord each other trading rights in their cities.

Israel suffered a severe defeat in the battle of Ramoth Gilead (I Kings 22.2–38). A word about it is necessary for a number of reasons. The 'king of Israel' fought alongside king Jehoshaphat, who was a contemporary of Ahab and Ahaziah of Israel. Before the battle an enquiry was made of the prophets of Israel, who numbered about 400 men. They were to advise whether it was a good thing to go into battle. The prophets said yes. However, Micaiah ben Imlah, another prophet who was asked for advice, prophesied disaster. For the first time we find the question of true and false prophecy among competing prophets of Yahweh, or more exactly, the question of the validity of professional prophecy[29] over against genuine charisma.[30] Despite the advice of Micaiah ben Imlah, the expedition took place. The 'king of Israel' fell in the battle. The context seeks to make it clear that this king was Ahab. But I Kings 22.40 says that he 'slept with his fathers', and this formula is used regularly when the king died a natural death.[31] These and other indications in the text make it highly probable that the battles in I Kings 22 should not be connected with Ahab but with one of the later kings of Israel, perhaps Joram.[32]

In a welcome way, an original document of the period from outside the Old Testament affords us a reliable perspective on the relationship between Israel and southern Transjordania, where it touched on the borders of the state of Moab. This is the 'Moabite stone', with an inscription by king Mesha of Moab.[33] The inscription itself is not dated, but it gives us the extremely significant information that Omri, the king of Israel, during his reign and that of his sons, occupied part of the land of Moab, until 'Israel perished' and Mesha was able once again to rule over the full extent of his land[34] and to fortify his cities. Now a Moabite king named Mesha is also mentioned in II Kings 3.4–27, where the allied kings of Israel, Judah and Edom mount an expedition against him. The Mesha inscription says nothing about this, but it does shed decisive light on the relationships and tensions which existed between Israel and Moab at the time of the dynasty of Omri, and at least fits admirably into the wider context of the time.[35]

The great stele which bears the Mesha inscription, the (restored) fragments of which are in the Louvre, was discovered as early as 1868 by a missionary named Klein in *dībān*, ancient Dibon. On it, Mesha describes himself as a Dibonite, so he will have ruled from Dibon. The city lies in the border territory of Moab north of the Arnon. In the fashion of Syrian inscriptions, after an introduction, Mesha speaks in the first person: 'I am Mesha, the son of *Kmš(yt)*,[36] king of Moab, the Dibonite.' He describes his relations with Israel in this way: 'As for Omri, king of Israel, he humbled Moab many years, for Chemosh (the Moabite god) was angry at his land. And his son followed him and he also said, "I will humble Moab." In my time he spoke (thus), but I have triumphed over him and over his house, while Israel has perished for ever! (Now) Omri had occupied the land of Medeba and (Israel) had dwelt there in his time and half the time of his son, forty years, but Chemosh dwelt there in my time.'

This information supplements what we know from the Old Testament. Under Omri, Israel penetrated into the area south of the Jabbok and north of the Arnon and by virtue of its military superiority now ruled these territories which were once under the lordship of the house of David. The situation continued under Ahab, and probably under his successors. When Mesha talks about Israel 'perishing', he seems to mean the end of the dynasty of Omri. At any rate, after the death of

Ahab, the Old Testament records a Moabite revolt (II Kings 1.1; 3.5) along with heavy tribute which had to be paid (II Kings 3.4). The invasion of Moab by Ahab's son Joram (3.7), and his alliance with Jehoshaphat of Judah including Edom, which was a dependency of Judah, presuppose a Moabite uprising after the death of Ahab. However, it is within the realms of possibility that at that time Mesha was already fighting against Israel, but was only in a position to win back the territory occupied by Israel after the fall of the house of Omri. He boasts of this in his inscription, which also lays particular stress on his building activity in numerous places. While details of the synchronization with II Kings 3 are unsatisfactory, on the whole the texts complement each other. Moab suffered under the Israelite expansion during the reign of the house of Omri; there were battles, in which Judah took part; but nevertheless Mesha succeeded in winning back the area north of the Arnon and perhaps even banishing the threat posed by the Edomites in the south. This can only have happened during the last years of the house of Omri. That the 'fall of Israel' mentioned by Mesha refers to the end of the dynasty, is, of course, no more than an interpretation. The Mesha inscription need not presuppose the accession of Jehu, and in that case would fit much better with II Kings 3. It would be unnecessary to assign a late date to the events in this chapter, say towards the end of the century.

The reign of Jehoshaphat (about 874–849) in Jerusalem and Judah ran parallel to that of Ahab and some of his successors. During these twenty-five years, Jehoshaphat must have had considerable success in the south (I Kings 22.41–51). Like Solomon before him, he attempted to restore a link with the Gulf of Aqaba. But his ships were destroyed at Ezion-geber. Nevertheless, his undertakings seem to have been helped on by the fact that there were no kings in Edom, which was ruled by governors (22.48). The latter were surely dependent on Judah. This would be indicated by the combined levy from Judah and Edom against Moab in II Kings 3.

Jehoshaphat's successor Joram (about 849–842) married the Israelite princess Athaliah. This was a high-point of good relations between Israel and Judah. At the same time, however, Judah's favourable links with the Edomites were severed. Edom chose its own king, and thereafter we hear no more of Edomite dependence. Edom was able to assert itself against Judah.

The reign of Joram's successor Ahaziah is put at only a year. He fell victim to Jehu's bloodbath when visiting the Israelite king Joram in Jezreel.

Omri had inaugurated a new epoch in Israel. He had stabilized the monarchy and at the same time had been able to create the presuppositions for a dynasty; he and his successors strove for accommodation with the Canaanite elements of the population. But while in this way the great stretch on the west side of Israel between the Phoenicians in the north and the Philistines in the coastal plain was secured, and there were excellent relations with Judah in the south through military alliances and marriage, a danger area was developing in the complex of Syrian city states which extended into eastern Transjordania. Behind them lurked the even greater danger of a stronger Assyria; its kings made systematic thrusts to the south-west and threatened the whole of Syria and Palestine. Here were the two main problems with which Israel and Judah were burdened after the forties of the ninth century: the expansionist policies of Syria and Assyria, and the tensions between Canaanites and Israelites within the state. These must be discussed next. Towards the end of the forties, crises arose in Israel and Judah, the outcomes of which were both characteristic of the states in which they occurred. It is customary to speak of the 'revolutions' of Jehu and Athaliah.

NOTES

1. See A. Alt, 'Der Stadtstaat Samaria' (1954), *KS* III, esp. 262f.; for the archaeological character of the site see R. Bach, 'Zur Siedlungsgeschichte des Talkessels von Samaria', *ZDPV* 74, 1958, 41–54.

2. It is worth remembering the similar purchases of land from the Canaanites by Abraham (the cave of Machpelah as a burial place, Gen. 23) and David (the threshing floor of Araunah, II Sam. 24); each time the tradition is based on the land that is bought. David, of course, took possession of the city of Jerusalem by right of conquest.

3. Alt, 'Stadtstaat', esp. 266–70.

4. But see the phrase used once by Isaiah, who puts 'Ephraim' and the 'inhabitants of Samaria' side by side (Isa. 9.8); cf. Alt, *KS* III, 300.

5. Pictures of the hill are usually taken from the west side: P. Volz, *64 Bilder aus dem Heiligen Lande*, 34; H. Bardtke, *Zu beiden Seiten des Jordans*, 1958, 62. Two different pictures, which are most impressive, appear in L. H. Grollenberg, *Atlas of the Bible*, 1957, 78; these are an impressive aerial photograph and a view from the south, which shows clearly how the hill falls away to the west.

6. Alt, op. cit., 270–83; id., 'Archäologische Fragen zur Baugeschichte von Jerusalem und Samaria in der israelitischen Königszeit' (1956), *KS* III, 303–25; bibliography of excavations in K. M. Kenyon, *Archaeology in the Holy Land*, [2]1965, 320f.

7. J. W. Crowfoot and G. M. Crowfoot, *Early Ivories from Samaria*, 1938 = *Samaria-Sebaste* II; J. W. Crowfoot, G. M. Crowfoot and K. M. Kenyon, *The Objects from Samaria*, 1957 = *Samaria-Sebaste* III; see also *ANEP*, 129, 130; there is an echo of the splendour in Amos 3.15.

8. For the religious questions see O. Eissfeldt, 'Jahwe und Baal' (1914), *Kleine Schriften* I, 1–12; H. Gese, in Gese/Hofner/Rudolph, *Die Religionen Altsyriens, Altarabiens und der Mandäer*, Die Religionen der Menschheit (ed. C. M. Schröder), 10, 2, 1970, esp. 182–215; see also *RGG* I, 805f. (lit.); R. Rendtorff, 'Die Enstehung der israelitischen Religion als religionsgeschichtliches und theologisches Problem', *TLZ* 88, 1963, 735ff.; G. Fohrer, *History of Israelite Religion*, 1973, 130–6.

9. Noth, *Personennamen*, 137f.

10. G. Fohrer, *Elia*, ATANT 53, [2]1968; O. H. Steck, *Überlieferung und Zeitgeschichte in den Elia-Erzählungen*, WMANT 26, 1968.

11. The exact location is unknown; cf. the remarks by M. Noth, *Aufsätze* 1, 367, 374, 519–22.

12. Present-day *ṣarafand*, about 7 miles south-west of Sidon on the road to Tyre; *BHH* 3, 2204 (Elliger).

13. A. Alt, 'Das Gottesurteil auf dem Karmel' (1935), *KS* II, 135–49; earlier scholars

retold the events in dramatic fashion, reading in later ideas; for an example see the section 'Elias und die Religiosen', in R. Kittel, *Gestalten und Gedanken in Israel. Geschichte eines Volkes in Charakterbildern*, 1925, 159–82.

14. Tacitus, *Hist.* II, 78, 3 (ed. Klostermann, 1950, 94); cf. also Suetonius, *De Vita Caesarum* VIII, 5 (ed. Roth, 1865, 228); for both passages see O. Eissfeldt, 'Der Gott Karmel', *Sitzungsberichte der Deutschen Akademie der Wissenschaften*, Kl. Sprachen, Literatur, Kunst, 1953, no. 1, 8–10.

15. O. Eissfeldt, 'Der Gott Karmel'; K. Galling, 'Der Gott Karmel und die Ächtung der fremden Götter', *Geschichte und Altes Testament* (Alt Festschrift), 1953, 105–25.

16. Mention might be made of Melkart or Ba'al-Šamēm; for the problems see Eissfeldt and Galling, op. cit.

17. For discussion of more recent views see now K. Seybold, 'Elia am Gottesberg. Vorstellungen prophetischen Wirkens nach I Könige 19', *EvTh* 33, 1973, 3–18.

18. Exod. 33.18–23, where Yahweh passes in front of Moses; he does not allow Moses to see his divinity, but Moses is allowed to see his 'back'. G. von Rad once regarded this passage as an image of the whole of the Old Testament. We cannot see God in the Old Testament, but we can see the characteristics of his activity; G. von Rad, in Alt/Begrich/von Rad, *Führung zum Christentum durch das Alte Testament, Drei Vorträge*, 1934, 70f.

19. No completely satisfactory explanation of the passage has yet been given. The idea of 'calm' does not quite cover what is meant; cf. the survey and explanation in J. Jeremias, *Theophanie*, WMANT 10, 1965, 112–5; see also O. H. Steck, *Überlieferung und Zeitgeschichte*, 117f.

20. In II Kings 8 the beginning of the kingdom of Hazael of Damascus is connected with Elisha; it is therefore impossible to give an exact date for the event; cf. A. Jepsen, 'Israel und Damaskus', *AfO* 14, 1941–44, esp. 158.

21. II Kings 9.1–10.

22. This is the source of the proverbial phrase the 'mantle of the prophet'.

23. 'Of course 7000 is a round number for quite a respectable minority', R. Kittel, *Die Bücher der Könige*, HK 1, 5, 1900, 154.

24. I Kings 21.17ff. reports a saying of Yahweh which was addressed to Elijah, but the connection with the circumstances in which it was uttered is not established. From v.20b on, the speech by Elijah is composed of phrases which already appear in I Kings 14.10f., sometimes word for word; R. Kittel, op. cit., 158f. For an assessment of the whole story of Naboth's vineyard and its relationship to II Kings 9 see J. M. Miller, 'The Fall of the House of Ahab', *VT* 17, 1967, 307–24, esp. 309–17.

25. K. Baltzer, 'Naboths Weinberg (I Kön. 21). Der Konflikt zwischen israelitischen und kanaanäischem Bodenrecht', *Wort und Dienst* (Jahrbuch d. Theol. Schule Bethel), NF 8, 1965, 73–88; F. J. Anderson, 'The Socio-Juridical Background of the Naboth Incident', *JBL* 85, 1966, 46–57; P. Welten, 'Naboths Weinberg (I Kön. 21)', *EvTh* 33, 1973, 18–32.

26. B. D. Napier, 'The Omrides of Jezreel', *VT* 9, 1959, 366–78.

27. Cf. the considerations whether and when Elijah had a personal confrontation with king Ahab in S. Herrmann, *Die prophetischen Heilserwartungen im Alten Testament*, BWANT 85, 1965, 51f.

28. *TGI*, 50; for further details see ch. 7 below.

29. J. Lindblom, 'Zur Frage des kanaanäischen Ursprungs des altisraelitischen Prophetismus', *Von Ugarit nach Qumran* (Eissfeldt Festschrift), BZAW 77, ²1961, 89–104; for the prophets in the entourage of king ZKR of Hamath, *KAI*, no. 202, see also S. Herrmann, *Heilserwartungen*, 58–60.

30. G. Quell, *Wahre und falsche Propheten*, 1952; E. Jacob, 'Quelques remarques sur les faux prophètes', *TZ* 13, 1957, 479–86; E. Osswald, *Falsche Prophetie im Alten Testament*, SGV 237, 1962; id., 'Irrende Glaube in den Weissagungen der alttestamentlichen

Propheten', *Wissenschaftliche Zeitschrift Jena*, Sonderheft, 1963, 65ff.; H. Seebass, 'Micha ben Jimla', *KuD* 19, 1973, 109–24.

31. G. Hölscher, in *Eucharisterion* (Hermann Gunkel zum 60. Geburtstag) I, 1923, 185; B. Alfrink, *OTS* 2, 1943, 106–18; C. F. Whitley, 'The Deuteronomic Presentation of the House of Omri', *VT* 2, 1952, 137–52, esp. 148.

32. C. F. Whitley, op. cit., 148–51; see also O. H. Steck, *Überlieferung und Zeitgeschichte*, 131–47.

33. *KAI*, no. 181; *AOT*, 440–2; *ANET*, 320f.; *TGI*[1], 47–9 (original text); *TGI*[2], 51–3 (translation).

34. Particularly the Moabite possessions on the northern frontier, over which there were disputes with Israel. Even in favourable circumstances this northern frontier is hardly likely to have extended beyond the latitude of the north end of the Dead Sea.

35. This is true, albeit with qualifications, of the Old Testament accounts also; see K.-H. Bernhardt, 'Der Feldzug der drei Könige', in *Schalom* (Jepsen Festschrift), 1971, 11–22.

36. The expansion of the second element of the name, the interpretation of which is uncertain, is based on an inscription from *el-kerak*, published in an article by W. L. Reed and F. V. Winnett, *BASOR* 172, 1963, 1–9; cf. *KAI* II, 170. The first element in the name denotes the Moabite deity Chemosh.

37. *KAI* II, 168 translates: 'and half the days of his sons, forty years'; *TGI*, 52: 'and the period of the reign of his sons – forty years'. The substitution of 'period' for 'half' is meant to ensure that the years of the reigns of all the sons of Omri (Ahab, Ahaziah and Joram) are covered; in this way the forty years run exactly parallel to the chronology of Israel from Omri on; thus G. Wallis, 'Die vierzig Jahre der achten Zeile der Mesa-Inschrift', *ZDPV* 81, 1965, 180–6.

6 | Two Revolutions – Jehu in Israel and Athaliah in Jerusalem

ACCORDING TO THE account in II Kings, the prelude to the downfall of the dynasty of Omri in Israel was the anointing of a new man from quite a different family, at the instigation of a prophet. The charismatic ideal of the northern state came to the fore again, just as it had before Omri ascended the throne. This is sufficient explanation for the Old Testament author. We can only guess at further reasons for the change of ruler. The new man made profound and radical changes in the conditions of the state; as far as we know, he was a supporter of that view of Israel which saw that Yahweh must be given the supremacy. We may assume that the last members of the house of Omri were weaklings, and that after the death of Ahab they were increasingly influenced by the 'queen mother'[1] Jezebel, who still lived at court. In addition, the increasingly difficult battles against the Aramaeans in Transjordania called for energetic leadership.

It seemed likely that all hopes and expectations would be fulfilled by an officer and commander named Jehu. He was anointed at the army camp and then made use of his authority without delay, taking over control of the state in a number of decisive steps. Were he really the anointed one, Israel would have had to acknowledge him in any case. So why did so much depend on the exercise of his personal efforts? What happens suggests that Jehu had an interest in seizing power and in the preparations for it, in which he played an active part.

Events are described at length in II Kings 9 and 10. It is possible to follow the course of events step by step so well that we can draw quite fundamental conclusions for the internal political constitution of Israel. The Deuteronomistic redactor incorporated such a detailed account of Jehu's rise to power in his work because he recognized that Jehu pursued the worshippers of Baal more vigorously than anyone before him. On the other hand, about a century later the prophet Hosea was critical of what happened (Hos. 1.4f.). It is worth going into the events in some detail here, because in many respects they are symptomatic of circumstances in Israel.

Events were set in train by a disciple of the prophet Elisha. The Israelites were fighting against the Aramaeans of Damascus and were encamped at Ramoth Gilead.

Jehu was there, surrounded by his troops. Joram, the king of Israel, was sick in his secondary residence at Jezreel. At the decisive moment Ahaziah, the king of Judah, was staying with him on a visit. Meanwhile the disciple of the prophet was on his way to Jehu. He summoned him from the group of officers and anointed him in private. The secrecy of the proceedings, without any witnesses, is reminiscent of the anointing of Saul by Samuel (I Sam. 9.27; 10.1). While Saul is said to have kept his secret to himself for a long time, Jehu was immediately asked by his officers, who had recognized the prophet's disciple, what 'this mad fellow'[2] wanted with him. After an initial hesitation, Jehu told them. He had been anointed king over Israel.[3] The officers immediately spread out their garments under him, blew the trumpet and proclaimed, 'Jehu has become king!'[4] In this way he was officially acclaimed by the army in their camp.

Given this official confirmation, Jehu did not delay in seizing the reins of power. He did it with unsuspected vigour. The Old Testament account is given in masterly fashion. The watchman on the tower of Jezreel sees Jehu's company approaching in chariots over the plain. It is not yet possible to identify them. Joram sends two messengers on chariots to discover what is going on. Jehu keeps them with him. The watchman gives the news to the king; now he adds, 'It looks as if it is Jehu, he is driving like a madman.' Tension is built up to a climax. The two kings, Joram of Israel and Ahaziah of Judah, mount their chariots. The two sides meet at Naboth's property, just before Jezreel. Joram asks what is up. Jehu roars, 'Your mother Jezebel is a whore and her sorceries keep increasing!' A significant comment. Joram turns his chariot, shouting 'Treachery!' to Ahaziah. Then Jehu's arrow hits the king of Israel; Ahaziah attempts to escape to the south, but is wounded while escaping and finally dies at Megiddo.

Meanwhile Jehu has reached the palace of Jezreel. Jezebel, in her finery, is looking through the great window into the courtyard as Jehu enters. She calls, 'What is it, you Zimri, murderer of your master?' A tradition is recognized here. The former seven-day king, the commander who so unsuccessfully sought the crown, has not been forgotten (I Kings 16.9–20). But Jehu is not concerned with history; only with the needs of the moment. 'Throw her down,' he calls. Two servants seize Jezebel and throw her into the courtyard. Jehu thunders over her in his chariot. Her blood spurts high up on the wall. He climbs down from his chariot, enters the palace and sits down to a meal as the reigning king.

In unusually brief and decisive strokes we are given a picture whose clarity and brutality leave nothing to be imagined. The end of Jezebel is quite justifiably painted in garish colours. She was the most inexorable foe of those circles which were faithful to Yahweh. But in occupying Jezreel Jehu has not yet finished his work. Jezreel was a secondary residence, perhaps a summer palace. Samaria was the capital: the royal family lived there, as did the aristocratic upper class, and there was a real risk that they might organize resistance. Jehu now adopted another approach; to begin with, he did not appear in the capital in person. He sends letters to the aristocracy of Samaria, pointing out that they have members of the royal house in their midst and that chariots and a fortified city are at their disposal. Finally he bids them select the best of the royal house and set him on the throne.

One may suspect sinister intentions behind such words, but the fact remains that Jehu could not take Samaria at a stroke, as he had taken Jezreel. Samaria was a fortified city, and had considerable political and military resources. At any rate, this must have been his view. But in fact the administration of Samaria surrendered unconditionally. Jehu now laid down his conditions. He asked that the heads of all the members of the royal family should be sent to him in Jezreel on the following day. Jehu spared himself the task of personally exterminating the family of his predecessor, which had been carried out by the other kings before him; he made others do it for him, and used his move for a piece of even more macabre demagogy. Samaria had acted by return; Jehu had the heads laid in two heaps before the gate of Jezreel and delivered a speech. He had killed the king, but who had killed these men? In his triumph, his cynicism knew no bounds. He claimed that he was the instrument of the divine will and had to perform judgment on the house of Omri and Ahab. Without doubt Jehu had perverted the power with which he had been entrusted.

Once the capital had surrendered, the king set out to take possession of it. Two scenes on his way form a marked contrast. All unsuspecting, and without knowledge of what had happened, a group of princes of Judah, brothers of king Ahaziah who had meanwhile died, were on their way to visit Joram at the palace. Jehu had them killed on the spot. Was he afraid of Athaliah in Jerusalem? She was an Israelite princess, and as queen mother had considerable influence after her son's death. Might she lay claim to the throne and make plans for vengeance as a member of the dynasty of Omri? We do not know what was in Jehu's mind. But by now the royal house of David, too, had suffered great losses at his hands.

Jehu's meeting with Jonadab ben Rechab, before he reached Samaria, had a different character. Jonadab was a leading personality among the Rechabites, whose religious ideal was nomadic (cf. Jer. 35); the two joined forces. Jehu invited him into his chariot to be witness of his actions in Samaria. A new stage in the programme was to be carried out.

The first thing that Jehu did in Samaria was to round up all the surviving members of the old royal house. It is said that he slew them all (II Kings 10.17). Then he gave the appearance of wanting to follow an entirely different course. To an assembly of the people he proclaimed, 'Ahab served Baal a little; but Jehu will serve him much.' He invited all the prophets of Baal and all the priests throughout the land, and not just from the capital, to a great sacrifice, assembled them in the great temple of Baal in Samaria and gave them festal garments. They came in large numbers, confident in the hope that the king would demonstrate his reverence for Baal in a new act and continue the policy of compromise introduced by Omri and Ahab. Hardly had they assembled in the temple when he had the house sealed off; immediately after the burnt-offering the slaughter began. The worshippers of Baal were massacred, the sacred objects were destroyed, the temple went up in flames and its site was defiled. The abolition of the sanctuary of Baal in Samaria is the climax of the account of Jehu's rise to power. Here we have the beginning of a religious policy which met with the sympathy of the Deuteronomistic redactors.

It is hard to dismiss the suspicion that the picture of the battle against the Baal cult in Samaria has been overdrawn. It was certainly impossible to put an end to Canaanite cultic practices throughout the land by means of a limited local action. The brief report on the reign of Jehoahaz, who followed Jehu, contains the remark that 'the Asherah also remained in Samaria' (II Kings 13.6). Nor is it conceivable that Jehu could have reigned so long and so successfully had his policy been based on brute force. Certainly, after the death of Jezebel he may have made a considerable contribution towards reviving the cult of Yahweh in Israel; the foreign queen's fanatical persecutions of the worshippers of Yahweh ceased. It is also significant that no prophet appeared in Israel for a long period after Jehu's accession, at any rate of the stature of an Elijah. Perhaps the groups of prophets who appear in the stories of Elisha as 'sons of the prophets' or 'disciples of the prophets' may have continued at the sanctuaries of the land. Perhaps the state cult at Bethel and Dan continued without interruption. At any rate, we hear of no clashes. It therefore seems likely that Jehu left existing cults in the land untouched, and that this course of action contributed substantially to the inner stability of the state. Jehu was able to become the founder of a new dynasty in Israel.

It is regrettable that we do not know more of Jehu's domestic policies. II Kings 10 praises the bloodstained usurper for what he did to 'the house of Ahab'. Consequently we cannot detect whether Jehu did away with the dualism which had hitherto existed between the capital Samaria and the rest of the Israelite territory.[5] It is certain that he dismantled the entire apparatus of power set up by the house of Omri in Samaria, but it is possible that he replaced it with something different. We do not know, for example, whether he did away with some of the special rights of Samaria and simplified the administration in the interest of stronger links between the capital and the rest of the state. Such a conclusion is by no means compelling; simply by virtue of its location and its position as capital, Samaria had not ceased to have an aura of its own,[6] and continued to be influential in very different circumstances.[7]

The Old Testament says virtually nothing about Jehu's foreign policy. All we hear of is defeats that he suffered against the Aramaean Hazael over a broad front in Transjordania (II Kings 10.32f.). A later discussion of the general political situation will, however, show that he must have taken steps against the Assyrian threat in company with the Syrian states. At this point we must go on to consider what was happening in Judah or, more accurately, in Jerusalem.

Jehu's bloodbath had also affected the house of David. He had killed king Ahaziah, who had only just come to power in Jerusalem, along with Joram before the gates of Jezreel, and he had not spared the princes of Judah on their visit to the northern state (II Kings 10.12–14). Who was left in Jerusalem capable of governing the state? Athaliah, mother of king Ahaziah, was still alive. She was an Israelite princess, who had been married to king Joram at the time when relations with the house of Omri were good.[8] Now that her son was dead and in view of the fact that there was no successor of age, she took over the rule herself. Coming from the northern kingdom, she may have seen this as her right; acting like a usurper she followed the custom of her own land and slew all the members of the royal house in Jerusalem (II Kings 11.1). In fact she succeeded in holding power in Jerusalem for six years (842/41–837/36). Hers was probably a tyrannical reign which went unchallenged because there was no adequate opposition. At first, at any rate. For in the long term Athaliah had miscalculated. It could only be a question of time before provision was made in Jerusalem for putting a son of David on the throne. And a son of David was still alive.

Jehosheba, a sister of king Ahaziah, had succeeded in rescuing one of his sons, Joash, who was still an infant, from the queen's bloodbath. The high priest Jehoiada hid him in the temple precinct. Significantly, this priest at the Jerusalem sanctuary regarded himself as the guardian of the Davidic tradition. He made all the necessary preparations for the enthronement of the young king. II Kings 11 gives a vivid account of what happened, even if some of the details are rather confused.[9] The measures which were taken step by step are clear enough. First the priest Jehoiada made sure of the loyalty and silence of the temple watch. He put them under oath in the temple and then showed them the royal prince Joash. Then he sealed off the temple precinct and evidently utilized the time of a change in the guard to anoint Joash. At this moment most of the able-bodied men of the temple guard would be inconspicuously concentrated at one point.

In heavy concealment the young prince was introduced into one of the forecourts of the temple, as far as we can see into the innermost court between the temple itself and the altar (II Kings 11.11). There Jehoiada put the crown on his head, gave him the 'royal protocol'[10] and anointed him. The anointing was followed by the acclamation of those present. The king was standing in a particularly prominent place. This coronation in extraordinary circumstances gives us a relatively complete picture of the elements in the royal ritual of Judah.[11]

The jubilation over the coronation in the temple brought Athaliah on the scene. She appeared in the temple, looked at what was happening, saw the king by the pillar and recognized the conspiracy. The temple guard took her out and killed her outside the holy precinct. Athaliah's rule came to an end; a son of David was again seated on the throne, brought to power by the help of a high priest working in the royal sanctuary.

After the coronation Jehoiada is said to have made a special covenant to bind 'the people' expressly to the new ruler and his dynasty (II Kings 11.17). The very general form of the text, the predominance of the idea of the people of God after the fashion of Deuteronomic theology, the isolated position of the verse and not least the remarkable tradition of such an act in the context of an enthronement scene do not encourage us to see the text as a reflection of a covenant formula firmly rooted in the royal ritual of Judah. Rather, it is a piece of later theological reflection.[12] It is in keeping with the pattern of Deuteronomic thought that after the mention of the treaty with the 'people' we hear of their actions, or more exactly, of the actions of the people of Judah, who do away with the cult of Baal introduced or tolerated by Athaliah. Thus the 'ideal harmony' so to speak is restored in Jerusalem. Yahweh, king and people form an inseparable unity on the basis of the covenant which has proved itself in action against the alien cult. This is the Deuteronomistic interpretation of events in Jerusalem.

II Kings 11.20 concludes the account with the observation that the 'people of the land',[13] i.e. the agricultural population of Judah, rejoiced after the king had been enthroned, and that the city (Jerusalem) was quiet. This seems to have been the real situation, in contrast to what is reported in vv. 17f. Stress is laid on the distinction between the city and the people of the land. Whereas the capital, the scene of the events, waited to see what would develop, the news was received in the country with unalloyed delight. The dynastic idea was evidently deeply rooted there; now it had led to victory. This text by itself hardly speaks of dissatisfaction with the rule of Athaliah.

Jehu's rigorous action even against members of the royal house of Judah led to the outbreak of crises of government in both states simultaneously. In Israel, anointing at the hands of a prophet led to an undisputed victory; even the acts of violence committed by Jehu did not stand in the way of a continuation of his rule. Matters were different in Jerusalem, where the bold ambitions of an energetic woman who, as queen mother, had some degree of justification for her claims, were still unable to shake the principle of dynastic succession. We can hardly have a clearer indication of the fundamental difference between the constitutions of the states of Israel and Judah. Judah asserted its independence from the tribes in the hill country of Ephraim in a way which had begun at the time when David was chosen as king, and was unwilling to surrender this independence. We can see from this how difficult it is to judge the states of Israel and Judah against the background of the idealistic unity of an ancient tribal alliance which had later been shattered. Judah and Israel were independent entities, each concerned to maintain its own character.

NOTES

1. See the pertinent remarks in O. H. Steck, *Überlieferung und Zeitgeschichte in den Elia-Erzählungen*, WMANT 26, 1968, 59–71.
2. The dialogue seems convincing. Army and clergy sometimes have little time for each other.
3. Why not *nāgîd*? II Kings 9.6, 12.
4. It is impossible to say for certain whether the spreading out of garments was a rite

of subservience. For the garment as an expression of power see I Kings 19.19. They were also spread in the way on Jesus' entry into Jerusalem, Matt.21.8; we cannot exclude the possibility that this passage echoes a rite associated with the kingship.

5. See the remarks by A. Alt, 'Der Stadtstaat Samaria', esp. 291–300.

6. Samaria was often the subject of sayings of the eighth-century prophets, but the number of these sayings is limited: cf. Amos 3.9f.; 4.1; 6.1ff.; Hos.7.1; 10.5, 7; 13.15b–14.1; Isa.8.4; 28.1–4; Mic.1.2–5a + 6, 7; 5.8f.

7. See the summary remarks in Alt, *KS* III, 300–2; id., 'Die Rolle Samarias bei der Enstehung des Judentums', *KS* II, 316–37 = *Grundfragen*, 418–39.

8. There is a dispute as to whether Athaliah was the daughter of Omri (II Kings 8.26; II Chron.22.2) or of Ahab (II Kings 8.18; II Chron.21.6). See also II Kings 8.27, where Ahaziah is called son-in-law to the house of Ahab. From what we can gather of her age, Athaliah was probably Ahab's daughter. This is challenged by J. M. Miller, 'The Fall of the House of Ahab', *VT* 17, 1967, 307–24, esp.307; H. T. Katzenstein, 'Who were the Parents of Athaliah?', *IEJ* 5, 3, 1955, 194–7.

9. The measures organized in II Kings 11.5–8 are difficult to understand, especially as we have no exact idea of the localities mentioned. For the whole text see W. Rudolph, 'Die Einheitlichkeit der Erzählung vom Sturz der Atalja (2. Kön.11)', in *Festschrift A. Bertholet*, 1950, 473–8.

10. The Hebrew word 'ēdūt in II Kings 11.12 is often understood to denote a document which contained the titles and honorific names of the king, for which there is also evidence in the context of Egyptian enthronements; G. von Rad, 'The Royal Ritual in Judah' (1947), in *The Problem of the Hexateuch*, 1966, 222–31, esp.226; E. Kutsch, *Verheissung und Gesetz*, BZAW 131, 1973, 56 n.29, argues on the basis of other presuppositions.

11. G. von Rad, op. cit.; there is now perhaps a parallel for the special place of the king in the courtyard of the temple in the form of a basalt base which has come to light in the late Bronze Age temple of Kāmid el-Lōz. Cf. the remarks by M. Metzer in the context of the contribution of Kumidi and the excavations at Tell Kāmid el-Lōz, SVT 22, 1972, esp.162–6.

12. Greater significance is attached to the covenant in M. Noth, 'Old Testament Covenant-making in the Light of a Text from Mari' (1953), in *The Laws in the Pentateuch*, 1966, 115f.; G. Fohrer, 'Der Vertrag zwischen König und Volk in Israel', *Studien zur Alttestamentlichen Theologie und Geschichte 1949–1966*, BZAW 115, 1969, 330–51; E. Kutsch, op. cit., esp. 163–5.

13. For this part of the population of Judah see E. Wurthwein, *Der 'amm ha 'arez im Alten Testament*, BWANT 4. Folge, 17, 1936.

7 | *Israel and Judah under the Shadow of the Struggle for Power in Syria*

THIS CHAPTER SETS out to cover a period of about a century. The revolution of Jehu took place between 845 and 840, and in 745 Tiglath-pileser III ascended the throne of Assyria and a short time afterwards inaugurated his great policy of expansion, which posed an immediate threat to Israel and Judah. We are relatively well informed about events in world history for the century before Tiglath-pileser III, in particular about the growth of Assyrian power after about 900 BC. Texts and pictorial representations from Assyria and neighbouring lands provide a variety of evidence. For conditions in Israel and Judah during this period, however, we are rather badly informed. This is one of the dark centuries in the period of the monarchy. Only three chapters, II Kings 12–14, give us any real information, supplemented by II Kings 15.1–12. The reports mostly have the character of annals; details are only touched on superficially and are seldom developed further.[1] This sparseness of Old Testament sources for conditions within Israel during the period is all the more regrettable since this is the century preceding the appearance of the great 'writing prophets', Amos, Hosea, Isaiah and Micah, and even including the beginning of their activity. This means that it is impossible to trace the growth of the conditions which these prophets encountered in Israel and Judah, which they criticized and which formed the background to their message, and to pass judgment on them.

The situation outlined here has consequences for any account of the period. In what follows we shall first give a brief survey of the sparse Old Testament accounts, which are oriented on the dates of the reigns of individual kings. Then we shall give a self-contained account of external developments. Finally, it should be possible to make at least a few remarks about internal developments within Israel and Judah, particularly about social problems, which play an important part in any assessment of the earliest classical prophecy.

The kings of Israel and Judah are shown in a synoptic table to which the kings of Assyria have been added:

Israel	Judah	Assyria
Jehu 842/41–815/14	Athaliah 842/41–837/36	Shalmaneser III 858–824
	Joash 836/35–797/96	Shamshi-Adad V 823–810
Jehoahaz 815/14–799/98		
Joash 799/98–784/83	Amaziah 797/96–769/68	Adad-nirari III 809–782
Jeroboam 784/83–753/52	Uzziah 769/68–741/40	Shalmaneser IV 781–772
		Asshur-dan III 771–754
Zechariah 753/52–752/51		Asshur-nirari V 753–746
Shallum 752/51–751/50		
Menahem 751/50–742/41		Tiglath-pileser III 745–727
Pekahiah 742/41–741/40		
Pekah 741/40–730/29	Jotham 741/40–734/33	
Hoshea 730/29–722/21	Ahaz 734/33–715/14	

There are reports of losses of territory throughout Transjordania from as early as the time of Jehu (II Kings 10.32f.). During the reign of his son and successor Jehoahaz (II Kings 13.1–9), too, the Aramaeans remained Israel's dangerous opponents in the north east. Mention is made of king Hazael and king Benhadad of Damascus. Israel suffered heavy losses of cavalry, chariots and infantry. The king of Aram scattered them like dust on the threshing-floor. True, a particular 'saviour' (*mōšīʿa*) arose against the Aramaeans,[2] but he did not have any lasting effect. The image of the Asherah remained in Samaria; this indicates that even under Jehu's successor, Canaanite influences again asserted themselves in the capital.

Jehoahaz was succeeded by his son Joash (II Kings 13.10–25; 14.14f.). He is said to have clashed with Amaziah, king of Judah. At Beth-shemesh (*rumēle* near *ʿēn šems*), where it descends to the coastal plain at the latitude of Jerusalem, he defeated the men of Judah in a battle, advanced on Jerusalem, broke down part of the city wall, made inroads on the treasure in the temple and the palace and finally returned home to Samaria (II Kings 14.8–15). This was the only time that troops from the northern state reached and plundered Jerusalem. The tradition remains obscure: it is quite isolated; the events have no recognizable consequences, nor is it possible to determine what gave rise to them.[3]

Joash is also said to have had successes in Transjordania. It is true that we hear once again of a Moabite invasion (II Kings 13.20), but on the death of king Hazael, Joash was able to take back from Hazael's successor, Benhadad, the cities which his father had lost.

Elisha makes one last appearance (II Kings 13.14–21). Joash had a last encounter with him before he died, presumably during Joash's reign.

Joash was succeeded in Israel by his son Jeroboam (II Kings 14.23–29), usually called Jeroboam II to distinguish him from the king of the same name who succeeded Solomon.[4] He already brings us down to the middle of the eighth century. The prophet Amos certainly made his appearance during Jeroboam's reign, and probably Hosea too. Jeroboam is the ruler whom the high priest of Bethel informed of Amos' arrival (Amos 7.10–17). His reign was extremely long, and is usually portrayed as a happy period, the calm before the great Assyrian invasion under Tiglath-pileser III. Consideration of the wider political context of the period will show that this judgment is only partly right. However, it may be assumed that the Aramaeans of Damascus were largely prevented from making thrusts to the south. The neighbouring kingdom of Hamath represented a serious threat. It had attained a dominant position which compelled Damascus to concentrate on its northern boundary. Thus we can understand how Jeroboam once again managed to bring under control territory from Lebo-Hamath to the Sea of the Arabah (II Kings 14.25). This information is, of course, somewhat imprecise. It could mean that Jeroboam won back a stretch of territory east of the Jordan, as in the time of David and Solomon.

The southern boundary of Israel, the 'Sea of the Arabah', should be located in the region of the Dead Sea. Possibly a new frontier was established against the Moabites, either on the heights at the north end of the Dead Sea or further south, as far as the Arnon. 'Lebo-Hamath' in the north hardly refers to a place connected with the state of Hamath;[5] on the contrary, it is the northern frontier of a territory in Transjordania which once belonged to Israel.[6] We may assume that Israel advanced far into the north and regained control of all the territories as far as Damascus which had been disputed since the time of Solomon.[7]

Jeroboam II was succeeded by his son Zechariah (II Kings 15.8–12). He reigned for only six months. We hear briefly that a certain Shallum conspired against him and that he was assassinated. But Shallum was no more fortunate. He was killed only a month later by Menahem, who made himself king (II Kings 15.17–22).

This introduces another revolutionary phase in Israel. Shallum, who killed Zechariah, was not a member of the dynasty of Jehu, which consisted of only five kings: Jehu, Jehoahaz, Joash, Jeroboam II and Zechariah.

On the whole, the reports on the contemporaneous kings of Judah are even shorter. Joash, who was rescued from Athaliah, is given a long reign: forty years. We hear in great detail about a new regulation for income to be used for improvements to the temple (II Kings 12.5–17). A more important point is that during his reign Hazael, king of the Aramaeans, occupied Gath, one of the cities on the Philistine coastal plain.[8] He also wanted to move on Jerusalem, but by paying a large sum from the temple treasury in tribute, Joash succeeded in ransoming the city (12.18f.). This supplements information which we have about his contemporary Jehoahaz of Israel, Jehu's successor. Jehoahaz suffered severe losses in Transjordania (II Kings 13.3–7). We can now see that the Aramaean attacks must also have been made on the western territory of Israel, so that even Jerusalem itself will have been directly threatened.

There is some obscurity about the fate of Joash, who was so miraculously rescued from Athaliah and crowned in so striking a way. He fell victim to the rebellion of two people, probably from his immediate entourage, and was slain by them. However, neither of the assassins seems to have sought the crown.

Joash was succeeded by his son Amaziah (II Kings 14.1–22).[9] We are not given any specific information about the succession. However, there may be a brief reference to it in II Kings 14.5, which says that Amaziah killed his father's murderers once the royal power was firmly in his hand. Amaziah was evidently a vigorous character. He fought successfully against the Edomites in the south (II Kings 14.10). This seems to have made him arrogant, so that he also provoked a conflict with Israel, the campaign in which he succumbed to king Joash of Israel at Beth-shemesh (II Kings 14.8–14).[10] But Amaziah was to suffer the same fate as his father. There was a conspiracy against the king in Jerusalem; he managed to escape to Lachish, but was killed there. Nevertheless, he was given an honourable burial in Jerusalem. This time, too, we hear nothing about the background to the coup, but there must have been a critical situation over the succession. The people of Judah, the *ʿam hā-ʾāreṣ*, banded together and made sure that Amaziah's son became king.

This son was Azariah, or, to call him by another form of his name, Uzziah (II Kings 15.1–7). He is assigned a very long reign. However, he was smitten with leprosy, so that Jotham, who was later to succeed him, had to act for him. Because it is impossible to fix firm dates here, there have been many hypothetical calculations of the reigns of kings during this period, producing a number of different results.[11] This has also influenced the dating of the activity of the prophet Isaiah and an assessment of his work, since according to Isa.6.1 he is said to have been called in the year of the death of king Uzziah.

These brief notes on the kings of Israel and Judah over this questionable period are just not enough to provide an adequate picture of the historical context. However, we can draw certain conclusions from them for the setting of events in world politics after the first half of the ninth century. The relative independence enjoyed by the two states of Israel and Judah, which they were able to maintain, was overshadowed by severe struggles in Syria which broke out among the city states there. These states also attempted to contest the growing power of the Assyrian empire, of course with differing success.

After the Aramaeans had penetrated along a broad front as far as the fertile crescent, towards the end of the tenth century, Assyria began to gain new strength under Asshur-dan II (932–910). The aim of the new Assyrian policy was to reconquer Aramaean Mesopotamia. The spirit of Tiglath-pileser I seemed to have come to life again. During the ninth century, at first in local skirmishes and then in much more extensive operations, carried out with unusual severity, the Assyrians succeeded in achieving military successes which terrified nations far beyond Mesopotamia. Asshur-nasir-pal II (883–859) should be regarded as the real founder of the neo-Assyrian empire.[12] All the fearful practices of Assyrian conquest and their techniques of domination can be seen in his methods, which later held together the Assyrian apparatus of state, despite high losses. The supreme aim was the extermination of any adversaries, either through extensive massacres or through deportations of the population to other territories in the Assyrian empire. In this way whole areas were depopulated, though elsewhere unusual enterprises proved to be possible. Asshur-nasir-pal II first broke the resistance of neighbouring countries in Mesopotamia. Beyond these territories he did not have the same degree of success. Nevertheless, he penetrated as far as northern Syria and received tribute from the Phoenicians.[13] Incidentally, it should be noted that Asshur-nasir-pal II was not only a conqueror, but also to a considerable extent an architect. In addition to Asshur and Nineveh, he was also interested in the city of Calah near where the upper Zab enters the Tigris (present-day Nimrud). Not only was the imposing palace there adorned with numerous alabaster and limestone reliefs and inscriptions, but its entrances were flanked with more-than-lifesize images of bulls, lions and all kinds of composite beings with human heads and eagles' wings. These became so to speak symbols of Assyrian art and were intended above all to ward off demons and evil powers.[14]

The wide-ranging expeditions of Shalmaneser III (859–824) were even more spectacular than the successes of his father Asshur-nasir-pal. Shalmaneser should be seen as the great Assyrian conqueror of the middle of the ninth century BC. His expeditions were often aimed at central and southern Syria, but they were not always successful. Despite everything, the Syrian city states were still in Aramaean hands; they were associated in a great coalition with independent power, and were more than a match for the impetuous foe, who did not seem to be as skilful as his father in assessing the realms of the possible. A great reputation was won by the coalition of Syrian princes which included not only the kings of Damascus and Hamath but also 'the Israelite Ahab' (*Aḫabbu Siri'lā'a*). The text can be found on the so-called 'monolith inscription' of Shalmaneser III.[15] In 853 there was a battle at Karkar, in the region of Hamath (*ḫirbet qerqūr* in the valley of the Orontes, immediately east of the Nuseiriyeh mountains). However, this battle, in which Shalmaneser claimed the victory, does not seem to have brought any lasting success. Battles with Syrian coalitions do not seem to have ceased during his lifetime.[16]

Shalmaneser's so-called fourth expedition against Damascus (in 842/41) was to be particularly significant in Israelite history.[17] The main thrust of his attack was directed against the territory of Damascus. At about the time of Jehu's revolution, king Hadadezer (*Adad-idri*) was succeeded there by king Hazael, a contentious man, who seized the throne by force. We hear of this in II Kings 8.7–15, and it is confirmed by Assyrian sources.[18] In his fourth expedition, Shalmaneser fought against Hazael, who had made Hermon, 'a summit facing the Lebanon', into a fortress. He laid siege to the king of Damascus and destroyed his plantations. These must have been the plantations at the fertile oasis of Damascus. However, we are not told that the city itself was captured. On the other hand, the Assyrians penetrated south of Damascus into the Hauran, and then moved westwards 'as far as the hills of Ba'lira'si over against ths sea'. 'There,' Shalmaneser remarks, 'I set up the pattern of my kingdom.' This can only have taken place in the foothills by the mouth of the present-day *nahr el-kelb*, about six miles north of Beirut.

Even today, the striking rock-formation of these foothills attracts tourists. Reliefs of Egyptian and Assyrian rulers can be found on its rock faces. One of them must be that of Shalmaneser (probably the one formerly taken to be Esarhaddon).[19] The images are life-size, but many of them have suffered severely from the weather. Nevertheless, one can understand why such memorials were made at that particular place. The foothills fall impressively towards the sea and to some degree form a natural boundary. At an earlier date the road led over the rock-formation, and passed immediately in front of the reliefs.[20] Today a good road by-passes the rock below the historic monuments. The consequent blasting of the rock has meant that some effigies, particularly that of Rameses II, are difficult to get at. At the foot of the hill one can see how the tradition has been continued: modern events are commemorated by similar monuments.

In the very inscription in which Shalmaneser speaks of setting up an effigy of himself, he speaks of a tribute paid not only by the people of Tyre and Sidon but also by Jehu of Israel: Jehu is called Iaua of *bīt-ḫumrī*, i.e. Jehu of the 'house of Omri'. This designation for Israel can also be found at a later date, despite the fact that 'the house of Omri' no longer existed as a dynasty. We have a pictorial account of Jehu's payment of the tribute on the so-called 'black obelisk', a basalt monument erected by Shalmaneser in Calah (Nimrud). This shows a series of scenes in individual stages. In the second row Jehu is depicted in a position of obeisance: the inscription reads, 'The tribute of Jehu, of *bīt-ḫumrī*; I received from him silver, gold, a golden *saplu*-bowl, a golden vase with pointed bottom, golden tumblers, golden buckets, tin, a staff for a king and wooden *puruhtu*.'[21]

From the year 838 we hear of further conquests in the 'land of Damascus' and of tribute from Phoenician cities.[22]

In short, Shalmaneser III may be said to have made impressive incursions into Syrian territory including Damascus, and even into the hill-country of the Hauran, but he did not gain a firm footing there and could not regard the land as an assured possession. Above all, the Assyrians were still kept at a remove from the territory of Israel; it can be shown that Ahab fought against them at Karkar in Syria, and Jehu was able to ward off the enemy by paying tribute. Israel's neighbour, the kingdom of Damascus, was bound hand and foot. Nevertheless, so II Kings 10.32f. reports, Hazael defeated Jehu throughout the border territory of Israel. This brief note fits the time of Jehu's successors better. Significantly, we do not hear in the Old Testament of bitter struggles against Damascus during Jehu's own reign. Shalmaneser III was not able to sustain his successes in Syria. The last years of his reign were burdened by internal struggles in Assyria itself; he retreated to Calah and had difficulty in maintaining his position there up to his death. Such changes of ruler were often occasions when subject peoples and tribute-paying nations could draw breath and reassert their independence. It was therefore only natural that the rulers of Damascus should have attempted to rebuild their power and should once again have directed their gaze southwards. This explains the severe Aramaean wars from the time of Jehu's successor Jehoahaz, which are reported in the Old Testament (II Kings 13.3–7). 'The king of Aram destroyed them and made them (the Israelites) like the dust at threshing.' But the Aramaean advance was not limited to the traditional battlefields in Transjordania; if it is true that Hazael occupied the city of Gath and that king Joash of Judah, the contemporary of Jehoahaz, had to purchase the freedom of Jerusalem with a considerable amount of tribute, he must also have invaded Philistine territory (II Kings 12.18f.).

In this way, then, the Old Testament account of the period and the information from outside the Old Testament overlap and support each other in an impressive way. Times must have become better for Israel when Damascus was attacked again. This happened about the turn of the century.

Shalmaneser III's successor, his son Shamshi-adad V (824–810), was so preoccupied with the situation in Assyria itself and with his relationship to Babylon that he had no time to attempt expansion into Syria. He married a Babylonian woman, Shammuramat, whose significance led to the legend of Semiramis. This woman later administered affairs for her son Adad-nirari III (810–782) while he was in his minority; he struck a decisive blow against the Aramaean state of Damascus. He compelled the king[23] to subject himself and to pay tribute; in addition, the same inscription points out that Tyre, Sidon, (the land of) Ḥumri, Edom and Philistia had also paid homage to him. This looks like an extensive expedition which reached beyond the coastal plain far into the south of Palestine, and even brought Israel into the sphere of Assyrian power. However, this raid to the south was not a matter of decisive significance, if it took place at all. Much more credible is the statement on a stele of Adad-nirari III which was only discovered in 1967: it mentions Damascus, Tyre and Sidon as the southernmost tributaries, but also adds king Joash of Samaria.[24] This was hitherto unknown. The offerings of the king of Israel will have been comparable to those from Jehu listed on the 'black obelisk'. But this means that Adad-nirari III was hardly able to extend his sphere of influence further than that of Shalmaneser III. Only Damascus seems to have yielded to his superior power, much to the advantage of its northern neighbour, the state of Hamath.

This situation of conflict within Syria, coupled with some disturbance on the northern frontier of Israel, has led to the often-repeated judgment that during the time of king Jeroboam II of Israel and Azariah (Uzziah) of Judah there was a lessening of tension, and Israel enjoyed a kind of 'Indian summer' before the invasion of the Assyrians under Tiglath-pileser III. This view has been challenged in more recent times, chiefly on the ground that too little attention had been paid to certain events in world politics which involved the Assyrians and also the states in northern Syria.[25]

Not least the opening chapters of the book of Amos (Amos 1.3–2.16) have been thought to indicate that towards the end of the sixties, the years in which the prophet's activity has been set, Israel became involved in new conflicts, brought on by the Aramaeans of Damascus and the Ammonites. The Syrian states at this time no longer felt themselves to be under direct threat from the north and began to take action on their own initiative. This view certainly has some truth in it, though the immediate effect on Israel remains uncertain. Nor can it be indicated with any degree of certainty from what period the above-mentioned verses of Amos come or to which particular events they refer. Given that the sequence of verses is authentic,[26] the transgressions of the Aramaeans, Philistines, Ammonites and Moabites (not to mention those of Israel) which they record are highly generalized in form, for all the efforts to be specific. Consequently they need not refer to new clashes in Amos' own time, but may cover the whole period of the dynasty of Jehu. This would give a more extended interval, from the second half of the ninth century almost to the middle of the eighth.

Other important events in international politics in this period are the first clash between the Assyrians and the Medes near Lake Urmia and the significant rise of the kingdom of Urartu on the plateau round Lake Van.[27] Urartu harassed the Assyrians during the time of the three weak kings Shalmaneser IV (781–772), Asshur-dan III (771–754) and Asshur-nirari V (753–746), when the real strong man was the field-marshal (*turtan*) Shamshi-ilu. It is clear that he had to cope with Urartu. Urartu reached a position of great power under its king Sardur III (810–743), hemming in the Assyrian empire and prevented the Assyrians from having access to the Mediterranean.

Other information that we have fits this situation well. A petty ruler in northern Syria, king Mati-ilu (Matiel) of the land of Agusi near Arpad, who had sworn loyalty to Asshur-nirari V about 754, went over to Urartu and fought with it against Asshur. This Matiel is known to us from a series of treaty texts on stelae which were discovered at *sefîre*, near Aleppo.[28] These are agreements concluded with other Aramaean partners, indicating a closing of the ranks among the Aramaean states. Apart from the fact that stelae I and II are probably earlier than stele III, it is difficult to date them, and there is dispute over their relationship with Matiel's treaty of 754 with the Assyrians on the one hand and that with Urartu on the other.[29] However, these details are relatively unimportant for an assessment of the general situation. This is characterized by the weakness of the Assyrians, the rise of Urartu and its influence on the Aramaean city-state system in northern Syria, which made it possible for the smaller states in southern Syria to attain a relative independence. This at least explains why in his series of threats Amos is exclusively dealing with Israel's immediate neighbours and not with the Assyrians. They were a danger on the distant horizon, but by the nature of things did not become an acute threat until the advent of Tiglath-pileser III in 745. This makes it feasible to put the appearance of this earliest writing prophet in the Old Testament towards the end of the reign of Jeroboam II. Asshur does not play a part in Amos' considerations, although it is impossible to know whether he did not nevertheless fear the mounting danger from the north. In view of the activity of Urartu, however, it remained uncertain when the decisive blow would come and who would strike it. We must leave aside here the question how far a prophet from Judah like Amos, appearing in Israel, could have been 'well informed' about international politics. But we should not underestimate antiquity in this respect.

At this point we should turn our attention to conditions within Israel and consider particularly social developments during this middle period of the monarchy. Almost exclusively, these are the background to the earliest written prophecy known to us, handed down in the books of Amos and Hosea, who was probably a slightly younger contemporary of Amos. Today we can see that the world of that time was being shaken by an extremely turbulent military and political situation. However, the international politics in which Israel was involved were hardly occasion enough to lead to the formation of the prophetic conceptions which acquired world significance with the writing prophets of Israel. Interpretation of history and vague prognoses of future events were not what prompted the great prophets of Israel to speak, nor did they dictate what these prophets had to say. The basic foundation of the prophetic message was Israel's own spiritual attitude, associated with its assurance of God, sense of justice and expectation of the future. This made the prophets see Israel's weakness in its fateful involvement with the stronger forces in its environment. They recognized the distortions of society among their contemporaries, and in an approach which has also become alien to our day, they associated them with international crises: they saw Israel's guilt punished by a foreign conqueror. But the prophetic speeches were also prompted by crises within Israel itself, and this gave them their weight; the reason for them must therefore be explained and understood in terms of Israel's very nature. The main difficulty that stands in our way is that the background of and the occasion for the appearance of the prophets must be inferred from their own writings. In form and content the sayings of, say, Amos are 'finished' works addressed to a particular situation, even before we analyse their cause and effects. This is something on which we have to reflect.

The most striking thing in a study of the classical prophecy of the eighth century is the way in which it is directed at a whole series of serious social injustices which are evidently connected with the attitudes of a well-to-do middle class. There is talk of oppression and deprivation of rights, of corruption and indebtedness, of a social disorder which there seems neither the will nor the ability to right. The historical books of the Old Testament give us no information here at all. As a result the social and political basis of the two states of Israel and Judah has to be reconstructed with a great deal of caution. We are compelled to infer some details from the prophetic books themselves, but these can be confirmed to a substantial degree by the law books. Relatively few detailed works have so far appeared on this group of problems.[30]

The best starting-point for an assessment of developments generally is the legal situation about property in Israel and Judah. As the incoming tribes invaded, they simply appropriated the land they occupied. The basis of law presupposed in the Old Testament was the conviction that this was the land which Yahweh had promised to the tribes and had given them for a heritage.[31] We are to conclude from this that in Israel the land really belonged to Yahweh; every free Israelite who had land of his own administered it as the gift of Yahweh to himself and his family. This conviction led to the view that the land could not be sold, and had consequences for the distribution of land and for the right of inheritance within families. This situation clearly obtained during the period of the tribal constitution. The situation changed with the advent of the monarchy. As a result, parts of Canaan were added to Israelite territory by conquest. The Israelite law of inheritance did not apply to them. Often the first kings acted with great caution. They did not apply the right of conquest at all rigorously. They purchased land for themselves, as was the case with David when he bought the threshing floor of Araunah in Jerusalem (II Sam. 24), or Omri when he bought the hill of Samaria (I Kings 16.24). These well-known purchases were possible and necessary because Canaanite land was involved, rather than the genuine territory of an Israelite tribe. The royal ownership of land increased in the course of time, even within Israelite territory itself. Family possessions fell vacant; dynasties and their claims changed. The story of Naboth's vineyard casts a good deal of light on particular circumstances. Kings may have assumed the right of intervening in the possessions of others. Further legal cases, of which we have no knowledge, may have brought changes in the old land law of Israel.

It followed from such developments that agriculture and administration in lands owned by the king had to be set on a new basis. An officialdom developed in the service of the king in favour of the court, which was responsible for administration and for the produce from the royal domains and from the land in the possession of Israelite tribes and families. This officialdom came into being when the monarchy became an established institution. Unmistakable testimony to this is provided more by the official lists of Solomon (I Kings 4.1–6), and his establishment of administrative districts with the express purpose of providing for the king and his house, than by those of David (II Sam. 8.15–18; 20.23–26). These officials were either retired military men or people who had entered the service of the king because they had no rights of inheritance. It was only a matter of time before these official circles were extended and completed.

It is clear how a new pattern of the distribution and administration of land consistently and systematically overlay the old tribal alliance with its legal principles. In terms of the conditions obtaining in the early period, the old system could be termed genuinely Israelite, whereas the newer approach was essentially an economic system. It was not just concerned with the tilling of Yahweh's land; it also set out to create a way of tending it which furthered the well-being of the court and the apparatus of state. This development was strengthened in those areas which were settled by Canaanites, because it was possible to make official purchases of land.

These were so to speak the new 'structures' introduced along with the monarchy, to the consequences of which allusion is already made in I Sam. 8. There Samuel, supposedly before the introduction of the monarchy, is made to warn the Israelites against the new institution. He speaks of a 'king's law' which will apply once kings are in power. It describes the conscription of young men into royal service, compulsory military service, their tasks in agriculture and in case of war. There is also mention of the numerous and demanding claims which the king will make on agricultural resources and on land, which he will hand over to his officials. The king appears as the centre of an organic state, all of whose functions are directed towards the monarchy, which it is arranged to serve. No matter in what period I Sam. 8 was finally conceived, it reflects experiences which grew out of the emancipation of the monarchy and which make it possible to draw some conclusions about the economic and social structure of the period of the monarchy in Israel and in Judah and about the principles on which it was based. Indeed it serves as a vivid illustration. These problems could well be made the subject of a wider and more detailed investigation. We might also ask, for example, about the expenditure on sanctuaries or about workers who devoted themselves more or less exclusively to handicrafts, including the production of weapons. However, there should be no forced answers to these questions. The important thing is to realize how many gaps there are in our knowledge of everyday affairs, and of day to day necessities, simply because of the lack of evidence.[32]

We may take it as certain that the cultivation of state domains developed alongside the land owned by free Israelites. These domains were subject to their own laws and obligations, and were administered by state officials; they in turn employed or supervised labourers. The roots of the exploitation lamented by the prophets may be sought in this extension of the administrative structure with its various grades of dependence; at any rate, this was the prime reason for a series of wrong developments and errors which undermined the older conceptions of Israelite law. As the administrative officials were exclusively subject to royal jurisdiction and in many respects acted in a context which it was hard for the ordinary person to comprehend, it was only natural that there should be resentment among those who still held to the early Israelite beliefs, which were largely stamped by the development of tribal order. The prophets also became the spokesmen of these groups. They took the side of the small people who had lost their defences, who were at the mercy of the 'apparatus' of state and who could not cope with it. Thus the upper classes, including the state priesthood and, at least in the northern state, even the monarchy, became the butt of prophetic criticism.

It must be emphatically stressed that this reconstruction of the economy and the administration of the period of the monarchy must unfortunately remain hypothetical in many respects, even though it is illuminated in many ways by the words of the prophets. However, a very few documents, found quite by chance, do serve to confirm the practices which had become prevalent. They are in the sober, bureaucratic form of administrative acts. Sixty-three ostraca have been found in excavations in Samaria, which in all probability come from the time of Jehu's dynasty. They are among the few documents written in Hebrew which we have from Israelite territory during the period of the history of Israel, that is, apart from the Old Testament itself.[33]

The ostraca were found all together in Samaria in a site which was originally assigned to the time of Omri, or at least the time of Ahab. Consequently, there were attempts to date the ostraca also to the period of the dynasty of Omri. But they must be later. They come from either the time of Jehu or that of his successor, or possibly from the time of Jeroboam II. Y. Yadin's view must remain hypothetical.[34] He proposes the first period of Tiglath-pileser III and wants to associate the contributions listed on the ostraca with the tribute which the Israelite king Menahem had to pay to the Assyrians.[35] Yadin bases his argument on a different understanding of the signs for numbers used in the ostraca.

The ostraca are delivery notes for wine and oil which was evidently sent to Samaria from the royal estates. Here is an example of each of the two forms which appear, to give some idea of the character of the text. The shorter form gives the date, place of despatch, recipient and goods: 'In the tenth year. From Azah (present-day *zawāta*, north-west of Shechem) to Gaddiyau (name of the official who served as a delivery point). A jar of fine oil.' The longer pattern is like the shorter to begin with, but gives the name of the official to whom the item is being sent instead of naming the item itself: 'In the fifteenth year. From Helek to Isa, son of Ahimelech. Heles from *ḥṣrt.*' It is particularly interesting that designations of districts should appear here which are known to us from the genealogy of the tribe of Manasseh (Num.26.30–33). Was there a deliberate reference here back to the earlier tribal order, or is this an administrative structure which was only developed during the period of the monarchy in connection with the geographical basis of the settlement, and which later helped to fix precisely the territories of tribes and clans? A number of questions remain open here.

The ostraca record only deliveries of wine and oil. To some degree this may be pure coincidence. However, the Egyptian administration also provides instances of special deliveries of this kind from the royal estates. It is possible that the rest of the produce was brought in through a general levy for which we do not have similar records.

The Samarian ostraca can illuminate a small area of the economic practice and provisioning at the time of the monarchy; we know nothing comparable from the Old Testament. It is, however, very easy to see how members of an administrative class who gained power and status particularly during the long duration of the dynasty of Jehu, were also able to fill their own pockets and enrich themselves unscrupulously, not only in natural produce but also in land and in everything else which fell within the scope of their administration. It would be very easy for an Israelite peasant who fell behind with his payments to become dependent on a royal official; it would then be possible with some semblance of justice (e.g. on the basis of the regulations about slavery for debt, cf. Exod. 21.2–11) to challenge his right of possession and finally to annex his land to the royal estates. The chief transgressions which the prophets have to attack are speculation in land and extortion, not to mention the luxury and extravagance indulged in by those who could manipulate the system (cf. Amos 2.6ff.; 4.1ff.). In short, the original agricultural system, which was essentially one of smallholdings, was overlaid by a growing pattern of estates and large-scale agriculture which was developed with royal support. We must attempt to understand the sayings of the prophets largely against the background of this contrast.

There is not the space here to attempt a detailed exposition of prophetic sayings. But once we realize the social division which existed within Israel, we can better understand remarks of Amos like, 'Those who turn justice to wormwood, and cast down righteousness to the earth . . . they hate him who reproves in the gate, and they abhor him who speaks the truth' (5.7, 10). The ancient justice administered at the gate had long been the setting in which the traditional laws had been cherished. Those who were forced into a dependent position now sought justice in vain. Amos 5.11f. is even more evidently an address to the new lords in the land: 'Therefore because you trample upon the poor and take from him exactions of wheat, you have built houses of hewn stone, but you shall not dwell in them (here the analysis turns into a series of threats) . . . you who afflict the righteous, who take a bribe, and turn aside the needy in the gate.' Such sayings cannot refer to a general failure of all Israelites before Yahweh, but they do envisage particular conflicts within Israel, and a conflict within the population itself between unscrupulous exploiters and those whom they had exploited and left without rights. Against this background of the perversion of the Israelite social order we can see what was really sought on the part of the prophets, and what they meant when they spoke of righteousness, self-sacrifice and love. The prophets struggled to give voice to earlier demands of Yahweh and at the same time to make them understood more profoundly. In what they said, the prophets enriched and extended knowledge of Yahweh to an extent which had hitherto been unknown.

It would be too one-sided to consider the words of the prophets of this period as no more than the religious interpretation of a development which in reality could not be altered. As we know, such a division between the state and religion, between spiritual conceptions and those of power politics, was not characteristic of Israel. The prophets saw an Israel which had become the helpless victim of forces which had interposed themselves between the people and their God. These forces were in the first instance a corrupt middle class and a considerable part of the aristocracy. Amos and Hosea, and Isaiah and Micah at a later date, could not but see that because of this rottenness inside, the state would not be able to withstand the dangers that threatened it from outside. Here are to be found the roots of their message of disaster, about which they felt unable to be silent. From what source they drew their towering insights, which went so far beyond the average thought of their contemporaries, is a question which cannot be discussed here. We should not belittle the profound dimensions of prophetic activity which go beyond all rational considerations. But the insights gained and expressed in this way were finally confirmed not least by the further course of events. The states of Israel and Judah were exposed to the severest pressures from outside and from within, and their very existence was put in jeopardy. The cause of this was an Assyrian of unparalleled energy, whose efforts at expansion did not stop, as before, at the gates of Israel and Judah.

NOTES

1. The parallel report in Chronicles has expansions in some passages, but these are not historically reliable: on king Joash, II Kings 12, see II Chron. 24, where there is an independent revision of II Kings 12.5–16 in verses 4–14; for Amaziah, II Kings 14.2–14, 17–20 see II Chron. 25; for Azariah/Uzziah see II Kings 14.21f.; 15.2f., 5–7, cf. II Chron. 26.

2. We do not know who the man was, nor the circumstances in which he made an appearance. His designation as 'judge' primarily suggests a man from Israel. This will hardly have been in the time of the Assyrian king Adad-nirari III, thus M. Haran, 'The Rise and Decline of the Empire of Jerobeam ben Joash', *VT* 17, 1967, 266–97, esp. 267f.

3. In view of the mention of the temple, the tradition may come from the chronicles of Judah; cf. Noth, *Überlieferungsgeschichtliche Studien*, 76; id., *History of Israel*, ²1960, 237.

4. Cf. M. Haran, op. cit.

5. Of course, II Kings 14.28 can be wrongly understood in these terms. Damascus is even mentioned alongside Hamath there. However, we may rule out such an extension of Jeroboam's power.

6. For Lebo-Hamath as the designation of a particular locality at the northern end of Transjordania see M. Noth, *Aufsätze* 1, 271–5; K. Elliger, 'Die Nordgrenze des Reiches Davids', *PJB* 32, 1936, esp. 40–45, differs; see on the other hand Noth, 'Das Reich von Hamath als Grenznachbar des Reiches Israel', *Aufsätze* 2, 148–60, esp. 159; see also now A. Malamat, 'Aspects of the Foreign Policies', *JNES* 22, 1963, 4, and M. Haran, *VT* 17, 1967, 278–84.

7. Cf. M. Noth, *Aufsätze* 1, 463. According to II Kings 14.25–27, these conquests of Jeroboam correspond to the word of a prophet named Jonah ben Amittai; he is mentioned by the Deuteronomistic history work, but the prophet Amos is not. Cf. now F. Crüsemann, 'Kritik an Amos im deuteronomistischen Geschichtswerk. Erwägungen zu 2. Kön. 14.27', in *Probleme biblischer Theologie* (Festschrift von Rad), 1971, 57–63.

8. There is still a dispute about its location. *Tell eṣ-ṣāfi* seems most probable; cf. K. Elliger, *ZDPV* 57, 1934, 148–52; id., *BHH* 1, 515; cf. also the discussion in Y. Aharoni, *The Land of the Bible*, 161f., 250f.

9. The chronology of king Amaziah always causes difficulties. According to II Kings 14.2 he reigned twenty-nine years and according to 14.17 survived Joash of Israel by

fifteen years. Jepsen, *Untersuchungen*, 38, assumes on the basis of his calculations that he was deposed in 787, but had continued to live until 773; cf. also J. Begrich, op. cit., 49ff.; Andersen's chronology offers a doubtful solution.

10. According to II Kings 14.9, Joash first gave his answer to Amaziah's demand in the form of a plant fable reminiscent of the fable of Jotham in Judg. 9. Questions arise here about the tradition. Is it possible to imagine that the whole of II Kings 14.8–14 has been taken over from 'chronicles' of Judah? On this see Noth, *Überlieferungsgeschichtliche Studien*, 76.

11. Jepsen differs from Begrich in the dates he gives for this period. The dates are: Azariah: 785/4 – 747/6 (Begrich), 787–736 (Jepsen); Jotham: 758/7–743/2 (Begrich), 759–41 (Jepsen).

12. Cf. the brief and instructive account of his person and work in W. von Soden, *Herrscher im alten Orient*, 1954, 78–89; also Scharff/Moortgat, *Ägypten und Vorderasien im Altertum*, ²1959, 400–5; *Fischer Weltgeschichte* 4, 1967, 25–44 (including Shalmaneser III and his successors).

13. *AOT*, 339f.; *ANET*, 275f.

14. Pictures in W. von Soden, op. cit., 83; *AOB*, 378–80; *ANEP*, 646, 647, 651. R. D. Barnett and W. Forman, *Assyrische Palastreliefs*, 1960, gives a marvellous impression of Assyrian relief art with numerous pictures from Nimrud.

15. Col. II, 90–102. Translations in *AOT*, 340f.; *ANET*, 278f.; *TGI*, 49f.

16. See the textual material in translations in *AOT*, 340–4; *ANET*, 276–80; see also the series by E. Michel, *Die Assur-Texte Salmanassars* III (858–824), in WO from vol. 1 on.

17. *AOT*, 343; *ANET*, 280; *TGI*, 50f.; E. Michel, *WO* I, 1947, 265–8.

18. *AOT*, 344; *ANET*, 280; E. Michel, *WO* I, 1947, 57–63.

19. *AOB*, 146.

20. Cf. the older picture in *AOB*, 147. Even better is the old drawing in H. Winckler, *Das Vorgebirge am Nahr el-Kelb und seine Denkmäler*, AO 10, 4, 1909, 7 and the great edition by F. H. Weissbach, *Denkmäler und Inschriften am Nahr el-Kelb*, 1922, 20 pl. 5 and table 2.

21. *ANET*, 281; *AOT*, 343; *AOB*, 121–5; *ANEP*, 351–5, esp. 355; cf. also the detailed pictures of people bearing tribute in Barnett/Forman, *Assyrische Palastreliefs*, 33, 34.

22. *AOT*, 343.

23. Here the king of Damascus is called Mari', Aramaic for 'my lord'; the address of the king was confused with his name; *AOT*, 344f.; *ANET*, 281f.; *TGI*, 53f.

24. S. Page, 'A Stela of Adad-Nirari III and Nergal-ereš from Tell al Rimah', *Iraq* 30, 1968, 139–53, and pll. XXXIX–XLI; on this and chiefly on the chronological problems of the texts of Adad-nirari see H. Donner, 'Adadnirari III und die Vasallen des Westens', *Archäologie und Altes Testament* (Galling Festschrift), 1970, 49–59.

25. S. Cohen, 'The Political Background of the Words of Amos', *HUCA* 36, 1965, 153–60; M. Haran, 'The Rise and Decline of the Empire of Jeroboam ben Joash', *VT* 17, 1967, 266–97; H. W. Wolff, *Amos*, BK 14, 2, 1967, 105f., 183f.

26. It is highly probable that the sections on Tyre (1.9f.), Edom (1.11f.) and Judah (2.4f.) should be regarded as additions, on grounds of both form and content; cf. H. W. Wolff, op. cit., 184f.; W. Rudolph, 'Die angefochtenen Völkersprüche in Amos 1 and 2', *Schalom* (Festschrift Jepsen), 1971, 45–9; id., KAT XIII, 2, 1971, esp. 118–24.

27. A. Goetze, *Kleinasien*, Kulturgeschichte des Alten Orients III, 1, ²1957, 187–200, esp. 192; id., *Hethiter, Churriter und Assyrer*, 1936, 170–85.

28. *KAI*, nos. 222–4 (with bibliography); cf. esp. M. Noth, 'Der historische Hintergrund der Inschriften von sefire', *ZDPV* 77, 1961, 118–72 = *Aufsätze* 2, 161–210; J. A. Fitzmyer, *The Aramaic Inscriptions of Sefire*, 1967.

29. See *KAI* II², 272–4; M. Noth, *ZDPV* 77, 167–72 = *Aufsätze* 2, 206–10.

30. A. Alt, 'Der Anteil des Königtums an der sozialen Entwicklung in den Reichen Israel und Juda' (1955), KS III, 348–72 = Grundfragen, 367–91, should be mentioned in first place; also M. Noth, 'Das Krongut des israelitischen Könige und seine Verwaltung', ZDPV 50, 1927, 211–44 = Aufsätze 1, 159–82; H. Donner, 'Die soziale Botschaft der Propheten im Licht der Gesellschaftsordnung in Israel', Oriens Antiquus 2, 1963, 229–45; K. Koch, 'Die Enstehung der sozialen Kritik bei den Profeten', in Probleme alttestament- lischer Theologie (von Rad Festschrift), 1971, 236–57; O. H. Steck, 'Prophetische Kritik an der Gesellschaft', in Christentum und Gesellschaft (ed. von Lohff/Lohse), 1969, 46–62; Marlene Fendler, 'Zur Sozialkritik des Amos', EvTh 33, 1973, 32–53.

31. G. von Rad, 'The Promised Land and Yahweh's Land in the Hexateuch' (1943), in The Problem of the Hexateuch, 1966, 79–93; see now also Eckert, Levinson, Stohr (eds.), Jüdisches Volk – gelobtes Land. Die biblischen Landverheissungen als Problem des jüdischen Selbstverständnisses und der christlichen Theologie, 1970, which pursues numerous per- spectives right down to the present.

32. S. Morenz, Prestige-Wirtschaft im alten Ägypten, Sitzungsberichte der Bayerischen Akademie der Wissenschaften, Phil.-hist. Kl., 1969, vol. 4, is interesting and illuminating; cf. now H. Klengel, Beiträge zur sozialen Struktur des alten Vorderasiens, 1971, which has a wealth of material; also Gesellschaftsklassen im Alten Zweistromland und in den angrenzenden Gebieten, XVIII Rencontre assyriologique internationale, München, 29. Juni bis 3. Juli 1970, Abhandlungen der Bayerischen Akademie NF 75, 1972.

33. G. A. Reisner et al., Harvard Excavations at Samaria I, 1924, 233ff.; M. Noth, 'Das Krongut' (see n.30); KAI, nos.183–8; four selected texts in TGI[1], 1950, 50; cf. also Galling, BRL, 407f., and BHH II, art. 'Ostraka', 1359f.

34. Y. Yadin, 'Ancient Judaean Weights and the Date of the Samaria Ostraca', Scripta Hierosolymitana 8, 1961, 9–25.

35. II Kings 15.19f.

8 | *Assyrian Expansion down to the Fall of Samaria*

IN THE YEAR 745, after a rebellion in Calah, Tiglath-pileser III succeeded in taking power in Assyria. His policy was to build up the Assyrian empire in a systematic way. As far as Syria and Palestine were concerned, he was at first faced with the problems which confronted his predecessors Shalmaneser III and Adad-nirari III in the ninth century. The petty states of Syria had to be brought down. After that, in the course of further campaigns, the great king penetrated northern Israelite territory as far as the coastal plain of Palestine, fought against the Philistines and finally reached the so-called 'Brook of Egypt', the *wādi el-'arīsh* far to the south.

This subjection of the whole area over the course of years was not achieved in a consistent manner or with the same degree of severity. Not all districts were immediately incorporated wholly into the Assyrian empire. Some at first merely paid tribute; in others, the reigning kings became vassals of the great king. In some cases Tiglath-pileser III may have been content with tribute and declarations of loyalty. This seems to have happened in the case of Judah.

Once an area was firmly in the king's hands, however, the Assyrians might adopt their practice of deportation. This meant that they resettled particularly the ruling classes in distant parts of the empire, while tending to leave the peasant classes where they were. This virtually ruled out the possibility of rebellion in subject territories. The most important elements among the population of the northern state of Israel fell victim to this practice; not only did Israel completely forfeit its existence as a state, but we cannot even recognize the deportees as a coherent group at a later date. They were scattered among the countries to which they were sent and there became swallowed up in the indigenous population. This did not happen to the people of Judah, who were not completely deprived of their individuality in exile in Babylon a century later.

The Assyrian army had reached a high degree of competence. It was superior to all opponents in equipment, technique and tactics. No military power was feared more than the Assyrians in their time: we have an apt description of them in some sayings of the prophet Isaiah:

Isaiah 5.26–29 runs:

He (Yahweh) will raise a signal for a nation afar off,
and whistle for it from the ends of the earth;[1]
and lo, swiftly, speedily it comes!
None is weary, none stumbles,
none slumbers or sleeps,
not a waistcloth is loose,
not a sandal-thong broken;
their arrows are sharp,
all their bows bent,
their horses' hoofs seem like flint,
and their wheels like the whirlwind.
Their roaring is like a lion,
like young lions they roar;
they growl and seize their prey,
they carry it off and none can rescue.[2]

Every detail in this saying of Isaiah's is based on exact observation of Assyrian techniques and practices in war. This can be demonstrated even down to the equipment depicted in illustrations of Assyrian soldiers, where for example the high-laced Assyrian military boot can easily be recognized.[3]

One important reason for the extraordinary superiority of the Assyrians was that they had a standing army at their disposal. Small kingdoms, like those in Syria and Palestine, often had only the conscript levy to rely on. In emergencies every free man had to go out to fight, and agriculture came to a halt. Such armies were incapable of large-scale expansionist undertakings, and it was impossible for them to keep control over large distances; they could only manage defensive operations in a limited area. The Assyrians had professional soldiers who not only came from their own people but were also mercenaries of various nationalities. Over the years these troops developed their skill and methods through their great campaigns. The mercenary armies of conquered states could be taken over as a means of increasing Assyrian military strength.

The Assyrians also developed new methods in the extension and consolidation of their empire. They created various degrees of dependence, since it was not their predetermined aim immediately to deprive each state of its independence and its own life. On the outer periphery of their sphere of influence, in the outermost states of the empire, the Assyrians at first contented themselves with declarations of loyalty from the native rulers. The latter thus entered into a vassal relationship and had to pay tribute. If, however, they failed to pay tribute, or cherished ideas of revolution, or took part in anti-Assyrian coalitions, the Assyrians moved on to the second stage of their policy of expansion. They reduced the state concerned, made areas of it into provinces and appointed a vassal friendly to Assyria to govern what remained. The formation of provinces was regularly associated with deportations. Only when the vassal of a rump state dared to conspire against Assyria did the great king take the third and final step, completely exterminating the remnants of the state and making the fragment that remained into a province. We can easily see how these three steps followed each other in succession from the way in which the northern state of Israel was treated.

In this way there arose an empire which was unique in its time. It was well-organized and had been built up systematically; it was a system of states, with numerous provinces surrounding the heart of the empire and in turn protected by a chain of vassal states. With few exceptions, the Assyrians also succeeded in their aim of gradually incorporating even these vassal states. The victorious course on which the Assyrians after Tiglath-pileser III entered in the Near East must be seen against this background of a deliberate and well-thought-out policy of expansion, a systematic practice of subjection and military superiority.

Tiglath-pileser probably began in 740 with the conquest of northern Syria. However, as far as we know, the first extensive campaign there took place in 738.[4] He subjected the state of Hamath in northern and central Syria, which had super-seded Damascus as the chief power there some decades earlier. Numerous Syrian states and Phoenician coastal cities paid tribute once the power of Hamath had been broken; those who paid tribute included king *Raṣunnu* of Damascus, known to the Old Testament under the name Rezin,[5] and *Menihimme* of Samaria, king Menahem of Israel (II Kings 15.17–22). The Old Testament text mentions that Menahem paid tribute to 'Pul'; in this passage Tiglath-pileser is given his Babylonian throne-name. We must therefore look at developments in Israel.

King Zechariah, the son of Jeroboam II and the last representative of the dynasty of Jehu, only reigned for six months before being murdered by Shallum. But only a month later Shallum was murdered by Menahem, who came from Tirzah to Samaria. Menahem then made himself king. The background to this surprisingly rapid change in ruler remains obscure; the reports give us no more than the bare facts. Menahem managed to rule for ten years (751/50–742/41).[6] It is possible that he was able to survive through great brutality and harshness. Some details in II Kings 15.14ff. might indicate this. The chief event recorded of him is his tribute to Tiglath-pileser (II Kings 15.19f.). He paid a thousand talents of silver, and raised this sum by imposing a poll tax of a kind which we cannot find attested elsewhere. He made each of his *gibbōrē haḥayil* pay fifty shekels. These were free landowners who were liable for the levy. Their number has been calculated at 60,000 for the northern kingdom of Israel alone.[7] They may have included old-established Israelites as well as royal officials and administrators. The upper classes, once so autocratic, now began to feel the pinch. They were the people in Israel with resources, and Menahem knew how to compel them to raise the tribute money. Thus he bolstered up his rule with Assyrian support. Tiglath-pileser left on their thrones kings who paid voluntarily, when they were in the outer areas of his empire. As a vassal of the great king, Israel was now on the extreme edge of the Assyrian sphere of power.

It accords completely with what has just been said that during this period the southern kingdom of Judah still remained completely outside these events and still had nothing to do with the Assyrians.

Consequently it is improbable that the king Azriyahu of Ya'udi, said to have paid tribute in an Assyrian text about the campaign of 738, should be identified with Azariah (Uzziah) of Judah. Rather, he will have been king of the state of Ya'udi in north-west Syria, a state which we know well from inscriptions of the kings of Sam'al. One need only recall the inscriptions of Kilamuwa (Donner-Röllig, *KAI*, no.24; *AOT*, 442f.) and Panammuwa (*KAI*, no.215) which were discovered in the 1890s in the excavations of the Deutschen Orient-Comité at Zenjirli.[8] This state of Ya'udi was one of the first to pay tribute to the Assyrian king in northern Syria, and it therefore fits particularly well into the operations of 738, distant Judah is quite another matter.

Sources for events in the state of Judah are very sparse in this period. Uncertainty over the date of the death of Azariah/Uzziah and over the question whether, say, his successor Jotham acted as regent for him (cf. II Kings 15.5) has led to a great number of chronological calculations which need not be discussed here. In the end they do not have any significance for an assessment of the historical course of events.[9]

We hear virtually nothing about king Jotham of Judah (II Kings 15.32–38) apart from the fact that the Syro-Ephraimite (north-Israelite) coalition was in process of formation during his time. Andersen's chronology accords with this: he assigns the years 741/40–734/33 to Jotham, making him die shortly before the crucial events of 733 with which his successor Ahaz had to cope.

But this is to anticipate the course of history quite considerably. We must now take up events in the northern state of Israel once again. After the death of Menahem,[10] his son Pekahiah ascended the throne (II Kings 15.23–26), but could only sustain his position for a brief period. He was then assassinated by Pekah, who made himself king (II Kings 15.27–31). This Pekah, son of Remaliah, was a chariot commander. Isaiah simply calls him 'the son of Remaliah' (thus Isa.7.5, 9), probably intending the term to be derogatory. Pekah is said to have reigned twenty years (II Kings 15.27), but that is improbable. A comparison with the Assyrian sources shows that the last year of his reign must have been 733/32.[11] By the express permission of Tiglath-pileser, he was succeeded by Israel's last king, Hoshea.

So much for the internal situation in Israel and Judah during the thirties. We must now consider developments on the international scene.

As far as we know, after his campaigns of 738, Tiglath-pileser did not undertake another until 734, which brought him 'to Philistia', the land of the Philistines. This brief note from the Assyrian list of eponyms[12] has recently been confirmed with the addition of further details. During English excavations in the north-west palace of Asshur-nasir-pal (883–859) in Nimrud in 1950, the fragment of a tablet was found with some information about the campaign of 734.[13] During this year the Assyrian king already reached the 'Brook of Egypt', the *wādi el-ʿarīsh*, having penetrated the coastal plain through Syria and Israelite territory. He was thus able to enter the territory of the Philistine city states. We read of clashes around Gaza, whose king Hanun had even fled as far as Egypt to avoid falling into Assyrian hands and becoming a vassal.[14] It looks as though the Assyrian king was wanting to gain control of the routes into Egypt, and possibly also to cut off contacts between the Syrian states and the Nile. We hear nothing at all about this campaign from the Old Testament. Israel will not have been involved in the fighting, as it was proving its loyalty by paying tribute.[15]

The situation changed in the following year, 733. In alliance with a number of petty states, Damascus sought to make itself independent of the Assyrians and institute its own policy. The state of Israel under Pekah joined the alliance, but not Judah, where Ahaz reigned. It is impossible to see why the king in Jerusalem did not join the coalition of Israel and Damascus. Was he afraid of the distant empire? Did he have a completely different policy in mind? Whatever was the case, king Rezin of Damascus and Pekah the son of Remaliah joined forces and advanced against Judah; they besieged Jerusalem, but without success (II Kings 15.37; 16.5). This remarkable conflict between the alliance of Aramaeans and Israelites on one side and Judah on the other is usually called the 'Syro-Ephraimite war'; the word 'Ephraim' is used *pars pro toto* for the whole state of Israel.

This minor war, which has only indirect relevance to the movements of Assyria, and which was probably waged by the partners in coalition with only part of their forces, is interesting because the message of a great prophet is associated with it. Isaiah 7.1–9, and probably its continuation in vv. 10–17, are certainly connected with the war; Hosea 5.8–6.6 also seems to have details of the Aramaean–Israelite advance on Jerusalem and Judah as its background.[16] Isaiah 7 tells of the appearance of Isaiah in an extremely tense situation. King Ahaz was evidently at one of the important points for the defence of Jerusalem, part of the water system of the city where an enemy attack might have particularly severe consequences.[17] It is commonly assumed that he was inspecting the fortifications of the city, but this cannot be stated with certainty. Whatever the case may be, Isaiah wanted to warn the king against entering upon a trial of strength with his opponents: the king had no need to worry so long as he trusted Yahweh. For the malicious plans of Samaria and Damascus, the two partners in the coalition, and all their threats,[18] were utterly doomed to failure. The great saying, 'If you will not believe, surely you shall not be established' (Isa.7.9), has its historical context here. At the moment of supreme danger it is important not to put one's whole trust in preparedness for battle. As a result of the saying of a prophet, the local conflict between an apparently superior opponent and the tiny state of Judah becomes an example for world history. This is one of those moments when the politicians can differ over the right course of action, but some decision has to be made under the pressure of the hour; whatever the uncertainty, the die must be cast. The prophet can venture against all appearances to put a brake on action and go against the politics of the day. He acts neither as politician nor as tactician, but speaks through faith in his God, in the assurance that he has received. However, his view surely does not run contrary to all realistic assessments of the situation. With the hindsight of the historian we may legitimately ask whether Isaiah's advice was not completely justified in the context of historical events. It was only a matter of time before the alliance of Damascus and Israel would dissolve; any coalition attempted against the Assyrians would come to grief sooner or later. Judah could in fact note a development of this kind with equanimity; but it would only be in a favourable position if it was never a partner in coalitions directed against Assyria.

The course of events is paradigmatic in other respects also. We do not know why the alliance of Aramaeans and Israelites could not achieve anything against Jerusalem. At all events, Ahaz became active. He subjected himself voluntarily to the Assyrian king, sent him gifts in homage and thus became a vassal (II Kings 16.7–9). Without being required to do so, Ahaz entered into a relationship of dependence which was not based on trust, as Isaiah intended, but on the fear of the politician, who does not shrink from paying the highest price and putting his own freedom at risk to ward off the lesser evil.

Whether the movements of Tiglath-pileser were determined by the request of Ahaz expressed in II Kings 16.7 for the great king to extricate him from the situation or by Tiglath-pileser's own strategy remains an open question. In any case he was on his way south, and Israel was within his next sphere of concern. At all events, he seems to have attacked the northern kingdom of Israel before the kingdom of Damascus, which did not fall in 733, but hung on until 732.

Tiglath-pileser reports on his actions against Israel in an inscription from his annals:[19] 'In my former campaigns I had added all the cities of Bit-Humria to my land . . . continued and had only left Samaria (?), they cast down *Pa-qa-ha*, their king.' These few sentences sketch out in a surprisingly clear form the second stage of the policy of Assyrian expansion explained above. After his alliance with Damascus, Pekah of Israel had become one of those rebellious vassals from whom Tiglath-pileser was no longer content to accept tribute. He reduced the territory of Israel and left only the capital and its surroundings as an independent remnant. In fact he made the greater part of the state of Israel into three Assyrian provinces which were no longer under the king in Samaria. These were named Megiddo, embracing Galilee and the plain of Jezreel; Dor, the coastal plain as far south as the level of present-day Tel-Aviv, and Gilead, the part of Transjordania which belonged to Israel.[20] We hear more from another Assyrian text: 'Bit-Humria . . . all its inhabitants (and) their possession I led to Assyria. They overthrew their king *Pa-qa-ha* and I placed *A-u-si-*' as king over them. I received from them 10 talents of gold, (x) talents of silver as their tribute.' Again the deportation is mentioned, and the fall of king Pekah, and then we hear of the appointment of a new king, made by Tiglath-pileser himself. Without doubt the reference is to Hoshea, the last king of the northern state of Israel. He was confirmed as a tribute-paying vassal of the Assyrians.

II Kings 15.29, 30 confirms briefly these stirring events of 733 which are reported in Assyrian sources. The statement that Tiglath-pileser 'took away' Iyyon, Abel-beth-maacah, Janoah, Kedesh, Hazor, Gilead and Galilee and all the land of Naphthali and led them away captive to Assyria clearly refers to the creation of provinces. It is understandable that the Old Testament text only mentions districts, and not 'provinces'. In essentials, however, the information corresponds to the Assyrian records. The only difference is that Tiglath-pileser seems to presuppose that the Israelites overthrew Pekah, whereas II Kings indicates that Hoshea killed Pekah the son of Remaliah after a conspiracy. Of course, such a course of events was nothing new for Israel; the generalized Assyrian text does not put the matter in doubt, just as on the other side the Old Testament text knows nothing of the legitimation of Hoshea by Tiglath-pileser.

Apart from the 'rump state of Ephraim', Israel had become an Assyrian province. Judah remained untouched and probably protected itself against imminent Assyrian attack by tribute. Ahaz had negotiated that.

The reckoning with Damascus took place a year later, in 732. The city was taken and its territory devastated. We hear nothing more of further campaigns of Tiglath-pileser III. The great king may have been content with the results which he had achieved, since in fact the whole of the corridor of Syria and Palestine was now dependent on him, whether as a system of provinces or as faithful vassals in the more distant areas. The latter category included not only Judah but also the land of the Philistines in the west and the series of petty states in the east and south-east: Ammon, Moab and Edom.[22] This is also confirmed by further documents which came to light in the excavations at Nimrud in 1950.[23]

Tiglath-pileser died in 727. For a chronological picture of the following period down to the fall of the Assyrian empire its rulers are here set alongside those of the state of Judah; the last king of the northern state of Israel, Hoshea, reigned from 730/29–722/21.

Judah	*Assyria*
Ahaz 734/33–715/14	Tiglath-pileser III 745–727
	Shalmaneser V 727–722
	Sargon II 722–705
Hezekiah 715/14–697/96	Sennacherib 705–681
Manasseh 697/96–642/41	Esarhaddon 680–669
	Asshur-bani-pal 668–626
	(Sardanapalus)
Amon 642/41–640/39	Asshur-etil-ilani 625–621
Josiah 640/39–609/08	Sin-shar-ishkun 620–612

Changes of ruler in Assyria were an incitement to anti-Assyrian coalitions in Syria and Palestine. Tribute was withheld, and there was even hope of outside support, perhaps from Egypt. II Kings 17.1–6 reports tersely how Hoshea, the king of Israel, withheld payment of tribute and sought an alliance with 'So, king of Egypt', as the text has it.

It was earlier suggested that 'So' should be interpreted as the proper name of a person. More recently, however, a brilliant and perhaps even correct hypothesis has been put forward: the name refers to the delta city of Sais. This seems philologically possible: in Egyptian, Sais is *S'w* (Sa'u) and in Assyrian *Sa-a-a*; phonetically this could produce *Sō* in Hebrew instead of *Sā**.

It is historically the case that during the twenties of the eighth century, as a result of pressure from Ethiopia, an independent dynasty came into power in northern Egypt. The residence of its ruler was Sais in the eastern delta, and here the so-called Twenty-fourth Dynasty of Sais was formed. Tefnakhte reigned there from 730 to 720, first as governor and later probably as an independent king. Hoshea of Israel may have struck up an alliance with him. But we hear nothing of an Egyptian mobilization. Hoshea's call for help will have fallen on deaf ears.

If 'So' is in fact the name of a place, a small expansion of the Hebrew text might be considered: *'el so' el melek miṣraim*, 'to So = Sais, to the king of Egypt'. The second *'el* may have fallen out when the name of the city was confused with what was taken to be the name of a Pharaoh.[24]

According to II Kings 17.4, Hoshea's contact with Egypt and his failure to pay tribute were the grounds for putting him in prison. In this way, the last independent remnant of the state of Israel, the city of Samaria and its surrounding districts, was deprived of its king. Samaria is said to have been besieged for three years. It is assumed that Shalmaneser did not keep his forces there permanently. The city finally fell in the year 722/21. According to earlier views, its Assyrian conqueror was Sargon II, who records the fact in his annals.[25] It was assumed that Shalmaneser V must have died shortly beforehand. Today preference is given to a passage from the 'Babylonian Chronicle' which attributes the destruction of Samaria to Shalmaneser.[26] However, we are indebted to Sargon II for further important information about the treatment of Samaria and its inhabitants.[27]

27,280 people were deported. The great king also talks of 'people from countries which I myself had conquered', whom he settled there.[28] Here is evidence of the third and final stage of the Assyrian practice of occupation, the liquidation of the residue of the already decimated state, extensive deportation and the settling of foreign population from another part of the empire. This is confirmed in II Kings 17.6. Those who were deported were sent to Asshur, more particularly to Halah, in the region of the Habor, a tributary on the left bank of the Euphrates), and specially to the area of Gozan (near the source of the Euphrates).

They were also sent to Media, to the regions north of Mesopotamia. This is the last report we have of the Israelite population who once lived in and around Samaria. They never returned home.

II Kings 17.24 records the new population which was settled in the land of Israel. They were people from Babylon, from the Babylonian city of Cuthah, and from Avva and Sepharvaim, two places which are unknown to us. Finally, they also came from Hamath, in central Syria. This last piece of information is particularly interesting. Hamath only fell in 720, some time after the conquest of Samaria. Thus the resettlement took place in stages.

The deportations above all affected the upper classes. The great mass of the population remained to work on the land. According to Judg.18.30 the priests of the state sanctuary of Dan were deported. Amos had already threatened Amaziah, the high priest of Bethel, with such a fate (Amos 7.17). The priests belonged to the upper class as much as the state officials and the leading land-owners, those who had great estates and those who administered royal property. They were replaced by the new settlers, who as the privileged class had to make arrangements with those of the population who had been left behind. Notes in the texts of Sargon already cited give some information in this direction. 'I appointed my officers as governors over them (i.e. the new settlers) and imposed upon them tribute as (is customary) for Assyrian citizens.' Thus the new settlers were those responsible for the produce of the land. In another place, Sargon reports: 'But I made Samaria better than before and settled therein peoples from countries which I myself had conquered. I appointed generals as governors over them and incorporated them into the land of Assyria.'[29] The new settlers brought their gods with them and worshipped them in their accustomed fashion (II Kings 17.29ff.). In one particular instance, however, help was sought from Yahweh, the god of the land. A plague of lions had broken out. A priest of Yahweh was asked to help because he knew the law (*mišpāṭ*) of the god of the land. So one of the deported Israelite priests was allowed to return with the consent of the great king and from then on worked in Bethel. Unfortunately, we are not told how successful he was (II Kings 17.25–28).

Other documents for the same period, from Gezer and Samaria, illuminate life in the land. These are orders for purchase which indicate that the buyers and their witnesses must be new settlers. They have Babylonian names (compounded with the name of the god Nergal), whereas the sellers have Hebrew names like *Nātan-Ia-u*. The new settlers were in a position to buy, and bought from the indigenous population.[30]

Under Assyrian occupation, the different elements of the population in Israel must surely have intermingled. However, the process is made even more complicated by the fact that other groups were added in the course of time. Foreign colonists arrived under Esarhaddon, in the first half of the seventh century (Ezra 4.2). There is mention of another similar group in the time of Asshur-bani-pal (Ezra 4.10). Should we also add the gloss in Isa.7.8b that after sixty-five years Ephraim will cease to be a people? Taken from 733, it brings us down to the time of Esarhaddon.

In such circumstances it is understandable that we hear very little about further developments on the territory of the state of Israel after the fall of Samaria. The Old Testament is virtually silent. The country was robbed of its independence and ceased to be a political factor; the settlement of a foreign upper class also kept the people of Judah from official contacts with their northern neighbours. As an Assyrian vassal, Judah itself was inevitably concerned about its relative independence. We have to realize that the separate developments within Samaria and Galilee, which can be noted for the rest of the period of the monarchy and down to post-exilic times, ultimately have their roots and first beginnings in this period after the fall of Samaria. In the long run, the exclusion of all political independence, the miscegenation of the population with the newly arrived settlers and the different way of life which this produced, inevitably served to alienate the north from Judah in the south. In many respects the differences went much deeper than the earlier confrontation between the tribes in Israel and Judah after the settlement. The final cause of the later formation of an independent Samaritan community set over against Jerusalem, and the verdict on 'Samaritans' which followed and which can still be found in the New Testament, was the consistent practice of subjection applied by the Assyrian empire. There were numerous conflicts which made the opposition to Judah more acute in the post-exilic period, but they were only subsidiary. The Assyrian conquest brought about the end of the state of Israel, and produced a breach with far-reaching political and ethnic effects on the land that was left.

NOTES

1. Yahweh will use the Assyrians as his instrument to perform his will.
2. Translation follows O. Kaiser, *Isaiah 1-12*, OTL, 1972, 132.
3. See the illustrations in *AOB*, 132-141; *ANEP*, 336-73; there are particularly impressive illustrations in Barnett/Forman, *Assyrische Palastreliefs*, 51, 53, 76, 77, 85, 87, 123, 125.
4. *AOT*, 345f.; *ANET*, 282f.; a part in *TGI*, 55.
5. The name of the king should properly be vocalized Razon (cf. LXX). He is mentioned in Isa.7.1ff.; 8.6; 9.10; also II Kings 15.37; 16.5, 6, 9.
6. Menahem: according to Begrich 746/5-737/6, according to Jepsen 747-738.
7. Galling, *BRL*, 176, 185-8.
8. Excavations in Zinjirli: reports were edited and published under the auspices of the Deutsche Orient-Comité in Berlin in *Mitteilungen aus den orientalischen Sammlungen der königlichen Museen zu Berlin*, XI-XV, 1893-1943.
9. For details see the works of Begrich, Jepsen and Andersen. The call of Isaiah took place in the year of Uzziah's death (Isa.6.1); it can certainly be said that the prophet appeared at the latest under Ahaz.

10. Andersen puts the death of Menahem in 742/41. This is one of the weaknesses of his calculations. In that case, how could Menahem be mentioned as having paid tribute in the campaign report of 738? According to Begrich, Menahem died in 737/36; according to Jepsen in 738.

11. Begrich assigns Pekah the years 734/33–733/32, Jepsen 735–732; Andersen's 741/40–730/29 again raises problems here.

12. List of Assyrian state officials from the ninth century BC with short notes on the campaigns of particular years; further details in A. Ungnad, *Reallexikon der Assyriologie* II, 1938, 'Eponymen', 412ff.

13. Published by Wiseman, *Iraq* 13, 1951, 21ff., pl. XI; translation *TGI*, 56; for a historical evaluation see A. Alt, 'Tiglathpilesers III. erster Feldzug nach Palästina' (1951), *KS* II, 150–62; E. Vogt, *Bibl.* 45, 1964, 348ff.

14. Cf. also the inscription of Tiglath-pileser, *AOT*, 347f.; *ANET*, 283f.; *TGI*, 57f., 58f.

15. A. Alt, *KS* II, 155–7, differs. In lines 10–13 of the fragment found in 1950 he conjectures allusions to a military clash between Tiglath-pileser and the state of Israel, and possibly even to the formation of a province on the northern coastal plain of Palestine.

16. A. Alt, 'Hosea 5, 8–6, 6. Ein Krieg und seine Folgen in prophetischen Beleuchtung' (1919), *KS* II, 163–87; see also J. Begrich, 'Der syrisch-ephraimitische Krieg und seine weltpolitischen Zusammenhänge' (1929), *Gesammelte Studien*, 99–120. The placing of Isa. 10.27b–34 in the context of the Syro-Ephraimite war is disputed; it is supported by H. Donner, 'Israel unter den Völkern', SVT 11, 1964, 30–38; id., *ZDPV* 84, 1968, 46–54; H. Wildberger, *Jesaja*, BK 10, 1972, 423–35, differs. He conjectures an Assyrian threat in the time of king Hezekiah, when Jerusalem was sympathizing with Ashdod.

17. The description of the place, 'end of the conduit of the upper pool on the highway to the Fuller's Field', sounds quite specific, but it has still not been precisely identified. See the commentaries on Isaiah and the great works on the historical topography of Jerusalem: J. Simons, *Jerusalem in the Old Testament*, 1952; L. H. Vincent, *Jérusalem de l'Ancient Testament* I, 1954; II/III, 1956; M. Avi-Yonah, *Sepher Yeruschalayim*, 1956, with the different views given there. For the whole text see H. Donner, op. cit., 7–18, and now O. H. Steck, 'Rettung und Verstockung, Exegetische Bemerkungen zu Jes. 7, 3–9', *EvTh* 33,.1973, 77–90.

18. Among the threats made was, according to Isa. 7.6, one to remove the dynasty of David and put a man on the throne who would merely be called 'son of Tabeel'. Perhaps he was not of royal origin and promised the men of Damascus and Israel that he would join them against the Assyrians. Cf. H. Donner, op. cit., 12f., and H. Wildberger, *Jesaja*, 275 (both with bibliographies). The acute threat to the royal house could have inspired Isaiah to conceive of an ideal ruler for Jerusalem and to foretell his advent. This would be the cause of and the stimulus for the 'messianic' passages Isa. 9.1–6 and 11.1–5, and perhaps also the Immanuel promise in Isa. 7.10–17; on this see now R. Kilian, *Die Verheissung Immanuels Jes. 7, 14*, SBS 35, 1968.

19. Annals lines 227f.; *AOT*, 347; *ANET*, 283.

20. See E. Forrer, *Die Provinzeinteilung des assyrischen Reiches*, 1921, 59–69; A. Alt, 'Das System der assyrischen Provinzen auf dem Boden der Reiches Israel' (1929), *KS* II, 188–205; cf. also *KS* II, 209–12.

21. *AOT*, 347f.; *ANET*, 283f.; *TGI*, 58f.

22. *AOT*, 348; *TGI*, 59; here king Ahaz of Judah appears as one who pays tribute; his name is given in a full form, 'Jehoahaz' (Iauhazi), which is not attested in the Old Testament.

23. H. Donner, 'Neue Quellen zur Geschichte des Staates Moab in der zweiten Hälfte des 8. Jahrh. v. Chr.', *MIO* 5, 1957, 155–84.

24. R. Borger, 'Das Ende des ägyptischen Feldherren Sib'e = סוא', *JNES* 19, 1960, 49–53; H. Goedicke, 'The End of "So, King of Egypt" ', *BASOR* 171, 1963, 64–6.

25. *AOT*, 348; *ANET*, 284; *TGI*¹, 53f.

26. *AOT*, 359f.; *TGI*, 60, with further literature.

27. Cf. especially the text reported by C. J. Gadd, *Iraq* 16, 1954, 173ff. (col. IV, 25–49); translation *TGI*, 60.

28. *AOT*, 348; *ANET*, 284; *TGI*¹, 54.

29. *TGI*, 60.

30. For the documents from Gezer see K. Galling, *PJB* 31, 1935, 81–6; for those from Samaria see A. Alt, 'Lesefrüchte aus Inschriften 4. Briefe aus der assyrischen Kolonie in Samaria', *PJB* 37, 1941, 102–4.

As a result of the fall of the state of Israel, Judah was doomed to inactivity if it was to avoid the most serious dangers and was not to risk an Assyrian attack on its own land. However, the silence of the contemporary prophet Isaiah on the fall of Samaria is remarkable. He may have seen it as the sorry confirmation of earlier fears.[1] And in any case it was not in the nature of the prophets to use events which had taken place to justify themselves.

The period from the fall of Samaria to the end of the eighth century was disturbed by a series of rebellions and coalitions hostile to Assyria, in which even Hezekiah of Judah was finally involved. This compelled the Assyrian king to intervene, and on the whole he proved successful. Still, there must have been a great temptation, especially for the smaller states, to enter into alliances against the Assyrians, and even Judah was attracted by such advances. The prophet Isaiah was an eyewitness in Jerusalem who observed the scene and passed judgment· on it. He gave an emphatic warning. It may have been at this time of considerable political and diplomatic activity that he made his famous remark, 'In quietness and in trust shall be your strength' (Isa. 30.15). He was utterly convinced that Judah would only draw attention to itself by conspiracies and that in the end no one could help it. With hindsight, we can see that Judah was favoured not least by its geographical situation. It was outside the main battlefields, high in the hills and not on the coastal plain. It was far enough south not to incur the suspicion of being involved in the Syrian attempts at coalitions. The king of Assyria may have been quite content with tribute from Judah. So Judah was spared, despite the rebellions of Hamath and Gaza in 720 and of Ashdod in 713–711; it was only invaded when it showed a hostile attitude to Assyria, in 701, in connection with the rebellions in Ashkelon and Ekron.

In 720, Hamath in central Syria, or more accurately what remained of this state after it had been reduced in 738, rebelled against Assyria. Now the whole territory became part of the Assyrian empire as the province of 'Hamath'.

King Hanun (Hanno) of Gaza also rebelled, with the help of Egypt. In the Assyrian texts a 'supreme commander of the land of Egypt' appears in this connection. He was evidently the commander of a sizeable contingent of Egyptian troops in south-west Palestine. Attempts were made at an earlier date to connect his name *Sib'u/e* with 'So king of Egypt' mentioned in II Kings 17.4; this possibility must be excluded, not least because we should probably read *Re'e* instead of *Sib'u* or *Sib'e*.[2] The king of Gaza, in alliance with the Egyptians, fought at Rapihu (Raphia, *tell refah*), fourteen miles south-west of Gaza, against the Assyrians, and was taken prisoner. *Re'e* managed to escape. Gaza became an Assyrian province.[3] The remarkable thing is that Raphia was probably the first occasion on which a large detachment of Egyptian troops was face to face with the Assyrians.

There were further rebellions during 713–711, centred on the Philistine city of Ashdod. Ashdod refused to pay tribute, and stirred up other states to form a coalition against Assyria. Sargon reports that 'the land of Judah, the land of Edom and the land of Moab' were also involved in the hostilities.[4] Thus the disturbance extended far into the interior. In addition, there were constant attempts to rouse Egypt against the Assyrians: the Egyptians must have been interested in keeping the Assyrians away to protect their own land. The Egyptian king at this time was Shabaka (712–698 BC), a member of the Twenty-fifth Dynasty which is known as the 'Ethiopian'. He is also well-known because of other documents.[5] Now was the time when rulers from the deep south near the Sudan held power in Egypt. Even king Hezekiah of Jerusalem seems to have succumbed to the temptation to enter into an alliance with these kings.

In Isa. 18.1–6, Isaiah has to deal with a delegation which had evidently come to Jerusalem for negotiations over an alliance. But the prophet consistently attacks these diplomats. He calls down woe on them: 'Ah, land of whirring wings which is beyond the rivers of Ethiopia, which sends ambassadors by the Nile, in vessels of papyrus upon the waters! Go, you swift messengers, to a nation, tall and smooth, to a people feared near and far, a nation mighty and conquering, whose land the rivers divide . . . ' These are the characteristics of the Sudanese as they may have appeared to Isaiah. It is typical that he not only dismisses the ambassadors, but tells them with great conviction that a time is coming when the Assyrians will inevitably launch an inexorable attack.

At the time of the rebellion of Ashdod, then, Isaiah had demonstrated his views in a most vivid way, by going around naked and barefoot as a sign that the king of Assyria would lead away the Egyptians and the Ethiopians naked and barefoot, a warning against all those who thought of making a pact with Egypt (Isa. 20.1–6).

Ashdod was overthrown; its king fled to Egypt but was handed over by the Egyptians to the Assyrians.[6] Despite their hostility, Judah, Edom and Moab seem to have escaped once again. But it seems as though they only waited for a suitable opportunity before rebelling against the Assyrians once again. In 705 BC Sargon II died and his son Sennacherib (705–681) came to power. Now king Hezekiah of Judah also withheld his tribute; in addition he seems to have removed Assyrian cultic symbols, the token of Assyrian overlordship, from Jerusalem. He also did away with another symbol which had previously stood in Jerusalem, 'the brazen serpent which Moses had made', to which the Israelites offered incense and which bore the name 'Nehushtan' (II Kings 18.4).

This seems to have been an old snake symbol which was connected with Israel's time in the wilderness.[7] In all probability, however, this connection is secondary and it was taken over from the indigenous Canaanite cultic tradition.[8] Both actions, the removal of the Assyrian cult objects and that of Nehushtan, are sometimes called Hezekiah's 'reform', an anticipation of the wider-ranging reform carried out by Josiah. This verdict may rest on the fact that Hezekiah receives special praise from the Deuteronomistic redactor of Kings for his step. None of the kings before him trusted in Yahweh as he did (II Kings 18.5f.). We cannot exclude the possibility that everything done by the king of Judah had anti-Assyrian overtones. Hezekiah seems to have played a leading role in the movement against Assyria. II Kings 20.12–19 reports that Hezekiah received a delegation from the Babylonian king Merodach-Baladan (Marduk-apla-iddin II), a prince who was king of Babylon under Sargon II from 722–711 and later under Sennacherib in 703. Hezekiah showed his armoury in Jerusalem to the Babylonians. This visit, too, may have fitted into the overall plans against Assyria.

Above all, however, after Sennacherib became king the two Philistine cities of Ashkelon and Ekron rebelled. Sennacherib was first occupied with numerous uprisings in his empire. He only mounted a campaign in Syria and Palestine in 701. Before that he had succeeded in regaining control of Babylonia and driving out Merodach-Baladan (Marduk-apla-iddin II). We have extensive source material about the campaign in Palestine, not least from the Old Testament itself. The relevant passages are II Kings 18.13–19.37, largely identical with Isa. 36; 37,[9] and also sayings of Isaiah in Isa. 1.30 and 31; these must be sayings from a late period of the prophet's activity. The Assyrian accounts we have are the 'Bull Inscription', composed after the sixth campaign,[10] and the larger account of events on the 'Taylor Prism',[11] together with references in other inscriptions.[12]

Sennacherib rushed through Syria and Phoenicia without encountering any resistance worth mentioning, and then attacked the rebel Philistine cities of Ashkelon and Ekron with all his might. At the same time an Egyptian army appeared from the south. Sennacherib says that it was led by 'the kings of Egypt', but these were probably only Egyptian city and district commanders. Sennacherib defeated the Egyptians at Eltekeh (*Altaqū = ḥirbet el-muqanna'*), in the hill-country between the coast and the hills of Judah, roughly level with Jerusalem. He then overthrew the Philistine cities of Ashkelon and Ekron. After this, the Assyrian king did not keep to the coastal plain, as his predecessors had done, but took the unprecedented step of moving round eastwards into the hills of Judah, heading straight for Jerusalem. Hezekiah was one of the rebellious vassals; now a direct attack was made on his territory.[13]

> Sennacherib first occupied the land of Judah: 'forty-six fortified and walled cities and their villages', as he says. Some fortresses, including Lachish (*tell ed-duwēr*), offered resistance. Sennacherib depicted the siege and capture of Lachish on reliefs at Nineveh.[14] Thus there seem to have been quite extensive battles in this region. The Taylor Prism also speaks of earth-ramps, battering rams, mines, breaches and sapper work used in the capture of the cities of Judah. Sennacherib mentions 200,150 people as booty; of course this number is too high, and has prompted a number of explanations, none of them certain.[15]
>
> This all seems consistent with Assyrian procedure. Sennacherib first occupied the area without regard to the capital, evidently to make an Assyrian province out of it. But after that, remarkably, he pursued another policy. He detached these territories from Jerusalem, and distributed them among the Philistine rulers who had remained faithful on this occasion, the kings of Ashdod, Ekron and Gaza.[16] No province of Judah was made. It is not easy to see why the king adopted this novel procedure. It is possible that he felt that to strengthen Philistine power would protect his empire more effectively against Egypt than if he were to make a separate Assyrian province. He may not have wanted to extend his system of provinces too near to Egypt, so as not to provoke the Egyptians again.

There remained Jerusalem. The city and its king Hezekiah were hemmed in by Assyrian troops. In the Taylor Prism, Sennacherib remarks vividly: 'Himself (Hezekiah) I made a prisoner in Jerusalem, his royal residence, like a bird in a cage. I surrounded him with earthwork in order to make it impossible to go out from the city gate.'[17] The isolation of Jerusalem is expressed equally clearly in Isa. 1.4–9, which says that 'the daughter of Zion is left like a booth in a vineyard, like a lodge in a cucumber field'. There is an allusion to the situation of the rest of Judah in the remark, 'Your country lies desolate, your cities are burned with fire; in your very presence, aliens devour your land.' Nevertheless, Jerusalem itself was spared: it was not captured, and Hezekiah remained on the throne. Why the city was saved is a special question to which no satisfactory answer has yet been given. This is because the Old Testament account is contradictory, and a comparison with Assyrian texts does not lead to any compelling solution.[18]

> The best-known version is that in II Kings 19.35–37. The angel of Yahweh smote the Assyrian camp by night, leaving many dead. This has usually been thought to indicate a plague, and on the basis of Assyrian texts and other parallels W. von Soden has recently shown that this possibility cannot be ruled out.[19] On the other hand, in II Kings 18.13–16 the Old Testament also knows of a large tribute which Hezekiah paid to Sennacherib. This is also mentioned in the

Taylor Prism, but in a strange form: Hezekiah sent the tribute to the Assyrian king in Nineveh and at the same time offered his homage, in other words his loyalty, through an ambassador. All these details correspond with the correct behaviour for a vassal proving his allegiance and paying tribute. In the present instance, however, this seems to happen after the Assyrian king has departed. The favourite conjecture that Sennacherib was compelled to make a hasty departure by events in Babylon will not do.[20] Thus we must suppose that events in the Assyrian camp outside Jerusalem made it necessary to depart; we cannot exclude the possibility that Hezekiah sent his tribute and ostentatiously reasserted his allegiance, the withholding of which was the occasion for the Assyrian attack.

All this may have seemed a miracle to the people of Jerusalem. They suddenly found themselves safe, and their king Hezekiah still maintained a relative degree of independence. We should not dismiss the details of the Old Testament account without proper consideration, because even the negotiations of the Rabshakeh (*rab šāqē*), the high Assyrian official, who stands before the walls of Jerusalem and asks its inhabitants to surrender the city against the will of their king (II Kings 18.17–37), have some parallels in negotiations with the inhabitants of Babylon,[21] so that this feature of the Old Testament account is also based on Assyrian practices.

The Old Testament seems to indicate that shortly after his campaign in Palestine, Sennacherib was killed by his sons (II Kings 19.37). This remark could be understood to suggest that events in distant Mesopotamia required his return home. Sennacherib was in fact murdered, but twenty years later in 681.

We learn virtually nothing about the further course of the history of Judah after 701 BC. II Kings 21 is the only chapter with any information before the accession of king Josiah, or more accurately, before the cultic actions which are understood as his 'reform'. In all essentials, the period between 701 and 622, the greater part of the seventh century, is hidden from our view. This may, of course, be because of the special conditions in Judah which had been brought about by the Assyrians. The land of Judah, the territory of the state outside Jerusalem, had been lost and was under Philistine rule. However, during the course of the seventh century, on some occasion unknown to us, this land (or at least a large part of it) must have been returned to the control of the house of David. At any rate, we find that the kings of Jerusalem are again masters of it at a later date. The land may possibly have been regained during the long reign of Manasseh, who succeeded Hezekiah on the throne.[22]

II Kings 21 has nothing good to say about Manasseh. He introduced foreign cults, he shed innocent blood. Prophets rose up against him. All this can be understood against the background of a favourable policy towards Assyria, which included the recognition of Assyrian cults.

We hear later from the reign of Josiah that there were Assyrian cults in Judah and around Jerusalem: foreign priests worked there, and incense was offered to Baal, the sun and moon, the planets and all the hosts of heaven (II Kings 23.5). This sounds very much like the Assyrian astral cult. Josiah did away with it, but kings of Judah are said to have instituted it. That must have happened during this essentially Assyrian period in Judah, i.e. after 701. Manasseh will have played a leading role here.

A report in II Chron. 33.11–13 is remarkable. According to this, the Assyrians sent Manasseh in chains to Babylon (not to Assyria!), but he later returned to Jerusalem. Was this some kind of punitive action for disobedience?

The time of Assyrian occupation during the seventh century was certainly an unhappy period for Judah. Perhaps the final chapters of the book of Micah belong to this period (Micah 6; 7). We are given the impression that law and order are breaking down. There is talk of the way in which Omri and Ahab behaved, an unmistakable reference to the increase of Canaanite practices. There are very few just and pious people in the land. At all events, Judah was not in a position to pursue an independent policy; world politics had passed by the tiny Assyrian vassal state, which had no real share in them any more. Meanwhile, however, Assyria had reached the zenith of its power.

Sennacherib's son Esarhaddon succeeded in conquering Egypt. In 671 the kingdom on the Nile was overthrown by the supreme Assyrian commander, the *turtānu* Sha-nabushu. The Ethiopian king Tirhaka was defeated, and Memphis was taken virtually without a struggle. Esarhaddon had Egypt ruled by twenty-two district commanders each with an Assyrian governor. Victory stelae were set up in all the territories of the empire. One of the most famous has been found in Zinjirli; it is now in Berlin. It shows a more-than-lifesize picture of Esarhaddon, who is leading the kings of Ethiopia and Tyre by a halter.[23] However, there were soon uprisings in Egypt. Esarhaddon sent his supreme commander there and finally followed him in person, though he was a sick man. He died before reaching Egypt, in 669.[24]

Esarhaddon's son and successor Asshur-bani-pal did not continue his father's brilliant foreign policy. His name is associated with the collection of cuneiform writings in his library at Nineveh, to which we are indebted for a large part of the literature of Mesopotamia. Internal dissensions weakened the power of the great empire. Asshur-bani-pal waged a hard war against Babylon, where his own brother Shamash-shum-ukin had been appointed as regent. Asshur-bani-pal finally defeated Babylon and a number of hostile coalitions. Nevertheless, the decline of Assyria as a great power had begun. Egypt had to be surrendered. The kings of the Twenty-sixth Dynasty inaugurated a new period of Egyptian self-assertion, begun by Psammetichus I of Sais, and by 663 they had restored complete independence from Assyria to Egypt. The Assyrian forces certainly got as far as Palestine in this period, but at least the Old Testament sources are silent on the matter. Manasseh was subservient to Assyria to the end. There is mention of

Manasseh of Judah in a list of vassals from the time of Esarhaddon; he is preceded by the king of Tyre and followed by the kings of Edom and Moab.[25]

Manasseh was succeeded by his son Amon (II Kings 21.19–26), but only for a very short time. He fell victim to a court conspiracy. However, the royal officials did not achieve much, for again the 'people of the land' first killed the conspirators and then enforced the succession of Amon's son Josiah, although he was only eight years old. We do not know who acted as regent for him. His mother is mentioned by name, but there is nothing to indicate that she carried out any official duties. It is pure conjecture that the king's sons mentioned in Zeph. 1.8 were those who acted for Josiah during his minority. It is also conjecture that the fall of king Amon was connected with a clash between two parties, one friendly to Assyria and one hostile, at the time of that power's decline. Of course the possibility cannot be excluded.

King Josiah seems to have pursued a consistent policy aimed at making Judah independent of Assyria. He followed a quite independent line which was to help not only Judah but perhaps even all Israel to new prosperity. The so-called 'reform of king Josiah' is only one element in this context; he was probably concerned to bring about an extensive reform of the state both internally and externally. The decline of Assyria and its empire in fact promised a turning-point for the states of Syria and Palestine; the time seemed ripe for their own political plans. To begin with, it was not evident that events would turn out quite differently in the end.

NOTES

1. Cf. Isa. 28.1ff.
2. R. Borger, *JNES* 19, 1960, 49–53.
3. Texts *AOT*, 348f.; *ANET*, 284f.; *TGI*, 62.
4. *AOT*, 351; *ANET*, 287.
5. The inscription of one of the most important theological texts in Egyptian religion, probably going back to an original from the Old Kingdom, comes from his time. This is the 'Shabaka Stone', made known by A. Erman, 'Ein Denkmal memphitischer Theologie', *SPAW*, 1911, 916–50. It was later investigated in detail by K. Sethe, *Dramatische Texte zu altägyptischen Mysterienspielen*, Untersuchungen 10, 1928, and subjected to new examination from the perspective of the history of religion by H. Junker, 'Die Götterlehre von Memphis', *APAW*, 1939, no. 23, 1940; see also the English translation *ANET*, 4–6; for a comparison with the Old Testament see K. Koch, 'Wort und Einheit des Schöpfergottes in Memphis und Jerusalem', *ZTK* 62, 1965, 251–93.
6. *AOT*, 350f.; *ANET*, 286; *TGI*, 63f.
7. Cf. Num. 21.4–9.
8. See the article 'Schlange' by M.-L. Henry in *BHH* III, 1699–1701; also K. Galling, *BRL*, 458f.; *RGG* V, 1419f.
9. II Kings 18.13–19.37 = Isa. 36; 37 (II Kings 18.14–16 is missing after 36.1); there are legendary features in Isa. 38–39, parallel to I Kings 20; the 'Psalm of Hezekiah' (Isa. 38.9–20) is absent from II Kings. See Leo L. Honor, *Sennacherib's Invasion of Palestine*, 1966; B. S. Childs, *Isaiah and the Assyrian Crisis*, SBT II, 3, 1967, 69ff.; see also O.

Eissfeldt, 'Ezechiel als Zeuge für Sanheribs Eingriff in Palästina' (1931), *Kleine Schriften* I, 239–46.

10. D. D. Luckenbill, *The Annals of Sennacherib*, 1924, 68–70.

11. D. D. Luckenbill, op. cit., 29–34; *AOT*, 352–4; *ANET*, 287f.; *TGI*, 67–9.

12. Luckenbill, op. cit., 77, 86; *ANET*, 288.

13. Sennacherib invaded an area which also contained the home town of the prophet Micah, Moresheth-gath (*tell el-judēde*); Micah saw the Assyrian attack coming, cf. Micah 1.8–16 and on it K. Elliger, 'Die Heimat des Propheten Micha', *ZDPV* 57, 1934, 81–152 = *Kleine Schriften*, 1966, 9–71; H. Donner, *Israel unter den Völkern*, 92–105.

14. *AOB*, 137–141; *ANEP*, 372f.; Barnett/Forman, *Palastreliefs*, 44–9.

15. The reduction to 2,150 made by A. Ungnad in *ZAW* 59, 1942/43, 199ff., seems far too mechanical and too low in comparison with the 27,280 people deported from Samaria: *TGI*, 68; cf. also W. Rudolph, 'Sanherib in Palästina', *PJB* 25, 1929, 59–80, esp.67; also A. Alt, ibid., 81 = *KS* II, 242f.

16. A. Alt, 'Die territorialgeschichtliche Bedeutung von Sanheribs Eingriff in Palästina' (1930), *KS* II, 242–9.

17. The last part of this sentence was given an apt translation by W. von Soden, 'Sanherib vor Jerusalem 701 BC', *Antike und Universalgeschichte* (Festschrift H. E. Stier), 1972, 43–51, esp.45.

18. Cf. the reflections and remarks in Rudolph, op. cit., 75–80, which take account of Herodotus' reports; W. von Soden, op. cit., and W. Baumgartner, 'Herodots babylonische und assyrische Nachrichten', in *Zum Alten Testament und seiner Umwelt, Ausgewählte Aufsätze*, 1959, 282–331, esp.305–9.

19. W. von Soden, op. cit., 49–51.

20. Ibid., 45.

21. An Assyrian letter from the year 731 about Assyrian negotiations with the inhabitants of Babylon before the siege of the city. H. W. F. Saggs, *Iraq* 17, 1955, 23ff.; see also W. von Soden, op. cit., 46–8.

22. Cf. A. Alt, *KS* II, 248f.

23. *AOB*, 143f.; *ANEP*, 447; there is some dispute as to whether the kneeling figures are Tirhaka himself or his son Ushanahuru; similarly, whether the standing figure is the prince of Tyre or of Sidon. Cf. *Durch vier Jahrtausende altvorderasiatischer Kultur, Vorderasiatisches Museum der Staatlichen Museen zu Berlin* (detailed guide), [8]1962, 52–5.

24. For the Assyrian conquest of Egypt see the relevant accounts in the histories of Assyria and Egypt; see also especially H. von Zeissl, *Äthiopen und Assyrer in Ägypten*, Ägyptologische Forschungen 14, 1955; R. Borger, *Die Inschriften Asarhaddons, Königs von Assyrien*, AfO Beiheft 9, 1956 (reprinted 1967); J. Yoyotte, 'Les principautés du Delta', *Mélanges Maspéro* 4, 1961; see the texts in *ANET*, 290–7.

25. *AOT*, 357f.; *TGI*, 70.

10 | *Josiah's Reform and the End of the Assyrians*

EVENTS IN WORLD history during the reign of king Josiah (640/39–609/08) were extraordinarily significant not only for Judah and for the territory of Israel occupied by the Assyrians since 722/21, but also for all the nations involved with Assyria at that time. Now began the rise of Babylon to become an independent power, the beginning of so-called neo-Babylonian domination; now was the time of the aggressive advance of the Medes and the Umman Manda, a Scythian group from the hills of northern Mesopotamia. The Assyrian empire, which was already breaking up, would eventually fall victim to this concentration of power. At the same time, Egypt was strengthened by the emergence of the Twenty-sixth Dynasty of Sais, and especially by the appearance of its first vigorous kings Psammetichus I and Necho II. Events in Palestine cannot be separated from these great movements in international politics. All the undertakings of king Josiah were inevitably connected, directly or indirectly, with the pattern of world politics in his time. This pattern offered him the possibility of new independent domestic and foreign policies, but at the same time gave its seal to the greatness and the tragedy of this king.

Josiah's so-called 'reform' cannot be understood in terms of domestic policy alone. Its roots quite certainly lie in the events of world politics and the cultural situation of the time. We must therefore consider the great international movements of the day before directing our attention to Judah and the actions of the king within his realm. This is all the more important, since the sources that we have do not give an altogether clear picture. A wider survey is necessary if we are to find an adequate and convincing explanation of the relationship of the Old Testament to documents from outside Israel. For this period the Old Testament needs to be interpreted in the light of non-Israelite sources.

From the time of Asshur-bani-pal the empire of Assyria was in decline, and after Asshur-etil-ilani and his brother Sin-shar-ishkun, this decline turned into a complete collapse. It became increasingly difficult to keep control of the great system of provinces and to maintain their ties with the heart of the empire. Provinces detached themselves or took independent action where they had the initiative. This can be seen most persistently from developments in Babylon.

New elements of population had established themselves there, coming from an area south of the mouth of the Euphrates and usually given the name 'Chaldaeans'. One of them, Nabopolassar (*Nabū-apla-uṣur*), succeeded in gaining control of the throne of Babylon. He became king in 625 BC and is regarded as the founder of the 'neo-Babylonian' empire. He was the father of Nebuchadnezzar, who was to be so significant for later developments in Judah.

While Nabopolassar was seeking independence for Babylon, the Medes invaded the region of the Tigris from the mountains of Iran, led by Cyaxares as he is called in the Greek tradition. The Babylonian version of his name is Umak-ishtar. The Medes posed a direct threat to the heart of Assyria. The Scythian tribes of *Ummān-manda,* who also reached the area of the Tigris from the steppes of southern Russia, are not identical with them.

The detailed course of events is recorded quite extensively in the Gadd Chronicle, part of the Babylonian Chronicle which depicts events from the tenth year of Nabopolassar to the sixteenth, and thus covers the period from about 616 to 609.[1] This shows clearly how Assyria was weakened by perennial war, how year by year Babylon was breaking loose and how finally the Assyrians were left with only their own country and some land on the western border. Nabopolassar, as 'king of Akkad', and Cyaxares formed an alliance. The city of Asshur itself seems to have been occupied solely by the Medes and then destroyed, whereas Nineveh, where king Sin-shar-ishkun ruled, fell victim to a united attack of Babylonians and Medes. The city was destroyed in 612; the king perished with it. Nevertheless, Assyrian power was still not finally destroyed. A certain Asshur-uballit managed to become king over Assyria in Haran, in western Mesopotamia. His reign is usually given as 611–606. The Umman Manda and the king of Babylon allied themselves against him and occupied the city of Haran. But Asshur-uballit escaped; a little later he reappeared to win back Haran, remarkably enough with Egyptian support. However, the Babylonians finally asserted themselves.

The intervention of Egyptian troops on the Assyrian side is particularly interesting. There is mention of them in this role as early as the campaigns of 616, well before Nineveh had fallen.[2] They attempted to defend the Assyrians against the Babylonians and their allies. Their appearance in north-western Mesopotamia in alliance with their former opponents presupposes a lengthy political and military development in the second half of the seventh century which is not entirely clear to us. The decline of Assyrian power evidently encouraged the Pharaohs of the Twenty-sixth Dynasty to reoccupy positions which they had once held. They devoted particular attention to the corridor of Syria and Palestine, which they now sought to bring under control. This was not only because of their concern for expansion, but also to protect them against Assyria and the latter's new opponents. They will also have sought to develop the Syrian states as a buffer zone.

We have some particularly valuable information about the long reign of

Psammetichus I (664–610) in Herodotus II, 157. The Egyptian king laid siege to the city of Ashdod for twenty-nine years. The number twenty-nine does not seem very trustworthy, but the whole procedure is symptomatic of the Egyptian attempt to establish firm positions on the coast of Palestine. Herodotus I, 105, reports a Scythian thrust towards Syria and Palestine. Psammetichus I also clashed with them and forced them to retreat at Ashkelon. At least here Egypt was involved in countering the peoples coming down from the north and protecting its own land against them. After the decline of Assyria this became a matter of life and death. It finally led to the surprising change of front in which the Egyptians, once the enemy of the Assyrians and conquered by them, now went into the field alongside them against a new enemy. Of course we do not know any details of the alliance between Egypt and Assyria; but in 616, the first year covered by the Gadd Chronicle, we already find Egyptian troops on the Assyrian side, and they were still allied with Asshur-uballit in his attempt to regain Haran for the Assyrians.

This support for Asshur-uballit comes at the same time as the arrival of Pharaoh Necho in Palestine, a fact which is also attested by the Old Testament. Necho II (610–595) was the successor to Psammetichus I. Josiah, the king of Judah, fell in battle against him in 609. Here the biblical narrative dovetails with events in world history. To anticipate matters somewhat, the Egyptians did not succeed in their attempt to restore Asshur-uballit as ruler. He succumbed to the superior forces of the Babylonians and their allies. With this, the Assyrian empire, which sixty years earlier had been the greatest power in the Near East, was finally vanquished. From that moment on, however, Necho felt himself to be the master of at least Syria and Palestine. This is the development which was decisive for the period immediately after Josiah's death. It is the international context in which the time of Josiah is to be set. A remarkable revolution in world politics was in process. Josiah was right at its centre.

We can well imagine that the king of Judah would attempt to exploit the decline of Assyrian power for the benefit of his own state. According to the Old Testament, the emancipation from Assyrian supervision was particularly marked in the cultic sphere. The alien deities, which also symbolized the presence of the alien power, were removed. However, this purging of the Assyrian cults was not the only change which is described as Josiah's reform. It was only the precondition. But because cultic centres were done away with in the framework of the reform, it is appropriate to take the two actions, emancipation and reform, in close conjunction, even if they should not be confused.

The account in II Kings 23 must be suspected of not always having made a correct distinction between the two actions. Each time it is important to establish whether non-Israelite or Israelite cult centres and their personnel are being abolished.

Seen from this perspective, II Kings 23.4–7, 10–15, 19, 20 prove to be political actions on the part of Josiah with the aim of emancipation from Assyria; vv. 16-18 are an addition. The content of II Chron. 34.3-7 may be compared. This passage has not been worked into the account of the reform. Here the distinction between emancipation and reform seems to have been drawn more clearly.[3] Josiah first had the temple purified of all Assyrian cult objects and did away with the houses in which cultic prostitution was practised. He then set all the foreign priests in Jerusalem and in the cities of Judah to manual labour. In II Kings 23.5 these priests are described with an Akkadian loanword as kᵉmārim, Akkadian kumru(m). The report of these apparently extensive actions against the foreign cults finally takes a remarkable turn. It is not limited to Judah, but also mentions the altar at Bethel and the Asherah there, which is burnt. Similar onslaughts took place in the cities of Samaria, where they reached such a pitch that all the priests of the high places were massacred and burned. Here we can see the king moving out into Israel. There is no compelling reason for doubting the correctness of these reports. Josiah also wanted to see the principles of his anti-Assyrian policy realized in the territory of what was once the northern state of Israel. In fact this means that he was also in a position to extend his rule to the north. The Assyrian administration was evidently no longer capable of functioning in these areas. We cannot discover how far the king was motivated by the idea of restoring the old personal union between Judah and Israel. Nor do our sources allow us to infer with any degree of certainty how individual actions were related to one another in time. In all probability, what is described extended over quite a long period.[4]

On the other hand, the report of the king's so-called 'reform', in which he set out to re-establish the cult of Yahweh, has the character of a unique and special treatment. It comprises II Kings 22.3-23.3; 23.8, 9, 21-23, 24, 25; there is a parallel in II Chron. 34.8-35.19.

The whole event began almost by chance with a routine piece of administration, the payment of money for building work in the temple, which was carried out by a royal official there. On this occasion the high priest Hilkiah declared that he had found 'the book of the Law' (the 'book of the Torah') in the house of Yahweh. The book was immediately brought to the king and read to him. It caused great astonishment and led to a series of highly significant actions.

First of all the advice of the prophetess Huldah was sought. She prophesied bad things for Israel but good things for Josiah, because the king had humbled himself before the words of the book. As Josiah later fell in battle it is thought permissible to accept that the reported message of Huldah is genuine. A secondary formulation of her words would have taken account of the king's violent death.

After seeking the counsel of Huldah, the king is said to have resolved on a kind of state action which formed the real nucleus of his reform. The book, which is here called the 'book of the covenant' (sēper habbᵉrît), was read aloud in a great assembly of the leading men of Jerusalem and Judah and many inhabitants of both city and country. Josiah then stood 'by the pillar', i.e. in his place for state actions in the temple,[5] and made a covenant with Yahweh 'to keep his commandments and his testimonies and his statutes with all his heart and with all his soul, to perform the words of this covenant that were written in this book' (II Kings 23.1–3). Those present then entered into this covenant and became partners in a treaty between themselves and Yahweh in which the king was intermediary. The whole composition and arrangement of the scene recalls the sacral covenants which were made or were claimed to have been made in Israel from earliest times, on the mountain of God (Exod.24.6–8) and in the assembly at Shechem (Josh.24.25f.). From this perspective, Josiah's actions emerge as an act of restoration, in which the earliest traditions of Israel are repristinated and given new life. Of course we should not forget that Josiah acted as king and not as leader of the tribal alliance. To this degree his action had political as well as cultic significance. The question is how the king came to be involved in this whole act of restoration and what is its relationship to the book discovered in the temple.

It has long been argued that the book found in the temple must have been Deuteronomy,[6] or more exactly, the nucleus of this book, which contained the basic tenets of Deuteronomy. The details of the solemn action in the temple and the further account of its consequences is so unmistakably close to the essence and thought of Deuteronomy, even down to the wording, that the Deuteronomic material could be presented as being without question the real centre of Josiah's policy of reform. Of course, questions have long been asked about the real content of the 'book', where it came from and why it was 'found'. After all, it came to light in a most mysterious way, and was acted on with surprising rapidity. The 'discovery' in the temple itself raised a great many questions and was given as many answers.[7] We cannot go into them here. Finally, there is the question of the composition, origin and fate of Deuteronomy. An earlier view that the work was in fact composed in Jerusalem for Josiah's reform, perhaps even at the king's command, in other words that it was an *ad hoc* creation, has now been largely abandoned. The king's aims would in that case have been brought out more pointedly than happens in Deuteronomy. The conviction is more widespread that Deuteronomy preserves earlier – and indeed the earliest – traditions of Israel, which have been collected together in the light of a number of unitive tendencies.

More recently, and particularly by A. Alt, the thesis has been put forward and maintained[8] that Deuteronomy collects together traditions of the northern state of Israel, that it was composed there as an ideal programme, perhaps after the fall of Samaria, and that it found its way into the temple in Jerusalem in some unknown manner.[9] If this thesis is correct, it may also give us a key for a historical assessment of Josiah's reform. The book may have played into Josiah's hands, and he may have known it beforehand: in any event, he used it to support and establish his claim to the whole of Israel, including the territory of the northern state of Israel. Without doubt the basic demands of Deuteronomy served Josiah's purpose brilliantly. First they provided the basic principle that Yahweh might legitimately be worshipped only in one place,[10] which Josiah recognized as being the temple in Jerusalem (neither the temple nor Jerusalem is ever mentioned in Deuteronomy itself). Secondly, the demand for single-minded devotion to the one God Yahweh legitimated the removal of all foreign cults and the unrestricted circulation of all the traditions of Yahweh. Finally, the idea of a united Israel acting as a totality from the beginning of its history underlined Josiah's political intention to extend his influence also to the northern kingdom of Israel. This is what Josiah saw as a new historical perspective: a united Israel under the one God, who was prepared to accept the cultic offerings of his people at one sanctuary. At the same time these are the constitutive elements of Josiah's basic conception; the king of Jerusalem becomes the protector of the traditions of the former northern state of Israel. Jerusalem and the house of David bind themselves without qualification to the law of Israel; in short, there is a move back through David to Moses. Only now, with Deuteronomy and the law of Israel, does Moses achieve the status of the great lawgiver. The traditions of the north only seem to have gained unqualified significance for Judah also in full measure after the time of Josiah. The significance of this fact can hardly be overestimated, for both the outward and the inner course of the later history of Judah and Israel from Josiah on.

That Deuteronomy was not an *ad hoc* work of the king but had its roots in real Israelite traditions is shown not least by the fact that some of Josiah's demands were not fulfilled, but realized differently in view of the historical conditions of the time. The best-known of these discrepancies involves the right of priests. Deuteronomy 18.1–8 gives any priests of the land who come to the central sanctuary the same rights as the priests who regularly serve at this sanctuary, while in II Kings 23.9 this right is expressly restricted. The priests of the land may not serve at the Jerusalem sanctuary; as country levites they are expressly excluded from it. It is possible that we can trace here the wish of the priests of the temple of Jerusalem to enjoy a monopoly. This development acquired special importance, since according to II Kings 23.8a Josiah had the priests of Judah brought to Jerusalem, abolishing their sanctuaries with a view to the centralization of the cult in Jerusalem. Probably we should not reject the hypothesis that the levitical country priests were only employed in subordinate functions at the Jerusalem sanctuary. Here was the impulse for a momentous development in later times, which probably became fully effective only after the exile. This was the matter of the rights of the 'levites' in the temple at Jerusalem; a struggle was carried on to give these levites higher status, to give them a specific place in the rights and duties of the temple. The so-called constitutional outline in Ezekiel 44 already speaks of this, and the problem runs right through the books of Chronicles. The distinction between priest and levite is also to be found in the New Testament. The beginning of this complex development is connected with the acts of cult centralization in Jerusalem and the sequel to the cultic measures introduced by Josiah.

What has just been said applies to the country priests from Judah. The priests in the realm of the old northern state of Israel were treated in a different fashion. Unless the passage is completely misleading, II Kings 23.19f. means that the greater part of these country priests on the hills of Samaria were simply exterminated. The account seems to refer not only to the priests of foreign cults but also to the priests of Yahweh. It is possible to find confirmation of these measures in a number of lists, lists of places in which members of the tribe of Levi, and therefore priests, were to dwell: the relevant passages are Josh. 21 and I Chron. 6.39–66. In these lists there is a concentration of priests in the area of the city state of Jerusalem, whereas between Jerusalem and Hebron there is no mention of any place as a priestly abode in the land of Judah; there is also a great gap between Bethel and the plain of Megiddo, right in the heart of Israelite territory. It is extremely probable that we are to see this as a consequence of the measures of Josiah which stripped the land of priests.[11] But this is in contradiction to Deuteronomy, which planned for an equal distribution of levitical dwellings throughout the land, and not a concentration in the proximity of the central sanctuary.

It should also be noted that Josiah celebrated a remarkable passover in Jerusalem.[12] This feast was originally limited to a single family and connected with the slaughter of a lamb (Exod. 12); now it was transferred to the central sanctuary, the only place where sacrificial slaughter was permissible (cf. Deut. 16). Consequently a full official passover was only possible in Jerusalem. The roots of the pilgrimages to Jerusalem for passover may be sought here; as is well known, the practice was still carried on at the time of Jesus.

The principal problems of Josiah's reform have now been discussed on the basis of Deuteronomy. It has been asked whether Josiah accorded Deuteronomy the status of an official constitution. Alt inclined to this view; Noth dissociated himself from it, thinking that it was all the less likely because Deuteronomy was not a statute at all to begin with.[13] The problem takes us back to Josiah's entire domestic policy, which in turn cannot be seen apart from possibilities abroad. Josiah's efforts at emancipation from the Assyrians and the Deuteronomic reform work were surely two concerns which should be distinguished; for this reason they have been presented separately here and elsewhere. On the other hand, both were simultaneous developments and both extended over a long period of time. They supplemented each other. To this extent the tradition is not so far out when it describes emancipation and reform alternately, and not successively.

We must also understand the realization of Josiah's efforts in a similar reciprocal relationship. Josiah's emancipation measures surely came at the beginning of his reign and will have been set in motion soon after his accession; the discovery of the book in the eighteenth year of his reign followed in 622, when his reign was already half over. This fits in with the gradual establishment of Josiah's apparatus of state, which now underwent far-reaching changes. The programme of Deuteronomy both countered cultic innovations within the state and also supported the king's policy towards the northern kingdom. All this sounds plausible to some degree. Nevertheless, questions remain open, particularly over a literary analysis of II Kings 22; 23. Understandably, the Deuteronomistic editors of Kings stressed the 'reform' as a special action and had the basic conceptions of Deuteronomy sanctioned by the king. We cannot exclude the possibility that the dramatic and programmatic events of II Kings 22; 23, namely the discovery of the book and the covenant ceremony in the temple, were deliberately elevated to this status and depicted as vivid scenes. Just as the conclusion and the beginning of a development were associated with a binding covenant ceremony through sacral scenery at the assembly at Shechem in Josh. 24, so too Josiah's reform may have been written up in a particular form with the use of mysterious features like the discovery of the book. Without doubt the acceptance of the basic demands transmitted in Deuteronomy and the attempt at the same time to repristinate the idea of a greater Israel form the historical nucleus. But the concentration of the event on a single act of reform for programmatic reasons cannot have happened in this way. If one does not insist on the idea of a sudden reform of an obligatory and official character, then all sorts of questions simply disappear. There is no need to consider the character of Deuteronomy as a constitution; there is no need to speculate, say, on Jeremiah's relationship to 'Josiah's reform', and we can understand why memories of Josiah's reformation seem to have completely faded for his successors, who were involved with another foreign power, and why the whole matter seems to have been sunk without a trace. Finally, after Josiah's death and the fall of Assyria, the work of reform lost its anti-Assyrian impulse and the star of another great power rose on the horizon. This created a new internal situation. Possibly the prophets Jeremiah and Ezekiel were instrumental in seeing that Josiah's efforts were continued; this, however, was not as the fruit of a carefully directed reform, but as the basic presupposition of a new self-understanding for Israel.

The trend towards restoration which is characteristic of Deuteronomy and the revival of material from Israelite tradition after the time of king Josiah, however it may be associated with Deuteronomy, is by no means restricted to Israel. The same thing can also be found in Egypt and in Mesopotamia. There, too, earlier traditions were revived and resort was had to earlier texts and cultic practices. In Egyptian pictorial art the hieroglyphics of the Old Kingdom underwent a kind of renaissance. Moreover, old texts were not only given new validity, but copied even as far as their detailed legislature. The treatise containing the essence of Memphitic theology which is explicitly described as a copy of an earlier text on the Shabaka stone also belongs in this connection. In Mesopotamia we may compare the collection of cuneiform texts by Asshur-bani-pal in his library at Nineveh. Above all, in Babylon Nebuchadnezzar was to prove to be a great restorer of temples: great care was taken over the carrying out of cultic demands.

At all events, it does not seem to be entirely coincidence that at this particular period, when new attention was being paid elsewhere to the traditions of temple and cult, Josiah too should have carried out his work of reform, even if his motives grew out of presuppositions specifically characteristic of Israel and Judah in a politically favourable climate. The tendency is comparable, the reordering of domestic policies being coupled with a restoration of the cult in accordance with the standards of ancient – perhaps even the earliest – traditions. This is the cultural background against which the work of Josiah must be assessed.

King Josiah fell at Megiddo, in battle with Pharaoh Necho; the date of his death is generally accepted as 609. This was about three years after the fall of Nineveh, at the time when Asshur-uballit was trying to rescue the rump of an Assyrian state in Haran. Pharaoh Necho set out to support him and at the same time to prevent further perils in Mesopotamia. Whether Josiah knew of the Pharaoh's intentions or not, the appearance of Egyptian troops in Palestine must have displeased him. For even if the Assyrians had been defeated, the presence of foreign troops on the borders of Israel and Judah was a danger which threatened the independence of the states of Syria and Palestine. Josiah may have been afraid that the Assyrian domination of his country might give way to Egyptian rule. He met the Pharaoh's troops at Megiddo. The report of the encounter is extremely brief, and even gives rise to misunderstanding (II Kings 23.29).

The king of Egypt is said to have 'gone up' at that time against ('*al*) the king of Assyria against ('*al*) the river Euphrates. At one time this double '*al* tended to be regarded in a hostile sense. But that raised the question why Josiah did not join forces with the Pharaoh. Among other things, the Babylonian Chronicle has made it certain that Necho sought an alliance with Asshur-uballit.[14] It would therefore be more appropriate if the Hebrew text read '*el* each time instead of '*al*; Necho went 'up to' the king of Assyria, not against him. The parallel account in II Chron. 35.20–25 says in neutral fashion that Necho went up 'to fight at Carchemish on the Euphrates'. This fits the situation better, since at this time Carchemish was a kind of Egyptian base on the Euphrates, from which forward operations could be launched. The Pharaoh first headed for Carchemish: it is not necessary to speak explicitly of a 'battle of Carchemish'. In II Chron. 35.21, Necho enquires after Josiah's intentions. Necho does not plan to fight against Josiah, but has to go into battle 'against another (royal) house'. However, Josiah did not listen to this explanation, but 'went out to battle in the plain of Megiddo'. The brief dialogue betweeen the kings reported here fits the historical situation better. But there is some doubt as to whether there was a full-scale battle at Megiddo, as the account in Chronicles seems to presuppose (II Chron.

35.22), or whether there was only a brief skirmish, as II Kings 23.29 indicates with the words 'slew him when he saw him'. Perhaps there was a surprise attack, which might have taken place in the *wādi 'āra*, the narrow pass through which Thutmoses III once crossed to Megiddo.[15]

Josiah's death took place at a time when Judah, which probably also included Israelite territory, needed determined leadership more than ever. The king had introduced an independent policy which had a chance when the balance of power was shifting, provided it was carried out with a mixture of vigour and sagacity. Josiah seems to have possessed both; his successors could not replace him. The people of the land decided in favour of his second oldest son, Jehoahaz, and set him on the throne: probably because he promised to continue the work of his father. However, it was precisely this that was to bring about his downfall.

NOTES

1. The text was tracked down in the British Museum in 1923 by C. J. Gadd, who published it and edited it; C. J. Gadd, *The Fall of Nineveh. The Newly Discovered Babylonian Chronicle, no. 21901 in the British Museum*, 1923; translations in *AOT*, 362–5; *ANET*, 303–5; *TGI*¹, 59–63; *TGI*² (an extract), 72–4.

2. Gadd Chron. 10; *AOT*, 362; *ANET*, 304 (in the report on the tenth year); *TGI*¹, 60.

3. In addition to the analyses of the text in introductions to the Old Testament see A. Alt, 'Die Heimat des Deuteronomiums' (1953), *KS* II, 250–75 = *Grundfragen*, 392–417; he also makes use of and assesses the earlier work of T. Oestreicher, *Das deuteronomische Grundgesetz*, 1923; see also A. Jepsen, 'Die Reform des Josia', in *Festschrift Friedrich Baumgärtel*, 1959, 97–108; L. Rost, 'Zur Vorgeschichte der Kultusreform des Josia', *VT* 19, 1969, 113–20.

4. Jepsen, op. cit., esp. 108, reconstructs a relatively consistent chronological sequence which also takes in the account of the reform; for the political conditions at the time see also Cross and Freedman, 'Josiah's Revolt against Assyria', *JNES* 12, 1953, 56–9.

5. Cf. II Kings 11.14.

6. W. M. L. de Wette, *Dissertatio critico-exegetica qua Deuteronomium a prioribus Pentateuchi libris diversum, alius eiusdam recentioris auctoris opus esse monstratur*, 1805, is usually quoted as the originator of this thesis. His work only mentions in passing that the law book found in the temple was Deuteronomy. Jerome, Chrysostom, Procopius of Gaza, Hobbes and Lessing had already expressed this view before de Wette; see R. Smend, *Wilhelm Martin Leberecht de Wettes Arbeit am Alten und Neuen Testament*, 1958, 32–6.

7. There was certainly no question of a priestly fraud. Nor has there been any convincing demonstration of the influence of models from outside Israel, according to which the divine origin of the holy books is said to be confirmed by their sudden discovery; cf. J. Herrmann, 'Ägyptische Analogien zum Funde des Deuteronomiums', *ZAW* 28, 1908, 291–302.

8. A. Alt, 'Die Heimat des Deuteronomiums', op. cit., cf. more recently the thorough investigations of L. Perlitt, *Bundestheologie im Alten Testament*, WMANT 36, 1969, 279–84; see also A. C. Welch, *The Code of Deuteronomy*, 1924.

9. L. Rost, *VT* 19, 1969, 114, conjectures that it was brought to safety in Judah by fugitives from the doomed state of Israel in the last phase of the struggle against the Assyrians.

10. Deuteronomy itself does not say that there must be one exclusive sanctuary of Yahweh; however, Yahweh is only to be worshipped where he himself desires; cf. L. Rost, op. cit., 115.

11. A. Alt, 'Bemerkungen zu einigen judäischen Ortslisten im Alten Testament' (1951), *KS* II, 289–305, esp. 294ff.; id., 'Festungen und Levitenorte im Lande Juda' (1952), ibid., 306–15.

12. For this disputed account and its parallel in II Chron. 35 see L. Rost, 'Josias Passa', *Theologie in Geschichte und Kunst* (Festschrift Walter Elliger), 1968, 169–75.

13. See M. Noth, 'The Laws in the Pentateuch' (1940), in *The Laws in the Pentateuch*, 1966, esp. 41–9; Noth thinks that the Deuteronomic law was treated, 'quite against the actual sense of its contents, as a state law-code', op. cit., 48.

14. *AOT*, 365; *ANET*, 305.

15. For the routes to Megiddo see A. Alt, *PJB* 10, 1914, 70–88. A. Malamat, 'The Last Wars of the Kingdom of Judah', *JNES* 9, 1950, 218–27, thinks that the 'battle at Megiddo' was a deliberate military and political undertaking on the part of Josiah and that Necho principally wanted to remove the former province of Magiddu from Assyrian hands; his view is repeated in *The Military History of the Land of Israel in Biblical Times*, ed. J. Liver, 1964, 296–314; see also S. B. Frost, 'The Death of Josiah: a Conspiracy of Silence', *JBL* 87, 1968, 369–82.

The Babylonians and the End of the
State of Judah

11

AFTER THE BATTLE at Megiddo which cost Josiah his life, Necho went further north, but was not able to set Asshur-uballit on the throne in Haran. The struggle for the city lasted several months, according to the Babylonian Chronicle from June to September 609. 'A strong Egyptian army' crossed the Euphrates with Asshur-uballit to conquer Haran. The battles with the Babylonian troops were fierce, and in the end the Babylonians gained the upper hand. We hear nothing of the fate of Asshur-uballit; he does not appear again.

However, Necho must have moved quickly south again, to take final possession of Syria and Palestine. He wrested these lands from the Assyrians at almost the very moment when the final remnants of Assyrian independence were shattered before Haran. Egyptian supremacy took some time to have any effect on the royal house in Jerusalem. It is assumed that Jehoahaz wanted to continue the politics of his father Josiah; for this reason he was preferred to his brother Eliakim, who was two years older. The three months of his reign correspond almost exactly to the time which Necho spent in Mesopotamia and Syria. He then had Jehoahaz brought to his headquarters at Riblah, immediately north of the plain between the two Lebanons. There Jehoahaz was imprisoned. At the same time, Necho imposed a large tribute of silver and gold on the land of Judah. Johoahaz was not allowed back to Jerusalem; at a later date he was brought to Egypt, where he died. Jeremiah 22.10–12, which is devoted to king Jehoahaz, refers clearly to his fate, though in that passage he bears the name Shallum.

Josiah's older son Eliakim now took his place. Necho confirmed him in office and changed his name to Jehoiakim. This was a tardy demonstration of the un-qualified supremacy of the Egyptian king. Like Menahem of Israel before him, Jehoiakim raised the requisite tribute by a poll tax; the difference was that a fixed sum was not demanded from everyone, but each citizen paid in accordance with his ability.[1] This situation did not, however, last for long, as new events soon loomed on the horizon.

After their victory over the Assyrians, the Medes and Babylonians shared what was formerly Assyrian territory; as far as we can see, the Medes claimed the heart of what was formerly Assyrian territory and the hill-country adjoining it to the north. The Babylonians controlled the rest of Mesopotamia and soon also turned their attention to Syria and Palestine. By the nature of things, this meant that there were further conflicts with the Egyptians.

In 605 there was a battle between the Babylonians and the Egyptians in and around Carchemish. As a result, the Egyptians abandoned Carchemish and finally also had to yield Syria and Palestine to the Babylonians. Until recently we were inadequately informed on events at Carchemish: the chief sources of information were a disputed note in Jer. 46.2 and remarks in the *Antiquities* of Josephus. However, since 1956 a further section of the Babylonian Chronicle has come to light. It was published by D. J. Wiseman and contains valuable material for the years 608–595; in this way it follows directly on the Gadd Chronicle with its information for the years 616–609.[2] It emerges clearly from the Gadd Chronicle that after his victory over the last Assyrian Asshur-uballit in 609, Nabopolassar fought successfully against the northern hill-people. This gave him a free hand for his move against the Egyptians at Carchemish. These campaigns occupied the years 609-607. In 606 there were clashes with the Egyptians on the outskirts of Carchemish, which formed a kind of Egyptian bridgehead. At first the Babylonians had little success in finding a foothold on the upper Euphrates. Meanwhile Nabopolassar had become old and sick. He handed over supreme command of the army to prince Nebuchadnezzar, who moved immediately on Carchemish and surprised the Egyptians. The Wiseman Chronicle says that Nebuchadnezzar 'marched to Carchemish which lay on the bank of the river Euphrates. He crossed the river (to go) against the Egyptian army which was situated in Carchemish and . . . they fought with each other and the Egyptian army withdrew before him. He defeated them (smashing) them out of existence. As for the remnant of the Egyptian army which had escaped from the defeat so (hastily) that no weapon had touched them, the Babylonian army overtook and defeated them in the district of Hamath, so that not a single man (escaped) to his own country.'[3]

This clear information enables us to understand Jer. 46.2 appropriately. Nebuchadnezzar defeated Pharaoh Necho at Carchemish in the fourth year of Jehoiakim. This would be the year 605, which the Babylonian Chronicle demands. We can see how the short note in Jeremiah inevitably remained incomprehensible as long as its basis was sought in the events of the year 609, above all following II Chron. 35.20, where Carchemish is mentioned, perhaps wrongly, as the battlefield of the year 609. But if Jer. 46.2 clearly relates to 605, we can also understand the further saying about Egypt in Jer. 46.3–12, which speaks of a rapid despatch of aid from Egypt to the north and of a great Egyptian defeat. These events were evidently followed with some satisfaction in Palestine, as they went against the interests of the Egyptians, who had been overlords since 609. It also confirms the note in Josephus, *Antt.* X, 11. 1, which says among other things that Nebuchadnezzar was entrusted with the command of the army while his father lay sick, and won a victory over the Egyptians even before he became king. The biblical accounts, Josephus and the Babylonian Chronicle supplement each other in a remarkably exact way.

At this point it may be useful to add a brief survey of the individual tablets of the neo-Babylonian Chronicle on the basis of the discoveries made by Wiseman:

Tablet 1: Wiseman Chronicle 626–623, year of accession to the third year of Nabopolassar, 41 lines;
after a gap of six years (622–617) there follows
Tablet 2: Gadd Chronicle 616–609, tenth to seventeenth year of Nabopolassar, 78 lines;
Tablet 3: Wiseman Chronicle 608–606/5, eighteenth year of Nabopolassar, 28 lines;
Tablet 4: Wiseman Chronicle, 605–595/4, twenty-first year of Nabopolassar and year of accession to tenth year of Nebuchadnezzar, 47 lines.
There follows a gap of thirty-seven years (594–557), so the destruction of Jerusalem is not confirmed again (587/6).
Tablet 5: Wiseman Chronicle 557/556, third year of Neriglissar, 27 lines.
Tablet 6: Chronicle of Nabonidus, 555–539, year of accession to seventeenth year of Nabonidus, 42 lines with gaps.

After their victory at Carchemish, the way south lay open to the Babylonians, and without delay they advanced into Syria and Palestine. Egyptian domination which, at least since the time of Necho, had assumed fixed forms there, collapsed completely. II Kings 24.7 characterizes the new situation with incomparable clarity: 'The king of Egypt did not come again out of his land, for the king of Babylon had taken all that belonged to the king of Egypt from the Brook of Egypt (*wādi el-arīsh*) to the river Euphrates.' Of course, this is only the final result; no real historical sequence is indicated. Here the Babylonian Chronicle, in the parts published by Wiseman, is of further help. After the battle of Carchemish, the text continues: 'As for the remnant of the Egyptian army which had escaped from the defeat so (hastily) that no weapon had touched them, the Babylonian army overtook and defeated them in the district of Hamath, so that not a single man (escaped) to his own country. At that time Nebuchadnezzar conquered the whole of the land of Hatti.' The Egyptians fled immediately south of Carchemish through the fertile region of north Syria south of Aleppo to Hamath. There the Babylonians caught up with them. Nebuchadnezzar conquered 'the whole land of Hatti', though probably not all at once. For Ashkelon only fell in 604, and Judah surrendered at the earliest in the same year. 'Hatti' primarily denotes northern Syria: the Babylonians surely headed first for Riblah, where Necho had his headquarters, and Nebuchadnezzar later took the town. He was still in Syria when the news of the death of his father Nabopolassar reached him. According to the Wiseman Chronicle the exact date of the latter's death was 8 Ab in the twenty-first year of his reign, i.e. 16 August 605. Nebuchadnezzar immediately hurried back to Babylon and was enthroned there at the beginning of September on 1 Ulul (7 September).

Nebuchadnezzar ruled over Babylon and its subject territories for almost half a century (605–562). In its usual form 'Nebuchadnezzar' (*nbwkdn'ṣr*), his name does not completely correspond with the Babylonian *Nabū-kudurri-uṣur*. Thus the form Nebuchadrezzar (*nbwkdr'ṣr*), which is also attested in the Old Testament, seems preferable.[4] Shortly after his accession he returned to Syria. We know from the Wiseman Chronicle that in the following years he regularly undertook campaigns in Syria and Palestine. These took place from his first to his eleventh year (with the exception of the fifth and ninth years). He had the country under firm control, but in particular instances he had to guard against threats and uprisings. Two events in particular stand out: the occupation of Ashkelon and the capture of Jerusalem in 597, with the first deportation which followed. In the meanwhile, however, Nebuchadnezzar was defeated by the Egyptians.

In the year 604, when Nebuchadnezzar appeared in Syria, 'all the kings of Hatti came before him and paid heavy tribute'. Ashkelon finally fell into Babylonian hands after an attack which probably took place in December. The city was destroyed and the king taken prisoner. Nebuchadnezzar probably remained in Hatti until February 603. It is supposed, not unreasonably, that during this period he also moved against Jerusalem or at least required the obeisance of king Jehoiakim. A note in II Kings 24.1 which for long has been difficult to date is introduced at this point. According to it, Nebuchadnezzar 'came up' and Jehoiakim became his servant for three years; then he turned and rebelled against him. It was believed earlier that this was the occasion of Nebuchadnezzar's attack which began in 597. However, there are no compelling grounds for such a hypothesis. Jehoiakim's declaration of loyalty is more conceivable after the Babylonian victory over Ashkelon; his rebellion three years later will be connected with the defeat of the Babylonian king in Egypt, which followed at the beginning of 600.

Nebuchadnezzar must have prepared this expedition to Egypt for some years before his final decision in 601. The Wiseman Chronicle gives an account:[5] 'In the year (601) the king of Akkad called up his army and went to Hatti. He went through Hatti in power. In Kislev (Nov./Dec. 601) he put himself at the head of his troops and set out for Egypt. The king of Egypt heard of this and called up his troops; they joined in a battle and inflicted a great defeat. The king of Akkad and his host turned and went back to Babylon.' This defeat could have been the moment of weakness which Jehoiakim exploited in order to rebel from Nebuchadnezzar, having been his vassal for three years (II Kings 24.1). Above all from the narratives in the book of Jeremiah we know of Jehoiakim's frivolous and arrogant attitude, which may have been given further encouragement at this time. Under his rule conditions in Judah and Jerusalem were not at their best. Jehoiakim shed much innocent blood (II Kings 24.4); he is attacked by Jeremiah as a brutal, unjust king who was fond of splendour (Jer. 22.13–19). There is a well-known scene in the palace in Jer. 36 where a scroll with the sayings of Jeremiah is read: Jehoiakim cuts it in pieces and burns it. The words of a prophet leave him unmoved. How differently his father Josiah acted in such a situation!

Nebuchadnezzar must have suffered quite a considerable defeat at Egyptian hands, as it took him almost two years to reorganize and re-equip his army, above all his chariot force. 'In the fifth year the king of Akkad (remained) in his land and assembled chariots and horses in great numbers.'[6] From December 599 to March 598 he was again in Hatti. During this period he undertook expeditions in quite another direction, against tribes in the wilderness of Arabia (here described with the Aramaic word *madbari*). These must have been groups and tribes in the wilderness and steppe regions living eastwards of Syria and Palestine. An echo of these undertakings can be found in one of Jeremiah's sayings against foreign nations (Jer. 49.28–33). This mentions Kedar and the kingdoms of Hazor which Nebuchadnezzar king of Babylon smote. Kedar is in this area of the wilderness of north-western Arabia;[7] Hazor is probably not the Galilean city, but a reference to the semi-nomadic tent-villages (*hsr'm*) in this area. In all probability Nebuchadnezzar sought to secure Syria and Palestine from the east. To achieve this he moved round the flank through his vassals on the coasts of Phoenicia and Palestine, who had always been rebellious and had become fickle after the defeat of Egypt. These undertakings were also aimed indirectly against Judah.

II Kings 24.2 may also be more comprehensible in this context. In the time of Jehoiakim bands of Chaldaeans, Aramaeans, Moabites and Ammonites are said to have moved against Judah. They devastated the country. This sounds like a coalition of groups from east of Palestine and the area to the north, where Nebuchadnezzar extended his activity in the years 599/98. Palestine now seems to have been his next goal. From March to December 598 he remained in Babylon. After that, however, he set out again for Hatti, this time with Jerusalem as his chief goal: 'In the seventh year, in the month of Kislev, the Babylonian king mustered his troops, and, having marched to the land of Hatti, besieged the city of Judah, and on the second day of the month of Adar took the city and captured the king. He appointed therein a king of his own choice, received its heavy tribute and sent (them) to Babylon.'[8] The king's departure in the month of Kislev falls into the time between December 598 and January 597. The occupation of Jerusalem on 2 Adar in the seventh year (of Nebuchadnezzar) has been calculated exactly as 16 March 597. This means that the city was besieged at the end of January at the earliest, and occupied within a matter of weeks.

According to this account in the Babylonian Chronicle, Jerusalem fell into the hands of the Babylonians without any marked difficulty. We hear no mention of resistance and destruction, but that the king was captured and replaced by a man after the heart of the king of Babylon. This change of ruler may be seen as one of the chief aims of the whole expedition.[9]

The Babylonian text does not make it clear which kings in Jerusalem were involved. No names are given. II Kings 24.10–17 and II Chron. 36.10 seem to give some information. According to them, the king reigning at the time of the occupation of Jerusalem was the successor of king Jehoiakim (*yᵉhōyāqîm*), his son Jehoiakin, whose name is usually written Jehoiachin (*yᵉhōyākîn*) to distinguish him more clearly from his father. Jehoiakim seems to have died a natural death in January 597. Jehoiachin then ascended the throne; he ruled three months, until the occupation of the city in March. Now Nebuchadnezzar also left Babylon in January, at quite an unusual time, since his was a winter campaign. Thus it looks as if it was Jehoiakim's death, which perhaps came as a surprise, that prompted Nebuchadnezzar to leave Babylon earlier than usual. As Noth suggests, his aim may well have been to appoint a new ruler in Jerusalem, a man 'after his own heart'. However, the question remains whether the death of a relatively insignificant vassal like Jehoiakim can have been sufficient reason to cause the Babylonian king to set out early.

As a result of his chronological calculations, A. Malamat[10] has challenged Noth's thesis. The period of little more than three months between the enthronement of Jehoiachin and his deposition seem to Malamat too short to allow the news of Jehoiakim's death to reach Babylon, to muster the troops and then to make the long march of more than a thousand miles to Jerusalem through the rainy winter weather. He therefore supposes that Nebuchadnezzar set out to put down a rebellion begun by Jehoiakim. This thesis, too, can be challenged. At a critical moment, would it really be necessary to bring all the army down from Babylon? At least in the early stages of a crisis, might not troops be summoned from garrisons in the neighbourhood?

It is beyond question that Nebuchadnezzar wanted to assert his sovereignty over Jerusalem by appointing a new man as king. It is difficult to see what objections he had against Jehoiachin. Nebuchadnezzar does not seem to have attempted to obtain his allegiance as a vassal; he immediately took him prisoner. Perhaps he did not want the son of the rebel Jehoiakim to take over the reigns of government in Jerusalem. We cannot be certain. All the details in II Kings 24.10ff. confirm the rapidity of the capture of the city. Jehoiachin 'gave himself up' with his family, his servants and his officials, and the king of Babylon 'took' (*wayyiqqaḥ*) him. This indicates a regular surrender of the city.

The Old Testament also mentions the heavy tribute of which the Babylonian Chronicle speaks, the treasures of the temple and the royal palace. However, in II Kings 24.13 we hear of extensive plundering of the temple. Nebuchadnezzar either carried off 'all' the treasure and the vessels of the temple or cut them in pieces. Jeremiah 27.18ff. indicates that the temple was in fact plundered, but we should not suppose that it was completely emptied. According to II Kings 25.13–17, when the city was finally taken in 587/86, the temple was plundered once again.

The inroads made on the officials and the population of Jerusalem are much more important and of much greater consequence. King Jehoiachin, his mother, his wives and the palace officials were carried off to Babylon. So too were the men who exercised power in Jerusalem numbering seven thousand, together with craftsmen, smiths and metal-workers, numbering a thousand in all. In view of this detailed information the number of ten thousand captives given in II Kings 24.14 seems too high. It must refer not only to the people of Jerusalem, but also to substantial numbers from the leading classes in the land.

Perhaps the list of those deported which is given in Jer. 52.28–30 is the basis for the reconstruction of the number 10,000. This passage says that 3,023 men of Judah in all were deported in the year 597. These may have been people from the district around Jerusalem, landowners and officials, whereas the rest of the population, named 'the poorest people of the land' (*dallat 'am-hā'āreṣ*) in II Kings 24.14, remained behind. This would mean that about 7,000 people were deported from Jerusalem itself and about 3,000 from Judah; numbers of this dimension are quite possible.

Among those deported from Jerusalem was the priest Ezekiel, who later became a prophet. He counted the years of exile from the moment of Jehoiachin's captivity. The latter was obviously regarded as the last legitimate representative of the house of David, who now dwelt among the exiles. This could strengthen the view among the exiles that they were the true bearers of the traditions of Israel and Judah and that one day they would be able to enforce them again. Hope for a return might germinate in these circles, and they will have retained a consciousness that they were the people of Yahweh.

Nebuchadnezzar replaced Jehoiachin by a man named Mattaniah. According to II Kings 24.17 he was an uncle of Jehoiachin, that is, a son of Josiah and brother of Jehoahaz and Jehoiakim. At all events, II Chron. 36.10 is wrong in saying that he was a brother of Jehoiachin.[11] As an expression of his sovereignty, Nebuchadnezzar renamed this Mattaniah Zedekiah, under which name he entered history as the last king on the throne of Judah. He reigned 'over Judah and Jerusalem', as II Chron. 36.10 officially puts it, until the fall of Jerusalem in 587/86. The exiles in Babylon did not take him seriously.

Once again we add the exact dates of the last kings of Judah:
 Josiah   640/39–609/08
 Jehoahaz   609/608
 Jehoiakim   609/08–598/97
 Jehoiachin 598/97
 Zedekiah   598/97–587/86

All the sources for the history of Judah in the time of Zedekiah have gaps in them. In the form in which we have it, the Babylonian Chronicle goes only as far as 595 and tells us no more about Judah. In 596 there was a Babylonian campaign in Elam. Perhaps this sheds some light on the saying against Elam in Jer. 49.34–39.[12] The Old Testament remains the most important source. There are the historical books, and important information about the mood of the time can be inferred from the books of the prophets Jeremiah and Ezekiel.

At this time Jeremiah was engaged in many conflicts in Jerusalem, especially with those who were firmly convinced that the city would be saved and that the Babylonians did not really present any serious danger in the long run. The narratives in the book of Jeremiah which describe all this were certainly given their final form under the impact of the catastrophe which followed, but in essentials they will go back to experiences which aptly reflect the prophet's attitude. Jeremiah attacked the confident pronouncements of Hananiah, who is often presented as the model of a 'false' prophet (Jer.28); he wrote a letter to the exiles in Babylon in which he advised them to prepare for a long stay (Jer.29). He recommended to his compatriots and the king that they should bow their necks to the yoke of the king of Babylon and serve him and his people; this was the only way to survive (Jer.27.12). These messages naturally did not please the inhabitants of Jerusalem; they even suspected Jeremiah of treachery, and of making common cause with the Babylonians. In fact, however, he saw much too clearly that in the desperate circumstances of the state nothing could be better for Jerusalem than to keep quiet and await developments. We can understand that in these circumstances king Zedekiah, who had little room for manoeuvre, sought Jeremiah's advice, even if it was often in secret (Jer.37.17–21; 38.14–27).

Ezekiel lived among the exiles east of Babylon by one of the canals which even at that time probably served to irrigate the land; the place bears the name Tel-Abib (Ezek.3.15).[13] It was possible to assemble the elders of Judah there and to speak to them.[14] Evidently the exiles lived together in some form of loose community: they were not scattered among the indigenous population in the same way as those who had been deported earlier from the former northern state of Israel into Assyrian-occupied territory. At first the Babylonian exile seemed to those deported in 597 to be a provisional internment: it was this that fed their hope that they would return to Jerusalem in the foreseeable future. Jeremiah and Ezekiel vehemently challenged this attitude: Ezekiel portrayed the imminent final fall of Jerusalem in many ways and underlined his conviction by symbolic actions. The deeper reason for his call in 593 was not conditions in exile, but the course of events in Jerusalem and Judah.[15]

Zedekiah was originally appointed as a man after Nebuchadnezzar's heart, but he did not prove to have this character. He was foolish enough to rebel against the Babylonians one last time and draw down the wrath of their king upon him. It is impossible to tell precisely what happened. Assuming that a large part of the upper classes were deported in 597, a whole series of official and administrative posts must have become vacant, and consequently there must have been a fairly considerable change within the country and its administration. Alt and Noth in particular have wanted to infer from the note in Jer.13.18, 19, that 'the cities of the Negeb are shut up, with none to open them', that the southern parts of the land were already lost in 597.[16] In that case the southern frontier of Judah ran rather north of Hebron, like the southern frontier of the later Persian province of Judah, and the southern territory will have been left to the Edomites. There is nothing in the Wiseman Chronicle to confirm this theory; we must consider the possibility that at first Judah retained its old territory and that cities in Judah were detached from the rule of Jerusalem only towards the end of Zedekiah's reign, or even afterwards.

Zedekiah certainly did not venture to rebel completely on his own initiative; he will have been prompted and even perhaps supported by events known to him. There was unrest in Tyre and Sidon. Not least, there were hopes of Egyptian advances. Psammetichus II (595–589) appeared in Palestine at least once, though we do not have any exact details.[17] We know no more about a journey made by Zedekiah to Babylon, which is said to have taken place in the fourth year of his reign (Jer. 51.59). Perhaps he aimed to allay the suspicions of the Babylonian king. It is still most probable that Zedekiah was relying on help from Egypt (Jer. 37.5–11).

It was in the ninth year of his reign that Zedekiah broke away from Nebuchadnezzar. The Babylonians appeared before Jerusalem with an army and began to besiege the city (II Kings 25.1). The siege lasted until the eleventh year of Zedekiah's reign, i.e. until the year 587/86.[18] It is generally assumed that the siege varied in its intensity. We could do with more exact sources: the biblical account in II Kings 25 concentrates on the very last days of Jerusalem and especially on the destruction of the palace and the temple.

It is all the more notable that a fortunate discovery makes it possible for us to gain some authentic information about the further course of events, if only in a limited way. We have some inscribed ostraca which were found in the gateway of the Judaean fortress of Lachish (*tell ed-duwēr*) and are usually described as the 'Lachish letters'.[19] They were probably addressed to the commandants of Lachish and introduce us to the death-throes of the state of Judah. The letters are sent from outposts around Lachish to give reports on the movements of Babylonian troops and to provide a picture of the situation for the commander of Lachish, which was one of the leading fortresses in the land. The condition of the twenty-one ostraca varies, and it is difficult to interpret some of them. In addition to regular letters, i.e. writings with coherent content, there are also mere lists of the names of officials and possibly also of messengers.[20] One of the most illuminating and specific accounts, which is often quoted, is to be found in letter IV, 10–12, which is addressed to the commander of Lachish: 'And let (my lord) know that we are watching for the signals of Lachish, according to all the indications which my lord has given, for we cannot see Azekah.' Azekah is one of the fortresses north of Lachish, identified with *tell ez-zakarīyeh*. The note indicates how matters were going. While the Babylonian troops were on the march, the fortresses gave signs to each other, or sent messengers as long as that was possible. Azekah, lying further to the north, seems already to have been reached by the enemy, so that the correspondent, who was probably between Lachish and Azekah, could only keep in touch with Lachish. This situation should be compared with Jer.34.7. There Jeremiah speaks with Zedekiah at a time when the army of the king of Babylon was already fighting against Jerusalem and against 'the cities of Judah that were left, Lachish and Azekah; for these were the only fortified cities of Judah which remained'. Thus Lachish and Azekah were in fact the last strong centres of resistance in the country. The Lachish letters therefore fall quite certainly into the first period of the siege of Jerusalem by the Babylonians; the year 588 is usually given as their date.

Letter VI on the situation in Jerusalem is also worth mentioning: it must have reached the correspondent from the besieged city, and have come from the surroundings of the king and his officials. There are said to have been people in the city 'who weaken the hands of the land and make the city slack (*lrpt*) so that it fails.' Jeremiah 38.4 should be compared with this. Here are officials who complain to the king about Jeremiah in words which sound very similar. Jeremiah, they say, should be killed because he is 'weakening (*merappē'*) the hands of the soldiers who are left in this city and the hands of all the people'. This charge leads to Jeremiah's arrest, after which he is put in a cistern. We may conclude that there was a group of people in Jerusalem who regarded further resistance against the Babylonians as senseless, who said as much and consequently weakened the city's will to resist. The almost exact agreement between the words of the Lachish letter and the text of Jeremiah indicates the difference of mood in the city. The question was whether it would really be possible to resist the Babylonians successfully in the long term.

We learn from Lachish ostracon III that a *sar haṣṣābā'*, a high official of the army of Judah, was sent to Egypt. We do not hear more about his mission, but it must have been connected with the relief of the city of Jerusalem. According to Jer.37.5, an Egyptian army did in fact come out, though we do not know its strength; it must have caused the Babylonians to break off the siege, at least temporarily. Egyptian help was not slow in coming; by that time Pharaoh Apries (589–570), mentioned in Jer.44.30 as 'Hophra', may already have succeeded Psammetichus II on the throne.

The Babylonians did not withdraw from the city. It must have been at starvation point towards the end (II Kings 25.3). Probably in the summer of 586 the Babylonians succeeded in making a breach in the city walls and entered the city. Zedekiah and his immediate entourage are said to have succeeded in breaking out of the city by night and escaping first into the wilderness of Judah, in the direction of the Jordan valley. But the Babylonians caught up with him at Jericho and took him prisoner. He was immediately brought to Nebuchadnezzar, who was in his headquarters at Riblah, in central Syria.

Zedekiah's fate in Riblah is horrifyingly gruesome. He was dealt with so harshly because he, the ruler appointed by Nebuchadnezzar, had resisted the might of

Babylon for so many years in Jerusalem. In Riblah his sons were killed before his eyes; he himself was blinded, put in chains and brought to Babylon. One can only hope that he died soon afterwards. We do not hear any more of him.

Meanwhile, Jerusalem was plundered and largely destroyed.

It is worth noting that according to II Kings 25.8–17 the royal palace and the temple were only destroyed about a month after the occupation of the city. The work was carried out by a high-ranking Babylonian officer, Nebu-zar-adan, who had come to Jerusalem for this purpose. He acted on the instructions of the great king.

The city was extensively burnt; gaps were made in the walls, depriving Jerusalem of its fortifications. Above all, the temple vessels were taken to Babylon, along with some of its structure: the iron pillars, the stands and the so-called iron sea, a great bowl containing water for purification. It is remarkable that the ark is not mentioned in this connection; we must assume that it too was either destroyed or taken away.

Once again large parts of the population were carried away to Babylon; this was what is generally called the 'second deportation'. The information about it in II Kings 25 is not clear. Verse 11 speaks in quite general terms about a remnant of the people in Jerusalem who deserted to the king of Babylon and a further remnant who were carried off by Nebu-zar-adan. On the other hand, this officer left behind some of the 'poorest of the land' (*dallat hā-āreṣ*) to be vinedressers and ploughmen (v. 12). Nebu-zar-adan took further officials, priests, doorkeepers, scribes and others who were captured in Jerusalem to Nebuchadnezzar at Riblah, where they were executed (II Kings 25.18–21).

Thus we cannot obtain a clear picture of those who were deported. At any rate it is clear that the upper classes, who will have been the real leaders, were severely punished, and a large proportion of the population of Jerusalem was led into exile. However, some able-bodied peasants were left in the land, so that it still contained a broad stratum of native inhabitants. The best source for the numbers of those deported, Jer. 52.28–30, says that after the destruction of Jerusalem only 832 inhabitants were deported. This does not seem very many; but this number, by virtue of being so small, is more trustworthy than many larger ones. We must consider the possibility that interference with the natives of Judah was smaller than in the case of the northern kingdom of Israel in the Assyrian deportation. These figures are significant when we consider further developments in the land of Judah under Babylonian hegemony.

The fall of Jerusalem marks the end of autonomy for Judah; it is the provisional conclusion to a history of political independence which had developed from the days of the conquest and had achieved constitutional form in the states of Israel and Judah. Now the kings of these states had been overthrown, the capitals largely destroyed, the land was under the control of a foreign administration, the sanctuaries had been dismantled, worship had become a problem and the leading groups lived in exile. The state had totally collapsed, but here and there the defeated people remained, not so scattered, not so much the victims of the whim of their conquerors that they were in deadly peril of losing their very identity.

One cannot describe vividly enough the totality of the catastrophe which had befallen Judah with the fall of Jerusalem. However, the really important question in considering the history of Israel is the degree to which this catastrophe in fact imprinted itself on Israel's consciousness. All the pre-exilic traditions about belief in Yahweh have in fact survived the catastrophe and continued to regulate the life of Israel at a much later stage. How were they preserved, and where and how were they sustained? Did this happen, as has been thought for a long time, only in exile, or did the mother country also play its part? Were perhaps the most important historical traditions of the pre-exilic period preserved and given new form not only in Babylon, but also in Palestine during the exile?

This brings us to important questions asked by modern scholars in their study of the exile and the period that follows. The fall of Jerusalem may certainly be seen as one of the most momentous events in the history of Israel; the exile may be noted as a profound interruption in that history; the following period may be seen in a different light from the period of the monarchy which had now come to an end – but this 'national' catastrophe did not bring about the end of 'Israel'. It contributed to a change in the form and the nature of Israel, which perhaps only from this moment on attained the breadth and depth which made Judaism, and with it the Old Testament, the paradigm of the people of God and their experience of God which they are in world history. The tragedy and greatness of this people culminates in the way in which with the aid of their God they overcome history.

NOTES

1. Compare together II Kings 15.20 and 23.35.
2. D. J. Wiseman, *Chronicles of Chaldaean Kings (626–556 BC) in the British Museum*, 1956 (²1961); cf. the partial translations in *ANET Suppl.*, op. cit.; see especially E. Vogt, 'Die neubabylonische Chronik über die Schlacht bei Karkemisch und die Einnahme von Jerusalem', SVT 4, 1957 (Strasbourg Congress Volume), 67–96.
3. Wiseman, op. cit., 67–9 (BM 21946, r.2–7); Vogt, op. cit., 74; *TGI*, 73.
4. The form Nabukodonosor goes back to the Greek translation.
5. Wiseman, *Chronicles*, 70 (BM 21946, v.5–7); *ANET Suppl.*, 564; *TGI*, 74.
6. Wiseman, *Chronicles*, 70 (BM 21946, v.8); *ANET*, ibid.; *TGI*, 74.
7. Cf. also Isa.42.11.
8. Wiseman, *Chronicles*, 72 (BM 21946, v.11–13); *ANET*, ibid.; *TGI*, 74; for the chronological problem, cf. especially R. A. Parker and W. H. Dubberstein, *Babylonian Chronology 626 BC – AD 75*, 1956.
9. Thus M. Noth, 'Die Einnahme von Jerusalem im Jahre 597 v. Chr.' (1958), *Aufsätze* I, 111–32.
10. A. Malamat, 'The Last Kings of Judah and the Fall of Jerusalem', *IEJ* 18, 1968, 137–56, esp. 144 n.15.
11. Cf. Noth, op. cit., 118 n.24.

12. Of course the reading 'Elam' is uncertain, BM 21946, v. 17; Wiseman, op. cit., 72. Hitherto the saying against Elam has raised problems for the interpretation of Jeremiah. At any rate this possible threat to Babylon from the Elamites could not shake the empire.

13. The name served as the model for Tel Aviv, the present-day capital of Israel, which was founded in 1909.

14. Cf. Ezek. 14.1–11; 20;33.10–20.

15. On the presupposition that Jerusalem was occupied on 16 March 597, by the same reckoning Ezekiel's call took place on 31 July 593, according to the date in Ezek. 1.1; cf. W. Zimmerli, Ezechiel, BK 18, 15*.

16. A. Alt, KS II, 280f.; M. Noth, History of Israel, ²1960, 283.

17. We only know that the expedition took place in his fourth year; it perhaps lasted two years; the king then fell sick and died in the seventh year of his reign; see W. Helck, Geschichte des Alten Ägypten, HdO I, 1, 3, 1968, 254.

18. A. Malamat, 'The Last Kings', op. cit., esp. 150–6, deals with the chronological problems on the basis of other suggestions for dating. He does not put the accession of Zedekiah in Nisan 597 or 596 but in Tishri 597, and puts the Babylonian entry into the fortress of Jerusalem on 18 July 586 and the destruction of the temple on 14 or 17 August 586.

19. The letters were edited by H. Torczyner, Lachish I (The Lachish Letters), 1938; bibliography and most recent version of the text by D. Diringer in Tufnell, Murray, Diringer, Lachish III, 1, 1953, 21–3, 331–9; translations of the most important ostraca: ANET, 321f. (cf. also ANEP, 279); TGI, 75–8 (TGI¹, 63–5 has only the Hebrew text); KAI, nos. 192–9; see especially K. Elliger, 'Die Ostraka von Lachis', PJB 34, 1938, 30–58.

20. Cf. the list of names given in Galling, TGI¹, 63, which contains some personal names characteristic of the time, including 'Jeremiah' and the name 'Gemariah' attested in Jer. 29.3 and 36.10–12, 25.

PART THREE

Israel in the Hands of the Great Powers

I | *The Period of the Babylonian Exile*

FOR PART OF the population of Jerusalem and Judah, exile in Babylon became a harsh reality after the first deportation in 597 BC. As a rule, however, the exile is taken to begin ten years later, from the moment of the fall of Jerusalem, and it is the period from that date on which is the subject of historical discussion and evaluation of 'the exile'. It is not easy to determine precisely when the exile ends, because not all the deported Jews returned home after the fall of Babylon in 539. On the contrary, a special problem is posed by the question of the return of families who had formerly been carried off to Babylon, which the lack of clear evidence makes difficult to solve. At all events, by the twenties of the sixth century at the latest it was possible for those living in Jerusalem and its environs to develop their own community life to the stage of being able to think of rebuilding the temple to form a focal point. Strictly speaking, the 'period of the Babylonian exile' covers more than the final phase of Babylonian rule; it goes beyond and includes those efforts which may be regarded as the first steps towards restoring the Jerusalem cult and the temple community. We should also remember that this period should not be considered only from the perspective of the people of Judah deported to Babylon; we should pay just as much attention to those elements of the population who had remained behind in Judah.

Earlier scholars in particular thought that the real life of Israel continued in exile, not in Palestine itself, which they believed to have been largely depopulated and devastated. They therefore saw the exiles as those who really handed down and preserved Israelite tradition. But on a number of grounds it is improbable that life in the mother country of Palestine ceased completely. In his *Geschichte des Volkes Israel*, Rudolf Kittel was already warning against imagining Palestine during the exile to be a *tabula rasa*.[1] In more recent times, the voices of those who assume that independent developments took place in Palestine itself during the exile have increased, despite the difficulty of describing such developments in any detail.[2]

In these circumstances it is important to examine what sources are available for the time of the exile. The Old Testament accounts are scattered, and must be taken from a variety of literary works. The Deuteronomistic history work ends with the fall of Jerusalem in 587/86, and only touches lightly on further developments in Judah, without following them at all seriously (II Kings 25.22–26); right at the end there is a portrayal of a kind of pardon for Jehoiachin, the king of Judah, who lived in exile and was accorded privileges by the great king of Babylon (II Kings 25.27–30). This happened in 560 BC, i.e. well into the exile, but for us remains a quite isolated event which the Deuteronomistic historian probably put at the end of his work deliberately, to provide a happy ending.

Chronicles does not speak of the exile at all. In II Chron. 36.20–23 the period is emphasized as having been a dark age which was only ended by the rise of Cyrus the Persian; with his decision to rebuild the temple at Jerusalem, Cyrus provides a sign of hope.

The prose chapters in the book of Jeremiah (Jer. 39–44) run roughly parallel to the brief account in II Kings 25.22–26. They are concerned with events in Judah after the fall of Jerusalem, but concentrate on the fate of the prophet Jeremiah after he was carried off to Egypt. It is probably wrong to connect Lamentations with Jeremiah, but it too describes conditions immediately after the destruction of the temple, and chs. 2, 4 and 5 probably give an accurate picture of conditions in the land.[3]

Sayings of the prophet Ezekiel take us further into the period of the exile; Ezekiel will probably have died in exile about 570 BC. However, it is virtually impossible to infer particular historical events from the material. The pardon of Jehoiachin in 560 provides a *terminus a quo* for the composition of the Deuteronomistic history work; more recently, scholars believe that it was given its final form in Judah, and not in exile.[4] Consequently the fundamental theological questions with which the work is concerned are to be understood as an expression of discussion in Judah during the second half of the exilic period, when attempts were being made to understand the present in the light of the past.[5] We should therefore suppose that at least a start was also made at this time on the final editing of the prophetic books, running parallel to the composition of the Deuteronomistic history work, even if exact details cannot be established.[6]

Persian power grew during the fifties of the sixth century under Cyrus II (559–529), from the ruling house of the Achaemenids. Its significance for the Jews in exile was recognized by the prophet whose sayings have been incorporated into Isa. 40–55. He is known as Deutero-Isaiah and is usually thought to have worked in exile. Whether he survived to see the fall of Babylon in 539 is an open question.

We have a series of extra-biblical documents of different genres and tendencies about the reign of the last Babylonian king Nabonidus (*Nabū-nā'id*) and the fall of Babylon. There is much dispute over details. These documents chiefly comprise the Babylonian Chronicle for the years 555–539, mentioned earlier, the so-called Nabonidus Chronicle;[7] a taunt song against Nabonidus (composed about 538);[8] the Cyrus cylinder,[9] and a number of further documents which illuminate the history of Nabonidus but are of only moderate value for the history of Israel.[10]

To understand events in Judah after the fall of Jerusalem we should look again at the list in Jer. 52.28–30, which says that 832 inhabitants of Jerusalem were led into exile in the year in which the city fell. It also adds that in the twenty-third year of Nebuchadnezzar, that is, in 582, 745 men of Judah were carried away captive by Nebuzaradan at the order of the king. Whatever the accuracy of the figures may be, the account is an indication. On the basis of what it says, we must suppose that even after the fall of Jerusalem, further groups of the population were sent into exile at intervals, even if we cannot see the reason for this measure or the system behind it. On the whole, Babylonian deportation was less radical than Assyrian. The exiles seem to have remained together, and there is no evidence of any systematic settlement of foreign peoples in Judah. For this reason alone, unlimited deportations are improbable; whatever happened, it will have been necessary to keep enough people to work the land. Repeated attempts at uprisings may well have been one reason for deportations.

There is no express mention anywhere that Judah was made a regular Babylonian province. The country was put in the charge of a native official from Judah named Gedaliah, who already seems to have held office under Josiah and Jehoiakim (II Kings 22.12, 14; Jer. 26.24). We may conclude from II Kings 25.24 that he was submissive to the Babylonians and advised his compatriots to adopt the same attitude. He chose Mizpah as the seat of government, probably in place of destroyed Jerusalem. He put under oath a number of soldiers, army commanders and other men from Judah who seem to have been prepared to recognize his appointment by the Babylonian king, and required them to submit to Babylonian rule. A man of royal blood, Ishmael ben Nathaniah, agitated against this policy, allegedly even with the support of the king of the Ammonites (Jer. 40.14). He gathered others together to kill Gedaliah. Although he had been forewarned, Gedaliah received Ishmael and his people in Mizpah. A banquet turned into a bloodbath. Ishmael and his men slew not only Gedaliah, but also all the guests from Judah and Babylon.

This was not all. On the day after Gedaliah's murder, eighty men came to Mizpah from the territory of the former northern state of Israel to offer sacrifices and incense 'at the house of Yahweh'; thus they were probably on their way to Jerusalem. Accordingly there were groups in the northern territories who recognized the sanctuary at Jerusalem and made pilgrimages there. We are not told whether they did this under the influence of Josiah's reform law, and we do not know how they failed to hear of the destruction of the temple. Of course we might suppose that the cult was being continued in Jerusalem in a reduced form. They wanted to speak to Gedaliah, but they fell into the hands of Ishmael, who immediately killed them. Only ten men escaped, who were prepared to tell Ishmael where they had hidden stores of food (Jer. 41.8). This situation is characteristic of the lawlessness and poverty of a country after catastrophe. Those who can offer something to eat remain alive.

Ishmael then took captive all the people who were still living in Mizpah, including a number of princesses whom the Babylonian official Nebusaradan had left in Gedaliah's safe-keeping. We must also suppose that the prophet Jeremiah was in Mizpah; after being freed by the Babylonians, he went to Gedaliah of his own free will (Jer. 40.1–6). Ishmael attempted to go over to Ammonite territory with all the people who were now in his power. But his plan misfired. In southern Judah a group of leading men who had heard of Ishmael's actions had gathered round Johanan, the son of Kareah. They gathered their strength and met Ishmael's group at Gibeon (Jer. 41.12). The result was surprising, but understandable. Those whom Ishmael had brought from Mizpah immediately went over to Johanan and his men, leaving only Ishmael himself and eight of his men to go over to the Ammonites in Transjordania.

In the region of Bethlehem, Johanan and the group from Mizpah considered what to do next. They were afraid of the Babylonians, because Gedaliah had been killed by a man from Judah. Jeremiah's opinion was asked (Jer. 42), and after pondering the matter for ten days, he recommended that they should stay in the country. But he was overruled, because to go away to Egypt seemed to be a foregone conclusion. The travellers set off, taking Jeremiah and his companion Baruch with them. They reached Tahpanhes, an Egyptian border fortress east of the Nile delta near Pelusium.[11] We do not know what happened after that. Jeremiah will have died in Egypt.

Other people of Judah from the leading classes may have followed the example of Johanan's groups without our knowing it. In this way the land will have suffered a creeping depopulation. The deportation of 582 mentioned in Jer. 52 is the last report we have from Judah either after or in connection with the murder of Gedaliah. We do not know who followed him in office, nor what further measures were taken for the government of the country. Possibly Judah was put under the city of Samaria and its authorities. Most of the people who could have taken over the leadership will either have left or have been deported. At the same time, any possibility of active resistance will also have been removed. The situation increasingly began to return to normal. A time came when new hopes could blossom in Judah. The land would be restored, the cities would be rebuilt, the land would become fertile and the population would increase. We can read this in some chapters of Ezekiel with Deuteronomistic colouring; it is by no means certain that they were composed by the great prophet of the exile.[12] Nor can we rule out the possibility that a composition like Jer. 30; 31 was written in this mood and was crowned with the hope of a new covenant and a restoration of the city of Jerusalem.[13] Further fuel may have been added to these hopes when after the death of Nebuchadnezzar in 562 a number of less significant rulers occupied the throne in Babylon, and the expectations of a change increased.

At the time of the fall of Jerusalem, the neighbouring states in the east and south-east of Judah seem still to have enjoyed a relative independence. The king of Ammon was possibly behind the murder of Gedaliah; some people had fled to Ammon from Judah at the Babylonian invasion and returned in Gedaliah's reign (Jer. 40.11f.). However, in the course of time these states too must have been conquered by Babylon. Josephus reports that Nebuchadnezzar subjected the Ammonites and Moabites on the occasion of a campaign directed towards Egypt in his twenty-third year (582).[14] However, we have no further information.

What were the fortunes of those who had gone from Judah into exile in Babylon? They included the upper classes, the royal house with Jehoiachin at its head, the great landowners, high state officials and priests. Ezekiel, the priest and prophet, was often invited to talk with the 'elders of Israel', that is, with the leading figures (Ezek.14.1–11; 20.1ff.; 33.10–20). A special term appears in Ezekiel for the group who were led into exile, the word *gōlā*.[15] We are given little detail about conditions of life in exile. There may have been whole settlements where the deportees lived together, to which it was even possible to write letters (cf. Jer. 29). We know of the name of one such settlement, Tel-Abib (Ezek.3.15); it is perhaps the Hebrew version of a local place name.[16] Other names of settlements can be found in Ezra 2.59 = Neh.7.61. They were near the river Chebar = *nāru kabaru* (perhaps 'great river', 'canal'), probably one of the eastern tributaries of the Euphrates.[17]

A Babylonian court list which even mentions Jehoiachin and calls him 'king of the land of Judah (*Ja-a-ḫu-du*)' sheds interesting light on the way in which the exiles were provided for. There can be no doubt who is meant here: we have one of those rare pieces of good fortune when a foreign source unexpectedly provides confirmation for a detail of the Old Testament account. The list comes from the thirteenth year of Nebuchadnezzar (592 BC), and in particular mentions supplies of oil sent to Jehoiachin, five of his sons, and other men of Judah.[18] But it was only during the reign of Nebuchadnezzar's successor, king Evil-Merodach (Awil-Marduk), which only lasted from 562 to 560, that the king of Judah was accorded special treatment (II Kings 25.27–30). In the thirty-seventh year of his exile, Jehoiachin was freed from his internment and given the right to eat at the court of Babylon. From this we can at least conclude how long Jehoiachin spent in exile, since he must have left Jerusalem in 597. Of course we do not know the date of his death. Over this long period hopes for a restoration in Judah could be pinned on this descendant of the house of David. The years of exile were counted after him, at least in the book of Ezekiel, whether that was finally edited in exile or in Judah. In both places the king may have been seen as a pledge of a restitution of Judah.[19] But the change of fortune came from another direction. During the fifties, the Persian empire began to rise inexorably, as that of Babylon fell.

A number of rulers followed Nebuchadnezzar, none of whom had a long reign on the throne of Babylon. Awil-Marduk (Evil-Merodach) has already been mentioned several times: he ruled from 562 to 560 and was deposed by force; we have a short piece of the Babylonian Chronicle for the year 557/6 from the reign of his successor *Nergal-šar-uṣur* (Neriglissar), 559–556.[20] The ruling line broke off with the latter's son Labashi-Marduk (556/55). There must have been some great internal revolution. After him, the last king of Babylon was Nabonidus (*Nabū-nā'id*), who came from Haran in Upper Mesopotamia. He was son of a priestess of the moon-god Sin, who was worshipped there. He was able to maintain his reign from 555 until the fall of Babylon in 539, despite internal political difficulties and a strange foreign policy which he nevertheless pursued consistently. He must have come into conflict with the priests of Marduk in Babylon, because he sought to elevate the moon god Sin of Haran to be the god of the nation, thus probably favouring the Aramaean groups in the state. In foreign affairs, Nabonidus' wars against Arab tribes in the southern wilderness are remarkable; he stayed ten years in the oasis city of Tema, a centre for communication and trade in northern Arabia. In the meantime he handed over the rule in Babylon to his son Belshazzar.[21]

The situation abroad may be the reason why this capricious ruler was not overthrown. It may well have filled the leading groups in Babylon with fear and hope. The extension of Persian power in the north and west promised threatening developments for Mesopotamia. At the beginning of his reign Nabonidus formed an alliance with the Persian king Cyrus, who had ascended the throne in 559 after overthrowing Astyages, king of the Medes. The kingdom had extended as far as Asia Minor and was a dangerous presence in the west for the Persians as well as the Babylonians. In Ecbatana, the capital of the Medes, Cyrus took control of a great Persian empire. Nabonidus' alliance with Cyrus warded off the Persian threat from Babylon at least for a time. In fact, Cyrus next turned his attention westwards. Croesus of Lydia, a king proverbial for his riches, attacked Cyrus, but suffered an overwhelming defeat at his hands in 586; as a result, Persian power extended as far as the west coast of Asia Minor. During the second half of the forties, Cyrus secured his authority on the east side of his kingdom by gaining control of the inhabitants of the high country of Iran, to the north-east of Babylon. All that remained was the south, the kingdom of Nabonidus.

Cyrus must have been attracted by the thought of an attack on the neo-Babylonian empire. With it he would gain not only Mesopotamia, but also Syria and Palestine and possibly even parts of the wilderness of Arabia, over which Nabonidus had gained control. The corridor through Syria and Palestine also offered the possibility of a conquest of Egypt, which would mean that Cyrus would rule over all the then known world. Cyrus moved consistently in this direction; of course it was only in the time of his son and successor Cambyses, in 525, that the battle of Pelusium brought victory over the Egyptians.

The overthrow of the Babylonian empire must have regularly been expected with a considerable degree of confidence and certainty in Babylon itself. Those who chiefly drew hope from this prospect were the states and groups dependent on the Babylonians, including those in exile from Judah. There is nothing against putting the activity of Deutero-Isaiah in the forties of the sixth century. The expectations of this prophet found their crudest and most understandable expression in the idea that Yahweh would make Cyrus his instrument and give him victory over Babylon. Deutero-Isaiah mentions Cyrus by name and designates him, the ruler of a foreign nation, 'his (Yahweh's) anointed' (Isa. 45.1), his 'shepherd' (Isa. 44.28). There is an unmistakable description of the fall of Babylon (Isa. 47).

Cyrus did not find his victory over Babylon difficult. To begin with, he did not even make a personal appearance. In 539 he ordered his commander Gobryas to attack: Nabonidus fell. Babylon came into Persian hands virtually without a struggle. It seems as though the priests of Marduk welcomed the conquerors as liberators, for they brought an end to Nabonidus' rule. Finally, Cyrus himself entered the city in a triumphal procession.

In addition to brief notes in the Babylonian Chronicle,[22] we have two accounts of the fall of Babylon, both of which are, of course, tendentious. Unfortunately the edges of one text, contained in a 'taunt song' against Nabonidus, are badly damaged. In all probability it is the report of a Babylonian priest who welcomed Cyrus as the chosen ruler, and condemned harshly the iniquities of Nabonidus. It is particularly worth noting that Cyrus restored the old cults from the time of Nebuchadnezzar:[23] 'The images of Babylonia, male and female, he returned to their cellas, the [gods who] had abandoned their [cha]pels he returned to their mansions.' (Against Nabonidus): '. . . [these] deeds he effaced, . . . in all the sanctuaries the inscriptions of his name are erased. . . . [To the inhabitants of] Babylon a joyful heart is given now, [they are like prisoners when] the prisons are opened . . . [liberty is restored to] those who were surrounded by oppression, [all rejoice] to look upon him as king.' The dominant themes of this text are Cyrus' concern for the gods and the eradication of the remnants of Nabonidus' reign. Such an account may be attributed to a priest of Marduk. It is still more significant that Cyrus presented himself as a servant of Marduk, that he understood the Babylonian gods and claimed to act in their name. He used polemic against Nabonidus to bring out his own mission all the more clearly. This can be seen on the Cyrus cylinder, a clay cylinder with a cuneiform inscription. The extant text begins with a condemnation of Nabonidus; then it portrays Marduk looking for a true ruler whom of course he finds in Cyrus:[24] 'He scanned and looked through all the countries searching for a righteous ruler willing to lead him. Then he pronounced the name of Cyrus, king of Anshan, declared him to become the ruler of all the world.' Accordingly Cyrus designates himself 'eternal offshoot of the kingdom whose dynasty Bel and Nebo love, whom they want as king to please their hearts'.[25] Cyrus received his rule from the hands of the Babylonian gods and thus entered into the true succession of rulers of Babylon. This may be seen as no more than a special form of court style and a piece of Persian propaganda, but that was not all. Behind it lies the special way in which the Persians treated their subject peoples and ruled over them.

Unlike the Assyrians and Babylonians, Cyrus and his successors did not seek to rule over and preserve their empire by the eradication of the old order and the exchange of native populations; they kept and restored the laws which had once been observed in the subject territories and respected the institutions which had grown up there. The Persian empire based its policy on local administrative structures, which it restored when they had ceased to exist, either as a result of violent action or through the lapse of time. The Persians paid particular attention to the ordering of the cult and the care of sanctuaries. This is the background against which we must understand Cyrus and his approach to the rule of the former Babylonian empire. It was to accord with the will of the gods of the land. Cambyses later adopted the same approach in Egypt by taking Egyptian royal titles, so that the Persian kings in Egypt might be seen as legitimate successors of the Pharaohs; they were reckoned as independent dynasties (the Twenty-seventh and Thirty-first).

It is obvious that this revolution in the organization of the empire as a result of Persian administrative practice must also have had far-reaching consequences for the Jews in Babylon and similarly for the inhabitants of Palestine. After the fall of Babylon, the inhabitants of the mother country were subject to the same authorities as the exiles. On this basis, a restoration of former conditions in Judah now seemed possible. Two questions inevitably arose. Might the Jews in exile now return to Palestine? In Jerusalem itself, could the city and temple now be rebuilt and the cult be restored? These central problems occupied Jewish history for at least a century after the fall of Babylon.

NOTES

1. R. Kittel, *Geschichte des Volkes Israel* III, 1, 1927, esp. 66–78, does, however, devote three long chapters to 'the leading men in Babylon', which include even 'the Deuteronomic circle'.

2. M. Noth, *The History of Israel*, ²1960, 292: 'Nevertheless the tribes left behind in the old country continued to be the centre of Israelite history and Israelite life. For them the events of 587 BC did not in any way signify the end.' Cf. also E. Janssen, *Juda in der Exilszeit. Ein Beitrag zur Frage der Entstehung des Judentums*, FRLANT 69, 1956; S. Herrmann, *Prophetie und Wirklichkeit in der Epoche des babylonischen Exils*, Arbeiten zur Theologie I, 32, 1967.

3. H. J. Kraus, *Klagelieder*, BK 20, ³1968, in particular sees behind these songs the lament over the destruction of the temple in Jerusalem which hitherto had been the centre of cultic life.

4. M. Noth, *Überlieferungsgeschichtliche Studien*, ²1957, 97, 110 n. 1; E. Janssen, op. cit., 12–18.

5. H. W. Wolff, 'Das Kerygma des deuteronomistischen Geschichtswerkes' (1961), *Gesammelte Studien*, 308–24.

6. In particular, those collections of prophetic sayings which indicate the influence of Deuteronomistic language, especially in the closing sections. We should also note those which display the character of a dispute, which suggests a later revision of the material. This is particularly clear in the book of Jeremiah, namely in the composition of the prose passages, and also in individual sections of the book of Ezekiel. For Amos see W. H. Schmidt, 'Die deuteronomistische Redaktion des Amosbuches', *ZAW* 77, 1965, 168–92.

7. *AOT*, 366–8; *ANET*, 305–7; there is a short extract in *TGI*, 81f.

8. *ANET*, 312–5; *TGI*¹, 66–70.

9. *AOT*, 368–70; *ANET*, 315f.

10. C. J. Gadd, *The Harran Inscriptions of Nabonidus*, 1958; *ANET Suppl.*, 560–3, and the literature given there; also R. Meyer, *Das Gebet des Nabonid*, Sitzungsberichte der Sächsischen Akademie der Wissenschaften, Phil.-Hist. Kl., Vol. 107, 3, 1962, esp. 53–81; K. Galling, *Studien zur Geschichte Israels im persischen Zeitalter*, 1964.

11. Jer. 43.7; for Tahpanhes see A. Alt, 'Taphnaein und Taphnas', *ZDPV* 66, 1943, 64–8; W. F. Albright, *Bertholet Festschrift*, 1950, 13f. Jer. 44.1 mentions a series of further places in Upper Egypt where people from Judah settled in the course of time: Migdol, Noph (= Memphis) and the land of Pathros, which will be in essentials identical with Upper Egypt. Thus the exiles from Judah gradually spread themselves over a wide area, presumably depending on opportunities for work.

12. Above all Ezek. 34–37; it is much easier to imagine that these texts came into being in Palestine than to see them as visions in distant Babylon; but Ezek. 37.1–14, the vision of the bones on the plain, presents some difficulties. The interpretation in vv. 11–14 is based on a conception of the whole house of Israel which is at least akin to the basic idea of Deuteronomy. It is more difficult to decide whether the basis of Ezekiel's ideal picture (Ezek. 40–48) is also to be set in the central exilic period and where it was composed; see now W. Zimmerli, 'Planungen für den Wiederaufbau nach der Katastrophe von 587', *VT* 18, 1968, 229–55; G. C. Macholz, 'Noch einmal: Planungen für den Wiederaufbau nach der Katastrophe von 587', *VT* 19, 1969, 322–52.

13. Jer. 31.31–40.

14. Josephus, *Antt.* X, 9. 7, §181f. (ed. Niese).

15. Ezek. 1.1; 3.11, 15; 11.24f.; 12.4; see also Jer. 28.6; 29.1, 4, 20, 31; Zech. 6.10, etc.

16. In 1909, sixty Jewish families founded a Jewish colony north-east of Jaffa and named it Tel Aviv to recall what was once the chief centre of the Babylonian exile.

17. The *shatt en-nīl* in the neighbourhood of Nippur is usually suggested; W. Zimmerli, *Ezekiel* 1, Hermeneia, Philadelphia 1979, 16, 112.

18. E. F. Weidner, 'Jojachin, König von Juda, in babylonischen Keilschrifttexten', in *Mélanges Syriens offerts à M. R. Dussaud*, II, 1939, 923–35; *ANET*, 308; *TGI*, 78f.

19. R. Meyer speaks of a kind of 'exilic dynasty' which Jehoiachin must have founded and sees in it the beginnings of a 'legitimate Davidic tradition which can be traced in Babylonian Judaism in connection with the office of the exilarch (*rēš gālūṭā*) down to the tenth century AD! R. Meyer, *Das Gebet des Nabonid*, 1962, 68.

20. D. J. Wiseman, *Chronicles of Chaldaean Kings (626–556 BC) in the British Museum*, 1956 (²1961).

21. Cf. the two texts *TGI*, 79–81. Belshazzar also appears in Dan. 5.1–6.1, in the setting of a saga, but there he is called king of Babylon and is regarded as a predecessor of Darius.

22. The seventeenth year of the Chronicle of Nabonidus, *AOT*, 367f.; *ANET*, 306; *TGI*, 81f.

23. Cf. n. 8 above.

24. *AOT*, 369; *ANET*, 315; *TGI*, 83.

25. Ibid.

2 | The First Decades of Persian Supremacy. The Post Exilic Temple

CYRUS HAD CONQUERED Babylon and gained control of the former Babylonian empire including Syria and Palestine. However, the first years of Persian supremacy had little effect on the situation of the Jews in exile and at home. There was evidently no immediate return from Babylon, nor was it to be expected, in view of the state of things, that in Palestine the inhabitants of Jerusalem and Judah would experience a fundamental change in their fortunes. It is most regrettable that we have no sources from Syria and Palestine to give us more details about the transition from Babylonian to Persian rule in these areas. Ultimately, though, it is not surprising, when one thinks how differently the Persian administration worked and how little occasion there will have been for resistance or for dramatic climaxes.

The Persians ruled over Syria and Palestine for more than two centuries. They were displaced by Alexander the Great, who turned southwards after his victory at Issus in 333 BC and finally became master of Egypt. We do not have sufficient sources to provide us with information about the long period of Persian rule in Palestine. In particular, the second half of their supremacy, say between 440 and 333, and even later, was an especially dark age in the history of Palestinian Judaism. We are better informed about a series of events between 538 and 440 BC. But we have no consecutive accounts of them to offer some indication of the course of development. This is unfortunately the case even with the most important sources for the post-exilic period in the Old Testament, the books of Ezra and Nehemiah and parts of Haggai, Zechariah and 'Malachi'.[1]

True, within the framework of the Chronicler's history, the books of Ezra and Nehemiah follow immediately after II Chronicles, but they do not present a well-rounded account. They give the impression of being unrevised source-material for the completion of the work of the Chronicler, but in their present state offer no more than a juxtaposition of varied sources without much concern for coherent content or chronology.[2] Ezra 4.8–6.18 and 7.12–26 even preserve the language of what are presumably original Aramaic texts.[3] They make use of so-called 'imperial Aramaic', which was then the official language of north-west Mesopotamia, Syria and Palestine. Persian administrative practice also served to further the use of local languages.

Aramaic was on the increase in Palestine at least after the exile, and perhaps even earlier;[4] it gradually replaced even Hebrew as the spoken language. From now on, Aramaic spread throughout the eastern Mediterranean, but was spoken in numerous local dialects. The Aramaic parts of the book of Daniel (Dan.2.4b–7.28) have a different form of the language from 'imperial Aramaic'. This so-called biblical Aramaic of Ezra and Daniel[5] should be distinguished from numerous other forms, for example the Aramaic used in Syria and in the writings of members of the military colony of Elephantine in Egypt in the fifth century. Further development brought idioms which have been given different names. Palestinian Aramaic is to be classified as western Aramaic; the eastern branch is made up of Syrian, Mandaean and the language of the Babylonian Talmud. Finally, Aramaic displaced even Akkadian ,which lasted down to the first century BC in a 'late-Babylonian' form, but essentially only as a language used in writing by those specially inclined. Aramaic gained the upper hand.

This gradual unification of language, albeit in different forms, was substantially furthered by the formation of the Persian empire. The Aramaic documents in the Old Testament give eloquent evidence of that.

One of the most important concerns of the books of Chronicles is to stress the significance of the Jerusalem temple and its cult. In the same way, the problem of the temple stands in the foreground of Ezra 1, which follows on directly from the end of II Chronicles. Cyrus proclaims that Yahweh, the God of heaven, has charged him to build a house in Jerusalem. So those who belong to the people of this God are to go up to Jerusalem and to set up the temple at their own expense. In this way, Ezra 1 combines different factors together in a programme. Cyrus himself appears as the chief architect of the temple, acting by Yahweh's commission. The Jews undertake the burden of the actual construction, and for this purpose are released from captivity and allowed to return home. At that point they made preparations to return home (Ezra 1.5). Cyrus did something else. He gave back the vessels of the temple which Nebuchadnezzar had once taken from Jerusalem, but he did not hand them over immediately to the Jews; he entrusted them to a Babylonian official by the name of Sheshbazzar, who is designated *hannāśi' lihūdā*, meaning a Persian government official for Judah (Ezra 1.7–11). Thus far the account in Ezra 1.[6] It covers all the problems with which the men of Judah were faced after the fall of Babylon: 1. Cyrus himself, loyal to all local and national cults, gives the command for the building of the temple, for the restoration of the Jerusalem sanctuary. 2. The deportees are given permission to return, for the express purpose of rebuilding the temple. 3. Cyrus returns the temple vessels formerly plundered by the Babylonians. Admittedly this neat, unified picture from Ezra 1 is fascinating, and it was inevitable that a popular picture of the end of the exile should be developed in these terms: a happy homecoming for those who had been deported and a speedy rebuilding of the temple.

But the mere fact that the temple was not built immediately, that decades

passed before it was reconsecrated, should raise questions. Moreover, other documents from the same book of Ezra reveal that events took a different course. In
Ezra 6.3–5 we have a document which, according to Ezra 6.2, was preserved in the
royal citadel of the Median capital, Ecbatana. It appears in the first long Aramaic
section of the text and is known to modern scholars as the 'edict' or 'decree' of
Cyrus.[7]

> The wording is as follows: 'A record. In the first year of Cyrus the king, Cyrus
> the king issued a decree: Concerning the house of God at Jerusalem, let the
> house be rebuilt, the place where sacrifices are offered and burnt offerings are
> brought; its height shall be sixty cubits and its breadth sixty cubits, with three
> courses of great stones and one course of timber; let the cost be paid from the
> royal treasury. And also let the gold and silver vessels of the house of God, which
> Nebuchadnezzar took out of the temple that is in Jerusalem and brought to
> Babylon, be restored and brought back to the temple which is in Jerusalem,
> each to its place; you shall put them in the house of God.'
>
> The 'first year of Cyrus the king' can only mean the first year of his reign
> over the Babylonian empire(538 BC).

The more considered content of this document in comparison with Ezra 1,
and the particular setting of what it has to say, rule out any doubt about its authenticity. According to Ezra 5.6–6.12, the Cyrus edict played a decisive role when the
satrap of Syria-Palestine, presumably from his official headquarters in Damascus,
made a number of officious inquiries. However, this high Persian official, whose
responsibility is given as *ᶜabar nahᵃre*, 'beyond the river (Euphrates)',[8] was first
active under king Darius I, i.e. after 521 BC, a good twenty years after the edict of
Cyrus. At this time he discovered that there was zealous activity in the building of a
temple in Jerusalem without his knowledge, and he therefore asked with what
authority the work was being carried on. The answer from Jerusalem was that it had
been authorized by a decree of king Cyrus. The satrap mentioned this in a communication to king Darius, a search was made in the archives, and the decree was
discovered. The satrap beyond the Euphrates was officially informed, and at the
same time he was assured that Darius permitted the continuation of work in
Jerusalem; indeed, in some circumstances he was even prepared to help it on.

The story in Ezra may well have been abbreviated and simplified, but it doubtless
contains an element of truth, especially as it accords well with the Persian concern
to foster local traditions and cults. However, the report from the time of Darius
leaves open the interesting question how it could be that only a year after the fall
of Babylon, Cyrus could issue such a decree for a relatively small and insignificant
temple in Jerusalem. With some justification, it has been assumed that some of the
Jews in exile may have drawn the king's attention in Babylon to this temple and
obtained a hearing.

In details, the edict for the rebuilding of the temple follows certain basic principles. Measurements are given, and instructions for the foundations: three courses of stones and one of wood; it probably went without saying that the rest of the wall would be built of clay. Possibly the construction of Solomon's temple served as a model. There is also an order that the temple vessels are to be returned, and in addition that the cost of the rebuilding is to be paid from the royal treasury. According to Ezra 1, on the other hand, these costs were to be met by the Jews themselves. We can only guess at the reason for this discrepancy. Probably the Chronicler felt that a foreign power should not be seen to contribute to the building of the temple. Similarly, in II Chronicles the involvement of Phoenician craftsmen in the building of Solomon's temple is played down.

However, the Cyrus edict is completely silent about another point which was quite essential for Ezra 1: the return of the exiles from Babylon. It might be argued that the edict did not have to say anything about this and indeed did not mean to. It was quite a different matter. But we should reckon with the possibility that the return did not take place at once. In Ezra 1 the Chronicler may have antedated later events and improperly associated them with the edict of Cyrus. In principle, it is unlikely that Cyrus would have been interested in keeping Jews in Babylonia. It may have seemed appropriate that the Jewish families living there should return to their homeland to guarantee a new order in Jerusalem and its environs. The possibility of a return cannot be excluded. But after such a long period, who will have been ready to return? Most of the generation of those deported in 597 and 587/6 will no longer have been alive; many of the younger people may not have felt an urge to go to unknown Palestine, even if it was presented as the land of their fathers.

The question of the return is usually connected with another problem. Why was the temple not rebuilt immediately, when the edict of Cyrus was issued in 538? There must have been a series of difficulties in Judah itself. Of course, we can do no more than guess. The view of the book of Ezra itself, that the rebuilding of the temple was impossible because of inadequate means, seems plausible. It was necessary for the exiles to arrive to get the work of rebuilding the temple under way. Now as the rebuilding did not in fact begin until the beginning of the reign of king Darius in 521, we might conclude that the crucial return only took place during or towards the end of the twenties of the sixth century. Possibly the expedition of the Persian king Cambyses to Egypt in 525 was a specific occasion for the return of a large number of those who had been deported. It is conceivable that the Persians wanted to secure and consolidate the situation in Palestine by carrying out such an undertaking. It is also possible that in this situation renewed advances by the exiles to the Persian state government found a more ready hearing!

However, putting the return in the twenties of the sixth century does not solve all the difficulties. No matter when we date the return, there remains a fact pointed out by the prophet Haggai, speaking about the situation in Jerusalem in the second half of the year 520. He says that there is a widespread view that 'The time has not yet come to rebuild the house of Yahweh' (Hag. 1.2). At the same time, however, he asserts bitterly that there are enough people who live in fine 'panelled' houses, while the house of God lies in ruins (Hag. 1.4). Each is concerned for his own house and does not think of building the house of Yahweh (1.9). This sounds as though what is missing in Jerusalem is not men and material to build the temple, but the will to get on with the work. There is no mention at all of returned exiles. Nor is there any attempt to raise spirits by prophesying their arrival. The same is true of the sayings of the prophet Zechariah, who was almost contemporaneous with Haggai (Zech. 1–8). At no point in his book does he refer to the exiles as being expected or as having already returned home. So we seem to be able to conclude with some degree of certainty that those who were deported, or their descendants, did not return from Babylonia to Jerusalem at that time, at any rate in a substantial group.

> Of course, if we accept this interpretation, we are left with the problem of interpreting the two similar lists in Ezra 2 and Neh. 7, which claim to be those of the deportees.[9] There has been much puzzlement over them. The Chronicler certainly did not invent them, nor are they a survey of the population of the province of Judah in the time of Nehemiah and Ezra (Wellhausen, Albright, etc.). It seems most likely that the lists give members of the Jerusalem community who were living there after 538, whether they all came from Babylon together, or in individual groups; equally, it may be a community list made at some time for some unknown purpose. Galling regards it as a list made between 520 and 515, when the temple was being rebuilt, which was later presented to the Persian satrap Tatnai when he visited Jerusalem (Ezra 5.3ff.).[10]

The fact remains that whenever the families of the exiles returned to Jerusalem, if they did, their arrival did not have an essential or even a substantial influence on the building of the temple. Other forces must have been at work, which finally set the rebuilding of the temple in motion in a relatively short time and even brought it to a speedy conclusion. It makes sense to see a connection between this development and the appearance of the two prophets Haggai and Zechariah in Jerusalem, which must have been symptomatic of a new situation. These men will not have emerged as a result of their own initiative; it is most probable that they were prompted by some outside event.

An exact dating runs through the two prophetic books. Haggai appeared in the second year of king Darius (the reference is to Darius I Hystaspes, 521–486 BC), from the sixth to the ninth month (say the end of August to November 520). The most important part of Zechariah's activity was between the eighth and the eleventh month of the same year, thus between October/November 520 and January/February 519.[11] The accession of king Darius was a shock for the world of his time. Cambyses, the conqueror of Egypt, had died in 522 without leaving a son to succeed him. Darius came from a different line, from the ruling house of the Achaemenids, and had to guard against a variety of opponents and the danger of a rival king. He was able to overcome these difficulties during the course of the first year of his reign.[12] However, the upheavals at the head of the Persian empire had far-reaching effects and led to unrest in the more distant provinces. True, we know little about conditions in Judah at this time, but we must reckon with the possibility that the movements in international politics also aroused hopes and expectations in the little community. They should not be too hastily labelled 'messianic' or 'theocratic', but they will have been concerned with the restoration of Jerusalem as a political and spiritual centre, in accordance with pre-exilic tradition. It will have been important to mobilize those forces which were convinced that the renewal of the people, its constitution and its faith must in the long run be achieved in Jerusalem itself and not in the Babylonian *gōlā*. Jerusalem was to be restored to honour and to regain its dominant role. While Haggai was concerned almost exclusively with domestic politics, the book of Zechariah pioneered a new world of ideas and images which seem to be an anticipation of apocalyptic forms and which consider the wider sphere of world history and world politics. Haggai 1 makes some remarks about drought and bad harvests. This may have had a weakening effect. Haggai draws the conclusion that it is simply a punishment because the temple has not yet been built. More significantly, Haggai addresses two men who were among the leaders in Jerusalem: Zerubbabel, the 'governor of Judah', and Joshua, the 'high priest' (*hakkōhēn haggādōl*, Hag. 1.1). As in Zechariah, they embody secular and spiritual rule, though we cannot see whether they were absolutely equal from the beginning or whether at first one was dependent on the other.

While Zerubbabel had a Babylonian name (*Zēr-bābili*), he himself came from Judah. Indeed he was a grandson of Jehoiachin, the Davidic king who was deported in 597 and pardoned in 560.[13] He may have been appointed by the Persians as an official for the province. We can imagine that he rose during the exile, was given a Babylonian name there, and later gained preferment as a near relative of the king of Judah who had been restored to favour. Finally, it may have seemed appropriate to give him a leading position in his homeland. His descent from the house of David was certainly not without significance; it may have aroused sympathy and hope, above all in Judah.

Thus Haggai talks of him in particularly high-flown language (Hag. 3.23): 'On that day, says the Lord of hosts, I will take you, O Zerubbabel my servant, the son of Shealtiel, says the Lord, and make you like a signet ring; for I have chosen you.' This special choice of Zerubbabel may underlie another passage, the text of which is difficult, Zech. 4.9: 'The hands of Zerubbabel have laid the foundation of this house; his hands shall also complete it.' The wording seems baffling and it is often challenged. For according to the Aramaic source of the book of Ezra (Ezra 5.16), Sheshbazzar, the man to whom the temple vessels were to be given (Ezra 1, and also Ezra 5.14f.), laid the foundation stone of the temple. K. Galling has argued very strongly that Zerubbabel was the decisive figure: he laid the foundation stone and also saw to the completion of the temple.[14] Sheshbazzar's role should not be overestimated; on the other hand, we can also imagine that it was in the interests of the Chronicler to reduce the importance of Sheshbazzar in favour of Zerubbabel, so as to ascribe the foundation of the new temple to a true man of Judah from a distinguished family. At all events, Sheshbazzar was certainly not a man of Judah. His name is thoroughly Babylonian (*Shamash-apla-uṣur*). It may be that following the edict of Cyrus he became a kind of plenipotentiary and in the course of time delegated his functions to other officials, among whom Zerubbabel played a prominent role. He was probably concerned with the affairs of Judah in a different way. The second important figure alongside Zerubbabel is the high priest Joshua. It is significant that the names Zerubbabel and Jeshua (sic!) stand at the head of the list of returned exiles in Ezra 2 and Neh.7. This could support the view that these are community lists from the time of Haggai and Zechariah; the leading men came to be placed at the head. At the same time, it is not completely out of the question that a group from Babylon appeared here, when Zerubbabel, entrusted with the authority of the Persian central government, was to take over affairs in Jerusalem. As hypotheses, the two interpretations, a list of deportees and a community list, are by no means irreconcilable.

Taking everything together, the change of rule in the Persian empire, a new political grouping in Jerusalem arising through Zerubbabel and the high priest Joshua, and the appearance of Haggai and Zechariah, to be linked with the two events, we have a plausible picture into which everything can be fitted. An advantageous political situation rekindled nationalistic hopes in Jerusalem, united political expectations (Zerubbabel) and cultic requirements (the high priest Joshua) with some degree of tension, and not least called for prophetic intervention (Haggai, Zechariah). The situation was by no means easy, and there may have been disputes over areas of jurisdiction, especially between Zerubbabel and Joshua. Evidence of this may be found in the 'night visions' at the beginnings of the book of Zechariah (Zech. 1–6), which are so difficult to interpret. They reflect not only the changes in world politics but also difficulties in internal politics. A reference to the high priest Joshua seems problematical, but in the end is probably justified.[15] Not least, these chapters are concerned with problems about the future form of the Jerusalem community in which the offices of Zerubbabel and the high priest are heightened in an idealistic way and linked with expectations for the future. Secular and spiritual leaders were in fact to shape the internal scene in Jerusalem, and on occasion also to complicate it.

It is not out of keeping with this picture of limited political and sacral emancipation in Jerusalem that the satrap of Transeuphrates should at first remain in ignorance of the building of the temple. He is first aware of the situation when he visits Jerusalem (Ezra 5.6–6.12), and then makes the enquiries to the great king described above, which end with the confirmation of the edict of Cyrus. The continuation of the account in Ezra 6 is then able to report good progress in the work on the temple. Finally the house is completed and consecrated on the third day of the month Adar in the sixth year of Darius, that is, in spring of 515 BC. We are not told whether or not Zerubbabel was present; we do not hear of him again. This has given rise to several hypotheses. Perhaps his period of office expired and he was recalled in the normal way; perhaps he died. We cannot, of course, tell whether he was ordered back because his royal descent brought with it the danger of an unlimited extension of his authority by local forces.

From 515, Jerusalem again possessed a temple. The sanctuary of Yahweh had been restored to its old place. We do not know what the new building looked like; we have neither descriptions nor pictures. It may have been a modest construction in comparison with Solomon's temple, though the basic features will have been similar. We can conclude this with some degree of certainty from the plan of the later Herodian temple. However, in comparison with the temple of Solomon there were problems in another respect, over the status of the restored sanctuary. The old temple had been a royal precinct and had come into being in a close association with the royal palace; kings were its protectors. The monarchy was not restored after the exile. Who now had the supreme authority over the new sanctuary? One can understand the hopes that might be pinned on Zerubbabel in this respect; one can imagine that the Persian officials may have claimed rights of supervision. One thing, however, is quite clear. In this particular sphere, in a situation where tradition now offered no precedent, there was a new figure who could put forward strong claims, that of the high priest. With the continued absence of a monarchy he may have concluded that the function of a priest should be linked with the status of a king. In this connection the evidence that in the post-exilic period priests were anointed is particularly interesting.[16] The beginning of this development can already be seen in the book of Zechariah (Zech.6.9–15), which mentions a regular coronation for Joshua.

A delegation from Babylonia arrives bringing gifts of silver and gold from which a crown intended for Joshua is to be made. More accurately, 'crowns' in the plural are mentioned, but only Joshua is mentioned as the one who is to wear a crown. Since Wellhausen,[17] the view has been widespread that it is Zerubbabel, the governor, and not Joshua, the priest, who is being crowned here. The name Zerubbabel, it is argued, was later replaced by that of Joshua, because Zerubbabel did not live to see the completion of the temple. But there are no compelling reasons for assuming that the names have been changed round. Another suggestion is much more likely, not least because of the rather remarkable plural 'crowns'. Perhaps mention of a simultaneous coronation of Zerubbabel has been omitted to give the honour to the high priest alone. If this hypothesis stands, it serves to emphasize the royal status of the high priest in the post-exilic period. The only question now was whether in the future the high priest would also seek to gain political influence over the sanctuary, and how he would go about doing so.

The temple was standing again, but a new community had still to be built around it. Not only did tradition and law need to be strengthened; the city of Jerusalem itself still lay open and unfortified, and its walls were still thrown down. It was still to be several decades before this period of outward uncertainty also came to an end and there was a far-reaching change in conditions.

NOTES

1. It must remain an open question whether *mal'āki* in Mal. 1.1 is the prophet's proper name or should properly be translated 'my messenger'. Cf. the commentaries and introductions to the Old Testament.

2. In addition to commentaries and introductions to the Old Testament see M. Noth, *Überlieferungsgeschichtliche Studien*, ²1957, 110–80; S. Mowinckel, ' "Ich" und "Er" in der Ezrageschichte', in *Verbannung und Heimkehr* (Festschrift W. Rudolph), 1961, 211–33; P. R. Ackroyd, *Exile and Restoration*, 1968; see now id., *I & II Chronicles, Ezra, Nehemiah*, Torch Bible Commentaries, 1973.

3. For the authenticity of the documents see already E. Meyer, *Die Entstehung des Judentums*, 1896 (reprinted 1965).

4. See esp. II Kings 18.26, where the negotiations are carried on in Aramaic.

5. H. Bauer – P. Leander, *Grammatik des Biblisch-Aramäischen*, 1927.

6. K. Galling, 'Die Proklamation des Kyros in Esra 1', in K. Galling, *Studien zur Geschichte Israels im persischen Zeitalter*, 1964, 61–77; id., 'Das Protokoll über die Rückgabe der Tempelgeräte', op. cit., 78–88, gives a detailed discussion of the problem.

7. See L. Rost, 'Erwägungen zum Kyroserlass', in *Verbannung und Heimkehr*, 1961, 301–7.

8. Seen from Mesopotamia.

9. K. Galling, 'Die Listen der aus dem Exil Heimgekehrten', in *Studien*, 1964, 89–108.

10. K. Galling, op. cit.; cf. also *Studien*, 56–60.

11. In Zech.7.1 we have an even later date, from the fourth year of Darius.

12. Cambyses had a younger brother who was born in the reign of Cyrus, named Bardiya, whom he killed because he might prove a dangerous rival. However, after Cambyses' death a certain Gaumata took Bardiya's name and came forward to claim the throne. As this man enjoyed considerable respect in many parts of the kingdom, Darius had to spend a year fighting against his opponent and bringing rebellious provinces under control again; see P. J. Junge, *Dareios I, König der Perser*, 1944.

13. As son of Shealtiel (cf. Ezra 3.2; Neh. 12.1; Hag. 1.1 with I Chron. 3.17); we do not know whether Pedaiah, a brother of Shealtiel mentioned in I Chron. 3.19, was his father. There may well have been two men named Zerubbabel.

14. K. Galling, 'Serubbabel und der Hohepriester beim Wiederaufbau des Tempels in Jerusalem', *Studien*, 127–48.

15. Cf. esp. Zech.3. The 'two sons of oil' in Zech.4.14 is probably a reference to Zerubbabel and Shealtiel. For the problems of the night visions see the commentaries, the extensive monograph by L. G. Rignell, *Die Nachtgesichte des Sacharia*, 1950, and the independent interpretation by K. Galling, 'Die Exilswende in der Sicht des Propheten Sacharja', *Studien*, 109–26; see also L. Rost, 'Erwägungen zum Kyroserlass'.

16. M. Noth, 'Office and Vocation in the Old Testament' (1958), in *The Laws in the Pentateuch*, 1966, 229–49.

17. J. Wellhausen, *Die kleinen Propheten*, ³1898; see also B. Duhm, *Anmerkungen zu den Zwölf Propheten*, reprinted from *ZAW*, 1911, 84.

The Reconstruction of Post-Exilic Jerusalem. Ezra and Nehemiah

THE YEARS AFTER the consecration of the temple in 515 BC are quite obscure for us. There are no sources to give any account of this period. But developments cannot have gone as expected. The community was not consolidated, nor was the situation characterized by internal order and a steady reconstruction of the city of Jerusalem. Self-assertion and freedom, even in dealings with neighbouring peoples, gained the upper hand. To men concerned with stricter observances and conscious of tradition, this seemed to be a dangerous deviation, a digression from the way that had been indicated. The appearance in Jerusalem of Ezra and Nehemiah from the families in exile set strict limits to this development in the middle of the fifth century, but at the same time evidently also laid the foundation for an adequately secured continuation of the existence of Israel–Judah for centuries to come.

It is usually assumed that another prophet appeared before Ezra and Nehemiah, whose sayings have come down to us in the short book 'Malachi'. This gives us an approximate picture of conditions in the country which must have developed in the decades after the completion of the temple. Their most prominent feature is misuse of the cult. Animals with blemishes, blind and lame, are used for sacrifices (Mal. 1.6–14). Offerings to the sanctuary are in disorder; deceptions occur regularly (Mal. 3.7–12). The book of Malachi is even more concerned with another charge. It has to deplore mixed marriages, marriages entered into with women from neighbouring nations (Mal. 2.10–12), while Israelite women are frivolously set aside (Mal. 2.13–16). The problem of mixed marriages occupied Ezra and Nehemiah just as much at a later date.[1] Those who entered into such marriages were chiefly the upper classes, including priests and levites; the population on the land were less involved. Political interests of a kind were probably involved. The marriages probably represented an attempt by the upper class to improve their position by entering into relations with their counterparts in neighbouring countries. Even if a man went to Samaria with this intention, he was still going beyond the bounds of his own people. For even there the upper class had been imported; there were very few Israelites among them. We can easily imagine, though there is no proof, that marriages of this kind were prompted by a kind of internationalist and liberal approach which was furthered, or at any rate was not hindered, by the presence of a tolerant foreign administration. The chief fear of people like the author of the book of Malachi was a threat to the particular Israelite way of life, the danger of alienation at the very roots of the national character. There can be no doubt; here was the germ of later differences within the community of Jerusalem and Judah. We are on the threshold of a later period which is characterized by different spiritual approaches and a deliberate struggle for a distinctive self-understanding.

The next event that we can date with some degree of certainty after the redaction of 'Malachi' is a petition by the officials of the provincial administration of Samaria. They approach the central Persian government with the news that the people of Jerusalem are beginning to build city walls and to fortify the city. The answer was not long in coming. The building of the walls was to be stopped. The petition and the answer are displaced in the book of Ezra (Ezra 4.7–22) and form part of the Aramaic section which also contains the enquiry about the edict of Cyrus (Ezra 5; 6). The section combines a number of official documents, left in Aramaic, but unfortunately not put in the right chronological order. The petition of the Samarian officials is put in the rule of Artachshastha, as Artaxerxes is named in the Old Testament. It will date from the beginning of the reign of Artaxerxes I Longimanus (465–424). The problem of Samaria can also be seen in some passages of Haggai and Zechariah. The people of Samaria feared for the independence of their city, and perhaps even for the safety of the whole provincial alliance, in that at that time Jerusalem was in fact a regular part of the province of Samaria. Above all, once Jerusalem was fortified and again had a temple, it threatened to challenge the predominance of Samaria and cause it to lose prestige. At any rate, first the building of the walls in Jerusalem, or at any rate the first attempt was stopped; at this particular time questions of internal security were particularly important to the Persian government. We know of a satrap of Transeuphrates named Megabyzus, who led a rebellion about the middle of the fifth century. Against this background we can better understand the measures taken by the Persian government.

A decisive change in conditions in Jerusalem and Judah only comes about with the arrival of Ezra and Nehemiah. Both of them came from families who had been deported to Babylon; both had attained high office abroad; and, as is shown not least by the tasks assigned to them, both were prominent personalities, at least among their peers. Both came with the knowledge of and indeed largely in the service of the Persian state government. There is, of course, a dispute over who came first and over the sequence in which their measures were effected. It is difficult to come to any conclusions here, because it is impossible to establish any completely reliable chronological sequence from the only sources we have, the books of Ezra and Nehemiah. Moreover, not all the sources have the same degree of trustworthiness or probability. We must consider the possibility that the material has been worked over either by the Chronicler or, in individual instances, by redactors unknown to us. Understandably, the texts have been analysed often and assessed in very different ways.[2]

The following passages stand out from the traditional material as a whole as independent testimony: 1. Ezra's instructions (Ezra 7.12–26); 2. the so-called Nehemiah memoirs in Neh. 1.1b–7.5 (composed in the first person), to which should be added Neh. 11.1f. + 12.27–13.31 from the last part of the book of Nehemiah. The Ezra tradition in Ezra 7–10 is particularly hard to assess; Neh. 8; 9 is very closely connected with it. This arrangement of the material suggests that Ezra came to Jerusalem first, that Nehemiah arrived later with another commission and that Ezra was then able to appear again with complete success (Neh. 8; 9). It cannot be demonstrated that events must have taken place in this way, nor do the books of Ezra and Nehemiah say as much; the loose sequence cannot, of course, even be regarded as one of chronological succession and the final form intended by the redactors. Without accepting a particular theory, we shall attempt here to follow the course of events as indicated by the arrangement of the sources in their present form, on the assumption that the redactors will not have confused the events completely.

According to Ezra 7, in the seventh year of king Artaxerxes, in 458 BC,[3] Ezra came from the 'province of Babylon' to Jerusalem accompanied by a group of men from Judah, with special authority from the Persian king (Ezra 7.16). Ezra himself was a priest (7.12); his genealogy is traced back to Aaron (7.1–5). Thus he may have come from a family of exiles; perhaps he was even of Zadokite descent. He bears a second important title in addition to that of priest; it is given in its Aramaic form: 'Scribe (*sōpēr*) of the law of the God of heaven.'

The designation 'God of heaven' is a customary title for the God of Israel in documents of the Persian period. 'Scribe' should be understood to mean an official with a particular sphere of responsibility, not, say, the author or interpreter of particular documents. Ezra may be said to have been, with some qualification, administrator of the 'law of the God of heaven', that is, the man in the Persian state administration responsible for the religious affairs of Israel. In view of the complex Persian policy over religion and cult, such a position seems possible and conceivable. Ezra was probably also familiar with Israelite legislation. In Egypt the Persian administration had the land law specially codified, so that they could arrange the administration of the province correctly under appropriate local principles. We cannot exclude the possibility that Ezra had a competence in a similar direction; however, we do not know how far this competence went or whether Ezra himself played a part in the collecting or even codifying of Israelite law. The Hebrew version of Ezra's title in Ezra 7.6 suggests that this latter could have been the case; there Ezra is called 'a scribe skilled in the law of Moses which Yahweh the God of Israel had given'. Later, he is simply given the abbreviated title 'Ezra the scribe' (Ezra 7.11; Neh. 8.1ff.). We cannot rule out the possibility that the term 'scribe' was misunderstood in these passages and is not just used in the sense of an official title; no wonder that over the course of time the figure of Ezra was interpreted in quite a different way, even giving rise to the idea of 'Ezra the interpreter of scripture'.[4]

Without reading too much into the figure of Ezra, it may be asserted that he was an official with particular responsibilities who received a special commission for Jerusalem. Artaxerxes gave him a letter to deliver, the Aramaic wording of which may be read in Ezra 7.12–26. He is allowed to take with him a group of people who are particularly anxious to return. Then he is to make a special investigation of the observance of the law in the community of Judah and Jerusalem, as is specifically stated, 'according to the law of your God, which is in your hand' (Ezra 7.14). Moreover, he is given a financial contribution from the king towards the Jerusalem temple and its cult. He is authorized to acquire further means, and the treasurers of Transeuphrates are instructed to fall in with his requests. He is to appoint new judges and officials and see that both the law of God and the royal law are observed.

Doubt is sometimes expressed about the authenticity of the document. It may have been edited, though it has been handed down in Aramaic, but it does meet the situation for which it is intended and can be connected with the troubles which 'Malachi' had to deplore. We cannot discuss here whether it is legitimate to suppose that some of the exiles living in Babylon had asked for a review of conditions in the mother country, or whether Ezra had in fact requested such a review himself. This would presuppose very close and regular contact between Babylon and Jerusalem. It is, however, worth noting that the instructions given to Ezra do not imply a comprehensive reform; for all the stress on individual details, they simply have the character of a specific clarification of local conditions. The law of the God of Israel is to be given normative significance, and it is to be taught where it has fallen into neglect (Ezra 7.25).

When Ezra arrived in Jerusalem, he acted in accordance with the instructions which he had been given. He handed over the king's contribution to the temple, and the returned exiles offered sacrifice. Then he took stock of the situation in the country and had a detailed report on the problem of mixed marriages. As a result, we are told that he was beside himself. He asked for an investigation of particular cases and gave local leaders powers which even included divorce.

We do not hear of any other steps taken by Ezra, such as the appointment of new officials. The account of his activity ends provisionally in Ezra 10, and then begins again in Neh.8 with a great event. Between these two points the memoirs of Nehemiah have been inserted (Neh. 1.1b–7.5). We shall discuss him here, following the biblical account, leaving aside the chronological question. It may be that the Nehemiah text has been put here in order to introduce the figure of Nehemiah, who was later associated with Ezra in people's memories; or Nehemiah may in fact have come to Jerusalem when Ezra had taken first soundings, but had not completely fulfilled his commission.

Nehemiah's report is composed in the first person and is full of impressive pictures and scenes. The narrative character is striking, and cannot be a complete fiction. Nehemiah, too, probably came from a family of exiles; he had even become a cup-bearer at the court of the Persian king in Susa.[5] One day a group of men from Judah appeared at court. Out of interest, Nehemiah asked them about conditions in their homeland. He was deeply affected to learn that the city was still unfortified; its walls still lay in ruins. At the royal table, Nehemiah seized his opportunity to tell the king of the situation in Jerusalem. He sought, and in the end received, authority enabling him to begin work on rebuilding the walls with the king's support.

The tale is well told, and may be tailored to Nehemiah's later achievements, but it is not lacking in contemporary colouring, and cannot be dismissed entirely as fiction. If something was to be done in Jerusalem, it was evidently beyond the means of the inhabitants. The impetus had to come from outside; permission was required which was not easy to obtain. Middlemen were needed, energetic figures who knew how to get on with things, how to convince authorities and get hold of the necessary papers. Any people which has experienced an occupying power and its regulations, of any description, knows that!

Nehemiah was given authority and papers. He obtained a letter to the king's second-in-command in the area, the satrap of Transeuphrates, which was a kind of pass to guarantee him a smooth journey to Judah. In addition, he received a letter to the steward of a royal estate who would give him the necessary wood for the building work. Not least, he was given a military escort for his journey and thus made an impressive entry into Jerusalem. This happened in the twentieth year of king Artaxerxes, in 445; that is, if we are correctly informed, thirteen years after the arrival of Ezra.

Remarkably enough, Nehemiah seems at first to have concealed his intentions in Jerusalem. He travelled out of the city secretly by night and inspected the ruined walls.[6] Then he said quite openly that the work of rebuilding the walls had to be started and obtained the support he needed, doubtless through reference to the authorization he brought with him. He was in fact successful in preparing for the rebuilding of the city wall, a task which he accomplished throughout strict organization.

Nehemiah divided up the walls into sections and made particular Jerusalem families responsible for each section; these in turn made use of local overseers from Judah. The latter introduced further people, so that there were sufficient for the whole undertaking. The people of Jerusalem by themselves would have been too few. Nehemiah 3.1–32 gives a detailed list of those involved in the building.

Nevertheless, numerous difficulties arose, hindrances from within the city and outside it. They came first from the heart of the Jerusalem community itself. There were people who complained because they were expected to do forced labour (Neh. 5.1–13). They felt that as a result they were incurring losses in their own businesses. Moreover, they had mortgages and in addition had to pay taxes to the Persian government. Nehemiah succeeded in arranging a remission of debts within the community; he was also prepared to make a personal sacrifice and to forgo large gifts for himself (Neh. 5.14–19).

Difficulties from outside were much more threatening. Leaders in the neighbourhood watched the inexorable reconstruction of the walls with suspicion. Three men above all are mentioned over and over again as being hostile to Jerusalem and to Nehemiah: Sanballat, the governor of Samaria, who was evidently afraid that the province would be divided; Tobiah, probably the governor of the neighbouring province of Ammon; and finally Geshem the Arab, a man who seems to have posed a threat from the south. First of all the building of the wall merely provoked their mirth (Neh. 2.10; 2.19f.). Then, however, Sanballat also aroused the upper classes in Samaria (3.33ff.). Finally, when the work was so far advanced that it was bound to be completed, they went over to active resistance (Neh. 4.1ff.).

Sanballat, Tobiah, southern groups described as 'Arabs', Ammonites and Ashdodites made an alliance, sought to encircle Jerusalem and to launch a surprise attack on it. The plan failed. News reached Jerusalem in time. The attack was probably then called off. But an alarm had been given. Nehemiah had to provide military protection for the builders. Watches were appointed and those working on the wall were armed so that they could defend themselves. Nehemiah 4.18 aptly remarks, 'They worked with one hand and held a weapon in the other.' Nehemiah gave orders that the people from the villages should spend the night in the city. Special arrangements were made for the watch. Nehemiah and his entourage did not take off their clothes or wash (Neh. 4.23).

The failure of the enemy led them to make criminal plans. They attempted to capture Nehemiah (Neh. 6). Negotiations were suggested, with evil intent, outside Jerusalem, which was now almost entirely surrounded by its wall. Nehemiah resolutely refused. He sent away four messengers; a fifth brought a letter with political charges. It was claimed that by building the wall Nehemiah was seeking to overthrow the king and become king himself. He had set up prophets to proclaim him king! Nehemiah was able to reject this as sheer invention. Last of all a secret attack seems to have been planned on him (Neh. 6.10–14).

Nehemiah and the men of Jerusalem and Judah asserted themselves against all threats with remarkable tenacity. The building of the city wall was completed in the relatively short space of 52 days. Jerusalem was again fortified and able to defend itself, a city in the full sense. Nehemiah put it and its gates in the charge of a *śar habbīrā*, a 'city commandant',[7] as we might say. He gave orders for a close watch on the gates. Dangers remained and could not be ignored. The problem of mixed marriages had now taken on a difficult and dangerous aspect. The relationships involved in them encouraged contacts with the neighbouring peoples, provoked them and made them more difficult, and could not simply be ignored.

Nehemiah now turned to quite another problem. The city itself did not have enough inhabitants. It was great and wide, but few people lived in it and it did not even have enough buildings (Neh.7.4). Nehemiah ordained that a tenth part of the families in the country should move into Jerusalem. Where there were no volunteers, the decision was to be made by lot (7.4f.; 11.1f.). Similar resettlements also took place in ancient Greece, where they led to the rise of new city centres. In synoecism, as the Greek technical term goes, those involved learnt a new political unity. For Jerusalem this had one advantageous effect of some consequence. More than ever, the city and the land of Judah felt themselves to be a self-contained entity, linked also by administration and family ties, and this gradually reduced the old opposition between the country and the residence, the 'man of Jerusalem' and the 'man of Judah'.

The question is whether this internal organization which had proved necessary, this creation of an entirely new administrative structure for Jerusalem and Judah, lay within Nehemiah's original terms of reference. Probably it did not. Nehemiah will gradually have grown into, or been drawn into, the whole complex of problems confronting Jerusalem; in some cases further authority would be needed to carry on without arousing the suspicions of the central government. In Neh.5.14 Nehemiah is called 'governor' (*pehah*) in the land of Judah, and in 8.9 and 10.2 he even seems to bear an official Persian title (*hattiršātā'*). This information does not help us to determine Nehemiah's legal position, but they are an indication that he was not just an official in Jerusalem and Judah with short-term concerns. In Neh.5.14 his stay is dated from the twentieth to the thirty-second year of Artaxerxes, i.e. from 445 to 433. Nehemiah 13.6 can be regarded as confirmation of this; Nehemiah returned to the great king, but then came back again to Jerusalem to cope with the misdemeanours there.

Noth's view is that Nehemiah had held the position of governor of the province of Judah right from the beginning.[8] But is that probable? How can we understand the rivalry of Nehemiah's neighbours, above all that of Sanballat of Samaria, if he was in fact an official of the Persian central government with equal status? It is more probable that over the course of time, in view of his difficulties and also his success, he was given further powers and achieved a personal authority which later helped him to advance to the function and office of a governor, whether this designation was in fact officially conferred on him or merely ascribed to him.

Between the account of the completion of the building of the wall in Neh.7.1–5 and the synoecism and solemn consecration of the city wall in Neh.11 and 12 on the other, the extended account of a self-contained event has been inserted in Neh.8–10 which has Ezra rather than Nehemiah at its centre. In a great assembly of the people before the water gate in Jerusalem, Ezra reads 'the book of the law of Moses which Yahweh had given to Israel' (8.1). Ezra himself stands on a special wooden dais like a large pulpit, flanked by prominent representatives of the people on the right and on the left. By shouting 'Amen, Amen', the assembly takes a personal part in the reading. Finally, Nehemiah and the levites bring out and explain the meaning of this day: it is holy to Yahweh. The feast of tabernacles, itself accompanied by readings, is associated with the reading of the law. The feast lasts for seven days, and a final assembly takes place on the eighth. Nehemiah 9 reports a great act of penitence, a prayer of Ezra in which he lists Israel's past failings in some detail. An act of obligation follows in Neh. 10. By an oath the people present bind themselves to keep the law given through Moses. A list is given of those who set their seal to a special covenant document, with Nehemiah at their head. Special cultic regulations are summarized in Neh. 10.33–40. Nehemiah 13 reports further measures, though there is no obvious connection between them and the law read by Ezra in Neh. 8–10.

We can follow the tradition of events in the books of Ezra and Nehemiah thus far. Problems have already been hinted at, especially with regard to the arrangement of the material and the difficulties which stand in the way of an exact chronological reconstruction. The question is whether it seems advisable to understand individual traditions as independent actions and consider the possibility of a different sequence of events.

M. Noth consistently takes the second way in his *History of Israel*.[9] He puts Nehemiah before Ezra and believes that first Nehemiah had to see to the formation of a community in its outward form, after which Ezra was able to bring about an inward renewal by making the law binding.[10] Noth is not completely consistent in that on the one hand he regards the Aramaic instructions for Ezra in Ezra 7.12–26 as the only trustworthy Ezra tradition, whereas on the other hand he attaches considerable importance to the scene in Neh. 8–10, for all its indications of the work of the Chronicler, believing that it indicates the continuation and further internal development of the community of the people of Judah. On the one hand, then, Ezra 7 rates highly for credibility, while on the other the Ezra tradition in Neh. 8–10 with the Chronicler's influence is also greatly valued.

Granted, Noth also believes that the Artaxerxes mentioned in Ezra 7.12 must be identical with Artaxerxes I Longimanus and not with Artaxerxes II Mnemon (404–358 BC) or even Artaxerxes III Ochus (358–337). The essential actions in the reordering of the Jerusalem community cannot be put later than about the middle of the fifth century BC. Noth therefore regards it as certain that Nehemiah came to Jerusalem for the first time in 445. On the other hand, he sees the Ezra narrative as largely the work of the Chronicler; above all, the combination of Ezra and Nehemiah is to be attributed to him. Now the dating of the arrival of Ezra in Jerusalem in the seventh year of Artaxerxes I, that is in 458 BC, raises considerable difficulties, as it clearly supports an earlier appearance of Ezra. But Noth considers the dates given for Ezra to be unreliable and declares: 'It is not known why Ezra's mission was later placed in the 7th year of Artaxerxes' reign.' He then continues: 'But if the Aramaic Ezra document and the Chronicler's narrative place Ezra in the age of Artaxerxes (I) only in a general way, the question of his chronological relationship to Nehemiah still remains unsolved. It is true that we have the Chronicler's opinion that Ezra came to Jerusalem before Nehemiah; but again it can hardly be assumed that this opinion was based on a real tradition.'[11] For justification Noth goes back to a series of circumstantial considerations. The Chronicler put Ezra first because he considered his task to be more important. On the other hand, it must be noted that Nehemiah found a considerable state of disorder in Jerusalem, and therefore it is improbable that Ezra achieved anything with his law. But the degree to which the Chronicler has been involved in the redaction of the books of Ezra and Nehemiah is a very difficult question to answer, and even Noth stresses explicitly 'that it is impossible to reach an absolutely firm decision on this point because there is a lack of reliable and unambiguous evidence, and that all we can hope to attain is a limited degree of probability'.[12]

While one would not want to challenge the amount of editing that has been done to the books of Ezra and Nehemiah, in view of the general state of the text it would seem just as correct to say that the course of events in their present form is in principle the right one as to follow Noth in defending the chronological order which he considers probable. In other words, the activity of Ezra and Nehemiah may not have happened in a neat succession; it is highly probable that their work overlapped. Alt already assumed that in all probability Ezra's first measures were unsuccessful.[13] Ezra failed because he lacked the necessary powers of administration and organization. When he received his instructions, he may have had in mind no more than an inspection of conditions and a considerable lessening of abuses. From the beginning Nehemiah arrived with a more comprehensive brief and more comprehensive authority. In the end this also made Ezra's work easier.

It is necessary to make a final evaluation of the work of the two men.

It was the Babylonians who, after occupying Jerusalem in 587/6 BC, for the first time incorporated Judah into a provincial administration supervised by an empire. As heirs of the Babylonian kingdom, the Persians seem in essentials to have kept to the neo-Babylonian administrative units which had already been formed. This applied not least to Samaria, which was the seat of a governor. According to Neh. 3.1–32, in Nehemiah's time Judah must have been divided up further: the word *pelek* appears, which is connected with the Accadian *pilku*, 'district'. Such districts were formed round the cities of Jerusalem, Beth-zur (*ḥirbet eṭ-ṭubēqa*) in the more northerly environs of Hebron, and Keilah further to the west; Beth-herem (probably west of Jerusalem, if it is identical with *'ēn kārim*) and Mizpah. We may conclude from this that in Nehemiah's time the territory of Judah was very limited, and did not even reach as far as Hebron in the south or Bethel in the north. The territory he took over was even smaller than the former kingdom of Judah. At any rate, the south seems to have been lost to the Edomites as early as 587 and they maintained their hold on that territory.

This narrow territorial basis on which the new community rested, so closely linked to the name Jerusalem, is an evident explanation of the small number of people, even measured by families, who appear in the traditions of Ezra and Nehemiah; from it we can also understand why the people of the land needed a close connection with the city. On the other hand, in so restricted an area it was also possible to take in hand centrally such delicate questions as that of mixed marriages. Nehemiah seems to have been less anxious for divorces, but in the future he wanted marriages between the people of Judah and Ammonites or Moabites to be avoided (Neh. 13.23–27). Nehemiah also had to deal with the sanctuary, and found specific problems there. Some levites were unable to remain at the temple because there was not enough food, so they had left the sanctuary. Offerings were not made in adequate quantities. Nehemiah had to appoint his own commission to see to a more equitable distribution of the gifts coming into the sanctuary (Neh.13.10–14).

Individual priests were in sympathy with neighbouring countries and claimed rights of their own. The priest Eliashib, a kinsman of the hostile Ammonite Tobiah, had irregularly prepared accommodation for him in the temple precinct; Nehemiah had to reverse the arrangement (13.4–9). One high priest was even son-in-law of Sanballat of Samaria. Nehemiah reports briefly and tersely, 'I chased him from me' (Neh. 13.28). In this case Nehemiah was dealing with a mixed marriage which might even have had political consequences.

One of Nehemiah's further measures was his 'market order' (Neh. 13.15–23). It was connected with the observance of the sabbath commandment, which was acquiring increasing significance in the post-exilic period. Nehemiah discovered that work was being done on the sabbath; in particular, people from the countryside of Judah and fish merchants from Tyre were coming to Jerusalem and even offering their wares on the sabbath. Nehemiah simply had the gates of the city shut and guarded on that day. Nevertheless, all kinds of people remained in front of the city wall and seem to have staged some kind of demonstration. Nehemiah warned them not to return on the sabbath.

These occurrences and individual measures shed some light on the complex picture of the time; it was these everyday details in particular which needed careful regulation. In a decisive way, Ezra and Nehemiah must have consolidated conditions in Jerusalem and Judah after the exile for generations to come. Not least of their measures was the reading of the law by Ezra. If one does not exaggerate this event and sees it in the narrow context of the new community, then Ezra's solemn reading was a renewed acceptance of the obligations of tradition, an attempt to regulate not only the cult but also the forms of community life in the widest sense by the law legitimated by Yahweh. What the detailed contents of Ezra's reading may have been is a piquant question, but no satisfactory solution is possible. We might think of the smaller collections of law which are recorded in the Pentateuch, the 'Holiness Code' (Lev. 17–26) or even parts of earlier law like the Decalogue and the Book of the Covenant (Exod. 20–23); it hardly consisted of purely cultic laws like Lev. 1–7, but will have comprised texts which were also concerned with individual conduct.

It was inevitable that Ezra should be seen not only as a man who preserved and furthered the use of the Israelite books of the law but also as author or at least redactor of Pentateuchal writings. It is worth mentioning in passing that no less a person than Spinoza, in his *Tractatus theologico-politicus* of 1670, chs. 7 and 8, developed a literary theory of his own which he associated with Ezra. In his view the whole of the Pentateuch, along with the books following it, as far as II Kings, was a great historical work composed by Ezra himself. Ezra, Spinoza argued, used a variety of sources, but at the same time worked them over, accommodating them to the needs of his time. Spinoza's theory is worth consideration, because it is in fact a possibility that post-exilic tradition and post-exilic interests were determinative in the selection of part of the Pentateuchal tradition, within the source which is normally known as the Priestly writing. Understandably, however, it is no longer possible to ascertain Ezra's share in this literary activity.

It is certainly the case that the activity of Ezra and Nehemiah should be seen against a complex background in which a number of interests conflict with each other.[14] Tensions within the community of Jerusalem/Judah were the consequence of decades of attempts at self-determination both internally and over against the neighbouring populations; without a competent authority in command, there were rivalries and disputes which made it difficult for Nehemiah to achieve the twin tasks of fortifying the city and improving the organization of the province. In the end, it was inevitable that he should also have intervened in the laws of the city and the countryside, just as he tried to exercise a determinative influence on the concerns of the sanctuary and its officials, the priests and levites. The tradition about these tensions offers hints rather than detailed descriptions and accounts of their causes, but it cannot wipe out the permanent achievement of Nehemiah's independent personality, alongside which the work of Ezra became possible. Unfortunately there is no evidence to indicate whether Nehemiah was recalled after twelve years (Neh. 5.14) because together with a group of people he was steering too radical a course, which did not contribute to peace within the city and probably lost him the favour of the great king.[15] We cannot assert with any certainty that in the end his work 'came to grief in a tragic way because his own party was overstretched and the theocratic ruling class resisted the political emancipation effected by the Diaspora'.[16] In the course of time, tradition saw him in another light and valued his work in another way. It was right that this should happen. The results of the limited activity of Ezra and Nehemiah tower far above the rest of the period of Persian rule over Palestine, for which the sources elsewhere are so poor. Nehemiah had given Judah a new administrative order and had built up and fortified Jerusalem, albeit in a modest way;[17] furthermore, in conjunction with the work of Ezra he had promulgated a legislation on which more could be constructed. It remains a matter for regret that the scanty accounts do not allow us to see the immediate effects of this brief period. So in the end the work of Ezra and

Nehemiah lies in a brief patch of light during a long process in which Jerusalem and Judah, now shrunk to a tiny compass, had to find new life amidst the tensions of the world around them. Thanks to their leading men, however, the tradition did not collapse; in the end it gave a foundation for this small community and guaranteed it a way of life.

NOTES

1. Ezra 9; 10; Neh. 6.18; 10.31; 13.4ff.; 13.23f.

2. Some titles from the extensive literature are: E. Meyer, *Die Enstehung des Judentums*, 1896 (reprinted 1965); C. C. Torrey, *The Composition and Historical Value of Ezra-Nehemiah*, BZAW 2, 1896; id., *Ezra Studies*, 1910; S. Mowinckel, *Ezra den skriftlaerde*, 1916; id., *Stattholderen Nehemia*, 1916; W. F. Albright, 'The Date and Personality of the Chronicler', *JBL* 40, 1921, 104–24; G. Hölscher, *Die Bücher Esra und Nehemia*, HSAT II, ⁴1923, 491–562; M. Haller, *Das Judentum*, SAT II, 3², 1925; M. Noth, *Überlieferungsgeschichtliche Studien*, 1943 (²1957), 110–80; A. Kapelrud, *The Question of the Authorship in the Ezra Narrative, A Lexical Investigation*, 1944; W. F. Albright, 'A Brief History of Judah from the Days of Josiah to Alexander the Great', *BA* 9, 1946, 1–16; W. Rudolph, *Esra und Nehemiah*, HAT 20, 1949; H. H. Rowley, 'The Chronological Order of Ezra and Nehemiah', in *The Servant of the Lord and Other Essays on the Old Testament*, 1952, 129ff.; H. Cazelles, 'La mission d'Esdras', *VT* 4, 1954, 113–40; K. Galling, *Die Bücher Chronik, Esra, Nehemia*, ATD 12, 1958; S. Mowinckel, ' "Ich und" "Er" in der Ezrageschichte', in *Verbannung und Heimkehr* (Festschrift W. Rudolph), 1961, 211–33; id., *Studien zu dem Buche Ezra-Nehemiah* I, II, 1964; III, 1965; K. Galling, *Studien zur Geschichte Israels im persischen Zeitalter*, 1964; U. Kellermann, *Nehemia. Quellen, Überlieferung und Geschichte*, BZAW 102, 1967 (see the more detailed bibliography of literature on Nehemiah there, 205–19); id., 'Erwägungen zum Problem der Esradatierung', *ZAW* 80, 1968, 55–87; 'Erwägungen zum Esragesetz', ibid., 373–85; id., *Messias und Gesetz*, Biblische Studien 61, 1971.

3. Assuming that the reference is in fact to Artaxerxes I Longimanus and that this date can be trusted.

4. For details see H. H. Schaeder, *Esra der Schreiber*, 1930.

5. The rise of prominent Jews in court circles may have a historical basis and may have occurred now and then. The narratives of the experiences of these men have certainly been elaborated at a later date. The figure of Daniel and his men in Dan. 1–6 is further evidence of this literary theme; these stories are more involved in didactic material than is the case with Nehemiah.

6. For details see A. Alt, 'Das Taltor von Jerusalem', *KS* III, 326–47, esp. 340–7; cf. the different view of J. Simons, *Jerusalem in the Old Testament*, 1952, 437ff.

7. Earlier called a 'captain of the fortress'; so too Noth, *History of Israel*, ²1960, 324.

8. With reference to the summary remark in Neh. 5.14; Noth, *History of Israel*, 321.

9. Noth, op. cit., 316–37.

10. A van Hoonacker, 'Néhémie et Esdras, une nouvelle hypothèse sur la chronologie de l'époque de la restauration', *Le Muséon* 9, 1890, 151–84, 317–51, 389–401, was the first to attempt to demonstrate at length that Ezra only came to Jerusalem after Nehemiah, under Artaxerxes II. In his *Geschichte des Volkes Israel*, ³1914, 292, H. Guthe tended to the view that Ezra arrived during the period of Nehemiah's second stay in Jerusalem, i.e. not until after 433 BC; on the presupposition that Ezra 7.7 refers to the seventh year of Artaxerxes II, Galling supposes that Ezra mission lasted from 400 to 397, *Studien*, 158–61.

11. Noth, *History*, 320.

12. Noth, *History*, 320.

13. Thus Alt in his lecture 'Geschichte des Volkes Israel in der Spätzeit' (my lecture notes from the summer semester of 1948). He regarded the year 444 BC (the year after Nehemiah's arrival in Jerusalem) as the year of the birth of a Jewish sense of community in and around Jerusalem. Similarly H. Guthe, *Geschichte*, 293, though he did not put the decisive year for the 'formation of the post-exilic Jewish community' until 430. R. Kittel, *Geschichte des Volkes Israel* 3, 2, 1929, 607f. makes Ezra fail before Nehemiah even appears on the scene.

14. U. Kellermann, *Nehemiah*, BZAW 102, 1967, especially the historical outline, 192–204. One must be sceptical about the assurance with which Kellermann makes assertions about parties and tendencies during the time of Nehemiah and in particular seeks to draw a distinction between a Zionistic/pro-Hasmonean line of tradition, which bears witness to a picture of Nehemiah after the pattern of Zerubbabel, and another line of tradition which starts from the theology of the Chronicler and presents Nehemiah as no more than a Persian official with responsibility for supervising the building of the walls, who 'had no significance for the real concerns of the cultic community' (op. cit., 174f.). It must remain a hypothesis that Nehemiah was descended from a branch of the house of David, though Kellermann is convinced of this (op. cit., 158, 182). Statements like this must be equally hypothetical: 'We must therefore suppose that Nehemiah fell victim to a controversy between Zionism and theocracy' (op. cit., 190).

15. Kellermann, op. cit., 203.

16. Kellermann, op. cit., 203f.

17. For the archaeological evidence following the excavations in the sixties see K. M. Kenyon, *Jerusalem – Excavating 3000 Years of History*, 1967, 108–12; see also id., *Archaeology in the Holy Land*, ²1965, 299f.

4 | The Second Half of the Persian Period and the Emergence of the Greeks in the Near East

WE HAVE VIRTUALLY no Old Testament sources which inform us about external conditions in Jerusalem and Judah for the period from the activity of Ezra and Nehemiah about the middle of the fifth century BC down to the Seleucid king Antiochus IV Epiphanes (175–164 BC). On the presupposition that the prophetic canon of the Old Testament was only closed in the third century BC,[1] there is at least the possibility that some passages in the prophetic books refer to prominent events in these centuries, insofar as they also affected Judaea and Samaria. This includes the expedition of Alexander the Great and his armies, which passed through Syria on their way to Egypt. However, they chiefly used the coastal plain and seem to have carried out only limited operations in the hill-country of the interior.[2] Finally, however, there is a high degree of probability that in the century of Persian rule following Ezra and Nehemiah, and before the Samaritans split off to become an independent community, not only was the Pentateuch given its final form in Jerusalem but at the same time the ground must have been laid for the complicated system of cultic ordinances and measures which have been recorded in the books of Chronicles.[3] Regretfully, many details in the text of Chronicles are very obscure. We know too little about the occasion for the various ordinances and their more immediate circumstances. Often cultic practice and theoretical requirements may stand cheek by jowl. According to the view of Chronicles, the institution and function of the priestly classes and the Levites in the Jerusalem temple were established and laid down once for all at the time of David. The king himself outlined the model for the sanctuary (I Chron.28.11–21), and Solomon was entrusted with carrying out the plan. Chronicles unfolds the history of Judah, but does so in such a way that contemporary claims and needs are set out in classic form and are made to seem the earliest tradition. The author has incorporated very different sources. He knew the Deuteronomistic history work (Joshua to II Kings), but left out all the parts of it that related to the northern kingdom of Israel. He replaced the early period of Israel with outline lists relating to the tribes and their composition, beginning his historical account only at the death of Saul (I Chron.10). The focal point is formed by David and the kings of Judah.[4]

All this means that Chronicles understands Jerusalem and its temple as the historical and cultic centre of Israel, and provides legitimation for them. The rebuilding of the temple after the exile and the work of Ezra and Nehemiah had provided the presuppositions for such an understanding. As far as we can discover, from the time of Josiah the sanctuaries outside Jerusalem, at least in the territory of Judah, had ceased to function. There was not the personnel for them to do so. These places of worship were not restored in the post-exilic period, not least because of the demands of Deuteronomy for centralization. This approach had now gained unqualified acceptance. Jerusalem was to remain the one legitimate place of worship in Israel. The central Persian government had allowed the rebuilding of the temple; thus it was an authorized and privileged sanctuary. Its monopolistic position seemed unassailable. Nevertheless, from the time of Ezra and Nehemiah and probably even earlier, rivalry had broken out between Jerusalem and Samaria, so that the old northern kingdom was standing out against its southern neighbours. Tendencies towards independence and cultic autonomy in the former Assyrian provinces of Megiddo and Samaria must have grown, especially after the time of Nehemiah, when Judah's position also seemed politically more established. Megiddo and Samaria may have continued as hyparchies under the Persians,[5] whereas Judah only formed an independent hyparchy with its own rights following the measures of Nehemiah.[6] The separation of Samaria from Jerusalem, which finally came about in the so-called 'Samaritan schism', the formation of an autonomous Samaritan cultic community, probably even before the arrival of Alexander the Great in Syria, was the inevitable result of a development which had been a long time in the making. We may only conjecture that it was launched by individual Samaritan figures, who pursued their policy zealously; the sources do not provide us with the exact means for proof.

National and political circumstances in the Persian empire form the framework of these developments in Judaea and Samaria. The Old Testament does not provide us with any information, but we are in a position to draw some conclusions about conditions in Judaea and Samaria, as in Syria, from non-Israelite sources. To provide a chronological framework for events, here is a list of the Persian kings with the dates of their reigns:

Cyrus II	558–530	Sogdianus	424
Cambyses	530–522	Darius II Nothus	424–405
Gaumata	522	Artaxerxes II Mnemon	404–358
Darius I	522–486	Artaxerxes III Ochus	358–337
Xerxes I	486–465	Arses	338–336
Artaxerxes I Longimanus	465–424	Darius III Codomannus	336–331
Xerxes II	424		

As a parallel to this it is useful to know that some of these rulers appear in the role of Pharaohs of Egypt.[7] The Twenty-Seventh Dynasty is made up of 'eight Persian kings', from Cambyses to Darius II. An Artabanus is inserted after Xerxes I, but he never ruled. Xerxes II and Sogdianus fell victims to disputes over the throne and therefore are insignificant.

During this period the Egyptians often rebelled against the Persians. After earlier attempts had failed,[8] towards the end of the fifth century Amyrtaeus of Sais succeeded in ruling for six years,[9] while Artaxerxes II was entangled in disputes with his brother Cyrus. Amyrtaeus of Sais is the sole representative of the 'Twenty-eighth Dynasty' (404–399). Those who led rebellions in Egypt had neither worked-out plans nor unanimity. They fought for power. Amyrtaeus was followed by four kings who formed the Twenty-ninth Dynasty and together reigned for about twenty years (399–380), substantially supported by alliances with Athens and Sparta. These four kings (Nepherites I, Psammuthis, Achoris and Nepherites II) came from Mendes in the Delta.

They were followed by the Thirtieth Dynasty with three kings from Sebennytus. Their first ruler, Nectanebes I (380–363), succeeded in carrying through an economic reorganization of the country and handed on the rule to his son Teos (Tachos). During his short reign (362–361), Teos raised a considerable army with the help of Greek mercenaries and advanced on Syria with it.[10] However, his nephew, with many followers, left him and became Nectanebes II (360–343), the last ruler at the end of the thirty illustrious Egyptian dynasties. Teos himself fled to the Persians. In 343, Artaxerxes III Ochus again succeeded in bringing Egypt firmly under Persian control. In the Christian period the names of the last three kings of Persia, Artaxerxes III, Arses and Darius III were added to Manetho's list of kings as the Thirty-first Dynasty. In 332 Alexander the Great conquered Egypt.

Thus the last Egyptian dynasties together form the following pattern:

Twenty-seventh Dynasty	The 'eight Persian kings'.	
	Cambyses	525–522
	Darius I	522–486
	Xerxes I	486–465
	Artabanus	—
	Artaxerxes I	465–424
	Xerxes II	424
	Sogdianus	424
	Darius II	424–405
Twenty-eighth Dynasty	Amyrtaeus of Sais	404–399
Twenty-ninth Dynasty	'Four kings of Mendes':	
	Nepherites I	399–393
	Psammuthis	393
	Achoris	393–380
	Nepherites II	380
Thirtieth Dynasty	'Three kings from Sebennytus':	
	Nectanebes I	380–363

	Teos (Tachos)	362–361
	Nectanebes II	360–343
Thirty-first Dynasty	Artaxerxes III Ochus	343–337
	Arses	337–336
	Darius III Codomannus	336–332

Within this chronological framework we can now put events and documents which shed at least some light on the Jewish communities and their fates both inside and outside the homeland. First, mention should be made here of the so-called Elephantine papyri, a collection of manuscripts written in Aramaic, which were found as fragments in the ruins on the island of Elephantine (Aramaic, *Jēb*, Egyptian '*bw*), in the Nile near Asswan in Upper Egypt. The bulk of the texts came to light in the systematic excavations carried out there in the years 1906–8.[11] In Elephantine[12] there was what is usually called a 'Jewish military colony', where Jewish mercenaries were encamped, along with troops of other nationalities posted there in the Persian period, probably to protect the southern frontier of Egypt. However, these people in the south of Egypt did not lead an isolated life, cut off from their homeland. They kept in touch with other Jewish groups in Egypt and even turned to Jerusalem and Samaria over cultic matters, to seek information and permission from the governors and leading figures. This makes the question of the significance and origin of this Jewish group an interesting one.

In all probability the Persians found this colony already established. There are indications that at the earliest from the seventh century, and certainly from the sixth century, people from Israel and Judah went abroad, partly under compulsion and partly voluntarily, as a consequence of the Assyrian and Babylonian occupation of the country. The law of the king in Deut.17.16 speaks of exchanging men for horses from Egypt. We cannot rule out the possibility that people already went from Israel to Egypt as soldiers on such deliveries. And after 586, it is possible that men from Judah not only remained in Lower Egypt, like Jeremiah and his group, but finally came to live dispersed over the whole of Egyptian territory.

The writings from Elephantine are dated. The earliest date is the twenty-seventh year of Darius I, i.e. 495 BC; the latest has been calculated as 1 October 399. The content of the documents is very varied. The bulk of them are private contracts, for marriage, the transfer of property, loans, the liberation of slaves. From various indications in the papyri it has been calculated that by the year 420/19 the group amounted to about 350 people, including women and children. The most interesting documents are those which report on the worship of the community and give some indication of the fortunes of particular people.

The group had its own temple, the temple of Yahu (*yāhū*), 'the God in the fortress of *Jēb*', 'the Lord of heaven'.[13] It is beyond question that this was a temple of Yahweh.[14] It was destroyed about 410 BC at the prompting of Egyptian priests, with the collusion of the local governor; evidently they took advantage of the temporary absence of the satrap responsible for the area.[15] However, it was possible for the temple to be rebuilt a little later.[16] The details of these events emerge from a lengthy petition in which the governor Bagohi (Bagoas) in Jerusalem is asked for permission and support for the rebuilding.[17] The Jews from Elephantine point out that Cambyses found the temple already established when he invaded Egypt. The temples of Egyptian gods were without exception torn down, but not this Jewish temple. Perhaps it was this preference for the Jews which annoyed the Egyptians and led to the destruction of the strange house of God; the Jews in Elephantine were regarded as privileged, not least because they were in the service of the Persians. However, they themselves did not feel independent and sovereign in all matters. In cultic matters at any rate, not only did they think it necessary to make enquiries in Jerusalem; they look for consent and permission from there – and not just from there. For at the end of their petition to Bagohi the authors remark: 'We have also communicated the entire matter in a letter in our names to Delaiah and Shelemiah, the sons of Sinuballit, the governor of Samaria.'

This opens up an interesting prospect. In all probability Sinuballit is identical with the Sanballat of the book of Nehemiah, who there appears as a harsh opponent of all the undertakings in Jerusalem. Now his sons are in power and the Jews of Elephantine also turn to them, without seeming to be aware of the tensions that exist between Jerusalem and Samaria. They evidently believed the matter to be in the competence of the officials in Samaria. At any rate, there was an agreement between Bagohi and Delaiah, which was put down in writing and sent to the Egyptian satrap Aršam.[18] The rebuilding of the temple was sanctioned, and so was the cult in its previous form. However, there is mention only of food offerings and incense offerings, and not of burnt-offerings and sacrifices; the two last were probably limited to Jerusalem. This situation is interesting not only for the relationship between the Diaspora and the mother country, but also because it confirms that towards the end of the fifth century it was still possible to arrange negotiations between Samaria and Jerusalem, specifically on cultic matters.

There is another document which is comparable with the character of this decision. Already in 419 BC, Darius II had allowed the Jews of Elephantine to celebrate the feast of unleavened bread.[19] As is well known, this feast is the second half of the passover. According to Ex.12, eating the unleavened bread was preceded by the killing of the passover lamb, a sacrifice which the Jews of the Diaspora were evidently not allowed to perform. The right of offering sacrifices involving blood was restricted to the sanctuary at Jerusalem. Here we have evidence of the binding character of the conception, taken over from Deuteronomy, of the central place for worship and sacrifice, which in the post-exilic period was now also extended to the Diaspora. The passover lamb could only be killed in Jerusalem.

The end of the military colony in Elephantine is obscure. The last document comes from the year 399 in which Amyrtaeus of Sais was replaced by the rulers of the Twenty-ninth Dynasty. It is a matter of pure conjecture whether these events within Egypt led to the abolition or transfer of the military colony. In the end, did it fall victim to further attacks?[20]

Resistance against the Persians became more vigorous in Egypt; Syria became the front line for Persian campaigns against Egypt, and was also the scene of numerous attacks against Persia. The Egyptian kings of the Twenty-ninth and Thirtieth Dynasties, who had achieved some degree of independence, attempted to meet the Persians there and weaken their military strength. They succeeded in doing so for a limited time, but ultimately without any decisive success. After the failure of the attempt of Artaxerxes II Mnemon in the years 389 to 387 to bring Egypt once again firmly under Persian control, from 380 onwards the Persians began to take extensive precautionary measures. Pharnabazus, one of their supreme commanders, assembled an army at Acco; however, no attack was launched against Egypt until 374, and then it failed. The campaign had to be broken off. The Egyptian king Teos (Tachos) achieved by far the most considerable success in 361 when he in fact seized the southern coast of Syria; however, he was so weakened by the defection of his nephew Nectanebes that he sought refuge with the Persians. The fact that this nephew became his successor, under the name of Nectanebes II, may possibly be connected with support from the later Artaxerxes III Ochus (358–337). However, the latter felt compelled to launch a new offensive against Egypt in 353, the failure of which incited the Phoenician cities to rebellion, in particular Sidon in 351. The not inconsiderable success of these revolts led Ochus to engage in a campaign against Syria in 348. Sidon fell through the treachery of its own king Tennes, and the rest of the Phoenician cities submitted voluntarily. The way to Egypt again seemed open for the Persians. However, their advance in 346 came to a standstill even before they reached the Nile Delta. The Sirbonian sea, at one time probably the scene of the miracle connected with the exodus of the Israelite tribes from Egypt, again showed how dangerous it could be. A large part of the Persian host perished there. Ochus finally succeeded in subjecting Egypt only in 343.

Did these conflicts pass over the Jews in Samaria and Judah without leaving any trace? Were there also anti-Persian activities among them? This possibility cannot be excluded. We have indications of it. However, the few literary indications and the archaeological evidence do not allow us to make any reliable detailed interpretation. The capture and the destruction of the city of Jericho, where Jews had gathered and rebelled against the Persians, can be seen in connection with the second expedition made by Ochus against Egypt in 353. That was even connected with the deportation of Jews to Babylonia and Hyrcania on the Caspian Sea.[21] These reports in later writers are based on earlier sources which are unknown to us,[22] but they have recently been connected with the rebellion of Phoenician coastal cities, in particular that of the city of Sidon in 351. It has been conjectured[23] that round about the middle of the fourth century BC, Judah, and also Samaria and Galilee, was drawn into the rebel movement against Persia; this would explain a series of indications of destructions of which there is archaeological evidence in

Hazor, Megiddo, Atlit, Lachish and Jericho.[24] However, the notion of so wide-spread a rebellion must remain pure conjecture, and the destruction mentioned may be connected with local events, for each of which there were different reasons.[25]

With some justification, in recent times there has been particular interest in the question of administration in Judah and Samaria during the Persian period. More than an assessment of the activity of Ezra and Nehemiah depends on the answer to this question. There must have been some reason for the vigorous and apparently irreconcilable differences between Jerusalem and Samaria, and the cause for them must be sought not least in issues related to local politics and questions of legal administration. The deportation of the majority of the population of the old northern state of Israel by the Assyrians, and the settlement there of new non-Israelite groups (II Kings 17.24), certainly contributed towards emphasizing the opposition between the inhabitants of the old northern state and Judah.[26] The Assyrian provincial divisions were largely taken over by the Babylonians, and were not changed in principle by the Persians. However, when Jerusalem and Judah fell to the Babylonians, the capital was in ruins, and Gedaliah ruled as governor in Mizpah, it was obvious that under Persian supremacy the real provincial capital of this region could not be Jerusalem, far less the insignificant Mizpah. Judah along with Jerusalem was added as a sub-district to the Persian province, which was controlled from Samaria. However, when the people of Jerusalem received permission from Cyrus, after the exile, to rebuild the temple, and with this boost to their identity in fact began the work, a conflict ensued. By virtue of its position as capital of the province, Samaria sought to influence what was going on in Jerusalem, but came up against resolute resistance. Jerusalem insisted on original and exclusive rights when it came to the building of the temple. The people of Samaria were to be excluded from its reconstruction. There was an irresolvable conflict between cultic rights in Jerusalem and the administrative role of Samaria.

It has long been argued that a change set in with Nehemiah.[27] He describes himself as the governor 'in the land of Judah' (Neh.5.14), appointed by the great king.[28] Thus the far-ranging powers with which Nehemiah came to Jerusalem must finally have led to the political independence of Jerusalem and Judah, that is, within the framework of existing possibilities, giving Judah the status of an independent province. We may see confirmation of this new status in those coins and jar handles which have meanwhile been found in large numbers and which bear the names *yhd*, 'Judah', or *yršlm*, 'Jerusalem', and indeed even 'Judah – the governor': they are chiefly to be dated to the fourth century.[29] They bear witness to the status of Judah as an independent province, evidently with the right to mint its own coins. After its political status was defined, the situation of rivalry between Jerusalem and Samaria seems gradually to have been relaxed, as is evident from the reaction to the enquiry from the Jews at Elephantine in 408 BC. The governors of Samaria and Jerusalem, to whom the enquiry was made, could agree without any obvious difficulties.[30]

The extent of the territory of Judah must of course have remained unchanged down to the end of the Persian period. There is no indication that the districts of the time of Nehemiah, already mentioned,[31] were abolished or changed.[32] Thus the frontier in the south continued to run between Beth-zur and Hebron, while in the north Mizpah and Bethel still formed part of Judah, as did Jericho in the east and Keilah in the west. The situation was different with Lachish, where not insignificant remains of a Persian palace (end of the fifth or beginning of the fourth century) were found.[33] Lachish, once one of the significant Judaean fortresses in western Judah, was now part of the province of Edom and was one of its administrative centres, if not the seat of a Persian governor.[34]

However, we must return to the situation in Jerusalem–Judah and in Samaria. With the elevation of Judah to be an independent province, Samaria lost all possibility of exerting political influence on Jerusalem, but the question of the cultic significance of Jerusalem and its temple remained open. The question of cultic independence for the Samaritan community was therefore only a matter of time; it was inevitable, given the political independence of Jerusalem. Contrary to many earlier assumptions, it probably did not come about only in connection with the arrival of Alexander the Great; as far as we can see it was in the making from the time of Nehemiah on. The transition of rule from the Persians to the Greeks simply seems to have sealed the division.[35]

In fact the preparation for this so-called 'Samaritan schism', ending with the building of the Samaritans' own temple on Mount Gerizim south of Shechem, seems to be connected with developments which can be ascertained with only relative probability from very different sources. In the book of Nehemiah, Neh.13.28 is particularly crucial. There it is reported that Manasseh, the son of the high priest Jehoiada, married a daughter of Sanballat (I) and was therefore exiled from Jerusalem. This was regarded as a mixed marriage; at the same time, however, there may have been an underlying fear that this marriage might make Samaria's claims on the privileges of Jerusalem unavoidable.

The account by Josephus in *Antt.* XI, 8 (304ff.) is much more detailed at this point. He divides up personal happenings among the leading families without concern for chronological possibilities, and in this way produces a single dramatic story. Sanballat (I) promises Manasseh, who is exiled at the time of Nehemiah, that a sanctuary will be built on Gerizim. This same Sanballat is said to have asked Alexander the Great for permission to build this temple, since he hastened to his aid at the siege of Tyre. In fact the Sanballat here must have been Sanballat III, and not the governor of the same name who lived a hundred years earlier. In that case, however, it is quite impossible that the offer should have been made to Manasseh. What does remain historically conceivable is that the masters of Samaria sought official sanction from the Greeks for their own cult. However, that does give us more certain information about the history of the origin of this cult. Recently it has been supposed that the exiling of Manasseh in Neh.13.28 is just one instance among many, and that whole groups of priests must have left Jerusalem, whether they wanted to or not. They will have gone to

Shechem and founded the Gerizim cult there. Of course this is only a hypothesis, and there is no certain evidence.[36]

Because it is so difficult to shed light on conditions, the discovery of new sources is extremely important. The so-called 'Samaria Papyri' from the fourth century BC, discovered in 1962, make it possible to confirm and to complete the list of governors of Samaria.[37] This in turn allows a revision of the list of contemporaneous high priests of Jerusalem, which had been constructed at an earlier stage.

The reconstruction of the Samaritan list made and put forward by F. M. Cross is based on the hypothesis that the governor was named on the principle of papponymy, i.e. that each son was given the name of his grandfather. A Sanballat was followed by Delaiah, who was followed by a further Sanballat; then came son X and, following him, another Sanballat. The gap between the second and third Sanballat can be filled at the result of a discovery of a papyrus with the name Hananiah.[38] On this presupposition the list of governors of Samaria put forward by Cross runs as follows (conjectured years of birth have been added in each case):[39]

Sanballat I	*c.* 485 BC
Delaiah	*c.* 460 BC
Sanballat II	*c.* 435 BC
Hananiah	*c.* 410 BC
Sanballat III	*c.* 385 BC

Comparison of this list with contemporary people and events which are already known to us confirms that in principle it can be used. Sanballat I will have been the contemporary of Nehemiah; Delaiah will have been the governor mentioned in the Elephantine papyri; Sanballat III, the contemporary of Alexander the Great. To this extent we now seem to be able to speak with some certainty.

Cross has similarly attempted to enlarge the list of Jerusalem high priests, reconstructed earlier,[40] following the same principle of papponomy, but here, although he has indicated other parallels outside Jerusalem,[41] we seem to be on very hypothetical ground.[42] Here is a list with the supposed dates of birth (the individuals added by Cross are in brackets):

Cross:	*Guthe:*
1. Jehozadak, before 587	
2. Jeshua, *c.* 570	Joshua ben Jehozadak, Hag.1.1
3. Jehoiakim, *c.* 545	Jehoiakim ben Joshua, Neh.12.10f.
[3. Eliashib I, *c.* 545, brother of the former]	
[4. Johanan I, *c.* 520]	
5. Eliashib II, *c.* 495	Eliashib ben Jehoiakim, Neh.3.1
6. Jehoiada I, *c.* 470	Jehoiada ben Eliashib, Neh.13.28 (?)

7. Johanan II, *c.* 445	Johanan (Neh.12.22) ben Jehoiada, according to the Elephantine papyri under Darius II (424–405); according to the erroneous information in Josephus, *Antt*.XI, 7.1 (297) under Artaxerxes III
8. Jaddua II, *c.* 420	Jaddua ben Johanan, according to Josephus, *Antt*.XI, 8.2–5, 7 (306–39, 346) Alexander the Great, but to be dated earlier
[9. Johanan III, *c.* 395]	
[10. Jaddua III, *c.* 370]	
11. Onias I, *c.* 345	Onias I, son of Jaddua, Josephus, *Antt*.XI, 8.7 (347)
12. Simon I, *c.* 320	Simon I, the Just (*c.* 250), Josephus, *Antt*. XII, 2.5 (43)

If we compare the material given here and connect it with the account in the book of Nehemiah, the Elephantine papyri and finally also the dramatized and abbreviated account in Josephus, despite all the difficulties over detail we have at least some criteria for an approximately appropriate chronological framework in which above all we can put the gradual preparation of the 'Samaritan schism', and not least the final break in the time of Alexander.

I have already said that caution should be exercised in reading Josephus' report of the appearance of Alexander in Syria and the neighbouring countries to the south.[43] The account is closely bound up with the ambitions of Sanballat of Samaria and finally comes to a climax with the appearance of the Macedonian king in Jerusalem. However, the Old Testament knows nothing of such a visit to Jerusalem by Alexander. Its historicity is doubted. Generally speaking, the following features should be regarded as reliable: after his victory over Darius III Codomannus at Issos in the extreme north-west corner of Syria in 333 BC, Alexander turned west along the coast with the intention of reaching Egypt. For seven months he is said to have laid siege to Tyre, the city built on an island off the Phoenician coast. Eventually he took the city after constructing a causeway from the mainland (which is still in existence today, though considerably extended in the meantime), which gave him access to it. There was again resistance at Gaza; the siege lasted two months. Then his route lay open through the wilderness of Sinai direct to Egypt. This course of action is understandable. The king went through the coastal plain and did not bother with the interior, which he left to his general Parmenio. Parmenio took Samaria by force, but possibly Jerusalem surrendered of its own accord.

Josephus has a different account, which goes further. According to him, immediately after taking Gaza Alexander turned towards Jerusalem (going northwards again!), and there received the homage of the high priest (Jaddua) who came out to meet him. (To put it more precisely, Alexander went to pay homage to the high priest, the God of Israel and the temple.) Sanballat, on the contrary, died suddenly after the capture of Gaza. According to a report in Q. Curtius Rufus,[44] the Samaritans burned alive their prefect Andromachus, who had been appointed by the Macedonians. Thereupon Alexander returned from Egypt and appointed Meno.[45] Furthermore, the Samaritans are said to have been punished by the introduction of a Macedonian settlement under the leadership of Perdiccas.

These accounts suggest that because Samaria put up considerable resistance against Greek occupation, it was spared less than Jerusalem, which was more amenable. Further developments seem to confirm this. Samaria became a Hellenistic city. The centre for those Samaritans who remained faithful to the Law was transferred to Shechem. There is even possible archaeological evidence of this: it seems that from 330 BC new efforts were made to reconstruct the city of Shechem.[46] This may also have been the time when the community which was gathering in Shechem built itself the sanctuary on Gerizim. Possibly the remains of a Samaritan temple found at *tell er-rās*, by Gerizim, also belong to this early period.[47] No temple from Hellenistic times was found in Shechem itself. The central importance which accrued to Shechem in this way is also reflected by Josephus.[48]

The Samaritans took over the Pentateuch as their holy scripture; it was probably the part of the Old Testament canon which had been completed at this time. In a remarkable way the Samaritan community has remained in existence down the ages until the present, though of course its numbers are limited and it is essentially confined to the area of Shechem, modern Nablus.[49]

The version of the Samaritan Pentateuch in a manuscript discovered in Damascus in 1616 is still important for Old Testament criticism. This manuscript differs from the Massoretic text in 6000 instances, though most merely concern orthographic details. In 1900 cases, however, the text agrees with the Greek translation against the Massoretic text. Thus the Samaritan Pentateuch is a very early witness to the text, which cannot be dependent on our Massoretic text. Its influence can be traced not only in the Greek version of the Septuagint but also in individual readings in the Qumran text, the New Testament and in Jewish texts which were not edited in line with the Massoretic text.[50]

It is not easy to produce a summary picture of conditions in the second half of the Persian period, not only in the community centred upon Jerusalem but also as they may have developed in the Diaspora, which was growing all the time. In the time of the Maccabees, i.e. in the second half of the second century BC, there was a considerable Jewish Diaspora in Galilee and in Transjordan. It is improbable that these groups were formed there only in Hellenistic times; their beginnings may go back to the Persian period. Indirect confirmation of this may be provided by accounts in Chronicles which presuppose relations between the community in Jerusalem and Galilean groups, and people from Asher, Manasseh and Zebulon (cf. II Chron.30; 15.9–15). At all events, it is interesting that in these texts we find the term *nērîm*, the 'strangers', and that Jewish belief is also accepted by those who were not originally Jews. This could mean that this Diaspora gradually grew from small beginnings. Circumstances in the Persian period may not have hindered such a growth.

Generally speaking, the judgment of Hermann Guthe, that 'the time between Nehemiah and Alexander the Great was a time of growth for the Jewish people', is true.[51] This was connected with their establishment and consolidation, with. the development and final fixation of historical and cultic traditions. This must have been the time in which the Pentateuch received its final form. Many of the ordinances fixed in the so-called 'Priestly Writing', the last stratum of the Pentateuch, were recognized in the Persian period as valid law. The practice of the cult became increasingly significant. So too did the conviction that membership of the community of the Jewish people could not primarily be linked with political and administrative ordinances, but had to be related to a general cultic law; it was this that created the real 'community' (*qāhāl*).[52]

The link with sacral ordinances guaranteed the solidarity of the people, no matter what military or political forces had them in their grasp. The idea of the 'people of God' did not disappear with the end of national sovereignty. Under foreign rule, loyalty to worship and the law became the way in which the Jews could show themselves to be the people of God, by fulfilling cultic ordinances in daily life and by recognizing normative principles of common life. We might call this the 'ossification of the post-exilic community in a piety centred on the Law', the decay of living faith into mechanical practice. However, such a judgment would be a great mistake. The Law does not represent the ossification of faith, but the means of preserving it and protecting it from collapse in the face of attacks from foreign powers and from the temptation to give in to them. By establishing and observing cultic regulations, this post-exilic community made an extraordinary contribution. It connected devotion to the God of Israel with fixed forms of lasting value, and in so doing created the possibility for the faith of Israel to resist all trials, whenever and wherever they came upon a community which, while having no significance as a nation, was becoming increasingly decisive in religious terms. In this connection our standard of judgment must certainly not be a deep-rooted Protestant mistrust of the Law, nor must it be based on those maxims derived from evolutionary thought to the effect that the later period represents the decay and stagnation of an original dynamism. Given the atmosphere of the time and the predominant degree of alienation, we may see the force of creative reception and reformation in the preservation and safeguarding of the essential content of the tradition that had been handed down. Despite inner tensions within the Jewish community and the controversies associated with the formation of groups, the Persian period brought with it a strengthening of the Law and of religious conviction, which proved strong enough to resist the onset of new ideas and customs in the Hellenistic period which began with Alexander. While we cannot give exact dates to these developments or outline their limits, it is clear that after Alexander, Judah was faced with new demands and bitter controversies which compelled Judaism to further defence and resistance. Now it found time and strength to reflect on the tradition and develop a consistent view of it, as happened in the Pentateuch and the historical work of the Chronicler. It is no coincidence that the Pentateuch, which was finally given canonical form in the Persian period, became the foundation document of Judaism and the bulwark against the alienation of Jewish faith.

This is also the context of the question of the origin of the synagogue, which has still not been clarified. Its beginnings probably go back into the Persian period.[53] The presuppositions for it lie in the centralization of the cult prescribed by Deuteronomy, which was carried through in the post-exilic period on the terms in which it had been understood since Josiah. Jerusalem alone was to be the place of legitimate sacrificial worship; the sanctuary of the people was there. With the completion of the Pentateuch, the idea of periodic readings of the Torah, which was also rooted in Deuteronomy (31.9–13), must also have gained ground. In this form of worship connected with a book there emerged a liturgy which was independent of the sacrificial cult, the centre of which was formed not by the altar on which the sacrifice was offered, but by the presentation of the holy book, in the form of scrolls which were later contained in the shrine of the Torah. Along with the sabbath and circumcision, this gathering around the Law became one of the essential characteristics of Jewish life, not only in the homeland but also above all in the Diaspora. In these three institutions Judaism created for itself those forms of religious life, independent of the temple and capable of being put into practice everywhere, which strengthened the community and made assimilation, which was particularly likely in the later Hellenistic Diaspora, difficult or impossible. We still do not know whether the first synagogues were built in the Diaspora, say in Babylon, or whether this had already happened in Judaea or Galilee.[54]

The consequence of the centralization of the cult and the Diaspora was the development of pilgrimages to Jerusalem and with them the development of festivals at the temple. The observation of the festal calendar contributed to a deepening of religious consciousness; however, after the centralization of the cult, the passover lamb could no longer be killed in the family circle. Passover became the corner-stone of the notion of pilgrimage. We should not overlook the interplay between the central sanctuary and the Diaspora which began in the post-exilic period. The pilgrim who wanted to offer his sacrifice, whether at one of the festivals or independently of them, needed to be taught about the nature and the time of the sacrifice. The refinement of cultic regulations and the fixing of them in writing partly resulted from the need to lay down exactly the rights and duties pertaining to the central sanctuary, to make the priestly Torah binding and thus to educate the pilgrim who was strange to the country and the place.

We can understand why Chronicles occasionally goes beyond the laws and customs fixed in the Pentateuch, as for example in the account of the Passover in II Chron.30.13–26 and 35.1–19, on the one hand from the growth of the whole cultic apparatus, especially through the Levites, who play so prominent a part in Chronicles, and on the other from the increasingly strict regulation of worship.

The fixing of laws and cultic regulations in writing and the development of them, along with the 'scribalism' to which this led, is not the product of an increasingly inward-looking 'piety' of the post-exilic period in a community which had been robbed of political independence. They helped to form this community afresh and to endorse the authority which Jerusalem already had in the eyes of the Diaspora. The enquiry made by the Jews of Elephantine sheds special light on this development. The political impotence of tiny Judah did not prevent an increase in the authority exercised by Jerusalem, the temple and its leading men, who were strengthened in their conviction that the Torah really does go out from Zion. The only way in which we can understand this is by realizing that this post-exilic, Persian period saw the rescue and enrichment of Israel's traditions, and that it laid the foundation for the creation of a Judaism which could withstand Hellenism. With the final redaction of the Pentateuch and the acceptance of it as a binding document, this period erected a monument for all time.

The formative power exerted by this era on the tradition stamped Jewish awareness in a special way and led to the hypothesis of an independent institution between the last prophets and the earliest scribes known by name. This was a college of men who had been entrusted with handing down the Law, the so-called 'Great Synagogue', or more exactly the 'men of the Great Synagogue' (*'anšē keneesset haggadōlā*).[55] The historical existence of this institution is largely questioned. Its historical starting point was thought to be in the great assembly of the people in Neh.8–10, which was later understood in a different way, namely as an assembly of learned scribes; these therefore became the real bearers of the tradition. The spiritual authority of the Great Synagogue was claimed chiefly by the Pharisees, and it became an ingredient of their tradition. Whatever the specific historical situation may have been, the idea of this Great Synagogue bears witness to an awareness that in the course of the Persian period, following the undertakings of Ezra and Nehemiah, something decisive happened which rescued the tradition, protected it and even provided it with an institutional safeguard. We may understand H. D. Mantel's judgment in this sense:[56] 'The significance of the Men of the Great Synagogue in the history of Judaism derives from their success in accelerating the process, begun by Ezra, of first limiting and then abolishing the religious authority of the hereditary priesthood.'

NOTES

1. O. Eissfeldt, *The Old Testament. An Introduction*, 1965, 565; J. A. Soggin, *Introduction to the Old Testament*, ²1980, 16; R. Smend, *Die Entstehung des Alten Testaments*, 1978, 18.

2. B. Duhm supposes that Alexander's expedition through Syria and Palestine to Egypt forms the background to Habakkuk 1 and 2. Instead of the word 'Chaldaeans' in 1.6 he wants to read 'Kittim', which would apply to the Greeks. However, quite independently of this conjecture, we may endorse the possibility that the people depicted, who are going 'through the breadth of the earth', are in fact meant to be the Greeks; B. Duhm, *Das Buch Habakuk, Text, Übersetzung und Erklärung*, 1906, 21–3. Details of Zech.9.1–8 can also be related to Alexander's expedition, cf. K. Elliger, 'Ein Zeugnis aus der jüdischen Gemeinde im Alexanderjahr 332 v.Chr. Eine territorialgeschichtliche Studie zu Sach.9,1–8', *ZAW* 62, 1950, 63–115; M. Delcor, 'Les allusions à Alexandre le Grand dans Zach.9,1–8', *VT* 1, 1951, 110–24; of course the connection between the Zechariah passage and Alexander's expedition has not been established beyond all doubt; see A. Malamat, *IEJ* 1, 1950/51, 149–54; J. G. Baldwin, *Haggai, Zechariah, Malachi*, Tyndale Old Testament Commentaries, 1972/76, 157–62; Elliger's thesis is accepted by Ina Willi-Plein, *Prophetie am Ende*, BBB 42, 1974, 105–8.

3. The Chronicler's history (I and II Chronicles, Ezra and Nehemiah) is thought to have been finished about the year 300 BC, though some later additions may have been made in the Maccabean period. M. Noth, *Überlieferungsgeschichtliche Studien* I, 1943, 150–5; W. Rudolph, *Chronikbücher*, HAT 21, 1955, X, differs on some details; K. Galling, *Die Bücher der Chronik, Esra, Nehemia*, ATD 12, 1958, 14–17; P. R. Ackroyd, *I & II Chronicles, Ezra, Nehemiah*, Torch Bible Commentaries, 1973, 24–29. See also the Introductions to the Old Testament.

4. The methodological difficulty in making a historical evaluation of the Chronicler's work lies in distinguishing between the historical source and later revision of it made from the perspective of establishing an aetiological connection between the contemporary period and the earlier evidence. Thus the account of the monarchy in the kingdom of Judah, and also the material in the books of Ezra and Nehemiah, must be read through the eyes of an author writing towards the end of the fourth century BC. For differences of degree in assessing these almost insoluble questions see T. Willi, *Die Chronik als Auslegung*, FRLANT 106, 1972 (who suggests a far-ranging revision of the texts of Samuel and Kings where they are parallel to Chronicles), and P. Welten, *Geschichte und Geschichtsdarstellung in den Chronikbüchern*, WMANT 42, 1973 (the Chronicler has given a new form to old material). Cf. also P. R. Ackroyd, *The Age of the Chronicler* (supplement to *Colloquium – The Australian and New Zealand Theological Review*, 1970); G. von Rad, *Das Geschichtsbild des chronistischen Werkes*, BWANT 54, 1930.

5. For the Assyrian province of Megiddo and its later fate see A. Alt, *Kleine Schriften* II, 374–84; cf. also K. Galling, *PJB* 34, 1938, 74f.

6. A. Alt, 'Die Rolle Samarias bei der Entstehung des Judentums', *Kleine Schriften* II, 316–37.

7. There is an instructive survey in W. Wolf, *Das alte Ägypten*, 1971, 249–51.

8. Details in E. Otto, *Ägypten – der Weg des Pharaonenreiches*, ⁴1966, 246–50; W. Helck, *Geschichte des alten Ägypten*, HdO I, 1.3, 1968, 258–68.

9. There are more details about this event and the subsequent period in F. K. Kienitz, *Die politische Geschichte Ägyptens vom 7. bis zum 4. Jahrhundert v.d.Z.*, 1953, 76–112; *Fischer Weltgeschichte 5, Griechen und Perser*, 1965, 318–29.

10. W. Helck, op. cit., 266; F. K. Kienitz, op. cit., 96f.; *Fischer Weltgeschichte* 5, 326f.

11. E. Sachau, *Aramäische Papyri und Ostraka aus einer jüdischen Militärkolonie zu Elephantine*, 1911; A. Cowley, *Aramaic Papyri of the Fifth Century* BC, 1923; further

documents have been published in: E. G. Kraeling, *The Brooklyn Museum Aramaic Papyri*, 1953. Translation of individual texts: *AOT*, 450–62; *ANET*, 222f.; 491f.; *ANET Supplement*, 633; *TGI*, 84–8. Some important literature: E. Meyer, *Der Papyrusfund von Elephantine*, 1912; A. Vincent, *La religion des Judéo-Araméens d'Elephantine*, 1937; K. Galling, *Studien zur Geschichte Israels im persischen Zeitalter*, 1964, 149–84; H. Bardtke, 'Elephantine und die jüdische Gemeinde der Perserzeit', *Das Altertum* 6, 1960, 13–31, gives a summary account with a description of the place illustrated by his own photographs; see also id., *Zu beiden Seiten des Jordans*, 1958, 89. Further literature in *RGG* 2³, 1958, 415–18. The Elephantine papyri are discussed against a wider background in P. Grelot, *Documents araméens d'Egypte*, 1972; for Persian administrative practice see also G. R. Driver, *Aramaic Documents of the Fifth Century* BC, ²1965.

12. This is the way in which Herodotus translates the name of the island (II.9,17f., 28–31, 69, 175; III,19f.). It means something like 'Elephant City', because it was a trading post for Nubian ivory.

13. *AOT*, 450f.; *ANET*, 491f.; *TGI*², 84–7; Grelot, op. cit., 406–15.

14. The writing and pronunciation of the divine name 'Yahweh' are the subject of constant academic discussion. For the way in which it is written in the Elephantine papyri see already E. Meyer, op. cit., 35; cf. now the remarks by M. Rose, *Jahwe. Zum Streit um den alttestamentlichen Gottesnamen*, Theologische Studien 122, 1978, 16–22.

15. This was a Persian official by the name of Aršam, for whom there is also good evidence elsewhere; cf. the documents discussed by Driver, op. cit., and the instances given by him, 88–96.

16. Probably about 405 BC; cf. Kraeling, op. cit.; *TGI*², 88.

17. See n.13 above and K. Galling, *Studien*, 149–84.

18. *AOT*, 452; *ANET*, 492; *TGI*², 88 (which gives more details). Grelot, op. cit., 415–17.

19. The so-called 'Easter Letter' of Darius II: *AOT*, 453; *ANET*, 491; *TGI*¹, 1950, 73 (only the Aramaic text); there is a version with a commentary in P. Grelot, op. cit., 378–86. The content of the royal message was passed on by a Jewish intermediary called Hananiah. We cannot discover any immediate occasion for the message.

20. It is impossible to give a detailed account at this point of everything contained in the Elephantine documents. A list of the items in the temple tax (*AOT*, 453f.; *ANET*, 491; Grelot, op. cit., 363) has always attracted particular attention; here we have the name 'šm-Bethel and Anath-Bethel, and elsewhere (Grelot, 93) Herem-Bethel, alongside Yahu (Yahweh). Presumably this is the continuation of a form of syncretism of the kind which was once to be found in the northern state of Israel and was eventually fiercely combatted in Judah after Josiah's reform. See Grelot, op. cit., 365f. The deities mentioned were hardly hypostases of the God Yahweh (against W. F. Albright, *Archaeology and the Religion of Israel*, ²1963, 174).

21. Eusebius, *Chronicon*, ed. Schöne, II, 112f.; Solinus, 35.4; Orosius, *Adversus paganos* III, 7.6f.; for the interpretation of these events see now G. Widengren, *IJH*, 500.

22. Josephus, *Contra Apionem* I, 22 (194), refers to Hecataeus of Abdera for the fact that in the Persian period Jews were deported to Babylonia. Orophernes is said to have been a leader of the Persian troops (Diodore 31.19). It is doubtful whether he gave his name to the Holophernes of the book of Judith. Cf. H. Guthe, *Geschichte des Volkes Israel*, ³1914, 309.

23. D. Barag, 'The Effects of the Tennes Rebellion on Palestine', *BASOR* 183, 1966, 6–12.

24. The archaeological material which is to be assigned to the Persian period is discussed by E. Stern, 'Eretz-Israel in the Persian Period', *Quadmoniot* II, 1969, 110–24 (in Hebrew); id., *The Material Culture of the Land of the Bible in the Persian Period, 538–332 BCE*, 1973 (in Hebrew).

25. For details see the arguments and viewpoints presented by G. Widengren, *IJH*, 501f.

26. This is the widely accepted view, though there are many differences over details. R. J. Coggins, *Samaritans and Jews. The Origins of Samaritans Reconsidered*, 1975; see also G. Widengren, *IJH*, 511–14.

27. A. Alt, *Kleine Schriften* II, esp. 332f.

28. In Neh. 5.14 *phh* should probably be read instead of *phs*.

29. Earlier discoveries: E. L. Sukenik, *JPOS* 14, 1934, 182–4; 15, 1935, 341–3; W. F. Albright, *BASOR* 52, 1933, 20; 53, 1934, 20–2; also K. Galling, *PJB* 34, 1938, 75f. The later discoveries at Ramath-rahel, south of Jerusalem, proved particularly fruitful; here in addition to jar handles of the well-known type there were also some with the inscription *yhd* (also in plene, *yhwd*) *phw'*, 'Judah the governor', some even mentioning names of people from Judah. We may conclude from this that in the fourth century BC people from Judah and not Persians were in charge of the province. Y. Aharoni, *BA* 24, 1961, 108–12; cf. also K. Galling, *Studien*, 182f.; *BRL²*, 233f. See more recently L. Mildenberg, 'Yehud: A Preliminary Study of the Provincial Coinage of Judaea', in *Greek Numismatics and Archaeology. Essays in Honor of M. Thompson*, 1979, 183–96, and plates 21,22. I am grateful to Dr T. Fischer for bringing this article to my attention.

30. See p. 324 above.

31. See pp. 315f. above.

32. See map 8 below, p. 413; also the survey of the districts in Y. Aharoni, *The Land of the Bible*, 364; E. Meyer, *Die Enstehung des Judentums*, 1896 (reprinted 1965), 105–8.

33. W. F. Albright, *The Archaeology of Palestine*, rev. ed. 1960, 144f. (with an outline); for this and further finds from the Persian period see K. M. Kenyon, *Archaeology in the Holy Land*, ²1965, 300–4.

34. This province was the southern neighbour of Judah, and included parts of the territory which once belonged to Judah about the level of the southern end of the Dead Sea and beyond, on the other side of the Arabah: see M. Noth, 'Eine palästinische Lokalüberlieferung in 2.Chron.20', *ZDPV* 67, 1943/45, 45–71, esp. 62f.; see also Kenyon, op. cit., 300–2.

35. I have attempted here to understand the constitutional problem of the separation of Samaria from Jerusalem and Judah, which is connected with the formation of the province of Judah, as the presupposition for the cultic consequences which followed later. The formation of the so-called Samaritan community was a lengthy process which was not limited to the Persian period. R. J. Coggins, *Samaritans and Jews*, 164, concludes: 'All the evidence suggests that the decisive formative period for Samaritanism was the epoch from the third century BC to the beginning of the Christian era . . . There is no evidence that any one decisive event played a special part in widening the breach between Jews and Samaritans.'

36. H. G. Kippenberg, *Garizim und Synagoge*, Religionsgeschichtliche Versuche und Vorarbeiten 30, 1971.

37. There are about twenty papyri and a great many fragments from a cave in the *wādi ed-dālīyeh*, about nine miles north of Jericho and three miles south-west of *ḥirbet fasāyil*, in fairly inaccessible rocky country about 1500 feet above the Jordan. They were discovered by Ta'amire Bedouins, who also found the Qumran caves in 1947. They offered papyrus fragments for sale in Jerusalem. After finding out where the discoveries had been made, the American Schools of Oriental Research made systematic investigations of the caves in 1963 and 1964 under the direction of P. W. Lapp. P. W. Lapp and Nancy L. Lapp, *Discoveries in the Wâdi-ed-Dâliyeh*, AASOR 41, 1974; for the papyri see F. M. Cross, ibid., 17–29; id., 'The Discovery of the Samaria Papyri', *BA* 26, 1963, 110–21 (with illustrations); id., 'Papyri of the Fourth Century BC from Daliyeh. A Preliminary Report on their Discovery

and Significance', in *New Directions in Biblical Archaeology*, ed. Freedman and Greenfield, 1969, 41–62; for the historical consequences cf. F. M. Cross, 'Aspects of Samaritan and Jewish History in Late Persian and Hellenistic Times', *HTR* 59, 1966, 201–11; id., 'A Reconstruction of the Judean Restoration', *Interpretation* 29, 1975, 187–203. The Aramaic texts were written in Samaria and are all legal documents of a private and administrative kind. They presumably come from inhabitants of Samaria who sought refuge from the troops of Alexander the Great. However, they were tracked down to the cave, where their skeletons were found alongside the papyri.

38. Papyrus 8; see F. M. Cross, *New Directions*, 1969, 43 and n.4.

39. F. M. Cross, *JBL* 94, 1975, 17.

40. Cf. the survey in H. Guthe, *Geschichte des Volkes Israel*, ³1914, 317f., which is based on the Old Testament and Flavius Josephus, with Cross, op. cit., 17.

41. F. M. Cross, op. cit., 6f.

42. See now the critical remarks by G. Widengren, *IJH*, 506–9. He regards the presuppositions on which Cross bases his reconstruction as methodologically consistent, but questionable from a historical point of view (508).

43. Josephus, *Antt.* XI, 8.2–6 (317–45); cf. also appendix C, 'Alexander the Great and the Jews', in Josephus, LCL VI, 512–32.

44. Q Curtius Rufus, *Life of Alexander* IV, 8, 9–11.

45. Cf. Josephus, LCL VI, 523.

46. G. E. Wright, *Shechem*, 1965, 170ff.; id., in *Archaeology and Old Testament Study*, ed. G. Winton Thomas, 355–70; R. J. Coggins, *Samaritans*, 1975, 104–11.

47. R. J. Bull, 'An Archaeological Context for Understanding John 4, 20', *BA* 38, 1975, 54–9.

48. Josephus, *Antt.* XI, 8.6 (340–5).

49. For the traditions of the Samaritans from a later period, the so-called 'Chronicles' (especially 'Chronicle II', according to the numbering by J. Macdonald) and the Samaritan Pentateuch, see R. J. Coggins, op. cit., 116–61 (with further literature); see also J. Jeremias, *Die Passahfeier der Samaritaner*, 1932. Leading members of the community have from time to time found their way into modern collections of photographs; cf. e.g. B. G. Eichholz, *Landschaften der Bibel*, 1963, 52f.; C. Hollis and R. Brownrigg, *Holy Places: Jewish, Christian Monuments in the Holy Land*, 1969, 43, 47.

50. E. Würthwein, *The Text of the Old Testament*, ²1980, 42–4; O. Eissfeldt, *The Old Testament. An Introduction*, 1965, 694ff.; J. D. Purvis, *The Samaritan Pentateuch and the Origin of the Samaritan Text*, 1968; P. Sacchi, 'Studi Samaritani I', *Rivista di Storia e di Letteratura Religiosa* 5, 1969, 413–40; Coggins, op. cit., 148–55; there is an edition of the text in A. von Gall, *Der hebräische Pentateuch der Samaritaner*, 1914–18 (reprinted 1962).

51. Guthe, *Geschichte*, ³1914, 309.

52. The word *qāhāl* is preferred in the Persian period, and occurs particularly frequently in the books of Chronicles (thirty-two times). Its original meaning was 'invitation', 'summons to an assembly', but particularly from the time of Deuteronomy it acquired theological connotations, so that it came to mean the 'cultic assembly'. In the end, however, in addition to this special use it was extended to all those entitled to take part in an assembly in the name of God. Thus in Chronicles the ideal model of a 'popular assembly of the Jewish worshipping community' can be connected with *qāhāl*. L. Rost, *Die Vorstufen von Kirche und Synagoge im Alten Testament. Eine wortgeschichtliche Untersuchung*, BWANT 76, 1938, 11–32; with some differences, *THAT* II, 1976, 606–19 (H.-P. Müller).

53. For the synagogue and synagogue worship, though largely from a later period than this, see S. Krauss, *Synagogale Altertümer*, 1922, 2ff.; E. Schürer, *The History of the Jewish People in the age of Jesus Christ*, § 27.II, new ed. by G. Vermes and F. Millar, II, 1979, 423–54; E. Meyer, *Ursprung und Anfänge des Christentums* II, 1921, 26–8; K. Hruby,

Die Synagoge. Geschichtliche Entwicklung einer Institution, 1971; M. Hengel, 'Proseuche und Synagoge. Jüdische Gemeinde, Gotteshaus und Gottesdienst in der Diaspora und in Palästina', in *Tradition und Glaube. Festgabe für K. G. Kuhn,* 1971, 157–84; J. Maier and J. Schreiner (eds.), *Literatur und Religion des Frühjudentums,* 1973, 391–413 (P. Schäfer); S. Safrai, in *WHJP* I, 8, 1977, 65–98.

54. Inscriptions from Egypt dating from the third century BC are the earliest evidence for the building of synagogues. The earliest inscription comes from the time of Ptolemy Euergetes (246–221 BC), with the transference of the right of asylum to a synagogue. S. Safrai, *WHJP* I, 8, 69, and the illustrations on p. 128. There is a list of further inscriptions and papyri in E. Schürer, op. cit., § 27.II, 425f.

55. The earliest and best-known example is in the Mishnah, Aboth 1.1.

56. H. D. Mantel, *WHJP* I, 8, 48: for the Great Synagogue see ibid., 44–52; also S. Kuenen, 'Über die Männer der grossen Synagoge', in Kuenen, *Geschichtliche Abhandlungen zur biblischen Wissenschaft,* 1894, 125–60; Schürer, op. cit., § 25. IV, 356–60.

The Rule of the Ptolemies and the Seleucids to the Accession of Antiochus IV

IT SEEMS VIRTUALLY impossible to give a distinctive profile of the political history of Israel in the period which now follows, between Alexander the Great and the Seleucid ruler Antiochus IV Epiphanes in the first half of the second century BC. The territory of Judah and Samaria, and the areas beyond the Jordan,[1] were dragged into the field of force generated by the power struggles which flared up violently among the successors of Alexander, the Diadochoi in Egypt and Syria, leaving the land first of all in Ptolemaic and then in Syrian hands. The Jewish Diaspora grew larger. In Egyptian Alexandria and later in Syrian Antioch it gained centres for its life outside the mother country. However, in Jerusalem quarrels between leading families increased, and we may see as one of the special dispensations of this time the fact that Jewish worship and Jewish life were able to keep themselves essentially free from the Hellenistic influence which was making itself felt everywhere. The Old Testament is virtually excluded as an independent source for this period. The few reports from the *Antiquities* of Flavius Josephus (XII, 1–4 = 1–236) cannot take the place of a proper historical account, and must be subjected to critical examination. Thus to a large degree we have to make use of non-Jewish sources to fill out our picture of the period and assess the effects of individual events on the members of the people of Israel and Judah.[2]

As a chronological framework for the political developments after Alexander, I shall list here the reigns of the Ptolemies and the Seleucids for the period with which we are primarily concerned.

Ptolemies:

Ptolemy I Lagi (Soter)

Satrap of Egypt	323–305
King	305–285
Ptolemy II Philadelphus	285–246
Ptolemy III Euergetes	246–221
Ptolemy IV Philopater	221–204
Ptolemy V Epiphanes	204–181
Ptolemy VI Philometor	181–145

Seleucids :

Seleucus I Nicator	312–281
Antiochus I Soter	281–261
Antiochus II Theos (Deus)	261–246
Seleucus II Callinicus	246–226
Seleucus III Ceraunus	226–223
Antiochus III The Great	223–187
Seleucus IV Philopator	187–175
Antiochus IV Epiphanes	175–164
Antiochus V Eupator	164–162
Demetrius I Soter	162–150
Alexander I Balas	153–145

It is generally agreed that the Hellenistic period began with the death of Alexander the Great in Babylon in 323. This development is characterized by a successive penetration of the Near Eastern and later also the Roman world with a Greek life-style, Greek city architecture, Greek language and philosophy.[3] Alexander had in fact laid the foundation for this development by his extensive expeditions, which took him to the Indus and what is now West Pakistan.[4] It was members of his troops, officers and soldiers, and also the Macedonian settlers who followed the troops, who settled in numerous cities in the lands which he had conquered, extended them, changed their names, developed them or went on to found new ones. 'Alexander's veterans' has become a stereotyped term which always comes up in any account of the foundation or the earliest history of such a city or settlement. Numerous cities were given the name 'Alexandria' in honour of the great conqueror. Of these, the Egyptian Alexandria west of the Delta was to acquire special significance, and it has remained a living testimony to the era even down to the present day.[5]

The founding of Alexandria in Egypt is connected with Alexander the Great himself. Its situation was not in the end decisive for the rise of the city. The city was connected with the Nile by a navigable watercourse from Lake Mareotis, an extensive stretch of water on its south side. Unlike the earlier ports to the east of the mouths of the Nile its harbour was protected from becoming sanded up by the direction of the flow of water. This favoured its rise under the Ptolemies and made it a centre of trade and commerce. Even under the first governor, Ptolemy I Lagi (Soter), and his successors Ptolemy Philadelphus and Euergetes, it had already become a centre for artists and scholars. This led to the foundation of the academy (the so-called Museion) of Alexandria, which served the arts and sciences; the famous library of Alexandria was connected with this.[6] At the same time the city became one of the most important centres of the Jewish Diaspora. The beginnings of the Greek translation of the Pentateuch are to be looked for there. The great significance of Alexandria remained down to Christian times;

it became a centre of Christian intellectual life and for the formation of Christian schools.[7]

Greek culture did not penetrate the area of Phoenicia and Palestine at the same time everywhere; to begin with, it affected the heart of old Israelite territory, in the hill-country of Samaria and Judaea, very little, if indeed at all. Hellenization began from Phoenicia and extended southwards into the coastal plain, where in addition to Acco (Ptolemais), Dor and Jaffa, above all Gaza and Ashkelon in the south adopted the new life-style. Furthermore, Greek culture developed special centres in particular places. West of the Jordan, Samaria had been occupied by Greek mercenaries. A later development in Transjordan was the so-called 'Decapolis', a series of cities chiefly south and south-east of Lake Tiberias, among which Gadara was particularly prominent. The successor of the old Rabbath Ammon was the city now called Philadelphia (after Ptolemy Philadelphus, 285–246). The cities east of the Jordan had connections with the old Beth-shean, now with the Greek name Scythopolis. The impressive buildings of Gerasa and Bosrah owe their origins chiefly to the Roman period, not before.[8]

In the century after Alexander, possession of Palestine and Phoenicia was at first hotly disputed. After Alexander's death, the division of all the land which he had conquered was only achieved after bitter struggles. To begin with, the individual governors of provinces were essentially as follows: Ptolemy I Soter governed Egypt; Seleucus the satrapy of Babylon; Antigonus the larger part of Asia Minor; Antipater, the last of the generals of Philip II, was governor of Macedonia and Greece. In the very year of Alexander's death, Ptolemy had the Syrian governor Laomedon driven out and took over Syria and Phoenicia for himself. According to Josephus' report,[9] Ptolemy himself is said to have appeared in Jerusalem in the year 320, on a sabbath, on the pretext of wanting to offer sacrifice in the temple. On this occasion he seized the city and took away numerous Jews to settle them in Alexandria. At the least, the account seeks to give an explanation for the beginnings of the Jewish population in Alexandria, which later became so numerous.

In the following years the whole corridor of Syria and Palestine became the scene of countless power-struggles between the 'Diadochoi', following the death of Alexander. The power of Antigonus and his son Demetrius Poliorcetes, who lived in Asia Minor, grew. Among others, Egypt under Ptolemy I and Seleucus as governor of Babylon allied themselves against him. The battles became fiercer between 315 and 301. In 312, Demetrius was defeated at Gaza. Thereupon Ptolemy penetrated even deeper into Syria, but eventually had to retreat before Antigonus. At the same time Seleucus was able to use this confusion to strengthen his position in Babylonia. His further return there became the real foundation for the Seleucid kingdom, in a twofold sense. Not only did the power of Seleucus seem to be decisively established, but with the year 312 BC people began a new basis for calculating time which extended far beyond the domain of the Seleucids. This was the so-called Seleucid era,[10] which alongside the numbering of years by Olympiads became one of the best known ways of calculating time in antiquity.[11]

Increasing suspicion that Antigonus was striving to take over the whole of Alexander's heritage led Ptolemy to make an alliance against Antigonus with Alexander's generals Lysimachus and Cassander, the son of Antipater. The decisive point was the battle at Ipsos in Phrygia in 301 BC. Antigonus was beaten and was killed in the fighting. Thereupon Seleucus received the greater part of Syria and Mesopotamia and built up Antioch into a capital city. Southern Syria, i.e. the whole area south of the Lebanon including the old territory of Israel and Judah, largely remained under Ptolemaic control. Nevertheless, this did not bring final peace. Ptolemies and Seleucids fought stubbornly for final possession of the whole territory of Syria and Palestine.

Only a few of the most important actions need to be mentioned here. The attack by Ptolemy II Philadelphus on Syria in the year 275 proved ineffective: he was forced to retreat. After Antiochus I was succeeded by Antiochus II in 261, the Seleucids struck back. A peace treaty was not made between the two parties in the dispute until 252; in connection with this, Antiochus II married Berenice, the daughter of Ptolemy II and Queen Arsinoe. It is generally agreed that Dan.11.6 refers to this event with the words: 'After some years they shall make an alliance, and the daughter of the king of the south shall come to the king of the north to make peace.'

The great vision in Dan.11.2–45 is a consecutive version of historical events from the Persian period; it goes on to Alexander and then outlines in a text full of allusions the turbulent events taking place between Ptolemies and Seleucids. To begin with it is in summary form, but eventually it gets more and more detailed, the nearer the author comes to the time of Antiochus IV Epiphanes. We also have further details of the subsequent course of the marriage of Antiochus II with Berenice, which reads almost like a dramatic opera libretto. To make his marriage possible, Antiochus II had cast off his wife Laodice. She took terrible revenge on behalf of her son Seleucus. In 246 she had Antiochus II poisoned and Berenice murdered. The way was not free for her son Seleucus, who in fact ascended the throne in the same year as Seleucus II Callinicus. A short time later, Berenice's father Ptolemy II died. Now his successor Ptolemy III Euergetes sought to avenge the murder of his sister. He invaded Syria, advanced far beyond Damascus, took a great deal of spoil and then had to break off the campaign because of a rebellion in Egypt. A counter-attack made later by Seleucus II was beaten off.

The book of Daniel also reports these events in connection with the verses quoted, in Dan.11.7–9: 'In those days a branch from her roots shall arise in his place (the reference is to Ptolemy III Euergetes); he shall come against the army and enter the fortress of the king of the north, and he shall deal with them and shall prevail.' There is probably an allusion to the penetration of the Egyptians as far as Antioch in v.8: 'He shall also carry off to Egypt their gods with their molten images and with their precious vessels of silver and of gold; and for some years he shall refrain from attacking the king of the north.' However, there is the addition of v.9: 'Then the latter shall come into the realm of the king of the south but shall return into his own land.' This is an allusion to the unsuccessful counter-attack by Seleucus II.

Seleucus III Ceraunus, who succeeded him in 226, was poisoned only three years later (223). His place was taken by his brother Antiochus III (223–187), generally called 'the Great'. He succeeded in driving the Egyptians even out of southern Syria, i.e. from Phoenicia and Palestine, and in bringing Jerusalem and Judah under Seleucid rule. That meant not only a change, but at the same time also an improvement for the situation in Jerusalem.

In 218 Antiochus went southwards along the coast and conquered cities in ancient Phoenicia and in the Palestinian coastal plain. However, in the following year, 217, he was defeated at Raphia on the north-eastern side of the Sinai peninsula by the Egyptians under Ptolemy IV Philopator. Ptolemy took back from Antiochus the territories which had been conquered, and in this connection is also said to have come to Jerusalem. Some extremely legendary material has become attached to this event, the historicity of which cannot be ruled out in principle; it has been preserved in what is known as III Maccabees.[13] King Ptolemy was prevented from entering the temple. After a number of miraculous events the king returned to Alexandria and there attempted to take vengeance on the Egyptian Jews. He had them shut up in the stadium and tried to have them trampled to death by elephants. This was prevented by the intervention of two angels. The raging elephants turned against the king's troops and annihilated them. Surprisingly, the king changed his mind and had the Jews celebrate a seven-day festival of joy which they wanted to repeat every year (III Macc.6. 22–41). Numerous details recall stories about persecutions of Jews, especially the book of Esther, which has its origin among eastern Jewish communities and ends up with the festival of Purim. The question is whether III Maccabees is meant to describe the western counterpart to the festival of Purim in the east. However, III Maccabees is a highly artificial composition which incorporates various elements which are also known from Josephus' work *Contra Apionem*, above all the alleged royal resolve to have Jews trampled under foot by elephants (*Contra Apionem* II, 5=53–55). It must therefore remain an open question whether and to what extent Egyptian Jewish communities were in fact exposed to acute threats which they had to endure amongst an alien population.[14]

In the lifetime of Ptolemy IV, Antiochus the Great did not venture any further expeditions southwards; only after the death of Ptolemy IV, in 201, did he attack his successor, Ptolemy V Epiphanes, lay siege to Gaza and capture it. His success did not last. In 198, Ptolemy's general Scopas advanced into the region of the upper sources of the Jordan. The contingent of Egyptian troops under his command was conquered by Antiochus at Paneas (*bānyās*). This battle marked a turning point. The Egyptians were definitively beaten. The whole of 'Syria', i.e. Phoenicia and the lands on both sides of the Jordan, indisputably came under Seleucid control. Seleucus I had already divided his kingdom into seventy-two satrapies, but these were smaller than the territories which had once been marked out by the Persians. The territories which had now been gained were added to the satrapy of 'Coele Syria'.[15] On the whole the Seleucids had a warm welcome in Jerusalem. There must have been a great deal of dissatisfaction under the Egyptians. Antiochus III renewed privileges for the city and the temple and stated these in a special decree.

This well known decree has been handed down by Josephus.[16] There have been many investigations into the wording and the authenticity of the document, which has indeed been put in question.[17] Whatever judgment may be made on it, whether it is a single decree or two decrees which Josephus has worked together, one part of the text (*Antt.* XII, §§138-9, 143-4) is concerned with urgent limited measures which relate to the city of Jerusalem, its restoration and its population. This text runs:

(138) 'King Antiochus to Ptolemy, greeting. Inasmuch as the Jews, from the very moment when we entered their country, showed their eagerness to serve us and, when we came to their city, gave us a splendid reception and met us with their senate (*gerousia*)[19] at their head, and furnished an abundance of provisions to our soldiers and elephants, and also helped us to expel the Egyptian garrison in the citadel (*akra*),[20] (139) we have seen fit on our part to requite them for these acts and to restore their city which has been destroyed by the hazards of war, and to repeople it by bringing back to it those who have been dispersed abroad. (143) And in order that the city may the more quickly be inhabited, I grant both to the present inhabitants and to those who may return before the month of Hyper-beretaios exemption from taxes for three years. (144) We shall also relieve them in future from the third part of their tribute, so that their losses may be made good. And as for those who were carried off from the city and are slaves, we herewith set them free, both them and the children born to them, and order their property to be restored to them.'

We should not overlook the fact that these are temporary measures which are directly connected with the war which has just been waged. This may explain not only the remarkable remission of tax but also the measure, recalling the time of Nehemiah, which consists of making up the population of the city once again from surrounding areas. However, over the longer term tribute is reduced only by one third.

In contrast to these immediate measures are promises about the temple and the cult which seem to have been intended to have a longer-term effect: this text, possibly an independent decree, has been inserted into the other ordinances in the version handed down by Josephus; it comprises §§140-142:

(140) 'In the first place we have decided, on account of their piety, to furnish them for their sacrifices an allowance of sacrificial animals, wine, oil and frankincense to the value of 20,000 pieces of silver [i.e. drachmae],[22] and sacred *artabae*[23]

of fine flour in accordance with their native law, and 1,460 *medimni* of wheat and 375 *medimni* of salt.[24] (142) And it is my will that these things be made over to them as I have ordered, and that the work on the temple be completed, including the porticoes and any other part that it may be necessary to build. The timber, moreover, shall be brought from Judaea itself and from other nations and Lebanon without the imposition of a toll-charge. The like shall be done with the other materials needed for making the restoration of the temple more splendid.'

The details of this text, which relate to the buildings of the temple, and especially the pillared halls, can no longer now be verified for this second post-exilic temple. All the buildings of that time were very probably replaced at a later stage by Herod's structure, which was on a much larger scale. Wood is emphasized because it was a particularly valuable material; it was used principally for roofing.[25] The last paragraph of the ordinances also deserves special attention.

(142) 'And all the members of the nation shall have a form of government in accordance with the laws of their country, and the senate, the priests, the scribes of the temple and the temple-singers shall be relieved from the poll-tax and the crown-tax and the salt-tax which they pay.'

The injunction to live in accordance with ancestral laws may have been addressed not only to Judaeans but also to the non-Jewish authorities in Jerusalem, who were to protect and guarantee the Israelite cult without qualification. Among the groups exempt from temple tax, the 'scribes of the temple' are particularly striking; here for the first time the designation *grammateis* appears. However, this is hardly a reference to those who are well versed in the scriptures, although later, and also in the New Testament tradition, the term was applied to those who were especially skilled in scripture and tradition. The 'crown-tax' may be a gift in homage to the ruler at a particular time.[26]

These wide-ranging material concessions to the cult and the sanctuary are comparable with the generous privileges once granted by the Persian government. Of course in some respects the Seleucids took over Persian administrative practices. For the most part, however, the measures in this decree by Antiochus III may have been strongly marked by the personality of the ruler himself. His successors acted differently.

After securing his kingdom in the south, Antiochus attempted to strengthen and extend his connections in Asia Minor. Events are confused. Asia Minor was also within the sphere of interest of Philip V of Macedon. He had allied himself with Hannibal in the Second Punic War. After Hannibal's defeat at Zama in 202 the Romans therefore turned to the East, fought in Greece and there also came up against Antiochus. He had arrived in Greece in 192, had conquered several places and now found himself face to face with Roman military power. The Romans put him to flight in the famous pass of Thermopylae in which the Spartans under Leonidas had once succumbed to the Persians (480 BC). In Asia Minor, to which the war was extended, they finally inflicted a heavy defeat on Antiochus at Magnesia in 190 BC. The Romans were under the command of Lucius Cornelius Scipio, who here earned his nickname 'Asiaticus', which was to distinguish him from his brother of the same name who had defeated Hannibal at Zama and went down in history as 'Africanus'. At the peace of Apamaea in Syria, Antiochus had to yield to the Roman conditions (188 BC). He lost all his possessions west of the Taurus and had to pay tribute of 15,000 talents. From this moment on the Seleucid empire went into decline. The Roman demands were a heavy burden on Syria and the Seleucid government, especially as important northern provinces like Parthia and Bactria were not contributors. From now on, too, the collection of money became one of the chief demands on the Syrian administration and also determined the military undertakings of the Seleucids. Antiochus III undertook an expedition to the distant area of Elam, to plunder temples there and lay hands on their treasure. It was there that he was killed, in 187 BC.

Seleucus IV Philopator (187–175) now took over the financial obligations of his father. His rigorous taxation policy also affected Coele Syria, including Judah. There is a very apt mention of this in the historical summary in Dan.11.20:

'Then shall arise in his place [viz., in place of Antiochus III] one who shall send an exactor of tribute through the glory of the kingdom; but within a few days he shall be broken, neither in anger nor in battle.'

The last words of this unusual but clear text already anticipate future developments, namely the treacherous murder of Seleucus IV by Heliodorus, who was finance minister and responsible for recovering taxes.

At this point we need to look at conditions in Jerusalem, where the two priestly families of the Oniads and the Tobiads, as they are usually called, were bitter rivals.[27] The Oniads were the Zadokite priesthood, those who claimed the status of high priest for themselves in direct succession. I have already given a list of these priests, as far as it can be reconstructed, down to Jaddua ben Johanan;[28] here I shall carry it further, with a few notes on each individual:

Jaddua ben Johanan, allegedly a contemporary of Alexander the Great (Josephus, *Antt.* XI, 8.2–5, 7=206–39, 346), but probably earlier

Onias I, son of Jaddua (*Antt.* XI, 8.7=346)

Simon I, the Just, son of Onias I (*Antt.* XII, 2.5=43), probably *c.* 250

Eleazar, son of Onias I (*Antt.* XII, 2.5ff.=40ff.), contemporary of Ptolemy II Philadelphus (?)

Manasseh, uncle of Eleazar (*Antt.* XII, 4.1=157), date uncertain

Onias II, son of Simon I the Just, according to *Antt.* XII, 4.1–10 (157–224) the contemporary of Ptolemy IV Philopator (221–204), Ptolemy V Epiphanes (204–181) and Antiochus III (223–187)

Simon II, son of Onias II (*Antt.* XII, 4.10f.=224, 229) (identical with Simon the Tobiad of II Macc. 3.4?)

Onias III, son of Simon II, possibly identical with Onias II; he died at the beginning of the reign of Antiochus IV Epiphanes (175/4: *Antt.* XII, 4.10; 5.1
=225, 237). He was the last legitimate high priest (Dan.9.25)

Jason, son of Simon II(?), 175–173; Antiochus IV replaced him by:

Onias (Menelaus), son of Simon II, 173–164 (*Antt.* XII, 5.1=238f.)

Jakim (Alcimus), appointed by Antiochus V Eupator, 163 (*Antt.* XX, 10.1
= 235) died 159

This Zadokite family was evidently in quite a strong position and, leaving aside
possible ups and downs, was able to maintain itself in power permanently. By
contrast, the Tobiads only held administrative offices within the temple organization. Their name comes from Tobias the Ammonite, who at one time was one of
Nehemiah's powerful opponents. He associated himself through marriage with the
leading circles in Jerusalem. One of Tobias' descendants with the same name was
commander of an international military colony in Ammon round about the time of
Ptolemy Philadelphus (285–246), had direct contact with the Egyptian court and
was married to a sister of the Jerusalem high priest Onias (II). He was one of the
most influential people in the house of Tobias, which used the Egyptians to rein-
force its strength in the area east of the Jordan.

The activity of this Tobias was surpassed by his son Joseph, who was able to
exploit the tensions which had arisen between Onias (II) and the Ptolemaic authorities. He was tax concessionaire for the Egyptian government in Judah and at the
same time had authority over Samaria and the cities with a predominantly Greek
population. His relations with Alexandria, his influence over local conditions east
and west of the Jordan, and his executive strength in all financial questions made
him a key figure in the economic life of Judaea and far beyond its boundaries. As
only part of the population benefited from his rigorous taxation policy, there were
bitter controversies and enmities, particularly also with the non-Jewish inhabitants
of the country.

The rise of the Tobiads restricted the influence of the high priest in a noticeable
way. In the end there were also marked tensions even within Joseph's family. His
youngest son Hyrcanus took sides with the high priest Onias II, while his brothers
wanted to depose him. An event reported in II Macc.3.4–40, which occurred as
early as the time of Seleucus IV Philopator (187–175), should be connected with
these quarrels.

It is said that the captain of the temple administration, Simon by name (probably
another son of Joseph the Tobiad) quarrelled with Onias about aspects of the
supervision of the city market. Simon could not get anywhere with Onias.
Thereupon he went to Apollonius, governor of Coele Syria and Phoenicia, and
claimed that the Jerusalem temple contained boundless treasure. Apollonius reported this to the king; because of Roman demands he was extremely interested
in new sources of income and immediately sent his minister Heliodorus to
Jerusalem. There, however, the high priest explained to him that this was money

deposited by widows and orphans, and also that of a very prominent man named Hyrcanus, who was a son of Tobias. Despite this, Heliodorus demanded the money, referring to the royal command, and even went into the temple treasury, an action which provoked a popular revolt. In the temple precincts Heliodorus suddenly had a vision. He lay motionless on the ground. However, the high priest was able to restore him to life. Heliodorus withdrew his demand and later reported to the king that 'there certainly is about the place some power of God.'

Tendentious and exaggerated as this narrative evidently is, it nevertheless reflects the complicated situation. The incident was provoked by treachery between the competing priestly families; the Seleucid government greedily followed up every hint that promised them gain. Evidently all the skill of the Jerusalem priesthood was called upon to conceal the money they had and to parry undesirable questions. It is reported that in the end Onias even resolved to pay a personal visit to the king in Antioch. He arrived too late. Heliodorus had murdered Seleucus IV.

This murder had far-reaching consequences, not least for Judaea and Jerusalem. The idea behind it was to help quite a different man to the throne with Roman support. This was Antiochus, who had already spent twelve years in Rome as a hostage. However, because instalments of tribute were outstanding, the Roman government required that Seleucus' other son, Demetrius, should remain in Rome. In the interregnum brought about by the period of negotiation, Heliodorus attempted to take control of Syria. However, Antiochus, who in the meanwhile had been released from Rome, succeeded in overthrowing Heliodorus with the support of the troops of king Eumenes II of Pergamum. He now ascended the Syrian throne as Antiochus IV Epiphanes. He set his political aims very high. Evidently he wanted to blot out the shameful memory of the peace of Apamea and therefore acted more decisively and rashly than all his predecessors. He ushered in a new and highly unpleasant era for Judaea and Jerusalem, which was to unleash unsuspected forces there.

Despite the numerous upheavals of war and the inner tensions since Alexander the Great, down to the time of Antiochus IV the land had experienced growing, albeit limited, prosperity. Antiochus IV then made inroads into the internal conditions of Jewish social life in an unprecedented way. The Ptolemies and Syrians had involved the countries south of the Lebanon in trade and commerce which in the Hellenistic period had been favoured by international markets and the development of new routes. Syrian corn went by ship to Egypt; similarly, precious oil was brought from Phoenician and Palestinian harbours to Alexandria and from there into the interior of Egypt. Asphalt was another article of export; found in abundance particularly in the area of the Dead Sea, it was valued very highly as an adhesive and a preservative. In the other direction, wine from the Aegean was imported for the Greek population of Syro-Phoenicia and Palestine. This has been shown by the handles of amphoras which have come to light in Beth-zur, Gezer, Samaria and elsewhere. Syria and Palestine was also on the trade route for numerous goods from the east and south-east; one important route ran from southern Arabia, via what later became Petra of the Nabataeans, to Gaza. From there the goods could be forwarded to Egypt either on land or by sea.

In addition to economic links there were also military and technical administrative measures which the Ptolemies and Seleucids developed systematically. A large number of mercenary units were used in Syria and Palestine in addition to local soldiers, and some of these lived together in military colonies. In times of peace these people often worked on land which was either assigned to them by the central government of the time or was under their direct supervision and administration.

One interesting example of Ptolemaic administrative practice can be found in the so-called Zeno papyri.[29] The military colony of Philadelpheia came into being at the time of Ptolemy II Philadelphus (285–246) on the edge of the great oasis of *fayyūm*, south-west of the Nile delta in Egypt, as the result of the granting of portions of land to mercenaries. The king's finance minister, Apollonius (261–246), had been involved in its development, and he put the administration of his property in the hands of a man called Zeno, who came from Caria. Zeno's correspondence with Apollonius was found in the ruins of Philadelpheia in 1915. Of particular interest here are papyri relating to the estate which lay both west and east of the Jordan, and was probably assigned to Apollonius by his king. The exact extent of the estate does not emerge from this correspondence. However, we do find lists of names which, as far as they can be identified, belong not only to Transjordan but also to Judaea, Galilee and the coastal plains.[30] Zeno visited these areas on behalf of Apollonius as early as 261–258. The relevant papyri speak of the purchase of domestic products by the Egyptians, above all of oil, wine and even slaves. They also speak of the appointment of Greek officials who worked for the Ptolemaic administration, especially in the cities. It is interesting that a Tobias was one of Zeno's local agents; it is said of him that he inherited an estate near Jericho, but on the east bank of the Jordan, and settled it with Greeks and local people. This Tobias was certainly a member of the influential 'Tobiads'.

Of course the Zeno papyri illuminate only the conditions on estates belonging to foreign landowners. Nothing is said about the native population. However, we must suppose that it was chiefly the small farmers who suffered losses at the expense of the larger estates, and that as with conditions in the Persian period, very different kinds of land-owning could exist side by side.

When the Seleucids took over rule of Coele Syria and Phoenicia, the territory was subject to a governor with a rank of *strategos*,[31] who had both military and civil authority. In all probability he had his residence in Acco (Ptolemais). No change in administration and government was introduced until the time of the Hasmoneans.

The influence of Hellenism on Coele Syria became stronger towards the year 200 BC, though it took different forms. It governed life in the cities on the coastal plain and in those places in the interior which were inhabited by Greek settlers. To a remarkable degree Judaea still remained free of this influence. Of course, Greek names gradually also became more frequent in Jewish circles. However, we can hardly say that Greek established itself everywhere as a language. It merely had a role in administration. As the real centres of the old Israelite tradition, Judaea and Jerusalem managed, as far as we can tell, to stave off the incursion of Hellenism with some success. That does not mean, however, that the Greek spirit remained completely unknown, or that some Jewish circles were not open to it. However, resistance and conflict were much more serious and problematic here than elsewhere. We may take the book Ecclesiastes (Koheleth), from the Old Testament, and Jesus Sirach (Ben Sira, or Ecclesiasticus), which doubtless goes back to a Greek original, as evidence for the end of the third and the beginning of the second centuries.[32] Both works appeared against the background of this time, still before the Maccabean revolt. In their own way each is concerned to come to terms with ancestral faith. Koheleth, the Preacher, complains about an ordering of the world which he feels to be unjust;[33] Jesus Sirach is aware of ideas of a universal humanity and wisdom, though these are inseparable from the God of Israel who has spoken authentically to his people in the Law and through the fathers.

The book Jesus Sirach itself contains the information that it was translated into Greek by a grandson of the author in Egypt, for the Jews there. Similarly, we may put the beginnings of the translation of the Pentateuch into Greek some time during the third century, in Alexandria. The community there had grown much larger, not only as a result of numerous immigrants from the home country of Judah, but also because it took in people who wanted to submit to the 'Law' independently of their racial origins. These 'newcomers' (*prosēlytoi*=proselytes) for the most part did not understand either Hebrew or Aramaic, but they did take part in the regular readings of the Torah. For them a translation of the Pentateuch into Greek was begun, at first in sections; eventually it took in the whole work. Other Old Testament writings were only translated later, during the process of their canonization.

Thus the beginnings of this activity of translation are to be found in liturgical practice' and to begin with very different recensions may have been in circulation. The idea that the translation of the Pentateuch was the result of a single piece of activity in which seventy-two scholars, working in isolation, arrived at a text which corresponded word for word, is an attractive legend which was recorded in the final section of the so-called Letter of Aristeas, a pseudepigraphical writing from about the second half of the second century BC; in all probability its purpose was to establish the authority of the Greek texts generally, and at least the recension which was produced in Alexandria, making it understandable as a work of divine co-operation and inspiration.[34]

According to the Letter of Aristeas, Ptolemy II Philadelphus (285-246) was interested in Judaism and its writings, which he wanted to include in the great library in Alexandria. However, in the opinion of Demetrius of Phaleron, who was in charge of the royal library, these needed to be translated. A court official named Aristeas was sent off to Jerusalem. The high priest is supposed to have given him six elders from each of the twelve tribes of Israel, seventy-two in all. Their task was to translate the whole Torah, i.e. the Pentateuch, into Greek, in Alexandria, in seventy-two days. This was a great enterprise, which was carried out on the island of Pharos, outside Alexandria: 'There he assembled them in a house, which had been built on the sea-shore, of great beauty and in a secluded situation, and invited them to carry out the work of translation, since everything they needed for the purpose was placed at their disposal. So they set to work comparing their several results and making them agree, and whatever they agreed upon was suitably copied out under the direction of Demetrius.'

It should at least be pointed out that according to this text the agreement in the wording of the translation did not, as is often said, come about in a 'miraculous' way, as though each individual translator arrived at the same result independently; the agreement was arrived at by comparing individual renderings together. The designation 'Septuagint' for the Greek translation of the whole of the Old Testament is based on this legend of the seventy (seventy-two) scholars working together in common, who only translated the Pentateuch. The historical circumstances reported by the Letter of Aristeas are to be judged fictitious, including the claim that the translation was carried out by Jews from Jerusalem or Judaea. They surely came from Alexandria. We cannot question in principle the assertion that they formed a committee and worked on the island of Pharos; however, we have no reliable indications which could confirm this. Still, the legend is right, in that the translation of the Pentateuch must have been begun in Alexandria in the third century BC. It is reckoned that the prophetic canon of the Old Testament, including the historical books, was similarly translated in the course of the first century BC.[35]

It emerges from all this evidence that in the Ptolemaic and Seleucid period, writing and worship were the real unitive factors for Jews in the home country and the Diaspora; they even exerted some attraction on their environment, where proselytes came to accept the law. This process should not be underestimated. At a time of increasing Hellenization, of great revolutions in almost all areas of culture and daily life, the spirit and life-style and above all the religion of the people of Israel made itself felt in this almost 'world-wide' fashion. The religious ideas of Israel were able to compete with those of other nations and religions, even in a variety of transformations within the Diaspora, a long way from Jerusalem, where the Greek language became a new medium for the transmission of the Israelite and Jewish tradition. This proved possible without the central core of these ideas becoming assimilated. The attempt by the Seleucids in the first half of the second century BC to force the metropolis of Jerusalem to accept Greek culture was to prove an utter failure. Antiochus IV's undertaking came to grief in the face of the resistance of Jerusalem, and conjured up the fighting spirit of the Maccabees.

NOTES

1. It is difficult to find a historically exact way of describing the former states of Israel and Judah at this time. The Ptolemaic documents talk of Syria and Phoenicia. In connection with the Persian division into satrapies, Herodotus (III, 91) speaks of the 'fifth province' Phoenicia, Palestine in Syria and Cyprus. The term 'Palestine' appears here for the first time, and stretches beyond the 'land of the Phillistines', the coastal plain, to the whole of the territory occupied by the old states of Israel and Judah. However, it primarily remains a designation of territory without a clear political and administrative demarcation. Y. Aharoni, *The Land of the Bible*, 1967, 357f.; Ben-Sasson (ed.), *Geschichte des jüdischen Volkes* I, 1978, 232f.

2. The extant works of the following ancient authors are relevant for this chapter and those which follow: Appian (second century BC); Polybius from Megalopolis in Arcadia (second century BC); Strabo from Amaseia (first century BC – first century AD); Nicolaus of Damascus (first century BC), who is the source which Josephus prefers to use, which is preserved in extensive fragments. Cf. also the great survey of sources in E. Schürer, *History*, § 3, new ed., I, 1973, 17–122; M. Stern, *Greek and Latin Authors on Jews and Judaism* I, 1974; G. Hölscher, *Die Quellen des Josephus für die Zeit vom Exil bis zum Jüdischen Krieg*, 1904; M. Hengel, *Judaism and Hellenism*, 1974; *IJH*, 539–49.

3. W. Tarn and G. T. Griffith, *Hellenistic Civilisation*, ³1952; *Fischer Weltgeschichte* 6: *Der Hellenismus und der Aufstieg Roms*, 1965; M. Cary, *A History of the Greek World 323 to 146 BC*, ²1951 (last reprint 1977, with a new bibliography); V. Tcherikover, *Hellenistic Civilization and the Jews*, 1959. For the Greek influences on Palestine before Alexander see D. Auscher, 'Les relations entre la Grèce et la Palestine avant la conquête d'Alexandre', *VT* 17, 1967, 8–30.

4. The classical account is that by J. G. Droysen, *Geschichte Alexanders des Grossen*, 1833, which has been reprinted many times since then; for Alexander's conquest of the Persian empire see H. Bengtson, in *Fischer Weltgeschichte* 5, 1965, 283–310; id., *Griechische Geschichte*, ⁵1977; more recently, P. Jouget, *Alexander the Great and the Hellenistic World. Macedonian Imperialism and the Hellenization of the East*, 1979.

5. One can count ten cities with this name, including Alexandria in Egypt. For the latter see now the brief survey in E. Brunner-Traut and V. Hell, *Ägypten*, ³1978, 284–306; further literature and the earliest example in *Lexikon der Ägyptologie* I, 1972, 134f.; there are impressive pictures of the antiquities with a short introduction to the history of the city in K. Michalowski, *Alexandria*, 1971.

6. This was burnt by Julius Caesar when he laid siege to Alexandria and sacked it. At the time it contained about a million scrolls, but these were partially replaced by the library of Pergamum, which consisted of 200,000 scrolls. This was given by Cleopatra. It was completely destroyed at the time of Theodosius the Great by Archbishop Theophilus in 389. The Museion provided accommodation for distinguished scholars, It was destroyed in connection with the operations of the Emperor Aurelian (270–275) against Alexandria.

7. The present-day capital of the country , Cairo, was only founded in AD 641, in the neighbourhood of earlier Egyptian fortifications, by champions of Islam, as a new capital of the country which, in contrast to Alexandria, would be free from Christian elements.

8. However, the foundation of Gerasa is put back to the time of Alexander. In the Seleucid period the city was known by the name of Antioch on the Chrysorhoos, a small stream which flowed in the neighbourhood. In 84 BC Alexander Jannaeus sacked it, and in 63 BC Pompey added it to the Decapolis. See the brief account of the history of the city and its buildings in G. L. Harding, *Antiquities of Jordan*, ²1967, 79–105; there is a comprehensive account in C. H. Kraeling, *Gerasa, City of the Decapolis*, 1938; see now M. Avi-Yonah (ed.), *Encyclopaedia of Archaeological Excavations in the Holy Land* (*EAE*) II, 1976, 417–28.

Bosrah (*boṣra eški ām*), for which there is evidence as early as the second millennium BC (A. Negev, ed., *Archaeological Encyclopaedia of the Holy Land*, 1972, 56f.), owed its rise first to its elevation to be capital of the province of Arabia (AD 106). See the instructive accounts by H. Guthe, *Griechische und römische Städte des Ostjordanlandes*, 1918; id., *Gerasa*, 1919.

9. Josephus, *Antt.* XII, 1.1 (4).

10. F. Finegan, *Handbook of Biblical Chronology*, 1964, 117–23. According to the Macedonian calendar the Seleucid era began on 7 October 312, but according to the Babylonian calendar, taking into account the New Year's Day on 1 Nisan, it began only on 3 April 311. See also H. Lietzmann, *Zeitrechnung*, 1946, 6f. and tables.

11. The Seleucid system of calculating time remained in use until after the rise of Christianity, and is still known even today among the Syrian Christians in the Lebanon.

12. O. Plöger, *Das Buch Daniel*, KAT 18, 1965, 152, 158f.; A. A. Di Lella, *The Book of Daniel*, AB 23, 1978, 257, 289; A. Lacocque, *The Book of Daniel*, 1979, 214–18.

13. In fact the book has nothing to do with the Maccabees. However, the name 'Maccabees' was later used in a very general way of all protagonists of Jewish faith over against Greeks and other non-Jews, including Jews in the pre-Maccabean period. The Greek text is part of the Alexandrian canon of the Septuagint, but was not taken into the Catholic canon of the Vulgate. There is an English version in *AP* I, 155–73; see also Riessler, *Altjüdisches Schrifttum*, 1928, 682–99; further literature in Eissfeldt, *The Old Testament*, 1965, 581f.; Soggin, *Introduction*, ²1980, 471, 473.

14. H. Ewald, *Geschichte des Volkes Israel*, ³IV, 611f., draws the opposite conclusion, namely that 'by composing and elaborating his narrative the author wanted to prove that in Egypt the Jews had always been good subjects and therefore were granted many honours, rights and freedoms by the Ptolemies.'

15. The term 'Coele Syria' (from the Greek *koilos*) really denotes flat or 'hollow' Syria, and was used by Strabo only to describe the plain between the two Lebanons. However, the term also includes further areas of southern Syria, in the narrower sense the area in the neighbourhood of the hill-country of Lebanon; in the wider sense the satrapies of Idumaea, Samaria and Phoenicia, together with Coele Syria proper, could be included in the general term 'Coele Syria'. G. Holscher, *Palästina in der persischen und hellenistischen Zeit*, 1902, 6–12, 51–5.

16. Josephus, *Antt.* XII, 3.3 (138–144).

17. See Appendix D in R. Marcus, *Josephus* 7 (LCL), 743–64; this also contains a discussion of earlier literature. A. Alt notes two different versions of the decree which have been worked together: *ZAW* 57, 1939, 283–5. Text in K. Galling, *TGI*, ¹1950, 76f. (only in Greek); ²1968, 89f. (which has a German translation but no Greek text).

18. This Ptolemy is one of the Egyptians who went over to the Seleucids; Antiochus entrusted him with affairs in the satrapies of Coele Syria and Phoenicia.

19. This 'council of elders' was a body subordinated to the high priest, corresponding to the later Sanhedrin. Cf. E. Schürer, *History*, § 4, new ed., I, 1973, 138–40.

20. The 'Acra' is the 'citadel' of Jerusalem. The Acra mentioned here, in the time of Antiochus the Great, was probably north of the site of the temple and was built up further by the Hasmoneans and Herod. At the time of Herod it was called the 'Antonia citadel'. According to an earlier theory, which was proposed by G. A. Smith, Schürer and more recently again by Simons, a distinction is to be made between this and the Acra built by Antiochus IV Epiphanes. The latter is to be sought in the south-east of the temple area, possibly in a place which has now been built over by Herod's levelling of the temple area. E. Schürer, *History*, § 4 n.39, 154f. More recent comments in this direction can be found in Y. Tsafrir, 'The Location of the Seleucid Akra in Jerusalem', in *Jerusalem Revealed*, Jerusalem 1975, 85f.; cf. also J. Simons, *Jerusalem in the Old Testament*, 1952, 148ff.

21. Probably the month Tishri (September/October) in the Israelite and Jewish calendar; J. Finegan, *Handbook of Biblical Chronology*, 1964, 73.

22. This is probably the value of the goods in kind mentioned earlier.

23. The *artaba* was an Egyptian measure of capacity, originating in Persia, of about forty litres; it thus corresponds to the Old Testament ephah. The term 'holy' added here possibly relates to the measures used in the temple.

24. The Attic grain *medimnus*, which we should probably also assume here, was a wide-spread measure of capacity, differing in size from city to city. It amounted to about fifty litres.

25. We know nothing of the existence of a building which was adorned with pillars and perhaps also with wood-panelling, after the fashion of Solomon's 'House of the Forest of Lebanon'.

26. Often attested after the time of Alexander (Arrian I, 12.1). In the Roman world this obligatory gift is called the *aurum coronarium*. Cf. T. Klauser, *Römische Mitteilungen* 59, 1944–46, 129ff.

27. There is a select bibliography on these priestly families in the LCL edition of Josephus, translated by R. Marcus, 7, Appendix E, 767f.; see also *The Hellenistic Age*, ed. A. Schalit, *WHJP* I, 6, London 1976, 96–105; *IJH*, 242–4.

28. See pp. 328f. above.

29. M. Rostovtzeff, *A Large Estate in Egypt in the Third Century* BC, University of Wisconsin Studies in the Social Sciences and History 6, 1922; the papyri are published in V. A. Tcherikover and A. Fuks, *Corpus Papyrorum Judaicarum* (CPJ) I, 1957; there are earlier publications and a short account in J. Herz, *PJB* 24, 1928, 105–9; see further F.-M. Abel, *Histoire de la Palestine* I, Paris 1952, 65–71; *IJH*, 571–3; there is a good reproduction of a papyrus in M. Avi-Jonah (ed.), *A History of the Holy Land*, 1969, 115.

30. There is an instructive survey in J. Herz, op. cit., 107; further topographical details in S. Mittmann, 'Zenon in Ostjordanland', *Archäologie und Altes Testament* (Galling Festschrift), 1970, 199–210.

31. Usually 'general', but here the designation of a senior administrative office.

32. For Koheleth see most recently A. Lauha, *Kohelet*, BK 19, 1978, 3. For Jesus Sirach see the Introductions to the Old Testament and especially Eissfeldt, 1965, 595–9. In Sir.50.27–29, Jesus ben-Eleazar is mentioned as author of the Hebrew text. His grand-son translated the work into Greek in Egypt (after 117 BC). Soggin, *Introduction*, ²1980, 450–7 (with more recent literature); F. Vattioni, *Ecclesiastico*, Naples 1968, refers to the Hebrew, Greek, Latin and Syriac texts and translations. Extensive fragments of a Hebrew text were found in the Geniza of the Ezra synagogue in Cairo in 1896; however, there is dispute as to their authenticity. Still, some fragments of the Hebrew Sirach found in Qumran, which show agreements with the text from Cairo, have at least suggested that a more positive answer might be given to the question of a continuing Hebrew textual tradition. Nevertheless, whether or not this Hebrew text is directly connected with the original version produced by the author at the beginning of the second century BC remains open.

33. Lauha, op. cit., 23, comments: 'For all his peculiarities, Koheleth serves as the guardian of some fundamental biblical ideas.'

34. There is an English version of the Letter of Aristeas in *AP* II, 83–122.

35. On the question of an original basic text of the Septuagint and its reconstruction see P. Kahle, 'Die Septuaginta. Prinzipielle Erwägungen', in *Festschrift O. Eissfeldt zum 60. Geburtstag*, 1947, 161–80; more recent discussion can be found in F. M. Cross, *The Ancient Library of Qumran*, rev. ed. 1961, ch.IV; R. Hanhart considers the significance of Septuagint study for scholarship in 'Die Bedeutung der Septuagintaforschung für die Theologie', in *Drei Studien zum Judentum*, Theologische Existenz heute, NF 140, 1967,

38–64; for the contribution made by Egypt see S. Morenz, *Ägyptische Spuren in den Septuaginta*, 1964; now in S. Morenz, *Religion und Geschichte des alten Ägypten*, 1975, 417–28; M. Görg, 'Ptolemäische Theologie in der Septuaginta', in *Das ptolemäische Ägypten, Akten des internationalen Symposions Berlin 1976*, ed. H. Maehler and V. M. Strocka, 1978, 177–85.

6 | *Antiochus IV and the Maccabees*

AFTER THE DEATH of Antiochus III the Great in 187 BC, the whole of the eastern Mediterranean, including Greece, entered a period of upheaval and the uncertainties associated with it. Rome began to extend its influence on the East. After the end of the Second Punic War in 201 BC, Rome dictated peace terms to the Carthaginians and rose to become the chief military power; she had become mistress of the Western Mediterranean. Then began the attack on the East, first on Macedonia; subsequently it turned against Asia Minor and Syria. Rome's link with Egypt also posed a direct threat to the Seleucids in Syria. There, however, Antiochus IV was now a ruler as ambitious as he was reckless, breaking down barriers in his attempt to extend and develop his power in a way unparalleled by any previous Seleucid ruler. He attempted also to impose Hellenism on Jerusalem and Judah by the use of political and military force, thus subjecting the Judaeans to the most severe trial that they had had to undergo since the Babylonian exile.

At this point opinions began to diverge. It will emerge that under the massive pressure of these new developments some Jews displayed a readiness to open themselves up to Hellenistic influences. Those faithful to the Law, however, regarded this as an acute challenge and decided upon resolute resistance. The Maccabees offered this resistance and for the whole era became a symbol of uncompromising struggle; for all their success, however, in view of existing power relationships this also led to tensions and the formation of new groupings. Thus this period already establishes the presuppositions for the many strata of early Judaism in the first century BC. In addition to the Pharisees, the representatives of orthodoxy, the subsequent period would also see the appearance of the Sadducees, a group with greater political and cultural mobility, which was more ready to compromise. Special developments also proved possible, among them the Qumran community. Different verdicts have been passed on the relationship between this group and the Essenes, who also gained ground. However, this already takes us beyond the limits of the present chapter.

We are better informed about the period after Antiochus IV than about the preceding period. I Maccabees is the chief source for conditions in Judaea. Originally it was written in Hebrew, but it has come down to us only in Greek.[1] It reports events between the accession of Antiochus IV in 175 and the death of the Hasmonean Simon in 134 BC. The narrative is in chronological sequence and has a fairly reliable basis in contemporary sources.[2] II Maccabees is a different matter. This only covers the period between 175 and 161 BC, and from 2.19 is an extract from the historical work of Jason of Cyrene, which otherwise is unknown to us. Jason came from Hellenistic Diaspora circles and may have written in Greek. Because of the numerous legendary elements which it includes, II Maccabees is not to be rated so highly as a source.[3] Both books of Maccabees, which found their way into the Apocrypha of the Old Testament, are therefore concerned to extol the merits of the Maccabaean movement, which remained faithful to the Law. Of the other writers whose accounts are significant for this period, Josephus and Polybius deserve special mention.[4]

It is not easy to describe individual events in the history of Judaea during this period because of the complexity of the motives involved and the way in which they are bound up with non-political conceptions and the dangers posed by the Seleucids. Seleucus IV Philopator (187–175), the predecessor of Antiochus IV, who fell victim to Heliodorus, had already attempted to abolish the financial autonomy of the sanctuary at Jerusalem, which had been guaranteed by Antiochus III. The unscrupulous Antiochus IV resorted to very different means to meet the extraordinary contributions which Rome exacted from him. He sold the office of the high priest to the highest bidder. The result was that in Jerusalem the high priests changed in rapid succession. First of all Antiochus IV deposed the high priest Onias III (about 175 BC), and replaced him with his brother Jason, because the latter promised him not only a large sum of money, but also that the Greek life-style would be imposed throughout Jerusalem. However, as early as 173 a rival to the high priesthood by the name of Menelaus,[5] who was probably one of the Tobiad family, made the king an even higher offer and himself became high priest. Menelaus occupied the office until 164 with one interruption, during Antiochus IV's first expedition to Egypt in 169, when Jason tried to drive him out. He recklessly sold temple vessels in order to be able to keep his financial promises to the Syrians.[6]

After 170, Antiochus was involved in bitter controversy with the Egyptians. They again laid claim to Coele Syria. However, Antiochus anticipated their attack and also had considerable success in two campaigns against Egypt. He had himself acclaimed king by his troops and was crowned Pharaoh in Memphis. In the meantime, however, the Romans emerged as victors in the Third Macedonian War at the battle of Pydna (168 BC). They looked on Antiochus' goings on in Egypt with the utmost suspicion. They now forced the Seleucids to leave Egypt and made their own claim on the country. Antiochus had to yield to the superior Roman strength. This caused revolts in various places in the Seleucid empire, and also in Jerusalem.

Antiochus himself had already appeared in Jerusalem in autumn 169,[7] on his return from his first Egyptian campaign; he had entered the temple and had it plundered, which had been his practice with sanctuaries elsewhere in his wide domain. When he finally had to leave Egypt under Roman pressure during his second Egyptian operation in 168 and there were disturbances in Jerusalem, the dispossessed high priest Jason once again assumed office, as has already been mentioned; however, his rebellion was put down and he had to flee. First of all he remained in Transjordan, but later he went to Egypt. Menelaus was restored to office under the protection of Syrian arms. Antiochus did not make another personal appearance in Jerusalem. He sent Apollonius, the 'chief collector of tribute' (I Macc.1.29; cf. II Macc.5.24) to Hellenize the city completely and to take precautions so that it had a sound military defence.[8] In connection with this the 'Acra', the fortress-like citadel in Jerusalem, was either expanded or completely rebuilt for the Seleucid garrison.[9] This now virtually permanent Seleucid occupation of Jerusalem did away with practically all the privileges which Antiochus III had granted to Jerusalem. There is a certain analogy between this whole procedure and the settlement of Samaria with Macedonian colonists after the city had rebelled against Alexander the Great. Apollonius had the Acra in Jerusalem occupied not only by a Syrian garrison but also by Hellenized Jews who were particularly well disposed to him. In I Maccabees they are called 'godless people'.[10]

In a series of further measures, some months after the establishment of the Acra, Antiochus also prohibited the temple sacrifices. He banned circumcision and other cultic requirements. But the most monstrous thing of all was the institution of the cult of Olympian Zeus in the sanctuary itself (167 BC), where he also had his own altar. The notorious but sufficiently clear designation 'abomination of desolation' in the book of Daniel (Dan.9.27; 12.11) is probably a reference to this altar of Olympian Zeus.[11] In addition, altars were built outside, in the Judaean countryside, on which anyone could sacrifice to the alien religion. Observance of Jewish cultic practices and ancestral religion carried the death penalty. This applied principally to the observance of the sabbath and other festivals.[12] Antiochus used such measures as a punishment for the practice of Jewish customs and rites, which were regarded as political offences, as rebellion against Seleucid rule. In fact by so doing he abolished the Torah, which had not been attacked by any foreign power since Judaea lost its political independence after the exile. The magnitude of the conflict for the Jews in and around Jerusalem cannot be exaggerated. It was an inescapable dilemma. One had either to refuse to obey the Seleucid king and thus be exposed to persecution, or be compelled to disregard ancestral religion, which was a betrayal of the cause dearest to one's heart; to deny the decisive religious force which hitherto had also largely laid the foundation for political independence and had made it possible. It was inevitable that this conflict should come to the boil.

The outward course of events described above, following from the accession of Antiochus IV, was made all the more oppressive by the fact that this Seleucid championed a systematic Hellenization which was by no means limited to the cultic sphere. Of course the erection of an altar to Zeus in the sanctuary at Jerusalem was without doubt the most monstrous sacrilege in the whole history of the temple. A foreign ruler had made a place of worship for a foreign deity in the very grounds of the temple. There is a vivid expression of the dismay that this caused in the books of Maccabees. And in fact there will have been few people who did not feel this sacrilege to be what it was. However, the fundamental hostility towards the Hellenistic life-style was not directly connected with this. Even some members of the priesthood were not completely opposed to the process of Hellenization. I Maccabees depicts the beginning of all the troubles with words which might be taken as a kind of scenario, even if they represent the viewpoint of those faithful to the Law: 'In those days lawless men came forth from Israel, and misled many, saying, "Let us go and make a covenant with the Gentiles round about us, for since we separated from them many evils have come upon us" ' (I Macc.1.11). We are then told that some of the people in fact received royal authorization to build a gymnasium in Jerusalem along Greek lines, and even underwent operations to disguise the fact that they had been circumcised (1.12–14). The gymnasium, in which athletes followed the Greek practice of competing in the nude, was in fact the symbol and the corner-stone of the whole Hellenistic way of life, and was particularly prized by younger people. All sporting competitions were held under the aegis of the gods and were meant to honour them; thus they were necessarily bound up with the cult of Heracles or Hermes, or claimed divine legitimation from the ruler in power at the time. It is understandable enough that this posed most serious problems for the majority of Jews who might want to be receptive to Hellenistic civilization. An episode related in II Macc.4.18–20 is illuminating in this respect. A group of Hellenistic Jews travelled to Tyre as a delegation from Jerusalem. Jason, the high priest at the time, gave them money for the sacrifice to Heracles. However, the men asked that the money might be used for other purposes because it was 'inappropriate' to use it for a sacrifice to Heracles.

This account is interesting in two ways. It shows the unscrupulousness of a high priest, but also the deeply-rooted feeling among the representatives of Jerusalem chosen here for what was 'appropriate'. In view of such events one may well ask how it could be that some of the priests could also apparently be inclined to accept compromises in cultic matters, apart from any obvious political opportunism. Of course the tradition should not be forgotten; however, at the same time there was a concern to assimilate the religion of Israel as far as possible to Hellenism, so that in the context of Greek education it, too, might be understood as one of the factors contributing to a universal human culture. The extremely complex process of the Hellenization of Judaea took place in an exceedingly tense political atmosphere. The attempts of the Seleucid leader, driven on by the spirit of the age and lacking in any understanding of the character and strength of the Jewish way of life, to achieve assimilation by force, could not but offend many people and provoke powerful opposition. We should assume that convinced Hellenists remained in the minority, and that at all events they were to be found in Jerusalem, whereas people in the outlying districts looked upon the revolution with mistrust.

The counter-attack did in fact come from groups among the unsettled country population. It began at a small place called Modein, between Beth-horon and Lydda to the north-west of Jerusalem. As the account has it, a Syrian official appeared there and required the country population to take place in alien sacrifices. He was opposed by a man from a priestly family, by the name of Mattathias,[13] who not only killed the official, but also a Jew who performed the sacrifice required (I Macc. 2.15–28).

Thereupon Mattathias fled with his five sons to the lonely neighbourhood on the eastern slopes of the hill-country of Judaea, where he gathered other like-minded people about him. These people made a foray, destroyed the altars which had been put up by the Seleucids, killed Jews who were favourably inclined to the Hellenistic spirit and the alien cult, and circumcised children who had not yet been circumcised. In this first period there seem to have been only small skirmishes with Seleucid troops. They mostly attacked on the sabbath, because on this day the pious Jews refused to put up any resistance. Finally Mattathias permitted fighting on the sabbath, in order to make possible organized defence.

Mattathias himself died in 166, in the first months of this battle for the Law of Israel against the alien spirit of Hellenism. One of his sons, Judas, surnamed Makkabi, 'the hammer' (Greek 'Makkabaios'), who went down in history as Judas the Maccabee (Judas Maccabaeus), continued the battle: as a result of his memorable surname, the revolt of those who remained faithful to the Law came to be known as the 'Maccabaean revolt'. Under Judas the scope of the fighting increased considerably, because now units of Syrian troops played a much greater part in the conflict.

Judas won his first battles in the immediate neighbourhood of Modein, at Bethhoron, and later to the south-west, in the region of Emmaus.[14] These actions now began to alarm the Seleucid government, which ordered the governor, Lysias, to march against the rebels. There was a battle at Beth-zur, about eighteen miles south of Jerusalem; again, Judas and his followers were victorious (I. Macc.4. 26–35). Lysias now attempted to engage in proper peace negotiations with the Judaeans in Beth-zur. The reason for this was, of course, that Antiochus IV was fighting the Parthians in the east and therefore could not release substantial contingents of troops to fight against the rebellious Judaeans. There was in fact a cease-fire which turned out well for the victors, if only to a limited extent. According to II Maccabees 11.19, Lysias required the Judaeans to acknowledge the authority of the Syrian central government. At the same time, a Roman delegation was on the way which wanted to make contact with the king in Antioch and was prepared to plead the Jewish case (II Macc.11.34–38).[15] Finally, even the high priest Menelaus seems to have intervened to appease the king (II Macc.11.29), probably because he recognized that the pious but combative Jews, who were really his opponents, had the upper hand.

In view of the manifest successes of the Maccabees, Antiochus IV yielded. In a royal decree, the text of which has been handed down in II Macc. 11.27–31, and the content of which may be taken to be reliable, a complete pardon is promised to all those who are prepared to return home at an appointed time. It is explicitly stated that the Judaeans are to be allowed to prepare their own food and observe their own laws as before. In fact that meant the end of the persecutions and the capitulation of the king, recognizing the failure of his attempt forcibly to impose Hellenistic culture and a Hellenistic life-style in Jerusalem. Of course, this did not solve the central problem, the Jerusalem cult and its sole orientation on the God of Israel. Menelaus was still in power as high priest. Judas therefore resolved to expel him and the Hellenizing priests in Jerusalem from office by force (I Macc.4.36–61). So in December 164 he occupied the city, purified the temple of all innovations and structural alterations, and changed the priesthood. He also managed to barricade the Seleucid garrison and their loyal followers in the Acra. The event longed for by those faithful to the Law took place on 14 December (25 Chislev) on the year 164, three years after the desecration of the temple:[16] it could again be consecrated with a purified altar to the God of Israel (I Macc.4.36–61; II Macc.10.1–8; Josephus, *Antt.* XII, 7.6f.=316–326). The celebrations lasted for eight days, and I Macc.4.59 ordains that this festival shall be repeated annually. It is the present-day feast of Hanukkah, which keeps alive the remembrance of these events.

According to I Macc.5, the restoration of Israelite worship in Jerusalem led many peoples living around Judaea to attack and even kill the Jews living in their midst. So Judas and his brother Simon are said to have engaged in a series of battles in the context of which there were victories over the Edomites and Moabites in Transjordan. Those faithful to the Law were even able, under the leadership of Judas and Simon, to rush to the aid of the oppressed inhabitants of Gilead and Galilee. The battles are said finally to have extended to the coastal plain and to Judaea. Hebron was subdued, as was Marisa, which lay west of it on the coast. Here we probably have a summary report which has brought together a large number of individual operations to make them seem a single campaign. Of course we cannot establish when one enterprise or another actually took place.[17]

It will have been only a few days after the consecration of the temple[18] that Antiochus IV died on a campaign against the Parthians. His eight-year-old son Antiochus V, later called Eupator, was not capable of succeeding him on the throne; so it seems that even while Antiochus IV was still alive, his general Philip was entrusted with the regency. These uncertainties over the question of the succession were to prove remarkably beneficial to Jerusalem and to Judas Maccabaeus. He increased the pressure on the Acra, so that the garrison turned to the Syrian king for help. Lysias, who at the time was host to the young Antiochus V, advanced to relieve the garrison. Judas withdrew and took up a battle position at Beth-zachariah, about six miles south-west of Bethlehem, where he was beaten. However, he succeeded in escaping to the fortifications of Jerusalem. Lysias pursued him and laid siege to the city. The situation for those under siege was extremely threatening, and Judas and his followers seemed lost. At that point, however, Lysias received the news that Antiochus IV had entrusted the regency to Philip and not to him. Philip was said to be on his way to Antioch, to take over the reins of government. This produced the turning-point (I Macc.6.55–63). Lysias was anxious to make a speedy departure and was ready for a compromise (163 BC).

The temple precincts were restored to those faithful to the Law, and they were again allowed to practise their ancestral religion.

II Maccabees 11.22–26 contains an official-looking document relating to this in the form of a letter to Lysias. It mentions the fact that 'the Jews do not consent to our father's change to Greek customs' and says that their old rights will now be given back to them. This seems to blot out the shame which Antiochus IV had brought on the people of Judaea and Jerusalem. Jerusalem regained its independent position and had that confirmed, though of course there were limitations, as will soon emerge. Quite unexpectedly, and against the agreements, Lysias had the fortifications of the temple precincts razed, killed sixty of the erstwhile Jewish rebels, and even had the high priest Menelaus (who had been removed from office) executed. As Lysias pointed out, he was to blame for all the troubles (II Macc.13.4).

In connection with this, Josephus observes (*Antt.* XII, 9.7=384f.) that Menelaus had caused the king's father to compel Jews to apostatize from worshipping the God of their ancestors. Surprising though this verdict may seem, and so far removed from actual circumstances, it may well be historical evidence for a political strategy to justify the Seleucids. They wanted to shift the blame for earlier developments from Antiochus IV and make one of the Jews responsible. At least this was a way in which the Syrians could demonstrate their resolution to take a new course of action.

The high priest was now Alcimus, evidently a member of the Zadokite family, who was also recognized by those faithful to the Law.[19] He had already been nominated by Demetrius I Soter (162–150 BC), after Antiochus V and Lysias had been murdered in Antioch. This was the Demetrius, son of Seleucus IV, who had once lived in Rome as a hostage. Nevertheless, the apparent complete change of circumstances in Jerusalem did not lead to general satisfaction. There was still a Syrian garrison in the Acra, and sacrifices were offered in the temple for the Seleucid ruler (I Macc.7.33). Judas Maccabaeus had played no part in the redistribution of power in the new constitution, and looked on developments with mistrust. He again withdrew into the hill-country of Judaea, accompanied by other dissatisfied followers. History again took a threatening turn.

Alcimus, originally supported by the armed forces of the Syrian governor Bacchides, felt threatened by this withdrawal of Judas and his supporters. He asked Demetrius I for help. Demetrius ordered his general Nicanor to go to Jerusalem and break the power of Judas if that were possible. This enterprise came to a surprising end. There was a battle well before the gates of the city, between Bethhoron and Adasa, in which Nicanor fell. Judas occupied Jerusalem and declared the day of the victory over Nicanor a festival (13 Adar=27 March 161). At the request of Alcimus the Syrians again intervened, this time under the leadership of Bacchides himself (I Macc.9.1–22). There seemed to be cause enough, because according to I Macc.8.17–32, Judas had sought to establish links with Rome.[20]

However, he was killed in the battle against Bacchides. At Elasa, the exact location of which is unknown, but which is presumably in the region of Beth-horon, Judas succumbed to the superior might of Syria (161/160 BC).

The fate of a bold and resolute man was sealed. After the restoration of the cult in Jerusalem, Judas had apparently achieved his aims. Was it the case, as was often said later, that in the last resort he was obsessed with power, and that this led him to further fighting and thus to his downfall? Did he ultimately fail to recognize that Alcimus in alliance with the Syrians represented a permanent threat which might again be directed at any time against the city and the temple? Rudolf Kittel's judgment is worth bearing in mind:[21]

'The death of Judas Maccabaeus saw the end of the last great man in Israel. . . . Without Judas the Hammerer, Judaism would have succumbed to force, at home and then necessarily in the Greek cities of the Diaspora. Where it might have continued among small groups, it would have been forced into obscure and remote corners. Thanks to Judas, Nehemiah's creation lived on and lasted down the centuries. When he eventually went, defeated, to the grave, he had not lived in vain.

The place of Judas was taken by his youngest brother Jonathan. He and his followers were pursued and at first could only survive by going into the Judaean wilderness near Tekoa. Bacchides controlled the country, Alcimus remained in office, and the cult remained untouched. Nevertheless, Jonathan and his people remained a resistance to be reckoned with. Alcimus died in 159, and to begin with his office was left empty. In the end Bacchides could not cope with Jonathan and therefore made him a peace offer (157 BC). With the consent of the Seleucids, Jonathan settled in Michmash, on the outskirts of Jerusalem, about eight miles from the city, in that territory to the north-east which once belonged to Benjamin. There he acted as a kind of 'judge', administering a form of local government; he was chiefly opposed to those friendly with the Greeks, with their Hellenistic tendencies. However, the majority of the Judaeans seem to have been on his side. These were the circumstances which helped Jonathan at an appropriate moment to an unexpected and unusual career.[21]

Demetrius I, threatened in 153 by Alexander Balas, who made himself out to be a son of Antiochus IV and laid claim to the throne, made a treaty with Jonathan and granted him the right to have his own troop of armed men. Jonathan went with them to Jerusalem, fortified the temple hill again and forced the Syrian garrison right back to the Acra. Then Alexander Balas went even further and nominated Jonathan high priest (152 BC). Jonathan does not seem to have lost any time in changing allies; he took office and joined Alexander's side. His calculations worked out. Demetrius fell to Alexander on the battlefield and the new ruler showed his gratitude to Jonathan. He invited him to his wedding with Cleopatra, a daughter of Ptolemy VI Philometor, in Ptolemais (Acco), and there made him *stratēgos* and *meridarchēs* (general and part-governor) of Coele Syria, so that in fact he had the status of a provincial governor with military and civil rights over Judaea. Of course this also obliged him to go to war on behalf of the Syrians. Jonathan put up successful resistance in the southern coastal plain between Joppa (Jaffa) and Ashkelon against the troops of Demetrius II, who was setting himself up as a rival king. As a result, Alexander Balas granted Jonathan the city of Ekron and its territory.

A series of turbulent events, in which Ptolemy VI Philometor (181–145 BC) was also involved, finally compelled Alexander Balas to flee to Arabia. Ptolemy had sent a contingent of troops to Syria to support Demetrius II Nicator, and after the death of Ptolemy in the same year, Demetrius II Nicator came to power (145–139). Jonathan's boldness in again laying siege to the Acra in Jerusalem provoked the wrath of the new ruler. Jonathan was summoned to Ptolemais, but there he must have succeeded in pacifying the king and securing the fulfilment of other wishes. These were related to an extension of Judaean territory northwards, by taking in the three districts of the province of Samaria,[23] which at the same time were granted far-reaching exemptions from tax and tribute (I Macc.11.34–36).

Jonathan regarded this only as partial success. There were still Syrian troops in the Acra and in Beth-zur. However, Demetrius II did not seem prepared to make further concessions, even when Jonathan had played an active and successful part in a rebellion against the king in Antioch (I Macc.11.41–53). New complications helped Jonathan on, but ultimately turned out to his disadvantage. One Diodotus Trypho from Apamea set up the son of Alexander Balas, still a minor, as a rival king, Antiochus VI. Jonathan and his brother were prepared to fight for Trypho in southern and central Syria to secure a territorial base for the potential ruler. The great successes which the brothers had there and the contacts which Jonathan made with Rome and Sparta (I Macc.12.1–23) must have seemed all too dangerous to Trypho. He himself had an eye on the crown, though of course he could not achieve a decisive success over king Demetrius. By a stratagem he succeeded in luring Jonathan with a small escort to Ptolemais, and after giving them a ceremonial welcome, took them prisoner. Jonathan's brother Simon immediately rushed to Jerusalem, where he was able to enlist a large number of people to continue the struggle. Although Trypho even had Jonathan with him as a captive, in his advance against Judaea he had to yield to Simon; however, Simon was not in a position to free Jonathan. On the retreat through Gilead, Trypho had Jonathan murdered at Baskama.[24] Simon is said to have brought his bones back to Modein for honourable burial.

Jonathan was certainly quite different from Judas Maccabaeus. However, they both had one thing in common, the resolution and harshness to break down resistance, pursue decisively the goals they had in mind, take advantage of favourable opportunities and make the most of even the most unfortunate situations. Here Jonathan proved even bolder than Judas in dealing with his opponents at the level of diplomacy, and was skilled in gaining sympathy when he felt that this would lead to success. However, despite his flexibility, in his dangerous intrigue with the Seleucid rulers, who ultimately gained the upper hand, he became a tragic figure who, useful though he have seemed at times, could not completely be trusted, and finally fell victim to the interests of sheer power politics.

Greatness and tragedy are combined in the Maccabaean struggle. The wild resolution of Mattathias and Judas had been kindled by zeal for the Law of the God of Israel, and they saved this Law and the prescribed forms of temple worship from the severest crisis since the exile, in the face of all the trials and attempts at alienation. However, it was impossible to break the political and military strength of the Seleucids, which markedly limited the room for manoeuvre to Jerusalem and Judaea. Here was the goad which did not allow the Maccabees to be content with their religious interests and concern for the Law. The apparently invincible Syrian garrison in the Acra and at Beth-zur was constantly before their eyes, and forced them on from zeal for the Law to power politics. Only a lack of resolution or weakness on the part of the Syrian central government could have helped the Maccabaeans towards their goal of religious and political independence. A favourable opportunity allowed Simon to discover and exploit a balance of power, in order to help Jerusalem and Judaea to arrive at a surprisingly new and independent status.

NOTES

1. The book is very close to the events described and in view of its closing words (I Macc.16.23f.) was most probably finished in Jerusalem during the time of the Hasmonean Hyrcanus (134–104 BC), or shortly after his death. For further details see the Introductions to the Old Testament and the short survey in *IJH*, 541–4.

2. K. D. Schunck, *Die Quellen des I. und II. Makkabäerbuches*, 1954, attempts to identify several contemporary strands of tradition; this is criticized by G. O. Neuhaus, 'Quellen im I Makkabäerbuch? Eine Entgegnung auf die Analyse von K.-D. Schunck', *JSJ* 5, 1974, 162–75.

3. The historical narrative proper is prefaced with two letters (II Macc.1.1–9; 1.10–2.18), the authenticity of which is particularly disputed. The whole book was probably finished in the first century BC. For the sources of the work see Schunck, op. cit.; J. G. Bunge, *Untersuchungen zum Zweiten Makkabäerbuch*, Bonn Dissertation 1971. See further J. R. Bartlett, *The First and Second Books of the Maccabees*, CBC, 1973; F.-M. Abel and J. Starcky, *Les Livres des Maccabées*, La Sainte Bible 27, 1961.

4. Relevant passages are parts of Books XII and XIII of the *Antiquities* of Josephus and the beginning of Book I of his *Jewish War*, which starts with Antiochus Epiphanes. Polybius' account of Roman history in forty books (only the first five of which are complete; the rest are in fragments) mentions Antiochus Epiphanes from Book XXVI on. Polybius, *The Histories* V, VI, LCL, 1927 (reprinted 1975). See also the survey of the literary and archaeological source material in *IJH* 538f.; see also E. Bickermann, *Der Gott der Makkabäer*, 1937, 143–53.

5. According to Josephus, *Antt.* XII, 5.1 (238f.) he was a son of Simon (II ?) and brother of Jason. Menelaus originally bore the name Onias.

6. According to II Macc.4.32–38 this came to the ears of Onias III, who had withdrawn to the vicinity of Antioch. Onias made bitter complaints, so Menelaus had him killed by the governor, Andronicus. The more exact circumstances of this event are unconfirmed, and they are improbable, given the place to which Onias is said to have fled, and where he is supposed to have been murdered. I. L. Seeligmann, *The Septuagint Version of Isaiah. A Discussion of its Problems*, 1948, discusses critical problems from the final stage of Onias

III's life (in an excursus); for the alleged exile of Onias III in Syria see 93f. Details of an account by Diodore (30.7.2) of the murder of the son of Seleucus IV by Andronicus have probably been transformed to Onias III. Thus Wellhausen, to whom Seeligmann (op. cit.) refers.

7. Since the discovery of the 'Seleucid List', in the British Museum, the chronology of the Seleucid kings, and along with them that of the Maccabean period has been largely assured. Translations in *ANET*, 566f.; *Bibl.* 36, 1955, 261f. The text is published in A. J. Sachs and D. J. Wiseman, 'A Babylonian King List of the Hellenistic Period', *Iraq* 16, 1954, 202–11. For an evaluation see J. Schaumberger, 'Die neue Seleukidenliste BM 35 603 und die makkabäische Chronologie', *Bibl.* 36, 1955, 423–35; there is a detailed study by R. Hanhart, 'Zur Zeitrechnung des I. und II. Makkabäerbuches', in A. Jepsen and R. Hanhart, *Untersuchungen zur israelitisch-jüdischen Chronologie*, BZAW 88, 1964, 49–96.

8. The causes and the sequence of the events described here are disputed. This is because there are different accounts in I Macc.1.20–23; II Macc.5.1–26; Josephus, *Jewish War* I, 1.1 (31–33); *Antt.* XII, 5.1–4 (237–256); Dan.11.28–31. There is disagreement as to whether Antiochus twice appeared in Jerusalem in person, i.e. also after his second campaign in Egypt, or whether he simply sent Apollonius the second time. In connection with this there is disagreement as to when Jason's rebellion took place, as early as 169 or a year later, so that intervention in the state of affairs in Jerusalem after the second campaign in Egypt could have a causal connection with Jason's rebellion. P. Schäfer has made a survey of the various points of view and their defenders in *IJH*, 564–6. The account given here starts from the presupposition that the occupation of Jerusalem and its temple and the Hellenization of the city and Judaea generally were among the Seleucid aims, and that therefore the various catalytic factors which the tradition reports are of secondary importance.

9. For the exact site of the Acra erected by the Seleucids see Y. Tsafrir in *Jerusalem Revealed*, 1975, 85f. He conjectures a place on the south-east side of the temple area. M. Avi-Yonah puts forward a different suggestion, that the Seleucid Acra is connected with the Hasmonean palace and should be located on the north-east side of the Jewish quarter: *EAE* II, 1976, 603. K. M. Kenyon's personal view is that the Acra was on the western hilll in the area of the citadel which was later built by Herod: K. M. Kenyon, *Jerusalem. Excavating 3000 years of History*, 1967, 113. See also above, p. 353 n.20.

10. I Macc.1.34.

11. For the translation 'abomination of desolation' cf. above all the Greek form in I Macc.1.54 (quoted in Mark 13.14; Matt.24.15); see also II Macc.6.2. Hartman and Di Lella, *The Book of Daniel*, AB 23, 1978, 252f.; A. Lacocque, *The Book of Daniel*, 1979, 198f.

12. There are arguments about the reason for the harsh measures against the religion of the Jewish people which are depicted here. Bickermann in particular argues that the Syrians will have undertaken to support an active Hellenistic party in Jerusalem itself, possibly under the leadership of Menelaus. Tcherikover differs. He explains the measures as a reaction against the Hasidim, who rebelled against the Acra and the elevation of Jerusalem to the status of a *polis*. Bunge adopts an intermediate position. He regards the refusal to offer sacrifice for the king after the erection of the altar to Zeus as the contributory factor leading to the Seleucid measures. E. Bickermann, *Der Gott der Makkabäer. Untersuchungen über Sinn und Ursprung der makkabäischen Erhebung*, 1937; V. Tcherikover, *Hellenistic Civilization and the Jews*, 1959; J. G. Bunge, *Untersuchungen zum Zweiten Makkabäerbuch*, Bonn Dissertation 1971. There is a short account of the various standpoints in *IJH*, 562–4.

13. He was one of the 'sons of Joarib' (I Macc.2.1), and was therefore a member of the priestly order named after Joarib; this is the first of the orders described in I Chron.24.7ff. It was probably his grandfather or great-grandfather who bore the name Hasmon (cf. the

details in Josephus, *Antt*. XII, 6.1 = 265 with *BJ* I, 1.3 = 36). So the whole family is also usually called 'Hasmonean' (in the narrower sense the designation 'Hasmonean' is usually applied to members of the dynasty after Simon, to distinguish them from the 'Maccabees', the sons of Mattathias). They were joined by the Hasidaeans (Hebrew *ḥasidîm*, 'the pious': I Macc.2.42), who must already have been an independent group before the Maccabaean revolt.

14. I Macc.3.1–4.25. Judas' opponents were Apollonius, whose exact function is unknown (he is perhaps identical with the chief tax concessionaire, II Macc.5.24); Seron, the supreme commander of Coele Syria; and Gorgias, a general in the service of Lysias.

15. Different verdicts are passed on the historically and binding force of the contacts between Jews and Romans in the second century BC. For the events mentioned here see T. Liebmann-Frankfort, 'Rome et le conflict judéo-syrien (164–161 avant notre ère)', *L'antiquité classique* 38, 1969, 101–120; Bunge, op. cit., 392–5, 421f.

16. The period of three years might be substantially correct. It is, however, improbable, also taking into account Dan.8.14; 12.11f., that the temple was reconsecrated on the very day on which it had been desecrated three years before (cf. I Macc.1.54 with 4. 52–54).The desecration of the sanctuary may already have taken place in the summer of 167. R. Hanhart, op. cit., 83f. II Macc.10.3–5 cuts down the three years to two; for the whole problem see Hanhart, op. cit., 76–84.

17. Furthermore this summary account in I Macc.5 clearly separates the account of the consecration of the temple (ch.4) from the events surrounding the death of Antiochus IV (ch.6), both of which must have followed in very close chronological succession. See Hanhart, op. cit., 82. For problems relating to the history and topography of I Macc.5 see K. Galling, 'Judäa, Galiläa und der Osten im Jahre 164/3 v.Chr.', *PJB* 36, 1940, 43–77.

18. I Macc.6.1–17; II Macc.9; Seleucid List, verso 14. Despite some uncertainties, it is highly probable that the news of the death of the king had already reached Babylon by 18 December 164. Hanhart, op. cit., 79f.

19. Alcimus is the Hellenized form of the Hebrew name Jakim. Instead of Alcimus, Onias, a nephew of Menelaus and son of Onias III, should have been high priest. However, after the appointment of Alcimus this Onias IV fled to Egypt. There Ptolemy VI Philometor allowed him to build a temple for the God of Israel in Leontopolis, in the district of Heliopolis. This, at any rate, is what Josephus reports in *Antt*. XII, 9.7 (387f.); XIII, 3.1–3 (62–73). However, in *BJ* I, 1.1 (33) and VII, 10.2f. (423–32), Josephus is of the opinion that this temple was founded not by Onias IV but by Onias III after he had fled to Egypt on the appointment of Menelaus as high priest (about 173 BC). For the greater credibility of the latter account see I. L. Seeligmann, op. cit., 91–3; similarly now Bunge, op. cit., 561–6; id., 'Zur Geschichte und Chronologie des Untergangs der Oniaden und des Aufstiegs der Hasmonäer', *JSJ* 6, 1975, 9–11. According to Seeligmann, groups in Jerusalem hostile to the Oniads were perhaps the cause of the other account in the *Antiquities*. Cf. also the observation pointing in this direction in *BJ* VII, 10.3 (341), where Onias is said to have had sinister motives, directed against Jerusalem.

20. For the authenticity and legal character of the treaty documents given here see D. Timpe, 'Der römische Vertrag mit den Juden von 161 BC', *Chiron* 4, 1974, 133–52. For an assessment of relationships between Judaea and Rome see also pp. 370f. below.

21. R. Kittel, *Gestalten und Gedanken in Israel*, 1925, 481.

22. I Maccabees is silent about events in the time between 157 and 152 BC because there were evidently no revolutionary changes in which Jonathan was involved.

23. These were districts which stayed loyal to the Jerusalem sanctuary and did not feel an obligation to the Samaritan cult on Gerizim, namely Aphaerema (presumably in the area north of Bethel), Lydda (Lod) and Ramathaim on the west side of the hill-country of Ephraim, facing the coast.

24. Situation unknown.

The Hasmonean Dynasty and the Beginning of Roman Rule in Jerusalem and Judaea

WITH JONATHAN'S brother Simon a new epoch began. He succeeded in doing what none of these men from the family of Mattathias and Judas had so far managed to achieve. He regained almost unlimited independence for Jerusalem and Judaea, he overthrew the Jerusalem Acra, the apparently invincible symbol of Seleucid presence among the people of Judaea, and finally he managed to become the founder of a dynastic rule which lasted down to the first century BC. Religious themes and stimuli faded almost completely into the background in the style with which the Hasmoneans exercised their rule, and considerations of strategy and power politics gained an almost intolerable importance. These were a feature of the Hasmonean dynasty in which it came to reflect the whole period. For we can only understand its rise and the possible courses it could pursue against the background of developments in world politics during the second half of the second century BC.

The first condition for the rise of the Hasmoneans was the gradual collapse of the power of the Seleucids and the Ptolemies. Syria and Egypt, the natural neighbours of Israel and Judah, and therefore always the greatest threat to them, were torn apart internally and hampered by conflicting forces; at the same time they lived in fear of Rome's steady advance eastwards. In Rome itself, the period of the civil wars began in 133 BC with the disturbances caused by the Gracchi; it only came to an end in 31 BC with the establishment of the principate by Augustus. Rome's forces were occupied constantly in conflicts represented by the wars against Jugurtha of Numidia (111–105 BC), against the Cimbri (113–101), and finally against the Italian Confederation (91–88 in the 'Social War'), together with the debilitating wars against Mithridates of Pontus.[1] In view of these developments, to begin with, the eastern lands were in fact preserved from the direct intervention of Rome, but their strength wasted away from within so that they could no longer cope with harsher external attacks. Between 83 and 69 BC, Syria succumbed to the rule of the Armenian king Tigranes, a son-in-law of Mithridates, and in Judaea a power-struggle developed until Pompey intervened and irrevocably brought about the end of Seleucid and Hasmonean independence.

At the time of the conflict between Demetrius I Soter and Alexander Balas, Ptolemy VI Philometor had intervened in Syrian affairs.[2] Balas defeated Deme-

The chronological framework provided below may help to make events in this chapter clearer:

Ptolemies

Ptolemy VI Philometor	181–145
Ptolemy VIII Euergetes II ('Physkon')	169–164
Ptolemy VIII Euergetes II ('Physkon')	145–116
Ptolemy IX Soter II Lathyros	116–107
Ptolemy X Alexander I	107–89
Ptolemy IX Lathyros (again)	89–81
Ptolemy XI Alexander II	80
Ptolemy XII Neos Dionysos Auletes	80–51
Cleopatra VII	51–30

Seleucids

Demetrius I Soter	162–150
Alexander I Balas	153–145
Demetrius II Nicator	145–139
Antiochus VI Dionysus	145–141
Antiochus VII Sidetes	139–129
Demetrius II Nicator (again)	129–125
Seleucus V	125
Antiochus VIII Grypos	125–113
Antiochus VIII Grypos	111–96
Antiochus IX Cyzicenus	113–95
Struggle for the succession	95–83
Syria under Tigranes of Armenia	83–69
Antiochus XIII Asiaticus	69–65
Syria a Roman province	from 65

Hasmoneans

Simon	142/1–134
John Hyrcanus I	134–104
Aristobulus I	104–103
Alexander Jannai	103–76
Salome Alexandra	76–67
Aristobulus II	67–63
Hyrcanus II	63–40

trius (150 BC) and married a daughter of Ptolemy's in Acco. This was the last attempt of a Ptolemy to gain influence in Syria, a bold move in view of Rome's constant mistrust of all arbitrary expansion by rulers on the periphery of its sphere of influence. Ptolemy finally turned away from Alexander Balas and recognized Demetrius II Nicator, to whom he gave his daughter Cleopatra as wife and with whom he finally succeeded in defeating Balas. However, Ptolemy died shortly afterwards as a result of wounds which he had received in battle (145 BC).

In Syria, Diodotus Trypho now rebelled and set up a son of Alexander Balas as king under the name of Antiochus VI. However, he himself was ambitious for power and murdered Antiochus in 141. Regardless of this, Demetrius II remained in power, but the northern flank of the Mesopotamian part of his empire was threatened by the Parthians and so he was interested in stabilizing conditions in the south. In this situation, Demetrius promised Simon independence and freedom from tribute for Judaea. In the 170th year of the Seleucid era[3] (142/1 BC), Simon was recognized in Jerusalem as 'great high priest and commander and leader of the Jews' (I Macc.13.42), and dated the years of his rule from that point. Thus the year 142/1 is the first of his era. In his second year he succeeded in subduing the Acra (141) and celebrated the appearance there of Jews faithful to the Law. Again a year later (140) he officially became ethnarch of Judaea. The priests and leaders of the people bestowed on him the rank of priestly commander (I Macc.14.25–49) with the right to hereditary succession (14.41). This laid the foundation for the continuation of Hasmonean rule as a dynastic line.

Simon was able to extend the territory of Judaea in a number of ways. The most important development was that he captured the port of Joppa (Jaffa) and thus gained direct access to the sea (I Macc.14.5). In addition he was able to establish himself in the former Samaritan territory south-east of Shechem, in the district of Akraba, thus extending his rule substantially northwards.[4] The conquest of Bethzur and Gazara (Gezer) are mentioned in a hymn which in an unusual way also depicts Simon's contributions to the welfare of the country (I Macc.14.6–15), and is written against the background of a tradition the models for which may be found in the Egyptian royal ideology.[5]

Simon's power was threatened once again. Antiochus VII Sidetes ascended the throne in 139 BC after his brother Demetrius II had been taken prisoner by the Parthians. Sidetes eventually besieged Trypho in Dora (Dor), the old port south of Mount Carmel, after battles in southern Syria, but with doubtful success. Trypho managed to escape by sea and was later killed at Apamea in central Syria.[6] Although to begin with he had been well disposed to Judaea, Antiochus VII rejected Judaean help at the siege of Dora. Now he demanded the restoration of Judaean territory, in particular Joppa and Gezer, and the Acra in Jerusalem. Simon opposed the demand. Thereupon the Syrian general Cendebaeus made an appearance and began an attack on Judaea from the coastal plain, in the neighbourhood of Jamnia. Simon's sons Judas and John defeated him near Modein, drove him back on to the plain, and thus again secured the independence of Judaea (I Macc.15.25–16.10).[7]

One important sign of the inner insecurity and conflicting forces which were still to be found within this newly-won state which Simon had founded so successfully was the attack made on Simon by his son-in-law Ptolemy, a provincial governor in the area round Jericho, in 134, to which Simon and his sons Mattathias and Judas fell victim. This happened during a tour of inspection made by Simon, while he was staying in the small fortress of Dok[8] which Ptolemy had built for himself. Doubtless the reason why Ptolemy murdered his successful father-in-law was his unscrupulous concern to gain sole rule for himself. For after the triple murder at Dok, he bent every effort towards removing Simon's sole surviving son John, who lived in Gazara (Gezer). However, John was warned in time and was able to escape the attack. He arrived in Jerusalem before Ptolemy, and there people accorded him the same rights as his father.

> Ptolemy was turned back at the very gates of the city. Thereupon he retreated to the fortress of Dok, near Jericho, where Simon had been murdered, but where John's mother still lived. John laid siege to the fortress, but did not take it quickly because he was concerned about his mother and other relations. Despite this, Ptolemy killed them all and managed to escape to Philadelphia, the old Rabbath Ammon.[9]

John adopted the ruling name of John Hyrcanus I, and continued to rule over Judaea from 134 until his death in 104 BC. However, hardly had he taken control than bitter struggles again broke out which showed how insecure was the autonomy of the Jewish state which Simon had achieved. Ptolemy, who had fled to Transjordan, succeeded in persuading Antiochus VII Sidetes to intervene in the affairs of the Hasmonean kingdom. He was also needled by the failure of his general Cendebaeus in the time of Simon, and this was an extra reason for him to subdue Judaea. Antiochus occupied the country, laid siege to John Hyrcanus in Jerusalem and exerted extreme pressure on the city. Finally, however, he relaxed the pressure and confirmed the autonomy of Judaea. But he razed the fortifications of Jerusalem and required tribute from the territories in the west and north-west, viz. from the port of Joppa. Weapons had to be handed in, and hostages were taken who are said to have included John Hyrcanus' brother.[10] Judaea again suffered the fate of a conquered nation.

Relief came for John Hyrcanus when Antiochus VII fell in a battle against the Parthians in 129.[11] Demetrius II, who had been taken prisoner by the Parthians in 139/8, had previously been freed in order to fight against his brother; now he himself again succeeded to the Seleucid throne (129–125 BC). From now on the Hasmonean Hyrcanus again considered himself to be an independent ruler, and retained this independence over the next decade, when numerous disputes over the throne in Syria considerably weakened the Seleucid apparatus of state. Hyrcanus rebuilt the fortifications on the north side of Jerusalem. These included the so-called 'Baris', a fortification on the north-western side of the temple platform, the predecessor of the later citadel Antonia.[12]

In the sphere of foreign policy Hyrcanus attempted to safeguard himself from the Romans by the renewal of earlier declarations of protection on the part of the Senate,[13] and above all to win back the city of Joppa. It is extremely difficult to reconstruct the history of the individual delegations sent to Rome and the decrees connected with them. After the death of Antiochus Sidetes in 129 BC, the so-called decree of Fannius in all probability secured the independence of Judaea, but it did not restore Joppa. That only happened towards the end of Hyrcanus' rule, between 114 and 104, as is evident from a decree which Josephus quotes within the framework of a popular resolution of the Pergamenes (the so-called Pergamene decree).[14]

Hyrcanus' long reign is generally regarded as having been successful, not least because he succeeded in giving Judaea a firm military base and in subjecting his immediate neighbours. To achieve this he enlisted paid mercenaries. This step was thought to be unusual at the time, but it helped Hyrcanus towards greater independence and mobility, regardless of popular feeling in Judaea. He pentrated deep into the south, advanced on ancient Edom and conquered the cities of Adora (*dūra*) and Marisa (*tell sandaḥanne*) south of Hebron. In this area, which from then on was known as Idumaea, he required the population to accept circumcision and to observe the Law, thus attaching the Idumaeans to the cultic community of Jerusalem. In the north of the erstwhile Israelite territory, Hyrcanus destroyed the Samaritan sanctuary on Mount Gerizim near Shechem, and finally also attacked the city of Samaria. The Samaritans summoned the Seleucids to their aid, but without success. After a one-year siege, Hyrcanus took the city and destroyed it (107 BC).[15]

It is hard to assess the internal effect of Hyrcanus' military success. The independence gained by Judaea must be seen against the background of the Seleucid struggles for power. The coins minted by Hyrcanus are often seen as a sign of his view of himself: on them he called himself, *inter alia*, 'The high priest John and the community of the Judaeans'.[16] However, the view that has been generally accepted is that Hyrcanus only minted his own coins towards the end of his reign, and then did so only in bronze.[17] However, according to the account in Josephus his claim to be high priest is said to have been the cause for his rejection by the Pharisees.[18] Underlying this account in dramatic form there may have been more extensive criticism by the Pharisees of the way in which the Hasmoneans ran the state, which may have resulted in Hyrcanus eventually coming closer to the Sadducees, after initial sympathy for the Pharisees. At this point it may be worth saying a few words about the groups which had been formed within Judaism at that time.

The starting-point for the formation of groups was the antipathy of Judaean circles towards the Hellenistic spirit of the age. Rather than suppose that the inner divisions within the community were only brought about by Antiochus IV, we might well accept the evidence that the group of Hasidim, the 'pious', is earlier than the religious persecutions of the Seleucids.[19] On the other hand, it is unsafe to regard the Hasidim as the immediate predecessors of the Pharisees. Certainly the Hasidim represented a group with a strict attitude towards the observance of the Law, which was opposed to the Seleucids, but on the other hand they also directed their opposition inwards against those Jewish groups which belittled the ancestral Law. The latter included the high priests who held office with the consent of the Seleucids. According to I Macc. 7.1–22, when Demetrius I made Alcimus high priest (162 BC), some of the Hasidim were prepared to come to an agreement with the ruling priesthood (7.13f.). However, the behaviour of Alcimus was not such as to win over the Hasidim. Possibly events of this kind led to a decisive break between Hasidim circles and the priesthood: the Hasidim called for strict observance of the Law and increasingly came to form an independent group, apart from the ruling priesthood. The laity could also flourish in this movement. In all probability, the Greek term 'Pharisee' is modelled on the Aramaic plural *perīsayyā*, 'the separated ones', but was certainly not used by the group to describe themselves; it would usually have been applied to them in a derogatory sense: they were the separatists.[20]

Others, who were open to the spirit of the age and with it to Hellenistic-style policies, rejected the strict observance of the Law required by the Pharisees. To a large extent this group also included the priesthood. The term 'Sadducee', by which it is usually known, may be connected with the old word Zadokite, which saw the priests as office-bearers deriving from Zadok, who was once priest in the time of David. As many of the members of the Jerusalem priesthood now sympathized with the Greeks and with Hellenistic innovations, 'Sadducee' became a kind of designation for a particular disposition and party loyalty. While the Sadducees recognized the written Torah, they rejected attempts to adapt it to the circumstances of the time because they were afraid that this might limit their potentialities. On the other hand, in their expositions of the Torah the Pharisees put forward a number of doctrines which had been handed down as oral tradition and were especially cherished. In the course of time this led to the restriction of Sadduceean views essentially to priestly and aristocratic circles, whereas the Pharisees, with their outward-looking concerns, had closer ties with the populace. Nevertheless, they did not represent a separate party, especially as they lacked the resources for power politics. Rather, they remained a movement within Judaism which was not just limited to Judaea, but also exercised some influence on the Diaspora. The Pharisees were not a leading class, as the Sadducees were. As a result of this they were freer in developing their thought and succeeded in arriving at a creative reshaping and development of the written tradition.[21]

These groups began to emerge in outline during the Hasmonean period. The interest of the Hasmoneans in power and the way in which they pursued it inevitably sharpened opposition in Judaea. It is therefore no coincidence that the first clear emergence of the Pharisees in our sources is to be found during the reign of John Hyrcanus I, where they are depicted as those who, while not disputing

Hyrcanus' status as ruler, nevertheless criticize him as high priest. It is difficult to say what direct consequences followed from this. However, the foundations of the conflict between the Hasmoneans and the Pharisees had been laid, and this was also to influence the history of Hyrcanus' successors.[22]

John Hyrcanus died in 104 BC. He had made provisions for his consort to succeed him on the throne. However, his oldest son Aristobulus succeeded in usurping rule for a year and was even to be the first Hasmonean to assume the title of king.[23] This ambitious and cruel man went down in history as Aristobulus I (104–103 BC). He had his mother starved to death in prison. He also imprisoned three of his brothers; to begin with he gave a free hand only to Antigonus, who was his favourite. However, Antigonus, too, fell victim to a plot, either because Aristobulus feared for his own safety as a result of his brother's military successes, or because he believed calumnies aimed at alienating the brothers. Despite the brevity of his reign, Aristobulus had successes in the north against the Ituraeans.[24] Presumably he succeeded in extending his influence further, beyond Samaria and Beth-shean, where his father John Hyrcanus had been successful in forcing some of the Galilean population to observe the cultic Law of Jerusalem. He required them to be circumcised.

After the sudden death of Aristobulus I, his consort Salome Alexandra released his imprisoned brothers. She made one of them king and married him. He was Alexander Jannai (103–76 BC), whose Hebrew name was in fact Jonathan. However, he took the Greek name Alexander and added the Jonathan in the shortened form Jannai.[25] He seems to have been an unstable personality who lacked the gift of regular planned government, but who nevertheless succeeded in conquering the whole of the ancient territory of Judah and Israel through countless campaigns, and in getting the better of his enemies both at home and abroad. His coins show him to have taken the title of king.[26] The influence which Salome Alexandra had on his rule is certainly not to be underestimated. After his death she herself succeeded to the throne.

Alexander Jannai succeeded in extending and securing his territory in a series of bitter battles which brought him to the verge of defeat. First of all he advanced into the northern coastal area and besieged Ptolemais (Acco) while the Seleucids Antiochus Philometor and Antiochus Cyzikenus were embroiled in battle. In sore straits, the inhabitants of Ptolemais appealed to Ptolemy Lathyros for help; he was meanwhile living in Cyprus, having been exiled from Egypt by Cleopatra (III). Ptolemy came to Syria by ship with a fighting force, and after Alexander had given up the siege for fear of him, succeeded in joining battle with Alexander at Asophon[27] in the middle reaches of the Jordan and defeating him. However, in Egypt there was mistrust about the extension of Ptolemy's power, so with an eye to the dangers threatening him from there Ptolemy left the country and returned to Cyprus.

Now Alexander Jannai again had a free hand and went on the rampage in central and northern Transjordan, where he took the cities of Gadara[28] and Amathus.[29] Later he turned to the southern part of the coastal plain and in particular took

Raphia and Gaza. His successes were not always permanent. He had to capture the city of Amathus a second time before going further to the north-east. There he was interested in the district of Gaulonitis (present-day Golan), north of the river Yarmuk. However, the Nabataean king Obodath (Obedas) was advancing against Damascus, in the same area, and Alexander, in an almost hopeless position, had to retreat: he fled to Jerusalem. There, he came up against the resistance of his own people. His arrogance, his warfare and probably also his religious indifference had made him a hated figure. He sought to take his revenge by persecution and murder, but in so doing only made the inhabitants of Jerusalem even more angry, so that they asked the Seleucid Demetrius III Eukairos for help. His troops inflicted an annihilating defeat on Alexander at Shechem. However, Alexander himself escaped and amazingly enough, once again found a great many supporters. Demetrius withdrew, and Alexander again felt himself to be strong enough to take cruel and bloody revenge on his Judaean opponents. The only way in which he could establish his power was by spreading fear, thus securing a base from which he could embark on new military enterprises.

To the south and south-east the Nabataeans presented severe dangers. They were a people from that part of the Arabah south of the Dead Sea and the hill country bordering it to the east, who came under the rule of Alexander at its full extent. Aretas, king of the Nabataeans, advanced into western Transjordan and defeated Alexander at Adida, in the neighbourhood of Lydda. However, Alexander came to a friendly arrangement with Aretas. The Nabataeans must again have withdrawn from this region. Alexander himself again advanced into Transjordan, where he was able to take a number of important cities, including the famous Gerasa.

We should also note that in all probability the foundation of the so-called Maccabaean or Hasmonean fortresses of Alexandreion and Machaerus, and possibly also Masada, goes back to Alexander Jannai. He probably used them chiefly as bases against the Nabataeans and began to develop them. They only became really important in subsequent decades, especially from the time when Herod the Great (37–4 BC) equipped them as real fortresses, adorned them with some attractive architecture and from time to time himself withdrew into one or other of them.[30]

Alexander Jannai died in Transjordan at the siege of the fortress of Ragaba, present-day *rajīb*, north or the Jabbok, in 76 BC. He was forty-nine years old. Josephus records that he had become an alcoholic and foresaw his death. He advised his consort to accord privileges to the Pharisees because they had great influence on the people. He had made himself so hated that he could not count on having a decent burial. He decreed that Salome Alexandra should be his successor.[31]

It is difficult to judge Alexander Jannai fairly. People are fond of saying that with him the degeneration of the Hasmoneans reached its terrible nadir. However, we should realize that it was not easy for this late heir of the Hasmonean power to retain the territorial possessions of Judaea and the neighbouring areas which belonged to it and to defend them against the growing threat posed by the Nabataeans. This ambitious, violent and doubtless also unstable character was not capable of carrying on balanced government in all directions. He was unable to overcome internal conflict, given his confrontation with the Pharisees. Right up to his last hours, violence and terror seemed to him to be the only way of binding Judaea together so that he could continue his wars. Overwhelmed by the demands of the time, constantly threatened with dangers, Alexander ultimately did not succumb to the superior strength of his enemies but to himself. M. Stern's judgment indicates the tension in his circumstances: 'But even Alexander Jannai realized that in the long run he could not rule against the will of the people, and at the end of his rule he made many concessions, in order to make a good impression on at least some of his Jewish adversaries. Furthermore, his last victories brought him great sympathy in Judaea.'[32]

Salome Alexandra succeeded in coming to terms with the Pharisees during a reign of nine years (76–67 BC). This safeguarded her authority and gave the country some peaceful years. She could keep her sons, who were no match for her, in check. She bestowed the high priesthood, which as a woman she could not occupy by law, on her oldest son Hyrcanus (II). Her younger son Aristobulus tried to exploit the discontent of the Sadducees, who felt at a disadvantage as a result of the increasing regard and protection for the Pharisees. The contribution made by Salome Alexandra should be rated very highly. Not only had she supported and influenced Alexander Jannai, but she was flexible enough to begin a new series of measures in domestic policy. She maintained the Hasmonean state without waging war, and she did not allow the opposition between her sons to come to open conflict. When she died at the age of seventy-three, it was inevitable that her sons should fight for power. At the same time the threats from outside increased. The Nabataeans again advanced from the south and the Romans came from the north and west. With Pompey the time had come for the Near East finally to be delivered into the hands of the great power in the west.

After the death of his mother Salome Alexandra, the high priest Hyrcanus II was made king. However, after a short siege of Jerusalem and with the help of the Sadducees, his energetic brother Aristobulus persuaded him to renounce the throne. Through the mediation of Antipas, governor of Idumaea, Hyrcanus sought refuge and help from the Nabataeans. He succeeded in winning over their king Aretas III, in his residence at Petra, though at the price of the territory of Moab, which he promised to him. With Nabataean support, Hyrcanus appeared before Jerusalem and laid siege to the city with Aristobulus in it. The population was largely on the side of Hyrcanus, and in so doing took sides against the Sadducees. Something unexpected happened in this extreme trial of strength between the heirs of the Hasmonean might, the people of Jerusalem and the Nabataean allies at thr gates of the city. Hyrcanus and Aristobulus both turned for support to Pompey's representative in Damascus, the Roman legate Scaurus. This man took the side of Aristobulus. On the orders of the Romans, the Nabataeans had to withdraw. Aristobulus continued to rule in Jerusalem, but he was no longer sole master of the situation; he had become a dependent of the Romans.

The earlier history of the emergence of Roman power in Syria is closely bound up with the rise of Pompey. The unfortunate L. Licinius Lucullus, who had come to grief in Armenia and could no longer be certain of Roman support, was replaced by Pompey at the beginning of 67 BC. Pompey was given extraordinary powers. After he had succeeded in ridding the Mediterranean of pirates in about three months, in 66 he was given the provinces of Bithynia and Cilicia, against the will of the Senate but with the support of Caesar. He was urgently concerned to end the war against Mithridates. Pompey demanded unconditional surrender, but the war went on. The troops of Mithridates were beaten near the Euphrates, and the king committed suicide after attempting a counter-attack (63 BC). Pontus and Bithynia became a double province. A treaty was made with the Armenian Tigranes. Pompey had already sent the legate M. Aemilius Scaurus to Syria in 65 BC, thus in fact doing away with the Seleucid state. In Damascus he learned of the dispute between Hyrcanus and Aristobulus in Judaea, but evidently could not yet make a final decision. Pompey spent the winter of 64/63 BC in Syria and arrived in Damascus in spring 63. There Aristobulus and Hyrcanus appeared in person to win the favour of the Romans. Antipater sent an envoy who pleaded for Hyrcanus, while a delegation from Jerusalem required the end of Hasmonean rule altogether and argued that the priesthood should be strengthened.[33]

To begin with, Pompey hesitated to involve himself in the complicated problems of Judaea. The Nabataeans evidently seemed to him to be the greater danger. However, at this point Aristobulus seemed in fact to be in a position to unite all the forces in Judaea around him and was organizing resistance in Jerusalem., So to begin with Pompey did not penetrate further into Transjordan, but took the direct route to Jerusalem. He must have crossed the Jordan at Scythopolis (Bethshean) and reached the *wādi fār'a*, which is otherwise only rarely mentioned, in a southerly direction. Near to the place where he left the Jordan rift there rises the Alexandreion, a citadel built and developed by Alexander Jannai, in a unique setting on a high pinnacle. Aristobulus had entrenched himself there, but had to surrender the citadel. He was hard pressed by Pompey, who followed close on his heels and pursued him beyond Jericho to the immediate vicinity of Jerusalem. Aristobulus appeared in the Roman camp and promised to hand over the city. But when Gabinius, sent on in advance by Pompey, was refused entry into the city, the whole Roman army advanced on it. Aristobulus, whom Pompey had kept with him since he appeared in the Roman camp, was now treated as a prisoner. In the face of this ultimate danger, the population of the city opened the gates. However, bitter resistance was offered in the fortified temple precincts. After a three-month siege, that too fell into the hands of the Romans. Pompey entered the temple and the holy of holies, a desecration in the eyes of those faithful to the Law. However, nothing was destroyed or plundered. The sacrifices continued to be offered the next day, and Hyrcanus again functioned as high priest. Thus, in 63 BC, Roman rule began in

Jerusalem. The city became subject to tribute. As a member of the Hasmonean house, Hyrcanus played only a limited role in his capacity as high priest. His impetuous brother Aristobulus was brought to Rome and featured in Pompey's triumphal procession in 61 BC.

It went almost without saying that the Romans would provide a new administration for their subject territories. However, the districts they created took account of the conditions which had developed over the course of history. Judaea continued to go with Jerusalem, along with the southern districts of Samaria which had once been taken by Jonathan the Maccabee, and Idumaea in the south, which had been conquered by John Hyrcanus I. In addition, part of southern and central Transjordan was added to Judaea and was given the name Peraea; so too were central areas of Galilee in which the Jerusalem cult and the Jerusalem Law were observed. Samaria was directly subject to the Roman provincial administration in Syria. The same thing went for the key cities in the coastal plain and for the group of Hellenistic cities in the north of Transjordan which began to play a distinctive part of their own under the designation 'Decapolis'; they even founded a 'Pompeian' era of their own.[34] The whole of Syria and 'Palestine', which in fact made up the western part of the old Seleucid imperial alliance, became the province of Syria, in the charge of the governor. The first to be appointed was M. Aemilius Scaurus.

> This territorial and administrative arrangement was maintained in essentials down to the Christian era. However, in 57 BC the governor Gabinius once again altered the situation in Jerusalem. Hyrcanus lost all political power and had to limit himself to cultic matters. Furthermore, five independent districts were created, which were directly subject to the governor.[35] However, the new ordering made by Gabinius was again given up in subsequent years, during the course of serious disputes between the Romans on the one hand and the last members of the Hasmonean house on the other, in particular with Aristobulus' son Alexander.[36] The high priest was again given authority over the whole area. Crassus, who became famous through the triumvirate of 60 BC, took over the province in 54, but shortly afterwards he fell in battle against the Parthians. From 53–51 BC his quaestor C. Cassius Longinus administered the province of Syria.

With the arrival of the Romans in the old territory of Israel and Judah and the formation of the province of Syria, the history of Israel in Old Testament times comes to its ultimate limit. The struggles of Aristobulus and his sons once again to exert influence on conditions in Judaea, the clashes between the high priesthood and the Roman authorities of the time, and not least the rise of Herod and his descendants, form a completely new period of history, the details of which I cannot go into here.[37] The people of Israel and Judah, now divided between different administrative regions and subservient to the interests of particular authorities, were deprived of their independence and their ancestral rights to an extreme degree. Roman rule was one of the hardest burdens that Israel ever had to bear.

The reason why the people found so elemental a will and power t resist the Romans was not just that Rome enjoyed such political and military sup.emacy, but in the last resort because the Roman ethos was so deeply opposed to Israel's conceptions of state and religion, and in comparison with the Seleucid attempts at Hellenization was more serious and more fundamental. Rome was a Western military power which had nothing to offer the East, but could and would exact a high price from it. This could have led to the maiming of Israel's innermost strength. However, instead it spurred Israel on to extreme resistance. It also made people in the country ready to listen to and accept statements from the earliest tradition in a new version and in a changed form. The emergence and the ministry of Jesus Christ must be seen against the background of this period of history and its extreme turbulence, and cannot be detached from it. At the same time, however, the words and actions of Jesus also heightened long-cherished expectations which had been prepared for at least since the intervention of Antiochus IV Epiphanes. So in conclusion I must say something about the spiritual developments in Jerusalem and Judaea from the days of the Maccabees.

It is hard to envisage in detail the burdens imposed on the Jewish community in Jerusalem and Judah after the time of Antiochus Epiphanes, in the context of the interplay of political and spiritual controversies. Nor can we easily assess their effects on the consciousness of the Jewish people. The continual fighting and the dangerous incursions of foreign powers on the relatively small territory west and east of the Jordan must have led not only to a successive physical decimation of the people, but also to a sapping of the will to resist and of the spiritual presuppositions on which that will was based. Nevertheless, it remains remarkable to what degree the will to resist was summoned up, and a battle was carried on to continue the life of the community, which was threatened on all sides. It was only natural that in view of the political fluctuations and the constantly new demands there were deep-seated divisions within the people of Jerusalem and Judah: this led increasingly to the formation of parties and groups. So we can understand that groups like the Hasidim, and ultimately the kindred Pharisees on the one hand and the Sadducees on the other, only become really evident in connection with the Maccabaean wars and the Hasmonean rulers, when each begins to play its own role. Controversy over ancestral belief, the fight for the Law and the question of the righteousness of God in the face of so hostile and tumultuous an environment led the new groups which were coming into being and establishing themselves to arrive at solutions of their own, and resulted in the creation of new forms of literary expression.[38]

Because of this complex development, we do not have enough information about the beginnings and the backgrounds of different groups and movements. Even extensive writing can only hypothetically be assigned to one group or another, with greater or lesser degrees of certainty. At least from the middle of the second century BC, in the form of 'apocalyptic' literature we find one such new manifestation of Israelite spirit which can be understood as an expression of the new experiences of

world politics from the perspective of the Jewish people. The second half of the
book of Daniel (chs. 7–12) may be the earliest example of this genre of literature;
at the same time, it is the only one to have found a place in the Old Testament.
Later works of this kind are usually included in the Apocrypha and Pseudepigrapha;[39] apocalyptic literature has found a way into the New Testament in the
form of the Revelation of John the Divine.[40]

With its great visionary images and the reflections connected with them, apocalyptic offers interpretations of world history, and is one of the most remarkable
attempts to understand present and future in spiritual and theological terms. Its
beginnings can already be found in the brief visionary accounts known as the
'night visions' of the prophet Zechariah (Zech.1.7–6.8). These are pictures and
brief accounts of symbolic actions, the subject of which is both Jerusalem's position
within the world of nations and the internal constitution of the city.[41] The apocalyptic of the book of Daniel is concerned almost exclusively with the great events of
world history and is introduced symbolically in Dan.7 by the picture of the four
beasts which rise out of the sea of chaos and embody four world empires. This is a
version of an old pattern presenting a sequence of world empires of different
character, originally the conception of different ages of the world. Here it is taken
over by Israel, though it probably goes back to early Greek (Hesiod) and Indo-
Iranian models.[42] The same pattern also forms the basis for the tradition incorporated in Dan.2, where the sequence of the kingdoms is presented symbolically, not
by the appearance of different animals, but by the different materials of which a
statue is made (the 'colossus on feet of clay'). In all probability we may assume that
the beasts and the statue in Daniel allude to the last four great world empires under
which the Jews lived and their direct or indirect influence on the people of Israel
and Judah. These were the kingdoms of the Babylonians, the Medes, the Persians
and the Greeks from the time of Alexander the Great, including the Hellenistic
states formed by the Diadochoi. At any rate, there is no consideration of the Roman
empire. The fourth beast in Dan.7.7f. is particularly interesting:

> [7]After this I saw in the night visions, and behold a fourth beast, terrible and
> dreadful and exceedingly strong; and it had great iron teeth; it devoured and
> broke in pieces, and stamped the residue with its feet. It was different from all
> the beasts that were before it; and it had ten horns. [8]I considered the horns, and
> behold, there came up among them another horn, a little one, before which three
> of the first horns were plucked up by the roots; and behold, in this horn were
> eyes like the eyes of a man, and a mouth speaking great things.

The interpretation of this fourth beast with its horns is given in Dan.7.19ff.,
from which it emerges very clearly that the little horn, which comes last, must be
Antiochus IV Epiphanes, who 'made war with the saints and prevailed over them'
(7.21), who 'changed the times and the law' (7.25). In that case the ten horns are
the Seleucids,[43] and the three horns who are plucked up to make room for the last
little horn must be interpreted as three supplanted kings. Apart from a few un-

certainties, the sequence of rulers is: (1) Alexander the Great himself; (2) Seleucus I; (3) Antiochus I; (4) Antiochus II; (5) Seleucus II; (6) Seleucus III; (7) Antiochus III, the Great.[44] We can be reasonably sure that the three supplanted kings after Antiochus III are: (1) Seleucus IV, the predecessor of Antiochus IV, murdered by his finance minister Heliodorus; (2) Demetrius the son of Seleucus IV, who was exchanged for Antiochus IV and lived in Rome as a hostage; (3) Antiochus, another son of Seleucus IV who died prematurely or was murdered by Antiochus IV. Thus these three would in fact have had a claim to the throne, but were prevented from succeeding by special circumstances and thus helped Antiochus IV, the little horn with the big mouth, to power. So the apocalyptic writer must have had a vivid impression of the events of the most recent past, and contributed to the creation of this fantastic picture.[45]

Daniel 7 became a prototype for apocalyptic literature, not only as a result of the visionary symbolism of its picture of world politics expressed in the form of the beasts, but also by virtue of its brief description of a scene in heaven which in solemn grandeur portrays the transcendent worlds in terms appropriate to the spirituality of later Israelite religion, and eventually influenced the first chapter of Revelation. Hardly has the little horn come up on the fourth beast than there is a complete change of scene. The heavenly throne room becomes visible, thrones are brought, and God himself, here called 'the Ancient of Days', takes his place. A heavenly judgment begins; the kingdoms of the world are condemned and brought to nothing. And then there comes with the clouds of heaven someone who looks like a man, like 'a son of man',[46] i.e. in contrast to the beasts he is a human figure, who is presented to the ancient of days. Daniel 7.14 says of him: 'And to him was given dominion and glory and kingdom, that all peoples, nations and languages should serve him; his dominion is an everlasting dominion which shall not pass away. . . .' This human figure who comes on the clouds of heaven is the symbol of the exercising of a new lordship over the world. In the further course of the chapter it is said that this coming kingdom is to belong to 'the saints of the Most High'.[47] We are not told any more about who these saints are. But if we do not understand them as absolute, ideal types of the distant future, they are at least those who see the evil in the great-power politics of the time, which must be overcome. God will have his will done on earth by the 'saints of the Most High' and the nations must receive their deserts. That is the expectation of the so-called 'apocalyptists', whose criticism of the present is absolute, and whose hope is therefore completely directed towards the future. What they see 'revealed' and 'expounded' is the plan of God with his people, whose members, faithful to the Law and loyal to the God of Israel, will at the same time concentrate upon themselves the blessing of future times. However, it remains completely open who in fact cherished such hopes, whether these were organized and distinct groups, or whether apocalyptic conceptions were common to all groupings and were even possible, or could find a footing, in whatever degree of intensity, inside the Pharisaic camp.[48] So it is not surprising that there should be talk of 'apocalyptic circles' or an 'apocalyptic movement', in which we should assume very specific ideas and conceptions to have been implanted, amounting virtually to a philosophy of history.

From ch. 10 on, the book of Daniel gives a detailed analytical outline of history which with its precise knowledge puts the schematic picture of the four world empires in the shade. In 11.3–39 there is a detailed survey of history from the time of Alexander the Great; from 11.21 we are to presuppose events after the accession of Antiochus IV. Daniel 11.29–39 also goes up to Antiochus' second campaign in Egypt in 167. The death of the king is mentioned, but we should assume that Daniel 11 was composed before this event, which took place in December 164.[49]

Criticism of the great political powers is evident in the apocalyptic view of the world; they must wear themselves out and find an end before the kingdom of God can dawn. Thus one of the consequences of the historical experiences of the community in Judah that we must note is a virtually dualistic view of the world, in which the rule of the world and the rule of God diverge. The question asked by apocalyptic is whether and to what extent the rule of God is still normative for world history and for the fate of Israel itself, so often divided within, or indeed whether it can again become normative. This approach provided decisive elements of future theological thought. The idea of the kingdom of God as a factor which overcomes the world inevitably raised in urgent form the question of the time when it begins, of those who represent this kingdom and are its chosen witnesses, of the criteria for their selection, and of the particular circumstances which will accompany the dawn of the kingdom of God. In this way we see the development of the elements of an 'eschatological drama' which extends from the annihilation of the enemies of God through judgment on the lawless and the appearance of the Messiah to a perfect and ideal time of salvation. Each of these elements will become an independent feature with a tradition of its own.

This is clear from a further collection of apocalyptic traditions which did not find is way into the biblical canon, the so-called Ethopic Enoch.[50] This is evidently a composite work; the dating of individual elements is hotly disputed.[51] The so-called 'Ten Weeks' Apocalypse' in chs. 93 and 91.12–17 of Enoch seems to be the earliest part; it apparently dates from before the Maccabaean revolt. So this passage could be almost contemporaneous with parts of the Daniel apocalypse. Other parts of Enoch can hypothetically be dated to the time of Judas Maccabaeus, to the reign of John Hyrcanus I, or even later to the reign of Alexander Jannai in the first century BC. The thought-world of apocalyptic has here developed much further. It is not just limited to the opposition between the power of the world and the rule of God, but seeks to discuss the ordinances and laws of the kingdom of heaven, so that to a large extent we have the rise of a real apocalypse, in the sense of 'disclosures' of the mysteries of the kingdom of heaven. The so-called Similitudes in chs. 37–71 are of supreme significance; here the symbolic figure of the son of man in Dan.7 is developed into an independent eschatological 'saviour', thus giving powerful stimulus to the characterization of the functions of the 'Messiah'.[52]

All these traditions and conceptions raise the question of authorship. Who composed them and handed them down, and what contribution did they make towards forming communities, which must be regarded as the vehicles of such highly-developed theological potential? In this connection it was a surprise, though not an unqualified solution to all outstanding problems, when in 1947 a chance discovery, followed up by later intensive archaeological research, brought to light the remains of a community the beginning of which must similarly lie in the second century BC. This is the astonishing discovery of manuscripts in caves on the eastern edge of the Judaean wilderness. Beneath them, in *ḥirbet qumrān* (Qumran), on the plateau of a marl terrace on the north-west shore of the Dead Sea, about a mile north of the spring *ʿēn feshka*, where were found the remains of a settlement which in all probability belonged to this community. Later it safeguarded its sacred texts against any attack, in particular, presumably, from the Romans, by placing them in the caves bordering on the terrace and the neighbouring side of the mountain. Above all, the manuscripts stored in jars have survived the centuries reasonably well.[53]

Despite specialist literature about the Qumran discoveries which is almost impossible to master,[54] and intensive work on the text material which has come to light,[55] when this is taken in conjunction with archaeological discoveries within the site[56] there can no longer be any doubt that this place was at one time the site of a monastic-type community which was kept together by a common life, study and the copying of sacred texts,[57] together with a binding form of doctrine. However, the attempt to identify this community directly with one of the groups already known to us either in Judaea or in the Diaspora has yet to prove successful. One cannot even identify them with the group of the Essenes, which is widely known and has been thoroughly investigated by a long tradition of research, though that is often assumed.[58] Agreements between fragments which have been discovered and a writing of a 'community of the new covenant in the land of Damascus',[59] discovered somewhat earlier, which had been recognized not long after the discovery of the manuscripts, indicate that from the second century BC individual Jewish groups could evidently have existed in large numbers and in individual cases could even have been interconnected. Their life-styles differed, and convictions took written form along the lines of quite independent traditions. As Qumran reveals, these communities could also require a form of common life which protected their existence in self-chosen withdrawal from the political and military undertakings of the time. Nevertheless, as archaeological discoveries in particular have shown, the Qumran community was not safe from surprises. The place must have been uninhabited for a long time, perhaps as the result of an earthquake, the traces of which can still be seen, most impressively on a staircase leading down to a cistern, which has an oblique break in it.[60] Presumably the settlement was uninhabited between 31 BC, the year of the earthquake, and about 4 BC, i.e. down to the end of the reign of Herod the Great, as can be reasonably established by discoveries of coins.

It is evident from the writings of the Qumran community that their expectations of the future were different and that their doctrinal conceptions were based on particular authorities, among which the 'teacher of righteousness' played a prominent role. This teacher, who is portrayed as a priest, was persecuted by a 'wicked priest', whose features are possibly modelled on the priestly rulers of the Hasmonean house, on whom the community passed a harsh judgment. As 'sons of light', the community felt itself to be engaged in battle with the 'sons of darkness', the other Jews and the Gentile nations. Members lived together in a close-knit group: everyone was supposed 'to bring their knowledge, powers and possessions into the community of God'.[61] Goods were held in common and people competed to fulfil the Torah to the supreme degree, 'to practise truth and humility in common, and justice and uprightness and charity and modesty in all their ways'.[62] Formulations of this kind obviously have links with the tradition of the law and the prophets. The Hymn Scroll (*Hodayot*) in particular gives the impression of strict piety; it follows the form of the psalms. The sacral fellowship of the group, which was also expressed in a common meal, at the same time had an eschatological stamp. The present is the end time. People were expecting 'the battle between the sons of light and the sons of darkness'.[63] Two messianic figures were regarded as the instruments of future salvation, a priestly Messiah, descended from Aaron, and a secular Messiah, from Israel.[64] This expectation corresponds to the manifold dualistic conceptions of the community, its sacral and secular ideals. The latter also includes the ideal of poverty and unqualified readiness to help.

The community identified itself with the true sanctuary of the temple. In view of the physical segregation of the Jerusalem temple, which was in the hands of others, this community had to develop an equal counterpart, so as to make room for the notion of expiation. Here we find a thoroughly priestly element: the priests are also those who preserve the covenant and discover the divine will.[65] It is clear from this complex of conceptions, in which on the one hand we find a link with the Torah and on the other a link with the eschatological traditions of prophecy and apocalyptic in a departure from the Israel of the present day, why it is not easy to identify the Qumran community with other groups beyond all question. There have been many attempts to establish connections between Qumran and the beginnings of Christianity. Generally speaking, the real roots of Qumran are in the tradition of the Old Testament and early Judaism, and cannot be seen as a forerunner of, or a transition to, the formation of later communities, despite the comparability of individual ideas in its general pattern. Comparison is also made difficult by the esoteric and isolationist strain in these Qumran people, who were so markedly concerned for their own particular way of life.

Among the writings found in and around Qumran were copies and parts of copies of biblical and apocryphal works. One of the first remarkable finds was an Isaiah scroll.[66] We may assume that all these writings had a significance for the community, which confirms the degree of its roots in traditional forms. One particular outstanding question is where the creative contribution of the community begins in this far-reaching process of acceptance. Despite its deliberate isolation, for a time the Qumran community remained a lively example of the manifold assimilation of traditional and contemporary ideals in the shade of world politics, and in faith in the true Israel of the future.

While the Qumran writings do not allow us to draw any direct conclusions about the events of the time, and we are largely forced to reconstruct the fate of the group from what can be found on the site of the settlement, another document gives clear indications which are to be connected with the events at the end of the Hasmonean period of rule and the appearance of Pompey in Jerusalem in 63 BC and his death on the Egyptian coast near Pelusium in 48 BC. This consists of the so-called Psalms of Solomon, handed down in Greek and Syriac translations. There is a series of eighteen psalms which, with a considerable degree of unanimity, scholars suppose to have been composed within the Pharisaic tradition.[67] Psalms 17 and 18 are of special significance here; they depict the accession of a ruler portrayed as Messiah, with numerous well-known traditional features, who is at the same time called 'Son of David',[68] and whose word smites and judges the peoples.[69] It is said of him (Ps.Sol.17.36–38):

And he himself (will be) pure from sin, so that he may rule a great people.
He will rebuke rulers, and remove sinners by the might of his word:
And (relying) upon his God, throughout his days he will not stumble;
For God will make him mighty by means of (his) holy spirit,
and wise by means of the spirit of understanding, with strength and righteousness.
And the blessing of the Lord (will be) with him: he will be strong and stumble not.[70]

Within the context of the Psalms of Solomon, in the middle of the first century BC, these words express expectations and hopes for a Messiah whose superiority is, and is to be, far greater than that of the militaristic politicians of all shades, one of which Jerusalem had just experienced in the form of Pompey. But it is also clear that the individual features of this messianic tradition, as it is expressed here, also point in the direction which will later also be taken by Christianity. On the other hand, it is not enough for us to derive the movement brought into being through Jesus solely from one of the political or spiritual groups within Judaism in the last centuries before the Christian era. Rather, with Jesus, and in the framework of the tradition connected with him, many different forms of Jewish piety are taken over, selected or transformed, so that there is also no future in attempting to establish close connections between the Qumran community and the first followers of Jesus. There is no doubt at all that Jesus and earliest Christianity drew directly on the tradition of the Old Testament and early Judaism. However, from a historical perspective the question which must remain open here is why and on what basis the way of thinking shaped by Jesus differed so decisively from other Jewish groups and traditions, and in the end became independent. At all events, the horizon of theological expectations against which the sayings of Jesus are to be seen was prepared for by the theology of his time, and caused by the harsh political pressures to which the country was exposed. The fact that Jesus did not attempt to exercise any political influence, but all the more resolutely turned towards people who were threatened on all sides to the point of despair, opened up to him the hearts of those who heard him. The failure of his undertaking might have made his death inevitable; the rise of independent belief in a Risen Lord strictly speaking lies outside all historical calculations.

We have now followed the history of the people of Israel and Judah beyond the period of the Old Testament down to the beginning of Roman rule over Jerusalem and Judaea. From this point on it comes to face its harshest trials. The Romans succeeded in subjecting the country completely, so that in the second century AD it completely lost its independence; it did not, however lose its existence, far less its spiritual and religious force, which it passed on to the West and to the world. As Christianity developed, it adopted the Old Testament as holy scripture and made it a fixed part of the canon of the Bible. To this degree the early church took over the tradition of the people of Israel, but in the doctrinal controversies of the first centuries it also became indebted to Western, Greek thought. At the same time, Judaism adopted a course which safeguarded its existence and helped to preserve its culture, through the tradition of interpretation contained in the Mishnah and Talmud, and later in a highly individualistic philosophy and literature. The history of the Israel of the Old Testament thus forms the presupposition for understanding Jewish religion and Christian thought. For in the course of its history Israel experienced the working of the one God who is common to both Jews and Christians.

NOTES

1. Mithridates VI, king of northern Cappadocia, owed his rise to the decline of the Seleucid kingdom. He sought to become ruler of the territories bordering on the Black Sea. Hence the name 'Pontus' given to his empire. On the Bosphorus he clashed with Roman interests; he occupied the province of Asia and like Antiochus III before him carried the attack over to Greece. Sulla succeeded in winning back the Roman territory in the First Mithridatic War (88–85 BC). The Second Mithridatic War (83/82) was indecisive. In the meanwhile king Tigranes of Armenia, a son-in-law of Mithridates, came into the ascendant. The Third Mithridatic War broke out over the possession of Bithynia (74–64). While the consul L. Licinius Lucullus was successful against Mithridates, his campaign into the highlands of Armenia failed because his troops mutinied.

2. See p. 363 above.

3. The year 170 of the Seleucid era is the year from 26 March 142 to 21 April 141 BC. R. Hanhart in BZAW 88, 1964, 95.

4. Thus he advanced beyond the three districts of Aphaerema, Ramathaim and Lydda which had been promised to Jonathan in 145 BC. For this see p. 367 n.22 above; also M. Noth, *History of Israel*, ²1960, 380f.

5. This is an example of the extraordinary sphere of influence of the Egyptian royal cult.

The Ptolemies had taken over its traditions, and its terminology continued to have a formative effect in the Hellenistic world, even in Jewish Hellenistic Judaea. Elke Blumenthal and S. Morenz. 'Spuren ägyptischer Königsideologie in einem Hymnus auf den Makkabäerfürsten Simon', *ZÄS* 93, 1966, 21–9.

6. According to Strabo 14.5.2, p. 668, Trypho was forced to commit suicide.

7. Simon's contacts with Sparta (I Macc.14.20–23) and Rome (I Macc.14.24; 15.15–21) present a special problem. Both the passages cited have details about diplomatic communications from Sparta and Rome, along with the note that Simon sent a great golden shield to Rome. At all events, the concern was to strengthen relationships between the Judaeans and Sparta and Rome. The authenticity and date of these documents are disputed, as is that of the similar-sounding decree of Valerius, which Josephus quotes (*Antt.* XIV, 8.5 = 145–8), though he assigns it to the time of Hyrcanus II. A. Giovannini and H. Müller, 'Die Beziehungen zwischen Rom und den Juden im. 2. Jahrhundert vor Christus', *Museum Helveticum* 28, 1971, 156–71, regard the document in I Macc.15.15–21 as a forgery; they put the Valerius decree in 134 BC, in the time of Hyrcanus I. T. Fischer, *ZAW* 86, 1974, 90–3, defends the authenticity of the documents in an attractive way with independent conjectures as to their dates. He sees the writings as examples of the way in which the Maccabaeans and the Hasmoneans increasingly became independent of the Seleucids, but in close connection with this joined the 'Roman clientele'. D. Timpe, 'Der römische Vertrag mit den Juden von 161 BC', *Chiron* 4, 1974, 133–52, esp. 146–52, assesses the texts in question in connection with the problem of 'treaty renewals' with Rome.

8. The name of this fortress is still recalled by the spring '*ēn dūk*, north-west of Jericho on the upper course of the *wādi en nuwē 'ime*. I Maccabees ends with Ptolemy's murder of Simon and his sons and the escape of John (I Macc.16.11–22).

9. Josephus, *Antt.* XIII, 8.1 (230–5); *BJ* I, 2.3–4 (54–66).

10. Josephus, *Antt.* XIII, 8.2–3 (236–48).

11. There is a detailed study of this in T. Fischer, *Untersuchungen zum Partherkrieg Antiochus' VII im Rahmen der Seleukidengeschichte*, Dissertation Munich and Tübingen 1970.

12. Josephus, *Antt.* XV, 11.4 (403). Closer attention in the most recent archaeological research has found traces of building activity in Jerusalem during the Hasmonean period, from the time of Simon and even more from the time of Hyrcanus I. Kathleen M. Kenyon, especially in her excavation on the south-east hill in 1961–1967, discovered that the construction of wall and towers almost on the top edge of the hill which were once called the 'Jebusite bastion' or the 'Jebusite ramp', and were thought to be the earliest walls in Jerusalem, will come from the second half of the second century, from the time of Simon or Hyrcanus I. Even in Hasmonean times the city must have extended beyond the tops of these hills towards the west and north. Recent Israeli excavations have confirmed this: in the Jewish Quarter of the Old City of Jerusalem, courses of walls from the Hasmonean period have come to light. The Hasmonean palace was probably also there. K. M. Kenyon, *Jerusalem. Excavating 3000 Years of History*, 1967, ch. VI; id., *Digging up Jerusalem*, 1974, 188–204; *EAE* II, 599–603. See further Y. Yadin (ed.), *Jerusalem Revealed*, 1975, 11f., 22f.; T. Kollek and M. Pearlman, *Jerusalem. Seine Geschichte in vier Jahrtausenden*, 1976, 85–93; A. Sharon, *Planning Jerusalem*, 1973, 18f., 178f.

13. The so-called decree of Valerius (Josephus, *Antt.* XIV, 8.5 = 145–8) and the letter to Ptolemy (I Macc.15.15–21); see n.7 above.

14. The decree of Fannius: Josephus, *Antt.* XIII, 9.2 (259–66); the Pergamene decree: *Antt.* XIV, 10.22 (247–55). The identity or the dependence of the decrees are disputed, but renewed attention has been paid to them in more recent times. See above all T. Fischer, *Untersuchungen*, Munich and Tübingen Dissertation 1970, 64–73 (decree of Fannius); 73–85 (Pergamene decree); there is a summary by Fischer in *ZAW* 86, 1974, 90–93. D. Timpe

reviews these documents in the context of a discussion of treaty renewals, *Chiron* 4, 1974, 147f.

15. Josephus, *Antt*. XIII, 10.2–3 (257–83).

16. See M. Noth, *History of Israel*, ²1960, 388, and the literature cited there, especially A. Reifenberg, *Ancient Jewish Coins*, ²1947, 13f.; 40f. pl.II.

17. B. Kanael, 'The Beginning of the Maccabean Coinage', *IEJ* 1, 1950/51; id., 'Altjüdische Münzen', *Jahrbuch für Numismatik und Geldgeschichte* 17, 1967, 166f. Y. Meshorer argues that Hasmonean coins began to be minted only in the time of Alexander Jannai; cf. U. Westermark, 'Syria', in *A Survey of Numismatic Research 1966–1971*, Vol. 1, 1973, 184f., 187. Y. Meshorer, 'The Beginning of the Hasmonean Coinage', *IEJ* 24, 1974, 59–61. See also the survey of Hasmonean coins, based on Meshorer, in *IJH*, 560–2. Cf. also T. Fischer, 'Johannes Hyrkan I. auf tetradrachmen Antiochos' VII? Ein Beitrag zur Deutung der Beizeichen auf hellenistischen Münzen', *ZDPV* 91, 1975, 191–6 and table 19.

18. Josephus, *Antt*. XIII, 10.5, 6 (288–298). Hyrcanus was to renounce the high priesthood and content himself with governing the people. This is what an individual Pharisee said to Hyrcanus at a feast, though without winning the assent of the other Pharisees. However, Hyrcanus supposed that the man had deliberately been put forward with his remark, in order to say what they all thought.

19. Cf. I Macc.2.42, where the Hasidim are distinguished from the Maccabaeans.

20. The literature on the Pharisees is extensive and the views about their origins are numerous. Reference should be made here in particular to R. Meyer, *Tradition und Neuschöpfung im antiken Judentum. Dargestellt an der Geschichte des Pharisäismus. Mit einem Beitrag von H.-F. Weiss, Der Pharisäismus im Lichte der Überlieferung des Neuen Testaments*, Sitzungsberichte Sächsischen Akademie der Wissenschaften, Phil.-hist. Kl.110/12, Berlin 1965; cf. also the summary account by C. Thoma, 'Der Pharisäismus', in J. Maier and J. Schreiner (eds.), *Literatur und Religion des Frühjudentums*, Würzburg 1973, 254–72.

21. For the history and form of these two groups see H. D. Mantel, 'The Sadducees and Pharisees', *WHJP* I, 8, 1977, 99–123; also G. Baumbach, 'Der sadduzäische Konservatismus', in Maier and Schreiner, op. cit. (n.20), 201–13; S. Safrai, *Das jüdische Volk im Zeitalter des Zweiten Tempels*, 1978, 106–12.

22. Later assessments of Hyrcanus are necessarily controversial. Rabbinic literature stresses his anti-Pharisaic attitude (cf. Sota 9.10): Josephus puts him in a surprisingly favourable light and describes his reign as happy, particularly in comparison with the actions of his sons. As Josephus says, Hyrcanus had three of the greatest privileges: the rule of his people, the high priesthood and the gift of prophecy (*Antt*. XIII, 10.7 = 299f.; *BJ* I, 2.8 = 67–9).

23. Josephus, *Antt*. XIII, 11.1 (301); *BJ* I, 3.1 (70). Strabo, *Geographica* 16.2.40, differs. None of the coins attributed to Aristobulus mentions his royal title or his Greek name Aristobulus. His Hebrew name was Jehuda (Judas).

24. Josephus, *Antt*. XIII, 11.3 (318f.). In this paragraph it is said that Aristobulus was called a 'friend of the Greeks' (Philhellene). E. Meyer assumes that this was not an incidental designation but a fixed title, i.e. 'he had the surname Philhellene'; he cites the Parthian kings as an example. E. Meyer, *Ursprung und Anfänge des Christentums* II, 1921, 277.

25. Greek or Latin tradition calls him Alexander Jannaeus.

26. On earlier types of coins the inscription runs 'The high priest Jonathan and the community of the Judaeans'. There are also bilingual coins: 'The king Jonathan' (Hebrew); 'King Alexander' (Greek). A. Reifenberg, *Ancient Jewish Coins*, ²1947, 14f.; 41; pl.II; M. Avi-Yonah (ed.), *A History of the Holy Land*, 1969, 123.

27. Asaphon or Asophon has often been identified with Zaphon (Josh.13.27; Judg.12.1) and this in turn with *tell es-sa ʿidīye* on the southern spurs of the *wadi kufrinjeh*, just over a

mile east of the Jordan. Cf. F.-M. Abel, *Géographie de la Palestine* II, ³1967, 448. However, more recent American excavations since the winter of 1964 have still not made it possible to identify the site definitively with a biblical location. J. B. Pritchard, *EAE* IV, 1028–32 (with bibliography).

28. Gadara (*umkēs*), city of the Decapolis, south-east of Lake Tiberias in a hilly region, on the south side of the Yarmuq. F. M. Abel, *Géographie de la Palestine* II, ³1967, 323.

29. Amathus ('*ammata*) in the central Jordan valley, near where the *wādi rājib* comes out of the hills. F.-M. Abel, *Géographic de la Palestine* II, ³1967, 242f.; cf. a different view in J. Schmitt, *ZDPV* 91, 1975, 50–4.

30. O. Plöger, 'Die makkabäischen Burgen', *ZDPV* 71, 1955, 141–72, reprinted in O. Ploger, *Aus der Spätzeit des Alten Testaments*, 1971, 102–33. For Masada see Y. Yadin, *Masada. Herod's Fortress and the Zealots' Last Stand*, 1966 (with bibliography), principally an account of excavations. Only a few remains in Masada could be dated with any probability to the pre-Herodian period. For Machaerus see A. Strobel, 'Machärus. Geschichte und Ende einer Festung im Lichte archäologisch-topographischer Beobachtungen', *Bibel und Qumran. Festschrift H. Bardtke*, Berlin 1968, 198–225; see further in *ZDPV* 90, 1974, 128–84; 93, 1977, 247–67. For the fortress of Hyrcania (*ḫirbet mird*) see O. Plöger, *Aus der Spätzeit*, 109–12.

31. For the end of Alexander Jannai and the designation of his wife to succeed him see Josephus, *Antt.* XIII 15.5 (398–404).

32. M. Stern, in Ben-Sasson (ed.), *Geschichte des jüdischen Volkes* I, 1978, 294.

33. Josephus, *Antt.* XIV, 3.2 (37–45; on the rejection of the monarchy: 41). In view of earlier treaties between Rome and the Maccabees and Hasmoneans before the latter had established a monarchy, there was at least apparent justification in the argument of the Jerusalem delegation that the people needed only to obey the priests. On this question, with reference to a tradition in Diodore, see T. Fischer, 'Zum jüdischen Verfassungsstreit vor Pompejus (Diodor 40.2)', *ZDPV* 91, 1975, 46–9. E. Bammel, 'Die Neuordnung des Pompejus und das römisch-jüdische Bündnis', *ZDPV* 75, 1959, 76–82, sees Pompey's measures in a wider context; despite energetic Roman implementation they will have been opposed by the Judaeans, which will have secured for them special treatment within the framework of the Roman policy over alliances.

34. H. Bietenhard, 'Die Dekapolis von Pompeius gis Traian. Ein Kapitel aus der neutestamentlichen Zeitgeschichte', *ZDPV* 79, 1963, 24–58; S. T. Parker, 'The Decapolis Reviewed', *JBL* 94, 1975, 437–41.

35. These were the districts of Jerusalem (including the hill country of Judaea and Idumaea); Gazara with the western hill country (Kanael differs, conjecturing the name Adora instead of Gazara and making it the centre of an independent district of Idumaea); Jericho with part of the hill country bordering on the south and north-west; Amathus, including the territory of Peraea; and Sepphoris in central Galilee. Cf. Josephus, *Antt.* XIV, 5.4 (90f.). See also H. Guthe, *Bibelatlas*, ²1926, map 10. B. Kanael, 'The Partition of Judea by Gabinius', *IEJ* 7, 1957, 98–106; E. Bammel, 'The Organization of Palestine by Gabinius', *JJS* 12, 1961, 159–62; E. M. Smallwood, 'Gabinius' Organization of Palestine', *JJS* 18, 1967, 89–92.

36. This Alexander was taken to Rome with Aristobulus, but managed to get away. Another son, Antigonus, lived with Aristobulus in Rome .

37. Reference should be made here to the classic account by E. Schürer, *Geschichte des jüdischen Volkes im Zeitalter Jesu Christi* I–III, Leipzig ⁴1901–9 (reprinted Hildesheim 1964); the first two volumes have now appeared in a revised and expanded English edition, *The History of the Jewish People*, Revised English Version by G. Vermes and others, 1973, 1979. Cf also J. Leipoldt and W. Grundmann, *Umwelt des Urchristentums* I–III, 1965–76, which contains a historical account, texts and pictures; A. Schalit (ed.), *The Hellenistic*

Age. Political History of Jewish Palestine from 332 BCE to 67 BCE, WHJP I, 6, 1976; F. F. Bruce, *Israel and the Nations from the Exodus to the Fall of the Second Temple*, 1963 (a detailed account of the period of the Second Temple). Earlier works: E. Meyer, *Ursprung und Anfänge des Christentums* II, 1921; A. Schlatter, *Geschichte Israels von Alexander dem Grossen bis Hadrian,* ³1925.

38. The three-volume work by E. Schürer, mentioned in the previous note, gives a detailed account of conditions after Antiochus IV: the first volume, §§ 1–21, deals with political history from 175 BC to AD 135, the second, §§ 22–30, with the constitution and institutions at home; the third, §§ 31–34, discusses conditions in the Diaspora and Jewish literature. Shorter surveys of the same period can be found in S. Safrai, *Das jüdische Volk im Zeitalter des Zweiten Tempels*, 1978; N. H. Glatzer, *Anfänge des Judentums*, 1966; D. S. Russell, *Between the Testaments*, ²1963. Two extensive works reflect more recent research: M. Hengel, *Judaism and Hellenism*, 1974; M. Avi-Yonah and Z. Baras (ed.), *Society and Religion in the Second Temple Period, WHJP* I, 8, 1977.

39. Translations: R. H. Charles (ed.), *Apocrypha and Pseudepigrapha of the Old Testament*, 1913 (2 vols, cited as *AP*); P. Riessler, *Altjüdisches Schrifttum ausserhalb der Bibel, übersetzt und erlautert*, 1928; W. G. Kümmel (ed.), *Jüdische Schriften aus hellenistisch-römischer Zeit* I–V, 1973ff., is still in course of publication; cf. also O. Eissfeldt, *The Old Testament. An Introduction*, 1975; L. Rost, *Einleitung in die alttestamentlichen Apokryphen und Pseudepigraphen einschliesslich der grossen Qumran-Handschriften*, 1971.

40. For the apocalyptic movement see J. Schreiner, in Maier and Schreiner (eds.), *Literatur und Religion des Frühjudentums*, 1973, 214–53, with further bibliography; above all see also J. M. Schmidt, *Die jüdische Apokalyptik. Die Geschichte ihrer Erforschung von den Anfängen bis zu den Textfunden von Qumran*, Neukirchen 1969; H. H. Rowley, *The Relevance of Apocalyptic*, ²1946; for the emergence and background of apocalyptic see O. Plöger, *Theocracy and Eschatology*, 1968; K. Koch, *The Rediscovery of Apocalyptic*, SBT II 22, 1972, gives an attractive, if polemic, account.

41. H. Gese, *Anfang und Ende der Apokalyptik, dargestellt am Sacharjabuch*, 1973; reprinted in *Vom Sinai zum Zion*, Munich 1974, 202–30.

42. K. Koch, 'Spätisraelitisches Geschichtsdenken am Beispiel des Buches Daniel', *Historische Zeitschrift* 193, 1961, 1–32; M. Noth, 'The Understanding of History in Old Testament Apocalyptic', *The Laws in the Pentateuch and Other Studies*, 1966, 194–214.

43. One contributory factor which may have inspired the apocalyptic writer to represent the Greek empire by the symbol of a beast with four horns could be that on coins both Alexander the Great and the first Seleucids were depicted as wearing horns; by contrast, we find nothing of this kind with the Ptolemies. This connection has been pointed out by S. Morenz, 'Das Tier mit den Hörnern. Ein Beitrag zu Dan.7,7f.', *ZAW* 63, 1951, 151–4, reprinted in S Morenz, *Religion und Geschichte des alten Ägypten*, 1975, 429–32.

44. The sequence remains hypothetical. If one does not want to include Alexander the Great, even more venturesome constructions seem required, for example the insertion of Antiochus Hierax, who played a role as rival king to Seleucus II between 240 and 227. For the view presented here see O. Plöger, *Das Buch Daniel*, KAT 18, 1965, 116f.

45. Other attempts have been made at interpreting the three horns which are plucked out, but they seem artificial. The advantage of the solution presented here is that it takes account of people who have a clear affinity to one another and who might also claim dynastic rights. For this and further problems see O. Plöger, op. cit.

46. The translation is a literal version of the Aramaic original. What is meant is that there is the appearance of someone who 'looks like a man'. The term 'son' denotes that he is one of the genre 'man'. Only later did the term 'son' of man take on independent significance, becoming something like a messianic title. Furthermore, in Dan. 7.13 the

figure is only compared with a human form; in no way, therefore, is he the 'Messiah' as a person in the eschatological sense.

47. M. Noth, 'The Holy Ones of the Most High', *The Laws in the Pentateuch*, 215–28.

48. For the different ways of understanding these developments see D. Rössler, *Gesetz und Geschichte. Untersuchungen zur Theologie der jüdischen Apokalyptik und der pharisäischen Orthodoxie*, WMANT 3, 1960.

49. For questions and problems of biblical chronology in connection with apocalyptic see K. Koch, 'Die mysteriösen Zahlen der judäischen Könige und die apokalyptischen Jahrwochen', *VT* 28, 1978, 433–41.

50. Only the Ethiopic translation has come down to us complete. The original text was Hebrew or Aramaic and was translated into Greek; the Greek text was the basis of the Ethiopian version. Translation in *AP* II, 425–69.

51. However, the earliest traditions are not to be put before Antiochus IV Epiphanes; it is generally accepted that the work was completed round about the middle of the first century BC. The chief point of dispute is whether the Similitudes in chs. 37–71 have undergone a Christian revision. For details see Eissfeldt, *The Old Testament*, 1965, 617–22.

52. E. Sjöberg, *Der Menschensohn im äthiopischen Henochbuch*, 1946. Cf. also the comprehensive account by P. Volz, *Die Eschatologie der jüdischen Gemeinde im neutestamentlichen Zeitalter*, 1934; there is more recent information in J. Klausner, *The Messianic Idea in the Apocryphal Literature*, *WHJP* I, 8, 1977, 153–86.

53. For details about the first discoveries and an introduction to the whole complex of problems see M. Burrows, *The Dead Sea Scrolls*, 1956; id., *More Light on the Dead Sea Scrolls*, 1958. Further details may be found in H. Bardtke, *Die Handschriftenfunde am Toten Meer*, 1953; id., *Die Handschriftenfunde am Toten Meer. Die Sekte von Qumran*, 1958; id., *Die Handschriftenfunde in der Wüste Juda*, 1962 (he gives an account of the discovery of further textual material in the area of the wilderness of Judah, in the *wādi murabbaʻāt*, on *ḥirbet mird*, and elsewhere). There is a short account of the settlement at Qumran and the most important discoveries in G. L. Harding, *Antiquities of Jordan*, [2]1967, 187–200.

54. This literature keeps on growing! In addition, further texts have been published recently. 1977 saw the publication of the so-called 'temple scroll', known since 1960 and given this title by the editor, Y. Yadin, *Megillat ham- Miqdaš. The Temple Scroll* (Hebrew Edition), 1977, Vols. I–IIIA. There are further details about Qumran literature in some of the Introductions to the Old Testament, especially that of Eissfeldt; see also Rost, *Einleitung in die alttestamentlichen Apokryphen und Pseudepigraphen einschliesslich der grossen Qumran-Handschriften*, 1971. See also the bibliographies on Qumran by C. Burchard, 1959 and 1965, and B. Jongeling, 1971.

55. For a translation of the texts see G. Vermes, *The Dead Sea Scrolls in English*, [2]1975. Among the numerous monographs see especially F. M. Cross and S. Talmon (eds.), *Qumran and the History of the Biblical Text*, 1975.

56. M. Noth, 'Der alttestamentliche Name der Siedlung auf chirbet kumrān', *ZDPV* 71, 1955, 111–23, conjectures that the place, or a previous settlement, may possibly be mentioned in the Old Testament under the name 'the city of salt', Josh.15.62.

57. This is indicated by the tables and benches of the scribes which were found in a special room in Qumran: see Burrows, *The Dead Sea Scrolls*, pl. IX. We cannot prove that all the scrolls discovered were written in Qumran. However, we can at least reckon on continuous scribal activity within the community.

58. The Essene thesis has been widely accepted, but is not without its critics; qualifications are offered by J. Maier and K. Schubert, *Die Qumraner – Essener*, 1973; there is a careful assessment by J. Licht, 'The Qumran Sect and its Scrolls', *WHJP* I, 8, 1977, 125–152, esp. 145–7. K. H. Rengstorf, *Hirbet Qumrân und die Bibliothek vom Toten Meer*, Studia Delitzschiana 5, 1960, conjectures that this was not an Essene settlement but the

location of a department of the Jerusalem temple which had transferred part of the temple library to Qumran; id., 'Erwägungen zur Frage des Landbesitzes des zweiten Tempels in Judäa und seiner Verwaltung', in *Bibel und Qumran, Festschrift H. Bardtke*, Berlin 1968, 156–76. S. Wagner, *Die Essener in der wissenschaftlichen Diskussion vom Ausgang des 18. bis zum Beginn des 20. Jahrhunderts*, BZAW 79, 1960, does not discuss the Qumran problem.

59. Usually called the Damascus Document for short. First discovered by S. Shechter in the Genizah of the Ezra synagogue in Old Cairo in 1896. Fragments of the same writing appeared in Caves 2, 4, 5 and 6 of Qumran. Eissfeldt, *The Old Testament*, 1975, 649–52. L. Rost, *Einleitung*, 1971, 127–30.

60. There are numerous pictures of it. A good one can be found in G. L. Harding, *Antiquities of Jordan*, pl. 31C (facing p. 195). There are splendid colour pictures in *Jerusalem und seine grosse Zeit*, 1977, 85–102, 255.

61. Community Rule (1 QS) I, 12; Vermes, *The Dead Sea Scrolls*, 72.

62. Community Rule V, 3, 4; Vermes, 78.

63. Because of its content, Sukenik gave this title to the text known as the 'War Scroll' (1 QM); Vermes calls it 'The War Rule', 122–46.

64. Damascus Document (Dam) XX, 1 (or XIV, 19); Vermes, 117.

65. Community Rule V, 9; Vermes, 79.

66. The Qumran copies – there is also a second copy of Isaiah – are the earliest witnesses to the text of the Old Testament in canonized form. They confirm the reliability of the tradition and give a glimpse of a stage of the text which is about a thousand years earlier than the Massoretic traditions, which formerly were all that was known to us. Some of the texts found in Qumran are now in the Israel Museum in Jerusalem, in the so-called 'Shrine of the Book'; the Isaiah scroll in particular is accessible here. See the series of pictures in M. Avi-Yonah, *Jerusalem – Die Heilige Stadt*, 1974, 120–5; there are two good pictures in C. Thubron, *Jerusalem* (The Great Cities), 1976, 179.

67. *AP* II, 625–52; Riessler, *Altjüdisches Schriftum*, 881–902, 1323f. Greek text also in the edition of the Septuagint by Rahlfs, II, 471–89. Cf. Eissfeldt, *The Old Testament*, 610–3; Rost, *Einleitung*, 1971, 89–91. In connection with its Pharisaic origin, differences are noticed within the Pharisaic movement which are also recognizable in the Psalms of Solomon; thus Eissfeldt, op. cit., 613, and more recently, in connection with a detailed analysis of the text, J. Schupphaus, *Die Psalmen Salomos*, 1977.

68. Ps.Sol. 17.21–25, using themes from Isa.11.1ff. and Ps.2.

69. Ps.Sol. 17.34f.

70. Translation from *AP* II, 650.

Bibliography

A. GENERAL

General Accounts

W. F. Albright, *From the Stone Age to Christianity*, New York ²1957

G. W. Anderson, *The History and Religion of Israel*, Oxford 1966

E. Auerbach, I. *Wüste und Gelobtes Land. Geschichte Israels von den Anfängen bis zum Tode Salomos*, Berlin ²1938

    II. *Wüste und Gelobtes Land. Geschichte Israels vom Tode Salomos bis Ezra und Nehemia*, Berlin 1936

H. H. Ben-Sasson (ed.), *Geschichte des jüdischen Volkes*. I. *Von den Anfängen bis zum 7. Jahrhundert*, Munich 1978

J. Bright, *A History of Israel*, London and Philadelphia ³1981

F. F. Bruce, *Israel and the Nations. The History of Israel from the Exodus to the Fall of the Second Temple*, Exeter 1963

E. L. Ehrlich, *Geschichte Israels von den Anfängen bis zur Zerstörung des Tempels (70 n.Chr.)*, Berlin 1958

G. Fohrer, *Geschichte Israels. Von den Anfängen bis zur Gegenwart*, Heidelberg 1977

A. H. J. Gunneweg, *Geschichte Israels bis Bar Kochba*, Stuttgart ²1976

J. H. Hayes and J. M. Miller (eds.), *Israelite and Judaean History*, London and Philadelphia 1977

M. Metzger, *Grundriss der Geschichte Israels*, Neukirchen ⁴1977

M. Noth, *History of Israel*, London and New York ²1960

R. de Vaux, *Ancient Israel*, London and New York 1961

— *The Early History of Israel*: I. *To the Exodus and Covenant of Sinai*; II. *To the Period of the Judges*, London and New York 1978

The World History of the Jewish People. I, E. A. Speiser (ed.), *At the Dawn of Civilization*, 1964; II, B. Mazar (ed.), *Patriarchs*, 1970; III, B. Mazar (ed.), *Judges*, 1971; VI, A. Schalit (ed.), *The Hellenistic Age. Political History of Jewish Palestine from 332 BCE to 67 BCE*, 1976; VIII, M. Avi-Yonah and Z. Baras (eds.), *Society and Religion in the Second Temple Period*, 1977

Earlier Accounts

H. Guthe, *Geschichte des Volkes Israel*, Tübingen ³1914

R. Kittel, *Geschichte des Volkes Israel*, Stuttgart, I, ⁵⁻⁶1923; II, ⁷1925; III/1, ¹⁻²1927; III/2, ¹⁻²1929

A. T. Olmstead, *History of Palestine and Syria*, New York 1931

E. Sellin, *Geschichte des israelitisch-jüdischen Volkes* I, Leipzig ²1935; II, 1932

J. Wellhausen, *Prolegomena to the History of Israel*, Edinburgh 1885
— 'Israel', *Encyclopaedia Britannica*, 9th ed., XIII, 1881, 396–431

Collected Works on the History of Israel

A. Alt, *Kleine Schriften zur Geschichte des Volkes Israel* I–III, Munich I, [4]1968; II, [3]1964;
    III [2]1968. A selection is available in English translation: *Essays in Old Testament
    History and Religion*, Oxford and New York 1966
O. Eissfeldt, *Kleine Schriften* I–V, Tübingen 1962–73
D. N. Freedman and J. C. Greenfield (eds.), *New Directions in Biblical Archaeology*, New
    York 1969
D. N. Freedman, G. E. Wright and E. F. Campbell (eds.), *The Biblical Archaeologist
    Reader*, Vols. 1–3, New York 1961–1970
K. Galling, *Studien zur Geschichte Israels im persischen Zeitalter*, Tübingen 1964
A. Kuschke and E. Kutsch (eds.), *Archäologie und Altes Testament, Festschrift für Kurt
    Galling*, Tübingen 1970
A. Malamat, *Mari and the Bible. A Collection of Studies*, Jerusalem 1973
B. Mazar, *Canaan and Israel: Historical Essays*, Jerusalem 1974 (in Hebrew)
— *Cities and Districts in Eretz-Israel*, Jerusalem 1975 (in Hebrew)
M. Noth, *Aufsätze zur biblischen Landes- und Altertumskunde*, Vols. 1 and 2, Neukirchen-
    Vluyn 1971
— *The Laws in the Old Testament and Other Essays*, Edinburgh and Philadelphia 1967
M. Noth (ed.), *Geschichte und Altes Testament, Festschrift A. Alt*, Tübingen 1953
O. Plöger, *Aus der Spätzeit des Alten Testaments. Studien*, Göttingen 1971
R. Rendtorff, *Gesammelte Studien zum Alten Testament*, Munich 1975
L. Rost, *Das kleine Credo und andere Studien zum Alten Testament*, Heidelberg 1965
J. A. Sanders (ed.), *Near Eastern Archaeology in the Twentieth Century. Essays in Honor of
    Nelson Glueck*, New York 1970
J. A. Soggin, *Old Testament and Oriental Sudies*, Rome 1975
R. de Vaux, *Bible et Orient*, Paris 1967
G. E. Wright (ed.), *The Bible and the Ancient Near East. Essays in Honor of W. F. Albright*,
    New York and London 1961

Handbooks and Lexicons

M. Avi-Yonah and E. Stern (eds.), *Encyclopaedia of Archaelogical Excavations in the Holy
    Land*, Vols. I–IV, English Edition, Oxford and Jerusalem 1975–78
Dictionnaire de la Bible, Suppléments 1–10, Paris 1928–74 (to be continued)
K. Galling, *Biblisches Reallexikon*, Tübingen [1]1937; [2]1977
J. Hastings, *Dictionary of the Bible*, revised by F. C. Grant and H. H. Rowley, Edinburgh
    [2]1963
Interpreter's Dictionary of the Bible, Vols. 1–4, New York and Nashville 1962; *Supplemen-
    tary Volume* 1976
K. Koch et al. (eds.), *Reclams Bibellexikon*, Stuttgart 1978
A. Negev (ed.), *Archaeological Encyclopaedia of the Holy Land*, London and Jerusalem 1972
M. Noth, *The Old Testament World*, London and Philadelphia 1966
B. Reicke and L. Rost, *Biblisch-historisches Handwörterbuch*, Göttingen I–III, 1962–66;
    IV, 1979
R. de Vaux, *Ancient Israel*, London and New York 1961

Collections of Texts

W. Beyerlin (ed.), *Ancient Near Eastern Texts Relating to the Old Testament*, London and
    Philadelphia 1978

J. H. Breasted, *Ancient Records of Egypt*, Vols. 1–5, Chicago 1906–7
H. Donner and W. Röllig, *Kanaanäische und Aramäische Inschriften*, Vols. 1–3, Wiesbaden ²1966–68
J. B. Frey, *Corpus Inscriptionum Judaicarum*, two vols., Rome 1936–52
K. Galling, *Textbuch zur Geschichte Israels*, Tübingen ¹1950; ²1968
G. L. Gibson, *Textbook of Syrian Semitic Inscriptions*, two vols., Oxford 1971–75
A. K. Grayson, *Assyrian Royal Inscriptions*, Wiesbaden, Vol. 1, 1972; Vol. 2, 1976
— *Assyrian and Babylonian Chronicles. Texts from Cuneiform Sources*, Vol. 5, New York 1975
H. Gressmann (ed.), *Altorientalische Texte und Bilder zum Alten Testament*, two vols., Berlin ²1926–27
D. D. Luckenbill, *Ancient Records of Assyria and Babylonia*, two vols., Chicago 1926–27
J. Maier, *Die Texte vom Toten Meer*, two vols., Munich 1960
— *Die Tempelrolle vom Toten Meer*, Munich 1978
J. B. Pritchard (ed.), *Ancient Near Eastern Texts relating to the Old Testament*, Princeton ³1969
— *The Ancient Near East in Pictures relating to the Old Testament*, Princeton ²1974
V. A. Tcherikover, A. Fuks and M. Stern, *Corpus Papyrorum Judaicarum*, Vols. 1–3, Cambridge, Mass. 1957–64
G. Vermes, *The Dead Sea Scrolls in English*, Harmondsworth ²1975

Atlases

Historical Geography

Y. Aharoni and M. Avi-Yonah, *The Macmillan Bible Atlas*
L. H. Grollenberg, *An Atlas of the Bible*, London 1959
H. Guthe, *Bibelatlas*, Leipzig ²1926
H. G. May (ed.), *Oxford Bible Atlas*, London ²1974
J. H. Negenman, *Grosser Bildatlas zur Bibel*, Gütersloh 1969
Tübinger Atlas des Vorderen Orients (in preparation)
G. E. Wright and F. V. Filson, *The Westminster Historical Atlas to the Bible*, Philadelphia and London ²1956

Maps and information predominantly on the State of Israel

Atlas of Israel. Cartography, Physical Geography, Human and Economic Geography, History, published by the Survey of Israel, Ministry of Labour, Jerusalem, Second (English) Edition 1970
Atlas of Jerusalem (Editorial Board D. H. K. Amiran, A. Shachar, J. Kimhi), Jewish History Publications, English Edition, Berlin 1973
Pictorial Volumes
(A small selection, usually containing a detailed text)
M. Avi-Yonah, *Jerusalem, die Heilige Stadt*. Photographs: W. Braun, Geneva 1974
— (ed.) *A History of the Holy Land*, London 1969
H. Bardtke, *Zu beiden Seiten des Jordans*, Berlin 1958
— *Vom Roten Meer zum See Genazereth*, Berlin 1962
— *Vom Nildelta zum Sinai*, Berlin 1967
G. Eichholz, *Landschaften der Bibel*, Neukirchen ³1972
E. and Z. Goldmann and H. Wimmer, *Israel. Seine Legende und seine Geschichte*, Lucerne and Frankfurt 1974
H. Gressmann, *Altorientalische Bilder zum Alten Testament*, Berlin ²1927
C. Hollis and R. Brownrigg, *Holy Places: Jewish, Christian and Moslem Monuments in the Holy Land*, London 1969

Jerusalem und seine grosse Zeit. Leben und Kultur in der Heiligen Stadt zur Zeit Christi, Würzburg 1977

E. Lessing (illustrations) and C. Westermann (text), *Gott sprach zu Abraham. Die Geschichte des biblischen Volkes und seines Glaubens*, Freiburg im Breisgau 1976

E. Lessing, with the collaboration of H. Cazelles, J. Bottéro et al., *Vérité et poésie de la Bible*, Fribourg and Paris 1969 (the illustrations presented here in large format are mostly identical with those in the work by Lessing and Westermann)

F. Lupsen, *Sehen wirst du das Land. Unterwegs zu biblischen Stätten*, Witten and Berlin 1973

J. Prawer and P. Meyer (photographs), *Heiliges Land. Seine Geschichte in Text und Bild*, Berne and Stuttgart 1975

L. Preiss and P. Rohrbach, *Palästina und das Ostjordanland*, Stuttgart 1925

J. B. Pritchard (ed.), *The Ancient Near East in Pictures Relating to the Old Testament*, Princeton 1969, ²1974

H. Reich (pictures) and M. Tavor (text), *Jerusalem. Ein terra magica Bildband*, Munich 1968

C. Tubron and the editorial staff of Time-Life Books, with J. Maizel (photographs), *Jerusalem* (in the series The Great Cities), Amsterdam 1976

P. Volz, *64 Bilder aus dem Heiligen Land*, Stuttgart n.d.

B. Literature on the Main Parts of the Present Book

Introduction

The Scene

A. M. Abel, *Géographie de la Palestine*, two vols., Paris 1933, 1938

Y. Aharoni, *The Land of the Bible*, Philadelphia and London ²1980

M. Avi-Yonah, *The Holy Land from the Persian to the Arab Conquests (536 BC to AD 640), A Historical Geography*, 1973; rev. ed. 1977

D. Baly, *Geography of the Bible*, rev. ed. London 1974
— *Geographical Companion to the Bible*, London 1963

M. du Buit, *Géographie de la Terre Sainte*, Paris 1958

H. Donner, *Einführung in die biblische Landes- und Altertumskunde*, Darmstadt 1976

H. Guthe, *Palâstina*, Bielefeld and Leipzig ²1927

M. Noth, *The Old Testament World*, Philadelphia and London 1966

E. Ormi and E. Efrat, *Geographie Israels*, Jerusalem 1972

J. Simons, *The Geographical and Topographical Texts of the Old Testament*, Leiden 1959

P. Thomsen, *Die Palästina-Literatur. Eine internationale Bibliographie in systematischer Ordnung mit Autoren- und Sachregister*, Vols. I–VI (cover the literature of the years 1895–1939); Vol. A, Berlin 1960, covers the literature from 1878–1894. Vol. VI and Vol. A edited by L. Rost, in collaboration with F. Maass and O. Eissfeldt. The bibliography is comprehensive and takes into account not only geography but history, economics and society up to the present day.

The Time

The Cambridge Ancient History, Vols. 1, 2, Third Edition, Cambridge 1970–75; Vol. 3, Cambridge 1929

Fischer Weltgeschichte: Vols. 2–4, *Die altorientalischen Reiche*, Frankfurt 1965–67; Vols. 5–8, *Die Mittelmeerwelt im Altertum*, Frankfurt 1965–66

E. Drioton and J. Vandier, *L'Egypte*, Paris ⁴1962

A. H. Gardiner, *Egypt of the Pharaohs*, Oxford 1961

C. H. Gordon, *The World of the Old Testament*, rev. ed. of *Introduction to Old Testament Times*, Garden City, New York 1958

W. W. Hallo and W. K. Simpson, *The Ancient Near East - A History*, New York 1971

W. Helck, *Geschichte des Alten Ägyptens*, Leiden 1968

— *Die Beziehungen Ägyptens zu Vorderasien im 3. und 2. Jahrtausend v. Chr.*, Wiesbaden ²1971

A. Jepsen (ed.), *Von Sinuhe bis Nebukadnezar*, Berlin ³1979

H. Junker and L. Delaporte, *Die Völker des antiken Orients*, Freiburg im Breisgau 1953

K. A. Kitchen, *Ancient Orient and Old Testament*, London 1966

— *The Third Intermediate Period in Egypt (1100–650 BC)*, Warminster 1973

E. Meyer, *Geschichte des Altertums*, five volumes in 8, reprinted Darmstadt 1965–69

S. Moscati, *Ancient Semitic Civilizations*, London 1957

— *The World of the Phoenicians*, London 1968

A. T. Olmstead, *History of the Persian Empire*, Chicago 1948

E. Otto, *Ägypten - der Weg des Pharaonenreiches*, Stuttgart ⁴1966

H. W. F. Saggs, *The Greatness that was Babylon*, London 1962

A. Scharff and A. Moortgat, *Ägypten und Vorderasien im Altertum*, Munich ³1962

H. Schmökel, *Geschichte des Alten Vorderasien*, Leiden 1957

— *Kulturgeschichte des Alten Orient*, Stuttgart 1961

D. J. Wiseman (ed.), *Peoples of Old Testament Times*, Oxford 1963

W. Wolf, *Das alte Ägypten*, Munich 1971

Witnesses and Evidence

W. F. Albright, *The Archaeology of Palestine*, Harmondsworth 1949

R. Amiran, *Ancient Pottery of the Holy Land*, New Brunswick, NJ 1969

M. Avi-Yonah and E. Stern (eds.), *Encyclopaedia of Archaeological Excavations in the Holy Land*, I–IV, Oxford 1975–78

— *Palaestina*, Munich 1974 (offprint from *Paulys Realencyclopädie der classischen Altertumswissenschaft*, Vol. 13, 322–454)

H. Bardtke, *Bibel, Spaten und Geschichte*, Leipzig 1969

K. H. Bernhardt, *Die Umwelt des Alten Testaments I. Die Quellen und ihre Erforschung*, Gütersloh 1967

K. Galling, *Biblisches Reallexikon*, Tübingen ¹1937; ²1977

M. Görg, *Untersuchungen zur hieroglyphischen Wiedergabe palästinischer Ortsnamen*, Bonn 1974

J. Gray, *Archaeology and the Old Testament World*, London 1962

G. L. Harding, *Antiquities of Jordan*, London ²1967

A. Jirku, *Die Ausgrabungen in Palästina und Syrien*, Halle/S. 1956

Z. Kallai, *The Tribes of Israel*, Jerusalem 1967 (in Hebrew)

K .M. Kenyon, *Archaeology in the Holy Land*, London 1960

— *Digging up Jericho*, London 1957

— *Digging up Jerusalem*, London 1974

M. Noth, *The Old Testament World*, Philadelphia and London 1966

D. Winton Thomas (ed.), *Archaeology and Old Testament Study*, Oxford 1967

P. Thomsen, *Palästina und seine Kultur in fünf Jahrtausenden*, Leipzig 1932

G. E. Wright, *Biblical Archaeology*, Philadelphia ²1962

Y. Yadin, *The Art of Warfare in Biblical Lands*, two vols., Jerusalem and Ramat Gan 1963

— (ed.), *Jerusalem Revealed. Archaeology in the Holy City 1968–1974*, The Israel Exploration Society, Jerusalem 1975

PART ONE   *The Birth of the People of Israel*

W. F. Albright, 'Abram the Hebrew', *BASOR* 163, 1961, 36–54
— *Yahweh and the Gods of Canaan*, London 1968
O. Bächli, *Amphiktyonie im Alten Testament. Forschungsgeschichtliche Studie zur Hypothese von Martin Noth*, Basle 1977
J. J. Bimson, *Redating the Exodus and Conquest*, Sheffield 1978
J. Bright, *Early Israel in Recent History Writing*, SBT 19, London 1956
M. Buber, *Königtum Gottes*, Heidelberg ³1956
H. Cazelles, 'Patriarches', *Dictionnaire de la Bible*, Supplément 7, 1961, 81–156
— 'Les localizations de l'Exode et la critique littéraire', *RB* 62, 1955, 321–64
O. Eissfeldt, 'The Exodus and the Wanderings', *CAH* 2, 3, Cambridge ³1975, 307–30
C. H. J. de Geus, *The Tribes of Israel*, Amsterdam 1976
R. Giveon, *Les bédouins Shosou des documents égyptiens*, Leiden 1971
A. Haldar, *Who were the Amorites?*, Leiden 1971
S. Herrmann, *Israel in Egypt*, SBT II 27, London 1973
K. Jaros, *Sichem. Eine archäologische und religionsgeschichtliche Studie mit besonderer Berücksichtigung von Jos.24*, Freiburg, Switzerland and Göttingen 1976
Y. Kaufmann, *The Biblical Account of the Conquest of Palestine*, Jerusalem 1953
K. M. Kenyon, *Digging Up Jericho*, London 1957
— *Amorites and Cananites*, London 1966
H. Klengel (ed.), *Beiträge zur sozialen Struktur des alten Vorderasien*, Berlin 1971
R. A. S. Macalister, *The Philistines*, London 1914
A. Malamat, 'Conquest of Canaan: Israelite Conduct of War according to the Biblical Tradition', in *Encyclopaedia Judaica Yearbook 1975/76*, Jerusalem 1976, 166–82
— 'Charismatic Leadership in the Book of Judges', in F. M. Cross and P. Hanson (eds.), *Magnalia Dei: The Mighty Acts of God. Essays . . . in Memory of G. E. Wright*, Garden City, New York 1976, 152–68
— *Early Israelite Warfare and the Conquest of Canaan*, Oxford 1978
A. D. H. Mayes, *Israel in the Period of the Judges*, SBT II 29, London 1974
B. Mazar, *The Philistines and the Rise of Israel and Tyre*, Proceedings of the Israel Academy of Sciences I/7, 1964
E. Meyer, *Die Israeliten und ihre Nachbarstämme*, Halle/S. 1906 (reprinted Darmstadt 1967)
H. Müller-Karpe (ed.), *Jahresbericht des Instituts für Vorgeschichte der Universität Frankfurt am Main 1976*, Munich 1977; this includes W. Helck, 'Die Seevölker in den ägyptischen Quellen'; H. Müller-Karpe, 'Zum Ende der spätkanaanäischen Kultur'; G. A. Lehmann, 'Die Seevölker-Herrschaften an der Levantkuste'
E. W. Nicholson, *Exodus and Sinai in History and Tradition*, Oxford 1973
M. Noth, *Das System der zwölf Stämme Israels*, Stuttgart 1930
E. Osswald, *Das Bild des Mose in der kritischen alttestamentlichen Wissenschaft seit Julius Wellhausen*, Berlin 1962
G. von Rad, *Der heilige Krieg im alten Israel*, Zurich 1951
D. B. Redford, *A Study of the Biblical Story of Joseph*, Leiden 1970
H. H. Rowley, *From Joseph to Joshua*, London 1950
N. K. Sanders, *The Sea Peoples*, London 1978
J. Sellnow (ed.), *Das Verhältnis von Bodenbauern und Viehzüchtern in historischen Sicht*, Berlin 1968
J. van Seters, *Abraham in History and Tradition*, New Haven 1975
R. Smend, *Das Mosebild von Heinrich Ewald bis Martin Noth*, Tübingen 1959
— *Jahwekrieg und Stämmebund*, FRLANT 84, Göttingen 1963

A. Strobel, *Der spätbronzezeitliche Seevölkersturm*, Berlin 1976
E. Täubler, *Biblische Studien. Die Epoche der Richter*, Tübingen 1958
R. de Vaux, *The Early History of Israel*: I. *To the Exodus and Covenant of Sinai*; II. *To the Period of the Judges*, London and New York 1978
— 'Les Patriarches hébreux et les découvertes modernes', *RB* 53, 1946, 321–48; 55, 1948, 321–47; 56, 1949, 5–36
— 'Les Patriarches hébreux et l'histoire', *RB* 72, 1965, 5–28; Eng. trs., 'The Hebrew Patriarchs and History', *Theology Digest* 12, St Mary, Kansas 1964, 227–40
H. Weidmann, *Die Patriarchen und ihre Religion im Licht der Forschung seit J. Wellhausen*, FRLANT 94, Göttingen 1968
M. Weippert, *The Settlement of the Israelite Tribes in Egypt*, SBT II 21, London 1971
— 'Abraham der Hebräer? Bemerkungen zu W. F. Albrights Deutung der Väter Israels', *Bibl* 52, 1971, 407-2
C. Westermann, *Genesis 12–50*, Darmstadt 1975
G. E. Wright, *Shechem – The Biography of a Biblical City*, New York and Toronto 1965
The World History of the Jewish People, Vol. II, *Patriarchs* (ed. B. Mazar), Israel 1961, London 1970; Vol. III, *Judges* (ed. B. Mazar), Israel 1961, London 1971
Y. Yadin, *Hazor*, London 1972
S. Yeivin, *The Israelite Conquest of Canaan*, Istanbul 1971
H. J. Zobel, *Stammesspruch und Geschichte*, Berlin 1965
B. Zuber, *Vier Studien zu den Ursprüngen Israels. Die Sinaifrage und Probleme der Volks- und Traditionsbildung*, Freiburg in Switzerland and Göttingen 1976

PART TWO *The Kingdoms of Israel and Judah*

Y. Aharoni, *Arad Inscriptions*, Judean Desert Studies, Jerusalem 1975 (in Hebrew)
A. Alt, *Kleine Studien zur Geschichte des Volkes Israel*, Vol. 2, Munich ³1964; Vol. 3, Munich ²1968
K. T. Andersen, 'Die Chronologie der Könige von Israel und Juda', *Studia Theologica* 23, 1969, 69–114
J. Begrich, *Die Chronologie der Könige von Israel und Judah und die Quellen des Rahmens der Königsbucher*, Tübingen 1929
Z. Ben-Barak, *'The Manner of the King' and 'the Manner of the Kingdom'. Basic Factors in the Establishment of the Israelite Monarchy in the Light of Canaanite Kingship*, Jerusalem Dissertation 1972
— 'The Mizpah Covenant (I Sam.10.25) – The Source of the Israelite Monarchic Covenant', *ZAW* 91, 1979, 30–43
J. A. Brinkman, *A Political History of Post-Kassite Babylonia, 1158-722 BC*, Rome 1968
G. E. Bryce, *A Legacy of Wisdom. The Egyptian Contribution to the Wisdom of Israel*, London 1979
M. Buber, *Prophetic Faith*, New York 1949
— *Königtum Gottes*, Heidelberg ³1956
G. Buccellati, *Cities and Nations of Ancient Syria. An Essay on Political Institutions with Special Reference to the Israelite Kingdoms*, Rome 1967
T. A. Busink, *Der Tempel von Jerusalem*, I. *Der Tempel Salomos*, Leiden 1970
B. S. Childs, *Isaiah and the Assyrian Crisis*, SBT II 3, London 1967
M. Cogan, *Imperialism and Religion: Assyria, Judah and Israel in the Eighth and Seventh Centuries BC*, Missoula, Montana 1974
H. Donner, *Israel unter den Völkern*, Leiden 1964
— *Herrschergestalten in Israel*, Berlin 1970
O. Eissfeldt, *'The Hebrew Kingdoms'*, *CAH* II-2, 1975

M. Elat, 'The Campaigns of Shalmaneser III against Aram and Israel', *IEJ* 25, 1975, 25–35
— *Economic Relations in the Lands of the Bible: c. 1000–539 BC*, Jerusalem 1977 (in Hebrew)
I. Eph'al, 'The Penetration of Arab Tribes to the Periphery of Palestine and Southern Syria in the 8th Century BC', in *Fifth World Congress of Jewish Studies, 1969*, Vol. I, Jerusalem 1971, 145–51 (in Hebrew)
E. Forrer, *Die Provinzeinteilung des assyrischen Reiches*, Leipzig 1920
K. Galling, *Die israelitische Staatsverfassung in ihrer vorderorientalischen Umwelt*, Leipzig 1929
J. H. Gronbaek, *Die Geschichte vom Aufstieg Davids (1 Sam.15–2. Sam.5). Tradition und Kompostition*, Copenhagen 1971
D. M. Gunn, *The Story of King David. Genre and Interpretation*, Sheffield 1978
E. W. Heaton, *The Hebrew Kingdoms*, Oxford 1968
T. Ishida, *The Royal Dynasties in Ancient Israel*, Berlin 1977
A. Jepsen, 'Israel und Damaskus', in *AfO* 14, 1941–4, 153–72
— *Die Quellen des Königsbuches*, Halle/S. ²1956
— and R. Hanhart, *Untersuchungen zur israelitisch-jüdischen Chronologie*, Berlin 1964
H. J. Katzenstein, *The History of Tyre*, Jerusalem 1973
R. Kittel, *Gestalten und Gedanken in Israel*, Leipzig 1925
J. Lindblom, *Prophecy in Ancient Israel*, Oxford 1962
D. J. McCarthy, 'The Inauguration of Monarchy in Israel', *Interpretation* 27, 1973, 401–12
A. Malamat, 'Organs of Statecraft in the Israelite Monarchy', *BA* 28, 1965, 34–50
— 'Aspects of the Foreign Policies of David and Solomon', *JNES* 22, 1963, 1–17
— 'Kingship and Council in Israel and Sumer; A Parallel', *JNES* 22, 1963, 247–52
— 'Jeremiah and the Last Two Kings of Judah', *PEQ* 83, 1951, 81–7
— 'The Last Kings of Judah and the Fall of Jerusalem', *IEJ* 18, 1968, 137–56
— 'Josiah's Bid for Armageddon', *Journal of the Ancient Near Eastern Society of Columbia University* 5, 1973, 267–79
— 'The Twilight of Judah: In the Egyptian-Babylonian Maelstrom', *SVT* 28, 1974, 123–145
T. N. Mettinger, *Solomonic State Officials – A Study of Civil Government Officials to the Israelite Monarchy*, Lund 1971
— *King and Messiah. The Civil and Sacral Legitimation of the Israelite Kings*, Lund 1976
A. R. Millard and H. Tadmor, 'Adad-Nirari III in Syria', *Iraq* 35, 1973, 57–64
N. Na'aman, 'Sennacherib's "Letter to God" on His Campaign to Judah', *BASOR* 214, 1974, 25–39
J. Naveh, 'A Hebrew Letter from the 7th Century BC', *IEJ* 10, 1960, 129–39
M. Noth, *Aufsätze zur biblischen Landes- und Altertumskunde*, two vols., Neukirchen 1971
— *Überlieferungsgeschichtliche Studien* I, Tübingen ³1967
— *Könige*, BK IX/1, Neukirchen 1968
B. Oded, 'The Phoenician Cities and the Assyrian Empire in the Time of Tiglath-pileser III', *ZDPV* 90, 1974, 38–49
A. L. Otero, *Cronologia e historia de los reinos hebreos (1028–587 a.C)*, Lugo 1964
R. A. Parker and W. H. Dubberstein, *Babylonian Chronology 626 BC–AD 75*, Providence, Rhode Island 1956
R. Rendtorff, 'Beobachtungen zur altisraelitischen Geschichtsschreibung anhand der Geschichte vom Aufstieg Davids', in *Probleme biblischer Theologie, Festschrift G. von Rad*, 1971, 428–39
M. Rose, *Der Ausschliesslichkeitsanspruch Jahwes. Deuteronomische Schultheologie und die Volksfrömmigkeit in der späten Königszeit*, Stuttgart 1975
L. Rost, *Die Überlieferung von der Thronnachfolge Davids*, Stuttgart 1926, reprinted in

L. Rost, *Das kleine Credo und andere Studien zum Alten Testament*, Heidelberg 1965, 119–253

J. Scharbert, *Die Propheten Israels um 600 v.Chr.*, Cologne 1967

K.-D. Schunck, *Benjamin*, BZAW 86, Berlin 1963

W. von Soden, *Der Aufstieg des Assyrerreiches als geschichtliches Problem*, Leipzig 1937
— *Herrscher im Alten Orient*, Berlin 1954

J. A. Soggin, *Das Königtum in Israel*, BZAW 104, Berlin 1967
— *Old Testament and Oriental Studies*, Rome 1975

H. J. Stoebe, *Das erste Buch Samuelis*, KAT VIII/1, Gütersloh 1973

H. Tadmor, 'Azriyahu of Yaudi', *Scripta Hierosolymitana* 8, 1961, 232–71
— 'The Southern Border of Aram', *IEJ* 12, 1962, 114–22
— 'Philistia under Assyrian Rule', *BA* 29, 1966, 86–102
— 'Assyria and the West: The Ninth Century and its Aftermath', H. Goedicke and J. J. M. Roberts (eds.), *Unity and Diversity*, Baltimore 1975, 36–48

E. R. Thiele, *The Mysterious Numbers of the Hebrew Kings*, Grand Rapids, Michigan 1977
— *A Chronology of the Hebrew Kings*, Grand Rapids, Michigan 1977

T. Veijola, *Die ewige Dynastie*, Helsinki 1975

G. Wallis, *Geschichte und Überlieferung: Gedanken über alttestamentliche Darstellungen der Frühgeschichte Israels und der Anfänge seines Königtums*, Stuttgart 1968

M. Weber, *Das antike Judentum. Gesammelte Aufsätze zur Religionssoziologie*, Vol. 3, Tübingen 1920 (reprinted 1976)

M. Weippert, 'Menahem von Israel und seine Zeitgenossen in einer Steleninschrift des assyrischen Königs Tiglathpileser III. aus dem Iran', *ZDPV* 89, 1973, 26–53

A. Weiser, *Samuel. Seine geschichtliche Aufgabe und religiöse Bedeutung*, Göttingen 1962

P. Welten, *Die Königs-Stempel. Ein Beitrag zur Militärpolitik Judas unter Hiskia und Josia*, Wiesbaden 1969

R. N. Whybray, *The Succession Narrative: A Study of II Sam.9–20 and I Kings 1 and 2*, SBT II 9, London 1968

G. Widengren, *Sakrales Königtum im Alten Testament und im Judentum*, Stuttgart 1955

D. J. Wiseman, *Chronicles of Chaldaean Kings (626–556 BC) in the British Museum*, London 1956

E. Würthwein, *Der 'amm hā'ārez im Alten Testament*, Stuttgart 1936
— *Die Erzählung von der Thronfolge Davids – theologische oder politische Geschichtsschreibung?*, Zurich 1974
— *Die Bücher der Könige, 1. Könige 1–16*, ATD 11, 1, Göttingen 1977

R. Zadok, 'Geographical and Onomastic Notes', *The Journal of the Ancient Near Eastern Society of Columbia University* 8, 1976, 113–23

PART THREE   *Israel in the Hands of the Great Powers*

(*a*) *The Persians, the Greeks, the Romans, Israel's neighbours*

E. Badian, 'Rom und Antiochos der Grosse. Eine Studie Über den Kalten Krieg', in *Die Welt als Geschichte* 20, 1960, 203–25

A. R. Bellinger, *The End of the Seluecids*, Transactions of the Connecticut Academy 38, New Haven 1949

H. Bengtson, *Griechische Geschichte. Von den Anfängen bis in die römische Kaiserzeit*, Handbuch der Altertumswissenschaft, 3. Abt., 4 Bd., Munich [5]1977; there is a special edition without notes and bibliography under the same title, Munich [5]1979
— *Zur Geschichte des Niedergangs des Ptolemäerreiches*, Abhandlungen der Bayrischen Akademie der Wissenschaften 17, Munich 1938
— *Die Strategie in hellenistischer Zeit*, three vols., Munich 1937–52

E. Bickermann, 'Bellum Antiochicum', *Hermes* 67, 1932, 47–76

The Cambridge Ancient History, Vols. 7–12, Cambridge 1928–39

M. Cary, *A History of the Greek World from 323 to 146 BC*, London 1932, reprinted with new bibliography 1963

K. Christ, *Krise und Untergang der römischen Republik*, Darmstadt 1979

A. Dietrich, G. Widengren and F. M. Heichelheim, *Orientalische Geschichte von Kyros bis Mohammed*, HdO I, 2, 4, 2, Leiden and Cologne 1966

T. Fischer, *Untersuchungen zum Partherkrieg Antiochos' VII im Rahmen der Seleukidengeschichte*, Diss. Munich and Tübingen 1970

Fischer Weltgeschichte Vols. 5–7, *Die Mittelmeerwelt im Altertum I–III*, Frankfurt 1965–66

D. Flach, 'Der sogenannte römische Imperialismus. Sein Verständnis im Wandel der neuzeitlichen Erfahrungswelt', *Historische Zeitschrift* 222, 1976, 1–42

P. M. Fraser, *Ptolemaic Alexandria*, three vols., Oxford 1972

A. Giovannini and H. Müller, 'Die Beziehungen zwischen Rom und den Juden im 2. Jh. v.Chr.', *Museum Helveticum* 28, 1971, 156–71

E. S. Gruen, 'Rome and the Seleucids in the Aftermath of Pydna', *Chiron* 6, 1976, 73–96

A. H. M. Jones, *The Later Roman Empire*, three vols., Oxford 1964

F. K. Kienitz, *Die politische Geschichte Ägyptens vom. 7. bis zum 4. Jahrhundert v.d.Z.*, Berlin 1953

T. Liebmann-Frankfort, *La frontière orientale dans la politique extérieure de la République romaine depuis le traité d'Apamée jusqu'à la fin des conquêtes asiatiques de Pompée (189/8–63)*, Académie Royale de Belgique, Classe des Lettres, Mem.3,59, Brussels 1969

A. H. McDonald, 'The Treaty of Apamea (188 BC)', *Journal of Roman Studies* 57, 1967, 1–8

A. Momigliano, *Alien Wisdom, The Limits of Hellenization*, Cambridge 1975

O. Mørkholm, *Antiochos IV of Syria*, Copenhagen 1966

A. Poláček, 'Le traité de paix d'Apamée', *Revue Internationale des Droits de l'Antiquité* 18, 1971, 591–621

G. Posener, *La première domination perse en Égypte. Receuil d'inscriptions hiéroglyphiques*, Cairo 1936

M. Rostovtzeff, *The Social and Economic History of the Hellenistic World*, Vols. I–III, Oxford 1941

H. H. Schmitt, *Untersuchungen zur Geschichte Antiochos' d. Gr. und seiner Zeit*, Wiesbaden 1964

H. E. Stier, *Roms Aufstieg zur Weltmacht und die griechische Welt*, Cologne 1967

— *Welteroberung und Weltfriede im Wirken Alexander d. Gr.*, Opladen 1973

W. W. Tarn, *Hellenistic Civilisation*, London ³1952

F. W. Walbank, *A Historical Commentary on Polybius* II, Oxford 1967

— *Polybius*, Berkeley 1972

— 'Polybius and Rome's Eastern Policy', *JRS* 53, 1963, 1–13

R. Werner, 'Das Problem des Imperialismus und die römische Ostpolitik im zweiten Jahrhundert v.Chr.', in *Aufstieg und Niedergang der römischen Welt* (ed. H. Temporini and W. Haase) I, 1, Berlin 1972, 501–63

E. Will, *Histoire politique du monde hellénistique*, two vols., Nancy 1966–67

(b) *Israel between the Babylonian exile and Roman rule*

F. M. Abel, *Histoire de la Palestine, depuis la conquête d'Alexandre jusqu'a l'invasion arabe*, two vols., Paris 1952

— *Géographie de la Palestine*, two vols., Paris 1933–38; ³1967

— *Les livres des Maccabées*, Paris ²1951

— with J. Starcky, *Les livres des Maccabées*, Paris ³1961

P. R. Ackroyd, *Exile and Restoration*, London 1968

— *Israel under Babylon and Persia*, Oxford 1970
G. Alon, *Jews, Judaism and the Classical World. Studies in Jewish History in the Times of the Second Temple and Talmud*, Jerusalem 1977
J. R. Bartlett, *The First and Second Books of the Maccabees*, London 1973
E. Bickermann, *Der Gott der Makkabäer*, Berlin 1937
— *Institutions des Séleucides*, Paris 1938
— *From Ezra to the Last of the Maccabees: Foundations of Post-Biblical Judaism*, New York 1962
— 'La charte séleucide de Jérusalem', *Revue des études juives* 100, 1935, 4–35
W. Bousset and H. Gressmann, *Die Religion des Judentums im späthellenistisichen Zeitalter*, Tübingen ³1926, reprinted 1966
J. G. Bunge, *Untersuchungen zum Zweiten Makkabäerbuch*, Diss. Bonn 1971
V. Burr, 'Rom und Judäa im 1. Jh. v.Chr. (Pompeius und die Juden)', in *Aufstieg und Niedergang der Römischen Welt* (ed. Temporini and Haase) I, 1, Berlin 1972, 875–886
M. Burrows, *The Dead Sea Scrolls*, London 1956
— *More Light on the Dead Sea Scrolls*, London 1958
R. J. Coggins, *Samaritans and Jews. The Origins of Samaritanism Reconsidered*, Oxford 1975
F. M. Cross, 'A Reconstruction of the Judean Restoration', *JBL* 94, 1975, 4–18= *Interpretation* 29, 1975, 187–203
L. Finkelstein, *The Pharisees: The Sociological Background of their Faith*, Philadelphia 1938; ³1946
T. Fischer, 'Zu den Beziehungen zwischen Rom und den Juden im 2. Jahrhundert v.Chr.', *ZAW* 86, 1974, 90–3
— 'Johannes Hyrkan I. auf Tetradrachmen Antiochos' VII?', *ZDPV* 91, 1975, 191–6
K. Galling, *Studien zur Geschichte Israels im persischen Zeitalter*, Tübingen 1964
C. Habicht, 'Hellenismus und Judentum in der Zeit des Judas Makkabäus', *Jahrbuch Heidelberger Akademie der Wissenschaften*, 1974, 97–110
M. Hengel, *Judaism and Hellenism*, London and Philadelphia 1974
— *Jews, Greeks and Barbarians*, London and Philadelphia 1980
C. Herzog and M. Gichon, *Battles of the Bible*, London 1978
E. Janssen, *Juda in der Exilszeit: Ein Beitrag zur Frage der Entstehung des Judentums*, Göttingen 1956
A. Jepsen and R. Hanhart, *Untersuchungen zur israelitisch-jüdischen Chronologie*, Berlin 1964
Josephus, in 9 vols. with an English translation by H. St John Thackeray, R. Marcus and others, LCL, Cambridge and London 1926–65
A Complete Concordance to Flavius Josephus, Three parts, ed. K. H. Rengstorf, Leiden 1969ff.
U. Kellermann, *Nehemia: Quellen, Überlieferung und Geschichte*, Berlin 1967
H.-G. Kippenberg, *Religion und Klassenbildung im antiken Judäa*, Göttingen 1978
K. Koch, 'Ezra and the Origins of Judaism', *JSS* 19, 1974, 173–97
T. Liebmann-Frankfort, 'Rome et le conflit judéo-syrien (164–161 avant notre ère)', *L'antiquité classique* 38, 1969, 101–20
J. Maier, *Das Judentum*, Munich 1973
J. Maier and J. Schreiner (eds.), *Literatur und Religion des Frühjudentums*, Würzburg 1973
K. Matthiae, *Chronologische Übersichten und Karten zur spätjüdischen und urchristlichen Zeit*, Berlin and Stuttgart 1978
B. Mazar, 'The Tobiads', *IEJ* 7, 1957, 137–45; 229–38
H. E. Del Medico, 'La prise de Jérusalem par Pompée d'après la legende juive de la ville inconquise', *Bonner Jahrbücher* 164, 1964, 53–87
E. Meyer, *Der Papyrusfund von Elephantine*, Leipzig ³1912

— Ursprung und Anfänge des Christentums (three vols.), 2. Die Entwicklung des Judentums und Jesus von Nazaret, Stuttgart and Berlin 1929

R. Meyer, Tradition und Neuschöpfung im antiken Judentum, Dargestellt an der Geschichte des Pharisäismus, Berlin 1965

R. A. Parker and W. H. Dubberstein, Babylonian Chronology 626 BC-AD 75, Providence, Rhode Island 1956

O. Plöger, 'Die Feldzüge der Seleukiden gegen den Makkabäer Judas', ZDPV 74, 1958, 158–88 = O. Plöger, Aus der Spätzeit des Alten Testaments, Göttingen 1971, 134–64

C. Rabin, 'Alexander Jannaeus and the Pharisees', JJS 7, 1956, 3–11

G. von Rad, Das Geschichtsbild des chronistischen Werkes, BWANT 54, Stuttgart 1930

M. Rappaport, 'La Judée et Rome pendant la règne d'Alexandre Jannée', Revue des Études Juives 127, 1968, 329–45

D. Rössler, Gesetz und Geschichte. Untersuchungen zur Theologie der jüdischen Apokalyptik und der pharisäischen Orthodoxie, Neukirchen 1960

D. S. Russell, Between the Testaments, London ²1963

— The Jews from Alexander to Herod, London 1967

S. Safrai, Das jüdische Volk im Zeitalter des Zweiten Tempels, Neukirchen 1978

H. H. Schaeder, Esra der Schreiber, Tübingen 1930

A. Schlatter, Geschichte Israels von Alexander dem Grossen bis Hadrian, Stuttgart ³1925

K. Schubert, 'Die Entwicklung der eschatologischen Naherwartung im Frühjudentum', in Vom Messias zum Christus, Freiburg and Basle 1964, 1–54

— Die jüdischen Religionsparteien im neutestamentlichen Zeitalter, Stuttgart 1970

K. D. Schunck, Die Quellen des I. und II. Makkabäerbuches, Halle/S. 1954

E. Schürer, Geschichte des jüdischen Volkes im Zeitalter Jesu Christi I–III, Leipzig ⁴1901–9, reprinted Hildesheim 1964. New English edition, The History of the Jewish People in the Age of Jesus Christ (175 BC–AD 135), Vol. I, Edinburgh 1973; Vol. II, Edinburgh 1978

S. Segert, 'Aramäische Studien I. Die neue Editionen von Brooklyn Papyri und Aršâms Briefe in ihrer Bedeutung für die Bibelwissenschaft', Archiv Orientalni 24, 1956, 383–403

E. M. Smallwood, The Jews under Roman Rule, Leiden 1976

M. Stern, 'The Hasmonean Revolt and Its Place in the History of Jewish Society and Religion', Journal of World History 11, 1968, 92–106

— Greek and Latin Authors on Jews and Judaism, Vol. 1, Jerusalem 1974

— Documents on the History of the Hasmonean Revolt, Tel Aviv ²1972 (in Hebrew)

V. Tcherikover, Hellenistic Civilization and the Jews, Philadelphia and Jerusalem 1959

D. Timpe, 'Der römische Vertrag mit den Juden von 161 v.Chr.', Chiron 4, 1974, 133–52

W. C. van Unnik. Flavius Josephus als historischer Schriftsteller, Heidelberg 1978

S. Wagner, Die Essener in der wissenschaftlichen Diskussion vom Ausgang des 18. bis zum Beginn des 20. Jahrhunderts, Berlin 1960

H. F. Weiss, 'Pharisäismus und Hellenismus. Zur Darstellung des Judentums im Geschichtswerk des jüdischen Historikers Flavius Josephus', OLZ 74, 1979, 421–33

A. C. Welch, The Work of the Chronicler, London 1939

P. Welten, Geschichte und Geschichtsdarstellung in den Chronikbüchern, WMANT 42, Neukirchen 1973

T. Willi, Die Chronik als Auslegung, Göttingen 1972

The World History of the Jewish People I, 6: A. Schalit (ed.), The Hellenistic Age. Political History of Jewish Palestine from 332 BCE to 67 BCE, London 1976; I, 8: M. Avi-Yonah and Z. Baras (eds.), Society and Religion in the Second Temple Period, Jerusalem and London 1977

S. Zeitlin, The Rise and Fall of the Judaean State, two vols., Philadelphia 1962–67

H. Zucker, Studien zur jüdischen Selbstverwaltung im Altertum, Berlin 1936

MAPS

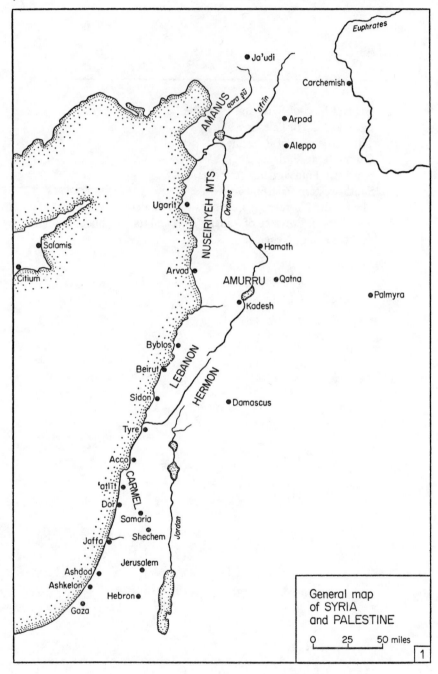

General map
of SYRIA
and PALESTINE

0   25   50 miles

1

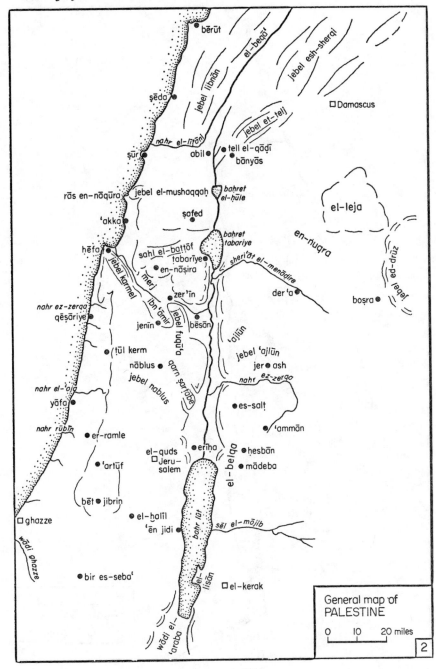

bērūt

el-beqā'

jebel libnān

jebel esh-sherqi

jebel et-telj

šēda

☐ Damascus

nahr el-lītāni

šūr

abil

tell el-qādi

bānyās

rās en-nāqūra

jebel el-mushaqqah

baḥret el-ḥūle

el-leja

'akka

safed

en-nuqra

baḥret tabariye

jebel ed-drūz

ḥēfa

sahl el-baṭṭōf

tabarīye

jebel karmel

ibn 'āmir

en-nāṣira

sheri'āt el-menādire

zer'īn

der'a

boṣra

nahr ez-zerqa

qēṣārīye

jenīn

jebel fuqū'a

bēsān

'ajlūn

jebel 'ajlūn

ṭūl kerm

jer ● ash

nāblus

qarn ṣarṭabe

nahr ez-zerqa

jebel nablus

nahr el-'ōja

es-salṭ

yāfa

'ammān

nahr rūbīn

er-ramle

el-quds

eriḥa

ḥesbān

'arṭūf

☐ Jeru– salem

el-belqa

mādeba

bēt ● jibrin

el-ḥalīl

☐ ghazze

'ēn jidi

bahr lūṭ

sēl el-mōjib

wādi ghazze

bir es-seba'

el- lisān

☐ el-kerak

wādi el- 'araba

General map of PALESTINE

0   10   20 miles

2

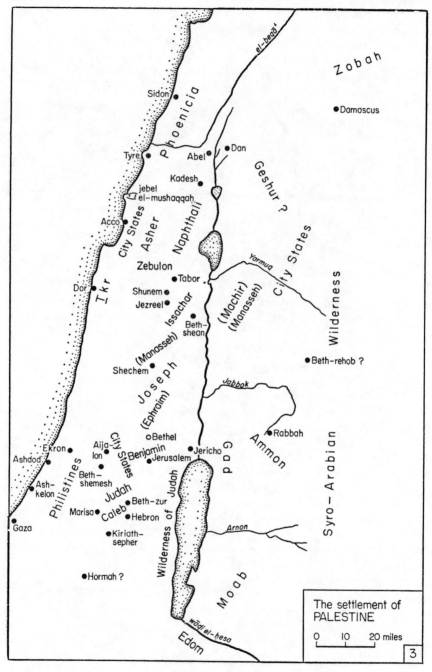

The settlement of
PALESTINE

0   10   20 miles

3

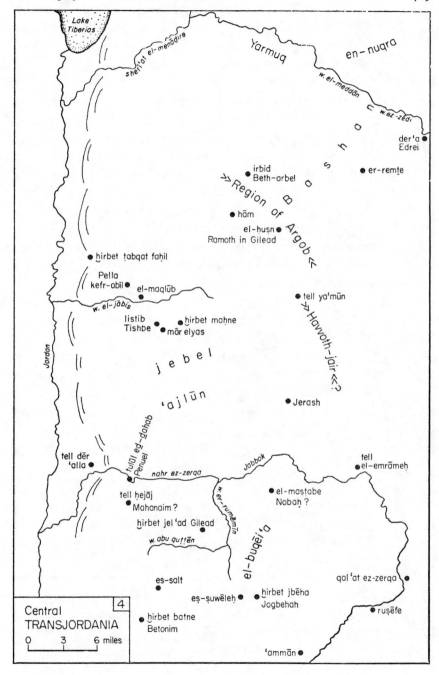

Lake Tiberias

Yarmuq

en-nuqra

sherīʿat el-menādire

w. el-meddān

w. ez-zēdi

der'a
Edrei

irbid
Beth-arbel

er-remte

>> Region of Argob <<

hām

el-huṣn
Ramoth in Gilead

ḥirbet ṭabqat faḥil

tell ya'mūn

Pella
kefr-abīl

el-maqlūb

w. el-jābis

>> Hawwoth-jair <<?

listib
Tishbe

ḥirbet mohne

mār elyas

j e b e l

'a j l ū n

Jerash

Jordan

tell dēr
'alla

ṭulūl ed-ḍahab
Penuel

nahr ez-zerqa

Jabbok

tell
el-emrāmeh

tell hejōj
Mahanaim ?

w. er-rumemīn

el-maṣtabe
Nobaḥ ?

ḥirbet jel'ad Gilead

w. abu quṭṭēn

el-buqēi'a

es-salt

qal'at ez-zerqa

eṣ-ṣuwēleḥ

ḥirbet jbēha
Jogbehah

ruṣēfe

ḥirbet baṭne
Betonim

'ammān

Central
TRANSJORDANIA

4

0   3   6 miles

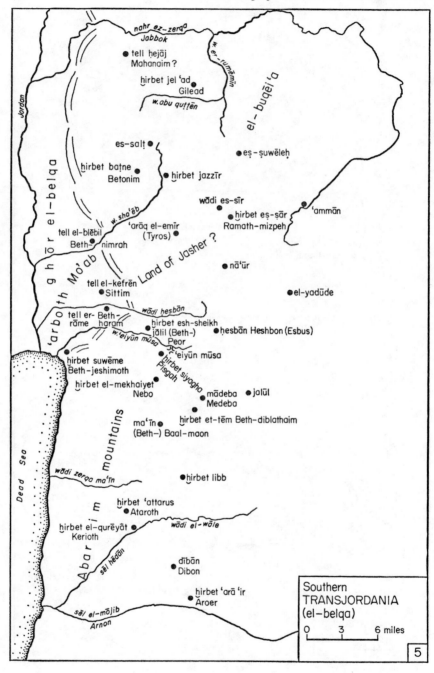

Southern
TRANSJORDANIA
(el-belqa)

0   3   6 miles

5

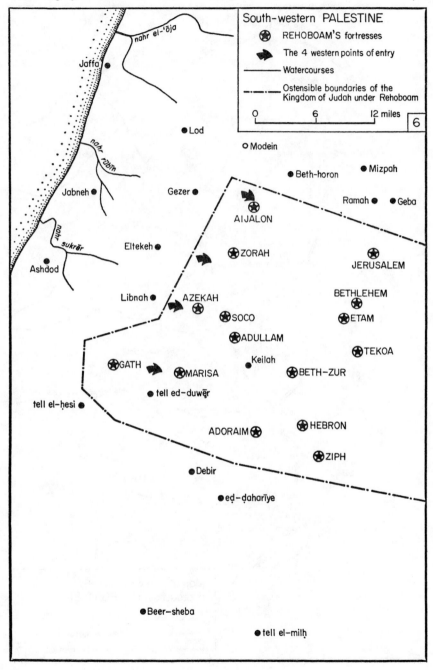

South-western PALESTINE

⊛   REHOBOAM'S fortresses

The 4 western points of entry

Watercourses

Ostensible boundaries of the
Kingdom of Judah under Rehoboam

0   6   12 miles

6

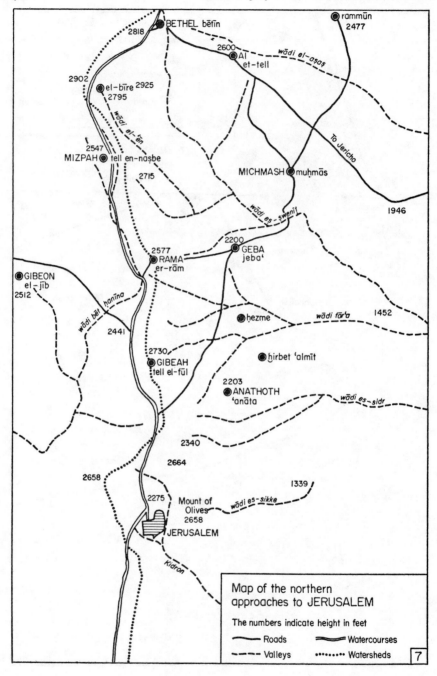

Map of the northern
approaches to JERUSALEM

The numbers indicate height in feet

—— Roads   ≈≈≈ Watercourses
- - - Valleys   •••••• Watersheds

7

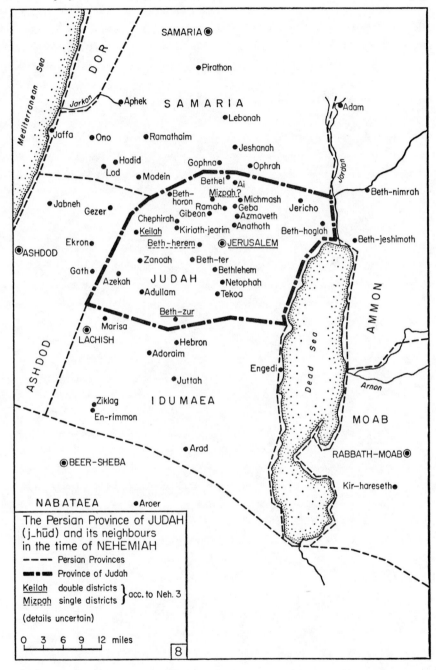

The Persian Province of JUDAH
(j_hūd) and its neighbours
in the time of NEHEMIAH

- - - - - Persian Provinces

■■■-■-■ Province of Judah

<u>Keilah</u> double districts } acc. to Neh. 3
<u>Mizpah</u> single districts }

(details uncertain)

0   3   6   9   12 miles

8

Index of Names

(The figures in *italics* after the main references indicate the maps on which places may be located)

Index of Biblical References

OLD TESTAMENT

Genesis		Genesis		Exodus	
2	182	28.10	52	1.2–4	168
2.11, 12	52	28.10–22	204	1.9	56
3	182	29.4	52	1.11	59
10	41ff.	29.31–30.24	45, 82, 99	1.15, 16, 19	66
10.22	51	29.34	109	2.1	84
11.10ff.	43	30.9–13	109	2.1–10	66
11.10–32	43	30.18	107	2.6, 7	66
11.20ff.	43	31	102	2.10	66
11.28	44	31.42	53	2.11, 13	66
11.29	44	31.53	53	2.11–22	66
11.31f.	52	32.2f.	47	2.23	67
12.1–3	50, 53	32.23–33	47, 51, 110	3	66, 71, 75, 77
12.4f.	52	34	84	3f.	125
12.6	47	35.4	47	3.8	55
13	106	35.23–26	168	3.13–15	75f.
14	49, 55, 171	36.10–14	43f.	3.14	77
14.7	84	36.31–39	85	3.18	60, 66
14.18–20	55	37	57	5.3	66
14.22	53	37.17	47	6.4	56
15	53	37.25–27, 28aβ	64	6.13ff.	67
15.12, 17	82	37.28aα	64	7.16	66
15.13, 16	67	39–50	57	8.18	66
17	53	45.10	66	9.1, 13	66
17.1	53	46.31–34	66	9.26	66
18.23	47	47.4, 6, 11	66	10.3	66
19.30–38	45	49	148	12	62, 269, 324
22.20–24	43f.	49.5	109	12.37	67
23	47, 170, 217	49.5–7	84	12.40f.	67
25.1–4	43f.	49.14, 15	93, 107	13.17f.	64
25.2	64	49.19	109	13.17–18a	67
25.3	52	49.24	53	13.20	67
25.12–18	64	49.27	121	14	67, 70
25.13–16	43f.	49.28	168	14.2	63, 67
25.18	52			14.5	67
26	47	Exodus		15	67
27.43	52	1–15	60, 66	15.1–22	70
28	47	1.1–7	56	15.1–21	67

APOCRYPHA AND PSEUDEPIGRAPHA

NEW TESTAMENT